W9-BIE-978

1001

Things Everyone Should Know About

AFRICAN AMERICAN HISTORY

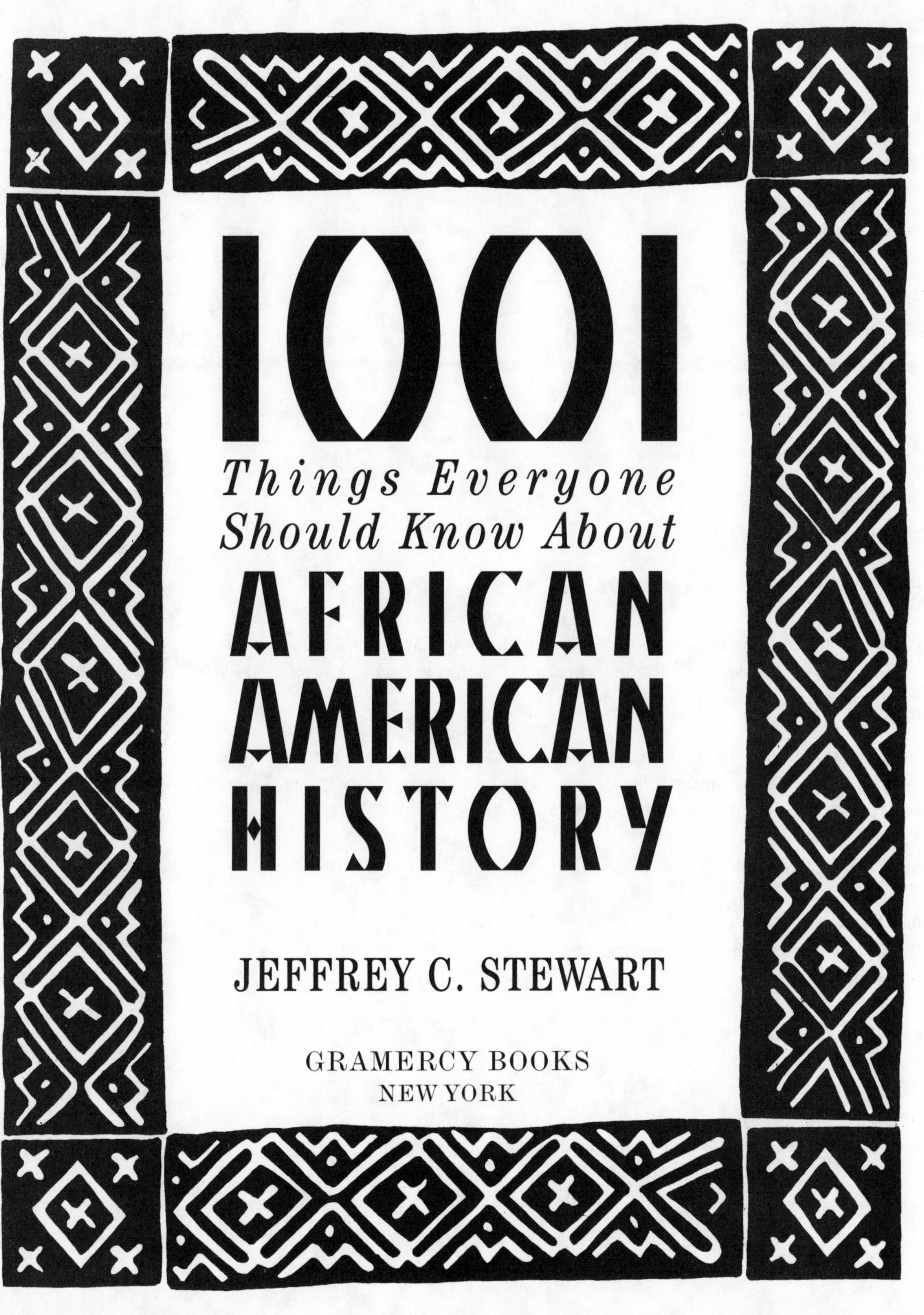

1001 Things Everyone Should Know About AFRICAN AMERICAN HISTORY

JEFFREY C. STEWART

GRAMERCY BOOKS
NEW YORK

This 2006 edition is published by Gramercy Books, an imprint of Random House Value Publishing, by arrangement with Doubleday Broadway, both divisions of Random House, Inc., New York. A previous edition of this book was originally published in 1996 by Doubleday.

Gramercy is a registered trademark and the colophon is a trademark of Random House, Inc.

Random House
New York • Toronto • London • Sydney • Auckland
www.randomhouse.com

Book design by Bonni Leon-Berman

Printed and bound in the United States.

A catalog record for this title is available from the Library of Congress.

ISBN 0-517-22840-8

10 9 8 7 6 5 4 3 2 1

To James A. Jones, my grandfather, an inventor and an entrepreneur, who inspired me and my family by his accomplishment.

Also honored in fondest memory is Jacqueline Reid Davis, my sister-in-law and supporter of my work in Black history, and Loki, my faithful companion during work for this book.

CONTENTS

Introduction ix

Part I
Great Migrations 1

Part II
Civil Rights and Politics 61

Part III
African Americans in the Military 181

Part IV
Culture and Religion 225

Part V
Invention, Science, and Medicine 319

Part VI
Sports 351

Select Bibliography 385
Index 389

INTRODUCTION

I can do no better than my colleague, John A. Garraty, in introducing this work than to repeat what he said about his book, *1001 Things Everyone Needs to Know About American History*: Garraty asserted that his book, like Charles A. Beard's *An Economic Interpretation of the Constitution of the United States*, was an *interpretation* of American history. So is mine, although I am taking aim at a particular part of American history in looking more closely and intensely at African American life and experience in America. But the main point is that I have presented here what I believe is most important and compelling about the African American experience in America—and not what others might select either before or after reading this book. Quite frankly, there is so much to know about African Americans that it would be quite impossible to provide anything truly exhaustive in one volume such as this—especially with such a numerical limit. At the same time, I have tried to be comprehensive rather than idiosyncratic in those topics that I have chosen to explore here. My book is designed to inform as well as to entertain, and to provide those completely unfamiliar with the topic something they can rely upon. While I do not think that these books are substitutes for textbooks in the field, I do believe that this book is an excellent supplement to textbooks and other materials used in high school and college courses. One of the things that I discovered in working on this book is how many contemporary academic books omit the kind of details that students—and I—am interested in finding out, such as when something occurred. I hope, therefore, that the book will be a useful reference work as well as a diverting one.

Actually, this book vibrates with a long tradition in African American history of providing popular histories to a select audience, a tradition that is perhaps most associated with the work of Joel Rogers, whose *World's Great Men of Color* is a classic. Here, however, I have extended considerable effort to overcome an obvious bias of such a work by including the innumerable women who have been not only great, but enormously influential in African American political, social, and cultural affairs. Another popular form of African American historicizing is the books and articles that document the "first" Black person to achieve a distinction. Although denigrated in some academic circles, such books have had an important function in Black popular culture of proving, often to an imaginary and skeptical audience, that Blacks *have* achieved, accomplished, or entered some activity historically associated with whites. Given the history of racism, being the first *inside* some restrictive arena has been important. But in this book, with the exception of sports, where racial barriers have been the stuff of American sports, I have tried to avoid overloading readers of this volume with the first Black persons, and to focus a bit more on the social processes involved. Similarly, in the section on inventions, I am just as interested in the process of invention as the inventor him- or herself. This is especially true in the first section, Great Migrations, which perhaps suggests that migration is a governing metaphor, a trope, as my colleague, Arnold Rampersad, would put it, for the African American experience as a whole.

One word on nomenclature is appropriate. In this work, as in other works of mine, I have used African American to designate Americans of African descent wherever possible, and have capitalized Black, because it refers to an ethnic group, such as Jewish, Chicano, Puerto Rican, etc. White is not capitalized because it does not refer to such an ethnic group. Finally, I also believe, again like Garraty, but perhaps for different reasons, that readers may find this book inspiring. It documents more than three hundred years of change and struggle in African American life that comprises one of the great stories in American history.

Acknowledgments

Finally, I would like to thank Marie Brown, Rob Robertson, Kelly Ryan, Maureen Mineham, Nancy Craig, Melynda Williams, Stefanie Tildon, Deborra Richardson, Betsy Rowe, Larry Hunter, Denise Hawkins, Richard Long, Karin Wisansky, Richard Korn, Kathy Ward, Fath Davis Ruffins, Suzanne Smith, Barbara and Nicholas Natanson, Elizabeth Turner, Martha Jackson Jarvis, Jarvis Grant, Beverly Brannon, Rita Waldron, Mary Lou Hultgren, Ann Stetser, Kelli Bronson, Dorothy Dow, Annie Brose, Richard Powell, Anthony Ruiz, Lawrence Jones, Tom Richards, Jamesetta Verela, Fay Acker, Shirley Tildon, Reginald Clark, David Potter, Tjark and Renate Reiss, Marion Deshmukh, Portia James and, most of all, my wife, Marta Reid Stewart, for help and support on this project.

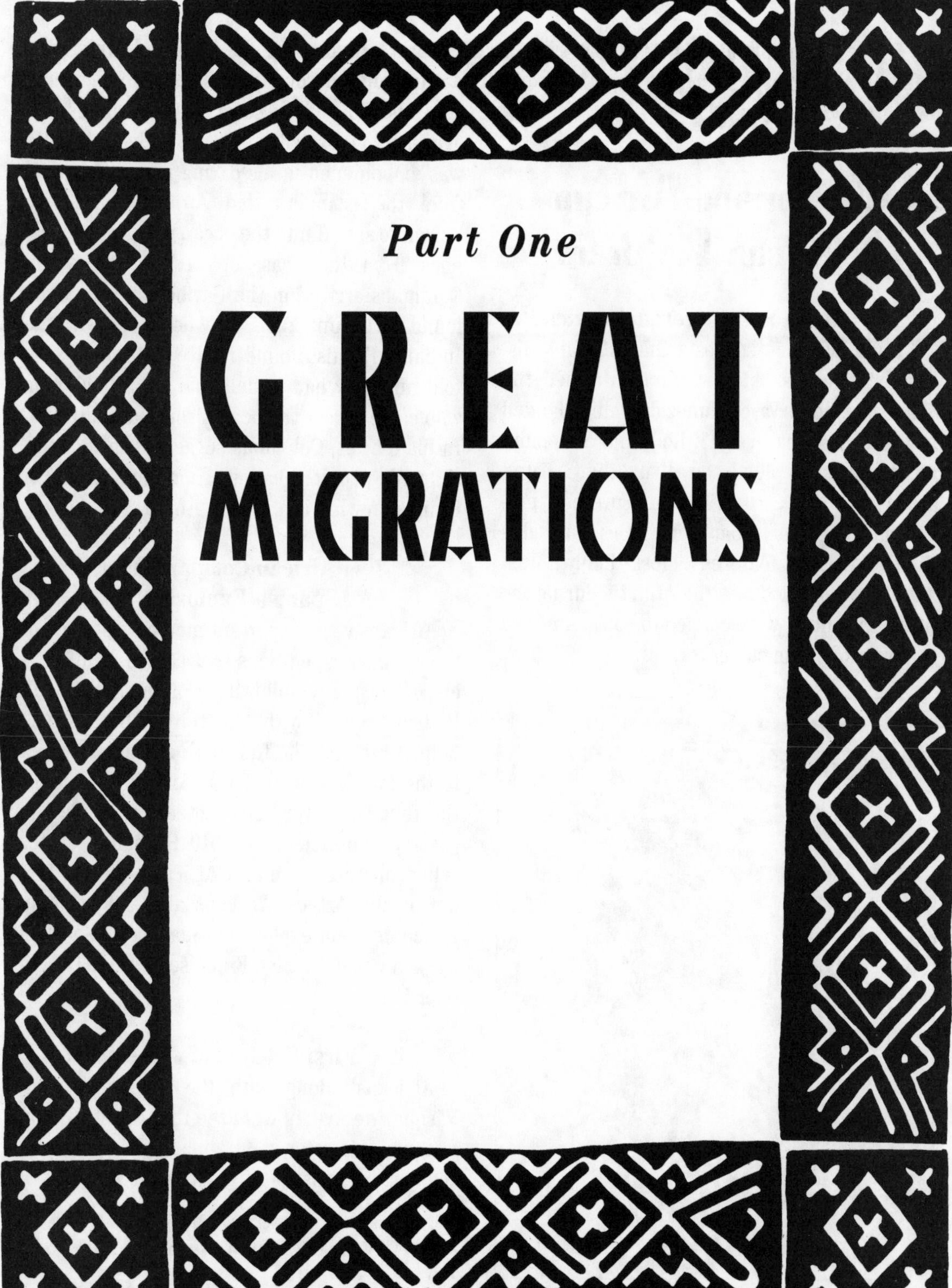

Part One

GREAT MIGRATIONS

FROM AFRICA TO AMERICA

African and African American Explorers

1 • Africans Discovered America

Strong evidence suggests that Africans discovered America before Columbus. When the Spanish explorer Vasco Núñez de Balboa landed in South America in 1513, he found a community of Black people already living there. Later, archaeological excavations uncovered pre-Columbian pottery that bore faces with distinctly African features. Most likely, West Africans who sailed into the Atlantic during the fifteenth century were carried to South America by powerful ocean currents.

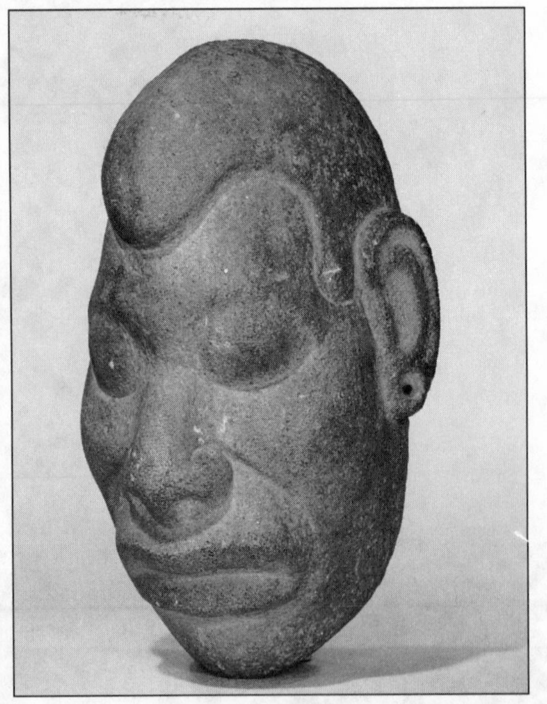

Negro stone head from Veracruz, Mexico. Classic period, c. A.D. 900. Courtesy of American Museum of Natural History, New York

2 • Columbus in the Wake of Africans

Christopher Columbus stopped in the Cape Verde Islands off the coast of Africa on his voyage west to find a shorter route to the Indies. He was emboldened in his daring journey by news from the islanders that Africans had been known to set off into the ocean going west in canoes from the coast of West Africa. When Columbus arrived in the Caribbean islands, he found dark-skinned people who traded with the Indians. He also found Native Americans who told him they had traded gold with Black men who came across the ocean from the southeast. In his diaries, Columbus suggested these dark-skinned peoples hailed from the coast of Guinea, in what is now West Africa.

3 • African Companions of Spanish Explorers

Africans were important members of each of the Spanish expeditions that came to the Western Hemisphere following Columbus. In 1513 Balboa brought with him thirty Africans who helped him cut the first path through Panama to the Pacific Ocean. These Africans also built the first ship ever constructed on the Pacific coast by foreigners. In 1519 Hernando Cortés relied on three hundred Africans to help him defeat the Aztecs. Africans also helped Juan Ponce de León explore Florida; they also filled the army that enabled Francisco Pizarro to conquer Peru.

4 • First Settlers of Jamestown

Africans, along with the Spaniard Lucas Vásquez de Ayllón, were the first to settle what is today Jamestown, Virginia. Ayllón explored the eastern coast of Virginia in the early 1500s

and was the first to bring Africans into what is now the United States. Ayllón founded San Miguel de Guadalupe, a colony that flourished until 1527, when Ayllón died and was replaced by a more repressive ruler. Eventually the Africans rebelled, burning the settlement and forcing the Spanish to retreat to Haiti. Many of the Africans who fled the Spanish settlement established their own colony in the area. One could say, then, that this community of Africans was, after those of the Native Americans, the first permanent colony in Virginia.

5 • Estevanico

The most important African explorer of America was Estevanico (also known as Little Stephen), the first foreigner to discover New Mexico. Born in Morocco around 1500, Estevanico left Spain on June 17, 1527, as the slave of Andrés Dorantes, a Spanish explorer. Dorantes and Estevanico had joined a disastrous Spanish expedition led by Pánfilo de Narváez, the Spanish governor of Florida, to explore his new territory. Soon after their arrival in Tampa Bay in 1528, the party fell victim to disease, animal attacks, and Indians vigorously defending their land. When the army of two hundred Spaniards tried to sail from Florida to Mexico, they shipwrecked in Texas. Eventually the party of two hundred was reduced to only four: Dorantes, Stephen, and two other Spaniards. Of these, Stephen was the most important to the success of their eight-year search for the Spanish settlement in Mexico City. Because of his facility for learning new languages quickly, Estevanico became the spokesperson and negotiated for food, shelter, and directions from the Indians. Once the group reached Mexico City, Estevanico was rewarded by appointment to another expedition, led by Father Marcos Niza, to travel northward and locate the legendary "Seven Cities," later called the Seven Cities of Cíbola (or Gold). Although Marcos later claimed to be the first to discover New Mexico, he had in fact sent Estevanico ahead of him as a scout. Disobeying Marcos's orders, Estevanico did not wait for his slower compatriot, but pushed on to become the first non–Native American to cross what today is the international border and explore Arizona and New Mexico. In May 1539 Estevanico reached the ridge of the Huachuca Mountains and surveyed much of southern Arizona. But upon reaching his destination, the city of Cíbola, Estevanico was murdered by the Zuni Indians in 1539, seeking to protect their land from further incursions. Although his death allowed others to claim they had discovered Cíbola, Estevanico remains the first foreign explorer of the southwestern United States.

6 • Black Explorer with Lewis and Clark

Lewis and Clark's 1804 expedition through the West from Missouri to Oregon was made easier by York, a Black slave owned by Clark. Over six feet tall and weighing more than two hundred pounds, York was the first Black man that many of the Native Americans had seen. York patiently allowed the Indians to examine his skin to see if the color would rub off. As one Flathead Indian explained, his dark skin inspired respect: "Those who had been brave and fearless, the victorious ones in battle, painted themselves in charcoal. So the Black man, they thought, had been the bravest of his party." York also entertained the Indians with athletic stunts. His antics helped ease the hostility and communication difficulties between the Indians and the exploration party. Clark recorded in his diary that York "amused the crowd very much, and Somewhat astonished them, that So large a man should be active." Some historians believe that York was freed by Clark after they returned to St. Louis and became an Indian chief in the West. Others believe he was never freed and his future after the expedition remained unknown.

7 • James Beckwourth (1798–1866)

Born a slave in Virginia, James Beckwourth ran away from his master in St. Louis, and headed West, where he worked for several years for the Mountain Fur Company and learned the ways of the fur trapper. Always an aggressive, resourceful individual, Beckwourth had his first big break when he stumbled into a Crow village and was claimed by one of the women as her son. Quickly accepting the Crow identity, he also accepted a Crow wife, and thereafter led the Crows in numerous wars against the Blackfeet Indians. Slated to succeed the chief upon his death, Beckwourth bolted to fight in the Seminole wars in Florida. But his greatest contribution came in 1850 when he located a pass through the Sierra Nevada and led the first wagon train through it. Located north of Reno, Nevada, Beckwourth's pass still exists as an example of the resourcefulness of this African American warrior-explorer.

James Beckwourth, one of the most famous of the mountain men. Photograph and Print Division, Schomburg Center for Research in Black Culture, New York Public Library, Astor, Lenox and Tilden Foundation

8 • Matthew A. Henson (1866–1958)

Matt Henson, as he was known to friends, was the man Robert Peary chose to accompany him on his "final dash" to the north pole in the spring of 1909. The orphaned son of Charles County, Maryland, parents who was already an accomplished seaman and well-read adventurer when Peary met him, Henson had accompanied Peary on his 1887 trip to chart a canal route through Nicaragua and on numerous previous arctic trips before Peary's last attempt to locate the north pole. Donald B. MacMillan, one of Peary's white companions left behind on the final leg of the 1909 attempt, recalled that Henson was

> *indispensable to Peary and of more real value than the combined services of all four white men. With years of experience equal to that of Peary himself, an expert dog driver, a master mechanic, most popular with the Eskimo, talking the[ir] language like a native, he went to the pole with Peary because he was easily the most efficient of all Peary's assistants.*

Henson actually reached what Peary had first projected as the north pole (later called Camp Jesup) forty-five minutes ahead of Peary, but Peary claimed he later crossed over the actual north pole a day later with two Eskimos. After their return to the United States, Peary distanced himself from Henson, who worked at menial jobs in the navy and the New York Customs House. Congress granted Henson a medal, along with Peary's other four assistants, for his efforts. Years after his death, Henson's body was moved to Arlington Cemetery from an unmarked grave in New York, and now rests next to that of Peary.

Matthew A. Henson. The Winold Reiss Collection of Portraits and Studies, Fisk University, Nashville, Tennessee. Photo courtesy of National Portrait Gallery, Smithsonian Institute

The Slave Trade

9 • Africans in the Slave Trade

During its four centuries of operation, the Atlantic slave trade removed approximately 11.7 million people, mostly from West and Central Africa, with the intention of settling them as slaves in Europe, the Americas, or on islands off the coast of Africa. Only about 9.8 to 10 million made it to their destination. The rest perished in port, at sea, or upon arrival in a new land.

10 • Slave Trade Numbers Debate

Controversy over the total number of Africans transplanted by the Atlantic slave trade has raged since Philip Curtin's *The Atlantic Slave Trade: A Census,* the first modern quantitative study of the slave trade, was published in 1969. Some felt Curtin's estimate of 9.8 to 10 million Africans arriving in the New World was too low. But recent revisions tend to uphold Curtin's overall figure, though his numbers for individual nations as destinations are still disputed. Some of the controversy comes from those who feel that calculating the number of Africans who were brought to the New World at only 10 million devalues the scope and horror of the slave trade. Some historians have suggested as many as 100 million men and women were removed from Africa! But such numbers are

Africans of the slave ship *Wildfire*. Prints and Photographs Division, Library of Congress

grossly exaggerated. Nevertheless, whether it was 10 million or 100 million, the slave trade was still one of the most devastating events in world history. Such a massive population transfer profoundly influenced the development of the American cultures we know today.

11 • Variation over the Centuries

The number of Africans removed by the Atlantic slave trade varied greatly over the centuries. From 1450 to 1600, about 367,000 Africans were taken out of Africa; another 1.868 million were removed in the seventeenth century. The number ballooned to 6.133 million human beings taken from their homeland in the eighteenth century. Then, after 1800, another 3.33 million were removed from Africa, even though the slave trade was outlawed in the United States after 1808.

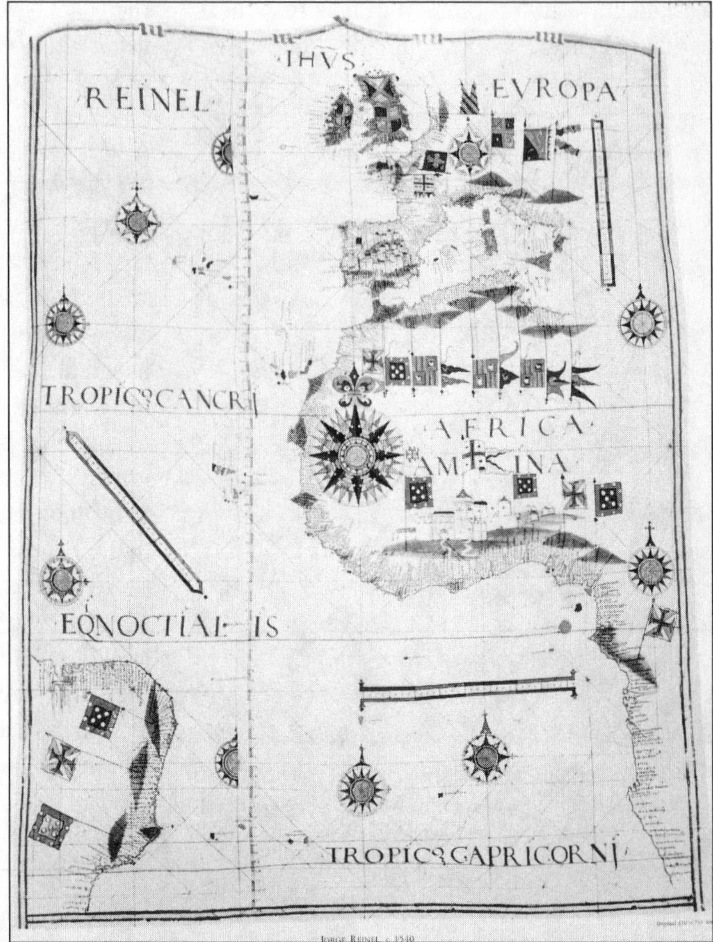

Portuguese chart of Africa c. 1540 by Jorge Reinel. Map and Geography Division, Library of Congress

12 • Portuguese Start Slave Trade

It was the Portuguese who first learned to sail down the Atlantic Ocean to West Africa. As a result, the Catholic Church awarded Portugal the exclusive right to exploration and trade with the continent of Africa in two papal bulls or decrees issued in 1493. The Portuguese had not waited for the papal bulls, however. In 1481 they had built a fort at Elmina over the objections of the West African Asante king, Kwame Ansa. Neither this fort nor its early entry into the trade could ensure Portuguese monopoly, however. By the middle of the sixteenth century, the Dutch, the French, the English, the Swedes, the Danes, and the Prussians would challenge Portuguese dominance of the slave trade and build forts of their own on the West African coast.

13 • Asiento

Under the asiento system, Spain, and later Spain and Portugal, granted licenses that permitted the direct shipment of Africans to specified destinations, but only after paying a substantial sum to the crown. Such licenses

were highly prized, as they guaranteed their owners a huge profit, and the acquisition process was full of theft, intrigue, and murder. Frequently the asiento required international diplomatic skills, as wealthy merchants of Portugal, for example, obtained a license and subcontracted Dutch or English captains to obtain and transport the Africans to the New World.

14 • Africans React to Portuguese Offer to Build a Fort on African Land

I am not insensible to the high honor which your great master, the Chief of Portugal, has this day conferred upon me . . . but never until this day did I observe such a difference in the appearance of his subjects. They have hitherto been only meanly attired . . . and were never happy until they could complete their lading and return. Now I remark a strange difference. A great number of richly dressed men are eager to build houses and continue among us. Men of such eminence, conducted by a commander who from his own account seems to have descended from God . . . can never bring themselves to endure the hardships of this climate. . . . It is far preferable that both our nations should continue on the same footing they have hitherto done, allowing your ships to come and go as usual.

—West African Asante king Kwame Ansa, upon the occasion of the Portuguese request to build a fort at Elmina

15 • Las Casas Myth

One of the most enduring myths is that the African slave trade to the Americas began in 1517 when Bartolomé de Las Casas, an ordained Spanish priest, suggested that Africans be brought to Haiti to replace the Native Americans who were dying in Spanish mines and plantations. Actually Las Casas was not the first to recommend use of African slaves. Africans were already at work in the New World when Las Casas approached Charles I, the king of Spain, with his recommendation. As early as 1501, King Ferdinand of Spain decreed, "Negroes born in the power of Christians were . . . allowed to pass to the Indies." In 1505 Ferdinand promised the governor of Hispaniola to "send more Negro slaves as you request" and increased the number of Africans sent to Hispaniola on a yearly basis. In 1516, as Charles I took the throne in 1516 (as Charles I), the use of African slaves in Spanish colonies in the New World was an established practice. By 1528 there were nearly ten thousand Africans in the New World, and although some had come as free people and some as indentured servants, most were enslaved.

16 • Slavery Increased with the Discovery of the Americas

The discovery of the Americas and the building of the transatlantic system of mining and plantation agriculture in the Spanish colonies stimulated a demand for labor, and Portugal was well positioned to supply that labor with African slaves. Portugal remained the dominant slave trader until the end of the sixteenth century.

17 • Portuguese Sugar Plantations in Brazil

Brazil was the primary destination of Portuguese-traded slaves by the end of the sixteenth century. Conquered by Portugal in 1500, Brazil was first valued for its forests full of "brazilwood," not for its agricultural potential. But Portuguese entrepreneurs experimented with the possibility of growing sugar in Brazil, and by 1600 Brazil had thousands of plantations. The word "plantation" meant to "plant" Europeans on overseas land, but by the end of the fifteenth century, it meant a tropical estate that produced a single crop for external consumption and used involuntary labor. The Portuguese had first tried to use Indian labor, but when that failed because of Indian resistance, flight, and insurrections, the Portuguese sugar growers decided to replace Indian laborers with Africans. The rise of Black labor in Brazil began around 1570; although Blacks had been employed as skilled workers and servants before that date, the large number of Indian deaths necessitated the importation of Africans for agricultural work. By the end of the sixteenth century Brazil was the "largest slave importing region in the Atlantic world."

The high mortality rate of slaves in the West Indies derived from harsh work conditions. Here slaves are used to provide power to run the mills. Prints and Photographs Division, Library of Congress

18 • The Caribbean, the Seventeenth- and Eighteenth-Century Destination of Slaves

During the seventeenth century, the Dutch, the British, and the French set up plantation colonies in the Caribbean that were copied from the "Brazilian model." Of these, the British were the most important and the most aggressive. In the seventeenth century the British seized Spanish islands in the Caribbean, most notably Jamaica in 1655, and set up sugar plantations on Barbados and Jamaica that by the end of the seventeenth century were producing more sugar for export than Brazil. The Dutch, who established the Dutch West Indies in the early seventeenth century, yielded to the naval superiority of England and became the banker of the slave trade, supplying capital to trading companies in England and France that brought increasing numbers of Africans into the slave trade in the seventeenth and eighteenth centuries. France also established its plantation system during the middle of the seventeenth century on Martinique and Haiti. By the middle of the eighteenth century, the sugar produced by slaves on Haiti exceeded that of any other Caribbean island. Not surprisingly, the rise in the numbers of Africans forced into the slave trade in the eighteenth century reflected the rise of sugar plantations in the Caribbean and their increased demand for labor. No doubt exists that African labor made this agricultural system profitable. As King Louis XIV of France, on August 26, 1670, noted, "There is nothing which contributes more to the development of the colonies and the cultivation of their soil than the laborious toil of the Negroes." Similarly, George Downing said of Barbados in 1645 that Africans were the "life" of the Caribbean. Europe has seldom been as unanimous on any issue as it has been on the value of African slave labor.

19 • English Trading

Although relative latecomers to the Atlantic slave trade, the English emerged as the nation that transported the largest number of West Africans in the Atlantic slave trade. English slave exports were about 9,000 per year by 1700, and they surged to more than 45,000 per year by the end of the century. English preeminence in the trade was caused in part by her possession of Barbados, the most important sugar-producing island in the Caribbean. The Atlantic slave trade was key to the emergence of Bristol, and later, Liverpool, as the major trading ports in England in the eighteenth century. Indeed, Liverpool became the queen of English slave-trading cities, supplying almost half the ships used in the Atlantic slave trade by the end of the eighteenth century.

Slaves from the British ship *Undine*. Prints and Photographs Division, Library of Congress

20 • Most Slaves from Coast of West Africa

Most of the Africans transplanted to the Western Hemisphere by the Atlantic slave trade came from the coast of West Africa, from such areas as Senegambia, Sierra Leone, the Gold Coast, the Windward Coast, the Bight of Biafra, and the Bight of Benin. Approximately 80 percent of the slaves exported by the British from 1760 to 1807 came from coastal West Africa. But there were other origins as well. Approximately 40 percent of the Africans imported to South Carolina from 1733 to 1807, for example, were Angolans from Central and southern Africa.

21 • Slave Trade in West Africa Prior to European Contact

Slavery and slave trading were well-developed systems in West Africa before Europeans established contact in the fifteenth century. A trans-Saharan trade in gold and slaves had existed with the Muslims for centuries. The Sudanese empires had used slaves to work large plantations, to staff huge armies, and to serve as administrators in state bureaucracies. Slavery was also popular as one of the few ways that economically aggressive individuals could move up in West African societies where ownership of land was not a means of upward mobility. But the very variety of occupations held by slaves in West African societies shows how different a system it was from the one that emerged in the Atlantic system. West African slaves enjoyed a status similar to European peasants, in that they often worked their own plots of land, lived in their own towns and villages, paid tribute to their masters, and held positions of importance in West African societies. Nevertheless, because slavery was an extensive institutional, legal, and commercial system in West Africa, it was easy for outsiders like the Europeans to acquire African slaves in local markets.

22 • African's View of African Slavery

Those prisoners [of war] not sold or redeemed we kept as slaves but how different was their condition from that of the slaves in the West Indies. With us they do no more work than other members of the community, even their masters' food, clothing and lodging were nearly the same as theirs (except that they were not permitted to eat with those who were free born) and there was scarcely any other difference between them than a superior degree of importance which the head of a family professes in our state.

—Gustavus Vassa

23 • Africans Sell Africans

It is a myth that most Africans who became slaves in America were captured by Europeans in slave raids. Most of the Africans who became slaves were sold into slavery by other Africans. The Portuguese did raid unarmed West African fishermen and their villages in the fifteenth century, but African leaders had organized sophisticated military defenses and delivered costly, bloody defeats to the Portuguese. The Portuguese realized then that the only way to ensure a steady, predictable supply of slaves was to build extensive political connections with African leaders and make the trade work in their interest. By the end of the sixteenth century this had been accomplished. A lucrative trade for European goods, especially weapons, facilitated the selling of slaves to the Europeans. Afterward, most Africans crossing the Atlantic had been captured and traded by other Africans into the hands of Europeans. Most of these captured Africans had become captives as a result of war between rival ethnic groups.

Africans selling Africans on the coast of Africa. Prints and Photographs Division, Library of Congress

24 • Captain's View of Slaves

Those sold by the Blacks are for the most part prisoners of war . . . others stolen away by their own countrymen, and with some there are who will sell their own children, kindred and neighbors. . . . I was told of one who designed to sell his own son after that manner, but he understanding French dissembled for a while and then contrived so cunningly as to persuade the French that the old man was his slave and not his father by which means he delivered him up to captivity. . . . However, it happened that the fellow was met by some of the principal Blacks of the country as he was returning home from the factory with the goods he had received for the sale of his father all of which they took away and ordered him sold for a slave. . . .

—James Barbot

25 • Royals vs. Commoners

Slaves were taken from all classes of African society. Many nobles became slaves as a result of loss or capture in intertribal wars.

My father . . . was a king, and treacherously murdered by the sons of a neighboring prince. To revenge his death, I daily went a hunting with some men, in hopes of retaliating upon his assassins; but I had the misfortune to be surprized, taken and bound; hence these ignoble scars [around his wrists and ankles]. I was afterward sold to your European countrymen on the coast of Guiana—a punishment which was deemed greater than instant death.

26 • Africans Traded Slaves for Firearms

Some African leaders sold slaves to Euro-

peans out of military or political necessity. Once African trading with Europeans for guns and gunpowder expanded in the eighteenth century, West African nations sometimes rose or fell because of their access to European firepower. Some African nations had to engage in the slave trade to acquire weapons to defend themselves against other nations who might attack and make them slaves. The slavers, therefore, exploited the divisions between Africans, who were divided not only by geography but also by language. The 264 Sudanic languages, 182 Bantu languages, and 46 Hamitic languages found in the region made Africa more complex linguistically, culturally, and socially than Europe. Rather than one people, Africans were many peoples each with their own history and rivalries. Europeans seeking more slaves for an expanding Atlantic market capitalized on these preexisting national rivalries. But many of the Africans engaged in the trade believed they were exploiting the Europeans by selling them unwanted captives from rival groups in return for weapons and other valuable goods.

27 • Bacaroons

Bacaroons were rows of wooden shacks on the coast of Africa where captured Africans were kept while awaiting transport to the Americas.

28 • Coffle

Coffle was the term used for a string of slaves connected by a forked branch or rope. Later, chains were used. Often, slavers used coffles to lead slaves from the interior to the coast, adding newly captured or purchased slaves along the way.

29 • Comments from a Slave on a Slave Ship

. . . the first object which saluted my eyes when I arrived on the coast, was the sea, and a slave

Coffle. Prints and Photographs Division, Library of Congress

ship, which was then riding at anchor, and waiting for its cargo. These filled me with astonishment, which was soon converted into terror, when I was carried on board. I was immediately handled, and tossed up to see if I were sound, by some of the crew; and I was now persuaded that I had gotten into a world of bad spirits, and that they were going to kill me. Their complexions, too, differing so much from ours, their long hair, and the language they spoke, (which was very different from any I had ever heard) united to confirm me in this belief. Indeed, such were the horrors of my views and fears at the moment, that, if ten thousand worlds had been my own, I would have freely parted with them all to have exchanged my condition with that of the meanest slave in my own country.

The Middle Passage

30 • Africans Die in Transit

On the average, two out of every ten Africans who left the coast of Africa on slave ships died during the Middle Passage—the trip from Africa to the Americas. Yet death rates varied greatly from ship to ship and over the four centuries of legal and illegal slave trading. Average death rates declined somewhat during the eighteenth and early nineteenth centuries as methods of travel, ship speed, and medical science improved, but increased after the slave trade was outlawed in the United States in 1808. Average yearly percentages did not reflect the tremendous loss that frequently occurred on particular voyages, and while not typical, some boats lost over half their slave population before reaching America. On the late-eighteenth-century voyage of the *Elizabeth*, for example, 155 out of 602 slaves on board perished before the ship arrived at its destination. Another example was the *St. Jan*, which left the island of Anobón on August 17, 1659. By the time it reached the West Indies on September 24, 1659, 110 slaves had died and the rest were in such disastrous condition "from want" of food "and sickness . . . that we saved only ninety slaves, out of the whole cargo."

31 • Housing for Slaves on Ships

Once a group of African slaves were boarded onto a slave ship, "the men were shackled two by two, the right wrist and ankle of one to the left wrist and ankle of another. Then they were sent to the hold or, at the end of the eighteenth century, to the 'house' that the sailors had built on deck. The women—usually regarded as fair prey for the sailors—and the children were allowed to wander" around by day, though they slept in separate decks from the men. "All slaves were forced to sleep without covering on bare wooden floors, which were often constructed of rough boards. In a stormy passage the skin over the elbows might be worn away to the bare bones."

32 • Loose/Tight Packers

In the slave trade, one of two techniques was usually advocated by slave ship captains: "loose packing" and "tight packing." The "loose packers" believed that by allowing slaves greater room, air, and sanitary conditions, more would survive the journey and thus bring greater profit. But "tight packers," who tended to dominate the trade after the middle of the eighteenth century, believed that by squeezing more people into the hole, the greater number would offset the increased death rate. An example of the disparity between the two techniques was the *Brookes*, a vessel of 320 tons that was ordered by the Law of 1788 to carry 454 slaves, even though the chart that determined their lo-

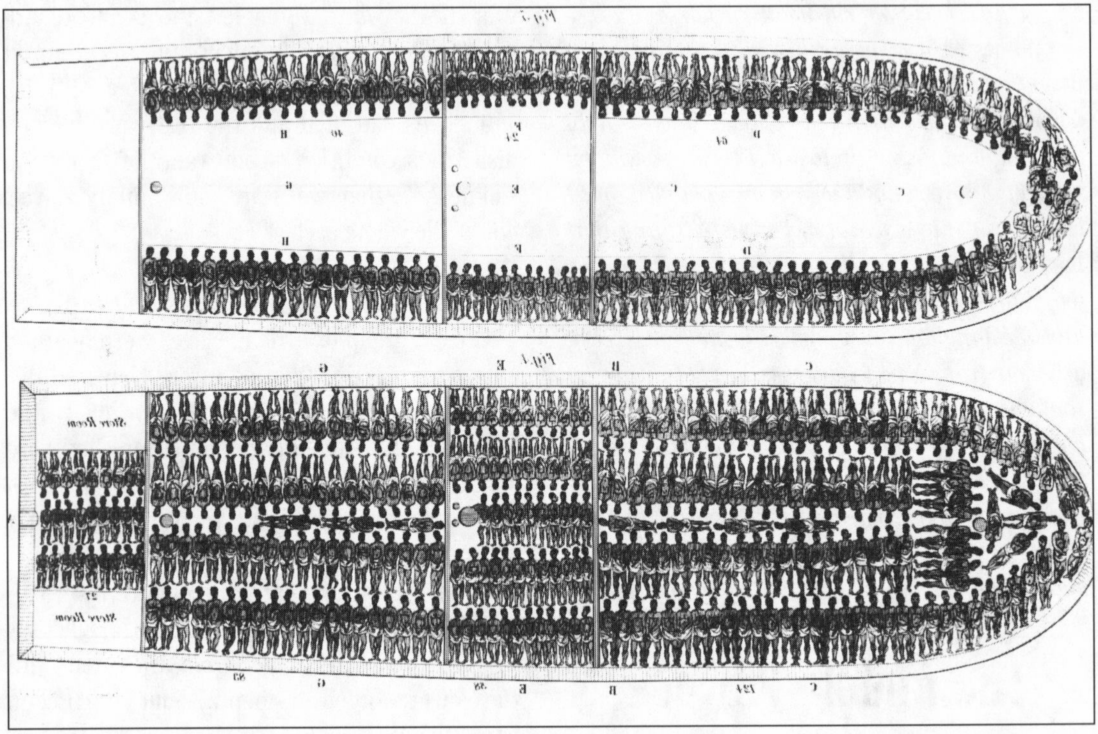

Diagram of the *Brookes*, a slave ship. Photograph and Print Division, Schomburg Center for Research in Black Culture, New York Public Library, Astor, Lenox and Tilden Foundation

cation could only find places for 451. But according to reliable witnesses, the *Brookes* had carried 609 on one voyage.

33 • Small Ships Transported Slaves

Although the famous diagram of the *Brookes* with 454 slaves aboard has created an indelible image of what the typical slave ship looked like, the reality is that most slave ships were much smaller than the 320-ton *Brookes.* In addition, most slave ships were not as completely filled or "tight-packed" before leaving Africa because it was difficult to acquire as many Africans as the 454 specified in the *Brookes* diagram. While the slave trade was a large, complex, and international enterprise, the actual ships were often owned and manned by small companies.

34 • No Link Between Packing and Mortality

Though "tight packing" was usually blamed for the high mortality rate among slaves in the Middle Passage, no proof exists that the practice resulted in dramatically higher deaths. A recent study of Dutch, French, British, and Portuguese slave ships arriving in Rio de Janeiro in the years between 1795 and 1811 did not show any correlation between the number of slaves per ton on each ship and the number who perished in the Middle Passage. In fact, some ships with smaller slave-to-ship tonnage ratios actually showed higher death rates than those with a higher ratio. While overcrowding certainly increased the misery of the slaves, it is debatable whether it actually increased deaths.

35 • Packing

The cargo of a vessel of a hundred tons or a little more is calculated to purchase from 220 to 250 slaves. Their lodging rooms below the deck which are three (for the men, the boys, and the women) besides a place for the sick, are sometimes more than five feet high and sometimes less; and this height is divided toward the middle for the slaves lie in two rows, one above the other, on each side of the ship, close to each other like books upon a shelf. I have known them so close that the shelf would not easily contain one more.

The poor creatures, thus cramped, are likewise in irons for the most part which makes it difficult for them to turn or move or attempt to rise or to lie down without hurting themselves or each other. Every morning, perhaps, more instances than one are found of the living and the dead fastened together.

—Rev. John Newton

36 • Voyage Length Linked to Mortality

The length of the voyage from Africa to the Western Hemisphere was the most important factor in slave mortality. A study of the French slave trade in the eighteenth century showed that ships that took 40 days to reach the New World port of delivery experienced roughly an 8.3 percent loss of slaves, but ships that traveled over 141 days had an average loss of 21.3 percent of their slaves. Even slight increases in distances could have an effect. Dutch slave ships that left Africa from the Guinea coast for the Caribbean instead of the nearer Angola averaged a 6.75 percent increase in the mortality of its slaves.

37 • Slaves Die Before Leaving Africa

Many captured Africans died before they were even loaded onto ships. The Portuguese crammed hundreds of slaves into the dungeon in Elmina, the first and best known Portuguese fort on the western coast of Africa. Often, the captured Africans were forced to wait in the dungeon for the arrival of more Africans so a larger cargo could be carried by the ships to the New World. A study of the Dutch slave trade calculated that an average of 3 to 5 percent of the slaves died before they left Africa, and during some waits, the percentage lost was much higher.

38 • Wait in Port Linked to Slave Deaths

Another factor that contributed to slave mortality was the long wait aboard ships anchored in port. The longer a slave ship remained in an African port, the larger the number of deaths that occurred among the slaves. The wait varied from place to place. At Bonny or Luanda, it might take a month or two to complete the loading process. But on the Gold Coast, where slaves were less numerous, loading of Africans could take from six months to a year. Such long waits had disastrous results, especially for the first people purchased. In 1677–78 the Royal African Company reported that on the *Arthur* fifty-five African men, women, and children died before the ship could leave for the New World.

39 • Psychological Trauma Linked to Slave Deaths

Psychological trauma caused the deaths of many Africans on the Middle Passage. Uprooted from their homelands, separated from their families, sold to Europeans who shackled and transported them to an ocean that many had never seen before, and then forced to inhabit squalid conditions during a long and tumultuous voyage, many Africans were overcome with despondency. On the *Elizabeth*'s tragic crossing, Isaac Wilson, the ship's physician, noted in his journal that many of the Africans were despondent and that he could not treat them. He also ventured that such despair made the Africans more susceptible to the effects of dysentery. Depression also contributed to the high rate of suicide among Africans when they were left unattended for any length of time up on deck.

40 • Greatest Cause of Slave Deaths—Disease

The greatest killer of Africans during the Middle Passage was disease. Scurvy, dysentery, smallpox, and a host of other contagious illnesses called "fevers" often spread like wildfire through the cramped, congested quarters of the slave ship. One French slave ship, *Le Rodeur,* was infected by ophthalmia in 1819. Not only all of the slaves but the entire crew were blinded by the disease. Most eventually recovered their sight. The thirty-nine who did not were thrown overboard, reputedly to avoid reinfecting the rest.

41 • Paying Head Money

Doctors on slave ships were paid a certain amount of money, called head money, for each slave that made it to America in reasonably good health. It was an incentive for the doctor to take good care of the slaves. Many of these men, however, were not doctors in the modern sense. Often, the title merely meant someone skilled in the use of leeches and other pharmacopoeia who could only practice aboard ship. Most of the captured Africans who survived the passage did so because of their own health and fortitude, not because of the ministrations of the shipboard "doctor."

42 • White Man's Grave

Africans were not the only ones to die as a result of the Atlantic slave trade. Indeed, Africa was called the white man's grave because of the high mortality of white crew members both on

TO BE SOLD, on board the Ship *Bance-Yland*, on tuesday the 6th of *May* next, at *Afhley-Ferry*; a choice cargo of about 250 fine healthy

NEGROES,

juft arrived from the Windward & Rice Coaft. —The utmoft care has already been taken, and fhall be continued, to keep them free from the leaft danger of being infected with the SMALL-POX, no boat having been on board, and all other communication with people from *Charles-Town* prevented.

Auftin, Laurens, & Appleby.

N. B. Full one Half of the above Negroes have had the SMALL-POX in their own Country.

Broadside announcing arrival of Africans from the "Rice Coast" who have been kept "free from the least danger of being infected with the SMALL-POX." Prints and Photographs Division, Library of Congress

African soil and at sea. Disease, poor conditions, inadequate food and water, and exhausting work contributed to the high death rate. Three out of five white men working for the Royal African Company in Africa died between 1684 and 1732. A popular saying among white seamen was "Beware and take care, Of the Bight of Benin; For one that comes out, There are forty go in."

Prints and Photographs Division, Library of Congress

43 • Pinching Doctors

Africans found novel ways to protest the "tight packing" of slave ships. A Dr. Falconridge testified before Parliament that when he had to go down in the holds of tightly packed ships, he took off his shoes because he could not walk without stepping on human beings. But Dr. Falconridge also said the Africans bit and pinched him so much that he had bruises on his feet.

44 • Ship Captain Murders Slaves in Cargo

Slaves were sometimes murdered by the captains of the slave ships. The worst recorded case on a British vessel occurred in late 1781 on the ship *Zong,* commanded by Luke Collingwood. Leaving the African coast for Jamaica with four hundred Africans on September 6, the *Zong* lost several whites and sixty slaves to disease by November 29. Others became sick, and water stores soon became depleted. Thinking that many more would die before he reached port, constituting a big loss to the shipowners, and believing drowned slaves would be covered by insurers, Collingwood decided to throw overboard all those who were sick. First, fifty-four of the sickest slaves were cast into the ocean; soon, forty-two more were similarly drowned. Although a heavy rainfall allowed the crew to collect additional drinking water, twenty-six more Africans were pushed off the deck, and another ten, seeing their fate, jumped overboard with their hands bound. When the *Zong* reached port, the insurers refused to pay and the shipowners sued the captain. The case became a cause célèbre for abolitionists, who seized upon the murders as symbolic of the evils of the slave trade. The *Zong* episode eventually moved the British Parliament to pass laws regulating the terms under which insurance could be paid for losses of slaves during transport.

45 • Slaves Jump Overboard

Many slaves mutinied or committed suicide just before landing in the New World. When the *Prince of Orange* arrived in St. Kitts' Bay, Jamaica, in 1737, for example, at least one hundred Africans leaped overboard to their deaths. In this case, the captain claimed that rumors by Africans that they were about to be eaten by white men caused the suicide. Such suicides may have succeeded in part because the crew, happy to have the Middle Passage over, relaxed their guard as the ship approached port.

46 • Attempted Escapes During Passage

The negroes are so wilful and loth to leave their own country, that they often leap'd out of the canoos, boat and ship, into the sea, and kept under water till they were drowned, to avoid being taken up and saved by our boats, which pursued them; they having a more dreadful apprehension of Barbadoes than we can have of hell, tho' in reality they live much better there than in their own country; but home is home, etc. We have likewise seen divers of them eaten by the sharks, of which a prodigious number kept about the ships in this place, and I have been told will follow her hence to Barbadoes, for the dead negroes that are thrown overboard in the passage.

—Captain Thomas Phillips

47 • The *Little George*

Sometimes slave rebellions at sea were successful despite the overwhelming odds. In early 1730, for example, the ninety-six Africans aboard the *Little George* wrested control of the ship away from the crew. Some crew members were tossed overboard, and the remainder sequestered themselves in a cabin armed with firearms and ammunition, hoping the Africans would be unable to navigate the unfamiliar ship. Although the journey took longer than usual due to the new crew's inexperience, the Africans successfully piloted the ship back to Africa, where they escaped.

48 • Suicide to Escape Punishment

On the English ship *Don Carlos,* the Africans attempted to overtake the crew with pieces of iron they had torn off the ship and with the shackles they had broken off their feet. One crew member recalled

. . . they fell in crouds and parcels on our men, upon the deck unawares, and stabb'd one of the stoutest of us all, who received fourteen or fifteen wounds of their knives, and so expir'd. Next they assaulted our boatswain, and cut one of his legs so round the bone, that he could not move . . . others cut our cook's throat to the pipe, and others wounded three of the sailors and threw one of them overboard in that condition.

Eventually, however, the crew's firepower overwhelmed the slaves and as the slaves scattered, the ship's captain reported: "many of the most mutinous, leapt over board, and drowned themselves in the ocean *with much resolution, showing no manner of concern for life.*"

49 • Mutinies on the Coast

Mutinies were also typical on the coast of Africa. The following incident took place at Old Calabar.

This Mutiny began at Midnight. . . . Two Men that stood Centry at the Forehatch way . . . permitted four [slaves] to go to that Place, but neglected to lay the Gratings again, as they should have done; whereupon four more Negroes came on Deck . . . and all eight fell on the two Centries who immediately called out for help. The Negroes endeavoured to get their Cutlaces from them, but the Lineyards (that is the Lines by which the

Handles of the Cutlaces were fastened to the Men's Wrists) were so twisted in the Scuffle, that they could not get them off before we came to their Assistance. The Negroes perceiving several white Men coming towards them, with Arms in their Hands, quitted the Centries and jumped over the Ship's Side into the Sea. . . . After we had secured these People, I called the Linguists, and ordered them to bid the Men-Negroes between Decks be quiet; (for there was a great noise amongst them). On their being silent, I asked, "What had induced them to mutiny?" They answered, "I was a great Rogue to buy them, in order to carry them away from their own Country, and that they were resolved to regain their Liberty if possible." I replied, "That they had forfeited their Freedom before I bought them, either by Crimes or by being taken in War." . . . Then I observed to them, "That if they should gain their Point and escape to the Shore, it would be of no Advantage to them, because their Countrymen would catch them, and sell them to other Ships." This served my purpose, and they seemed to be convinced of their Fault.

50 • Fattening Up Slaves

If a surplus of food existed at the end of the passage, captains and crew often overfed the Africans in order to "fatten them up" for market.

51 • Fear of Cannibalism

Many of the captive Africans feared they would be eaten by the Europeans. Cannibalism provided a logical explanation for the failure of the captured to ever return. Traders exploited this fear by threatening to eat the slaves, or turn them over to another group who would, if the slaves did not obey. These cultivated fears led to such expressions of dread that the white slavers eventually relented. Olaudah Equiano recalled that during his experience aboard ship

there was much dread and trembling among us, and nothing but bitter cries to be heard all night from these apprehensions, insomuch that at last the white people got some old slaves from the land to pacify us. They told us we were not to be eaten but to work, and were soon to go on land where we should see many of our country people. This report much eased us.

Landing in the New World

52 • Marching Skeletons

When a captain sold Africans upon arrival in the New World, he often brought them ashore in small boats, forced them to line up onshore, and marched them, like a ragtag army, into town, where they would be taken to market. On some occasions, such marches would be accompanied by the playing of bagpipes. A witness to one of these processions commented, "The whole party was . . . a resurrection of skin and bones . . . risen from the grave or escaped from Surgeon's Hall."

53 • Examination of the Enslaved

Most often, captains sold Africans in consultation with a factor, or broker, who, along with the captain, looked over the assembled Africans and selected out those who were ill, crippled, or near death. These would often be sold separately as "refuse" slaves, sometimes for as low as a dollar. The rest of the Africans were sold at set prices for men, women, boys, and girls. Once the prices were set for all of the purchases, the buyers "scrambled" to select the best-looking prospects. Such a rush of purchasers often frightened the Africans, especially those who

Inspection and sale of a slave. Prints and Photographs Division, Library of Congress

believed they were to be eaten once they landed.

North America

54 • First Twenty Africans as Indentured Servants

In 1619, a year before the landing of the *Mayflower*, the first Africans arrived in British North America aboard a Dutch ship that landed at Jamestown, Virginia. The "twenty Negers," as they were called by the Dutch, were sold not as slaves, but as indentured servants who worked for a term of service, usually seven years. By 1651 several of these original twenty Africans had completed their term of service and received land as part of the usual "freedom duties" that masters gave freed servants, white or Black. One of these twenty, Mr. Anthony Johnson, rose to become a prosperous farmer and master of several white indentured servants. But by the end of the seventeenth century, all Africans brought into or born in Virginia were declared slaves, and any upward mobility like Johnson enjoyed became a near impossibility. In a span of eighty years, Virginia society had evolved into one of the harshest and most severe legal systems of slavery in the Americas.

55 • Africans in Massachusetts

Africans arrived in New England prior to the settling of the Massachusetts Bay Colony in 1629. Records show that Samuel Maverick, the region's first slaveholder, arrived in 1624 and owned two Africans. By the time John Winthrop, later the colony's governor, arrived in 1630, Africans had been living and working in Massachusetts for some time.

Landing at Jamestown, 1619. Prints and Photographs Division, Library of Congress

56 • Slave Trade Latecomers

North Americans were relative latecomers to the slave trade, which had been under way for two hundred years before it became a factor in the development of North America. For the most part, Americans were not involved in the slave trade until the middle of the eighteenth century. This was largely because of the relatively late development of a plantation agricultural system in North America.

57 • The Royal African Company

The formation of the Royal African Company dramatically altered the slave trade to North America. Before its incorporation, British North Americans had to get their slaves from other carriers—Portuguese, Dutch, or French—who had direct contact and bases in Africa. But with the incorporation first of the Royal Adventurers in 1663, and its later incarnation as the RAC in 1672, the British colonies could obtain slaves directly from British traders. Even then, the percentage of slaves coming to British North America was very small. Before the beginning of the eighteenth century, British North America received only a tiny percentage of all slaves being transported by the British to the New World. Most went to the British West Indies, especially Jamaica, which took fully one-third.

58 • Tobacco Cultivation Demanded Slave Labor

It was the successful cultivation of tobacco in Virginia and Maryland that created a demand for labor and ultimately a lucrative trade in slaves to North America in the late seventeenth century. As tobacco shipments to England increased in volume to 105 million pounds in 1771, the demand for slaves increased as well. Tobacco cultivation is extremely labor-intensive, and the tobacco farmers could not persuade enough Englishmen to migrate to North America, so they turned to African labor.

59 • Rice Cultivation

The cultivation of rice in eighteenth-century South Carolina, North Carolina, and Georgia was, like tobacco, a stimulus for the Atlantic slave trade. Rice required not only intensive labor but also agricultural skills that few Englishmen had. People with growing skills from West and Central Africa were especially sought by tobacco planters, and there is considerable evidence that enslaved Africans taught the slave owners how to cultivate rice, since rice did not grow in the colder climate of Great Britain.

60 • Variations in North American Slavery

The daily life of enslaved Africans in North America varied according to what region they

lived in and what type of crop they cultivated. The most common system, the "gang-labor method," was found in regions growing tobacco and cotton. Under this system, slaves worked the entire day in groups controlled by a driver or overseer. In South Carolina and Georgia, however, where rice was the predominant crop, a "task system" operated that allocated a certain amount of work to each slave per day. After a slave's task was completed, he could do what he wished with the rest of the day. Many slaves used this time to tend their own crops, which they used to supplement their diets, and if there was a surplus, to sell to other slaves or local traders. Corn, potatoes, tobacco, peanuts, sugar, watermelons, and pumpkins were commonly grown.

61 • Puritans Ardent Slave Traders

Once North Americans entered the international commerce in Africans, the Puritans of New England became some of the most ardent slave traders. After Captain William Pierce of Boston successfully traded captured Pequot Indians for Africans in the West Indies in 1638, other Boston merchants began a lucrative trade between New England and the West Indies. Then, in 1644, Boston traders launched direct trade with Africa to import slaves—a commerce that mushroomed during the eighteenth century, after the British Parliament revoked the Royal African Company's exclusive monopoly on the slave trade. By the middle of the eighteenth century New England had become the biggest slave-trading region in British North America.

62 • Triangle Trade

The slave trade was vital to the emergence of New England as a trading, shipbuilding, and manufacturing center in the eighteenth century. On the famous triangular trade route, New England ships transported food, lumber, horses, and manufactured goods to the West Indies, exchanged them for rum, and then sailed for Africa, where the rum bought Africans, who were transported back to the West Indies. Often, the routes would be altered to meet current demand; but the important fact was that such trade undergirded the rise of the incredibly profitable rum industry which "became New England's largest manufacturing business before the Revolution." By 1774 there were over one hundred distilleries in Rhode Island and Massachusetts, with those in the latter producing over 2.7 million gallons of rum. On the West African coast, New England rum was bartered and traded more than English, French, and Dutch alcohol, weapons, trinkets, or dry goods.

63 • Slave Trade Fuels War of Independence

Many of the conflicts that led to the War of Independence had their origin in the Atlantic slave trade. Parliament's passage of the Navigation Acts was designed to force colonial planters to do business exclusively with British merchants. In 1723 the British Parliament overturned a Virginia act that reduced the number of Africans being imported into the colony on the grounds that such action would hurt other aspects of British trade with the colonies. In 1764 the Parliament passed the Sugar Act, which attempted to control the growing North American trade with the French West Indies, whose sugar was part of the infamous triangle trade of rum, sugar, and slaves. Not surprisingly, the colony that protested the Sugar Act most vociferously was none other than Rhode Island—the colony most involved in slave trading.

64 • Trade Boycott as Resistance to British

Opposition to the British slave trade was one

way for the North American colonists to resist British colonialism. When the 1774 British Parliament imposed the Coercive Acts on the colonials to punish them for resistance to the earlier Townshend and Tea Acts, the colonists boycotted the British slave trade to America. The First Continental Congress made the slave trade a cornerstone of its resistance against the British when it suspended trade with Britain in 1774, declaring that after December 1, the British could no longer import slaves into the colonies. The resistance continued even after the War of Independence. One of the first acts of the Continental Congress in 1776 was to vote that "no slaves be imported into any of the thirteen United Colonies." Rather than humanity, the cause of this act was a desire to hurt Britain where the colonies knew it would hurt the mother country the most—in the slave trade.

George Mason. Prints and Photographs Division, Library of Congress

65 • English Profit from the Slave Trade

That resistance by North Americans hurt the British economic interest is certain:

The slave trade is "indeed the best Traffick the Kingdom hath," John Cary affirmed, "as it doth occasionally give so vast an Imployment to our People both by Sea and Land." It was "a Trade of the most Advantage to this kingdom of any we drive, and as it were all Profit." It was linked, of course, with the West Indian trade "and [I] do joyn them together because of their dependence on each other."

66 • Slave Trade Drove a Moral Wedge Between Britain and the Colonies

In 1772 the Virginia House of Burgess declared to King George III: "The importation of slaves into the colonies from the coast of Africa hath long been considered a trade of great inhumanity, and under its present encouragement, we have too much reason to fear will endanger the very existence of your Majesty's American dominions."

After the war, the anti-slavery advocate George Mason concluded that the slave trade "was one of the great causes of our separation from Great Britain."

67 • Original Draft of the Declaration of Independence

The anti-slave trade sentiment influenced Thomas Jefferson's first draft of the Declaration of Independence, in which he indicted the King of England, George III, for foisting the slave trade on the colonists. As originally written, the Declaration of Independence claimed that King George

has waged cruel war against human nature itself, violating its most sacred rights of life liberty in the persons of a distant people who never offended him, captivating and carrying them into slavery in another hemisphere, or to incur miserable death in their transportation thither. The piratical warfare, the opprobrium of infidel *powers, is the warfare of the* Christian *king of Great Britain. Determined to keep open a market where MEN should be bought and sold, he has prostituted his negative for suppressing every legislative attempt to prohibit or to restrain this execrable commerce.*

But the Continental Congress struck this passage from the Declaration. Most likely, Congress did not wish to list slavery in the Declaration for fear that after the war, the new nation might be called on to abolish slavery. Moreover, Jefferson's characterization of slavery and the slave trade as being forced upon the colonists was a half-truth at best: the colonists avidly pursued the slave trade and slavery on their own and had not been blocked by the king from ending the slave trade. The passage remains significant, however, for showing that Jefferson, contrary to some later interpretations, did regard Africans as "MEN . . . bought and sold" who were subject to the Declaration's principles that all men "are created equal, that they are endowed by their Creator with certain unalienable Rights, that among these are Life, Liberty, and the pursuit of Happiness."

68 • Slavery Purchased America's Freedom

While the colonists resisted the British slave trade, they actually benefited from the slave system that depended on the trade. As one historian puts it, Americans actually purchased their freedom with products grown by slaves and then traded to the French during the War of Independence. Before the war, agricultural products such as rice, indigo, and tobacco—all produced by enslaved Africans—were British America's most valuable exports. Without the slave trade and slavery, British North America would never have been able to generate the wealth to gain its freedom from England, at least in the eighteenth century. As a member of the British Parliament acknowledged after the war: "I know not why we should blush to confess that molasses [produced by sugar cultivated by slaves] was an essential ingredient of American independence."

69 • States Dispute Slave Trade Limitations After Independence

Although the colonies made much of the inhumanity of the British slave trade during the conflict with England, the United States could not immediately agree to end the slave trade after the war was over. Virginia, along with several other states, voted to prohibit the future importation of slaves. But South Carolina and Georgia frustrated the effort by threatening to not join the Union if the slave trade was prohibited. The rest of the states capitulated in the interest of unity. But the agreement that the United States would not limit the slave trade before 1808 became the outer limit of tolerance for continuation of the slave trade.

70 • Fear of Rebellion Caused Slave Trade Limitations

South Carolina stopped importing slaves during the War of Independence, partly because it feared the huge concentrations of slaves already in the state and the possibility of a slave rebellion like that which was shaking St. Domingue, now known as Haiti. But in 1803 South Carolina reopened the slave trade to grab

as many slaves as it could before the national prohibition of slave trading went into effect in 1808. The new ability to resell slaves in the recently acquired Louisiana Territory also influenced the decision to reopen the slave trade.

71 • British North American Slave Trade Grows

In the period 1701–1810 the United States (and beforehand, British North America) imported only 5.8 percent of the slaves arriving in the Western Hemisphere and slightly more than 20 percent of the slaves that entered British American territories, including the West Indies. As the eighteenth century progressed, however, the American share of the British trade increased, and by the 1740s its trade in slaves exceeded that of Barbados. By 1760 Jamaica's preeminent role in the trade was challenged. In the last years of the slave trade, from 1761 to 1808, the United States received more than 166,900 slaves. Though a late starter in the trade and always a lesser destination for British imported slaves, British North America was quite a significant recipient of enslaved people in the second half of the eighteenth century.

72 • Diseases of Tropics and Sugar Cultivation Increase Slave Mortality

American reliance on the slave trade was relatively low compared to other New World slave societies for one particular reason: the high rate of natural increase of the African American population in British North America, in contrast to the low rate found in the British West Indies. "From 1700 to 1780 the Black population increased twice as rapidly as the rate of importation. In the year 1790 the Negro population stood at 757,000, and by that time perhaps no more than one-half that number of Negroes had been imported." By contrast, Jamaica, Barbados, and the Leeward Islands "held a population of about 387,000, although perhaps 1,230,000 had been imported. Diseases of the tropics and rigors of sugar cultivation exacted a heavy toll in the Caribbean." It was not climate, but the conditions of sugar cultivation and diseases in the tropics, that accounted for the demographic "holocaust" of the British West Indies.

73 • Britain and the United States Abolish Slave Trade

In 1807 Lord Grenville's bill to abolish the slave trade passed the House of Lords and the House of Commons, and was approved by the British crown. That same year, the United States Congress responded to President Jefferson's December 1806 annual message against the "violation" of the slave trade by passing a law prohibiting Americans from involvement in the international slave trade. But it was Britain that aggressively suppressed the slave trade with its powerful navy. Although abolitionist sentiment in Britain played a prominent role in the movement to end the trade, it succeeded in part because of the decline of mercantilism, the reduced profitability of plantation slavery, and the rise of industrialism in England.

74 • Slave Trade Continues

Despite British and American action against the slave trade, the forced migration of Africans continued. From 1780 to 1867, in the period when slave trading was reputedly in decline, more than 5 million Africans—roughly half of the total who arrived in the Americas—were removed forcibly from Africa to the Western Hemisphere. Because the United States possessed a largely self-reproducing slave population after 1800, the U.S. was not the major market for slave trading in the 1800s. But the expansion of sugar plantations in Cuba and coffee planta-

tions in Brazil during the 1800s kept demand for imported slaves high, and illegal slavers continued to meet that demand.

FROM SLAVERY TO FREEDOM

Rebellions

75 • Haitian Revolution Extends Slave Trade End

Britain might have outlawed the slave trade before 1808 if it had not been for the Haitian Revolution. That revolution effectively ended sugar production on St. Domingue (Haiti), a French colony, thereby increasing the value of sugar from the British West Indies. Profits to be made from sugar cultivation soared, and so did the demand for more slaves to work British West Indian plantations. Thus, in 1792, the House of Commons agreed only to the principle that the slave trade ought to be ended, and did not abolish the trade until 1808, four years after the Haitian Revolution was over.

76 • Internal Slave Trade—Rebellion

On October 25, 1841, 135 Blacks were put aboard the *Creole* in Hampton Roads, Virginia, for transfer to New Orleans. On November 7, as the boat neared the Bahamas, the slaves attacked the crew, appropriated all the weapons on board, and retrieved the documents that committed them to slavery. Forcing the crew to take them to an English colony, the ship arrived in Nassau on November 9. Boats piloted by Bahamian Blacks surrounded the ship in the Nassau harbor, permitting the slaves to escape.

77 • Amistad Rebellion

The most famous on-board slave rebellion in U.S. history was the Amistad Incident of 1839. On July 1 of that year, a group of Africans who had been illegally imported to Cuba murdered the captain and took control of the Spanish ship

Death of Captain Ferrer aboard the *Amistad*. Prints and Photographs Division, Library of Congress

Death of Capt. Ferrer, the Captain of the Amistad, July, 1839.

Don Jose Ruiz and Don Pedro Montez, of the Island of Cuba, having purchased fifty-three slaves at Havana, recently imported from Africa, put them on board the Amistad, Capt. Ferrer, in order to transport them to Principe, another port on the Island of Cuba. After being out from Havana about four days, the African captives on board, in order to obtain their freedom, and return to Africa, armed themselves with cane knives, and rose upon the Captain and crew of the vessel. Capt. Ferrer and the cook of the vessel were killed; two of the crew escaped; Ruiz and Montez were made prisoners.

Amistad while it was transporting them from Havana to plantations in Puerto Príncipe, Cuba. Their leader, twenty-five-year-old Joseph Cinque, tried to direct the boat back to Africa, but their purchaser, Montes, steered a course for the United States, where the USS *Washington* captured the vessel and took it and the Africans to New London, Connecticut. The case became a cause célèbre and gained enormous public attention, not only for the captured Africans but also for the abolitionist movement, which assembled an excellent team of lawyers to keep the Africans from being returned to Spain. Eventually Cinque and his fellow Africans were allowed to return to Africa after former President John Quincy Adams successfully argued the Africans' case before the United States Supreme Court.

78 • Fears of Slave Rebellions

Rebellions frequently occurred in the slave trade, especially while ships waited at anchor on the coast. The captain of the *Albion-Frigate* discovered this when he mistakenly allowed his slaves the use of knives to eat meat. After breaking down the forecastle door and breaking off their shackles, the slaves killed several whites before the crew could counterattack and regain control of the ship. Twenty-eight slaves were either killed or jumped overboard to freedom.

79 • Description by an English Captain

An English captain wrote in 1693:

When our slaves are aboard we shackle the men two and two, while we lie in port, and in sight of their own country, for 'tis then they attempt to make their escape and mutiny; to prevent which we always keep centinels upon the hatchways, and have a chest full of small arms, ready loaden and primed, constantly lying at hand upon the quarter-deck, together with some granada shells; and two of our quarter deck guns, pointing on the deck thence, and two more out of steerage.

80 • National Loyalty in Rebellions

The danger of rebellion on a slave ship increased dramatically if all or almost all of the slaves on board were from the same African nation or could speak the same language. The belief existed among slave ship captains that some peoples were more volatile and more revolutionary than others. People along the Gold Coast were considered to be particularly warlike and hateful of other Africans. Ship captains often put this knowledge to good use. "We have some 30 or 40 gold coast negroes, which we buy . . . to make guardians and overseers of the Whidaw negroes, and sleep among them to keep them from quarreling; and in order, as well as to give us notice, if they can discover any caballing or plotting among them, which trust they will discharge with great diligence."

81 • Rebellions in North America

Unlike rebellions in South America and the Caribbean, those that occurred in British North America had almost no chance of success. Slaves faced a numerically superior white population in all of the southern states, with the exception of South Carolina. Even when not outnumbered, slaves were poorly armed, usually with only sticks and knives, since slaves were prohibited from bearing arms as early as the late seventeenth century. Nevertheless, slaves still plotted and rebelled against southern slavery, even when it meant certain death.

82 • Revolt Causing 1712 Slave Act

In 1712 a slave revolt threatened to destroy New York City. In April twenty to thirty African

American slaves, along with two Indians, set fire to a building and ambushed several whites who came to put out the flames. When nine whites were killed and at least five more wounded, a general alarm was sounded and soldiers were brought to the scene. Within a day, the slaves' rebellion had been overcome and most of the rebels captured, except those who committed suicide. Following a trial, twenty-one slaves were executed for their participation. As a result of the revolt, New York passed the 1712 Slave Act to suppress insurrections, Massachusetts enacted a law against further importation of slaves into that colony, and Pennsylvania instituted high taxes to restrain African importations.

83 • Garcia and Fort Negro

After the War of 1812, over three hundred Blacks occupied an abandoned British fort on the banks of the Apalachicola River in what is now Florida. Known as Fort Negro, it was headed by an African American man named Garcia. The heavily armed fort became a symbol of Black independence and a threat to the southern slave system. The United States Government made destruction of the fort one of its highest priorities after the War of 1812. In the summer of 1816 the U.S. Navy and Army under Colonel Clinch surrounded Fort Negro and called on the community to surrender. Garcia refused. On July 27, 1816, an attack was launched, but the heavily fortified garrison repelled it. But a second attack succeeded in hitting the ammunition supply, and the fort exploded. Only sixty-four of the three hundred Blacks survived the blast, and only three of the sixty-four were uninjured. Garcia, unhurt, was executed by firing squad. The remaining survivors were returned to slavery.

84 • Slaves Blamed for Fires

Many suspicious or unexplained fires in southern and northern towns were attributed to rebellious slaves. On February 28, 1741, fearful whites in New York City regarded a series of fires as a sign that a slave rebellion was about to begin. Fueled by rumors of a plot, whites rampaged in New York and attacked the Black population. Thirteen Blacks were burned alive, eighteen hanged, seventy shipped to the West Indies, and thirty-three released for a conspiracy that was never proved to have existed. Setting fires was, however, a tactic favored by resistant slaves because it allowed the violent destruction of property valued by whites while avoiding a direct confrontation with slave owners. In the 1790s fires in Charleston, Albany, New York City, Savannah, and Baltimore were blamed on Blacks, and in 1803 Blacks in York, Pennsylvania, attempted to burn major sections of the city after a court convicted a Black woman of attempting to poison two whites. Eleven buildings were destroyed before the militia arrived and enforced a curfew.

85 • Slave Vandalism

The slaves destroyed tirelessly. Like the peasants in the Jacquerie or the Luddite wreckers, they were seeking their salvation in the most obvious way, the destruction of what they knew was the cause of their sufferings; and if they destroyed much it was because they suffered much.

86 • The Stono Rebellion

On September 9, 1739, approximately twelve slaves revolted at Stono, South Carolina, some twenty miles southwest of Charleston. Led by a recently arrived Angolan slave, the group killed two white men guarding a warehouse, took weapons they found inside, and marched south-

ward to escape to freedom in St. Augustine, Spanish Florida. As they marched, other Blacks joined the group, which swelled to more than seventy-five people. Unfortunately for the marchers, they were discovered by a Colonel Bull, lieutenant governor of the colony, who, after narrowly escaping capture by the rebels, rode off to sound the alarm. Bull returned with an armed militia which engaged the slaves, who had stopped ten miles from Stono, in a battle that decimated the rebel force. Some rebels escaped, but most were eventually caught. Twenty-five whites and fifty Africans were killed in the battle. The Stono Rebellion led to a temporary decline in the importation of Africans into a colony that was already described as a "Negro country."

87 • How Toussaint l'Ouverture Led Haitian Revolution

The Haitian Revolution, which began on August 22, 1791, and ended on January 1, 1804, was the only rebellion to liberate an entire slave population. Inspired by the ideals of the French Revolution, slaves on St. Domingue succeeded in overthrowing the white planter class, repulsing the French Army, and defeating Spanish and British forces (the latter invading the island in 1793). The Haitian Revolution's success was largely attributable to its outstanding leader, General Toussaint l'Ouverture, who outwitted all three European forces with tactics that foreshadowed modern guerrilla warfare. The island's mountainous terrain, the spread of yellow fever and malaria among the French, British, and Spanish, and the conflicts among whites and mulattoes on the island enabled this revolution to succeed where others did not. In addition, the huge numerical superiority of slaves ensured success. Though l'Ouverture did not live to see the end of the revolution, its success proved that Africans could achieve self-determination in the New World and gave a hope of freedom to millions of slaves in the Western Hemisphere.

Toussaint l'Ouverture. Prints and Photographs Division, Library of Congress

88 • Gabriel's Attack on Richmond, Virginia

When a twenty-four-year-old slave named Gabriel Prosser organized a large-scale attack on the city of Richmond in 1800, the entire state of Virginia was shocked. Owned by the barbaric Thomas H. Prosser of Henrico County, Virginia, Gabriel was a six-foot-two-inch man, who in the spring of 1800 began studying the layout of Richmond, recording the location of arms and ammunition, and stockpiling swords, pikes, and bayonets. Gabriel planned to organize slaves into three columns, one to take and hold the city, another to grab arms and ammunition at

the city's powder magazine, and another to kill all those who tried to stop them. When Gabriel communicated his plan to numerous slaves, two informed their master, who in turn alerted Governor James Monroe. Even though Monroe amassed six hundred troops in the capital, the one thousand slaves that Gabriel assembled outside of Richmond still had a chance to disrupt the city. But a violent thunderstorm that evening washed out a crucial bridge and the slave army broke up. In the following days, hundreds of Blacks were murdered or arrested. Gabriel was captured in Norfolk on September 25. Neither Gabriel nor his lieutenants would divulge their plans, even in the face of death, and all were executed.

89 • Trial a Mockery?

Gabriel Prosser at his trial for organizing a slave rebellion in 1800:

I have nothing more to offer than what George Washington would have had to offer, had he been taken by the British and put to trial by them. I have adventured my life in endeavoring to obtain the liberty of my countrymen, and am a willing sacrifice to their cause: and I beg, as a favour, that I may be immediately led to execution. I know that you have pre-determined to shed my blood, why then all this mockery of a trial?

90 • Henry Highland Garnet Encouraged Resistance

Some Black militants, like Henry Highland Garnet, exalted:

Brethren, arise, arise! Strike for your lives and liberties. Now is the day and the hour. Let every slave throughout the land do this and the days of slavery are numbered. Rather die freemen than live to be slaves. . . . Awake, Awake, no oppressed people have secured their liberty without resistance.

Henry Highland Garnet. Prints and Photographs Division, Library of Congress

91 • Revolt Led by Dislondes

On January 8, 1811, some thirty-five miles from New Orleans, a group of four hundred to five hundred slaves led by Charles Dislondes, a free mulatto from St. Domingue, revolted on the plantation of Major Andry, wounding the major and killing his son. Arming themselves initially with axes, knives, and clubs, the slaves eventually obtained firearms and marched from plantation to plantation in St. Charles and St. John the Baptist Parishes, wreaking havoc and sending whites fleeing to New Orleans. The next day Major Andry recovered enough to lead eight to ten heavily armed planters against the slaves, whom he claimed he slaughtered in great numbers. Actually it was the arrival of four hundred militiamen and sixty U.S. Army regulars from New Orleans, under the command of Brigadier General Wade Hampton, that routed the slave army. Sixty-six slaves were killed, sixteen more were captured, but seventeen escaped into the woods to die or find freedom. All those captured

were executed in the most brutal manner, with the heads of some displayed on the road from Andry's plantation to New Orleans as a message to other would-be rebel slaves.

92 • Denmark Vesey's 1822 Conspiracy

Denmark Vesey's 1822 conspiracy sent fear throughout the South. Vesey was an African-born seaman and former slave who had purchased his freedom and who carried himself as a prideful freeman. Vesey was intelligent, spoke many languages, and chastised other Blacks for obsequious behavior toward whites. Inspired by the Bible description of how the children of Israel were delivered out of Egypt from bondage, Vesey constructed a complex plan to overthrow the city of Charleston on July 14. He enlisted several lieutenants from the artisan class of slaves to spread the word carefully among only trusted slaves, not house servants. Vesey divided his army into divisions according to their presumed African tribal heritage and planned a six-pronged attack on Charleston. When a slave revealed the plan to white planters, two of Vesey's lieutenants were arrested on May 31 and Vesey advanced the day of the attack to June 16 to thwart his enemies. But on June 14 a Charleston slave spied on fellow slaves and revealed to his master that a revolt was planned. Vesey and other conspirators were arrested, and they were hanged on July 2, ironically for acts of rebellion that never occurred.

93 • Slaves Betraying Slaves

Many rebellions were thwarted because slaves told their masters about plots. Some betrayed their fellow slaves because it was one of the surest ways to obtain one's own freedom. One such informer betrayed an 1816 slave rebellion in Camden County and the South Carolina legislature purchased his freedom from his master for the sum of $1,100. Devany Prioleau, who revealed plans of the Denmark Vesey conspiracy, obtained his freedom and an annual pension of $50, which was raised to $250 in 1857.

94 • Rise and Take Your Freedom!

Some African Americans, mostly free people in the North, openly advocated violence as the best way for slaves to obtain their freedom. In 1829 *David Walker's Appeal,* a seventy-six-page inflammatory pamphlet, called on slaves to rise and kill their masters. "Remember Americans," Walker, the self-taught, dark-skinned tradesman wrote, "that we must and shall be free and enlightened as you are, will you wait until we shall, under God, obtain our liberty by the crushing arm of power? Will it not be dreadful for you? I speak Americans for your own good." Some attributed Walker's suspicious death in 1830 to the retribution of slavery supporters, but it did not end the influence of the pamphlet, which became a kind of bible to revolutionary-minded Black abolitionists of the period.

95 • Nat Turner's Rebellion

Not long after David Walker issued his radical appeal, the bloodiest slave revolt in U.S. history occurred: Nat Turner's rebellion in Southampton, Virginia, in 1831. Nat was a mystical slave who could read and write, and who interpreted the eclipse of the sun on February 12 as a sign from God that he should "arise and prepare myself . . . to slay my enemies . . . with their own weapons." Nat confided his plans only to four trusted slave allies until it was too late for them to be betrayed; then, on the evening of August 21, Turner and his band began their reign of terror by killing all white people they encountered, be-

Discovery of Nat Turner. Prints and Photographs Division, Library of Congress

ginning with Nat's master's family. The group gathered weapons, provisions, horses, and additional slaves. By August 23 the band consisted of seventy slaves, and they had slain more than fifty-seven white men, women, and children. When some in Turner's group went to recruit more slaves, Turner's party was attacked by whites. Though Turner's force initially repulsed this attack, reinforcements for the white forces eventually overwhelmed the group. As Turner's forces scattered, hundreds of white volunteers and militia rushed to the area and began massacring Blacks indiscriminately. Turner eluded capture for months by living in a little cave in the ground near his former home, until he was discovered by Benjamin Phipps on October 30. Unlike Gabriel Prosser and Denmark Vesey, Turner spoke openly during his trial about his role in the uprising. He pleaded not guilty, however, because "he did not feel so," having been directed by God. He was hanged on November 11.

96 • White Newspaper Comments on Nat Turner

Even a white newspaper could treat the subject of Nat Turner with cold sympathy:

Nat seems very humble; willing to answer any questions, indeed quite communicative, and I am disposed to think tells the truth. I heard him speak more than an hour. He readily avowed his motive; confessed that he was the prime instigator of the plot, that he alone opened his master's doors and struck his master the first blow with a hatchet. He clearly verified the accounts which have been given of him. He is a shrewd, intelligent fellow. [Richmond Whig]

97 • Nat Turner's Remains

The bodies of those executed, with one exception, were buried in a decent and becoming manner. That of Nat Turner was delivered to the doctors, who skinned it and made grease of the flesh. Mr. R. S. Barham's father owned a money purse made of his hide. His skeleton was for many years in the possession of Dr. Massenberg, but has since been misplaced.

—William Sidney Drewry

98 • Fear of Rebellions

To those who lived in the midst of slavery, "It is like a smothered volcano—we know not when, or where, the flame will burst forth but we know that death in the most horrid forms threatens us. Some have died, others have become deranged from apprehension since the South Hampton affair" (Mrs. Lawrence Lewis, niece of George Washington, to Mayor Harrison Gray Otis of Boston, October 17, 1831).

99 • Religious Slaves Fomented Rebellions

Sometimes the most religious slaves fomented rebellions. A local paper, writing about

the 1816 Conspiracy in Camden County, South Carolina, reported that "those who were most active in the conspiracy occupied a respectable stand in one of the churches, several were professors, and one a class leader."

100 • Hidden Slave Rebellions

If individual acts of revolt are included, it is unknown exactly how many slave revolts occurred in the United States. Hundreds of acts of physical resistance, poisonings, stabbings, shootings, house and plantation burnings, and acts of vengeance must have gone unreported or unrecognized as revolts.

Robert Smalls. Brady Collection, Library of Congress

101 • Frederick Douglass Resists Covey's Brutality

A typical example of individual rebellion was Frederick Douglass's act of resistance against Covey, the "Negro breaker." Douglass's master had hired him out for a year to Covey because Douglass was becoming a difficult slave. Covey succeeded in brutalizing Douglass to such an extent that Douglass ran away and hid in the woods. When he returned to Covey's farm on Sunday, Covey was friendly and forgiving. But on Monday morning, Covey grabbed Douglass in the barn and tried to tie him up, presumably for a whipping. In a split second, Douglass determined to resist, to strike no blow, but to parry all of Covey's and refuse to be beaten. After an hour of wrestling, during which Covey became exhausted trying to beat the younger and stronger Douglass, Covey withdrew and told him, "now, don't you let me get hold of you again." Douglass knew Covey spoke the truth—for Covey had been bested by his young slave. Even more remarkably, Covey never turned Douglass over to the authorities for resisting a white man, an act punishable by death. Admitting that Douglass had successfully resisted him, however, would have destroyed Covey's reputation and business as a Negro breaker. In numerous other instances, it must have been difficult for whites to admit to having been bested by their slaves.

102 • Slave Appointed Navy Captain of Stolen Ship

Rebellious slaves were found even within the Confederate Army. During the Civil War, the Confederacy often used slaves as crew members of its ships, and in at least one instance, the practice backfired. In 1862 the slave pilot Robert Smalls of the steamship *Planter,* along with other slave members of the crew, stole the ship out of the Charleston harbor. Smalls was able to navigate the ship northward into Union hands. As a reward for his accomplishment and in recognition of his skill, Smalls was made captain of the *Planter* when it again set sail under the Union flag.

103 • Punishment of Slaves Pleases God?

I am now to acquaint you that very lately we have had a very wicked and barbarous plott of the designe of the negroes rising with a designe to destroy all the white people in the country and then to take the town [Charles Town] in full body but it pleased God it was discovered and many of them taken prisoners and some burnt some hang'd and some banish'd.

—Anonymous letter to Mr. Boone in London, June 24, 1720

Runaways

104 • The First Runaways

Since the first arrival of Africans to British North America, enslaved men and women have attempted to escape bondage by running away. In the seventeenth century Black and white indentured servants often tried to escape together. In 1640 a Black slave who, with six white indentured servants, tried to steal a small ship stocked with food and weapons was charged with conspiracy to escape. That same year a Black servant ran away with two white servants and was sentenced to lifetime servitude for his action.

105 • Successful Runaways Living in Maroon Colonies

Until recently, Maroon colonies, or settlements of runaway slaves, were thought only to have existed in the Caribbean or South America. Certainly, the quilombos, as they were called in Brazil, and the Maroon colonies of the Dutch and British West Indies lasted longer, were larger, and were able to be more self-sustaining in terms of agriculture, and later, trade, than any such settlements in the United States. The Palmares Maroon colony in Brazil, which numbered thousands of runaway slaves, successfully fought off Portuguese troops that attempted to capture it, and forced the Portuguese to negotiate treaties with them. Similarly, Maroon colonies in Surinam maintained their independence for three hundred years and their descendants live today as the Djulea and Saramaccan peoples.

106 • Recapture of Maroon Colonies

Maroon colonies on the scale of those found in the Caribbean and Latin America did not exist in the United States. Nevertheless, in eighteenth-century Spanish Florida, smaller Maroon colonies, made up of runaway slaves and Indians, survived and maintained their independence until the Creek war of 1813. Other Maroon colonies made up of a dozen or more slaves existed in various southern communities into the nineteenth century and posed an annoying threat to the southern slave regime. In 1729, for example, a group of Virginia slaves escaped into the Blue Ridge Mountains, carrying guns, ammunition, and agricultural supplies. Their presence posed such a temptation to other slaves that eventually a small army of white men was raised and sent into the mountains where, after a fierce battle, the slaves were recaptured.

107 • Maroon Slaves Rather Die Than Be Captured

In Cabarrus County, North Carolina, a ferocious battle erupted in March 1811 when a band of slave catchers discovered a group of fugitive slaves. The fugitive slaves had established a Maroon colony in the area and had already declared their willingness to die rather than be captured and returned to slavery. In the battle that resulted, two African Americans were killed, one injured, and two African American women were captured.

108 • Black Seminoles

Many slaves of South Carolina and Georgia escaped bondage in the eighteenth century by running away to Florida, where, in the marshes and swamps of this Spanish colony, they eluded capture. These runaways eventually bonded with Indian survivors of local wars from the Creek and Cherokee Nations. Known as the Seminole Indians, they created a new ethnic group, the Black Seminoles, and numbered over 100,000 before 1750. Fiercely independent and excellent scouts and traders, the Black Seminoles assumed a prominent role as scouts in the Mexican War of the late 1840s. But their valor and loyalty to the nation were not rewarded with the land promised them, and they were eventually forced onto reservations in Florida and, later, Oklahoma.

109 • Fugitive Slave Act of 1793

In 1793 the United States Congress passed the Fugitive Slave Act that placed the authority of the federal government behind the recovery of slaves by masters. In a clear victory for the South, the law made it more difficult for slaves to escape bondage by allowing masters to follow slaves to the North, capture suspected fugitives, bring them before a judge, and claim them as

Slaves escaping from eastern shore of Maryland. Prints and Photographs Division, Library of Congress

escaped slaves. If convinced, the judge could award the slaves to their master without a trial or opportunity for the enslaved persons to present witnesses. Ironically, because the law was so tilted in favor of the master, it provoked considerable support and sympathy for runaway slaves in the North and led some whites to assist runaways in the underground railroad.

110 • Drapetomania

"Drapetomania, or the Disease Causing Negroes to Run Away" was how one southern doctor, Samuel Cartwright of the University of Louisiana, explained the fact that hundreds of African Americans were fleeing southern plantations in the 1840s. They must be sick! Apparently it did not occur to Dr. Cartwright that it might be slavery that made Black people flee to the North.

111 • Escape to Freedom Seemed Formidable

To look at the map and observe the proximity of Eastern Shore, Maryland, to Delaware and Pennsylvania, it may seem to the reader quite absurd to regard the proposed escape as a formidable undertaking. But to understand, *some one has said, a man must* stand under. *The real distance was great enough, but the imagined distance was, to our ignorance, much greater. Slaveholders sought to impress their slaves with a belief in the boundlessness of slave territory, and of their own limitless power. Our notions of the geography of the country were very vague and indistinct. The distance, however, was not the chief trouble, for the nearer were the lines of a slave state to the borders of a free state the greater was the trouble. Hired kidnappers infested the borders. Then, too, we knew that merely reaching a free state did not free us, that wherever caught we could be returned to slavery. We knew of no spot this side the ocean where we could be safe.*

—Frederick Douglass

112 • Ellen and William Craft

A talent for cross-dressing and masquerade helped Ellen and William Craft escape from slavery. Around 1847 the two Georgia slaves hit upon the idea of traveling as master and slave, with Ellen Craft, who was light-skinned enough to be mistaken for white, posing as a sickly gentleman. Putting on a man's black suit, cloak, and high-heeled boots, Ellen hid her beardless face by muffling it because of a feigned toothache. Unable to read or write, she placed her arm in a sling as if broken so she would not be asked to sign the register at hotels. She also pretended to be deaf in order to limit having to speak in her natural voice. All of these stratagems worked to perfection, as they were treated as gentleman and slave in first-class hotels in Charleston and in Richmond. But in Baltimore they were almost discovered when officials demanded that Ellen post a bond for William, since a bond was required "for all negroes applying for tickets to go North." But the quick-thinking William objected that he had to travel with his young master to care for him because of his very delicate health, which already threatened to cause the young man's demise before he could reach expert medical treatment in Philadelphia. This overcame the objections and the Crafts made it safely first to Philadelphia and then, after resting awhile, to Boston, where they openly told their story. The story of the escape was celebrated throughout the North and the South, but it also elicited the wrath of their owners, who sent slave catchers to Boston to retrieve them after the Fugitive Slave Act of 1850 was passed. William and Ellen Craft again fled for their lives, this time to London, where they remained until after the Civil War, when they returned, and purchased a plantation outside of Savannah, Georgia, near their old home.

113 • The Obstacles to a Slave's Escape

It is impossible for me now to recollect all the perplexing thoughts that passed through my mind during that forenoon; it was a day of heartaching to me. But I distinctly remember the two great difficulties that stood in the way of my flight: I had a father and mother whom I dearly loved,—I had also six sisters and four brothers on the plantation. The question was, shall I hide my purpose from them? Moreover, how will my flight affect them when I am gone? Will they not be suspected? Will not the whole family be sold off as a disaffected family? But a still more trying question was, how can I expect to succeed, I have no knowledge of distance or direction. I know that Philadelphia is a free state, but I know not where its soil begins, or where that of Maryland ends? Indeed, at this time there was no safety in Pennsylvania, New Jersey, or New York, for a fugitive, except in lurking-places. . . .

Within my recollection no one had attempted to escape from my master; but I had many cases in my mind's eye, of slaves of other planters who had failed, and who had been made examples of the most cruel treatment, by flogging and selling to the far South, where they were never to see their friends more. I was not without serious apprehension that such would be my fate. But the hour was now come, and the man must act and be free, or remain a slave for ever. How the impression came to be upon my mind I cannot tell; but there was a strange and horrifying belief, that if I did not meet the crisis that day, I should be self-doomed—that my ear would be nailed to the door-post for ever.

—James W. C. Pennington, *The Fugitive Blacksmith* (London, 1849)

114 • Fugitive Slave Act of 1850

As part of the Compromise of 1850, Congress passed a more aggressive Fugitive Slave Act that made it relatively easy for masters of slaves to reclaim them. The Fugitive Slave Act stated that a slave owner had to simply produce an affidavit that he or she had ownership of a slave, bring the affidavit to a judge, along with the slave, and the reputed slave would be remanded by the judge to the slaveholder's custody. The law also demanded that all sheriffs and marshals assist those who came North looking for fugitives and provided for the imprisonment, as an enemy of the government, of any person who assisted a runaway. Although the law was included in the Compromise of 1850 to satisfy the South that the North would cooperate in the return of fugitive slaves, the law so angered northerners, who resented the invasion of the North to serve the interests of slave owners, that opposition to slavery became even more fierce and widespread.

115 • First Arrested

The first person arrested under the Fugitive Slave Act of 1850 was James Hamlet, who was seized in New York and returned to the South by slave catchers. Although no firm number exists as to the number of slaves captured under this law, it certainly spread fear among the escaped slave population in the North that despite the best efforts of their abolitionist friends, they could easily be taken back into slavery.

116 • Henry "Box" Brown

Perhaps the most imaginative method of escape from slavery was that devised by Henry "Box" Brown, who mailed himself to freedom. In 1856 Brown, a slave in Richmond, Virginia, ordered a box three feet by two by two feet eight inches deep and put in it a jug of water, a few

The resurrection of Henry "Box" Brown at Philadelphia. Prints and Photographs Division, Library of Congress

biscuits, and a bar to open the box from the inside. His friend James A. Smith addressed the box to William H. Johnson's Philadelphia home on Arch Street, and marked the exterior "Handle with Care" and "This Side Up." Twenty-six hours later, after traveling several miles upside down, Brown arrived in Philadelphia. Abolitionists alerted to the unique cargo had the box picked up from the delivery station and brought secretly to the office of the Anti-Slavery Society. After the assembled Anti-Slavery men pried off the top, up jumped Mr. Brown, who exclaimed, "How do you do, my gentlemen?"

117 • William Peel Jones

In 1859 William Peel Jones succeeded in transporting himself to freedom by steamship from Baltimore to Philadelphia. Jones was moved to action because his master had been selling off his slaves and had threatened the slave with putting him on the market soon. Like Henry "Box" Brown, Jones obtained a box; unfortunately, it was smaller than Brown's and forced Jones to keep his legs folded throughout the trip. Jones almost cried out in pain during his ocean journey, and he suffered such cold from the sea air as to give him constant chills. But such suffering was matched by the devotion of Jones's white ally in his endeavor, who not only mailed Jones in Baltimore but also traveled by land to Philadelphia, where his ally discovered the box on the boat. When the box was transported to safety and opened an hour later, the men rejoiced at their successful teamwork for many hours.

118 • The Theft of Solomon Northrop's Freedom

Often, freemen and freewomen of color were arrested and taken South into bondage. The most celebrated case of a freeman of color being captured and taken South into slavery occurred even before the 1850 Fugitive Slave Act was passed. In this instance, the slave catchers made no pretense of a legal right of ownership. Rather, Solomon Northrop had the unfortunate luck to be spotted by two slave catchers at an evening social playing the fiddle. Realizing that such a good fiddler would bring a handsome price in the South, the two men approached Northrop with a proposition: come to Baltimore and work as a free musician of color. Frustrated by the lack of work in the North, despite his excellent carpentry skills, Northrop agreed, only to awake one morning and find himself in chains. Sold to the highest bidder, Northrop spent twelve years in the Deep South, working on plantations, first as a field hand and then as an artisan slave. A white fellow carpenter who befriended Northrop took pity on him and delivered a letter to his white benefactor back home, who issued legal proceedings that eventually freed Northrop. After returning North, Solomon wrote his famous autobiography, *Twelve Years a Slave,* which became an abolitionist classic, since it was written by an educated free northern Black who had experienced slavery and exposed the conditions of life under which most southern slaves lived.

119 • The Christiana Tragedy

Although most escaped slaves simply fled when slave catchers came North trying to find them, some, as William Still, the Philadelphia conductor of the underground railroad put it, "loved liberty and hated Slavery, and when the slave-catchers arrived, they were prepared for them." Such was the case in Lancaster County, Pennsylvania, on September 11, 1851, when slave catchers tried to capture seven presumedly fugitive African Americans. An Edward Gorsuch, his son, and a small party of armed white men had camped outside a house near Christiana where Gorsuch believed slaves belonging to him were staying. After chasing a Black man back into the house, the party threatened to storm the house by force, even though Gorsuch admitted that the two men he had seen were not his slaves. Gorsuch, however, would not relent in his belief that his slaves were inside the house, even after a body of thirty armed Black men had gathered outside. When one of the Black men inside the house attempted to leave, Gorsuch fired on him, at which point the assembled Black group returned fire, and a fight ensued. When it was all over, Gorsuch was dead and his son seriously wounded, but the Black group sustained only flesh wounds. Despite clear evidence that the group had acted in self-defense, newspapers condemned the "resisting of a law of Congress by a band of armed negroes." Although several Blacks were rounded up and arrested, the two believed to be fugitive slaves escaped, with, according to some, the assistance of the United States marshal supervising the case.

120 • Runaway Reward

Not even passage of the Fugitive Slave Act of 1850 and its compulsion of northern law enforcement officials to help with recapture could replace what had always been the most effective way for slave owners to learn the whereabouts of fugitive slaves: offering a financial reward for information leading to the capture of a slave.

$200 Reward.

RANAWAY from the subscriber, on the night of Thursday, the 30th of Sepember,

FIVE NEGRO SLAVES,

To-wit: one Negro man, his wife, and three children.

The man is a black negro, full height, very erect, his face a little thin. He is about forty years of age, and calls himself *Washington Reed*, and is known by the name of Washington. He is probably well dressed, possibly takes with him an ivory headed cane, and is of good address. Several of his teeth are gone.

Mary, his wife, is about thirty years of age, a bright mulatto woman, and quite stout and strong.

The oldest of the children is a boy, of the name of FIELDING, twelve years of age, a dark mulatto, with heavy eyelids. He probably wore a new cloth cap.

MATILDA, the second child, is a girl, six years of age, rather a dark mulatto, but a bright and smart looking child.

MALCOLM, the youngest, is a boy, four years old, a lighter mulatto than the last, and about equally as bright. He probably also wore a cloth cap. If examined, he will be found to have a swelling at the navel.

Washington and Mary have lived at or near St. Louis, with the subscriber, for about 15 years.

It is supposed that they are making their way to Chicago, and that a white man accompanies them, that they will travel chiefly at night, and most probably in a covered wagon.

A reward of $150 will be paid for their apprehension, so that I can get them, if taken within one hundred miles of St. Louis, and $200 if taken beyond that, and secured so that I can get them, and other reasonable additional charges, if delivered to the subscriber, or to THOMAS ALLEN, Esq., at St. Louis, Mo. The above negroes, for the last few years, have been in possession of Thomas Allen, Esq., of St. Louis.

WM. RUSSELL.

ST. LOUIS, Oct. 1, 1847.

Prints and Photographs Division, Library of Congress

121 • Whites Assist Underground Railroad

Some of the most famous conductors on the underground railroad were white. Levi Coffin, a Quaker, assisted close to two thousand runaway slaves. He often hid runaways in a special compartment built in his house. Thomas Garrett turned his home in Wilmington, Delaware, into one of the most famous stations on the underground railroad. And the Canadian-born physician Alexander Ross made trips throughout the South and rescued slaves from

Fugitives arriving at Levi Coffin's Indiana farm. Prints and Photographs Division, Library of Congress

New Orleans, Richmond, Nashville, and Selma. Not only did whites risk their lives and rescue many slaves, but white participation in the movement gave the underground railroad respectability in the eyes of many whites that it would not have had otherwise.

122 • Harriet Tubman (1820?–1913)

Black conductors on the underground railroad were quite effective at one of the more dangerous activities: going South and making contact with slaves who wanted to flee slavery. The most famous of these conductors was Harriet Tubman, who made dozens of trips into the South, going onto plantations in a variety of disguises and bringing hundreds out of the South. Reportedly Tubman carried a gun with her and more than once threatened a slave who suddenly became frightened and wanted to turn back. Such methods kept Tubman from ever being discovered or captured. Leonard A. Grimes, another Negro conductor, was not so fortunate. Working as a cab operator in Washington, D.C., he used his carriage to deliver runaway slaves to freedom as well as to transport wealthy white passengers. But during one of his trips into Virginia, he was arrested for helping a runaway family escape and spent two years in a Richmond prison.

Harriet Tubman. Brady Collection, Prints and Photographs Division, Library of Congress

123 • Runaway Assistance

Thousands of largely anonymous African Americans assisted runaways by providing them with overnight housing and food. In addition, the independent Black churches played a vital role as stops along the underground railroad. This was especially important because many escaped slaves had a tremendous fear of white people and were apprehensive about being betrayed by whites offering to hide them from authorities. Ellen Craft, for example, was terrified when she and William Craft were housed with a white man, Barkley Ivers, after reaching Philadelphia. "I have no confidence whatever in white people," she reportedly told William, because "they are only trying to get us back into slavery."

124 • Runaway Meets Adult Brother He Never Knew Existed

A remarkable meeting that occurred in 1850 illustrates the effect of slavery on African American families. William Still, a conductor—and later, historian—of the underground railroad, was working as a clerk in the office of the Philadelphia Anti-Slavery Society when a recently freed slave named Peter walked in. Through a helpful white man, Peter had pur-

William Still. Prints and Photographs Division, Library of Congress

chased his freedom from his master and then traveled from Alabama to Pennsylvania in search of his parents, Levin and Cidney, who had earlier escaped from slavery but had been forced to leave Peter behind. As Peter relayed this story of his search to William Still, the latter became excited: William Still's own parents were named Levin and Cidney, and as Peter talked further, William realized that he was talking to his long-lost brother, whom he had never met.

125 • Douglass's Intellectual Migration

Often escape to the North was not enough to ensure a runaway's freedom. That was the case for Frederick Douglass, who, with the assistance of a free African American woman, Anna Murray, who became his wife, escaped from Baltimore by sea in September 1838 by posing as a free Black sailor. But after Douglass became an infamous speaker with William Lloyd Garrison on the abolitionist lecture circuit and authored an autobiography, *Narrative of the Life of Frederick Douglass* (1845), in which he identified his former owners, Douglass again had to flee, this time to England, to escape recapture. His trip to England in August 1845 was a huge success, as he lectured to crowds on the evils of slavery, and his conversations with English intellectuals and activists led to his liberation from the Garrisonian idea that moral suasion was the only way to end slavery. When Douglass returned to the United States in August 1847, a freeman after English friends had purchased his freedom, he moved his family to New York from the Garrisonian stronghold in Boston, started his own newspaper, the *North Star,* and eventually broke with Garrison to advocate political action as a means of bringing slavery to an end.

Colonization Movements

126 • Thomas Jefferson, the Nation's First Colonizationist

Thomas Jefferson was one of the earliest advocates of African American colonization. Jefferson doubted whether whites and Blacks could live together in a multiracial society after slavery. He believed that even the friends of Negro freedom would hesitate if emancipation meant amalgamation of the races. The only way to secure white support for emancipation, in his mind, was to link it to colonization of African Americans outside of the United States. In his *Notes on the State of Virginia,* originally published in 1782, Jefferson described a plan

to emancipate all slaves born after passing the

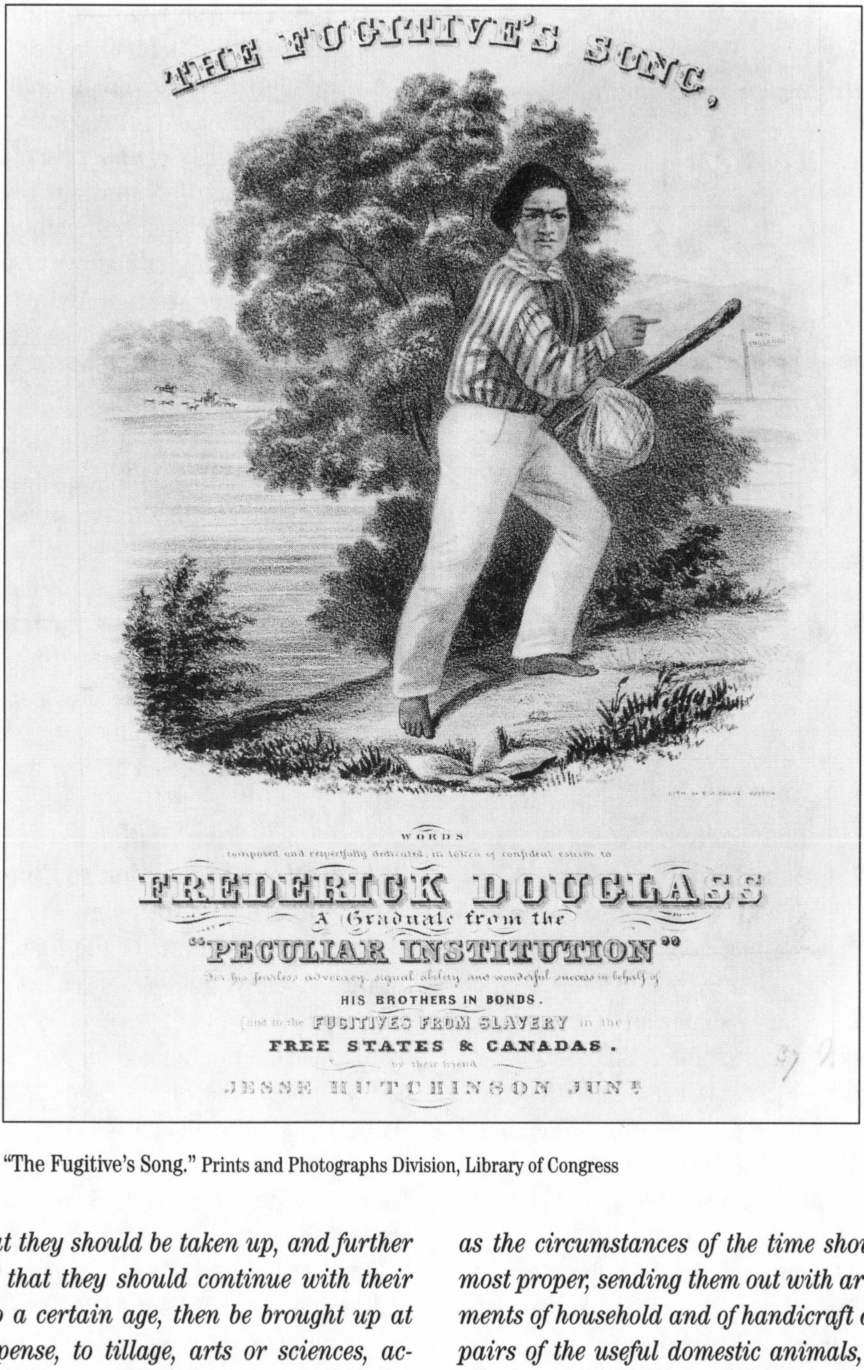

"The Fugitive's Song." Prints and Photographs Division, Library of Congress

act . . . that they should be taken up, and further directing, that they should continue with their parents to a certain age, then be brought up at public expense, to tillage, arts or sciences, according to their geniuses, till the females should be eighteen, and the males twenty-one years of age, when they should be colonized to such place as the circumstances of the time should render most proper, sending them out with arms, implements of household and of handicraft arts, seeds, pairs of the useful domestic animals, &c. to declare them a free and independent people, and extend to them our allegiance and protection, till they shall have acquired strength.

Paul Cuffee and his brig, *Traveller*. Prints and Photographs Division, Library of Congress

127 • Paul Cuffee, the First African-American Colonizer of Africa

The first man to successfully transport Black Americans to Africa was Paul Cuffee (1759–1817), a Black shipowner. Cuffee was a devout Quaker, and he wanted Blacks to return to Africa in order to help Christianize the continent. He was also a successful entrepreneur and saw colonization as a way to open trade with Africa. In addition, he wanted free Blacks to have the choice to return to Africa if they wished. Cuffee appealed to the federal government and free Blacks to support his plan, and he successfully transported thirty-eight African-Americans to Freetown, Sierra Leone.

128 • The American Colonization Society

A year before Paul Cuffee's death in 1817, the American Colonization Society was founded by white philanthropists, slave owners, and Henry Clay. Its goal was to find an outlet for free Blacks who were being manumitted by slave owners in the upper South after the turn of the century. The society transported 86 Blacks to Africa in 1820 and established the settlement of Liberia in 1822. By the end of the decade, the society had relocated 1,162 people to Africa at a cost of $100,000. Because revenue from subscriptions sold to the public was not enough to foot such expenses, Clay and the society lobbied Congress for financial support, but failed to get it. They did, however, receive $30,000 from the state of Virginia in 1850. By then, the society had spent $1.8 million to ship 10,000 African-Americans to Liberia, most of whom were former slaves who had been freed by their masters in order to be shipped out of the United States.

129 • Black Opposition to Colonization

Many free Blacks, including even Paul Cuffee, opposed the efforts of the American Colonization Society. Cuffee wanted emigration to open trade and help Africa and the settlers; but he did not like the implication that the society had to remove free Blacks from American society because they could not succeed and live amicably with whites in America, which was Thomas Jefferson's view. Some free Blacks thought the society was supported by those who believed that Blacks were biologically and socially inferior to whites and unassimilable into a free American society. Others believed that if the society gained federal support, free Blacks might be forced to repatriate to Africa. At the very least, many believed that the society

tended to undermine the antislavery effort by removing successful (and to white southerners, dangerous) free Blacks from the population. Ultimately colonization under the auspices of the ACS would threaten the efforts of abolitionists to bring a rapid end to slavery. Thus, many Black leaders organized national conventions against colonization.

130 • Douglass—We Are Here to Stay

We are of the opinion that the free *colored people generally mean to live in America, and not in Africa; and to appropriate a large sum for our removal would merely be a waste of the public money. We do not mean to go to Liberia. Our minds our made up to live here if we can, or die here if we must; so every attempt to remove us, will be, as it ought to be, labor lost. Here we are and here we shall remain. While our brethren are in bondage on these shores, it is idle to think of inducing any considerable number of the free colored people to quit this for a foreign land.*

For two hundred and twenty-eight years has the colored man toiled over the soil of America, under a burning sun and a driver's lash—plowing, planting, reaping, that white men might roll in ease, their hands unhardened by labor, and their brows unmoistened by the waters of genial toil, and now that the moral sense of mankind is beginning to revolt at this system of foul treachery and cruel wrong, and is demanding its overthrow, the mean and cowardly oppressor is mediating plans to expel the colored man entirely from the country. Shame upon the guilty wretches that dare propose and all that countenance such a proposition. We live here—have lived here—have a right to live here, and mean to live here.

—Frederick Douglass speech published in the *North Star,* January 26, 1849

131 • Peter Williams, a Black Minister, on Colonization

We are natives *of this country; we only ask that we be treated as well as* foreigners. *Not a few of our fathers suffered and bled to purchase its independence; we ask only to be treated as well as those who fought against it.*

132 • Black Leaders and William Lloyd Garrison

Black leaders in the antebellum North lobbied the famous white abolitionist William Lloyd Garrison to oppose colonization. "It was their united and strenuous opposition to the expatriation scheme that first induced Garrison and others to oppose it," commented Lewis Tappan, another famous white abolitionist.

133 • Blacks Drop "African" from the Names of Their Organizations

The American Colonization Society also had a more subtle, though no less profound effect on Black leaders and organizations in the antebellum North. Many of them dropped the word "African" from the names of their organizations and the letterheads of stationery, for fear that the use of "Africa" could be manipulated by colonizationists to imply that such Blacks or their organizations desired a return to Africa. Black churches and newspapers, for example, began to use terms such as "Colored American" in their titles.

134 • Abolitionist as Colonizationist

Some late-eighteenth- and early-nineteenth-century abolitionists supported the idea of colonizing African Americans outside of the United States. Benjamin Lundy, a respected abolitionist, even traveled to Upper Canada in January 1832 to scout a place to settle runaway slaves and free people of color from the United States.

He discovered that the Quakers had beat him to it. A settlement, Wilberforce Colony, already existed there, having been established some years earlier by the Society of Friends. Support of colonization was a moderate position of abolitionists before the 1840s that was consistent with their belief that emancipation and integration of the slaves into American society was not possible in the foreseeable future.

135 • Re-created America

Those African Americans who migrated to Liberia in the antebellum period did not leave their American culture behind. Indeed, they recreated an American lifestyle in Liberia. Most spoke the English language and built houses that resembled regal homes of the South. Indeed, the social life and customs of the migrants more closely resembled those of Victorian America than of West Africa. Many conceived of their role as that of a missionary bringing civilization to otherwise "backward" peoples.

136 • Colonization as Suppression of the Slave Trade

Efforts to expand Liberia before the Civil War were linked to efforts to suppress the continuing if illegal international trade in slaves. In 1849 Joseph Jenkins Roberts, the first Black president of Liberia, requested the United States to buy territories adjacent to Liberia so that his country could police the entire West Coast of Africa from Sierra Leone to Cape Calmas, thereby helping to end the international

House of Joseph Jenkins Roberts, first president of Liberia. Prints and Photographs Division, Library of Congress

slave trade. His proposal was rejected. But Congress did pass a law instructing the U.S. president to send a naval fleet to the coast of West Africa to capture slave ships and resettle Africans in bondage in Liberia. The president put this policy into motion, and by 1867 some 5,700 Africans had been resettled in Liberia.

137 • Emigration Sentiment in the 1850s

African American interest in emigration revived in the 1850s because of the passage of the Fugitive Slave Act, the South's zeal in pursuing runaway slaves, and the North's apparent acquiescence to slave power. Even those like Frederick Douglass who had opposed colonization in the past began to give colonization a second look. Others became convinced that the only salvation for African Americans lay outside of the territorial United States. Martin Delany, a Black doctor, seriously began to plan to transport African Americans to Africa, even though he opposed the work of the American Colonization Society. Rather than going to Liberia, Delany decided to try and establish a colony for emigrating African Americans in what is now Nigeria. Delany even traveled to Nigeria and signed a treaty with its Yoruba king, Abeokuta. But Delany's dream of an African American Nigeria foundered when the Civil War erupted and interest in emigration among American Blacks plummeted. Delany himself became a major in the U.S. Army.

138 • Abraham Lincoln Favored Colonization

At several points in his career, but especially in his annual address to Congress as president on December 1, 1862, Lincoln articulated his support for colonization by proposing an amendment to the Constitution to instruct Congress to appropriate money to colonize free Black people, "with their own consent, at any place or places without the United States." This amendment would accompany the amendment he also proposed to emancipate the slaves, and reflected his long-standing belief in the efficacy of colonization to solve the race problem. But in the same address, Lincoln sought to separate colonization from the arguments against free Blacks remaining in the United States. He discounted arguments that free Blacks would steal labor away from white laborers or demographically overwhelm the nation. He did believe that "deportation" of free Black labor would increase the demand for white labor, a positive in his view. But by February 1864 Lincoln seemed to realize that colonization was not a feasible way to deal with the problem of the freed slaves. That month he directed Edwin M. Stanton to outfit a ship to be sent "to the colored colony established by the United States at the island of Vache, on the coast of San Domingo, to bring back to this country such of the colonists there as desire to return." The experiment to settle free Blacks on Caribbean islands had failed, as most of the African Americans wanted to return. Though not a believer in the social equality of African Americans, Lincoln seemed in 1864 to be moving toward accepting the inevitability of a multiracial postwar American society.

139 • The Afro-American Steamship and Mercantile Company

Whether to Africa or to the American West, the cost of emigration was often prohibitive to potential migrants. When the Reverend Daniel E. Johnson of San Antonio created an all-Black stock company to buy and operate steamships, he hoped to raise the necessary capital by selling shares to Blacks nationwide. Calling the or-

ganization the Afro-American Steamship and Mercantile Company, Johnson hoped to encourage emigration, commerce, race organization, and responsibility. Local clubs designed to locate and unite interested people could be formed when one hundred shares were subscribed. People would subscribe to the ten-dollar shares, but then fall behind in the dollar-per-month payments. Ultimately, only Atlanta, Charleston, and Baltimore were able to maintain clubs.

140 • Postwar Revival

Having declined in the 1860s, African American emigration interest rose again after 1877 with the collapse of Radical Reconstruction and the withdrawal of federal troops from the South. Martin Delany and several South Carolinians formed the Liberian Exodus Joint Stock Steamship Company to transport African Americans to Africa. The company's first ship, the *Azor,* set sail for Africa in the spring of 1878. But it soon found its way into debtor's court, reputedly because of the disreputable activities of its white captain, and the ship was eventually sold for debts. Unfortunately the Liberian Exodus Joint Stock Steamship died quickly thereafter.

141 • The Congo Company

The Congo Company, as it was commonly known, was founded in 1886 in Washington, D.C., by three white men from Baltimore who believed it might be profitable to transport Blacks back to Africa. The Congo Free State had been recently established, and these enterprising men hit upon the idea of colonizing the state with African Americans. Its founder, Martin H. K. Paulsen, developed enough interest that the company was incorporated with a Black man from the District of Columbia as president and white men as secretary and treasurer. In a manner that foreshadowed Marcus Garvey's Black Star Line, Paulsen sold stock in the company to raise revenue; but when an attempt to exploit a neglected 1862 federal law granting proceeds from the sale of abandoned southern lands failed to net the company an immediate $500,000, the white shareholders abandoned the company to the Blacks. Once a Baptist preacher from Georgia got behind the project, interest among Georgia Blacks ran high. When the company sold tickets for one dollar plus postage to become "preferred passengers," thousands rushed forward to buy what they believed was passage to Africa when, in fact, it only allowed them to buy passage once a ship was secured. Although the company never transported anyone to Africa, the interest generated by the company proved how serious emigration fever was in the South of the 1880s.

142 • Fraud and Redemption

Many would-be emigrants were frustrated by seemingly fraudulent operators. The Congo Company, for example, convinced potential migrants that a ship had been chartered and would leave for Liberia from Savannah in November 1890. The departure date was repeatedly postponed, but in January 1891, fifteen hundred people converged on Savannah in expectation of transport to Africa. Eventually it became clear that no ship was coming. Some Blacks remained in Atlanta hoping it would soon arrive. Others yielded to the stiff pressure from labor agents urging them to move West. But for those who remained in Savannah redemption came in the form of the Danish steamer *Horsa*, which on March 19, 1895, departed Savannah for Liberia.

143 • Bishop Turner's Dream

The most outspoken advocate of emigration

before World War I was Henry McNeal Turner, who used his position as a bishop in the African Methodist Episcopal Church to lobby African Americans to emigrate to Africa. Turner believed that bringing Africans to the United States had been part of God's providential mission to allow American Blacks and whites to join together to redeem and civilize Africa. Whites, however, had reneged on their obligation by blocking Black efforts at improvement, such as education and economic development, in the American South. Ex-slaves, Turner believed, must now shoulder the burden by themselves and redeem Africa from the white missionaries overrunning the mother country. When Turner articulated his views in the AME journal, the *Christian Recorder*, in the 1880s, other Black leaders, including fellow ministers, vigorously opposed his idea. Benjamin Tanner argued that it was foolish for African Americans to abandon the United States when millions of immigrants, even visiting African students, were coming to and staying in the United States.

Marcus Garvey, 1926. Library of Congress, Prints and Photographs Division, NYWT and S Collection

144 • Marcus Garvey's Nightmare

The most famous Black emigrationist was Marcus Garvey (1887–1940), a Jamaican who came to the United States in 1916 and founded the American branch of his Universal Negro Improvement Association. Motivated by the perception gained on his travels around the Caribbean and in England that Black people were oppressed wherever he found them around the globe, Garvey believed that Black people would never be respected until they had their own independent nation in Africa. After he gained widespread support in the United States for his militant critique of imperialism and white racism, Garvey, on June 27, 1919, incorporated the Black Star Steamship Corporation, the practical basis for realizing his dream of a Black nation. Selling stock for five dollars a share, Garvey raised thousands of dollars, purchased three ships, the *Yarmouth,* the *Kanawha,* and the *Booker T. Washington,* and tried to establish the company as both a profitable shipping company and a propagandist symbol of Black Pride. Unfortunately these goals undermined the effort to repatriate African Americans back to Africa. Garvey's inexperience in running a shipping company, his incompetent assistants, and the real problems with the ships he purchased doomed his Black Star Line to financial catastrophe. Hundreds of thousands of African Americans had bought stock in a company that was bankrupt by the end of 1920, completely unable to send anyone back to Africa. Garvey's financial mismanagement, coupled with organized opposition from the United States attorney general and such other Black leaders as W. E. B. Du Bois and William Pickens, doomed Garvey, and he was arrested in January 1921 for mail fraud. He was found guilty in June 1923 and incarcerated in a federal penitentiary in Atlanta in 1925. Though his sentence was commuted by President Calvin Coolidge in 1927, he was deported back to Jamaica, where he was never again able to generate the kind of enthusiasm for his scheme that he had enjoyed in the United States. Actually the Back to Africa scheme was only one of many of Garvey's programs, but it was the one that brought down his entire operation.

"Go West, Young [Black] Man!"

145 • Horace Greeley's Favorite Saying

Horace Greeley, the nineteenth-century journalist, was fond of urging Americans to "Go West, Young Man." But he meant only young white men. He was adamant that the new lands "shall be reserved for the benefit of the white Caucasian race."

146 • African Americans First Settlers in Ohio Valley

Despite Horace Greeley's wishes, free Black people, like free whites, yearned to move West. African Americans were among the first non–Native American settlers of the Ohio Valley. When Knox County, Ohio, was incorporated in 1808, it already contained a famous Black man—Enoch Harris, known as "Knuck," who was an expert stable hand and handler of horses. Most Black migrants were servants in white households but generally were not slaves. Most eventually obtained and farmed small parcels of land.

147 • Jean Baptiste Point du Sable

A Black man, Jean Baptiste Point du Sable, was the first to settle what became Chicago, Illinois. Born in Haiti around 1745 to a wealthy Frenchman and an enslaved African woman, du Sable had been educated in Paris before becoming a seaman and sailing to New Orleans. In 1779 he left New Orleans for the Chicago River, where he engaged in fur trapping until he was arrested as war broke out between England and France. But because he spoke English well and had conducted his business and other affairs in an honorable way, he was released and allowed to return to Chicago, where he lived for sixteen more years. During that time he married an Indian woman, built a log cabin that was decorated with European paintings, and became well known to the Indians in the area with whom he traded. Most travelers habitually stopped at du Sable's post to trade their furs and get provisions. Du Sable resided there until he ran for election and lost. Unable to accept his loss, he sold his holdings and left Chicago in 1800. Never as successful afterward as he had been in Chicago, du Sable died in poverty in 1818. Nevertheless, he had established the first outpost in the area that became known as Chicago.

148 • Internal Slave Trade

The opening of passages over the Appalachians to slave owners in the late eighteenth and early nineteenth centuries brought about the first major internal migration of African Americans in American history. Approximately 100,000 African Americans were uprooted from settled communities in the upper South and forced West between 1790 and 1810. This western movement of slaveholders, combined with the closing of the international slave trade, created a strong internal market for slaves in the United States. The internal slave trade further developed as slaveholders in Virginia, South Carolina, and Georgia traded slaves to the burgeoning cotton kingdom of Mississippi, Alabama, Louisiana, and Kentucky in the early nineteenth century.

149 • Texas

As slavery became hotly contested in the South, many farmers took their slaves West in search of greater freedom and better economic opportunities. In 1845, when Texas entered the Union, it contained 100,000 white settlers and 35,000 slaves. By 1861, when it seceded from the Union, it had over 430,000 whites and 182,000 slaves. The movement of slaves and slave owners to the West spread Anglo-American and African American cultures across the continent.

150 • Mexican vs. U.S. Rule

Under Mexican rule, Blacks in Texas were free. The Black population before the mass influx of southerners was relatively small—450 in 1792 and 2,000 in 1834. Many Blacks had Spanish surnames. As southerners moved in, they brought their slaves with them and refused to manumit them as the law required. This led to growing friction between the Mexican and American governments. Many free Blacks supported the United States in the war against Mexico and found themselves in worse positions afterward. As Greenbury Logan recorded it:

My discharge will show the man[n]er in which I discharged my duty as a free man and sol[d]ier, but now look at my situation. Every previleg dear to a freeman is taken away and Logan is liable to be imposed upon by eny that chose to do it. No change to collect a debt without [white] witnesses, no vote or say in eny way. Yet Logan is liable for Taxes as eny other person.

151 • Deadwood Dick

Nat Love, or Deadwood Dick, as he called himself, was the most famous and outrageous of the thousands of Black cowboys who migrated West in the post–Civil War era and became cowpunchers. He remains famous today because he was the only Black cowboy to write his own autobiography, which allowed him to infuse his life story with Western myth. His idea for the autobiography as well as the name Deadwood Dick may have come from reading Edward Wheeler's dime novel, *Deadwood Dick,* published in 1877, which told the exploits of *the Black Rider of the Black Hills.* In his own autobiography, *The Life and Adventures of Nat Love, Better Known in the Cattle Country as "Deadwood Dick"* (1907), Nat relates how he was born a slave in Davidson County, Tennessee, in 1854, but left the South for Kansas, arriving in Dodge City in 1869. There his riding, roping, and shooting skills earned him a job on the cattle drives out of Texas to Midwest shipping points. He was also the roughest cowboy on the trail, claiming to have been shot at least fourteen times without being seriously injured and to have excelled at outlandish pranks. He once roped a United States Army cannon in an attempt to steal it. His most famous boast was that he once rode a horse into a Mexican saloon and ordered a drink for his horse and himself. He related that his nickname, "Deadwood Dick," was given to him when he won several roping and shooting contests in a rodeo on July 4, 1876, in Deadwood City in the Dakotas. Although exaggerated, Nat Love's autobiography conveys elements of Black cowboy life out West. There was little formal segregation of Blacks in frontier towns and a great deal of personal freedom. That life came quickly to

an end in the late 1880s when the railroad took over transportation of beef to market and ended the lifestyle of the cowboy. In 1890, Deadwood Dick became a Pullman porter.

152 • Free States Prohibit Black Immigration

Four northwestern states denied free Blacks the right to migrate into those states. Iowa passed an act in 1851 prohibiting the immigration of free Blacks into the state. Every free Black found in Iowa was to be given three days to leave the state once notified by a public official. Those that refused were taken to court and, if convicted, ordered to pay a fine of two dollars a day for every day they remained in the state. Then they would be put in jail until they paid the fine or agreed to leave. The other three states, Illinois, Indiana, and Oregon, adopted—in 1848, 1851, and 1857, respectively—anti-Black immigration clauses as part of their state constitution. Oregon went so far as to punish not only Blacks who entered, but also those who brought them. Although these laws were not always enforced, they symbolized the second-class citizenship endured by African Americans already living in those states.

Ho for Kansas!

Brethren, Friends, & Fellow Citizens:
I feel thankful to inform you that the
REAL ESTATE
AND
Homestead Association,
Will Leave Here the
15th of April, 1878,
In pursuit of Homes in the Southwestern Lands of America, at Transportation Rates, cheaper than ever was known before.
For full information inquire of
Benj. Singleton, better known as old Pap,
NO. 5 NORTH FRONT STREET.
Beware of Speculators and Adventurers, as it is a dangerous thing to fall in their hands.
Nashville, Tenn., March 18, 1878.

Broadside to entice African Americans to follow Benjamin "Pap" Singleton to Kansas. Prints and Photographs Division, Library of Congress

153 • Exodusters

One of the few freedoms that the Civil War brought to African Americans was the freedom to move. Once Reconstruction had ended, sharecropping had reinstalled slavery in a new form on Black farmers, and white terrorism made life and limb unsafe for Blacks in the South, two men—Louisiana's Henry Adams and Tennessee's Benjamin "Pap" Singleton—fired the enthusiasm of southern African Americans for migration to Kansas as the one place in America where the former slave could be free. Both men exhorted Blacks to migrate as early as 1877, but Adams led a large, en masse transplanting of between 20,000 and 40,000 African Americans from the South toward Kansas in 1879. The movement of African Americans westward did not go unnoticed: southerners reacted with alarm, claimed northern white Republicans were behind the "Exodus," and forced congressional hearings on the issue. During

testimony, Pap Singleton claimed that "I am the whole cause of the Kansas migration," but Adams was at least as significant. Ultimately, however, the cause of the "Exodus" was neither man, but the horrific conditions of life in the postwar South and the promise of better conditions in the West. Actually, though migrants to Kansas were not always met with outright hostility, the welcome was far from enthusiastic, especially as Kansas was forced to absorb close to 100,000 poor, landless African Americans in the late 1870s and early 1880s. In Lincoln, Nebraska, over 150 African Americans from Mississippi were banished from the town. But in other instances, the Freedmen's Relief Association and sympathetic whites from the East supplied food, clothing, and money to the destitute and enabled them to settle and not starve. Seldom did any of the migrants reverse their course and go back to the Deep South.

154 • Nicodemus

In July 1877 thirty Black colonists who had left Lexington, Kentucky, arrived in Kansas and built the town of Nicodemus. Located in Graham County, Nicodemus was one of the earliest Black towns established by former slaves during Reconstruction. The original settlers utilized wood they found along the Solomon River as fuel and as material to build small lean-tos and houses. As the town grew, other former slaves who were disenchanted with postwar life in Mississippi, Missouri, Kentucky, and Tennessee migrated to the town, which was inspired by a spirit of self-reliance. Citizens even went so far as to pass a series of resolutions in 1879 thanking the people of Kansas and other states for helping the town, but refusing any further charitable assistance. Because it was an all-Black town of former slaves, the town had received support from the neighboring communities. Some residents were afraid that charity would make their people unwilling to work and attract destitute, undesirable persons. By 1880 seven hundred residents populated Nicodemus, which had become quite prosperous. It contained its own post office, stores, hotels, and land office. Although the town declined in 1888 because the Kansas Railroad passed it by, Nicodemus was still a thriving farm community in 1910. Reputedly the town was named after a slave who came on the second slave ship who became an outstanding citizen after he purchased his freedom.

155 • Oklahoma

Some African Americans wanted to establish an all-Black state in the Oklahoma Territory, which had been created by the federal government in 1889. Edwin P. McCabe, a native of Kansas, wanted to settle a Black majority in each voting district of the territory. Over seven thousand Blacks entered the territory in its first year. Several all-Black towns were established, including Langston, named after John Langston, a prominent abolitionist, educator, and politician from Virginia. At its peak, Langston had a population over two thousand, and a university (Langston University) was established in 1897.

FROM RURAL TO URBAN AMERICA

156 • Urban Migration

African Americans have been moving toward cities since Blacks have enjoyed the opportunity to choose their residences. Urban slavery offered better conditions of labor, health, and per-

Migrant. Photograph by Jack Delano. Prints and Photographs Division, Library of Congress

sonal freedom for slaves than rural slavery. Often, urban slaves were domestic servants who lived in the master's house, or just behind it, in the better part of town and enjoyed the freedom to travel unsupervised through streets to carry out errands. In some cases, particularly in the 1840s and 1850s, masters allowed urban slaves to "hire out" their time and contract their own employment. Under such circumstances slaves paid their masters only a portion of their earnings. "Living out" also became popular, because masters found they could save on the costs of feeding, clothing, and housing slaves by allowing the slave to live in a separate residence and pay his or her rent out of earnings. Under such circumstances, slaves who were husband and wife could "hire out" and "live out" and thereby approximate the feeling that they were free. Even though Frederick Douglass hated the experience of having to give part of his wages to his master in Baltimore, Douglass agreed that living in the city was far superior to living in the rural countryside of Maryland.

157 • Urban Discrimination

Frederick Douglass documented the racism and hostility he experienced after he finally escaped from slavery. White workers refused to work with Black workers in many of the trades, and Douglass was beaten up on one occasion when he tried to work. Ironically, in southern cities under slavery, "white and Black carpenters worked side by side in the shipyards," but Douglass could not work as a caulker on a ship in a northern city because "I was told that every white man would leave the ship in her unfinished condition if I struck a blow at my trade upon her." In southern cities, there was plenty of work, but little freedom; in northern cities, there was plenty of freedom, but no work.

158 • Cityward During the Civil War

With the Civil War and the prospect of emancipating the slaves, some northern cities feared that thousands of newly freed slaves would suddenly rush northward and begin competing with white workers for jobs. Emancipation at the end of the war did encourage African Americans to go to the city, but not to the North; many more went to southern cities. The southern city held out the prospect not only of greater freedom but also of nonagricultural employment, and thus a sharp and symbolic break from the labor of plantation slavery. The relative lack of urban and industrial development in the South, the postwar devastation, and the concerted efforts of former planters and the Freedmen's Bureau forced many of the new migrants in southern

cities to return to their former plantations and their former jobs as agricultural workers.

159 • Post-Reconstruction Urban Migration

Although many southern Blacks tried to escape the oppression of the rural South by migrating in the period after 1877, most could not migrate to the urban North. The late-nineteenth-century American city experienced a tremendous influx of European immigrants who swelled the urban pool of unskilled laborers and reduced the need and demand for southern Black workers. Moreover, many freedmen still retained the dream of independent landownership as a symbol of their freedom, and there was a much greater chance of owning a farm if a southern Black migrated West. Small numbers of skilled and well-educated African Americans did migrate from southern to northern cities, from 1890 to 1910. But as late as 1910, 52.3 percent of migrants from the South were still going West. This changed with World War I.

160 • Blacks as Strikebreakers

African Americans had worked in northern industry prior to 1916. But they were generally only brought in as strikebreakers. In the Chicago stockyards in 1894, Blacks were hired for the first time in the meatpacking industry when thousands of workers in that industry conducted a sympathy strike with the American Railway Union strike against the Pullman company. That sowed the seeds of race hatred that continued well into the twentieth century in the meatpacking unions. Blacks did not always go along with the strikebreaking formula, however. When Latrobe Steel decided to transport 317 Black workers from Birmingham to break a strike, the workers refused to serve the owner's interest and asked to be returned to Alabama. Whether they were strikebreakers or not, the situation facing Black workers in the industrial North before 1916 was difficult. The major fact was that there was very little work for African American workers outside of the South before World War I.

161 • Great Migration

World War I transformed Black migration to northern cities into a real option. With the outbreak of hostilities in 1914, the European war dramatically reduced European immigration into the United States and jump-started American industry as it became a source of manufactured goods to the combatants. Suddenly a huge demand for unskilled labor in the urban North emerged, without a local source to supply it. Where years before, the color line in northern industry prevented African Americans from obtaining jobs, suddenly industrial leaders were so eager to hire Black workers that in 1916 recruiters went South to bring Black workers to such cities as Pittsburgh, Chicago, Detroit, and Indianapolis. Fueled by this early encouragement, migration North became a fever that spread by word of mouth throughout the South, and entire Black communities picked up and left Mississippi, Georgia, Alabama, and the Carolinas for good. Approximately 500,000 migrated to the industrial North in the period 1916 to 1919.

162 • Reasons for Leaving

Migrants who left the South during World War I felt pushed out of the South because of the deterioration in the quality of life for Blacks. In the 1890s Jim Crow segregation spread throughout the South, such that railroads, meeting houses, schools, and work sites became legally and drastically segregated. At the same time, laws disfranchising the Black voter through

"understanding clauses" that required voters to read and write, poll taxes that required voters to pay registration taxes, and outright voter intimidation dramatically reduced the number of African Americans voting in the South. As if that were not enough, a fever of lynching spread across the South in the 1890s, as Black males, especially businessmen or property owners, were targeted for speaking up or not behaving deferentially to whites. Those conditions, coupled with the lack of equal educational opportunities for Black youth, convinced many Blacks, especially those between the ages of eighteen and thirty-three, that the only future for the younger generation existed up North. As one group of migrants told W. E. B. Du Bois, the editor of the *Crisis,* the journal of the National Association for the Advancement of Colored People, migrants were "willing to run any risk to get where they might breathe easier."

163 • Letters in the *Chicago Defender*

Some southern Blacks wrote to the *Chicago Defender* to explain the brutal conditions of the South that made migration appealing but difficult:

. . . *We work but cant get scarcely any thing for it & they dont want us to go away & there is not much of anything here to do & nothing for it Please find some one that need this kind of a people & send at once for us. We dont want anything but our wareing and bed clothes & have not got no money to get away from here with & being to get away before we are killed and hope to here from you at once. We cant talk to you over the phone here we are afraid to they dont want to hear one say that he or she wants to leave here if we do we are apt to be killed. They say if we dont go to war they are not going to let us stay here with their folks and it is not any thing that we have done to them.* . . . [Letter from Daphne, Alabama, April 20, 1917]

164 • Boll Weevil

The devastation caused by the boll weevil also contributed to the Great Migration. The boll weevil, a grayish beetle approximately an inch long, infests cotton plants by depositing its larvae in the boll of the cotton plant. The larvae then feed on the boll, effectively destroying the plant. The boll weevil entered the United States via Mexico in 1892, and by 1903 had cut a swath through Louisiana; by 1907 the weevil had hit Mississippi. Black farmers in Louisiana were hit hardest in the period 1906–10, those in Mississippi in the period 1913–16, and Alabama after 1916. Its impact on Black farmers' attitudes toward the South can be best gauged in the refrain of a song:

De white man he got ha'f de crap
Boll weevil took de res'
Ain't got no home,
Ain't got no home.

165 • Migration North Swells with World War I Industry

In 1916 a trickle of African Americans moving from the rural South to the urban North swelled into a flood, as American industrial production jumped during World War I and European immigration fell. Even recent European immigrants to the United States returned home to fight for their countries. Suddenly an American industrial world that had been all but closed to African Americans was desperate for unskilled laborers and interested in hiring Negroes. And African Americans, tired of mistreatment and abuse in the South, were ready to leave and take a chance on life in the urban industrial North. Pennsylvania and Illinois gained more than 90,000 and

73,000 African Americans in the 1910s, while Michigan's Black population skyrocketed from a mere 17,000 to over 60,000 by 1920.

166 • Labor Agents

Labor agents were often blamed for the migration of large numbers of African Americans out of the South during the Great Migration. Though northern industrialists did initially send agents South to spread the word of work in the North, agents had ceased to be a major factor in the migration by 1917. Long before then, Black southerners had themselves taken over the role of informing their neighbors and friends that the opportunity and necessity to move North had come. Indeed, Black southerners had been ready to leave for years. Once it became widely known that jobs were available in the North, they left.

167 • Letters Home to the South

Those who had migrated and obtained well-paying jobs wrote letters to relatives and friends painting flattering pictures of life up North and encouraging people to follow in their footsteps. These letters were probably the single most important factor in making the decision to leave the South.

I should have been here 20 years ago. I just begin to feel like a man. It's a great deal of pleasure in knowing that you have got some privilege. My children are going to the same school with the whites and I dont have to umble to no one. I have registered—Will vote the next election and there isnt any "yes sirs" and "no sir"—its all yes and no and Sam and Bill.

168 • Migration After a Lynching

Very often a lynching, commonplace in the South of the early twentieth century, would be the catalyst that sent a family or an entire town's Black population up North. One group of African Americans from Florida told investigators that "the horrible lynchings in Tennessee" had prompted them to move. The Chicago Urban League noted that after lynchings, "colored people from that community will arrive in Chicago inside of two weeks."

169 • Black Mississippian Explains

Just a few months ago they hung Widow Baggae's husband from Hirshbery bridge because he talked back to a white man. He was a prosperous Farmer owning about 80 acres. They killed another man because he dared to sell his cotton "off the place." These things have got us sore. Before the North opened up with work all we could do was to move from one plantation to another in hope of finding something better.

Jesse Washington, eighteen years old, lynched and burned, May 15, 1916, Waco, Texas. Prints and Photographs Division, Library of Congress

170 • Economic Reasons for Migrating North

Ford worker. Photograph by Arthur Siegel. Prints and Photographs Division, Library of Congress

Black migrants were able to make as much for a day's work in the North as they made working for a week in the South. Jobs in the industrial North—from the stockyards in Chicago to the steel mills in Pittsburgh—offered dignified work that was nonagricultural. But just as important as good jobs was the sense of being able to live a real life for the first time, and to expect that they could finally begin to live the American Dream. Many Black migrants expressed the view that for the first time they could believe that life would be better for their children than it had been for them.

171 • *Defender* Help-Wanted Ads

The *Chicago Defender*, a Black-owned and edited newspaper, played a pivotal role in fostering the Great Migration. Numerous editorials appeared in the *Defender* during the 1910s urging southern Blacks to vote against southern racism with their feet and come North to work and freedom in Chicago. Perhaps most important, the *Defender* also published thousands of help-wanted ads that convinced those still skeptical that well-paying jobs were waiting for them in Chicago.

Wanted—Men and Women—architects, mechanics, cement masons, carpenters, painters and decorators; cement workers, electricians, plumbers, steamfitters, bookkeepers, steno-typewriters. All must be qualified to take charge of their positions. Apply by letter only, with self-addressed stamped envelope to International Ideal Home and Investment Bankers. Charles D. Basse, 183 N. Wabash Avenue.

172 • Looking for Work

Many people wrote the *Chicago Defender* looking for opportunities or to inquire about conditions in the North.

In reading the Defenders want ad I notice that there is lots of work to be had and if I havent miscomprehended I think I also understand that the transportation is advanced to able bodied working men who is out of work and desire work. Am I not right? with the understanding that those who have been advanced transportation same will be deducted from their salary after they have begun work. Now then if this is they proposition I have about 10 or 15 good working men who is out of work and are dying to leave the south and I as-

sure you that they are working men and will be too glad to come north east or west, any where but the south. [Letter from Port Arthur, Texas, May 5, 1917]

173 • Housing

Although industrial capitalists were willing to provide jobs for African Americans during World War I, none provided housing. This forced Blacks who migrated North during the Great Migration into slum areas of cities such as Chicago that were already overfilled with residents. Eventually such neighborhoods began to impinge on nearby poor white neighborhoods, usually those populated by immigrants. Black migrants were often charged higher rents, as this entry in the Philadelphia Urban League report indicates:

Russell Street Apartment—Ten-family apartment. Apartments taken over in 1923 by colored. Place formerly rented for $30.00 and $35.00 per month. Rent raised $10.00. Apartments each of four small rooms. Steam heat and electricity. General conditions of the interior bad. Needs redecorating. Paper on the walls very dirty and loose. Floors bad. Plumbing fair. Some apartments worse than others. Garbage and rubbish receptacles inadequate for the apartment house. Lawns bad.

174 • Restrictive Covenants

Restrictive covenants were agreements signed voluntarily or involuntarily by property owners in the early twentieth century to prevent Blacks from buying property. There were two distinctive types of restrictive covenants. One was an agreement between existing owners. In Harlem, for example, protective associations forced property owners to sign agreements not to rent apartments to African Americans for ten years. Some covenants even limited the number of African Americans hired to work in a home. The signers all paid one another a fee to make it binding, and the covenants were then notarized and put on file at the city hall of records. Blocks covered by such covenants were sometimes known as Covenant Blocks, and African Americans families took particular delight in being the first to bust a Covenant Block. The other major kind of restrictive covenants were clauses in real-estate deeds, passed from owner to owner of houses or apartment buildings, that prevented selling or subleasing the premises to an African American. Most of the first kind of restrictive covenants had no binding legal value, but constituted a powerful psychological device to enforce residential segregation in northern cities. Often, however, once a Covenant Block was broken, white owners sold to whomever they wanted without legal consequences. The second type was legally binding, although seldom enforced if an owner violated it.

175 • The Second Great Migration

African Americans continued to move northward and cityward after World War I in 1918. In fact, the migration increased during the 1920s as another million southern African Americans picked up their bags and left southern living conditions. The migration expanded in the 1930s as the New Deal Agricultural Adjustment Act of 1933 forced many more to migrate once the AAA paid white southern farmers not to produce crops and made it profitable to dispense with Black sharecroppers. Technological advances such as the cotton picker machine made large numbers of unskilled agricultural laborers obsolete in southern agriculture. Then, as World War II began, Black mass migration exploded

and nearly 5 million African Americans left the South for the North from 1940 to 1960. While migrants during the Second Migration were spread over a longer period of time and did not have the immediate impact on racial relations as the Great Migration during World War I, the Second Migration created huge ghettos in all of the major American cities. Whereas in 1890 close to 90 percent of African Americans lived in the South, by 1960 only 50 percent of African Americans still resided there. Moreover, the movement North was also a movement toward urban rather than rural living. By 1990 over 84 percent of African Americans lived in urban areas, making "African American" and "urban" almost synonymous in modern America.

176 • Southward Bound

Ironically, after the huge migration to the North prior to the 1960s, a desire to return to the South gripped the imagination of many African Americans in the early 1970s. Close to 1 million African Americans moved into the South during the period 1970–75. Although the tide slowed in the period 1975–80 to roughly 194,000 African Americans moving to the South, the lure of the southern United States continued. The end of public segregation in the South during the Civil Rights Movement of the 1960s contributed to the desire of African Americans to return to warmer climates and to a region with a closer sense of community.

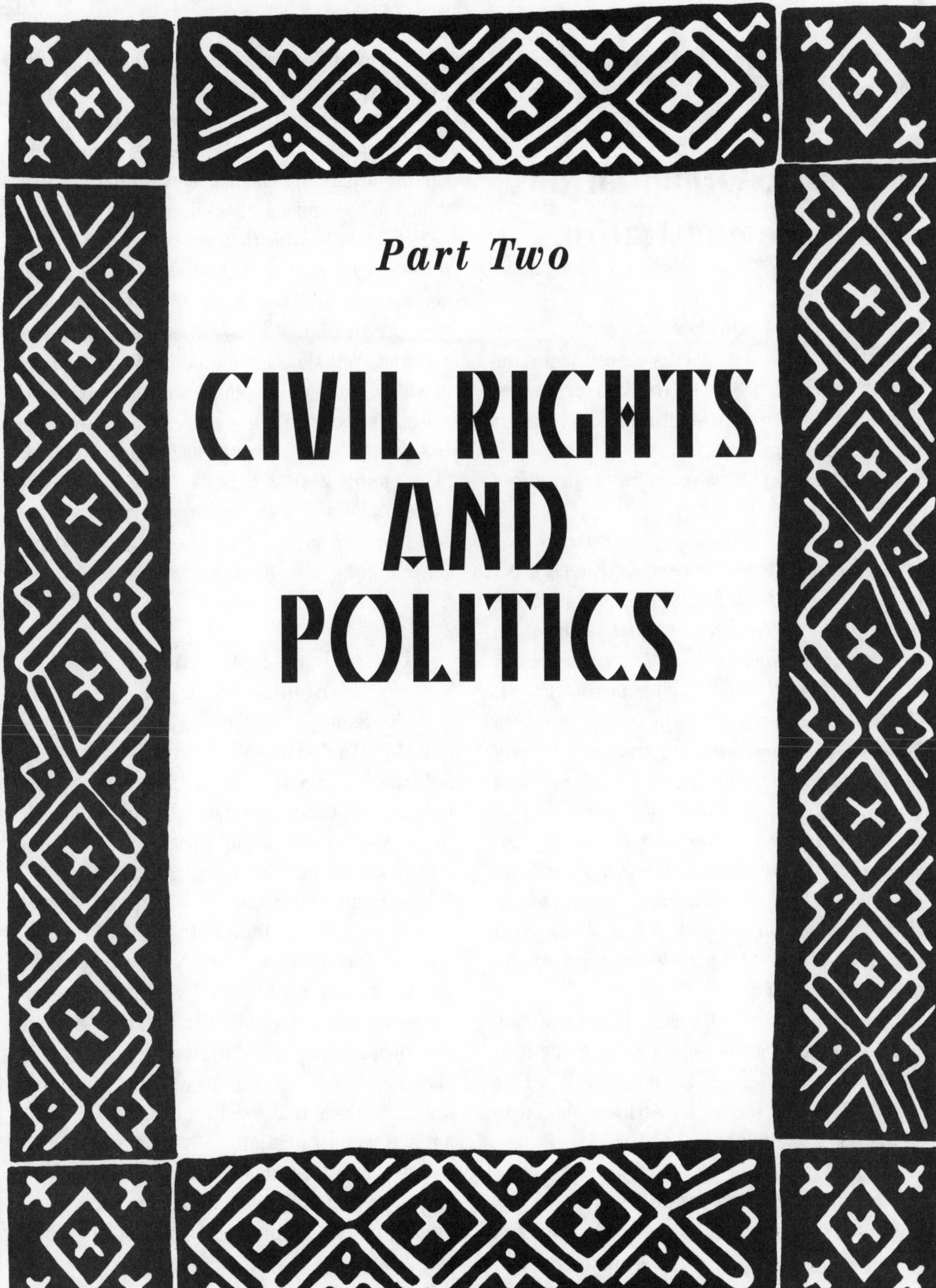

Part Two

CIVIL RIGHTS AND POLITICS

COLONIAL

Protests, Organizations, and Demonstrations

177 • Quaker Protest

Protest against slavery is as old as the institution in the United States. The Quakers issued the earliest recorded resolution against slavery on May 18, 1652.

Whereas their is a common course practiced among Englishmen, to buy negroes to that end that they may have them for service or as slaves forever; for the preventing of such practices among us, let it be ordered, that no black mankind or white being shall be forced, by covenant, bond, or otherwise, to serve any man or his assignees longer than ten years, or until they come to be twenty-four years of age, if they be taken in under fourteen, from the time of their coming within the liberties of this Colony—at the end or term of ten years, to set them free as the manner is with the English servants. And that man that will not let them go free, or shall sell them away elsewhere, to that end they may be enslaved to others for a longer time, he or they shall forfeit to the colony forty pounds.

The resolution is noteworthy for acknowledging that some Africans were already being held "as slaves forever" in 1652 and that it called for a limited term of service for Africans similar to what existed for indentured whites.

178 • Mennonites

An early protest against the slave trade was recorded in 1688 by Germantown Mennonites in the colony of Pennsylvania. The Mennonites believed the slave trade violated Christian principles. The Germantown Protest stated slavery was wrong because the Negroes were brought to the Americas against their will, that it was wrong to buy and sell them like cattle.

Pray, what thing in the world can be done worse toward us, than if men should rob or steal us away and sell us for slaves to strange countries, separating husbands from their wives and children. Now this is not done in the manner we would be done to; therefore, we contradict and are against this traffic of men. And we who profess that it is not lawful to steal, must, likewise, avoid purchasing things that are stolen, but rather help to stop this robbing and stealing, if possible. And such men ought to be delivered out of the hands of the robbers and set free. . . .

179 • Judge Sewall and the First Abolitionist Tract

Judge Samuel Sewall of Massachusetts wrote one of the first extensive abolitionist tracts, *The Selling of Joseph,* in 1700. As the judge who participated in the Salem witch trials, Sewall believed slavery was wrong because of its sinful effects on ruling whites and its inhumane effects on enslaved Blacks. This negative view of slavery would be reiterated throughout the history of opposition to slavery, even by nineteenth-century abolitionists who, like Sewall, opposed slavery but did not consider African Americans the equals of whites. Sewall's tract is also important because it was the first sustained analysis that used biblical passages for antislavery justifications. For example, Sewall noted that in Exodus 21:16, the Bible commands that "he that stealeth a man, and selleth him, or if he be found in his hand, he shall surely be put to death."

180 • Anthony Benezet on the Slave Trade

A forceful attack on the slave trade was delivered by Anthony Benezet, a Quaker from Philadelphia, who, as a schoolteacher and reformer, popularized the view that the slave trade was both anti-Christian and inhuman. His *Observations on the Inslaving, Importing and Purchasing of Negroes: With Some Advice Thereon, Extracted from the Epistel of the Yearly-Meeting of the People Called Quakers, Held at London in the Year 1748* attacked the abuses and cruelties of the slave trade. *"Did not he that made you, make them?"* his essay queried.

OBSERVATIONS

On the Inslaving, importing and purchasing of

Negroes;

With some Advice thereon, extracted from the Epistle of the Yearly-Meeting of the People called QUAKERS, held at *London* in the Year 1748.

Anthony Benezet

When ye spread forth your Hands, I will hide mine Eyes from you, yea when ye make many Prayers I will not hear; your Hands are full of Blood. Wash ye, make you clean, put away the Evil of your Doings from before mine Eyes Isai. 1, 15.

Is not this the Fast that I have chosen, to loose the Bands of Wickedness, to undo the heavy Burden, to let the Oppressed go free, and that ye break every Yoke, Chap. 58, 7.

Second Edition.

GERMANTOWN:

Printed by CHRISTOPHER SOWER. 1760.

Title page of Anthony Benezet's *Observations*. Prints and Photographs Division, Library of Congress

181 • John Woolman, Anti-Slavery Quaker

John Woolman, an itinerant Quaker minister, authored one of the most influential critiques of slavery in the colonial period. Woolman wrote *Some Considerations on the Keeping of Negroes: Recommended to the Professors of Christianity of Every Denomination* in 1746, after traveling through Virginia, Maryland, and North Carolina and observing the conditions and treatment of slaves. Although Woolman, like Judge Samuel Sewall, was concerned about the corrupting effect of slavery on the slave owners, it was the plight of the slaves that moved him to write his essay, for "the general disadvantage which these poor Africans lie under in an enlightened Christian country . . . often filled me with real sadness." There were some good slave owners, Woolman believed, but in general, treating another human being as a slave dimmed the master's spiritual vision. Another reason for Woolman's opposition to slavery was that it devalued the Quaker religion in the eyes of slaves. Woolman practiced his beliefs by individually proselytizing Quakers to give up their slaves. And his essay influenced far more Quakers when the Philadelphia Yearly Meeting, in 1754, distributed it to Quaker groups throughout Pennsylvania and New Jersey. The essay even made its way to England, where it led the London Yearly Meeting of June 1758 to condemn the slave trade. Woolman published a second and more forthright version, *Some Considerations on the Keeping of Negroes, the Second,* in 1762. When the Philadelphia Yearly Meeting, in 1776, finally prohibited Quakers from owning slaves, Woolman's essays were largely responsible.

Legal Decisions and Their Implications

182 • Hugh Davis Is "Whipt"

Africans and Europeans had been sexually involved with one another from the earliest years of the Virginia colony. The first mention of race in the colonies comes in the case of Hugh Davis, who was brought before the Court of Chauncery in Virginia in 1639 for having had sexual relations with a Black person. "Hugh Davis to be soundly whipt before an assembly of negroes & others for abusing himself to the dishonor of God and shame of Christianity by defiling his body in lying with a negro...." As historian Leon Higginbotham points out, the court record does not reveal the race of Davis or whether the African was enslaved or free, female or male. Probably, Hugh Davis was a free European who in sleeping with an African, whether free or not, violated the still informal English prohibition against interracial sex.

183 • Negro Woman Is "Whipt"

White men were not primarily the ones "whipt" for interracial sex in colonial Virginia. In the Robert Sweat case of 1640, a man who had fathered a child with an African American woman servant was brought to trial. But the "negro woman shall be whipt at the whipping post," while "Sweat shall tomorrow in the forenoon do public penance for his offence," surely a lighter penalty for the "offense." Was she punished more harshly because she was Black, a woman, or a servant? We do not know for certain.

184 • Runaway John Punch

Black and white servants often banded together to run away from servitude in colonial Virginia. It may have been to discourage such unions that John Punch received his severe sentence in 1640. Punch was brought to trial for trying to escape in the company of two white servants. The three were equally guilty, but when sentences were issued, the whites were sentenced to serve an additional year for their masters and three additional years for the colony. But John Punch, the Negro, was required to serve his master and his master's heirs for the rest of his life. Is this proof of racial discrimination? Not quite, since we do not know if John Punch was guilty of some previous infraction. But the trial of Punch is our earliest recorded instance of slavery or lifetime servitude existing in Virginia.

185 • Ambiguous Graweere

We know that Blacks in early seventeenth-century Virginia were utterly degraded, but the case of Graweere in 1641, in which an African American servant successfully secured the freedom of his child, shows that some Blacks were able to take advantage of the legal system. Because his master allowed Graweere to keep livestock and profit from it, Graweere was able to appeal to the court for permission to buy the freedom of his child. By the turn of the century, such a purchase would be largely unthinkable for a Black servant, who by then would be considered a slave, and his children also slaves—servants for life.

186 • The Problem Solved

The real problem English colonists had with interracial sex is that it produced children who were no longer servants or slaves according to English law. Traditional English law held that the status of any child followed that of the father. But in colonial Virginia, which had very

few white women, it was difficult to stop interracial relations between white men and Black women altogether. In a 1662 act, Virginia solved the problem: "Children got by an Englishman upon a Negro woman shall be bond or free according to the condition of the mother, and if any Christian shall commit fornication with a Negro man or woman, he shall pay double the fine of a former act." This Virginia act is one of the earliest examples of how the institution of slavery changed the English legal practice, a trend that would continue into the new country's legal apparatus.

187 • License to Kill Blacks

By the beginning of the eighteenth century, whites could legally kill Black slaves who resisted their "correcting," as it was called then. In a 1705 act, the Virginia council determined that if a master accidentally murdered his slave while "correcting" him or her for some offense, the master's act would "not be accounted [a] felony; but the master, owner, and every such other person so giving correction, shall be free and acquit[ted] of all punishment. . . ." Ironically this law was put into effect as the rights of white servants were being strengthened.

188 • Intermarriage Punished

Intermarriage between Blacks and whites in seventeenth- and early-eighteenth-century Virginia prompted the passage of a law in 1705 that prohibited the practice and imprisoned whites for six months. Although both white men and white women were punished for marrying African Americans, only white women could have their marriages annulled if it was discovered the woman had sexual relations with an African American prior to marriage. Usually the early birth of a "mulatto child" brought on the discovery. It was not until a 1967 Supreme Court decision that all state and local prohibitions against intermarriage were outlawed as unconstitutional (*Loving v. Virginia*, 1967).

"Ladies Whipping Girls." Woodcut from *Picture of Slavery*, by George Bourne (Middletown, Conn.: E. Hunt, 1834). Prints and Photographs Division, Library of Congress

189 • Want to Be Free

Perhaps the most important difference between slavery in North America and slavery in Latin America was the drastic curtailment of the possibility of freedom or manumission in North America. In 1691, for example, Virginia passed a law that prohibited the freeing of any African American by a master without first making arrangements for removing the freed Black out of the country within six months. In other words, the ideal society in late-seventeenth-century Virginia was one in which all the Blacks

were slaves and the whites were masters. In 1705 the colony reinforced the marginality of free Blacks by passing a statute that made it unlawful for any nonwhite person to own a servant or a slave. In a colony rapidly becoming a slave colony, exclusion from power to own slaves meant pauperism, and, if not migration out of the colony, perhaps slippage back into enslavement.

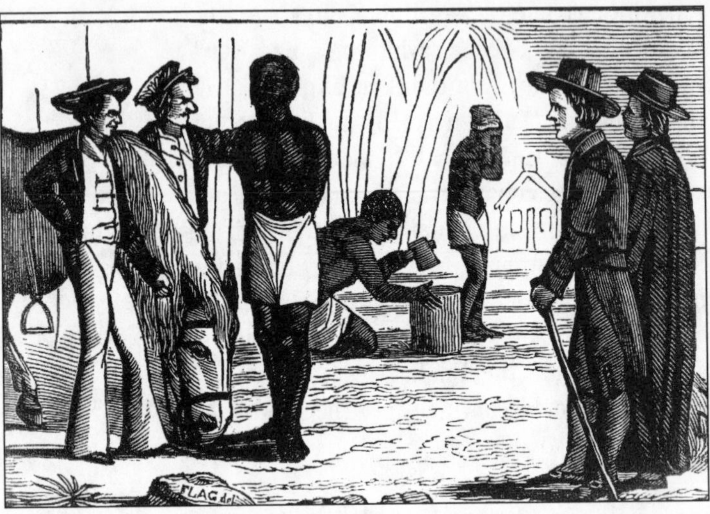
"Exchanging Citizens for Horses." Woodcut from *Picture of Slavery*, by George Bourne (Middletown, Conn.: E. Hunt, 1834). Prints and Photographs Division, Library of Congress

190 • Hogs or Real Estate?

A real dilemma for the colonial legal system in North America was how to rank slaves. In 1671 the case of an orphaned child who had inherited Black slaves prompted a decision. If treated like real estate, the slaves could not be disposed of until the child was twenty-one. But if the slaves were considered as hogs or other livestock which might die in the interim and hence lose their value, then the child could sell the slaves now. The court ruled that the latter was the more reasonable to protect the interest of the child. Slaves in North America were thus regularly treated as chattel, as movable and perishable livestock.

191 • 1712 Act: Decline of Rights, but Slave's Human Will Acknowledged

With the passage of the 1712 Slave Act, South Carolina instituted a repressive system of control over slaves who had once enjoyed certain liberties. Seventeenth-century slaves worked in a variety of occupations, such as cooperage, fishing, and cattle herding, and enjoyed a degree of personal freedom, but eighteenth-century slaves in South Carolina were more likely to be forced into rice cultivation and to suffer under a variety of controls on their personal freedoms. The 1712 code required slaves to have a written pass unless they were accompanied by a white person. Slaves who were caught without a pass were to be whipped. Slaves were also prohibited from trading without their master's permission, thus limiting the money that slaves could acquire on their own. Any property that the slave possessed, moreover, could be forfeited. The 1712 law commanded masters to search slave quarters every two weeks for weapons; and after 1722, justices of the peace could seize horses and other livestock owned by slaves without impunity. The ability of the slave to rise in society through the acquisition of property or wealth was thus severely limited, along with his or her personal freedom. But the 1712 Slave Act also recognized, indirectly, that slaves were human. For example, it stated "that if any Negroes or other slaves shall make mutiny or insurrection, or rise in rebellion against any authority and government of this Province," they would be tried and executed for their

crimes if convicted. Clearly slaves were considered responsible for their actions and capable of rebellion. Ironically the South Carolina law recognized that at least sometimes slaves were human.

192 • Impact of Rebellion

Outbreaks of slave rebellions generally led colonial legislatures to pass even more stringent laws that lowered the status of slaves in the legal system. A prominent example is the 1740 Slave Act passed in South Carolina after the Stono Rebellion of 1739. Rather than defining the slave as necessary to the economic livelihood of the colony, as earlier acts had done, the 1740 act declared that slaves were "mere subjects of property in the hands of particular persons" and thus destined to be "*kept in due subjection and obedience.*" While the code tried to suggest that owners needed to provide adequate food and housing to slaves, perhaps with the idea that less well kept slaves might be more likely to rebel, the code also stipulated that only another white person could bring a complaint against a master. It also made it a crime to teach a slave to read or write.

193 • Free Blacks Voted in Colonial South Carolina

Free Blacks voted in South Carolina elections held in 1701 and 1703. After the first election, an assembly was called to try and limit those eligible to vote. In discussing the election in 1701, "the dissenters of Colleton County charged that unqualified aliens, *i.e.* French Protestants, strangers, paupers, servants, and even free negroes, were allowed to vote." Protests were again raised after the 1703 election, because "aliens, Jews, servants, common sailors and negroes were admitted to vote. . . ." Such voting was allowed because the colony was under the control of the Lord Proprietors, a specifically commercial and British undertaking. Only after 1721, when South Carolina acquired a royal government responsive to the demands of the local white population, was voting limited to "Christian" whites, and even then some Blacks still voted. Free Blacks exercised their right to vote from the beginning of colonial America and only reluctantly relinquished it.

194 • Free Blacks Owned Slaves

Free Blacks owned property, one of the reasons they were able to continue to vote in colonial South Carolina, where voting began to be limited to those who were owners of property. Some free Blacks also owned slaves, an essential possession in an agricultural society rapidly becoming dependent on slavery to supply its spiraling labor needs. But as historian Leon Higginbotham suggests, free Black ownership of slaves might have had an additional motive: many free Blacks purchased slaves, sometimes family members, in order to protect them. As South Carolina tightened manumission laws in the early eighteenth century, it became increasingly difficult to free even relatives; transfer of ownership to a free Black was one way to circumvent the system.

195 • Taxation Without Representation

Even after free Blacks began to lose the right to vote, they were still taxed on their property. Indeed, sometimes free Blacks were taxed more than their white counterparts. In 1792 a law was passed imposing a tax of two dollars on free Blacks irrespective of their property.

196 • Decline of Status of Free Blacks

As the eighteenth century progressed, the legal status and rights of free Blacks declined, and increasingly the courts treated free Blacks

and slaves similarly. Free Blacks did continue to possess the right to bring civil suits in court in the eighteenth century, but by the early nineteenth century free Blacks were denied the right to have their testimony honored in court. Perhaps most important, the free Black population dwindled in number during the eighteenth century. The 1722 Slave Act in South Carolina demanded that owners who freed slaves had to transport them out of the state; and after the 1735 act, any manumitted person who returned to South Carolina could be reenslaved. By 1800 the South Carolina legislature passed a law that prohibited free Blacks from being brought into the colony. In the nineteenth century South Carolina's free Black population was limited in numbers and in location to tiny communities in such cities as Charleston.

197 • Georgia Outlaws Slavery!

Georgia, the last colony founded by the British, prohibited the transportation of Blacks into the colony after 1735 and denied its colonists the right to own or use slaves. On one hand, the prohibition of slaves reflected the views of James Oglethorpe, a trustee of the colony, who thought that "slavery . . . is against the Gospel, as well as the fundamental law of England." But as Leon Higginbotham shows, the banning of slaves from Georgia was far from a humanitarian act: it was part of a design to profit from slavery by permitting the government to capture all slaves found in the colony and to sell them into slavery in another colony. Thus, Georgia profited early from its close proximity to such slaveholding colonies as South Carolina. Moreover, the penalty for having slaves in Georgia was merely a fine, not the freeing of slaves. Not surprisingly, as Georgia matured as an agricultural colony in the 1750s, pressure from local planters repealed the prohibition and instituted in the slave codes of 1755, 1765, and 1770 some of the harshest laws governing slaves in British North America.

198 • Pennsylvania Slavery

Although life for slaves in Pennsylvania was considerably less harsh than in Virginia, South Carolina, or Georgia, it was still quite repressive. Slaves in Pennsylvania were tried before a special court in which the principal concern was to protect the master's property. In one trial two slaves were convicted of burglary and sentenced to death in 1707, but the charge was reduced to protect the masters from loss. The masters were permitted to "inflict on [their slaves] such corporal punishment as may be requisite for a terror to others of their color." The masters were then instructed to lead the slaves through the town "with their arms extended and tied to a pole across their Necks, a Cart going before them, and that they shall be severely Whipt all the way as they pass . . . [and] that this punishment shall be repeated for 3 market days successively." Afterward, the owners could transport them out of the colony.

REVOLUTIONARY PERIOD

Protests, Organizations, and Demonstrations

199 • Crispus Attucks

Crispus Attucks, a runaway slave, led a group of rowdy Boston citizens to pelt and taunt a regiment of British soldiers. On March 5, 1770, the British responded by shooting Attucks and ten

Crispus Attucks, the first American to die at the Boston Massacre, 1770. Schomburg Center for Research in Black Culture, New York Public Library, Astor, Lenox and Tilden Foundation

other persons. Though it has been commonly believed that Attucks was the first to die, there is no proof. What is known is that Attucks was believed to have been at the head of the crowd of citizens, and to have provoked the incident by striking one of the British soldiers, Hugh Montgomery.

The people seemed to be leaving the soldiers, and to turn from them, when there came down a number from Jackson's corner, huzzaing and crying, damn them, they dare not fire, we are not afraid of them. One of these people, a stout man with a long cord wood stick, threw himself in, and made a blow at the officer . . . the stout man then turned round, and struck the grenadier's gun at the captain's right hand, and immediately fell in with his club, and knocked his gun away, and struck him over the head. . . . This stout man held the bayonet with his left hand, and twitched it and cried, kill the dogs, knock them over. This was the general cry; the people then crowded in. . . . I turned to go off, when I heard the word fire . . . I thought I heard the report of a gun. . . . Do you know who this stout man was, that fell in and struck the grenadier? I thought, and still think, it was the mulatto who was shot.

Attucks was one of four men, including Samuel Gray, Samuel Maverick, and James Caldwell, killed that evening and celebrated afterward as America's first martyrs.

200 • Natural Rights Applied to AFAM Freedom

African Americans drafted petitions to be free utilizing the philosophy of the natural rights of man that white colonists used to justify separation from England. In Boston, on April 20, 1773, four slaves petitioned for their freedom by writing:

Sir, the efforts made by the legislative of this province in their last sessions to free themselves from slavery, gave us, who are in that deplorable state, a high degree of satisfaction. We expect great things from men who have made such a noble stand against the designs of their fellow-men *to enslave them. We cannot but wish and hope Sir, that you will have the same grand object, we mean civil and religious liberty, in view of our next session. The divine spirit of* freedom, *seems to fire every humane breast on this continent, except such as are bribed to assist in executing the execrable plan.*

The signers of the petition, Peter Bestes, Sambo Freeman, Felix Holbrook, and Chester Joie, went on to state that they did not demand their immediate release from their masters, but only a few days off a week to cultivate their own crops, with the prospect that at a future date, "we can, from our joynt labours procure money to transport ourselves to some part of the Coast of Africa, where we propose a settlement." Other similar petitions followed, including one in 1774, which stated explicitly in the language of John Locke that "your Petitioners apprehind we have in common with all other men a natural right to our freedoms without Being depriv'd of them by our fellow men as we are a freeborn Pepel and have never forfeited this Blessing by aney compact or agreement whatever."

201 • Revolutionary Antislavery Movements

From 1775 to 1804, numerous antislavery societies were founded in northern states. In 1775 the first Quaker antislavery society in America, the Society for the Relief of Free Negroes Unlawfully Held in Bondage, was established in Philadelphia. In 1785 the New York City Manumission Society was organized by John Jay and Alexander Hamilton. Benjamin Franklin founded the Pennsylvania Abolition Society in 1789. The first national antislavery society, the American Convention for Promoting the Abolition of Slavery, was founded in 1794. The latter went beyond earlier societies to protest the legal and political disabilities placed on free Negroes as well as slavery and the slave trade.

202 • The Anti-Slavery Society of London

Antislavery societies were not limited to the United States. In the late eighteenth century, in response to the move to abolish the slave trade, concerned English men and women founded the Anti-Slavery Society of London. Josiah Wedgwood (1730–95) of that society first published what became one of the most famous medallions of the antislavery movement, this picture of a praying slave.

A woodcut of the Anti-Slavery Society of London's Kneeling Slave Medallion, originally designed by Josiah Wedgwood in 1787. Prints and Photographs Division, Library of Congress

203 • Free African Society

African Americans organized their own societies in the revolutionary period as a way of combating racism and providing for their own survival. One such society was the Free African Society of Boston, which was formed in 1796. This society had more than one purpose: it was committed to the moral uplift of African Americans, but it was also committed to ensuring the economic survival of the Black community in Boston. Toward that end, the Free African Society provided burial insurance and legal representation for its members, the latter in case they might be the victim of reenslavement. The society also provided an opportunity for cultural enrichment, by sponsoring a "Charity Lecture quarterly." Such societies often maintained private lending libraries and offered educational instruction. These societies were needed because it was becoming increasingly clear that African Americans were generally excluded from similar societies that served the white community.

204 • Prince Hall Exhorts

Some African American organizers of fraternal organizations had a more militant agenda than the Free African Society of Boston. That was the case with Prince Hall's African Lodge, established in 1787 after Hall was refused a charter for a Black lodge from the American Masons. After his rejection by the Americans, Hall succeeded in obtaining a charter for a lodge from the British Masons and established the African Lodge, No. 459, in Boston, with Hall as its master. Delivering an address in 1797 to lodge members, Hall exhorted Black Masons to help one another and regard one another with the fellow feeling of the Mason.

205 • Plea for Protection

In 1787 four African American freedmen filed a petition in the House of Representatives to be absolved from having to comply with recent laws passed in North Carolina. Even though these men had been freed legally by their masters, they were still subject to capture and return because of the rewards under North Carolina law. Their petition offered a broader critique of the cruelty of the new nation's fugitive slave laws in practice.

In addition to the hardship of our own case . . . , we believe ourselves warranted, on the present occasion, in offering to your consideration the singular case of a fellow-black now confined in the jail of this city, under sanction of the act of General Government, called the Fugitive Law. . . . This man, having been many years past manumitted by his master in North Carolina, was under the authority of the aforementioned law of that State, sold again into slavery, and, after serving his purchaser upward of six years, made his escape to Philadelphia . . . has been lately apprehended and committed to prison.

Despite such evidence of abuse, the House of Representatives decided not to honor the petition.

206 • Antislavery Petitions Submitted to Congress

On January 2, 1800, a group of Pennsylvania Blacks, including James Forten and Absalom Jones, submitted an antislavery petition to the House of Representatives. The petition sought abolition of the slave trade and repeal of the Fugitive Slave Act of 1793. Congressional reaction was immediate and hostile, as the response of Harrison Gray Otis of Massachusetts illustrates: "To encourage a measure of this kind would have an irritating tendency, and must be

mischievous to America very soon. It would teach them [Blacks] the art of assembling together, debating, and the like, and would so soon, if encouraged, extend from one end of the Union to the other." Undaunted, African American organizations continued to submit petitions over the next several decades. In 1836 Congress adopted a rule preventing consideration of such petitions. The rule was finally rescinded in 1845.

207 • Elizabeth Freeman

No better example exists of how African American slaves utilized Republican ideology to free themselves than the case of Elizabeth Freeman, who was born of African parents around 1742. While working in the Sheffield home of one of the wealthiest merchants in Massachusetts, Colonel John Ashley, Freeman's face was scarred for life when the "lady" of the house attempted to strike Elizabeth's sister with a hot kitchen shovel, and Elizabeth jumped in between and took the blow instead. Furious at such treatment, Elizabeth left the house of Colonel Ashley forever, although Ashley had the gall to attempt to recover her through the law. But Freeman went to a Mr. Theodore Sedgwick, a lawyer, and asked if she could not argue for her freedom under the law. When he asked her what law that might be, she answered "that the 'Bill of Rights' said that all were born free and equal, and that, as she was not a dumb beast, she was certainly one of the nation." Sedgwick accepted her case and Freeman won her suit for freedom against Colonel Ashley. The jury that set her free even awarded her thirty shillings in damages; but the important precedent established by her case was that the Bill of Rights had in fact abolished slavery in Massachusetts.

Portrait of Elizabeth "Mumbet" Freeman by Susan Sedgwick, 1811. Massachusetts Historical Society

Legal Decisions and Their Implications

208 • Abolition Laws

Revolutionary-era antislavery sentiment culminated in a series of state laws passed from 1777 to 1804 in Vermont, Massachusetts, New Hampshire, Pennsylvania, Rhode Island, Connecticut, New York, and New Jersey that abolished slavery in those states. Pennsylvania became the first state to end slavery by an act of its legislature when it passed "An Act for the Gradual Abolition of Slavery" in 1780. But as was the case with many such acts, the Pennsylvania law left enslaved those who were already slaves, and freed only those born after the law. Even those freed were still obligated to serve an

additional twenty-eight years before they were freed.

209 • Right to Slave Property

The Constitution contains a provision for assisting slave owners in the recapture of fugitive slaves. "No Person held to Service or Labour in one State, under the Laws thereof, escaping into another, shall, in Consequence of any Law or Regulation therein, be discharged from such Service or Labour, but shall be delivered up on Claim of the Party to whom such Service or Labour may be due." This paragraph in the Constitution was part of the reason that Judge Roger B. Taney ruled against the freeing of Dred Scott in the *Dred Scott* decision of 1857.

210 • Constitution Says Slaves Count as Three-Fifths of a Person

That the southern states meant to keep their slaves can be seen from how determined they were to have the slaves counted for purposes of determining their representation. During the 1787 Constitutional Convention, the southern states, led by Georgia and South Carolina, proposed Blacks be counted as equals to whites for representation purposes. The northern delegates considered slaves property and thought they should not be counted at all. A compromise was finally reached whereby slaves would be counted as three-fifths of a person. As it appeared in Article I of the Constitution: "Representatives and direct Taxes shall be apportioned among the several States which may be included within this Union, according to their respective Numbers, which shall be determined by adding to the whole Number of free Persons, including those bound to Service for a Term of Years, and excluding Indians not taxed, *three fifths of all other Persons.*"

211 • The Northwest Ordinance

The Northwest Ordinance adopted in 1787 had two implications for African Americans. First, it outlawed slavery in new territories seeking admittance to the Union, thus incorporating Thomas Jefferson's proposal that slavery be confined to the states in which it already existed. Disappointingly the ordinance also allowed the capture of fugitive slaves found within these territories.

212 • Race and the Naturalization Act

When Congress passed the federal Naturalization Act in 1790, it declared that only "free white persons" of good character who had resided for at least two years in the United States and one year in the state from which they applied could be naturalized. But neither the Constitution nor the Naturalization Act defined citizenship or stated that any person currently living as a native of the United States could not be thought of as a citizen. Thus, the Constitution and the Naturalization Act left open whether free Negroes were in fact citizens and entitled to the enjoyment of all of the privileges of citizenship.

213 • Conflict Between Slave and Free States

The Fugitive Slave Act of 1793 did not answer the question of whether a slave remained a slave when both master and slave traveled from a slave to a free state to reside even temporarily in the free state. For example, the Maryland Court of Appeals ruled in 1799 that a slave who was hired out to work in Pennsylvania became free because of Pennsylvania's laws abolishing slavery. In the early national and antebellum periods, the laws of the state where a slave resided were thought to determine status.

ANTEBELLUM PERIOD

Protests, Organizations, and Demonstrations

214 • African American Celebrations

African Americans celebrated the most important event of the early nineteenth century when on January 1, 1808, the law abolishing the international slave trade took effect. Gathering in New York City, African Americans listened to Peter Williams, a well-versed orator, discuss the impact of the slave trade on Africa, the horrors of the Middle Passage, and the triumph of men like John Woolman, Anthony Benezet, and William Wilberforce over the forces of evil and profit in the slave trade. On July 4, 1827, all slaves became free in New York State under its gradual emancipation plan, originally passed in 1799. The African Zion Church was the festive center of the celebration that year, and was decorated with pictures of famous abolitionists, such as John Jay and Thomas Clarkson. Then, on August 1, 1834, African Americans and abolitionists celebrated the end of slavery in the British West Indies. That celebration was bittersweet, however, because of the realization that slavery was still alive and thriving in the United States.

215 • National Negro Conventions

Beginning in September 1830, African Americans held annual national political conventions until 1835, and then periodically afterward until 1855. Through the conventions, African Americans issued addresses to the nation, called attention to the plight of Black Americans, both free and slave, debated the merits of colonization, and issued calls for the immediate emancipation of all slaves. What these national conventions did was link Blacks from different cities into a national political community, and mark the emergence in the 1830s of a new presence in the American political arena—that of the Black abolitionist.

216 • David Walker's Appeal

Born a free Black in Wilmington, North Carolina, David Walker despised slavery. Migrating to Boston in 1785, he grew increasingly radical. His 1829 publication of an eighty-page pamphlet known widely as *David Walker's Appeal* created an uproar in the South. In the appeal, Walker asserted that American Blacks would not be free until Blacks worldwide were freed, so all must fight for universal emancipation:

Your full glory and happiness . . . shall never be fully consummated, but with the entire emancipation of your universal brethren all over the world. . . . For I believe it is the will of the Lord that our greatest happiness shall consist in working for the salvation of the whole body. When this is accomplished a burst of glory will shine upon you, which will indeed astonish you and the world.

217 • The Liberator

The *Liberator* was the preeminent abolitionist newspaper. Started by William Lloyd Garrison on January 1, 1831, the paper enjoyed immense support from African Americans. In the first edition, Garrison declared:

I will be as harsh as truth, and as uncompromising as justice. On this subject, I do not wish to think, to speak, to write, with moderation. No! No! Tell a man whose house is on fire to give a moderate alarm; tell him to moderately rescue his wife from the hands of the ravisher; tell the

William Lloyd Garrison, editor of the *Liberator*.
National Archives

mother to gradually extricate her babe from the fire into which it has fallen; but urge me not to use moderation in a cause like the present! I am in earnest—I will not equivocate—I will not excuse—I will not retreat a single inch—AND I WILL BE HEARD!

218 • American Anti-Slavery Society

The American Anti-Slavery Society was a benevolent and reform organization founded in Philadelphia on December 4, 1833. Dominated by William Lloyd Garrison, Theodore Weld, Lewis and Arthur Tappan, Henry B. Stanton, and James G. Birney, the society published four periodicals, sent more than seventy lecturers throughout the country, encouraged the formation of local chapters, and tried to dispense antislavery literature throughout the North and South. The multiracial society included five Black abolitionists on its board: Peter Williams, Robert Purvis, George B. Vashon, Abraham Shadd, and James McCrummell. Although the American Anti-Slavery Society did not create the new abolitionist movement, the organization came to symbolize the two major strains of antislavery activism in the 1830s and 1840s—a wide-ranging moral crusade and an intellectual movement.

219 • Interracial Tensions in the Movement

Even the antislavery movement contained instances of discrimination and segregation of African Americans. For example, when the Anti-Slavery Women met at their first convention in New York in 1837, the society debated the propriety of having African American women in the organization and only allowed them to join after considerable debate. Some African Americans criticized that most antislavery people wished to have all-white antislavery societies. Most antislavery societies were more concerned about ending slavery, and thereby removing its sin from the conscience of whites, than in fighting against the racial prejudice that shackled free Negroes in the North.

220 • The American and Foreign Anti-Slavery Society

A split occurred in the American Anti-Slavery Society in 1840 when William Lloyd Garrison, who had never held an office in the organization, seized control of the society by stacking the convention with votes from Boston, his base of support. The split occurred ideologically between those, like Lewis and Arthur Tappan, who believed in advocating political action as the best method for attaining abolition and those, like Garrison, who favored appeals based on moral principles. In addition, some in the American Anti-Slavery Society opposed the policy of allowing women to speak to the men at the meetings. Garrison supported the right of women as speakers, being a firm advocate of women's rights. Those that supported political action and opposed women speakers broke off to form the American and Foreign Anti-Slavery Society, which became the nucleus of the Liberty Party, which campaigned on an antislavery plank in the early 1840s. Blacks who committed to the American and Foreign Anti-Slavery Society included Christopher Rush, Samuel Cornish, Charles B. Ray, and James W. C. Pennington.

221 • Reaction of South to Antislavery

The Georgia legislature offered $4,000 for the arrest of William Lloyd Garrison. Arthur Tappan was worth $12,000 in Macon and $20,000 in New Orleans. Vigilance committees in North Carolina offered $1,500 for the arrest of anyone distributing the *Liberator* or *David Walker's Appeal.* A Georgian subscriber to the *Liberator* was dragged from his home, tarred and feathered, set afire, dunked in a river, tied to a post, and then whipped.

James W. C. Pennington. Prints and Photographs Division, Library of Congress

222 • The Murder of Elijah Lovejoy

Violent opposition to the abolition movement was not restricted to the South. Elijah Lovejoy, the white publisher of abolitionist literature, was forced to flee St. Louis after he criticized a judge's lenient treatment of defendants accused of burning alive an African American. William Lloyd Garrison was dragged through the streets of Boston with a noose around his neck on one occasion. These sorts of incidents, however, did not deter the bravest abolitionists, some of whom paid with their lives. In 1837 Lovejoy was murdered by a mob that attacked and destroyed for the fourth time the printing press he used to publish the *Alton (Ill.) Observer.* Even in death Lovejoy was a martyr for freedom, as many joined in the struggle not only against slavery but against those forces in American society that sought to curtail free speech.

223 • Garrisonians Abandon Political Action for Passive Resistance and Moral Force

Garrisonians began to advocate passive resistance and nonviolence. William Whipper published an "Address on Non-Resistance to Offensive Aggression" in 1828 that suggested that "the practice of nonresistance to physical aggression is not only consistent with reason, but the surest method of obtaining a speedy triumph of the principles of universal peace." Garrisonians also began to condemn "complexional institutions" such as Black churches, lodges, schools, newspapers, and conventions, thereby widening the gulf between Garrisonians and some of the more radical Black abolitionists.

224 • Frederick Douglass Splits with Garrisonians

When Frederick Douglass returned from England to America in August 1847, he found his freedom of expression and advancement limited by William Lloyd Garrison. Douglass returned from England with money to start his own newspaper, but Garrison opposed it. After a year of complying with Garrison's wishes, Douglass moved to Rochester, New York, began to publish one, and encouraged Blacks to take a more active role in the antislavery movement. Publishing a newspaper strengthened Douglass's connection with the Black community and deepened his sense of race pride. Douglass began to criticize the Garrisonians for their subjugation of Blacks within their organization and argued that "no people that has solely depended . . . upon the efforts of those, in any way identified with the oppressor . . . ever stood forth in the attitude of Freedom." Douglass also began to develop his own analysis of the antislavery struggle and finally rejected Garrison's insistence that abolitionists avoid political action. In developing his independent thinking, Douglass was not forced to segregate himself. The formation of the American and Foreign Anti-Slavery Society in 1840 as an alternative to the Garrison-controlled American Anti-Slavery Society brought Douglass new and powerful allies in Lewis and Arthur Tappan and Gerritt Smith.

225 • Divisions Within the Abolition Movement

Although ostensibly working toward the same goal, interracial and intraracial divisions developed within the abolitionist movement. Charles Lenox Remond, for example, was an early and prominent supporter of the Garrisonian philosophy of passive nonviolence and moral suasion, which rejected political action because the

Charles Remond. Prints and Photographs Division, Library of Congress

Constitution was deemed a proslavery document. When Douglass broke with Garrison over this issue and allied himself with the Liberty Party, his defection split the followers of the Garrisonian position. In a well-attended and well-publicized debate held at Shiloh Church in New York City in May 1857, Charles Remond challenged Douglass to prove that the Constitution was not a proslavery document. But even Remond eventually moved away from the Garrisonian position and even advocated slave revolts. Despite being highly regarded, Remond allegedly resented the greater attention accorded Frederick Douglass. On one occasion, Remond publicly thanked God that he was not a slave or the son of a slave. Douglass, upon hearing of Remond's remarks, replied: "I thank God I am neither a barber nor the son of a barber."

226 • Reaction to Fugitive Slave Law

Black abolitionists were even more divided by how best to respond to the aggressive Fugitive Slave Law passed as part of the Compromise of 1850. Suddenly the idea of settling outside of the territorial United States became a more appealing idea. Not only were former slaves at greater risk of easy capture and return to the South, but many Black abolitionists responded to the bill's passage as a sign that the federal government was not ready to end slavery or grant free Negroes basic civil rights. Although opposition to the American Colonization Society continued, men such as Martin R. Delany became convinced that leaving the United States, perhaps for the Caribbean, was necessary because of the lack of political rights. Others, like James Theodore Holly, believed in emigration regardless of the granting of political rights, because African Americans, in his view, would continue to encounter "a social proscription stronger than conventional legislation." Even staunch anticolonizationists like Frederick Douglass began to give support to the idea, and in the spring of 1861 Douglass accepted an invitation to visit Haiti. The firing on Fort Sumter kept him from making the trip, for he knew that both war and a radical transformation of slavery were imminent.

227 • Further Divisions

The tension between Frederick Douglass and Charles Lenox Remond was in part a tension between Black abolitionists who had been slaves and those who were freeborn. Often, those who had been slaves possessed a greater sense of entitlement to speak upon the issue of slavery, and that led to conflicts sometimes with free Negroes of the North. One such conflict emerged at a Massachusetts meeting of Blacks held on August 2, 1858, in reaction to the *Dred Scott* decision. Remond declared that he was ready to "spit" on Judge Roger B. Taney's ruling in the case and urged the assembly to issue a statement of defiance of the *Dred Scott* decision. He even proposed that the convention issue a call to the slaves to rebel, and though he realized it was bold, he did his best to make sure those assembled would not turn pale at the suggestion of rebellion. Josiah Henson, the subject of Harriet Beecher Stowe's *Uncle Tom's Cabin,* rose and stated that he believed that Remond would be the first to desert a fight to the death with the slaveholders if it ever came to that. Before the furious Remond could get to his feet to rebut the attack, Henson added that he had never in his life turned pale. Remond's proposal was voted down.

228 • John Brown's Raid at Harpers Ferry

John Brown, a fervent abolitionist, believed he was chosen by God to end slavery. Funded by New England antislavery organizations, Brown tried to establish a station in western Virginia to help fugitive slaves. On October 16, 1859, Brown, with fewer than fifty men, attacked the U.S. arsenal in Harpers Ferry hoping to acquire enough ammunition to launch an attack on Virginia slaveholders. After two days, the arsenal was recaptured by U.S. Marines commanded by Robert E. Lee, then a colonel in the U.S. Army. Brown was convicted of "treason, conspiracy, and advising slaves and others to rebel, and murder in the first degree." Although advised by his attorney to plead insanity, he refused and was sentenced to death by hanging. Five African Americans participated in the raid; two were killed in the fight with U.S. troops, two were hanged, and one escaped.

People and Politics

229 • Benjamin Lundy (1789–1839)

One of the most influential antislavery leaders of the early nineteenth century was the European American Benjamin Lundy, founder and editor of the *Genius of Universal Emancipation,* an antislavery newspaper published from 1821 to 1839. Early in his life Lundy was saddened by the sight of slaves in chains in Virginia and became a dedicated opponent who sacrificed a lucrative business to write and proselytize against slavery. Lundy recruited William Lloyd Garrison to the abolitionist movement. Garrison went to Baltimore in 1829 to work on the *Genius* and became its associate editor before going on to publish the *Liberator.* Garrison eventually moved away from Lundy's conservative antislavery views, such as his faith in gradual emancipation of slaves over years and colonization of free Negroes in Africa. Lundy also tried to develop a free-labor colony, possibly in Texas, in the 1830s, which would prosper by using free Black laborers and thereby convince southern planters that hiring free Black workers was even more profitable than slavery. Although Lundy failed to realize his scheme, he was one of the earliest and most inspirational of antebellum antislavery thinkers, and one of the first to successfully publish an abolitionist newspaper.

230 • William Lloyd Garrison (1805–79)

William Lloyd Garrison was a former white indentured servant who was at the forefront of the abolition movement of the 1830s. Garrison first joined the cause of antislavery agitation in Boston in 1828, when he met Benjamin Lundy, who was looking for subscribers for his *Genius of Universal Emancipation,* a quarterly journal of antislavery rhetoric. At the time, Garrison was a printer who had published the early writings of John Greenleaf Whittier and had edited the *Boston National Philanthropist,* a temperance newspaper, and later the *Bennington (Vt.) Journal of the Times.* Lundy recruited Garrison to serve as coeditor of the *Genius* in Baltimore, but their association was brief. Although influenced by Lundy's ideas, Garrison eventually broke away from Lundy, returned to Boston, began publishing the *Liberator,* and launched the New England Anti-Slavery Society in 1831. Over the next thirty years, Garrison would be the most influential intellectual leader of the abolitionist movement. Eventually he would define the new abolitionism as opposition to colonization, advocacy of immediate emancipation of the slaves, harsh attacks on American churches and the United States Constitution for complicity in slavery, and the belief that moral persuasion rather than political action would end slavery in America. Garrison was also responsible for linking abolitionism to the temperance, peace, and women's rights movements. Garrison was also the one white abolitionist who socialized easily with free Blacks in the North. Whereas many abolitionists advocated an end to slavery but eschewed any social contact with free Blacks in the North, believing, as Samuel Ringgold Ward put it, that it was best to "love the colored man at a distance," Garrison frequently dined at the homes of such free Blacks as James Forten, James McCrummell, and William Topp, and stayed with others during his frequent travels.

231 • Theodore Weld (1803–95)

The son of a white conservative Presbyterian minister, Theodore Weld was one of the architects of the agency system of the American Anti-Slavery Society that sent men out to lecture and

convert audiences to the cause of antislavery in the 1830s. As a young man, he was a well-known lecturer on temperance and moral reform, and was commissioned by the Tappan brothers to establish the Lane Theological Seminary, which he founded in Cincinnati in 1833. Weld organized the famous Lane Seminary Debate, held in January 1834, which systematized the antislavery argument, which Weld then standardized and made integral to the training of agents for the American Anti-Slavery Society. Weld was responsible for training and sending out men who became the backbone of the agency system. These men were paid to travel and convert audiences to the antislavery position. This education and persuasion campaign proved to be the key to the American Anti-Slavery Society's success in building antislavery sentiment in the United States during the 1830s. Though Weld and others like him were often heckled and sometimes stoned and beaten by crowds hostile to the antislavery position, eventually they converted large portions of the states to which they were sent. Still active as a speaker and lecturer in his nineties, Weld rendered invaluable intellectual service to the abolitionist movement.

James Forten, Sr. The Historical Society of Pennsylvania

232 • James Forten, Sr. (1766–1842)

James Forten was an early American success story as well as a prominent Black abolitionist. Having studied as a boy at a school run by Anthony Benezet, Forten served as a powder boy on an American ship in the Revolutionary War, apprenticed to a wealthy sailmaker, and then assumed control of the firm when the owner died. In 1832 Forten was worth over $100,000, employed white and black workers in his firm, managed considerable rental property, and lived in one of the best homes in his native Philadelphia. But Forten was also an active and influential abolitionist: the American Anti-Slavery Society was conceived at Forten's home by William Lloyd Garrison; Forten was a member of that society's board of managers; and Forten reputedly persuaded Garrison to oppose colonization. He sponsored a petition in 1832, with William Whipper and Robert Purvis, to block state legislature attempts to enhance enforcement of the Fugitive Slave Act in Pennsylvania. Beyond the abolition of slavery, Forten advanced women's rights, universal peace, and improvement for the free Negro. He authored a pamphlet of protest against a bill in the Pennsylvania senate to bar free Negroes from immigrating into the state, and founded and served as president of the American Moral Reform Society, an association of African American men devoted to moral and educational improvement of the race.

Robert Purvis, Sr. Prints and Photographs Division, Library of Congress

233 • Robert Purvis, Sr. (1810–98)

Born of mixed parentage—his father was a wealthy cotton broker, his mother a freeborn descendant of a native-born African—Robert Purvis came to Philadelphia from Charleston, South Carolina, at age nine, and at age sixteen, upon the death of his father, inherited $120,000. But Purvis's wealth and prominence did not deter him from becoming an avid abolitionist. Having met Benjamin Lundy and William Lloyd Garrison in 1830, Purvis developed a long-term friendship with Garrison, who often stayed at Purvis's home when Garrison stopped in Philadelphia. A number of runaway slaves stayed overnight at Purvis's home too, since as president of the Vigilance Committee of Philadelphia, he was engaged in the underground railroad. He espoused the "free produce movement," and only served food at his house that was not planted by slaves, supported women's rights, temperance, and prison improvement, and preferred integrated to racially segregated reform movements. Accordingly he was, until 1859, the only African American member of Benjamin Franklin's Pennsylvania Society for Promoting the Abolition of Slavery. Purvis also fought, unsuccessfully, against the proposal to eliminate Blacks from voting in Pennsylvania and successfully blocked the attempt of the school board in his township of Bayberry to bar Black children from public schools when he threatened to withhold the considerable sum he paid in taxes.

234 • William Whipper (1804?–76)

Known as the most articulate writer of the Philadelphia Black abolitionists, William Whipper was also a very successful businessman who pioneered the steam-scouring process into a lucrative dry-cleaning business and ran a successful "free labor and temperance" grocery in Philadelphia. Although not a great speaker, Whipper was very active in the national Negro convention movement, helped organize the American Moral Reform Society, which espoused education, economy, and temperance for all, not just free Blacks, and edited that society's journal, the *National Reformer,* becoming the first African American to edit a national magazine. Whipper was in demand when there was a need to write papers or resolutions. Some of his most important writings were "Address before the Colored Reading Society of Philadelphia" (1828), "Eulogy on William Wilberforce" (1833), and "Non-Resistance to Offensive Aggression," which was published in the *Colored American* in 1837. Whipper, who was a mulatto, was also active in the underground railroad, spending almost $1,000 a year to assist runaway slaves. Despondent over the treatment of

Frederick Douglass. National Archives

African Americans in the United States and the Fugitive Slave Act of 1850, Whipper purchased land in Canada in 1853, with an eye to migrating there. But the Civil War raised his hopes about justice in the United States. Along with Frederick Douglass, Whipper tried, unsuccessfully, to persuade President Andrew Johnson to extend civil rights to Black Americans.

235 • Frederick Douglass (1817–95)

The most famous of the Black abolitionists, Frederick Douglass was born a slave in Talbot County, Maryland, had received favored treatment as a gifted young slave, and eventually escaped to freedom in 1831 by impersonating a free Black sailor. Under the care of David Ruggles, the Black head of the New York Vigilance Committee, Douglass moved to New Bedford, Massachusetts, became an avid reader of the *Liberator,* and in 1841, at an abolitionist meeting in Nantucket, Massachusetts, rose and told his story of what it had been like to be a slave. Soon after, Douglass became one of the star attractions for the Massachusetts Anti-Slavery Society. Studying the style of exposition used by Garrison and Wendell Phillips, Douglass evolved from a slave storyteller to an outstanding speaker, whose diction and poise, wit, humor, and sarcasm transformed him into an engaging lecturer. Challenged by those who believed that no one who spoke that well could have been a slave, Douglass, who had taught himself to read and write, authored his autobiography, *Narrative of the Life of Frederick Douglass,* which was published in 1845. It immediately became a classic, for it was one of the few slave narratives authored by a slave himself. It also made Douglass a marked man for recapture by his former master, causing Douglass to flee to England, where he further enthralled audiences. After twenty-one months in England, Douglass returned to the United States with funds enough to purchase his freedom and to assume the reputation of the most highly regarded of the Black abolitionists.

236 • Sojourner Truth (1797?–1883)

Born in Hurley, Ulster County, New York, in 1797, Isabella grew up on a Dutch farm and was sold to a variety of masters before she escaped from her last master, John Dumont, when he reneged on his promise to release her from bondage following a year of particularly hard labor. She decided to leave when God, whom she spoke to often, advised her to leave. That special relationship with God gave her the courage to successfully sue Dumont for the return of a son that he had sold into slavery in the Deep South, which was illegal under New York law. It also gave her the power to change her name and

Sojourner Truth, Randall Studios, c. 1870. The National Portrait Gallery, Smithsonian Institute

transform herself into Sojourner Truth, who by the 1840s would become an abolitionist and a popular speaker in the revival movement then sweeping the Northeast. She became one of the abolitionist movement's most famous speakers, whose folk wisdom and wry humor disarmed angry anti-abolition crowds in Massachusetts, Connecticut, and even Indiana, where, on one occasion, when challenged by men who disbelieved that she was a woman, she bared her breast and embarrassed her critics. Perhaps most important, Sojourner Truth became one of the very few Black women to participate in the women's rights movement. According to witnesses, she rescued the Akron, Ohio, Women's Rights Convention in 1851 from collapsing under the withering assault of male ministers, who countered the call for women's equality with arguments based on the Bible. Sojourner, in her so-called "Ar'n't I a Woman?" speech, turned the arguments of biblical and intellectual superiority against the men, and asserted her equality with any of them.

237 • Wendell Phillips (1811–84)

Wendell Phillips was a wealthy Bostonian who dedicated himself to lecturing not only on Garrisonian abolitionism but also on the evils of industrial capitalism and the exploitation of labor in America. Like Sojourner Truth, he was regarded as one of the greatest orators of the nineteenth century. After the murder of Elijah Lovejoy, a meeting was called at Faneuil Hall, Boston, on March 26, 1837, to discuss Lovejoy's death. James T. Austin, the attorney general of Massachusetts, referred to Lovejoy's murderers as Revolutionary-era patriots and almost swayed the audience. But Phillips answered the outrageous comparison with a withering verbal speech that sealed his reputation as a first-class antislavery speaker. Phillips supported Garrison's demand that women be allowed the same rights in the American Anti-Slavery Society. He became increasingly militant in the 1840s and 1850s, vigorously opposing the Mexican War, the separation of the North from the South, and the slowness of Lincoln in freeing the slaves. After the Civil War, he became an advocate of a variety of reforms, from American Indian rights to women voting, and the increasing opposition of labor to the rise of moneyed corporations.

238 • Charles Lenox Remond (1810–73)

The son of a Salem hairdresser, merchant, and caterer, Remond was the first Black agent of the Massachusetts Anti-Slavery Society in 1838. Remond was a man of indefatigable energy who lectured every day, sometimes twice a day, to boisterous, hostile crowds, and was re-

puted to be a great speaker, on par with the great Wendell Phillips. Remond was an unwavering follower of Garrison and believed moral suasion was the only way to bring an end to slavery. He was chosen by the American Anti-Slavery Society as one of its four delegates to attend the 1840 World's Anti-Slavery Convention in London, where, to protest the segregation of women at the convention, he sat in the gallery and entertained Lady Byron, duchess of Sutherland. He remained in Great Britain for eighteen months, lectured in Ireland and Scotland, and brought back to the United States an "Address from the People of Ireland," signed by sixty thousand, urging their opposition to slavery. A frequent victim of Jim Crow segregation on trains, Remond was the first Black person to address the legislative committee of the Massachusetts House of Representatives in 1842, when he delivered the "Rights of Colored Persons in Traveling." Remond was opposed to the growing tendency of Blacks to form their own organizations, being critical of any association based on color. During the Civil War, he enlisted men for the famous 54th Massachusetts, which was the first unit to gain national respect for Black troops.

239 • Sarah Parker Remond (1826–94)

Sarah Remond was a physician and an abolitionist who began lecturing with her brother, Charles Remond, in Groton, Massachusetts, in July 1842 and went on to become a famous speaker and fierce fighter for African American civil rights on her own. She protested segregation in public places and more than once sued establishments that either segregated or removed her because of her color. In one case, she had the agent for Madame Henriette Sontag, who was singing in the Boston Atheneum's production of Mozart's *Don Giovanni,* arrested for assisting in forcibly ejecting Remond and her friends from the theater. She also sued the theater and won $500 in damages. Appointed a lecturing agent for the American Anti-Slavery Society in 1856, she went to England and lectured on the evils of slavery in Ireland, Scotland, and England, helping to encourage a boycott against purchasing slave-grown cotton. Regarded as a "living refutation to the theory of Negro inferiority," Sarah Remond eventually settled first in Florence and then in Rome, preferring to live abroad rather than face race prejudice at home.

240 • Formation of the Liberty Party

A year before members of the American Anti-Slavery Society left to form the American and Foreign Anti-Slavery Society, some abolitionists decided to create a national political party, the Liberty Party, to bring about the end of slavery. Formed in 1839 by James Birney, a former slaveholder and a prominent Alabama lawyer converted to antislavery by Theodore Weld in 1832, and by such African American abolitionists as Henry Highland Garnet and Samuel Ringgold Ward, the new party ran Birney for president in 1840. Although Birney only received 7,059 votes, the running of an antislavery presidential candidate was the beginning of a process of political activity on the part of antislavery forces that would culminate in the election of Abraham Lincoln in 1860. The Liberty Party was also the first political party to permit African Americans in any office, even nominating Frederick Douglass to run for New York secretary of state in 1855.

241 • White Women in the Antislavery Movement

White women made dramatic contributions to the abolitionist movement beyond the controversy that split the American Anti-Slavery

Society. Philadelphia's Lucretia Mott was one of the founding members of the American Anti-Slavery Society. She preached at a Quaker meeting in 1818 and was well received. But when Sarah Grimké did the same, some objected to having a woman "speak in meeting." In response to this opposition, her sister, Angelina Grimké, wrote an appeal to southern women to oppose slavery, and Sarah wrote a similar appeal to southern clergymen. This led to controversy within the American Anti-Slavery Society as to whether it was appropriate for women to speak to mixed audiences of men and women. When Angelina Grimké undertook a lecture tour in 1839, controversy swirled nationally about the role of women in the movement. Some felt that challenging the old prohibition against women speakers was diverting the resources of the antislavery movement. Much of the opposition came from the clergy, some of whom regarded women who spoke in public as being somehow unnatural. Many felt more comfortable with women playing a supportive role in the movement, confined to such activities as raising funds for the schools, making clothes for runaway slaves, and serving as teachers in schools for Blacks. But as Garrison recognized, abolitionism was part of a larger liberationist movement that could not be easily confined or limited simply to the problem of slavery.

242 • Free-Soil Party

In August 1848 in Buffalo, New York, antislavery Democrats and Whigs came together to form the Free-Soil Party, whose slogan was "Free Soil, Free Speech, Free Labor, and Free Men." The party chose as their presidential candidate Martin Van Buren, who had become an antislavery figure mainly because of his opposition to the annexing of Texas. The Free-Soil Party was not, however, an abolitionist party: it sought merely to keep slavery a state institution and restrain it from spreading into the western territories. The party's platform represented the minimum of slavery opposition—the desire to contain it rather than eliminate it—and lacked any expression of concern for African American civil or political rights. The party mainly reflected the prevailing ideologies of the states in which it emerged: Massachusetts Free-Soilers were far more militant in their opposition to slavery than Illinois Free-Soilers, who advocated internal colonization and separation of free Negroes from whites.

243 • Harriet Beecher Stowe (1811–96)

Called by Abraham Lincoln "the little woman who started the Civil War," Harriet Beecher Stowe contributed mightily to the abolitionist movement when she published *Uncle Tom's Cabin* in 1852, a denouncement of slavery that was particularly effective because of its sympa-

Harriet Beecher Stowe. National Archives

thetic portrait of the African American character Uncle Tom. Although the novel suffered from some of the melodrama typical of abolitionist tracts of the period, the portrayal of Tom as a human being with feelings evidently influenced many northerners to see slavery as an inhuman institution. Even more influential than the novel on antebellum audiences was the play, which toured throughout the North and brought the drama of Tom and Little Eva to life for many Americans.

244 • Republican Party and Slavery

In 1854 remnants of the Free-Soil Party, the Liberty Party, and the old Whig Party combined to form a new, centrist political organization, the Republican Party. In the election of 1860 the Republican Party ran as its presidential candidate Abraham Lincoln, who had a reputation for being opposed to slavery. But the Republican Party was not an abolitionist party. It proposed only to limit the expansion of slavery into the territories and preserve them for settlement by white men rather than for African Americans. Indeed, several of those territories already had ordinances prohibiting the in-migration of free Blacks. "Free soil" meant free of all Negroes, whether slave or free. Neither Lincoln nor the platform of the Republican Party promised to end slavery. As Horace Greeley, a Republican Party spokesperson put it, "Never on earth did the Republican Party propose to abolish slavery.... Its object with respect to slavery is simply, nakedly, avowedly, its restriction to the existing states."

245 • David Walker Condemns Whites

David Walker's Appeal was one of the first public documents to harshly condemn whites for their treatment of Blacks.

Yet those men tell us that we are the seed of Cain, and that God put a dark stain upon us, that we might be known as their slaves!!! Now, I ask those avaricious and ignorant wretches, who act more like the seed of Cain, by murdering the whites or the blacks? How many vessel loads of human beings have the blacks thrown into the seas? How many thousand souls have the blacks murdered in cold blood, to make them work in wretchedness and ignorance, to support them and their families? How many millions souls of the human family have the blacks beat nearly to death, to keep them from learning to read the Word of God, and from writing?

Southern reaction to the *Appeal* was swift and hostile. Special sessions of Virginia, Georgia, and North Carolina legislatures were called to discuss the tract, and some southern politicians demanded Boston officials arrest Walker immediately. Walker knew the publication threatened his life but declared himself "ready to be offered at any moment." In June 1830, soon after the third edition of the *Appeal* was published, Walker was found dead outside the clothing store he owned.

246 • New England Anti-Slavery Society Defines Immediate Emancipation

In its annual report of 1833, the New England Anti-Slavery Society explained what was meant by "immediate abolition."

What, then, is meant by immediate abolition?

It means, in the first place, that all title of property in the slaves shall instantly cease, because their Creator has never relinquished his claim of ownership, and because none have a right to sell their own bodies or buy those of their own species as cattle. Is there any thing terrific in this arrangement?

It means, secondly, that every husband shall have his own wife, and every wife her own husband, both being united in wedlock according to its proper forms, and placed under the protection of law. Is this unreasonable?

It means, thirdly, that parents shall have the control and government of their own children, and that the children shall belong to their parents. What is there sanguinary in this concession?

It means, fourthly, that all trade in human beings shall be regarded as felony, and entitled to the highest punishment. Can this be productive of evil?

It means, fifthly, that the tremendous power which is now vested in every slaveholder to punish his slaves without trial, and to a savage extent, shall be at once taken away. Is this undesirable?

It means, sixthly, that all the laws which now prohibit the instruction of slaves, shall instantly be repealed, and others enacted, providing schools and instruction for their intellectual illumination. Would this prove a calamity? . . .

247 • Why a Negro Convention Is Necessary

William Hamilton addressed the fourth Convention of the Colored Peoples in New York City in June 1834 and provided a rationale for the organization.

. . . alas for the people of color in this community! Their interest is not identified with that of other men. From them, white men stand aloof. For them the eye of pity hath scarcely a tear. To them the hand of kindness is palsied, to them the dregs of mercy scarcely are given. To them the finger of scorn is pointed: contumely and reproach is continually theirs. They are a taunt, a hissing, and a byword. . . . Ought they not meet to spread out their wrongs before one another? Ought they not to meet to consult on the best means of their relief? Ought they not to make one weak effort—nay, one strong, one mighty moral effort—to roll off the burden that crushes them? Under present circumstances it is highly necessary the free people of color should combine and closely attend to their own particular interest.

248 • First Editorial from the *North Star*

We solemnly dedicate the North Star to the cause of our long oppressed and plundered fellow countrymen. May God bless the undertaking to your good! It shall fearlessly assert your rights, faithfully proclaim your wrongs, and earnestly demand for you instant and even-handed justice. Giving no quarter to slavery at the South, it will hold no truce with oppressors at the North. While it shall boldly advocate emancipation for our enslaved brethren, it will omit no opportunity to gain for the nominally free complete enfranchisement. Every effort to injure or degrade you or your cause—originating wheresoever, or with whomsoever—shall find in it a constant, unswerving and inflexible foe. . . .

249 • Antislavery Attitudes Toward Free Negro Morality

Much of the antislavery sentiment among northern whites derived from a strongly moralistic and religious consciousness, which was reflected sometimes in moralizing advice to the northern African American community:

We have noticed with sorrow, that some of the colored people are purchasers of lottery tickets, and confess ourselves shocked to learn that some persons, who are situated to do much good, and whose example might be most salutary, engage in games of chance for money and for strong drink.

A moment's thought will show the folly, as well as wickedness of their course. Gambling strikes at the very vitals of society, and surely the laboring but rising classes of the community, have no time to waste, nor money foolishly to hazard. All persons of color who are keepers of places for dram drinking, gambling, lewdness and other infamy, should be faithfully remonstrated with; and continuing their practices should be regarded as most injurious of all your enemies.

250 • Proslavery Attack on the Right to Free Speech

During the 1830s the campaign against the abolitionist movement reached a fever pitch as abolitionist literature was seized by the United States Post Office and antislavery printing presses of James G. Birney were destroyed in Cincinnati in 1836 and those of Elijah Lovejoy in Alton, Illinois, in 1837. In the case of Lovejoy, the mobs not only destroyed his press but took his life. Edward Beecher wrote about that affair and the assault on the freedom of expression in antebellum America.

Resolved, 1. That the free communication of thoughts and opinions is one of the invaluable rights of man; and that every citizen may freely speak, write and print on any subject, being responsible for, the abuse of that liberty.... The committee then admit that Mr. Lovejoy has the right to print what he pleases; and to be deprived of this right only for abusing it; and that the question of abuse is to be settled by law, and not by a mob.... The simple fact is, and no sophistry can hide it, that Mr. Lovejoy's rights, and those of all his subscribers had been assailed by a mob; and nothing was needed to restore quiet but that the mob should let them alone. But the mob would not; and for this reason the friends of law armed themselves to repel illegal violence.

251 • Justification for the Antiliteracy Law

There might be no occasion for such enactments in Virginia or elsewhere, on the subject of negro education, but as a matter of self-defense against the schemes of Northern incendiaries, and the outcry against holding our slaves in bondage. Many now living well remember how, and when and why the anti-slavery fury began, and by what means its manifestations were made public. Our mails were clogged with abolition pamphlets and inflammatory documents, to be distributed among our Southern negroes to induce them to cut our throats.... These, however, were not the only means resorted to by the Northern fanatics to stir up insubordination among our slaves. They scattered far and near pocket handkerchiefs, and other similar articles, with frightful engravings, and printed over with antislavery nonsense, with the view to work upon the feeling and ignorance of our negroes, who otherwise would have remained comfortable and happy. Under the circumstances, there was but one measure of protection for the South, and that was adopted....

252 • Reaction of Bostonians to the Return of Anthony Burns Under Fugitive Slave Act

No martial music hear, only the dull tramp of feet and the clatter of horses' hoofs. The men gripped their muskets and stared stolidly down, closing their ears to the jeers and taunts of the crowd.

Windows along the line of the march were draped in mourning and lines of crepe were stretched across the streets. From the window opposite the Old State House was suspended a Black coffin on which were the words, "The Funeral of Liberty." Farther on, the American flag, the Union down, was draped in mourning. The

solemn procession was witnessed by fifty thousand people who hissed, groaned and cried, "Kidnappers! Kidnappers! Shame! Shame! . . ."

Burns was the last fugitive ever seized on the soil of Massachusetts.

253 • Sojourner Truth on Women's Rights

I want to say a few words about this matter. I am a woman's rights, I have as much muscle as any man, and can do as much work as any man. I have plowed and reaped and husked and chopped and mowed, and can any man do more than that? I have heard much about the sexes being equal; I can carry as much as any man, and can eat as much too, if I can get it. I am as strong as any man that is now. As for intellect, all I can say is, if woman have a pint and man a quart—why can't she have her little pint full? You need not be afraid to give us our rights for fear we will take too much, for we can't take more than our pint'll hold. . . . I can't read, but I can hear. I have heard the bible and have learned that Eve caused man to sin. Well if woman upset the world, do give her a chance to set it right side up again. . . . And how came Jesus into the world? Through God, who created him and woman who bore him. Man, where is your part? But the women are coming up, blessed be God, and a few of the men are coming with them. But man is in a tight place, the poor slave is on him, woman is coming on him, and he is surely between a hawk and a buzzard.

—Speech at Women's Rights Convention, Akron, Ohio, June 21, 1851

254 • The Meaning of July Fourth for the Negro

Frederick Douglass, among several others, commented on the alienation African Americans felt in regards to the celebration of the Fourth of July, the date of American independence, when he spoke at a Rochester, New York, celebration in 1852.

Fellow citizens, pardon me, allow me to ask, why am I called upon to speak here today? What have I, or those I represent, to do with your national independence? Are the great principles of political freedom and of natural justice, embodied in that Declaration of Independence, extended to us? and am I, therefore, called upon to bring our humble offering to the national altar and to confess the benefits and express devout gratitude for the blessings resulting from your independence to us?

But such is not the state of the case. I say it with a sad sense of the disparity between us. I am not included within the pale of this glorious anniversary! Your high independence only reveals the immeasurable distance between us. The blessings in which you, this day, rejoice, are not enjoyed in common. The rich inheritance of justice, liberty, prosperity and independence, bequeathed by your fathers, is shared by you, not by me. The sunlight that brought light and healing to you, has brought stripes and death to me. This Fourth of July is yours, *not* mine. You *may rejoice,* I *must mourn.*

255 • Douglass on the Philosophy of Reform

Let me give you a word of the philosophy of reform. The whole history of the progress of human liberty shows that all concessions yet made to her august claims have been born of earnest struggle. . . . If there is no struggle there is no progress. Those who profess to favor freedom and yet deprecate agitation are men who want crops without plowing up the ground; they want rain without thunder and lightning. They want the ocean without the awful roar of its many waters.

—"West Indian Emancipation," 1857

256 • John Rock at the Celebration of the Boston Massacre

John Rock (1825–66) was a dentist, physician, and a Black abolitionist who used the occasion of the celebration of the Boston Massacre of 1858 to attack the treatment of the African American in America.

Our fathers fought nobly for freedom, but they were not victorious. They fought for liberty, but they got slavery. The white man has benefitted, but the black man was injured. I do not envy the white American the little liberty which he enjoys. It is his right, and he ought to have it. I wish him success, though I do not think that he deserves it. But I would have all men free. We have had much sad experience in this country, and it would be strange indeed if we do not profit by some of the lessons which we have so dearly paid for. Sooner or later, the clashing of arms will be heard in this country, and the black man's services will be needed: 150,000 freemen capable of bearing arms, and not all cowards and fools, and three quarters of a million slaves, wild with the enthusiasm caused by the dawn of the glorious opportunity of being able to strike a genuine blow for freedom, will be a power which white men will be bound to respect.

257 • John Brown's Last Remarks

This court acknowledges . . . the validity of the law of God. I see a book kissed, which I suppose to be the Bible, or at least the New Testament, which teaches me that all things whatsoever I would that men should do to me, I should do even so to them. It teaches me further to remember them that are in bonds, as bound with them. I endeavored to act up to that instruction . . . I believe that to have interfered as I have done, as I have always freely admitted I have done in behalf of His despised poor, is no wrong, but right. Now, if it is deemed necessary that I should forfeit my life for the furtherance of the ends of justice, and mingle my blood further with the blood of my children and with the blood of millions in this slave country whose rights are disregarded by wicked, cruel and unjust enactments, I say let it be done.

258 • The Missouri Compromise

When the territory of Missouri applied for statehood, Congress had to decide whether slavery would be permitted or outlawed in the new state. Southern slaveholders had already migrated into Missouri lands, so the question was extremely difficult. In 1820 a two-part compromise was adopted. Missouri gained admission as a slave state, and Maine joined the Union as a free state at the same time, so the balance of slave and free states remained equal—twelve of each. But even more important, the compromise established the principle that slavery could expand into the portion of the Louisiana Territory below 36°30′ north latitude, but not into territory above that latitude. The compromise also reaffirmed that it was legal to capture fugitive slaves in the nonslave territory.

259 • Black Citizenship

Missouri's entry into the Union raised another contentious dispute over its constitution, because it barred free Negroes from entering the state. Barring free Negroes from interstate travel was unconstitutional, some in Congress argued, because free Negroes were citizens. Southerners howled at this suggestion, since they did not regard free Negroes as citizens: certainly they did not enjoy all the rights of citizens in those southern states where they resided in 1820. Some northern congressmen maintained that denying that free Negroes were citizens undermined the entire native basis of citizenship. "If being a native, and free born,

and of parents belonging to no other nation or tribe, does not constitute a citizen of this country, I am at a loss to know in what manner citizenship is acquired by birth," stated one. The Missouri Compromise did not resolve the question of whether free Blacks were citizens; and in the 1830s and 1840s not only would free Blacks be barred from entering more free territories and states but their civil rights, such as the right to vote, would be curtailed in many northern states. But since loss of any specific civil right did not mean the loss of all of one's rights as an American citizen and because the Constitution did not limit citizenship for native-born Americans, the argument over whether free Blacks were citizens was not resolved until the *Dred Scott* decision of 1857, and even that decision was soon challenged.

260 • Black Pennsylvanians Lose the Right to Vote

African Americans began to lose one of the principal rights of citizenship, the right to vote, in the 1830s, ironically during the Jacksonian Period when universal suffrage was being extended to white men. In the early National Period, just after the ratification of the Constitution in 1788, the right to vote was restricted to property owners in many states. But in making voting a privilege of class, the provision gave the vote to free Blacks as well as whites. In the 1830s, however, protest arose about the right to vote for unpropertied laboring whites; and when these Jacksonian-era provisions were discussed, the issue was often opposed by those who wished to keep laboring Blacks from obtaining the vote. As a result, in 1837, property-owning African Americans lost the right to vote in reform legislation that awarded the vote to all white men. Such disfranchisement of the well-to-do Black population actually satisfied the increasingly racist white working class in Philadelphia, which in several anti-Black riots of the 1820s and 1830s had targeted the homes and churches of wealthy African Americans.

261 • Prigg v. Pennsylvania

In *Prigg v. Pennsylvania* (1842) the United States Supreme Court ruled Pennsylvania's "personal liberty" law of 1826 unconstitutional because its sole purpose, in the opinion of the Court, was to block the apprehension and return of fugitive slaves. In doing so, the Court established that a master's right to the return of his or her slave from another state was a national right that could not be abrogated by state law, but could only be legislated by Congress. Since the Court argued that the return of a fugitive slave was essentially a federal responsibility, this decision, ironically, spurred abolitionists to pass even more "personal liberty" laws in such states as Pennsylvania, Rhode Island, Connecticut, Vermont, Massachusetts, and New Hampshire that prevented state authorities from assisting in the recovery of fugitive slaves because it was a federal responsibility. These laws set the stage for the passage of a fugitive slave law in the Compromise of 1850 to compel state authorities to assist the recovery of a master's fugitive slave from another state.

262 • School Segregation in Boston

Brown v. Board of Education (1954) is the most famous school desegregation case, but legal challenges demanding desegregation had been filed as early as 1849. In Massachusetts, for example, African Americans filed a suit (*Roberts v. the City of Boston*) asking the court to enforce the provision of the Massachusetts constitution that declared "all men, without distinction of color or race, are equal before the

law" and to allow Black attendance at white schools. Charles Sumner argued the case on behalf of the African American plaintiffs and delivered a famous address criticizing racial discrimination:

Who can say that this does not injure the blacks? Theirs, in its best estate, is an unhappy lot. Shut out by a still lingering prejudice from many social advantages, a despised class, they feel this proscription for the Public Schools as a peculiar brand. Beyond this, it deprives them of those healthful animating influences which would come from a participation in the studies of their white brethren. It adds to their discouragements. It widens their separation from the rest of the community, and postpones the great day of reconciliation which is sure to come. Although the court rejected his arguments and found that school segregation was "neither illegal or unreasonable," school segregation was abolished in 1855 in Massachusetts when the state legislature passed a measure outlawing racial segregation.

263 • The Wilmot Proviso

In 1846 David Wilmot, a Pennsylvania congressman, proposed a bill that would prohibit the extension of slavery into any new territories acquired as a result of the Mexican War. Wilmot opposed the extension of slavery not because he was ideologically opposed to the institution, but because he felt its practice in the new territories would be inimical to the interests of free labor. In arguing for his proviso, Wilmot reminded congressmen from slaveholding states that he had supported the inclusion of Texas in the Union as a slave state. "We are told," Wilmot said, "that the joint blood and treasure of the whole country is being expended in this acquisition, therefore it should be divided, and slavery allowed to share. Sir, the South has her share already. . . . Now, sir, we are told that California is ours; that New Mexico is ours—won by the valor of our arms. They are free. Shall they remain free? Shall these fair provinces be the inheritance and homes of the white labor of freemen or the Black labor of slaves? This, sir, is the issue. . . ." The Senate rejected the Wilmot Proviso in 1847, but its debate added to the contentiousness over slavery in the territories.

264 • Compromise of 1850

The Compromise of 1850 contained two important elements affecting African Americans. First, it included a new, more stringent fugitive slave law. The new law shifted responsibility for enforcement to federal authorities and permitted assistance from federal marshals and private citizens to pursue and return fugitive slaves. Once apprehended, the fugitive slave would not be allowed to testify on his or her own behalf, and a transcript of an owner's claim of loss was sufficient proof of ownership. The law offered considerable financial rewards to federal commissioners who remanded alleged fugitives back into slavery. The federal commissioners who determined the status of fugitive slaves, for example, received five dollars if the slave was declared free and ten dollars if declared a fugitive and returned to the "rightful" owner. In order to appease abolitionist leaders who were incensed by the Fugitive Slave Act, the second feature of the compromise abolished the slave trade in the District of Columbia. But abolitionists regarded this as woefully insufficient.

265 • Kansas-Nebraska Act

The Kansas-Nebraska Act in 1854 permitted the occupants of the territories seeking admission to the Union to decide for themselves whether the territories would be slave or free,

abrogating the agreement established in the Missouri Compromise that all territories above 36°30′ north latitude would be free. Instead, the Kansas-Nebraska Act reflected the belief of Stephen Douglas, its author, that once popular sovereignty became the test of whether a state was slave or free, the controversy over slavery in the territories would be put to rest. In practice, however, the Kansas-Nebraska Act set off a violent struggle between proslavery and antislavery forces as each tried to settle the territories.

266 • *Dred Scott* Case

In 1837 Dr. John Emerson left Missouri to spend four years as an army surgeon in Illinois, a free state. He brought his slave, Dred Scott, with him. Under the Missouri Compromise, Scott also should have been free in the part of the Louisiana Territory in which he had previously lived with Emerson. When he returned to Missouri from Illinois, Dred Scott sued for his freedom, but the court ruled that residence in a free state did not automatically make a slave free. In the meantime, Dr. Emerson had died and his widow became Scott's owner. She married Congressman Calvin C. Chaffee of Massachusetts, a well-known abolitionist. Because Chaffee did not want to be known as a slave owner, Scott was sold to Mrs. Emerson-Chaffee's brother. Scott tried to bring suit in federal court, but when the Supreme Court heard the case in 1857 it decided against Scott because (1) as an African American, Scott was not a citizen of Missouri as set out by the Constitution and had no rights in federal courts, (2) temporary residence in a free state did not make one free, and (3) the Missouri Compromise was unconstitutional. This last decree limited the power of Congress to exclude slavery from any Northwest territories that would subsequently apply for admission to the Union.

Engraving of Dred Scott. Prints and Photographs Division, Library of Congress

267 • Black Civil Rights in the North in the 1850s

Black civil and political rights declined in the 1850s. Although less than 2 percent of the population of the free states (fewer than 250,000 persons), African Americans were severely restricted in their movement and their exercise of basic rights. Blacks lived in the poorest, filthiest, and oldest neighborhoods, worked at the most menial of jobs, attended segregated public schools when they attended school at all, and lacked basic legal protection before the law. All states except Massachusetts denied African Americans the right to serve on juries. Indiana, Iowa, Oregon, California, and Lincoln's own state, Illinois, refused to allow African Americans to testify against whites in court. In California this led to the widespread abuse of Blacks by whites who knew they were immune to prosecution. Ironically the antislavery movement may have indirectly caused an intensifying of restrictions, for as some states witnessed the increasing power of the antislavery movement, fear spread that Blacks would leave the South in droves to compete with white labor in the North and the territories. Accordingly Oregon, Iowa, Indiana, and Illinois barred Blacks from immigrating into the state.

268 • Restrictions on Voting

Five New England states permitted African Americans to vote without restrictions in the presidential election of 1860. In New York, only Blacks who owned $250 or more in property could vote. In Ohio, only those African Americans who visibly appeared to have more Caucasian than African blood in their veins were allowed to vote. In the rest of the country, African American voters played no part in choosing Abraham Lincoln to be the thirteenth president of the United States.

CIVIL WAR

Toward the War

269 • Black Abolitionist View of Lincoln's Election

Most northern Blacks, especially Black abolitionists, approved of Lincoln's election, even if it did not mean he would work to end slavery. According to Frederick Douglass, the election was at least a step in the right direction.

What, then, has been gained to the anti-slavery cause by the election of Mr. Lincoln? Not much, in itself considered, but very much when viewed in the light of its relation and bearings. For fifty years the country has taken the law from the lips of an exacting, haughty and imperious slave oligarchy. . . . Lincoln's election has vitiated their authority, and broken their power . . . [and] . . . demonstrated the possibility of electing, if not an Abolitionist, at least an anti-slavery reputation *to the Presidency.*

270 • Southerners React to Lincoln's Election

Regardless of what Lincoln or the Republican Party platform stated, southern states believed the election of Lincoln as president meant the end of slavery. Immediately after the election in November 1860, several states began to hold conventions and debate secession from the Union. Before Lincoln took office on March 4, 1861, seven states had seceded from the Union. South Carolina (December 20, 1860) was the first to secede, followed by Mississippi (January 9, 1861), Florida (January 10), Alabama (January 11), Georgia (January 19), Louisiana (January 26), and Texas (February 1). Although Lincoln and other Unionists were angry that "the functions of the Federal Government were found to be generally suspended within" those states, Black abolitionists were glad to see them go. "Stand not upon the order of your going, but go at once," exclaimed H. Ford Douglass. "There is no union of ideas and interests in this country, and there can be no union between freedom and slavery." Likewise, most Garrisonians supported secession because it would remove the moral evil of slavery from the United States and the Constitution and free the United States from having to defend and protect slavery. Black abolitionists like Frederick Douglass also believed removal of the South from the Union would reduce the influence of the South in trying to erode northern Black political and civil rights, and ultimately prompt more slaves to escape the South and slavery for the North.

271 • Crittenden Compromise of Black Rights

Black abolitionists correctly assumed that compromise with the secessionist South to keep it in the Union would prolong slavery and hurt free Negroes in the North. That such fears were well founded became clear when Senator John Crittenden of Kentucky proposed what became known as the Crittenden Compromise in 1860. Among other things, Crittenden wanted a constitutional amendment that would allow slavery in territories below the 36°30′ line and guarantee that no additional interference with southern slavery would be permitted. Virginia, which was seeking ways not to secede, invited representatives from northern states to Virginia to discuss the proposal, but African Americans in Massachusetts protested. A key ingredient in the compromise was a demand that the few northern states that granted political and civil rights to African Americans rescind those rights and support colonization of free Blacks outside of the country. Black Bostonians wrote that "as citizens of the Commonwealth of Massachusetts who have heretofore felt perfectly secure in the enjoyment of the rights pertaining to such citizenship . . . pray your honorable body . . . to oppose and vote against every proposition which may have in view the withdrawal or injury of those rights." African Americans in the North breathed a sigh of relief when Massachusetts did not support the Crittenden Compromise and Lincoln scuttled it by refusing any extension of slavery into the territories.

272 • African American Reaction to Fort Sumter

African Americans in the North rejoiced when South Carolina's armed forces started the Civil War on April 12, 1861, by attacking Fort Sumter, the federal garrison in South Carolina. After the federal government called up troops and Virginia (April 17), Arkansas (May 6), Tennessee (May 7), and North Carolina (May 20) left the Union, most African Americans in the North approved of the war because they believed it would eventually end slavery. Many African Americans also saw the war as a way for Blacks to prove their citizenship and help liberate the slaves by fighting in the war effort. African Americans throughout the North formed militia companies, began drilling, and volunteered their services. But their offers were rejected. The secretary of war declared in 1861 that "this Department has no intention at present to call into the service of the Government any colored soldiers." The militia commander in Ohio declared inaccurately that "the Constitution will not permit me to issue the order" to raise African American troops. Others in Ohio put the matter more bluntly: "We want you d——d niggers to keep out of this; this is a white man's war." The Lincoln administration and most white northerners argued during its first two years that the Civil War was not a war over slavery, but a way to reunite the Union.

Toward Emancipation

273 • The Slaves as a Military Element in the South

Slavery was an asset to the South, as this article in the *Montgomery Advertiser* dated November 6, 1851, boldly asserted.

The total white population of the eleven states now comprising the Confederacy is 6,000,000, and, therefore, to fill up the ranks of the proposed army (600,000) about ten percent of the entire white population will be required. In any other country than our own such a draft could not be met, but the Southern States can furnish that number of men, and still not leave the material interests of the country in a suffering condition. Those who are incapacitated for bearing arms can oversee the plantations, and the negroes can go on undisturbed in their usual labors. In the North the case is different; the men who join the army of subjugation are the laborers, the producers, and the factory operatives. Nearly every man from that section, especially those from the rural districts, leaves some branch of industry to suffer during his absence. The institution of slavery in the South alone enables her to place in the field a force much larger in proportion to her white population than the North.

274 • Douglass on Lincoln's Early War Policy

In his *Douglass' Monthly* dated July 1861, Frederick Douglass questioned Lincoln's reluctance to emancipate the slaves.

Why? Oh! Why, in the name of all that is national, does our Government allow its enemies this powerful advantage?... The very stomach of this rebellion is the negro in the condition of a slave. Arrest that hoe in the hands of the negro, and you smite rebellion in the very seat of its life. ... Teach the rebels and traitors that the price they are to pay for the attempt to abolish this Government must be the abolition of slavery.... Henceforth let the war cry be down with treason and down with slavery, the cause of treason.

275 • Harriet Tubman Was More Positive

Harriet Tubman was more positive about Lincoln than Frederick Douglass in 1861.

God won't let Massa Linkum beat de South till he do de right ting. Massa Linkum he great man, and I'se poor nigger; but dis nigger can tell Massa Linkum how to save de money and de young men. He do it by setting de niggers free. S'pose dar was awfu' big snake down dar, on de floor. He bite you.... You send for doctor to cut de bite; but snake he rolled up dar, and while doctor dwine it, he bite you agin. De doctor cut out dat bite; but while he dwine it, de snake he spring up and bite you agin, and so he keep dwine, till you kill him. Dat's what Massa Linkum orter know.

276 • First Confiscation Act

The first emancipation act was issued by Congress, not by President Lincoln. On August 6, 1861, Congress passed the Confiscation Act, which stated that any slaves owned by masters who were aiding the insurrection against the national government could be captured and set free. This was an act that enabled generals to withhold captured slaves from their masters, in contrast to Union Army policy early in the war. Its impact was limited, however, as the Union forces in 1861 were mainly experiencing losses on the battlefield.

277 • Lincoln Edges Toward Emancipation

Lincoln's views on emancipating the slaves evolved during the Civil War, and on March 6, 1862, he recommended that Congress adopt a resolution to offer funding to any state that voluntarily adopted gradual emancipation. "Resolved that the United States ought to co-operate with any state which may adopt gradual abolishment of slavery, giving to such state pecuniary aid, to be used by such state in its discretion, to compensate for the inconveniences public and private, produced by such change of system." Unfortunately for Lincoln, the border states blocked Congress from passing such a bill.

278 • Lincoln Retreats with Hunter

On April 25, 1862, General David Hunter, commander of the Union forces, declared martial law in South Carolina, Georgia, and Florida. On May 9 he declared: "Slavery and martial law in a free country are altogether incompatible; the persons in these three States—Georgia, Florida, and South Carolina—heretofore held as slaves, are therefore declared forever free." But on May 19 Lincoln revoked Hunter's order.

I, Abraham Lincoln, president of the United States, proclaim and declare, that the government of the United States, had no knowledge, information, or belief, of an intention on the part of General Hunter to issue such a proclamation . . . and that the supposed proclamation, now in question, whether genuine or false, is altogether void, so far as respects such declaration.

I further make known that whether it be competent for me, as Commander-in-Chief of the Army and Navy, to declare the Slaves of any state or states, free, and whether at any time, in any case, it shall have become a necessity indispensable to the maintenance of the government, to exercise such supposed power, are questions which, under my responsibility, I reserve to myself, and which I can not feel justified in leaving to the decision of commanders in the field. These are totally different questions from those of police regulations in armies and camps.

279 • Abolitionists React

I come now to the policy of President Lincoln in reference to slavery. . . . I do not hesitate to say, that whatever may have been his intentions, the action of President Lincoln has been calculated in a marked and decided way to shield and protect it from the very blows which its horrible crimes have loudly and persistently invited. . . . He has steadily refused to proclaim, as he had the constitutional and moral right to proclaim, complete emancipation to all the slaves of rebels who should make their way into the lines of our army. He has repeatedly interfered with and arrested the anti-slavery policy of some of his most earnest and reliable generals. . . . To my mind that policy is simply and solely to reconstruct the union on the old and corrupting basis of compromise, by which slavery shall retain all the power that it ever had, with the full assurance of gaining more, according to its future necessities.

—Frederick Douglass

280 • Lincoln's Early Views

Lincoln seemed to answer Douglass's charges when Lincoln replied by letter (August 22, 1862) to similar criticisms published by his longtime supporter, the Republican Horace Greeley: "If I could save the Union without freeing *any* slave I would do it, and if I could save it by freeing *all* the slaves I would do it, and if I could save it by freeing some and leaving others alone I would also do that. What I do about slavery, and the colored race, I do because I believe it helps to save the Union."

281 • Second Confiscation Act and Other Pressures from Congress

In addition to the lobbying of abolitionists and Union generals, Lincoln was also increasingly pressured by Congress in 1862. Congress had already issued the first emancipation order that freed the slaves of the District of Columbia and compensated their owners up to $300 each. A resident of Baltimore brought the news to a District of Columbia slave.

Chambermaid at Smith's (my former place) . . . is a slave so this morning I went there to inform her of the passage of the Bill when I entered The cook her and another Slave woman who has a slave son were talking relative to the Bill expressing doubts of its passage & when I entered

they perceived that something was ahead and emeadiately asked me "Whats the news?" The Districts free says I pulling out the "National Republican" and reading its editorial when I had finished the chambermaid had left the room sobbing for joy. The slave woman clapped her hands and shouted, left the house saying "let me go and tell my husband that Jesus has done all things well."

In addition to the District bill, a second confiscation act was passed by Congress on July 17 that declared "forever free" the slaves of rebel masters when those slaves came into Union lines. This act did not have the impact of Lincoln's final Emancipation Proclamation, however.

282 • Preliminary Emancipation Proclamation

For largely political reasons—assuaging abolitionists in his party, destabilizing the South, enlisting desperately needed Black troops, preventing England from entering the war on the side of the Confederacy, and transforming a lackluster Unionist conflict into an idealistic war to end slavery—Lincoln decided to free the slaves by presidential decree. But Lincoln did not want to issue the proclamation before the North had won a major victory for fear such a proclamation would seem an act of desperation. Thus, Lincoln waited until the Union Army finally won a major battle at Antietam on September 17, 1862, issuing his preliminary proclamation on September 22.

That on the first day of January in the year of our Lord, one thousand eight hundred and sixty-three, all persons held as slaves within any state, or designated part of a state, the people whereof shall then be in rebellion against the United States shall be then, thenceforward, and forever free; and the executive government of the United States, including the military and naval authority thereof, will recognize and maintain the freedom of such persons, and will do no act or acts to

Lincoln reading the Emancipation Proclamation to his cabinet. Prints and Photographs Division, Library of Congress

repress such persons, or any of them, in any efforts they may make for their actual freedom.

Lincoln's proclamation was still tentative and something of a bribe: if any of the Confederate states ceased their resistance to the Union, their slaves would not be freed.

283 • Final Emancipation Proclamation

None of the rebellious states had ceased their armed resistance by January 1, 1863, so Lincoln issued the promised Emancipation Proclamation: "Now, therefore, I, Abraham Lincoln, President of the United States, by virtue of the power in me vested as Commander-in-Chief. . . . as a fit and necessary war measure for suppressing said rebellion, do, on this first day of January . . . declare that all persons held as slaves within said designated States, and parts of States, are, and henceforward shall be free," except the slaves in the four loyal slave states—Maryland, Delaware, Missouri, and Kentucky—thirteen parishes of Louisiana, including New Orleans, forty-eight counties in West Virginia, seven counties in Virginia, including Norfolk and Portsmouth, "which excepted parts are, for the present, left precisely as if this proclamation was not issued."

Actually Lincoln's proclamation did not really free any slaves. Left untouched were the numerous slaves in the border states that had remained loyal to the Union. Lincoln feared he would alienate those states if their slaves were freed, so he exempted them. And those slaves living in the Confederate states would be freed only when, or if, the Union Army won. The proclamation did free those slaves, called contrabands of war, already in Union lines, but this was redundant, as they had already been freed by the Confiscation Act of 1862. Despite this, Lincoln's proclamation was still pivotal. It gave needed meaning to the conflict as a war to end slavery in America. The Emancipation Proclamation also made it difficult for England to enter the war against a nation fighting to do what England had already done by freeing the slaves in the West Indies. But the most important part of the proclamation was basically neglected: it ordered that Blacks "be received into the armed service of the United States."

284 • Karl Marx on Lincoln and His Proclamation

Even revolutionary thinkers like Karl Marx were impressed with Lincoln's proclamation, which Marx argued represented the largest transfer of property in the history of the world. Marx was also impressed with the democratic style of the president, who, according to Marx,

> *always gives the most significant of his acts the most commonplace form. . . . Indecisively, against his will, he reluctantly performs the* bravura aria *of his role as though asking pardon for the fact that circumstances are forcing him to "play the hero." The most formidable decrees which he hurls at the enemy and which will never lose their historic significance, resemble—as the author intends them to—ordinary summonses sent by one lawyer to another on the opposing side. . . . And this is the character the recent Proclamation bears—the most important document of American history since the founding of the Union, a document that breaks away from the old American Constitution—Lincoln's manifesto on the abolition of slavery. . . . Never yet has the New World scored a greater victory than in this instance, through its demonstration that, thanks to its political and social organization, ordinary people of good will can carry out tasks which the Old World would have to have a hero to accomplish!*

285 • Southern Slaves Learn of the Proclamation

Most slaves in the Confederate South learned of the Emancipation Proclamation through the slave grapevine, a communication network between Blacks in the Union Army and slaves behind Confederate state lines. But some learned of it through the newspaper. In New Orleans free Blacks published their own bilingual newspaper, *L'Union,* which disseminated information about Lincoln's edict.

Brothers! The hour strikes for us; a new sun, similar to that of 1789, should surely appear on our horizon. May the cry which resounded through France at the seizure of the Bastille resonate today in our ears. . . .

Men of my blood! Shake off the contempt of your proud oppressors. Enough of shame and submission; the break is complete! Down with the craven behavior of bondage! Stand up under the noble flag of the Union and declare yourselves hardy champions of the right. Defend your rights against the barbarous and imbecile spirit of slavery; prove to the entire world that you have a heart noble enough to walk with civilization and to understand its benefits, and a spirit high enough to know and admire the imposing work of the Creator. . . .

286 • Slaves Learn from Union Soldiers

On the South Carolina Sea Islands, the former slaves who were already liberated and attending schools run by northern teachers held a celebration on January 1, 1863.

I wish it were possible to describe fitly the scene which met our eyes as we sat upon the stand, and looked down on the crowd before us. There were the black soldiers in their blue coats and scarlet pantaloons, the officers of this and other regiments in their handsome uniforms, and crowds of lookers-on,—men, women, and children, of every complexion, grouped in various attitudes under the moss-hung trees. The faces of all wore a happy, interested look. The exercises commenced with a prayer by the chaplain of the regiment. . . . Colonel Higginson then introduced Dr. Brisbane, who read the President's Proclamation, which was enthusiastically cheered.

Toward Equality

287 • Reaction in the North: Anti-Black Riots

Some whites in the North welcomed the Emancipation Proclamation. But many others, especially those from the lower classes and of foreign birth, reacted angrily to it. Many white workingmen feared that emancipation would bring job competition with freedmen who might migrate North. Others, many of them from the Irish working class, also reacted angrily to Lincoln's imposition of the draft, which to their minds committed them to fight in a war to free the slaves. On July 13, 1863, these feelings boiled over into four days of bloody rioting in New York City. The rioting started at the draft enrollment office, which was burned down, but it quickly shifted to attacks on the Black section of the city. Twelve hundred people, mostly African Americans, were killed, the Colored Orphan Asylum was set on fire, and hundreds of Blacks were forced to flee from their homes. The ferocity of the attacks on defenseless Blacks, in part a frenzy of anti-Republican feeling whipped up by local Democratic politicians, was unbelievable. "A child of 3 years of age was thrown from a 4th story window and instantly killed. A woman one hour after her confinement was set upon and beaten with her tender babe in her arms. . . . Children were torn from their

mother's embrace and their brains blown out in the very face of the afflicted mother. Men were burnt by slow fires." In the end, Union troops were required to quell the rioting.

288 • Northern Treatment of Former Slaves

Mistreatment of African Americans was not confined to the Irish working class in New York. Even soldiers in the Union Army stationed in the Sea Islands off the coast of South Carolina regularly abused and degraded African Americans in the community. But at the same time, many northerners, especially schoolteachers, volunteered to go South and educate the freedmen. These missionaries, both African American and European American, set up schools, provided religious instruction, and helped freedmen make the transformation from slave to free labor.

289 • Lincoln's Plan for Reconstruction

On December 8, 1863, Lincoln issued his Proclamation on Amnesty and Reconstruction for the restoration of the Confederate states into the Union. He offered them a full pardon and restoration of their rights if they were willing to take an oath of loyalty to the Union and accept the end of slavery. When 10 percent of a seceded state's population that had voted in the election of 1860 pledged their future loyalty to the Union, then that state could create a new state government and elect representatives to Congress, subject to the approval of each house of Congress. But Lincoln's proclamation did not demand that the Confederacy give civil or political rights to former slaves or free people of color or promise them the right to vote in the postwar South. As Wendell Phillips noted, Lincoln's plan "frees the slave and ignores the negro."

290 • The Miscegenation Controversy

During Lincoln's reelection campaign in 1864, Democrats sought to exploit the fears of white Americans about the social consequences of the Emancipation Proclamation. Two Democratic strategists, in one of the first examples of election "disinformation," published a pamphlet that they advertised as being produced by an abolitionist. Its title page graphically portrayed what the pamphlet argued—that the point of Lincoln's emancipation of the slaves was to promote "social equality" in general, and sexual intercourse in particular, between the races. The pamphlet introduced a new word in the language—miscegenation—for the latter

Cover of a pamphlet that falsely represents Lincoln as favoring miscegenation as a consequence of the Emancipation Proclamation, 1864. Prints and Photographs Division, Library of Congress

practice. Despite the boldness of its appeal to racist sentiments, the pamphlet was not believed to be authentic, and Lincoln was reelected despite an effective attempt by Democrats to use the Emancipation Proclamation against him.

291 • Lincoln on Postwar Black Voting Rights

Like most northerners, Lincoln's belief in the moral rightness of the abolition of slavery did not mean he supported the notion that Blacks were or ever would be the equals of whites. Indeed, Lincoln continued to advance plans for the voluntary colonization of African Americans outside of the United States as the best way to address their postwar status. Yet Lincoln, who showed himself flexible on the subject of emancipation, may have been flexible on the issue of suffrage for Blacks in Reconstruction had he lived to direct it. During the process of Reconstruction in Louisiana, representatives of the wealthy, educated, and cultivated freeborn Negro community in New Orleans met with Lincoln on March 12, 1864, to present a petition to obtain the right to vote in a reconstructed Louisiana. After that meeting, Lincoln wrote to Governor Michael Hahn:

Now you are about to have a Convention which, among other things, will probably define the elective franchise. I barely suggest for your private consideration, whether some of the colored people may not be let in—as, for instance, the very intelligent, and especially those who have fought gallantly in our ranks. They would probably help, in some trying time to come, to keep the jewel of liberty within the family of freedom.

Hahn, however, did not support Lincoln's notion.

292 • Civil Rights Change During the Civil War

The Civil War brought some changes in the civil rights of Blacks in the North, but not without a struggle. After the Emancipation Proclamation was issued in 1863 and Blacks were permitted to fight in the war, California began to allow African Americans to testify in criminal court. Ohio also struck down its Black Laws. But the Civil War also brought enforcement of the anti-immigration statute in Illinois which fined any African American who entered the state. Anyone who could not pay the fine could be arrested and sold into slavery at a public auction. Before the war, this statute was rarely enforced, but when Black migration into the state increased during the Civil War, the courts began to enforce the law vigorously. In 1863, for example, the year of Lincoln's Emancipation Proclamation, eight Blacks were convicted of illegal entry into the state and seven of them were sold into slavery. Black Chicagoans were outraged by the convictions and, led by the wealthy African American tailor John Jones, they prodded, lobbied, and petitioned the Illinois state legislature to eliminate the Black Laws. In February 1865 the laws that kept African Americans from entering the state, serving on juries, or giving testimony in Court were repealed. By the winter of 1865–66 even Indiana had struck down its anti-immigration law. But some things had not changed: only five New England states had allowed Blacks to vote with whites at the beginning of the war, and only those five still granted equal voting rights to Blacks at the end of the war.

293 • Black Convention of 1864

On October 4–7, 1864, more than a hundred African American men gathered at Syracuse, New York, for a "National Convention of Colored

Citizens" to plan a postwar political agenda for Blacks. In attendance were Jonathan C. Gibbs, Richard H. Cain, Francis L. Cardozo, Jonathan J. Wright, Henry Highland Garnet, and Frederick Douglass, who wrote the convention address, "Address to the People of the United States." Although Garnet, a strong Black nationalist, still argued that Blacks should pursue a separate identity, most participants read the events of the Civil War—the imminent demise of slavery, the employment of African American troops, and the success of the abolitionist movement—as signs that African Americans were on the verge of complete acceptance into the mainstream of American society. Among the list of convention recommendations were the abolition of slavery, support of women's rights, full civil and political equality in the law, and extension of the franchise to African Americans. To lobby for these ideas, the convention founded a National Equal Rights League, with the lawyer John Mercer Langston as president. In his "Address to the Colored People of the United States," he urged Blacks to found local auxiliaries of the Equal Rights League in their communities to fight for their rights.

294 • Discrimination on Philadelphia Streetcars

A sign of how far African Americans still had to go to receive equal treatment on public accommodations came in January 1865 when Robert Smalls, the Black Civil War hero who had stolen a Confederate ship and delivered it to the Union Navy, was thrown off a streetcar in Philadelphia because he was an African American. That incident sparked a nationwide outcry about segregation in public accommodations in the North. In May 1865 Massachusetts enacted the first public accommodations law in American history. Ohio soon struck down its Black Laws. But it was not until 1867, two years after the end of the Civil War, that Pennsylvania desegregated its public transportation and allowed African Americans like Robert Smalls to ride the Philadelphia streetcars like other American citizens.

295 • Rock at the Supreme Court

In February 1865 John Rock became the first African American to be accepted as a lawyer before the Supreme Court. Presented by Charles Sumner and accepted by Chief Justice Salmon P. Chase, Rock became a symbolic repudiation to the 1857 *Dred Scott* decision by the Supreme Court.

296 • Truth Desegregates D.C. Trolleys

In March 1865 a law was passed in the District of Columbia outlawing discrimination on streetcars. But it had not been tested in the streets until Sojourner Truth took on the forces of discrimination. Truth had moved to the nation's capital to work as a nurse tending to the injured and wounded from the war, and during her stay in Washington, she faced difficulty transporting articles for her patients because Blacks were only allowed to ride on a few Jim Crow cars on each line. Even on these cars, Blacks often had to stand because the cars were filled with whites, who, by custom, occupied the seats. After writing to the head of the street railroad, Sojourner believed the practice was ended until she tried to signal a car to stop. Several passed her until finally she began to yell, "I want to ride! *I want to ride!!* I WANT TO RIDE!!" When one car was blocked temporarily from leaving, Sojourner leaped on board to the cheers of the crowd. The conductor, angered by her victory, yelled that he would put her off, but she challenged him and remained on board. After several other conflicts with conductors

boarding cars, Truth was finally thrown against the door of a car by a streetcar driver in Georgetown. At the hospital she learned that her shoulder had been broken. Immediately she had the conductor arrested for assault and battery, and the driver lost his job. Sojourner recalled in her autobiography:

It created a great sensation, and before the trial was ended, the inside of the cars looked like pepper and salt; and I felt, like Poll Parrot, "Jack, I am riding." A little circumstance will show how great a change a few weeks had produced: A lady saw some colored women looking wistfully toward a car, when the conductor, halting, said, "Walk in, ladies." Now they who had so lately cursed me for wanting to ride, could stop for black as well as white, and could even condescend to say, "Walk in, ladies."

297 • Freedmen's Bureau

In the last months of the war, southern life was completely devastated. Crusading Union forces and fleeing Confederate stragglers decimated the remaining plantations, destroyed roads, bridges, and cities, and left thousands of people homeless without food or clothing. The pleas of former slaves and free people of color for relief were largely ignored by southern governments more concerned with the plight of former planters and with their own survival as state entities than with helping the newly freed Blacks. So African Americans turned to northerners and abolitionists, who responded by pressuring Congress to provide for the needy in the South. In March 1865 Congress established the Bureau of Refugees, Freedmen, and Abandoned Lands, more popularly known as the Freedmen's Bureau, to aid displaced former

A drawing by A. R. Waud to show the Freedmen's Bureau as a mediator between southern white and freedmen's interests.
Prints and Photographs Division, Library of Congress

slaves and white refugees. It provided food, clothing, supplies, job placement, education, and homestead land to people, and negotiated disputes over contracts between former masters and former slaves. From 1865 to 1869, the Bureau distributed over 21 million rations, set up forty-six hospitals, and spent over $2 million to treat illnesses. But despite its benefits to the South, white southerners denounced the Bureau as an agent of Republican control and an interference in local affairs. When Congress passed a bill to extend the operation of the Freedmen's Bureau in February 1866, President Andrew Johnson vetoed it, claiming that it would create an immense federal bureaucracy, injure citizen's rights, and make freedmen lazy. In July Congress overrode Johnson's veto, extending the life of the bureau until 1870.

298 • Assassination of Lincoln

When Lincoln was shot at Ford's Theater on April 14, 1865, and died the next day, the outlook for postwar African American civil rights changed dramatically. However, Lincoln's death may have improved the outlook for full black political rights. If Lincoln had lived, it is unlikely that the Radical Republican element in Congress would have taken over Reconstruction and pushed through legislation such as the Reconstruction Act of 1867 and the Fourteenth and Fifteenth Amendments. But Lincoln was replaced by the politically less flexible and less astute Vice President, Andrew Johnson, who steered the presidency into a showdown with congressional Republicans that he ultimately lost.

299 • The Wade-Davis Bill

Many of the Republicans in Lincoln's own party disagreed with his mild plan for Reconstruction of the nation, and expressed that dissatisfaction by passing their own plan in the Wade-Davis Bill on July 2, 1864. The bill called for a provisional military governor of a state to enroll all white citizens of a state, and after a majority of them took an oath of allegiance to the Union, a constitutional convention would be held to raise a state government. Any southerner who had been a member of the Confederate Army or served in the Confederate government was disqualified from voting or serving as a delegate. The states had to accept, of course, the end of slavery. This bill, by basing representation on a majority of loyal citizens, made it more difficult for states to return to the Union. Lincoln did not support the bill and let it die by simply failing to sign it in time. Given the clamor of Republicans about Lincoln's ignoring of Black rights in his plan, it is interesting to note that the Wade-Davis Bill contained no reference to Black voting rights.

Reconstruction Terms, Phrases, and Slogans

300 • Presidential Reconstruction

Presidential Reconstruction was the process begun by Abraham Lincoln and continued by President Andrew Johnson of bringing the Confederate states back to the Union. Termed a mild reconstruction by Republicans in Congress who proposed harsher terms in the Wade-Davis Bill (July 2, 1864), Presidential Reconstruction only required 10 percent of a seceded state's voting population to pledge their future loyalty to the Union and accept the end of slavery in order to rejoin. Although Lincoln did not sign the Wade-Davis Bill, he was willing to allow states to return to the Union under either his or Congress's plan, but southerners, not surprisingly,

preferred Lincoln's plan. Tennessee, Louisiana, Arkansas, and Virginia tried to return to the Union under his plan, but failed because of irregularities. When the less flexible Andrew Johnson assumed the presidency after Lincoln died on April 15, 1865, Johnson discounted Congress's view of Reconstruction and quickly brought all of the seceded states back into the Union while Congress recessed for the summer. When Congress met in December 1865, it noted that the South had returned as its new representatives to Congress old Confederates, including the vice president of the Confederacy. Moreover, the former slave South was passing Black Codes that reinstituted the controls of slavery, and northerners were being harassed on visits through the South. When Congress passed a civil rights bill for Blacks and extended the Freedmen's Bureau, Johnson vetoed both measures and declared Blacks were not ready for citizenship responsibilities. That led to a showdown between Johnson and congressional Republicans that he lost. In the election of 1866, an overwhelming majority of Republicans were reelected to Congress who ended Presidential Reconstruction by pushing through the Reconstruction Act of 1867 over Johnson's veto.

301 • Radical or Congressional Reconstruction

Radical Reconstruction, also known as Congressional or Black Reconstruction, reflected a broader definition of Reconstruction than Presidential Reconstruction. Republicans in the postwar Congress believed that a social and political reconstruction of the South was necessary in addition to bringing the seceded states back into the Union. Thus, in the main bill of Radical Reconstruction, the Reconstruction Act of 1867, the seceded states had to accept the right of Blacks to vote and to serve as representatives in the state and federal legislature. Southerners had to hold constitutional conventions in which Blacks were participants, draw up constitutions that ensured Black political and civil rights, and have those constitutions approved by Congress. Former Confederates were not allowed to vote in this process, or in state or federal elections. The former Confederate states also had to ratify the Fourteenth Amendment. Beginning in June 1868, Arkansas, North Carolina, South Carolina, Louisiana, Alabama, and Florida were reconstructed and readmitted to the Union. It was not until 1870 that Virginia, Mississippi, and Texas returned, largely because they initially refused to deny the franchise and officeholding to former Confederates. Each also had the additional requirement to ratify the Fifteenth Amendment. With the exception of Virginia, all the southern states were ruled by Republican state governments for varying periods of time: in South Carolina Republican Reconstruction lasted until 1877; in Texas it ended as early as 1874.

302 • The Myth of Black Reconstruction

James Pike and other chroniclers of Radical Reconstruction have called it Black Reconstruction and portrayed it as overwhelmingly negative. Their story of Reconstruction in states such as South Carolina describes illiterate, incompetent ex-slaves, greedy northern white carpetbaggers, and treasonous scalawags who dominated helpless southern white "civilization" in a period of fraud, corruption, and plunder. In truth, Blacks never dominated southern state institutions because, with the exception of South Carolina, Blacks never held a majority of state offices. And in South Carolina the Black elected officials with the most powerful state positions were not ex-slaves, but free Negroes,

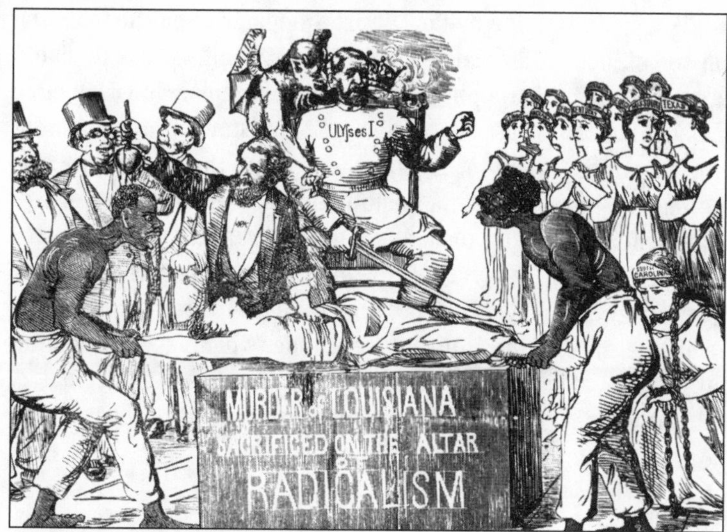

Racist 1871 engraving that characterizes Radical Reconstruction as the murder of southern states under President Ulysses S. Grant's administration. Prints and Photographs Division, Library of Congress

the majority of whom were of mixed-race backgrounds. Many of these mixed-race free people owned property, had some education, and were conservative in their political outlook and public behavior. In general, Blacks in the Congress and in state government served with ability and sometimes with distinction. Corruption *was* rampant in Radical Reconstruction, but it had also been widespread in pre- and postwar southern state government. Although Reconstruction state governments did incur large debts, such was probably unavoidable given the devastation of the postwar South: schools had to be built, roads repaired, railroads established, to bring the South back. And although the later Redeemer governments rewrote Radical Reconstruction state constitutions to delete provisions for Black suffrage, many of the southern states continued to use the constitutions written under Radical Reconstruction with few other changes.

303 • Free Negroes, or Free People of Color

"Free Negroes" and "free people of color" refer to those African Americans who were free before the Civil War and hence were not freed by the Emancipation Proclamation or the Thirteenth Amendment. Often such free Negroes were either mixed-race relatives or descendants of white masters and might possess money, property, or position because of such relationships.

304 • Freedmen

"Freedmen" refers to those African Americans who were formerly slaves and were emancipated by the Civil War.

305 • Freeborn

"Freeborn" refers to African Americans born before the Civil War whose parents were not slaves. The freeborn possessed the highest status in post–Civil War African American social circles, followed by the free Negroes, who were not freeborn, and then the freedmen.

306 • Mulatto

A mulatto is a person of mixed-race parentage, usually with one white and one African American parent. While not enjoying the kind of separate legal and political status of mulattoes in the Caribbean or Latin America, mulattoes in both pre- and postwar southern society often benefited when they were fathered by wealthy or prominent white planters or businessmen. The term is rapidly being replaced by "mixed race" in contemporary usage, since "mulatto" is derived from the Spanish word for mule.

307 • "Who Freed You?"

"Who freed you?" was a question sometimes asked of unknown persons of African descent to determine whether the person had been slave or free prior to the Civil War. If the answerer had been freed by the Civil War, then he or she was viewed by free Negroes as socially inferior. Such ranking of people by their pre–Civil War status was common in the Black Victorian social class that emerged in the post–Civil War era. Charleston, South Carolina, contained one of the wealthiest and most self-consciously free Negro communities. Many of the Charleston free Negroes were descendants of white masters, owners of considerable private property, and members of social clubs, such as the Brown Fellowship Society, which excluded all African Americans except those descended from mixed-race unions. Such social conflicts spilled over into the political realm where free Negro and ex-slave representatives clashed in the South Carolina state legislature over bills to redistribute the property of landowners and protection for Black laborers.

308 • Sharecropper

"Sharecropper" refers to the legal relationship between those who rented parcels of land from landowners in the postwar South. Initially, after the Black Codes were overturned by Congress, ex-slaves refused to work on large plantations in gang labor groups because these were too reminiscent of slavery. Landowners feared ex-slaves would not work without compulsive work routines. Yet landowners needed laborers and laborers lacked land, so sharecropping emerged as a compromise. Tenant farmers rented a parcel of land to work as their own in return for a percentage of their crop at the end of the growing season, usually one-quarter to one-half of the crop, depending on the tools and animals owned by the tenant. Although sharecropping began as a compromise that seemed to satisfy some of the freedmen's demands for autonomy, by the end of the Reconstruction period, a combination of falling prices for cotton, dishonest and unscrupulous planters, the inability of freedmen to read and write, and terroristic activities had transformed sharecropping into a system under which few tenants ever made enough by the year's end to get out of debt, let alone accumulate any capital.

309 • Carpetbagger

A carpetbagger was a northerner who came to the South during Radical Reconstruction (1867–77) to, according to the view of many southern whites at the time, pillage and profit from the economic policies of Republican-dominated state governments. Many white southerners believed the northerners allowed the "rape and pillage" of the South by Blacks in order to reap financial rewards. In reality, however, many northerners who came South devoted themselves unselfishly to helping the freedmen and dispossessed white southerners adjust to change. And some political carpetbaggers, such as South Carolina Governor Daniel H. Chamberlain, were conservative members of the Republican Party who helped undo Black Reconstruction.

310 • Scalawag

A scalawag was a native-born white southerner who joined or supported the Republican Party during Radical Reconstruction. Scalawags were viewed as siding with the freedmen, rather than with the white population, and thus as traitors to the Redeemers, who came after Radical Reconstruction.

311 • Louisiana Murders

The Louisiana Murders, a mass attack that occurred as a result of a disputed election, took place on Easter Sunday in 1873. In Grant Parish, Louisiana, Blacks, afraid white Democrats would take over after the election, "set up armed resistance around the county seat of Colfax." After three weeks, white supremacists overran Colfax, killing over three hundred blacks—many of whom had surrendered. It is called the worst incident of mass racial violence in the Reconstruction period.

312 • "Wave the Bloody Shirt"

Waving a bloody shirt was a practice Republican politicians used in the elections of 1866, 1868, 1872, and 1876 to draw public attention to southern violence against African Americans. The bloody shirt of a lynching victim, for example, would be displayed to whip up enthusiasm for the Republican Party in these elections. At the same time, southern racists who attempted to overthrow Reconstruction were creating such shirts through violent attacks on African Americans. Although Rutherford B. Hayes, the Republican presidential candidate in 1876, used the "bloody shirt" in his election campaign, he willingly complied when southern congressmen demanded he withdraw federal troops from the South to obtain their votes for president. Once the bloody-shirt tactic was no longer useful to Republicans politically, they completely abandoned concern for African American safety.

313 • Redeemers

The Redeemers were white Democrats who led the fight against Radical Reconstruction and replaced Republicans in positions of power in southern state governments after President Rutherford B. Hayes's withdrawal of federal troops from the South in 1877. Redeemers weakened Black political power, rewrote Reconstruction state constitutions, reduced state taxes and budgets, returned land to former planters, and created a legal system that ensured white supremacy and a controlled Black labor force.

314 • The Invisible Empire

The Invisible Empire was a name applied to the Ku Klux Klan, which emerged first in December 1865 as a fraternity of former Confederate officers living in Pulaski, Tennessee. As a *kyklos,* or circle of friends, the Klan practiced strange and mystical rituals, donning robes and masks and riding horseback around the countryside, whooping and yelling. Early Klan members noticed that African Americans were frightened by this cavorting, and the practice spread. But it was not until the passage of the Reconstruction Act of 1867 that the Ku Klux Klan found its real raison d'être and became a regional terrorist organization. Transformed at a meeting in Nashville, Tennessee, into a mystical "empire," with dukes and dominions, the new Klan was ruled by a grand wizard, a Confederate soldier named Nathan Bedford Forrest. While explicitly dedicated to defending the weak and the female, the Invisible Empire was mainly designed to intimidate and torture carpetbaggers, schoolteachers, Republican legislators, Freedmen's Bureau officials, scalawag judges, and all African Americans whose behavior violated southern "traditions." Klan beatings, maimings, and killings became so abhorrent that even Forrest was moved to disband the organization in January 1869. It continued to operate until 1872, however, when Reconstruction was all but over. Most of the upper class and Conservative Democrats sought to distance themselves from the Klan's activities, but many Redeemers praised the Klan as the

most important factor in the successful overthrow of Reconstruction.

Laws, Amendments, and Supreme Court Decisions

315 • Compromise of 1877

In the presidential election of 1876, the Republican and Democratic candidates, Rutherford B. Hayes and Samuel Tilden, received equal numbers of electoral votes, which threw the election into the House of Representatives. In the same election, the three states in which Reconstruction governments had not been overthrown—South Carolina, Louisiana, and Florida—reported fraudulent election results and the Democrats and Republicans both claimed victory. In order to gain the votes of southern states in the House to secure his election, Hayes promised to withdraw federal troops from the South and give control of remaining loyal Republican governments to the Conservative Democrats. Hayes also promised to assist the South in getting federal money for internal improvements. Upon his selection by the House as president, Hayes quickly removed the troops and left Black southerners at the mercy of southern white Democratic state governments.

316 • Thirteenth Amendment

Although Lincoln had issued the Emancipation Proclamation in 1863, it was not clear that this liberation of southerners' "property" would have the force of law. Thus, Congress passed the Thirteenth Amendment to abolish slavery throughout the Union on January 31, 1865, and sent it to the states to be approved. President Johnson then made its acceptance a prerequisite for readmission of the Confederate states into the Union.

317 • Black Codes

During Presidential Reconstruction, 1865–66, state governments throughout the South passed laws to regulate the status and conduct of the emancipated slaves. These laws, known as the Black Codes, affected almost every aspect of an African American's life. The Black Codes' key objective was to control African American workers by limiting their ability to secure employment outside of plantation work. Although the laws varied from state to state, the Black Codes also regulated mobility and interracial contact. Stiff fines and jail sentences were meted out to those who violated the codes. According to Benjamin F. Flanders, they were the product of state legislatures whose "whole thought and time will be given to plans for getting things back as near as slavery as possible."

318 • Mississippi's Black Codes

Mississippi had some of the toughest Black Codes. It required all blacks to have written proof of employment for the coming year each January. If an employee left a job before the end of a contract, he or she forfeited wages already earned. To discourage an employee's ability to barter for better employment, the state imposed a $500 fine on anyone who offered work to someone under contract. Blacks could not rent urban land. Vagrancy could be punished by fines or involuntary labor on plantations. Blacks were also punished for insulting whites, or, remarkably, preaching the Gospel without a license.

319 • South Carolina's Black Codes

While South Carolina's Black Codes retained a glimmer of the Old Regime's paternalism—

most notably the prohibition against evicting former slaves from plantations—the codes also forbade African Americans from working at nonagricultural jobs. If a Black person worked as anything other than a farmer or a domestic servant, he or she had to pay an annual tax as high as $100 a year. That made it almost impossible for Charleston's Black artisan class to earn a living at its trade. South Carolina's code also forced Blacks to sign annual employment contracts that specified the hours of work, usually from sunup to sundown, and prohibited workers from leaving the plantation during those hours without the owner's permission. Even traveling-circus performers and fortune-tellers could be hauled in for vagrancy and then forced to work on plantations for free.

320 • Northern Reaction to the Black Codes

While initially less concerned with granting Blacks the right to vote or any other civil rights, many white northerners believed the war had been fought to establish a free labor system in the South. The Black Codes convinced northerners that the South had not accepted this lesson of defeat. The suspicion that the South was restoring slavery through the Black Codes galvanized northern opinion against Presidential Reconstruction.

321 • Civil Rights Act of 1866

With the Civil Rights Act of 1866, passed on April 9, 1866, Congress conferred on African Americans all the civil rights enjoyed by whites, except for the vote, which was regarded as a privilege. The Civil Rights Act of 1866 defined citizenship as coming from the federal government and not the state, and its protection was not limited to the South or the former slaves. It forbade any discriminatory laws by states and it was enacted to render null and void the Black Codes. It also gave African Americans the rights to enter into contracts, to sue, to give evidence in court, and to own property.

322 • Fourteenth Amendment

Proposed in 1866, the Fourteenth Amendment was passed in 1867. "No State shall make or enforce any law which shall abridge the privileges or immunities of citizens of the United States; nor shall any State deprive any person of life, liberty, or property, without due process of law; nor deny to any person within its jurisdiction the equal protection of the laws." The Fourteenth Amendment made civil rights legislation permanent and guaranteed Blacks equal pro-

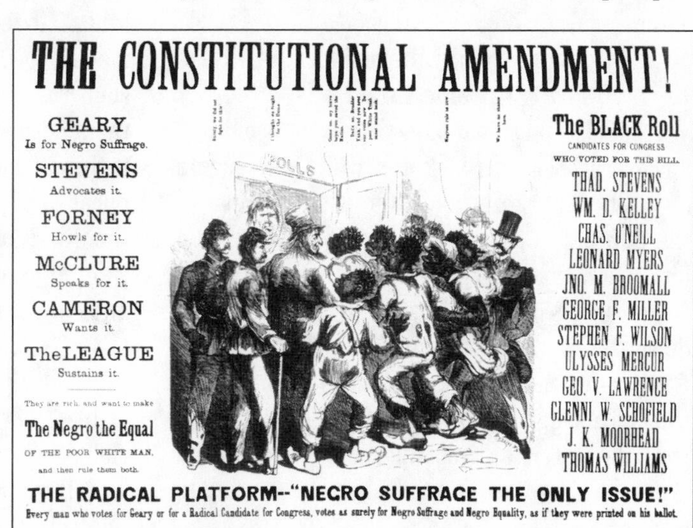

Racist 1866 Pennsylvania governor election poster that highlights northern white opposition to the Fourteenth Amendment and its guarantees of voting rights to African Americans. Prints and Photographs Division, Library of Congress

tection under the law. States were required to ratify the Fourteenth Amendment as a condition for readmission to the Union.

323 • The Reconstruction Act of 1867

With the Reconstruction Act of 1867, Congress wrested reconstruction of the South away from the president and imposed new requirements for the reentry of Confederate states to the Union. The act disfranchised former Confederates and divided the eleven Confederate states, except Tennessee, into five military districts under army commanders. It also required each state to elect, through universal male suffrage, a constitutional convention, which would write new constitutions that provided for Black voting in their state constitutions. Once the constitutions were approved by a majority of the voters in each state, and the states had ratified the Fourteenth Amendment, the states could reenter the Union and send representatives to Congress. The Reconstruction Act of 1867 also franchised Blacks in the District of Columbia and extended the term of the Freedmen's Bureau.

324 • Louisiana Liberalism and the Supreme Court

In 1869 Louisiana passed a law forbidding any segregation of Black and white passengers on public transportation. In a clear example of the Supreme Court's tendency to curtail state legislation that was pro–African American, the Court, in its *Hall v. DeCuir* decision, struck down this Louisiana law in 1878. The Supreme Court ruled in this case that the Louisiana law was an abridgment of the right of Congress to regulate interstate commerce, even though the Louisiana law only applied to intrastate carriers.

325 • Slaughterhouse Cases of 1873

In the Slaughterhouse Cases, the Supreme Court gutted the civil rights enforcement of the Fourteenth Amendment. In direct contradiction to the Civil Rights Act of 1866 and the Fourteenth Amendment, the Supreme Court ruled that two classes of citizenship existed—state and federal—and that the Fourteenth Amendment covered only those rights received under federal citizenship. Since most civil rights fell under state citizenship, this decision denied protection under the Fourteenth Amendment for Blacks whose rights were increasingly under attack in the South. When state and local authorities refused to protect Black voters in federal elections from beatings and murder, the Supreme Court denied those victims the right to claim that their voting rights had been violated under the Fourteenth Amendment.

326 • *United States v. Cruikshank*

In the *Cruikshank* decision, handed down on March 27, 1876, the Supreme Court ruled that the Fourteenth Amendment did not protect citizens who were exercising their constitutional right to peaceful assembly from intimidating other citizens. Such intimidation was a local matter, in the Court's opinion, since it believed such rights derived from state rather than national citizenship. What this decision did was to legitimize attacks on Blacks assembling for the purpose of political activity. After this decision, the Ku Klux Klan and other terrorist groups were able to attack Black Republican meetings and conventions in the South with impunity.

327 • Fifteenth Amendment

In 1868 the Republicans argued that the right to suffrage remained a state prerogative, so following Ulysses S. Grant's election, a Republican Congress offered a new constitutional

amendment to deal with the question of Black voting. According to the Fifteenth Amendment, "The right of citizens of the United States to vote shall not be denied or abridged by the United States or by any State on account of race, color, or previous condition of servitude." Unfortunately, even after the Fifteenth Amendment took effect on March 30, 1870, it did not insure that African Americans could vote. The Supreme Court had ruled previously that the rules governing suffrage were still the province of the states. States could keep Blacks from voting for nonracial reasons. That loophole was manipulated by southern state constitutions to limit Black suffrage through the understanding, grandfather, and other clauses.

328 • Civil Rights Act of February 28, 1871

Congress passed the Civil Rights Act of 1871 in response to the growing intimidation of Black voters in the South. Known as the "Ku Klux Klan Act" it gave the federal courts a wide variety of powers designed to combat violence if the violence curtailed a person's constitutional rights. Federal courts acquired the power to appoint persons to oversee and supervise elections, and it became a federal crime for anyone to interfere with their work. To specifically counteract the Ku Klux Klan, Congress also outlawed the wearing of disguises upon public highways or in another person's house for the purpose of depriving them of equal protection of the laws.

329 • Civil Rights Act of March 1, 1875

The Civil Rights Act of 1964 was not the first law in American history to guarantee equal access to public accommodations. The Civil Rights Act of March 1, 1875, curtailed the rise of Jim Crow laws in the South, and made as strong a statement of equal rights as the Civil Rights Act of eighty-nine years later. In unequivocal language the 1875 act declared that

all persons within the jurisdiction of the United States shall be entitled to the full and equal enjoyment of the accommodations, advantages, facilities, and privileges of inns, public conveyances on land or water, theaters, and other places of public amusement; subject only to the conditions and limitations established by law, and applicable alike to citizens of every race and color, regardless of any previous condition of servitude.

The act went on to state that anyone who deprived a person of such "equal enjoyment" because of his or her race could be fined $500, to be paid to the victim. District attorneys were compelled to arrest such violators, and if the district attorneys refused to act, they too could be fined $500, also to be paid to the victim. Federal courts were given jurisdiction in these cases to give federal protection to the civil rights. Unfortunately for American citizens, this landmark legislation was ruled unconstitutional a decade later by the Supreme Court in the 1883 Civil Rights Cases.

330 • *United States v. Reese*

Voter intimidation, in the form of murders and threats of murder against those attempting to vote, increased so drastically in the South during the 1870s that the entire nation became aware of the problem. Faced with an example of such intimidation in *United States v. Reese* (1876), the Supreme Court struck down the federal provisions guaranteeing voting rights. Such action by the Supreme Court sanctioned voter intimidation.

"The Union as it was," cartoon by Thomas Nast for *Harper's Weekly*, October 21, 1876. Prints and Photographs Division, Library of Congress

331 • Supreme Court Nullifies the "Ku Klux Klan Act"

In *United States v. Harris* (1883) the Supreme Court further limited the Fourteenth Amendment as a means of protecting Blacks from civil rights abuses. In this case, a mob had grabbed several African Americans from a Tennessee jail, killed one of them, and beat the others severely. The Supreme Court ruled this was not a violation of the Fourteenth Amendment's equal protection clause because that amendment asserted that no *state* could deprive a person of equal protection under the laws, and did not specifically claim that no *individual* could do so. Regulation of individual behavior was a state matter, the Court argued, and if the state did not deem Black rights important enough to protect, that was not the federal government's business. This decision struck down the Civil Rights Act of 1871, the so-called Ku Klux Klan Act, by holding that congressional action against private actions was not permitted by the Fourteenth Amendment.

332 • Supreme Court Nullifies Public Accommodations Protection of the Civil Rights Act of 1875

In the 1883 Civil Rights Cases the United States Supreme Court ruled that the Civil Rights Act of 1875 was unconstitutional. According to Justice Joseph P. Bradley, who wrote the majority opinion, the Fourteenth Amendment did not give Congress the ability to pass legislation against racial discrimination in public accommodations because "that amendment proscribed only deprivation of rights by *state action.*" In a radical reinterpretation of the Fourteenth Amendment, the Court argued that only discrimination by states, not individuals, was prohibited under the Fourteenth Amendment. Discrimination by private businesses amounted to infringement of the "social rights" of African

Americans, not their civil or political rights. The effect of this ruling was to sanction discrimination by individuals.

333 • Possession of Weapons Prohibited

Despite the pervasiveness of guns and other weapons in southern culture, under Section 1 of the Penal Laws of Mississippi, African Americans were unable to possess firearms without authorization from the local government. Rarely was such permission granted. No similar requirements applied to whites.

Quotations

334 • James Pike's View of South Carolina During Black Reconstruction

In a reputedly objective, but actually racist, account of Radical Reconstruction in South Carolina, James S. Pike, a Republican journalist, said:

In the place of this old aristocratic society stands the rude form of the most ignorant democracy that mankind ever saw, invested with the functions of government. It is the dregs of the population habilitated in the robes of their intelligent predecessors, and asserting over them the rule of ignorance and corruption. . . . It is barbarism overwhelming civilization by physical force. . . . We enter the House of Representatives. Here sit one hundred and twenty-four members. Of these, twenty-three are white men, representing the remains of the old civilization. These are good-looking, substantial citizens. They are men of weight and standing in the communities they represent. . . . This negro dense negro crowd . . . do the debating, the squabbling, the lawmaking, and create all the clamor and disorder of the body. . . . The Speaker is black, the Clerk is black, the doorkeepers are black, the little pages are black, the chairman of the Ways and Means is black, and the chaplain is coal black. At some of the desks sit colored men whose types it would be hard to find outside of the Congo; whose costume, visages, attitudes, and expression, only befit the forecastle of a buccaneer. It must be remembered, also, that these men, with not more than a half dozen exceptions, have been themselves slaves, and that their ancestors were slaves for generations. . . .

335 • Another View of Black Political Participation

Although controversial, African American participation in the constitutional conventions held after the Reconstruction Act of 1867 was often praised:

Beyond all question the best men in the convention are the colored members. Considering the influences under which they were called together, and their imperfect acquaintance with parliamentary law, they have displayed, for the most part, remarkable moderation and dignity. . . . They have assembled neither to pull wires like some, nor to make money like others; but to legislate for the welfare of the race to which they belong. [Charleston Daily News]

336 • Henry Turner's Rebuttal

One of the ways southerners undermined Reconstruction was to challenge the seating of African American representatives in the state legislatures. In Georgia in 1868, for example, several representatives were rejected by the state legislature because they were Black. In the following speech, delivered in the Georgia House of Representatives on September 3, 1868, Henry M. Turner attacks those in the legislature who questioned his right to a seat in the body.

Whose Legislature is this? Is it a white man's Legislature, or is it a black man's Legislature?

Who voted for the Constitutional Convention, in obedience to the mandate of the Congress of the United States? Who first rallied around the standard of Reconstruction? Who set the ball of loyalty rolling in the State of Georgia? It was the voice of the brawny-armed Negro, with the few humanitarian-hearted white men who came to our assistance. I claim the honor, sir, of having been the instrument of convincing hundreds—yea, thousands—of white men, that to reconstruct under the measures of the United States Congress was the safest and best course for the interest of the State.

Let us look at some facts in connection with this matter. Did half the white men of Georgia vote for this Legislature? Did not the great bulk of them fight, with all their strength, the Constitution under which we are acting? And did they not fight against the organization of this Legislature? And further, sir, did they not vote against it? Yes, sir! And there are persons in this Legislature to-day, who are ready to spit their poison in my face, while they themselves opposed, with all their power, the ratification of this Constitution.

337 • Violence Rebutted

The following is testimony taken by the Joint Congressional Committee on the Condition of Affairs in the Late Insurrectionary States, July 3, 1871.

Willis Johnson (colored) sworn and examined.

Q.: *Where do you live?*

Johnson: *At Leonidas Sims's, in Newberry County.*

Q.: *How long have you lived there?*

Johnson: *This year. I lived there one year since I have been free before this year. . . .*

Q.: *Have you been at any time visited by men masked and disguised—Ku Klux?*

Johnson: *Yes, sir.*

Q.: *When?*

Johnson: *Last night two weeks ago.*

Q.: *Go on and tell what you saw and what they said and did, telling it in your own way.*

Johnson: *When I awoke, as near as I can tell, it was between 12 and 1 o'clock. I heard some one call "Sims." I held still and listened, and heard them walk from his door to my door. I was upstairs, and I got up and came down-stairs. They walked back to his house again and asked him to put his head out. He did not answer, but his wife asked them who they were. They said they were friends. They walked back to my door again, and just as they got to the door they blew a whistle. Another whistle off a piece answered, and then men seemed to surround the house and all parts of the yard. Then they hallooed, "Open the door." I said nothing. I went to the head of the bed and got my pistol, and leaned forward on the table with the pistol just at the door. They tried with several surges to get the door open, but it did not come open. They went to the wood-pile and got the axe, and struck the front door some licks, bursted it open, and then went to the back door and burst it open. Nobody had yet come into the house; they had not come in. They said, "Strike a light." Then I dropped down on my knees back of the table, and they struck some matches and threw them in the house, and two of them stepped in the front door, and that brought them within arm's length of me as they stood there. As soon as they did that, I raised my pistol quickly, right up to one's back, and shot, and he fell and hallooed, and the other tried to pull him out. As he pulled him I shot again. As they were pulling, others ran up and pulled him out in the yard, and when the whole party was out in the yard I stepped to the door and shot again, and then jumped to the back door and ran. I got off. I staid away until the next morning; then I came back and tracked them half a mile where they had toted this man*

and laid him down. I was afraid to go further. Mr. Sims and I were together, and I would not go any further, and he told me to go away; that I ought not to stay there; that he saw the men and saw the wounded man, and was satisfied that he was dead or mortally wounded, and I must leave. Mr. John Calmes, the candidate of the democrats for the legislature, advised me to take a paper and go around the settlement to the white people, stating that I would never vote the radical ticket, and he said he did not think they would interfere with me then. He said that all they had against me was that on election day I took the tickets around among the black people; and he said: "You knocked me out of a good many votes, but you are a good fellow and a good laborer, and we want labor in this country." I told him I would not do that. . . .

People and Politics

338 • Early African American Political Aspirations

Despite the myth that African American Reconstruction leaders were tools of northern Republican leaders, Black political leaders with their own agenda for reconstruction existed in most cities of the Confederate South. Even before the end of the Civil War, African American political groups began to meet and demand political representation in the postwar world. In South Carolina, for example, the Sea Island community sent a group of representatives to the 1864 National Republican Convention, although they failed to be seated and recognized. After Union troops captured Charleston, African Americans met on March 30, 1865, to pass resolutions that publicly declared their support of the Union at a time when violent reprisals by Confederate stragglers were still common. When South Carolina whites convened to petition readmittance to the Union under Presidential Reconstruction in September 1865, Blacks lobbied unsuccessfully for the same rights accorded to white citizens. Then, in November, Blacks convened their own Colored People's Convention and demanded the state grant equal rights and voting rights to African Americans. Such assertions of and demand for political rights arose from the Black community prior to the Reconstruction Act of 1867 and the introduction of northern Republicans into South Carolina Reconstruction politics.

339 • Economic Insurgency

Along with political activism, African Americans also engaged in an economic struggle for just treatment in the postwar period. Hundreds of Blacks rebelled against exploitative labor contracts, and in some cases took physical possession of plantations and moved into the "big houses," claiming them as rightfully their own. Black urban laborers in Richmond, Virginia, laundry women in Mississippi, longshoremen in New Orleans, and mechanical workers in Georgia all struck for higher wages.

340 • The Constitutional Conventions

When Congress passed the Reconstruction Act of 1867, African American political activity accelerated. Each state of the former Confederacy had to hold constitutional conventions that included African Americans, though in practice the number of African Americans at the conventions varied greatly from state to state in proportion to the percentage of Blacks in the state population. In South Carolina Blacks were the majority at the constitutional convention; in Louisiana the ratio was fifty-fifty; but in Texas only nine of ninety members were African American. The conventions drew up constitu-

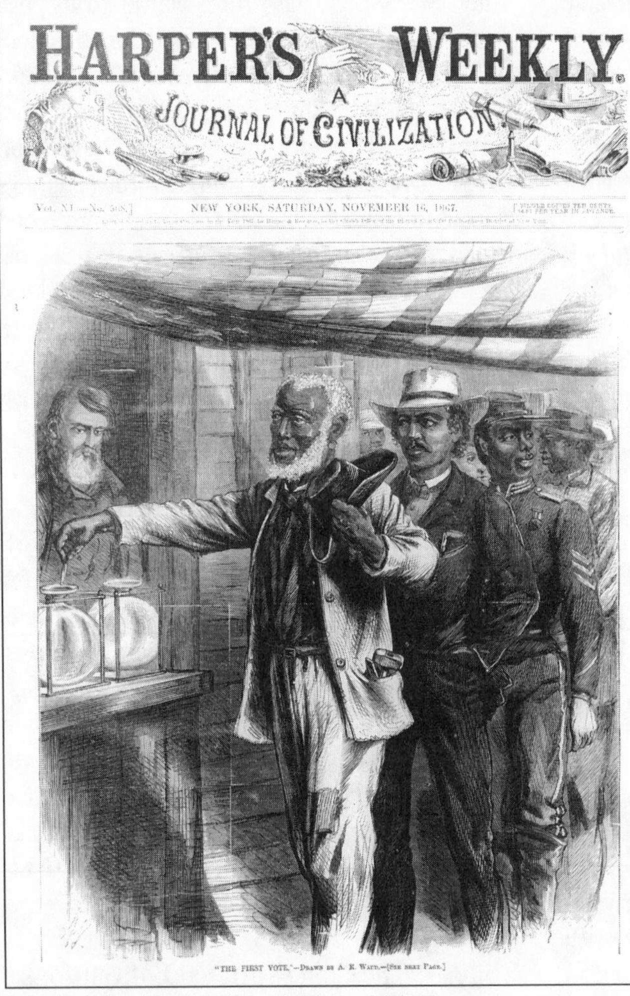

HARPER'S WEEKLY
A JOURNAL OF CIVILIZATION

Vol. XI.—No. 568.] NEW YORK, SATURDAY, NOVEMBER 16, 1867.

"THE FIRST VOTE."—Drawn by A. R. Waud.—[See next Page.]

"The First Vote," by A. R. Wand in *Harper's Weekly*, November 16, 1867. Prints and Photographs Division, Library of Congress

tions that abolished property qualifications for voting and holding office, extended the ballot to all male residents, banned slavery, and eliminated race distinctions in the possession and inheritance of property. By 1900 most of these constitutions were replaced by constitutions severely limiting the rights of Blacks.

341 • Black Civil Rights Protest After the Reconstruction Act of 1867

Passage of the Reconstruction Act of 1867 led to expectations that discriminatory southern social practices would change. Following the 1867 meeting to approve the Republican Party platform, several African American men climbed aboard a streetcar in Charleston, South Carolina, demanding the right to ride on the cars usually reserved for whites. In Louisiana the demands of Black soldiers of the 39th Infantry to ride on New Orleans streetcars reserved for whites forced General Sheridan to order the urban transit companies to integrate their cars. These accomplishments were not short-lived. When an African American woman was thrown from a streetcar on April 17, 1867, her formal complaint forced the streetcar company to allow Blacks to ride on the streetcars without discrimination until shortly after 1900, when a new wave of Jim Crow segregation was reinstituted.

342 • Thaddeus Stevens (1792–1868)

Thaddeus Stevens, a lawyer and one of the founders of the Republican Party, was perhaps the single most important congressman during the Reconstruction period. As a member of the House of Representatives, he was a vigorous critic of the Crittenden Compromise, of Lincoln for overruling General David Hunter's decision to free the slaves, and of Presidential Reconstruction, with its mild demand that only 10 percent of the southern state voting populations pledge loyalty to the Union. He was one of the

principal opponents, along with Charles Sumner, of President Andrew Johnson, and he led the congressional campaign to seize control of Reconstruction, treat the Confederate states as territories, and make them accept African American voting. In the latter, he was motivated not only by a sense of justice for the freedmen but also by practical political considerations: Stevens was shocked by the possibility that former Confederate states might send back Confederate leaders and unrepentant Democrats to Congress. He supported Black suffrage in part to ensure the dominance of the Republican Party in the Congress for years to come. Stevens was a shrill, tough-minded, sharp-tongued legislator who bullied and threatened his opponents to go along with his plan to make the South pay for its treason and to guarantee the political rights of African Americans.

343 • Charles Sumner (1811–74)

Charles Sumner, the United States senator most famous for having been caned by Congressman Preston S. Brooks of South Carolina after Sumner's speech attacking the Kansas-Nebraska Act of 1854 and its author, Stephen A. Douglas, was an outspoken opponent of slavery. For years Sumner spoke out against slavery, the Fugitive Slave Act, and the attacks on abolitionists by proslavery Whig politicians in his native Massachusetts. When he returned to the Senate after his beating in 1857, Sumner resumed his vitriolic, acid-tongued attacks on slavery and its defenders in one of the classics of antislavery speeches, "The Barbarism of Slavery," delivered on the eve of the presidential election. During the war, he was the first congressman to advocate the freeing of slaves and pressed for the granting of civil and political rights to the freedmen after the war. Like Thaddeus Stevens, Sumner demanded that Congress control Reconstruction, blocked Louisiana's readmission to the Union under Lincoln's 10 percent plan, and led the Senate in denunciations of Andrew Johnson. Like Stevens as well, Sumner demanded the extension of all political rights to African Americans while at the same time insisting that those Confederates who had committed treason should not enjoy the franchise in the postwar South.

344 • Blacks in Congress During Reconstruction

During the Reconstruction years, two African Americans served terms in the Senate and twenty African Americans were elected to the House of Representatives. In the House eight of the twenty representatives came from South Carolina, four from North Carolina, three from Alabama, and one each from Georgia, Mississippi, Florida, Louisiana, and Virginia.

345 • Hiram Rhoades Revels (1822–1901)

Hiram Revels was selected by the Mississippi state legislature in 1870 to fill the Senate seat vacated by Jefferson Davis. That made him the first African American chosen to be a member of Congress. Seated on February 25, 1870, he served in the Senate until March 3, 1871, when its short term ended. Born in Fayetteville, North Carolina, Revels was first an ordained minister of the African Methodist Episcopal Church in Baltimore. During the Civil War, he organized colored troops in Maryland and then went to Mississippi in connection with the Freedmen's Bureau effort to create schools for African American youth. After serving as an alderman in Natchez, Mississippi, in 1868, he became a state senator before being selected to represent Mississippi in the United States Senate. Revels was the epitome of politically conservative

Hiram Rhoades Revels, the first African American senator. Photograph by Matthew Brady. Prints and Photographs Division, Library of Congress

African American politicians who gained positions during Reconstruction. After leaving the Senate, Revels sensed the changing political winds of Mississippi and lobbied in 1875 in favor of a white conservative overthrow of the Republican state government.

346 • Blanche K. Bruce (1841–98)

In 1874 Blanche K. Bruce of Mississippi became the second African American selected to serve in the United States Senate. Bruce was the only African American to serve a full term in the Senate until 1972, when Edward Brooke of Massachusetts finished his first term as a U.S. senator. Bruce was a mixed-race slave born in rural Virginia. After running away to freedom in Kansas, attending Oberlin College, and working for a couple of years on a Mississippi riverboat, Bruce migrated to Bolivar County, Mississippi, in 1870, where he was elected sheriff and tax assessor. Those positions allowed him to acquire wealth and a palatial plantation lost by its owner to Reconstruction taxes, and eventually led to his selection as a U.S. senator. On his climb to power, Bruce made a few political enemies, one of whom was James L. Alcorn, the other Mississippi senator, who broke Senate tradition by refusing to escort Bruce to his Senate seat. New York Senator Roscoe Conkling escorted Bruce instead and became Bruce's lifelong friend. Unlike Senator Hiram Revels, Bruce used his Senate appointment to lobby successfully for colored people's rights: he opposed the Chinese Exclusion Act that was passed in 1878, introduced a bill to desegregate the U.S. Army, recommended federal support of the "Exodusters" migrating to Kansas, and successfully investigated and rescued from bankruptcy the Freedman's Savings Trust Company of Washington, D.C.

347 • Jefferson F. Long (1836–1900)

A vigorous fighter for African American political rights, Jefferson F. Long in January 1871 became the second African American, and the first from Georgia, to be elected to the House of Representatives. Although he served only until the end of the term on March 3, 1871, Long became the first African American to address the House of Representatives when he delivered a speech against a bill removing restrictions on the vote for Confederates. Long argued that Confederates would use the vote to restore white supremacy rule, depicted the rampant hatred expressed toward the American flag and its display, and exposed attacks on Blacks and Republican sympathizers by the Ku Klux Klan. Not until the election of Andrew Young to the House in 1972 would another African American from Georgia be sent to the House of Representatives.

348 • Governor P. B. S. Pinchback (1837–1921)

The first African American to serve as governor of a state was not Douglas Wilder, but P. B. S. Pinchback. His tenure as governor, however, was much shorter than Wilder's. Pinchback had been elected president pro tempore of the Louisiana senate in 1871 and promoted to lieutenant governor upon the death of Oscar J. Dunn. Pinchback was governor of Louisiana for just forty-six days, from December 9, 1872, to January 13, 1873, after the elected governor, Henry Clay Warmouth, was impeached. Pinchback was never able to reach the governor's mansion by election, but he retired to Washington, D.C., where, along with Blanche Bruce, he became a celebrity in Washington social circles.

P. B. S. Pinchback, governor of Louisiana. Photograph by Matthew Brady. Prints and Photographs Division, Library of Congress

349 • Robert Carlos De Large (1842–74)

A key myth of Reconstruction is that Black legislators tried to deny white southerners the right to vote. In reality, African American legislators generally lobbied for the removal of political debilities on Confederates. The best example of a conservative Black legislator was Robert De Large, who introduced a bill in the South Carolina legislature in 1868 to remove all political disabilities on former Confederates. Like many of his colleagues, De Large, a mixed-race ex-slave who was distinguished by his muttonchops, believed that the Black Republicans could not afford to appear too radical or vindictive toward the whites. At the same time, De Large, who later served in the House of Representatives and delivered an eloquent speech in favor of the Fourteenth Amendment, was not so conservative as to fail to demand that more of

Robert Carlos De Large, South Carolina legislator. Photograph by Matthew Brady. Prints and Photographs Division, Library of Congress

the positions of power in the Republican-controlled legislature be given to African Americans. "Why is it that we colored men have become identified with the Republican Party?" De Large asked in 1874.

Is it because there is loadstone which attracts and holds us there, or is it because we are deluded and follow blindly certain men? No! We joined this party because it professed equal rights and privileges to all. . . . We thought, on the ground of expediency we must do nothing to offend them, but some impudent scoundrels in the party now say: "You want too much; you want everything!" We placed them in position; we elected them and by our votes we made them our masters. We now propose to change this thing a little, and let them vote for us. It is no more than reasonable they should do so.

350 • Martin R. Delany (1812–85)

Martin Delany, the Black abolitionist and emigrationist, was one of the most effective nonelected African Americans to work with the South Carolina Freedmen's Bureau. From 1865 to 1868 Delany was effective in protecting African American rights in contracts with employers, in part because he used his reputation as a national Black leader to resist bureau attempts to water down his directives. His efforts included creating an independent cotton press for Black freedmen that circumvented the Charleston cotton factories which controlled cotton processing. This, of course, did not sit well with planters or merchants, and Delany was attacked in the press and in the bureau. Although his cotton press eventually failed because of economic reprisals, Delany continued to work for the freedmen.

JIM CROW

Terms, Phrases, and Slogans

351 • Jim Crow

"Jim Crow" was taken from a white performer named Thomas "Daddy" Rice who caricatured Black styles of walk, talk, and dress in the 1830s. Initially performing in Cincinnati, Rice brought his impressions to the New York Bowery Theater in 1832. His songs became popular American classics, in which he told his working-class white audience that "every time I weel a-bout I jump Jim Crow." "Jim Crow," Rice's portrayal of a handicapped Black man, became an urban stereotype of Black behavior almost as popular as "Uncle Tom." But in the late nineteenth century "Jim Crow" came to symbolize the wide-ranging system of segregation that separated Blacks and whites in almost every aspect of public life in the American South. In recent years the term "Jim Crow" has come to represent the entire system of Black oppression in the South, including not only segregation but also disfranchisement, lynching, rioting, and economic discrimination, which together carved out a place for the Negro in the South as a second-class citizen.

Historians debate the actual beginning of the Jim Crow system in the South. Almost all believe the first attempts at segregation began immediately after the Civil War, codified in the Black Codes. But these efforts were struck down by the Civil Rights Act of 1866, the Reconstruction Act of 1867, and the Fourteenth Amendment. One historian, C. Vann Woodward, has argued that after such suppression, the persuasive segregation of southern life that ap-

peared in the early twentieth century did not begin to develop until the 1890s and the struggle over populism in the South. Other historians, most notably Joel R. Williamson, however, have found evidence of segregation in public life in the South in the 1870s and 1880s, when Blacks began to be refused admittance to first-class cars on trains. That seems plausible, since Congress passed the Civil Rights Act of 1875 in response to the rise of public discrimination against African Americans. Still, that the law was passed and enforcement attempted indicates that segregation in public arenas was not the law of the South in the 1870s. Even after Rutherford B. Hayes, as part of a deal to seal his selection by the House of Representatives to be president, withdrew federal troops from the Confederate South in 1877, African American access to public accommodations varied throughout the South. But in 1887 Florida passed the first segregation statute ordering railroads to segregate their passenger cars. The next year, Mississippi followed suit, and in 1889 Texas passed its own Jim Crow law. The passage of the Florida laws began the Jim Crow period, one of government sanction of segregation, disfranchisement, and terror in the South that lasted until the 1954 *Brown v. Board of Education* (Kansas) decision that declared segregation unconstitutional.

352 • Peonage

Peonage, or the practice of holding people on land against their will, emerged in the late-nineteenth and early-twentieth-century South. Where people worked as sharecroppers, they often found themselves in debt to landowners or merchants at the end of the harvesting season when "settlin'-up time" came. Often they began the next year in debt and were prevented from leaving the plot of land they farmed until they paid that debt. Although peonage was a class system that affected white sharecroppers and tenants as well as Black ones, it was a particularly devastating form of social control on the former slave. One peon testified:

I am not an educated man. I will give you the peonage system as it is practiced here in the name of the law. . . .

I am brought in a prisoner, go through the farce of being tried. The whole of my fine may amount to fifty dollars. A kindly appearing man will come up and pay my fine and take me to his farm to allow me to work it out. At the end of the month I find that I owe him more than I did when I went there. The debt is increased year in and year out. You would ask, "How is that?" It is simply that he is charging you more for your board, lodging and washing than they allow you for your work, and you can't help yourself either, nor can anyone else help you, because you are still a prisoner and never get your fine worked out. . . . The court and the man you work for are always partners. One makes the fine and the other one works you and holds you, and if you leave you are tracked up with bloodhounds and brought back.

353 • Lynching

Between 1882 and 1901 over a hundred lynchings, almost all of them of African Americans, occurred each year, with several years topping two hundred. Lynching allowed the whites to retain a measure of control by instilling considerable fear among the Black community. By the early 1890s a pattern appeared. More lynchings tended to take place during the hotter months (July was the most popular) and most took place either at or near the scene of the alleged crime. Areas undergoing rapid or extreme economic and political changes were more likely to experience lynchings, and once one

Thomas Shipp and Abram Smith hanging from a tree, Marion, Indiana, 1930. Prints and Photographs Division, Library of Congress

lynching took place, more usually followed. Immediately after a lynching tensions remained high and the Black residential and commercial areas of the city often were burned and looted. Local authorities, if they did not actively assist in it, usually did nothing to stop a lynching. Officials at the highest level of southern governments announced their support of the practice. Cole Blease, for example, a former governor in South Carolina, planted the finger of a lynched man in the gubernatorial garden.

354 • Disfranchisement

Disfranchisement was the process of denying Blacks the right to vote, especially in the late-nineteenth and early-twentieth-century South. Disfranchisement required considerable ingenuity on the part of southern racists, since the Fifteenth Amendment prohibited denial of the right to vote to a person because of race or color. In order to disfranchise the African American, racists had to devise some other factor that would, in effect, exclude Blacks from the voting rolls. One of the earliest was the poll tax.

355 • Poll Tax

Poll taxes, which made payment of a tax a requirement for voting, first developed in Tennessee in 1890. Usually the voter had to pay the tax before he could vote, but often under confusing conditions that made it difficult for African Americans to pay it. For example, the poll tax might have to be paid on a certain date at a certain time, but the location would only be known by a select few. In addition, the tax was often beyond the restricted salaries of most Blacks. Even though the poll tax was effective in keeping Blacks away from the polls, it was not enough to satisfy the state of Mississippi, with its majority Black population. Mississippi devised an additional device to discourage Black voters, called the understanding clause.

356 • Understanding Clause

The understanding clause demanded that potential voters pass a literacy test to qualify to vote. Developed at Mississippi's 1890 convention, the understanding clause required all citi-

zens to be able to read and interpret a section of the state constitution to the satisfaction of polling officials. First proposed by white conservatives as a demand to elevate the educational qualifications of voters, the clause disfranchised many poor whites, but was mainly aimed at Black voters. In 1894 South Carolina, after years of prodding by Bill Tillman, adopted a similar clause in its constitution. Because of the clause's potential to disfranchise some illiterate southern whites, the grandfather clause was adopted in Louisiana.

357 • Grandfather Clause

Developed at the Louisiana convention of 1898, the grandfather clause exempted all males whose fathers or grandfathers could vote in the election on January 1, 1867, from having to pay poll taxes or pass the understanding test. Because southern Blacks had been denied the right to vote before 1867, they were ineligible for this exemption, which almost all whites enjoyed. Lacking such a qualification, any Black man desiring to vote would then have to pass the poll tax and understanding provisions. It was enormously effective: in 1896, 130,344 Black Americans had been registered voters in Louisiana. But in 1900, after the new clauses had been inserted in the state constitution, only 5,320 African Americans remained as registered voters in Louisiana.

358 • White Primaries

If some Blacks were able to register despite the myriad obstacles to registration, white primaries rendered their votes meaningless. In the solidly Democratic South, the candidate who won the Democratic primary was virtually assured of victory in the actual campaign. Many states adopted laws limiting participation in the primaries to whites only.

Protests, Organizations, and Demonstrations

359 • Ida B. Wells-Barnett Protests Lynching

Ida B. Wells (1862–1931) had been a radical for most of her life. In 1884 she sued the Cleveland and Ohio Railroad for making her leave the first-class accommodations for which she had paid. Wells won the case in state court, and even though it was later overturned by the Tennessee Supreme Court, she believed her protest had been the right thing to do. She became famous as an African American radical when she challenged the South's newest obsession, the lynching of Blacks, in an article published in the *Memphis Free Speech and Headlight,* a Black newspaper, on March 9, 1892. Her article protested the lynching of three young Black businessmen who had tried to defend their store from attack by local whites. "The city of Memphis," she wrote, "has demonstrated that neither character nor standing avails the Negro if he dares to protect himself against the white man or become his rival." These men had been attacked because they had become economic rivals of a local white business. Wells argued lynching was thus a form of economic reprisal. Such an argument was inflammatory enough in the South of 1892, but Wells went further and asserted it was a "thread-bare" lie that most Black men were lynched for raping white women. The white men of the South ought to stop using that excuse because, as she hinted, a closer examination would show that the white women associated with lynching victims had been voluntarily involved with Black men. For those remarks, in a May 1892 issue of *Free Speech* her newspaper office was destroyed, and Wells, traveling in Natchez, Mississippi, was told

Poster portrait of Ida B. Wells and her 1917 words: "I'd rather go down in history as one lone negro who dared to tell the government that it had done a dastardly thing." Prints and Photographs Division, Library of Congress

not to return to Memphis. She didn't, but instead launched a career of writing and agitation about lynching that galvanized an international awareness about the practice. Her books *Southern Horrors: Lynch Law in All Its Phases* and *A Red Record: Tabulated Statistics and Alleged Causes of Lynching in the United States,* published in 1892, were two of the first books to compile statistics on and analyze the causes of lynching. The statistics bore out her contentions: only one-third of those lynched were even accused of rape and most were lynched for acts of economic, educational, or political assertiveness. Ida B. Wells was politically allied with W. E. B. Du Bois and his Niagara Movement, and critical of Booker T. Washington's accommodationist posture toward southern violence.

360 • Booker T. Washington's Counsels Against Politics and Protest

At a Cotton States' International Exposition held in Atlanta, a Black man, Booker T. Washington (1856–1915), head of Tuskegee Institute in Alabama, delivered his famous "Atlanta Compromise" speech. Delivered on September 18, 1895, Washington's speech renounced the attempt of Blacks under Reconstruction to exercise their political rights and assert their social equality with whites. Rather than protest, Washington recommended that Blacks avoid challenging segregation and disfranchisement, work diligently at the agricultural and business occupations open to them, and acquire as much education and economic power as the South would allow them. Washington asked whites to grant Blacks the opportunity to advance independently and economically within their segregated sphere in exchange for Black willingness not to demand political rights. Washington argued that Blacks and whites in the South could be "as separate as the fingers in all things social, but united as a hand in all things fundamental," i.e., economic progress. Washington's speech was a tremendous success, in part because in the year of Frederick Douglass's death, it signaled the rise of a new Black leader and an alternative to Douglass's emphasis on protest as the best means to accomplish Black progress.

361 • Booker T. Behind the Scenes

Despite his public disavowal of Black political resistance and his obsequious manner of presenting himself to white people, Booker T. Washington actually worked behind the scenes to defend African American political and social rights. In 1898, for example, he not only asked the Louisiana legislature to ensure that the understanding clause and other restrictions on voting would be applied fairly, but he also lent

Booker T. Washington. Prints and Photographs Division, Library of Congress

his financial support to legal challenges to the constitutionality of Louisiana's grandfather clause. Secretly he financially supported efforts to end racial discrimination on Pullman cars in southern states. He also provided money to lawyers seeking to overturn statutes in Texas and Alabama that excluded African Americans from participation on juries. Washington did all of this secretly and quietly, usually through organizations like the Afro-American Council, to avoid alerting whites that he was working against segregation and disfranchisement.

362 • Black Opposition to Booker T. Washington

Booker T. Washington's moderate public stance against racism angered many African American intellectuals who formed organizations in the late nineteenth and early twentieth centuries. Richard T. Greener, the first African American to graduate from Harvard College, was one of the founders of the National Association of Colored Men, an organization of Black professionals. With a less avowedly political focus, the American Negro Academy was founded in March 1897 to promote "literature, science and art" among African Americans and also to foster "the defense of the Negro against vicious assault." Ida B. Wells was perhaps one of the earliest to publicly criticize Washington's singleminded public endorsement of Black economic advancement in the South. She argued that following Washington's counsel to forgo demand for civil rights and seek economic parity would increase one's chances of being lynched, as had been the case in Memphis in 1892.

363 • The National Association of Colored Women

Of considerable significance was the formation of the National Association of Colored Women, an outgrowth of the local women's club movement that had begun in earnest in the 1890s. Such clubs as the Phyllis Wheatley Club of New Orleans and the Woman's League of Washington, D.C., were independent associations devoted to self-help, education, and social reform. But in the spring of 1895 these clubs joined together to form the National Association of Colored Women, in part to respond to the increasingly negative portrayals of Black women in the press. Another reason for the formation of the National Association was the rise of segregation in white women's clubs, which before the 1890s had freely admitted African American women. When Mrs. Fannie Barrier Williams, an African American, was recommended for membership in the Chicago Woman's Club in 1894, it led to a national discussion in the media over the appropriateness of Black women in predominantly white women's clubs. While Mrs. Williams was eventually admitted, Mrs. Josephine Ruffin, of the Women's Era Club of Boston, an African American women's club, was refused admittance to the National Federation of Women's Clubs at its meeting in Milwaukee in 1900. Perhaps in response to these incidents, the National Association of Colored Women became increasingly political in the early twentieth century, inviting and hosting lectures from Black leaders from a variety of points of view.

364 • Horrific Lynching Mobilizes W. E. B. Du Bois

When W. E. B. Du Bois, the Harvard Ph.D. graduate and Berlin-trained social scientist, came to Atlanta University in 1897, he launched an impressive series of studies of African American life and culture and settled into a comfortable job as a university professor. But in 1899 Du Bois was shaken out of his academic complacency by the horrific lynching of Sam Hose in April of that year. Sam Hose had killed a white farmer during an argument and was brutally lynched and burned to death by a mob of over two thousand people. After his charred body was dragged to the ground, men, women, and children struggled with one another to take home pieces of his burned flesh as souvenirs. Learning of the lynching stopped Du Bois from working on his monographs to go down to the *Atlanta Constitution* to contribute a letter of mild protest to the editor. Afterward, he learned that Hose had been barbecued and that his burned knuckles were placed on display in a shopkeeper's window in Atlanta. Deeply disturbed by the incident, Du Bois began to pen his landmark book, *The Souls of Black Folk* (1903), in which he criticized Booker T. Washington's accommodationist and educational policies. Three years later, the eruption of the horrific Atlanta race riot would convince Du Bois that he could not confine himself to scholarly research, but must find some way to protest the worsening conditions of Black life in America.

365 • The Boston Riot

Most white Americans had no inkling of the growing dissatisfaction with Booker T. Washington in the ranks of America's Black intellectual class until a near riot broke out at a Washington address to a National Negro Business League meeting held at an African Methodist Episcopal (AME) Zion church in Boston in the summer of 1903. Boston was the intellectual stronghold of William Monroe Trotter (1872–1934), Washington's most outspoken African American critic. A dapper graduate of Harvard College, Trotter had a fiery disposition and a tremendous animosity toward Washington, devoting columns of his newspaper, the *Guardian,* to anti-Washington news and gossip. Washington had largely ignored Trotter and his group until the July 30 address, when William H. Lewis, another Harvard graduate and a Bookerite, tried to introduce Washington to the crowd of two thousand at the Columbus Avenue church. The audience erupted into commotion, catcalls, and whistles as Washington tried to take the podium. Police advanced into the crowd and were attacked by women with hatpins and pocketbooks, while Trotter stood up and read a series of questions for Washington that could not be heard over the din of the crowd. Trotter was arrested and convicted for conspiracy to disturb the peace. He was sentenced to thirty days in jail. But Washington was also hurt by the event. His wealthy white supporters and Black supporters were stunned by the reaction and looked for explanations. Washington was so embarrassed by the media coverage of the incident that he felt obliged to write to President Theodore Roosevelt to apologize for any concern the incident caused him. Afterward, it would be difficult for Washington to claim he alone spoke for the African American.

366 • The Niagara Movement

On July 10, 1905, thirty young African American professionals gathered at the Erie Beach Hotel in Ontario, Canada (racial discrimination prevented them from obtaining lodgings on the American side of Niagara Falls), to form the Niagara Movement. They were teachers, lawyers, doctors, ministers, and businessmen—whom W. E. B. Du Bois had earlier described as the race's "talented tenth"—who wanted to use their talents to fight for Black rights. Led by William Monroe Trotter and Du Bois, who was chosen the general secretary, the Niagara Movement opposed Booker T. Washington and his control of Black institutions but declined to favor any particular policy. Nevertheless, the group elected an executive committee and drafted a "Declaration of Principles" that celebrated the African American's right to protest. "We refuse to allow the impression to remain that the Negro-American assents to inferiority, is submissive under oppression and apologetic before insults. Through helplessness we may submit, but the voice of protest of ten million Americans must never cease to assail the ears of their fellows, so long as America is unjust." Although it met several more times and reached out to other groups, such as the National Association of Colored Women's Clubs, the Niagara Movement failed to gain much support, because of Washington's opposition and because membership was limited to the tiny "talented tenth." But the Niagara Movement prepared the way for the National Association for the Advancement of Colored People by advocating protest against terrorism and litigation against Jim Crow laws.

367 • The National Association for the Advancement of Colored People (NAACP)

In 1908 a riot broke out in Springfield, Illinois, after an African American shot and killed a white police officer. A mob broke into the jail where the accused was awaiting trial, killed him, hanged him from a telephone pole, and shot the body hundreds of times. After the lynching, the mob destroyed the Black section of the city. William English Walling, a well-known writer, reported from the scene of the Springfield riot in an article entitled "Race War in the North." Walling observed:

Either the spirit of the abolitionists, of Lincoln and Lovejoy, must be revived and we must come to treat the Negro on a plane of absolute political and social equality or [Senators J. K.] Vardaman and [Bill] Tillman will soon have transferred the Race War to the North. . . . Yet who realizes the seriousness of the situation and what large and powerful body of citizens is ready to come to their aid?

Mary White Ovington, one of the founders of the NAACP. Prints and Photographs Division, Library of Congress, Visual Materials from the NAACP Records

Walling answered his own question by issuing a call in 1909 for a select number of socialists, African American protest leaders, and concerned citizens to come together for the purpose of founding a large body to oppose such atrocities. Thus the National Association for the Advancement of Colored People (NAACP), an interracial organization to fight for equal rights for African Americans, was created. In addition to Walling, some of the more prominent founding members were Joel Spingarn, Mary White Ovington, and Dr. W. E. B. Du Bois.

368 • The *Crisis*

The *Crisis* was the official journal of the NAACP. Edited by W. E. B. Du Bois, it was to stand for "the highest ideals of American democracy, and for reasonable but earnest and persistent attempts to gain these rights and realize these ideals." Within several years of its first publication in November 1910, its circulation surpassed 100,000. Its features included a spotlight on African American "Men of the Month," a summary of news on domestic and international race issues, a recap of local and national NAACP activities, and substantial attention to African American literature.

369 • A Silent Antilynching Parade

On July 28, 1917, thousands of African Americans silently marched through New York City to Madison Square to protest lynching and the East St. Louis race riots. Without uttering a sound, the marchers carried antilynching banners and distributed leaflets that proclaimed: "We march because we want to make impossible a repetition of Waco, Memphis and East St. Louis, by rousing the conscience of the country and to bring the murderers of our brothers, sisters and innocent children to justice."

370 • NAACP Legal Defense Activities

From 1910 on, the NAACP devoted much of its activities to seeking legal remedies to the problems of de jure segregation and Black disfranchisement in America. In 1915 the NAACP successfully litigated *Guinn v. United States,* in which the Supreme Court declared the grandfather clauses in Maryland and Oklahoma restrictive to the Fifteenth Amendment and therefore null and void. Two years later the NAACP successfully obtained a Louisville ordinance declaring residential segregation unconstitutional. Then, in 1923, in *Moore v. Dempsey,* the NAACP successfully argued for a new trial of an African American accused of murder. The Supreme Court agreed with the NAACP that the accused had not received a fair trial because Blacks were excluded from the jury.

371 • UNIA Meeting in Madison Square Garden

In 1920 Marcus Garvey's militant organization, the Universal Negro Improvement Association, which he had founded in Jamaica in 1914 and launched in Harlem in 1917, held its first annual mass convention at Madison Square Garden. Thousands of African Americans attended, dozens of street marches and parades were held, and many Blacks joined an organization that advocated "Africa for the Africans," pride in the Black race, independent economic development, and repatriation back to Africa. Garvey's organization grew into the largest mass movement of African Americans prior to the Civil Rights Movement of the 1950s–1960s, but Garvey was handicapped by poor business practices in launching his boldest enterprise, the Black Star Line. The failures of that undertaking, coupled with increasingly hostile attacks by African American leaders and espionage by J. Edgar Hoover, resulted in Garvey's downfall. In

1925 Garvey was convicted of mail fraud and jailed in the Atlanta Penitentiary until 1927, when President Calvin Coolidge commuted his sentence and deported him from the United States as an undesirable alien.

372 • The Right to Self-Defense

In September 1925 hundreds of whites surrounded the Detroit home of Dr. Ossian Sweet, a Black physician. Sweet had, in the eyes of the crowd, overstepped his bounds by moving into the formerly all-white neighborhood. Dr. Sweet, his wife, two brothers, and seven friends decided to stay and defend their home. After the house was attacked with rocks and firebombs, the occupants, armed with guns, opened fire on the crowd. A white man in the crowd was killed, and all the occupants of the home, except Mrs. Sweet, were arrested. A defense team led by Clarence Darrow represented the Sweets and their friends, and the first trial ended in a hung jury. At the second trial, Henry Sweet, Dr. Sweet's brother, was tried first, separately. The all-white jury's verdict of not guilty set a precedent allowing self-defense by African Americans.

373 • Brotherhood of Sleeping Car Porters

In 1925 A. Philip Randolph founded the Brotherhood of Sleeping Car Porters, the first railway union to be open to Black membership. In addition to fighting for the rights of Black Pullman porters, Randolph used the organization to demand better treatment of Blacks within the American Federation of Labor and to agitate for social justice and civil rights for all African Americans. Moreover, Randolph utilized the porters as "civil rights missionaries," because they traveled from city to city and were able to spread and gather information about African American affairs nationwide.

374 • Antilynching Bill

In the early 1920s the NAACP launched a campaign to enact an antilynching law. In 1921 Representative C. C. Dyer of Missouri introduced an antilynching bill that passed the House by a vote of 230–119. Passage in the Senate, however, was much more difficult to attain. The NAACP sent the Senate a letter urging passage that was signed by twenty-four governors, thirty-nine mayors, twenty college presidents, and other important officials. Full-page ads were also placed in leading newspapers such as the *New York Times* and the *Atlanta Constitution.* Southern senators, however, successfully filibustered the bill and it never came to a vote.

The NAACP flew this flag outside its offices in New York every time a lynching took place in the South. Prints and Photographs Division, Library of Congress, Visual Materials from the NAACP Records

375 • Rejection of Judge Parker

Politically blacks exercised increasing influence, especially through the NAACP. President

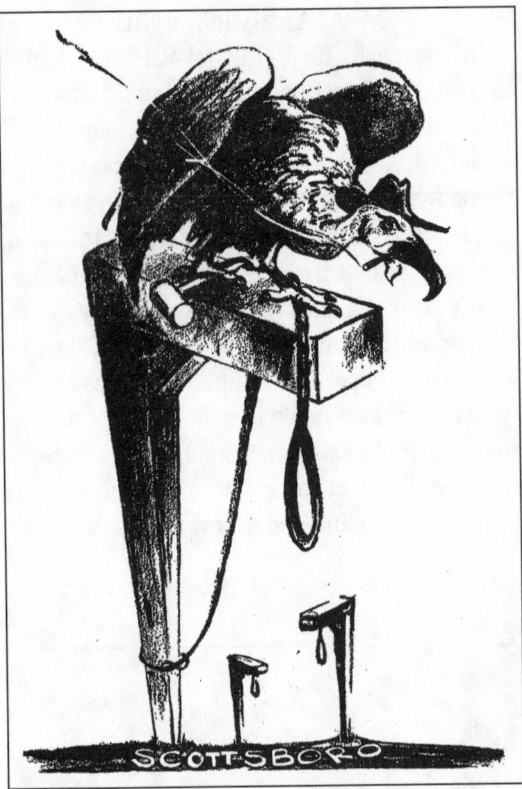

"The Higher Court," cartoon suggesting that the Supreme Court decision overturning the first Scottsboro conviction was part of the same system of injustice as existed in Alabama. Prints and Photographs Division, Library of Congress, Visual Materials from the NAACP Records

Herbert Hoover, for example, nominated Judge John H. Parker to a seat on the Supreme Court. The NAACP requested the withdrawal of Parker's nomination after it became evident that Parker had opposed black suffrage. When Hoover declined, the NAACP conducted mass meetings and write-in campaigns. Pressured, the Senate refused to confirm Parker. A *Christian Science Monitor* article described it as "the first national demonstration of the Negro's power since Reconstruction days."

376 • Scottsboro Case

In 1931 nine young Black men were arrested in Scottsboro, Alabama, on a charge of raping two young white women as they all rode together on a freight train through Alabama. The entire case rested on the testimony of the two women, one of whom was a prostitute, the other a semiliterate cotton mill worker who later recanted her story. Narrowly avoiding being lynched, the nine young men, some of whom were suffering from advanced syphilis, were convicted. But publicity generated by the U.S. Communist Party brought national attention to the case and a new trial. Although the nine were again convicted, several of the men did not serve their full sentence, in part because of the widespread belief in their innocence. The case not only gained favorable opinion for the Communist Party but also embarrassed the NAACP, which, under Walter White, lost the right to represent the "Scottsboro Boys" to the C.P. That embarrassment galvanized White, the executive secretary of the NAACP, to take action and revitalize the NAACP's legal challenge to racism and segregation.

377 • NAACP's Legal Strategy in the 1930s

In 1935 Walter White convinced Howard University Law School Vice-Dean Charles Houston to head up a new legal challenge to educational segregation. Houston's strategy was to test the constitutionality of segregated schooling by showing it was not equal. On tours throughout the South, Houston had previously documented with photographs the inequalities of segregated elementary and high school education. But Houston decided to focus on graduate and professional schools, for tactical reasons. Relatively few states had constructed separate facilities at the graduate level for Blacks, so that it would be easy to show unequal access. Early in the century, few Blacks demanded edu-

cation beyond the college level; but by the 1920s the number of Blacks entering graduate and law schools had risen. Houston decided to focus on law schools because he believed judges would easily see that makeshift separate law schools for Blacks were not equal in training or reputation to prestigious white law schools. His first victory came in the *Murray* case, where Donald Gaines Murray had been denied admission to the University of Maryland law school. With the assistance of Thurgood Marshall, Houston's former student and a man who himself had been rejected by the University of Maryland law school, Houston argued before the Baltimore city court that Murray ought to be admitted to the law school. Houston and Marshall were successful and the municipal court ordered the University of Maryland to admit Murray. By 1939, the legal work of challenging segregation had grown so much that White created a separate organization, the NAACP Legal Defense and Educational Fund, Inc., with Thurgood Marshall at the helm, to handle the work.

378 • "Buying Power" Movement

During the early 1930s African Americans began using their economic and political power. The "Buying Power" movement, begun in Chicago, used picketing and boycotts to force white employers, especially those with a large Black clientele, to employ Blacks in their businesses. In New York City Adam Clayton Powell, Jr., a future congressman, led a four-year effort that added ten thousand Black workers to the telephone company, the light company, the bus company, dime stores, department stores, and the 1939 World's Fair. Organizations employing similar tactics sprang up in other cities around the country.

379 • The New Negro Alliance

In Washington, D.C., the New Negro Alliance instituted a "don't buy where you can't work" campaign against several local chain stores. In a typical case, the Alliance surveyed a three-block area surrounding an A&P store that refused to hire blacks, and found only five white households. More than ten thousand blacks lived within that area and together they spent an average of $4,700 per month at the A&P, yet company policy prohibited black employees. Alliance leaders tried to negotiate with the A&P management, but after several unproductive meetings, they called on area residents to boycott and picket the store. Over 90 percent of the neighborhood complied, and as economic losses mounted, the A&P management capitulated. Eighteen black clerks were hired by A&P, and several other chains adopted similar policies in an effort to forestall any Alliance action against them.

380 • Southern Tenant Farmers' Union

Organizing against racism and economic subjugation was not limited to Black professionals in northern cities. Following the passage of the Agricultural Adjustment Act of Franklin Delano Roosevelt's New Deal administration, Black and white sharecroppers and farm laborers in Arkansas joined together in 1934 to form the Southern Tenant Farmers' Union (STFU). The organization was designed to fight the eviction of tenants and sharecroppers from land they had worked for years. Under the Agricultural Adjustment Administration (AAA), farmers were paid money not to bring land under cultivation in order to reduce the supply of farm products and drive up prices. But in practice, the AAA policy was disastrous for tenants and sharecroppers, since the AAA simply paid landowners, with the assumption that they would pass on payments to tenants, which did

not happen. The STFU also sought to obtain a fairer share of government parity payments for tenants. By 1935 over ten thousand tenants had joined the union; but the union had also come under attack from planters and local southern authorities who raided meetings, arrested members, and beat and shot some who refused to stop attending meetings. In 1936 the STFU organized a strike of cotton pickers in five states that brought national attention to the union. In this effort, African American tenant organizers were most effective in getting tenants to resist inducements to return to the fields. Unfortunately for the union, Roosevelt and those in the AAA administration refused to support the efforts of the STFU, being more concerned with keeping the goodwill of southern politicians to support New Deal legislation. Without that support, the STFU collapsed under the pressure from landowners and state authorities.

381 • Harlem Race Riot of 1935

On March 19, 1935, shoppers in a Kress dime store in Harlem saw a young Black boy grabbed by store workers and taken into a basement, where they believed he was violently beaten. Soon after, an ambulance pulled up in the alley behind the store, and the rumor spread that the boy had been killed. This set off angry protests fueled by six years of the Depression and unemployment in Harlem, neglect of its social services by New York government, and the bitter segregation that denied Blacks, even in Harlem, the ability to work in stores like Kress. When a group of radicals protesting conditions in Harlem assembled outside the store, a riot broke out, even though the boy, Lino Rivera, had been released. Roving bands of people began to break store windows, loot goods, and challenge police and store owners in two days of rioting. It was to be America's first modern race riot. Harlem radicals claimed that agitation against poor housing, poor city services, high unemployment, high rent eviction rates, and endemic racism even in Harlem had laid the groundwork for the riot.

382 • First March on Washington

The first March on Washington was proposed in 1941 by A. Philip Randolph in response to discrimination in war industries employment and segregation of the armed forces. With the beginning of World War II in Europe in 1939, the U.S. economy pulled out of the Great Depression as the United States began to supply the Allies, principally France, Great Britain, and the Soviet Union, with materials to fight the Axis powers. But as was so often the case in America, Blacks were the last hired in the industrial boom. Randolph, who was head of the Pullman porters' union, gathered together several civil rights leaders and proposed a March on Washington by 100,000 African Americans to focus national attention on the treatment of African Americans in the United States. Randolph had several points he wanted addressed and would not back down, even though President Franklin D. Roosevelt pleaded that a March on Washington would hurt the U.S. war mobilization. Finally, in order to get Randolph to call off the march, FDR issued Executive Order 8802, which banned discrimination in hiring by industries involved in the war effort and established the Federal Employment Practices Commission (FEPC) to hear complaints. Although some critics believed that Randolph sold out for too little and that the FEPC, which could only hear complaints and not impose fines, was a paper institution, establishing the principle of equal employment and the commission was a step forward. Even though industries could not be punished for discrimination, it was nevertheless

A. Philip Randolph. Photograph by Gordon Parks for Office of War Information, Washington, D.C., November 1942. Prints and Photographs Division, Library of Congress

embarrassing for companies to have to appear before the commission, a sign of their lack of patriotism.

383 • Formation of CORE

In April 1942 the Fellowship of Reconciliation (FOR) authorized James Farmer to start an organization to practice Ghandian nonviolent resistance to segregation in the Chicago area. Bob Chino, another of the group's founding activists, argued it should be called the Committee of Racial Equality, or CORE, "because it will be the center of things, the heart of the action." CORE moved away from the pacifist practices of FOR to advocate direct defiance of segregation, and succeeded in desegregating several eating and recreational establishments in Chicago. CORE may have conducted the first successful sit-in when twenty-eight members of the group took seats in booths and at the counter of the Jack Spratt restaurant, which eventually dropped its discriminatory policy of not serving African Americans. Other such successes followed, but CORE had difficulty raising money in the late 1940s and early 1950s until the Montgomery Bus Boycott jump-started the direct-action movement. CORE would again seize center stage in the civil rights struggle by launching the Freedom Rides in 1961.

Quotations

384 • Letter Warning Those Assisting Voter Registration

In 1920 a prominent white Florida lawyer urged African Americans to register to vote. He subsequently received the following message from the Ku Klux Klan:

We have been informed that you have been telling Negroes to register, explaining to them how to become citizens and how to assert their rights.

If you know the history of reconstruction days following the Civil War, you know how the "scalawags" of the North and the Black republicans of the South did much as you are doing to instill into the Negro the idea of social equality. You will remember that these things forced the loyal citizens of the South to form clans of determined men to maintain white supremacy *and to safeguard our women and children.*

And now you know that history repeats itself and that he who resorts to your kind of game is handling edged tools. We shall always enjoy white supremacy *in this country and he who interferes must face the consequences.*

Grand Master Florida Ku Klucks
Copy, Local Ku Klucks, Watch this man.

385 • Jim Crow Railroad Travel

The disparity between accommodations on the railroad for white and Black travelers repu-

diated the myth that separate did not mean unequal. In *A Black Man's Appeal to His White Brothers* Dr. R. S. Lovingwood, the president of Samuel Houston College in Austin, Texas, described the conditions facing an African American on the railroad during the Jim Crow era:

I went to a station to purchase my ticket. I was there thirty minutes before the ticket office was opened. When the ticket office opened I at once appeared before the window. While the agent served the white people at the other side I remained there beating the window until the train pulled out. I was compelled to jump on the train without my ticket and wire back to have my trunk expressed to me. Considering the temper of the people, the separate-coach law may be the wisest plan for conditions in the South, but the statement of "equal accommodations" is all bosh and twaddle. I pay the same money, but I cannot have a chair car, or lavatory, and rarely a through car. I must crawl out all through the night in all kinds of weather, and catch another "Jim Crow" coach. This is not a request to ride with white people. It is a request for justices, for "equal accommodations" for the same money. . . .

I rode through a small town in Southern Illinois. When the train stopped I went to the car steps to take a view of the country. This is what greeted me: "Look here, darkey, don't get off at this station." I put my head out of the window at a certain small village in Texas, whose reputation was well known to me. This greeted me: "Take your head back, nigger, or we will knock it off."

386 • March on Washington Movement

. . . our nearer goals include the abolition of discrimination, segregation, and jim-crow in the Government, the Army, Navy, Air Corps, U.S. Marines, Coast Guard, Women's Auxiliary Army Corps and the Waves, and defense industries; the elimination of discriminations in hotels, restaurants, on public transportation conveyances, in educational, recreational, cultural, and amusement and entertainment places such as theaters, beaches and so forth.

We want the full works of citizenship with no reservations. We will accept nothing less. . . . As to the composition of our movement. Our policy is that it be all-Negro, and pro-Negro but not anti-white, or anti-Semitic or anti-labor, or anti-Catholic. The reason for this policy is that all oppressed people must assume the responsibility and take the initiative to free themselves. Jews must wage their battle to abolish anti-semitism. Catholics must wage their battle to abolish anti-catholicism. Their workers must wage their battle to advance and protect their interests and rights.

And while the March on Washington Movement may find it advisable to form a citizens committee of friendly white citizens to give moral support to a fight against the poll tax or white primaries, it does not imply that these white citizens or citizens of any racial group should be taken into the March on Washington Movement as members. The essential value of an all-Negro movement such as the March on Washington is that it helps to create faith by Negroes in Negroes. It develops a sense of self-reliance with Negroes depending on Negroes in vital matters. It helps to break down the slave psychology and inferiority-complex in Negroes which comes and is nourished with Negroes relying on white people for direction and support. This inevitably happens in mixed organizations that are supposed to be in the interest of the Negro.

—A. Philip Randolph, keynote address to the Policy Conference on the March on Washington Movement, Detroit, September 26, 1942

387 • Residential Discrimination

The first edition of the *Crisis* in November 1910 applauded the citizens of Baltimore who attempted to break through the residential segregation separating the white and Black communities.

An inevitable step in anti-Negro prejudice is being taken in Baltimore, and threatened elsewhere. The colored folk of that city long ago became dissatisfied with a particularly bad system of alley homes. They saved their money and purchased nearly the whole length of Druid Hill avenue—one of the best colored streets in the world. Then they began to expand into parallel streets, one of which was McCulloh. They had been told that "money talks," and that the surest road to respect in America was financial success. The result was inevitable. The white people of McCulloh street rose in indignation and are importuning the City Council to pass an ordinance prohibiting colored people from "invading" white residential districts, and vice versa.

388 • Violent Attacks on Black Homes in Integrated Neighborhoods

Citizens from across the country appealed to the NAACP to send them legal assistance. The NAACP's second annual report quoted a Kansas City resident's letter that requested aid from the organization's legal department:

We desire to place before the legal department of the NAACP, the case of a group of Negroes of Kansas City, Missouri, who have suffered repeated attempts to destroy their property by an organization of white men who have demanded that they leave the neighborhood. There are nine Negro families in one block and twelve in the next who have purchased or are in process of buying their homes, ranging in price from $1,500 to $4,000. In the block in which I live five explosions of dynamite have occurred in the past year, causing considerable damage to our homes and much mental uneasiness on the part of our families. The last of these, which happened Saturday, November 11, was by far the most destructive of them all, completely wrecking the home of Mr. Hezekiah Walden. . . .

We have again and again appealed to the mayor and the chief of police to give us protection from these crimes, but the detectives have been of no help either in running the perpetrators to earth or in checking further threats and outrages. We feel that we have a clear case against the city, inasmuch as we have faithfully discharged our duties as citizens, and we are about to retain eminent legal counsel to defend our cause. In addition to this, we beg that we may have the assistance of some member of the legal department of the NAACP who will join us in vigorously prosecuting this case.

People and Politics

389 • John M. Langston (1829–97)

The election of John Mercer Langston to the House of Representatives in 1890 shows that African American political power did not evaporate completely with the end of Reconstruction in 1877. The son of a white planter and a mixed-raced mother, Langston had attended Oberlin College, studied law with a judge, and been admitted to the Ohio bar in 1854. After the Civil War, he organized the Law Department at Howard University before serving as its first dean and then as president from 1873 to 1875. Then, after a brief stint as resident minister and consul general to Haiti and chargé d'affairs to the Dominican Republic, he won the 1888 election to the House of Representatives, but took his seat on September 23, 1890, only after the House had determined that his Democratic rival

John M. Langston. Photograph by Matthew Brady. Prints and Photographs Division, Library of Congress

had cheated. He was a member of the House for less than six months, and his stint showed some of the difficulties of being an African American representative after Reconstruction. When Langston's term ended on March 3, 1891, he failed to get reelected.

390 • Booker T. Washington Dines at the White House

At the turn of the century, African Americans began to believe the federal government might renew its interest in their plight, especially after Teddy Roosevelt broke with segregationist decorum and invited Booker T. Washington to dinner at the White House on October 16, 1901. The meal infuriated much of the white South, but instilled pride and hope in the African American community. Roosevelt's image among Blacks was further bolstered by his support of William Crum as the collector of port in Charleston, South Carolina. Crum's appointment was vehemently opposed by white South Carolinians, but Roosevelt declared that unless the opponents of the appointment could come up with any reason for opposition other than color, then the appointment would stand. In addition, Roosevelt refused to accept the resignation of Minnie Cox, the postmistress in Indianola, Mississippi. Ms. Cox had been threatened with bodily harm if she did not relinquish her position, but Roosevelt refused to let the post office accept her resignation, and the office was subsequently closed for a period when she continued to decline to return.

391 • The Brownsville Riot

The burgeoning hope African Americans may have felt under Teddy Roosevelt waned with his handling of the Brownsville Riot. On the night of August 13, 1906, a bartender and police officer were wounded in Brownsville, Texas. The 25th Infantry (Colored) was stationed nearby at Fort Brown. Although an immediate roll call at the camp proved everyone accounted for, the Brownsville community suspected a Black military perpetrator. As the Black troops entered the town later that night, fighting broke out. One citizen was killed and another wounded. In response to a preliminary report that blamed the African American soldiers for the disturbances, President Roosevelt dismissed the entire battalion without honor and disqualified every member from civil or military service. In 1970 historian John Weaver published *The Brownsville Raid,* which proved that no Black soldier was responsible for the incident. In 1972, after further review, the dishonorable discharge was finally rescinded.

392 • Woodrow Wilson Preelection Letter to Bishop Walters

Woodrow Wilson wrote to Bishop Alexander Walters, regretting an invitation to address a mass meeting at Carnegie Hall sponsored by the National Colored Democratic League:

It is a matter of genuine disappointment to me that I shall not be able to be present at the meeting on Saturday night. . . . It would afford me pleasure to be present, because there are certain things I want to say, I hope that it seems superfluous to those who know me, but to those who do not know me perhaps it is not unnecessary for me to assure my colored fellow-citizens of my earnest wish to see justice done them in every matter, and not mere grudging justice, but justice executed with liberality and cordial good feeling. Every guarantee of our law, every principle in our constitution, commands this, and our sympathies also make it easy. The colored people of the United States have made extraordinary progress toward self-support and usefulness, and ought to be encouraged in every possible and proper way. My sympathy with them is of long standing, and I want to assure them through you that should I become President of the United States they may count on me for absolute fair dealing and for everything by which I could assist in advancing the interests of their race in the United States.

393 • Wilson Segregates Federal Departments

As with Theodore Roosevelt, African Americans' hopes dimmed with the actions of the newly elected president. Woodrow Wilson's first transgression was the segregation of federal government departments in Washington, D.C. Wilson purported his actions were in the best interests of African Americans because it would allow them to work in peace without fear of racial discrimination. In a letter to Wilson, August 15, 1913, the NAACP disputed this logic:

The National Association for the Advancement of Colored People, through its Board of Directors, respectfully protests the policy of your Administration in segregating the colored employees in the Departments at Washington. It realizes that this new and radical departure has been recommended, and is now being defended, on the ground that by giving certain bureaus or sections wholly to colored employees they are thereby rendered safer in possession of their offices and are less likely to be ousted or discriminated against. We believe this reasoning to be fallacious. It is based on a failure to appreciate the deeper significance of the new policy; to understand how far reaching the effects of such a drawing of caste lines by the Federal Government may be, and how humiliating it is to the men thus stigmatized.

394 • Wilson Meets with Trotter

Woodrow Wilson's second affront to the African American community was his reaction to William Monroe Trotter, editor of the *Boston Guardian.* Trotter and other members of a protest committee from the National Independence Equal Rights League met with Wilson in November 1914. Trotter, as chairman of the committee, served as spokesman. According to the *Chicago Defender:*

In the fervor of his [Trotter's] plea for equal rights for his people he forgot the servile manner and speech once characteristic of the Afro-American and he talked to the president as man to man, addressing the head of the government as any American citizen should, especially when discussing a serious matter. But the president did not like Mr. Trotter's attitude and said that if the committee came to him again it would have to get a new chairman. The president added that

he had not been addressed in such a manner since he entered the White House.

Afterward, the President confided to a colleague that he had lost his temper and that Trotter had spoken intelligently and manly.

395 • *The Birth of a Nation*

Perhaps the most striking example of Woodrow Wilson's insensitivity toward racial concerns was the screening of the film *Birth of a Nation* at the White House. Based on the best-selling novel by Thomas Dixon, Jr., *The Clansman,* the film extolled the virtues of the Ku Klux Klan. Using stereotypical portrayals of lusty Black men ravaging defenseless white women, the film exploited the prejudices of the time. After a private screening at the White House, Wilson is alleged to have said: "It is like writing history with lightning and my only regret is that it is all so terribly true."

Photograph of NAACP protest at theater showing *The Birth of a Nation*. Prints and Photographs Division, Library of Congress

396 • Charlotta Spears Bass (1880–1969)

Charlotta Bass was a bold African American newspaper editor and civil rights activist of the first decade of this century, whose arguments for civil rights were utilized by later spokespersons of the 1950s and 1960s movement. She was a journalist who in 1912 became editor of the *Eagle* (renamed *California Eagle*), the oldest West Coast newspaper for Blacks. Under her guidance (and that of her husband, John Bass), the paper directed its focus to social and political issues important to the Black community. Her motto was "win or lose, we win by raising the issues." She wrote against policies such as harsh sentencing of Black criminals, job discrimination, and the ever-present intimidation and mistreatment of blacks. She even faced down threats from the Ku Klux Klan, which was very strong in California in the 1940s and 1950s. After joining the Progressive Party in the 1940s—"the only party in which there is any hope for civil rights"—she became, in 1952, the first Black woman to run for the second highest political office in the nation when she was nominated as the Progressive Party's vice presidential candidate.

397 • Oscar DePriest Elected to Congress

In 1928 Oscar DePriest became the first African American elected to the House of Representatives in the twentieth century. Significantly he was not elected from the South, but from Illinois's 3rd Congressional District, making him the first African American elected to the House from the North. His election symbolized a Black political shift that would continue

through the first half of the twentieth century as more African Americans migrated out of the South, which denied them a right to vote, into the urban North, where they could vote. Eventually the growth of Black voting power in the North would force a shift in the racial agenda of the Democratic Party. DePriest was only a forerunner of that shift, because he was a Republican at a time when almost all African Americans voted the Republican Party, "the party of Lincoln."

DePriest used his position to fight for African Americans. His most notable success was passage of the amendment to eliminate racial discrimination in the Civilian Conservation Corps. He defied southern racism by speaking in the South, despite threats on his life, and challenged Senator James Heflin of Alabama by eating in the Senate restaurant. He tried but failed to pass antilynching legislation. DePriest's opposition to Roosevelt's public assistance programs spelled his end, and he was defeated by Arthur W. Mitchell, a Democrat, in 1934.

398 • William Edward Burghardt Du Bois (1868–1963)

William Edward Burghardt Du Bois was the leading African American intellectual and fighter for civil rights in the Jim Crow period. Born in Great Barrington, Massachusetts, educated at Harvard, Fisk, and the University of Berlin, Du Bois made groundbreaking contributions in numerous fields, from sociology to history to fiction to autobiography. While teaching at Atlanta University, he published his most moving work, the *Souls of Black Folk,* in 1903, and then left the university to found, first, the Niagara Movement and then the National Association for the Advancement of Colored People, for which he served as director of research and editor of the *Crisis.* He broke with the NAACP

W. E. B. Du Bois. Prints and Photographs Division, Library of Congress

in 1934 and returned to teaching at Atlanta University, continuing to publish widely in history and political theory. After World War II he committed himself to the cause of world peace, but became a target of government harassment during the cold war for his alleged connections to communists. In 1961, after the State Department was forced to return his passport, which had been seized unconstitutionally, he left the United States and settled in the West African nation of Ghana, where he resided until his death in 1963.

399 • Mary Church Terrell (1863–1954)

In 1884 Mary Church Terrell and two others became the first Black women to receive a B.A. from Oberlin College. Although one of the best educated of the growing African American middle class, she was early acquainted with racism when Matthew Arnold observed her classroom

at Oberlin. When Terrell recited several verses in Greek as requested by her teacher, Arnold said he was astounded because he had heard that African Americans could not recite Greek because of the physiological shape of their tongues! Remembering this incident in her autobiography, *A Colored Woman in a White World* (1940), as an example of the ignorance fostered by racism even among the so-called educated, she dedicated herself to uplifting her own race and educating white sensibilities. Moving to Washington, D.C., to teach school, she became a leader in Washington Black society following her marriage to the prominent judge Robert Terrell. But Mary Church was not one to allow her "wifely" duties to deter her from serving the cause of freedom. In 1895 she founded the National Association of Colored Women, which promoted respect and advancement of African American women. A charter member of the NAACP, Mrs. Terrell was also very active in local issues, becoming the first woman to serve on the District of Columbia Board of Education. Mary Church Terrell became a symbol of the cultural and political leadership exercised by African American women in the twentieth century.

400 • Walter Francis White (1893–1955)

Walter Francis White joined the staff of the National Association for the Advancement of Colored People in 1918, and because of the light color of his skin, was able to make a unique contribution to the fight against racism. White posed as a white journalist and traveled through the South to collect information on discrimination, segregation, and most important, lynchings without anyone suspecting that he was African American or a member of the NAACP. His reports helped the association pressure Congress to pass an antilynching law. In 1929 Walter White became acting secretary and then secretary of the NAACP and steered that organization through its difficult years in the 1930s, which included a losing struggle with the Communist Party for control of the Scottsboro Boys case, a failed attempt to win congressional passage of antilynching legislation, and an increasingly successful legal assault on segregation. He was also responsible, according to W. E. B. Du Bois, for forcing Du Bois to resign from the organization in 1934. During the cold war, when other African American leaders were suspected of communist sympathies, White was sufficiently safe to be appointed by President Harry Truman to the U.S. delegation to the United Nations. Forced to accept a ceremonial post of executive secretary of the NAACP in 1950, his death came in the year following the organization's greatest triumph, the Supreme Court decision in *Brown v. Board of Education.*

401 • Asa Philip Randolph (1889–1979)

Asa Philip Randolph was one of the most important but underappreciated African American leaders who made his mark in an area that is often ignored: African American labor. Randolph began to organize workers while a student in college, but became even more energetic in the cause of Black unionization during World War I. He believed that African Americans could not blindly give their loyalty to the United States war effort, but must take advantage of the situation to improve their working status. Toward that end, he founded the *Messenger* to publicize his unionization movement, as well as to provide a critique of organizations like the NAACP, who he believed were too conservative. As founder and head of the Brotherhood of Sleeping Car Porters, he was successful in winning recognition for the union from the Pullman

Company in 1925. He was one of the founders of the National Negro Congress in the 1930s, which sought to galvanize Black thinking on the left, and in 1941 he organized the first March on Washington to protest discrimination. That march was eventually called off when President Franklin Delano Roosevelt capitulated to Randolph's demands and issued Executive Order 8802. In 1963 Randolph was a leader in organizing the second proposed March on Washington, which actually took place.

402 • Henrietta Vinton Davis (1860–1941)

Although men are usually mentioned most prominently in connection with the Garvey movement, one of the most important organizers of the Universal Negro Improvement Association (UNIA) was a woman, Henrietta Davis. A promising actress during the 1880s and a popular public speaker (who was well known in New York City for her speaking recitals), she gave up her performing career to join Garvey in spreading his philosophy of Black nationalism and pride in African heritage. Following Garvey cost Davis her career and many of her friendships. Garvey's dislike of light-skinned African Americans and his calls for Black racial purity and superiority, ideas repugnant to much of the Black elite of the 1920s, made it difficult for her to keep her middle-class, professional friendships. She died in obscurity.

403 • Mary McCleod Bethune (1875–1955)

Mary McCleod Bethune was president of the National Council of Negro Women and a member of President Franklin Delano Roosevelt's "Black Cabinet" of advisers on racial matters after his election to the presidency in 1932. She was also the founder and president of Bethune-Cookman College, director of the Negro Affairs Division of the National Youth Administration, and one of the American observers who attended the 1945 conference in San Francisco to establish the United Nations.

404 • Paul Robeson (1898–1976)

Paul Robeson graduated from Rutgers University, where he was elected to Phi Beta Kappa and was twice named to Walter Camp's all-white All-American football team. Robeson went on to Columbia University, where he earned a degree in law, but although he worked in a law firm briefly in New York City, his heart was in acting. After appearing in several amateur stage productions, he decided to make the theater his career. After successful appearances in Eugene O'Neill's *The Emperor Jones* and *All God's Chillun Got Wings,* Robeson began to sing on the concert stage, excelling particularly in the singing of African American spirituals. By the mid-1930s his motion picture film credits, his performance of the title role of *Othello* in London, and his acclaimed singing had made Robeson an international star. But because Robeson would not repudiate his ties to the left as others did during the blacklisting of the 1940s and 1950s, his career suffered. He created considerable controversy in 1949 when he was misquoted by the press as stating that African Americans would not fight against the Soviet Union. Quickly Robeson was blackballed in the United States, targeted for harassment and investigation, and eventually deprived of his passport (along with W. E. B. Du Bois) by the State Department. His name was removed from the list of All-Americans for the years that he played college football, and the College Football Hall of Fame refused him membership, making him the only All-American not to be included. Still, Robeson never relented in his defense of

Paul Robeson, a world-renowned African American singer, leads Moore Shipyard workers in Oakland, California, in singing "The Star-Spangled Banner." "This is a serious job," he told them, "winning the war against fascists. We have to be together." September 1942. National Archives. Courtesy of A.P./Wide World Photos

his right to speak freely and criticize American racism. He died in Philadelphia in 1976, having seen the success of a new civil rights movement in America.

405 • Adam Clayton Powell, Jr. (1908–72)

The son of the founder of the Abyssinian Baptist Church in Harlem, Adam Clayton Powell, Jr., was a graduate of Cornell University, the pastor of his father's church, and, in 1944, the first representative elected to Congress from Harlem. Powell used his congressional seat, which he held for over twenty-four years, as a bully pulpit for improved civil rights for African Americans. He pressured several presidents and members of Congress to pass substantial civil rights legislation and criticized them for the weak compromise bills that were eventually passed. As a leftward-leaning politician, Powell brought national attention to the economic conditions of Black and white workers in America. During the 1950s and 1960s he worked closely with civil rights organizations such as the NAACP, the Student Nonviolent Coordinating Committee (SNCC), and CORE, and supported such efforts as the national boycott against five-and-dime stores that refused to serve African Americans at lunch counters in the South. His greatest contribution came after he became, in 1961, chairman of the Committee on Education and Labor in the House of Representatives, where he used his position to promote antipoverty legislation and block the proposals of others who did not support civil rights programs. He also supported legislation for the expansion of educational and artistic opportunities, proposing a National Foundation on the Arts and Humanities in the 89th Congress. But Powell's flair for expensive travel and flamboyant living, often paid for by

government funds, led to his expulsion from the Congress. In 1969, after a two-year stint in the Bahamas, he was reelected to Congress by his constituents after the Supreme Court ruled his expulsion unconstitutional. But in 1970 a Harlem newcomer, Charles Rangel, defeated Powell in the Democratic primary by 150 votes and ended the legendary congressman's political career. He died of complications from prostate surgery on April 4, 1972, having been African America's most outspoken congressman.

406 • Ralph J. Bunche (1904–71)

Dr. Ralph J. Bunche was awarded the Nobel Peace Prize in 1950 for his work to establish peace in the Middle East. He received a Ph.D. from Harvard in 1934 and later worked for the U.S. State Department, and still later, the United Nations. After the establishment of a Jewish state in 1948 and the resulting animosity between Jews and Palestinians in the region, Bunche helped design a tentative (and ultimately futile) peace agreement between the two groups in Israel. It was his work in this area that was recognized by the Stockholm committee.

407 • Thurgood Marshall (1908–93)

Thurgood Marshall successfully argued the case that became the Supreme Court's most important twentieth-century decision, *Brown v. Board of Education of Topeka, Kansas,* handed down on May 17, 1954. It was Marshall who decided to switch the Legal Defense Fund's tactics, pioneered under his mentor, Charles Houston, from trying to prove southern schools were unequal to making the case that segregated schooling was inherently unequal, despite the conditions of respective schools. Marshall successfully led the Legal Defense Fund's continued assault on segregation until 1967, when he was chosen by President Lyndon Johnson to become the first African American Supreme Court judge. Unlike many others who were appointed to the Supreme Court, Marshall did not abandon his ideological moorings, but continued the campaign for racial justice he had begun before his appointment to the Court. In 1991 he retired from the Supreme Court because of ill health, and he died on January 24, 1993.

Thurgood Marshall, right, leaves Birmingham, Alabama, courthouse with Autherine Lucy, 1956. Courtesy of A.P./Wide World Photos

Laws, Executive Orders, and Supreme Court Decisions

408 • "Force Bill" Fails

In January 1890 the Republican representative from Massachusetts Henry Cabot Lodge submitted a bill to Congress that would be the last congressional attempt of the Jim Crow period to protect African American voting rights

in the South. In what became known as the Force Bill, Lodge sought to obtain federal oversight for federal elections in the South. He brought before Congress extensive evidence of the abuses of Blacks who attempted to vote in such elections in the South. His statistics showed that the percentage of voters in many elections far underrepresented the total population, and in a bill that foreshadowed the Voting Rights Act of 1965, advocated federal intervention. But the bill encountered stiff resistance from southerners who characterized it as another example of the federal government trying to interfere with the state's prerogative to establish its own rules for voting within its boundaries. The bill passed the House, but failed in the Senate on January 26, 1891.

409 • Louisiana's "Act to Promote the Comfort of Passengers"

On July 10, 1890, Louisiana passed a law that "all railway companies carrying passengers in their coaches in this State, shall provide equal but separate accommodations for the white, and colored, races, by providing two or more passenger coaches for each passenger train, or by dividing the passenger coaches by a partition so as to secure separate accommodations." Any passenger who violated this provision could be fined twenty-five dollars and jailed for twenty days. This was the first state law to require segregation of this magnitude, even though other states had barred African Americans from first-class cars on railroads before.

410 • *Plessy v. Ferguson*

Early in the 1890s, Homer Plessy, a man of mixed racial heritage (one-eighth Black, seven-eighths white) refused to ride in the "colored" section of a Louisiana train and was arrested. Louisiana law stipulated "equal but separate accommodations for the white, and colored, races." Plessy sued to have the law overturned, contending it violated the Thirteenth and Fourteenth Amendments. In 1896 the Supreme Court rejected this argument and upheld Louisiana's contention that separate but equal accommodations did not violate the Fourteenth Amendment's equal protection clause. In doing so, the Court created a distinction between political rights and social discrimination.

The object of the [Fourteenth] amendment was undoubtedly to enforce the absolute equality of the two races before the law, but in the nature of things it could not have been intended to abolish distinctions based upon color, or to enforce social, as distinguished from political equality, or a commingling of the two races upon terms unsatisfactory to either. Laws permitting, and even requiring, racial separation in places where the races are liable to be brought into contact do not necessarily imply the inferiority of either race to the other, and have been generally, if not universally, recognized as within the competency of the state legislatures in the exercise of their police power. . . .

In the aftermath of this decision, state and local governments that had not passed segregation statutes felt free to do so.

411 • *Powell v. Alabama*

In this 1932 decision, the United States Supreme Court ruled that the Scottsboro Boys (nine poor young Black men who had been tried and convicted for rape of two white women migrants) had been denied the counsel of their choice. This was a violation of the Fourteenth Amendment's due process clause. This case was the first time that a conviction for rape of Black

men had been overruled by a higher court. It sent the case back to Alabama to be tried again, this time with lawyers representing the Scottsboro Boys supplied by the Communist Party's International Labor Defense. The decision also established that African Americans had a right to adequate legal counsel as part of their constitutional rights as citizens.

412 • *Gaines v. Missouri*

In 1938 the United States Supreme Court ruled that states have to provide equal educational facilities for all citizens *within the state.* Missouri had attempted to send Lloyd Gaines out of state to law school to preserve its "white only" Missouri law school. With this decision, the Supreme Court put the onus of responsibility on states to establish a separate but equal graduate and professional school system, if such a state wished to maintain segregated schooling. The problem for states such as Missouri was that increasing numbers of African Americans were graduating from undergraduate programs at Black colleges and universities.

413 • Executive Order 9808

In the aftermath of World War II, mob violence and lynching of African Americans, in conjunction with the continuing controversy about segregation in American society, led President Harry S. Truman to issue Executive Order 9808 on December 5, 1946, which set up a committee to study the protection of civil rights in the United States. In October 1947 the Committee on Civil Rights published its report, which established the four basic rights a government must protect: the right to safety, the right to citizenship, such as service in the armed service and the exercise of voting, the right to freedom of expression, and the right to equality of opportunity. The report stated that African Americans lacked these rights and recommended the President end discrimination and segregation in the armed forces.

414 • Executive Order 9981

In July 1948, four months after his civil rights message to Congress, President Harry Truman issued an executive order to desegregate the armed forces. In doing so, Truman took a bold political risk. Already far behind in the polls to the Republican challenger, Thomas Dewey, Truman needed a dramatic move to revitalize his bid for reelection. Desegregating the armed forces greatly angered the southern segregationists in the Democratic Party, many of whom abandoned the party during the summer convention to vote for Strom Thurmond, a States Rights Party presidential candidate. But Truman's gesture paid off: he edged out Dewey for the victory with majorities in northern urban areas and with support from 69 percent of the African American voters. Truman's victory signaled a shift in the locus of national power in the Democratic Party away from southern Dixiecrats and toward the northern, ethnic, and industrial coalition that Roosevelt's New Deal had built.

415 • *Sweatt v. Painter*

In 1950 the United States Supreme Court ruled that the law school of the University of Texas had to open its doors to a Black applicant despite the fact that the state maintained a separate law school for Blacks. The Supreme Court argued that the benefits of the University of Texas law school—its superior facilities, faculty, and postgraduate contacts—made it a significantly better school for the applicant, and to deny him access to such a school was a denial of his right to due process under the Fourteenth Amendment. This ruling undermined the southern states' strategy creating a dual educational

system, since now if inequality could be proved, Black applicants had to be admitted to previously "whites only" schools.

416 • *Brown v. Board of Education of Topeka, Kansas*

Brown v. Board of Education was the landmark decision by the United States Supreme Court that segregated educational facilities were a violation of the Fourteenth Amendment and thus unconstitutional. The Brown case was one of several suits brought by the National Association for the Advancement of Colored People's Legal Defense and Educational Fund on behalf of the parents of Black children in Kansas, South Carolina, Virginia, Delaware, and the District of Columbia, who had watched their children be bused long distances to dilapidated Black schools when quality white schools existed in their neighborhoods. The NAACP had decided to shift from challenging segregation in graduate or professional school education to challenging elementary education. The NAACP had also shifted from showing that segregated educational facilities were unequal to arguing that segregation was degrading to Black children and thus a violation of the Fourteenth Amendment's guarantee of equal protection. The United States Supreme Court agreed and ruled unanimously on May 17, 1954, that segregated schools were "inherently unequal," because to force Black children to attend separate schools purely because of their race "generates a feeling of inferiority as to their status in the community that may affect their hearts and minds in a way very unlikely ever to be undone." After this decision all aspects of segregated life in the South came under pressure, even though the *Brown* decision was limited to elementary school education. This decision overturned the *Plessy v. Ferguson* decision of 1896.

CIVIL RIGHTS MOVEMENT

Protests, Organizations, and Demonstrations

417 • Racist Reaction to *Brown v. Board of Education*

Despite the Supreme Court's 1954 ruling in *Brown v. Board of Education,* southern states refused to allow Black children into white schools, and refused to dismantle segregation in public accommodations. Resistance against desegregation, though, was not a view held only by state or local governments. White southerners took it upon themselves to organize opposition to desegregation. One manifestation of that opposition was the White Citizens Councils, made up of citizens who considered themselves more respectable than those engaged in Ku Klux Klan activities. The first meeting of a White Citizens Council occurred in Mississippi on July 11, 1954, at which the group laid plans for resisting the Supreme Court decision in Mississippi. It was this type of active resistance to the Supreme Court decision that made the direct-action Civil Rights Movement necessary. For without the willingness of African Americans and their sympathizers to challenge segregation, the desegregation of the South might not have taken place. Only by creating a crisis in southern segregation could African Americans force the government, especially executive and legislative branches of the federal government, to intervene in the South and force compliance.

418 • Montgomery Bus Boycott

The first salvo in the war against segregation in southern society was delivered by a diminu-

tive Black seamstress named Rosa Parks, who, on December 1, 1955, refused to vacate her seat on a Montgomery, Alabama, bus in order for a white passenger to sit. Mrs. Parks was an NAACP activist, who knew that local civil rights leaders were looking for a case to test Montgomery's bus segregation ordinance. But such concerns were secondary in her mind to the indignity of having to get up from her seat just because Montgomery segregation decreed that no African American could occupy a row on a bus with a white person. Contrary to popular misconception, Mrs. Parks was not sitting in the white section: she had taken a seat in the first row of the Black section; but when all the seats in the white section had been filled and a white man was left standing, the bus driver ordered her and two others to get up and let the white man sit. In truth, then, no "Black section" really existed. Upon the bus driver's order, the other two Blacks stood, but Parks refused to get up and was arrested for violating that ordinance. In response, members of the NAACP launched the Montgomery Bus Boycott. After electing the young Rev. Martin Luther King, Jr., as its president, the Montgomery Improvement Association organized a cab service for Black domestic servants and circumvented both the bus company and local officials who sought to break the boycott. The boycott was effective at hurting the bus company financially, but it did not force Montgomery to rescind its bus segregation statute. Again, the Supreme Court came to the rescue: a year after Mrs. Parks refused to give up her seat, the Court ruled that Montgomery's bus segregation ordinance was unconstitutional. Afterward, Black passengers could ride wherever they pleased on Montgomery buses.

419 • SCLC Formed

At a meeting held in Atlanta, Georgia, January 10–11, 1957, the Southern Christian Leadership Conference (SCLC) was founded with Dr. Martin Luther King, Jr., as its president and Ralph Abernathy as its treasurer. First called the Southern Negro Leaders Conference and then the Southern Negro Leadership Conference, the organization was primarily an assembly of ministers who wished to move beyond what the NAACP or the Urban League was doing in the area of civil rights. SCLC focused on building the momentum for direct action in civil rights created by the success of the Montgomery Bus Boycott. Over the next ten years, SCLC would become the most successful of the modern civil rights organizations in carrying out large-scale, well-coordinated, and well-financed demonstrations in a number of southern cities.

420 • Little Rock School Desegregation

In August 1957 nine Black students (later known as the Little Rock Nine) attempted to register at the all-white Central High School in Little Rock, Arkansas. They were denied access to the school by Arkansas Governor Orval Faubus. When the federal government ordered Faubus to allow their registration, he replied he could not guarantee the safety of the students. Local people turned out to taunt and terrorize the students, so much so that eventually their parents would not let them attend the school until the federal government guaranteed their safety. After much delay, President Dwight D. Eisenhower reluctantly ordered federal troops to Little Rock to protect the students and ensure that Faubus would comply with the school integration order.

421 • The Sit-in Movement

The sit-in movement began on February 1, 1960, when four African American students from the North Carolina Central Agricultural

and Technical College sat down at a Woolworth's lunch counter in Greensboro, North Carolina. The aim of the sit-in was to force Woolworth's to serve African Americans at the only lunch counter in the store, where they were not then allowed to sit. Soon after, the idea of the sit-in quickly spread to other cities in five states. Students sat in in Winston-Salem, Durham, Charlotte, and Fayetteville, North Carolina, as well as in Portsmouth, Virginia, and Chattanooga and Nashville, Tennessee. Other students organized nationwide demonstrations and protests outside of segregated Woolworth stores. The Greensboro students were cursed, spit on, and burned with cigarette butts by white youths, but maintained their sit-in until July 25, 1960, at 2:00 P.M., when, without prior notice, the four Black students were served. By 1962 thousands of lunch counters and other public accommodations had been desegregated in roughly 150 cities.

A sit-in at a Woolworth's lunch counter in Jackson, Mississippi, on May 28, 1963, turned ugly when whites attacked demonstrators John Salter, Jr., Joan Trumpeter, and Anne Moody, the latter the author of *Coming of Age in Mississippi.* State Historical Society of Wisconsin

422 • SNCC Founded

The Student Nonviolent Coordinating Committee, or SNCC (pronounced *snick*), was an organization of students who had become active in the sit-in movement. The organization was founded at a conference held April 16–18, 1960, in Raleigh, North Carolina, which Southern Christian Leadership Conference executive director Ella Baker organized. Baker believed that the students needed an organization of their own. Less hierarchical than either SCLC or CORE, SNCC pioneered a "cell" approach to leadership in which group consensus was needed to adopt policy. Critical of the tendency of some SCLC leaders to "invade" a southern city, call demonstrations, and then abandon the Black community afterward, SNCC pioneered a different approach, whereby members lived in and adopted the concerns of the Black community. This experience of close contact with rural Blacks in Mississippi and Alabama led to a radicalization of SNCC, which, along with rising Black anger in the middle 1960s, contributed to the election of Stokely Carmichael as SNCC president in 1966. Carmichael popularized the slogan "Black Power" and steered the organization away from its earlier commitment to interracial democracy toward the goal of separate Black community development. The organization declined in the early 1970s, a victim of governmental repression, white ostracism, and internal conflicts.

Ella Baker. Prints and Photographs Division, Library of Congress, Visual Materials from the NAACP Records

423 • Freedom Rides

The Freedom Rides began on May 4, 1961, when thirteen Blacks and whites who were trained in nonviolence left Washington, D.C., on a bus trip through the South to challenge segregation in interstate bus facilities. Organized by CORE, the Freedom Riders challenged segregated seating requirements, segregated bathrooms, and seating signs in bus terminals. A bus was bombed outside of Anniston, Alabama, and the Freedom Riders were attacked and beaten savagely in Anniston, Birmingham, and Montgomery, Alabama. They were arrested in Mississippi, but CORE eventually convinced the Supreme Court to order Mississippi to refund the Riders' bond money. At the insistence of Attorney General Robert Kennedy, the Interstate Commerce Commission issued a directive to end bus segregation in the South.

424 • Albany Movement

Begun on November 17, 1961, and lasting until August 1962, the Albany Movement was the first community-based civil rights demonstration. SCLC, SNCC, CORE, and the NAACP all contributed to the Albany Movement. The heart and soul of the movement, however, was a group of local Black professionals and townspeople determined to change the highly segregated southern town of Albany, Georgia. Their task was made difficult, however, by the intransigence and resourcefulness of local white leaders, especially Sheriff Laurie Pritchett, who had learned

Freedom Ride bus destroyed by southern white rioters in Anniston, Alabama, May 15, 1961. Prints and Photographs Division, Library of Congress. Courtesy of Bettmann Archives

from other confrontations with civil rights demonstrators and deliberately sought to minimize national publicity. Albany was also a crisis for the leadership of Martin Luther King, who came to Albany fully expecting a dramatic victory, but not only left without one but received some of the blame from younger activists who felt his unwillingness to defy federal court orders and his adherence to nonviolent methods hurt the Albany Movement. Nevertheless, Albany was an important experience for many young activists and local African Americans. Although it would take six more years to desegregate Albany—a town whose leaders closed parks rather than desegregate them and removed chairs from libraries before admitting Blacks—a grassroots activist movement had been started that eventually transformed even Albany.

425 • James Meredith Integrates Ole Miss

James Meredith's entry into the University of Mississippi was one of the most hard-fought victories of the Civil Rights Movement, mainly because "Ole Miss" symbolized the antebellum traditions of the South. On September 3, 1962, a federal court declared Meredith was eligible for entry into Ole Miss and the school must admit him. This led to a hysterical confrontation between Governor Ross Barnett, a segregationist who believed his reelection chances depended on his ardent defense of Mississippi's state rights, and the federal government. Using television, Barnett whipped up racial feelings among residents and at football games, all the while negotiating with President John F. Kennedy to find a way to comply with the federal order and yet remain an ardent defender of segregation. After Meredith was sneaked into a room in Baxter Hall on campus on September 30, white students attacked federal marshals and full-scale rioting erupted as Barnett took the radio to call all loyal southerners to Oxford, Mississippi, to defend the southern way of life. Kennedy ordered army troops to Oxford to rescue the federal marshals. When it was over the next morning, 160 federal marshals were injured and two innocent white bystanders were dead. At 7:55 A.M. Meredith was able to walk casually across a now deserted campus and register as a student.

426 • Birmingham April–May 1963

On April 3, 1963, SCLC and the Alabama Christian Movement for Human Rights (ACMHR) launched Project C, a series of demonstrations by Blacks in Birmingham, one of the South's most industrialized yet segregated cities. During the first stage, demonstrators marched to integrate lunch counters, drinking fountains, and downtown businesses, and were peacefully arrested. During the second stage, forty-five people marched to City Hall and kneeled in prayer every day for forty-five days. After Martin Luther King was arrested on April 12 (Good Friday) for violating an injunction against marching, he used his solitary confinement in jail to pen his now famous "Letter from a Birmingham Jail," his answer to eight white clergymen who urged him to stop the demonstration and to work peacefully through the courts. Declaring that to achieve the "positive peace" of the New Testament, social disruption was necessary, King put into practice the third and most controversial phase of the demonstrations as soon as he got out of jail. On May 2, 1963, nearly one thousand children marched every day from Sixteenth Baptist Church to City Hall, where they were arrested. As critics decried the use of children, the commissioner of public safety, Eugene "Bull" Connor, attacked demonstrators with police dogs and powerful fire hoses. Pressured by the Kennedy administration

and northern industrialists, Birmingham's business leaders signed an agreement that granted SCLC's and ACMHR's demands to desegregate lunch counters and rest rooms, to hire African Americans in sales and clerical positions, to release jailed demonstrators, who numbered about two thousand, and to form a permanent biracial committee. It was the SCLC's and Martin Luther King's most dramatic and effective victory in the movement since the Montgomery Bus Boycott victory of 1956.

427 • Governor Wallace's University of Alabama Schoolhouse Stand

Days after the successful ending of the 1963 Birmingham demonstrations, Governor George Wallace of Alabama precipitated another confrontation between those seeking to integrate southern institutions and those seeking to keep them segregated. The University of Alabama was ordered by federal court to admit Black students. Wallace believed he could circumvent the order by encouraging whites to stay away from the university. But eventually, on June 11, Wallace personally blocked the doorway to a university building and prevented two Black students, James Hood and Vivian Malone, from enrolling. Wallace then read a statement to Deputy Attorney General Nicholas B. Katzenbach, which argued that the attempt to register Black students at the University of Alabama was an "action in violation of rights reserved for the state by the Constitution of the United States and the Constitution of the state of Alabama." But a few hours after Wallace's "stand in the door" tactic, Wallace left the campus when asked by Alabama National Guard General Henry Graham, along with federal marshals, to remove himself. That same day Black students walked through the door Wallace had previously blocked, and desegregated the University of Alabama.

428 • 1963 March on Washington

Held on August 28, 1963, the March on Washington was organized by A. Philip Randolph, president of the Brotherhood of Sleeping Car Porters and an elder statesman of the Civil Rights Movement. In 1941 Randolph had called a similar march to protest discrimination in wartime hiring; in 1963 he again wanted to draw attention to Black unemployment, which stood at 11 percent, compared to 6 percent for whites. One of his original demands was for job training for Blacks, but after the Birmingham demonstrations and the attacks on Blacks by Bull Connor and his dogs, the March on Washington assumed much broader significance. President John Kennedy's civil rights bill was being argued in the Congress, and the march became a coming together of all of the major civil rights, labor, and religious organizations to urge passage of the Civil Rights Act, rapid integration of the public schools, and passage of a fair employment practices bill. President Kennedy initially tried to dissuade Randolph and Bayard Rustin, the deputy organizer of the march, from holding it, but once Kennedy realized it would take place, he endorsed it. Expecting 100,000 marchers, organizers were surprised when the numbers swelled to 250,000 people, at that time the largest demonstration in the nation's history. Although there was tension between the many different voices and organizations represented, the march went smoothly and was a remarkable show of unity. While some participants, such as SNCC's John Lewis, delivered speeches sharply critical of American practices, Martin Luther King best captured the mood of optimism and hope that day with his now classic "I Have a Dream" speech.

429 • Freedom Schools

As part of SNCC's effort to mobilize the Black

Civil Rights March on Washington, 1963. Prints and Photographs Division, Library of Congress

population in Mississippi, organizer Charles Cobb developed the idea of the "freedom schools" in 1963. Recognizing that Mississippi's educational system was not only inadequate but also counterproductive to the kind of intellectual curiosity and political thinking that SNCC wanted to foster in the Black population, Cobb decided to utilize the hundreds of young college-age students coming South to work in the movement as an educated "fifth column." The radical white professor Staughton Lynd directed a program of study in the spring and summer of 1964 that included academic subjects and also "movement" courses such as Black culture and leadership development. Although tensions developed that year between inexperienced white volunteers and seasoned Black organizers, the Freedom School was a success and a forerunner of later Black Studies curricula.

430 • Mississippi Freedom Democratic Party

Founded at a rally in Jackson, Mississippi, on April 26, 1964, the Mississippi Freedom Democratic Party was SNCC's attempt to create an alternative Democratic Party in Mississippi. The idea began when SNCC workers attempted to create separate voter registration requirements for Blacks who were otherwise prevented from registering to vote under the rules of the Democratic Party in Mississippi. But the idea quickly blossomed into a much more ambitious attempt to challenge the legality of the Mississippi delegation at the Democratic National Convention held that year in Atlantic City, New Jersey. During the Summer Project, SNCC workers encouraged seventeen thousand African Americans to register to vote, although only sixteen hundred were registered by authorities. Another eighty thousand Blacks registered as members of the MFDP, proof of the attractiveness of the alternative party in Mississippi. At the beginning of the

Fannie Lou Hamer speaking truth to power at the Democratic National Convention in Atlantic City, August 22, 1964. Prints and Photographs Division, Library of Congress, U.S. News & World Report Collection. Photo by Warren K. Leffler

national convention, nine Democratic state delegations and over twenty congressmen initially endorsed the MFDP. Fannie Lou Hamer, the charismatic SNCC organizer, electrified the nation when her impassioned request before the Credentials Committee to seat the Freedom Democratic Party was carried on network news. But in the end, President Lyndon Johnson refused to allow any challenge that might threaten his nomination, and when the MFDP refused to accept a White House compromise—"We didn't come all this way for no two seats," Hamer reputedly said—the MFDP effort to unseat the Dixiecrats was defeated.

431 • March from Selma to Montgomery

Beginning on January 2, 1965, SCLC launched a voting registration drive in Selma, Alabama, to dramatize the disparity in voter registration—only 1 percent of the fifteen thousand nonwhite population of Selma was registered to vote in that city. Selma was also important because its sheriff, Jim Clark, and his posse were ardent segregationists. The first month of registration was relatively calm, although Martin Luther King was attacked when he registered on January 18. The drive for voter registration became more violent during the next month. King was arrested on February 1, and after his release, he called on the federal government to enact a voting rights act. But the Selma campaign was going badly and in danger of collapsing when, on March 7, SCLC's Hosea Williams and SNCC's John Lewis led about five hundred people on a march from Brown Chapel African Methodist Episcopal Church in Selma to the state capital of Montgomery to present a petition to Governor George Wallace. King was in Atlanta preaching at his church when the group crossed over Pettus Bridge and was attacked from the front by Major John Cloud's Alabama state troopers and from behind by Jim Clark's tear-gas-throwing posse on horseback. In the chaos that ensued, John Lewis's skull was cracked, dozens of people were beaten and injured, and the marchers were forced back to the church, where Black residents, tired of weeks of harassment, armed themselves and threatened to engage Clark's posse in a shooting war. Through the efforts of Wilson Baker, Selma's director of public safety, who succeeded in getting Clark to retreat, and Andrew Young, who got armed Blacks to return to their homes, a bloodbath was avoided. But the attack was recorded by photographers from major national magazines, and the pictures showed the world southern justice in Alabama. A week later, hundreds of people, including many prominent whites in the religious community, traveled to Selma to participate in a second march along the same route, led this time by Martin Luther King. Bloodshed was avoided when King, by prearranged agreement, limited the march to crossing the Pettus Bridge and returning to Selma. That action was severely criticized by militants in the movement, who argued, in the words of Eldridge Cleaver, that King "denied history a great moment." For if King had attempted to march to Montgomery and the marchers had been attacked, many people—both white and Black—would have been injured. But King didn't want to risk further violence against the marchers either from police or from Ku Klux Klan snipers. The Selma marches did, however, force the federal government to intervene. And on March 1, in his address to Congress, President Lyndon Johnson said he was sending a voting rights bill to Congress and concluded with the movement's own salutation, "And we . . . shall . . . overcome."

432 • Organization of Afro-American Unity

Following his removal as a minister of the Nation of Islam and his trip to Mecca, Malcolm X (1925–65) formed the Organization of Afro-American Unity, a Black nationalist group designed with progressive, militant, and political goals. Beyond simply permitting Malcolm X greater political involvement than he had with the Black Muslims, the OAAU was part of Malcolm X's plan to bring the case of American racism before the United Nations as a human rights violation rather than simply a case of American civil rights. But shortly after forming this organization, Malcolm X was assassinated by two former Black Muslims.

433 • The Black Panther Party

Founded in Oakland, California, in October 1966 by Bobby Seale and Huey P. Newton, the Black Panther Party promoted the idea of militant self-defense for the Black community against police brutality. Originally named the Black Panther Party for Self-Defense, the Panthers advocated a "Ten Point Program" that demanded full employment of Black people in America, decent housing, release of Black prisoners (all of whom were political prisoners in the eyes of the Panthers), payment of the forty acres and a mule (in contemporary currency) promised to former slaves during Reconstruction, and the holding of a United Nations plebiscite for the Black community to determine its future relationship to the United States. Blending the ideas of Malcolm X, Franz Fanon, Karl Marx, and Mao Tse-tung, Seale and Newton rejected cultural nationalism and called for a revolution to address the colonial relationship of the Black community to the larger American society. In the Black community of Oakland, California, the Panthers were mainly known for wearing black berets and black leather jackets, and for creating a system of armed patrols that followed police whenever they stopped Black citizens. The Panthers gained the attention of the press in 1967 when Bobby Seale and twenty-five armed members marched to the capitol building in Sacramento, California, and read a statement of protest against a gun-control bill introduced by California Assemblyman Don Mulford to limit the Panthers' right to carry weapons in public. That incident also garnered the attention of FBI Director J. Edgar Hoover, who announced that the Black Panthers were "the greatest threat to the internal security of the country" and orchestrated a counterintelligence program to desta-

Huey P. Newton poster, artist unknown. "The racist dog policemen must withdraw immediately from our communities, stop their wanton murder and brutality." Permission granted by Gary Yanker

bilize the party. In 1968 Eldridge Cleaver, a former Black Muslim and in 1968 the Black Panther Party's Minister of Information, ran for U.S. president as a candidate of the Peace and Freedom Party. The Black Panther Party was the victim of police and FBI harassment, and numerous members were killed either in shootouts with police or in raids on the homes of Panther Party members. Although the party contained roughly three thousand members in 1972, it collapsed shortly afterward because of internal divisions and legal problems. Elaine Brown assumed the chairmanship of the party in 1974 when Newton left the United States for Cuba to avoid prosecution on murder charges; he eventually was killed in 1989 in a drug-related shooting. Bobby Seale was tried and convicted for traveling across state lines to incite a riot at the 1968 Democratic National Convention in Chicago. Eldridge Cleaver fled imprisonment by leaving the country, living for a while in Algeria and Cuba, and breaking with the party in 1971. Cleaver returned to the United States in 1976, become a political conservative, and apologized for some of his former statements. *Panther,* a film on the early years of the party, by Melvin and Mario Van Peebles, was released in 1995. The spirit of those years survives in the Dr. Huey P. Newton Foundation, run by Brown and David Hilliard, another former party officer.

434 • Poor People's Campaign

Shortly after the death of Dr. Martin Luther King, Jr., in 1968, Rev. Ralph Abernathy, the southern minister who succeeded King in SCLC, organized a protest demonstration in Washington, D.C., called the Poor People's Campaign. Thousands of African Americans trekked to the nation's capital to draw attention to the continuing problem of poverty and racism in America. Taking up temporary residence in the shadow of the Lincoln Memorial, protesters constructed a shantytown, called Resurrection City, while Martin Luther King's widow, Coretta Scott King, led a demonstration of welfare mothers from around the country. The Poor People's Campaign and Resurrection City symbolized a shift in the Civil Rights Movement politics away from mere racial discrimination toward what was later dubbed the Welfare Rights Movement.

Some Important People Not Yet Mentioned

435 • Daisy Bates (b. 1920)

Daisy Bates was the prime mover behind the Little Rock desegregation movement in 1957 that eventually resulted in the integration of Little Rock Central High School. As the president of the Arkansas chapter of the NAACP, Bates organized the Little Rock Nine, the first Black students to enroll at Central High in September 1957. She became the custodian, confidante, and adviser to the Little Rock Nine. In 1958 she and the nine students won the NAACP Spingarn Medal. Bates continued to struggle against bigotry and institutional prejudice, and in 1972 she organized a movement to expose and critique President Richard Nixon's cutting of funds for economic opportunity programs in Mitchellville, Arkansas.

436 • Fred Shuttlesworth (b. 1922)

Rev. Fred Shuttlesworth was the African American president of the Alabama Christian Movement for Human Rights (ACMHR) in Birmingham, Alabama, an organization founded in 1956. Shuttlesworth was also an active member of SCLC and one of the principal architects of the Birmingham campaign. On May 7, 1963, one

of the most violent days of the Birmingham demonstration, Shuttlesworth was seriously injured when water from a fireman's hose slammed him into a building. According to his own account, he returned to the front lines from his hospital bed just in time to veto a deal between Martin Luther King and President John Kennedy to cancel the demonstrations before the demands had been met. More militant than King and some other southern ministers, Fred Shuttlesworth once walked, as James Farmer later recalled, right through a crowd of violent white youths who had surrounded a Baptist church during a riot in 1961. Farmer recalled that "I was scared as hell, but Shuttlesworth . . . shoved his way through the incredulous whites. These goons were standing there, thousands of them with clubs. 'Out of the way, Go on. Out of the way,' he said. He didn't have any trouble. They stopped and looked at him and said: '*That nigger's crazy.*' And I was standing right behind him trying to be little. And we got to the church and got in. . . ."

437 • Diane Nash (b. 1938)

Diane Nash was an undergraduate at Fisk University in 1960 when she became a leader of the student sit-in movement at downtown lunch counters in Nashville, Tennessee. Her most important contribution to the subsequent boycott of downtown stores came on the steps of City Hall when she asked Nashville Mayor Ben West, "Do you feel that it is wrong to discriminate against a person solely on the basis of his race or color." The mayor responded "as a man and not as a politician" that he could "not agree that it [is] morally right for someone to sell them merchandise and refuse them service." Once the mayor had sanctioned the rightfulness of the protest, white resistance wilted, and less than a month later, African Americans were served at lunch counters in Nashville. Nash also revived the Freedom Rides in 1961, after the first riders were beaten and their buses burned in Anniston, Alabama. Fearing that to end the Freedom Rides would signify that violence could thwart the movement, Nash led a large contingent of Nashville students who boarded new buses in Birmingham and rode to Montgomery, Alabama, and then to Jackson, Mississippi. Eventually the renewed Freedom Rides forced Attorney General Robert Kennedy to make the Interstate Commerce Commission issue tough new guidelines to thwart segregation in interstate travel facilities.

438 • John Lewis (b. 1940)

As a Fisk University student, John Lewis became, along with Diane Nash, one of the organizers of the Nashville Sit-in, and later one of the founders of SNCC. Lewis was savagely beaten by southern whites during the first Freedom Rides in Montgomery, Alabama, in 1961. As chairman of SNCC, Lewis delivered the most militant speech at the 1963 March on Washington, even after it had been edited down to comply with other civil rights organizations. Then, on March 7, 1965, Lewis led the most important

John Lewis, SNCC chairman, at the meeting of the American Society of Newspaper Editors, April 16, 1964. Photo by Marion S. Trikosko. Prints and Photographs Division, Library of Congress, U.S. News & World Report Collection

event of the Civil Rights Movement, the fateful Selma to Montgomery march that elicited attacks from Alabama state troopers. In 1966 Lewis lost the leadership of SNCC to Stokely Carmichael and his more militant Black Power rhetoric. After resigning from SNCC, Lewis worked with the Southern Regional Council and directed the Voter Education Project. In 1986 he ran successfully for Congress from Georgia.

439 • James Farmer (b. 1920)

James Farmer founded CORE in 1942. A student of nonviolent resistance, a technique first developed by Mahatma Gandhi, Farmer served as national director of CORE from 1961 to 1966. Farmer was one of the original organizers of the Freedom Rides that successfully challenged segregated bus facilities along interstate routes in the South. He was succeeded at CORE by Floyd McKissick, who moved the organization in the direction of the Black Power movement. After touring the lecture circuit and teaching, Farmer worked for a short time as an assistant secretary of administration in the Department of Health, Education and Welfare under Richard Nixon from March 1969 to December 1970. In 1985 he published his autobiography, *Lay Bare the Heart.* He now teaches at Mary Washington College in Fredricksburg, Virginia.

440 • Stokely Carmichael (b. 1941)

In 1966 Stokely Carmichael, one of SNCC's most energetic field-workers in Mississippi, became chairman of the organization. Carmichael was most famous for coining the slogan "Black Power," which caught on among young Black militant activists who felt that neither integration nor nonviolence was viable in the Civil Rights Movement of the 1960s. In his transformation of the previously interracial organization into a Black Power organization, Carmichael kicked whites out of SNCC, a move that alienated many veteran SNCC activists. Leaving SNCC in 1967 (H. Rap Brown became the new chairman), Carmichael joined the Black Panthers and then left the United States for residence in Africa. Changing his name to Kwame Toure, in honor of Dwame Nkrumah and Sekou Toure, the former head of SNCC became a Pan-Africanist, but ironically was arrested in Guinea in West Africa for expressing his desire for revolutionary change. During the 1980s and 1990s Toure has traveled and lectured around the world, organizing chapters of the All African Peoples Revolutionary Party, which he founded in 1969.

441 • Julian Bond (b. 1940)

Julian Bond was one of the organizers of SNCC, the Student Nonviolent Coordinating Committee, for which he also served as communications director from 1960 to 1966. In 1965 Bond was elected to the Georgia state legislature by a predominantly Black district, but he was denied his seat for a year because the legislature refused to seat him: its members objected to his public opposition to the Vietnam War. Many in the Black community argued that Bond's antiwar views were simply an excuse to deny an African American a seat in the Georgia House. Eventually the United States Supreme Court ordered the Georgia House of Representatives to seat Bond. Later, he ran unsuccessfully for a seat representing Georgia in the U.S. House of Representatives, losing to another SNCC leader, John Lewis, in part because Bond refused to accept Lewis's challenge to take a drug test. Bond narrated the voice for the PBS documentary *Eyes on the Prize* and has taught civil rights history at American University in Washington, D.C., and now at the University of Virginia at Charlottesville, Virginia.

442 • Marion Barry (b. 1936)

A superb community organizer, Marion Barry was one of the original founders of SNCC, and one of the people most active in teaching Black teenagers in Mississippi. That expertise came in handy when Barry became the second Black mayor of Washington, D.C., in 1979. In his three terms as mayor, Barry developed summer youth programs, tax relief programs for the elderly, and revitalized the downtown area; he also increased the debt of the nation's capital to pay for such programs during a period of declining revenues. The debate over Barry's performance as mayor was interrupted in 1990 when he was arrested on drug charges after he was videotaped smoking crack cocaine in a hotel room in a FBI sting operation. Convicted for misdemeanor possession of cocaine, Barry served a six-month prison sentence. After his release, he returned to Washington and successfully ran for a seat on the City Council representing the city's most desolate sector, Ward 8. In 1994 he stunned his critics and opponents by winning the Democratic primary mayoral election with 47 percent of the vote, employing the same kind of grassroots organizational strategy he had developed in SNCC, and going on to win reelection to a fourth term as mayor.

Marion Barry as mayor, 1995. Courtesy of the Mayor's Office, District of Columbia

Quotations

443 • Rosa Parks Remembers

I had had problems with bus drivers over the years, because I didn't see fit to pay my money into the front and then go around to the back. Sometimes bus drivers wouldn't permit me to get on the bus, and I had been evicted from the bus. But as I say, there had been incidents over the years. One of the things that made this get so much publicity was the fact the police were called in and I was placed under arrest. See, if I had just been evicted from the bus and he hadn't placed me under arrest or had any charges brought against me, it probably could have been just another incident. . . . I had almost a life history of being rebellious against being mistreated because of my color.

444 • The Significance of Courageous Lower-Court Judges

Elbert Tuttle was chief judge of the U.S. Fifth Circuit Court of Appeals and an Eisenhower appointee when the 1954 *Brown v. Board of Education* decision was handed down.

You see, the school case dealt with education, and the court said, "Education is somewhat unique, and education is per se unequal if it's segregated." Well, there was the feeling expressed, the clear import, that segregation in any public area must be looked at with great suspicion. But it wasn't said . . . didn't become a precedent that

bound anybody, except in school litigation. So when the suits were brought with respect to golf courses and courthouses, voting, jury duty, we faced these problems before the Supreme Court ever reached them.

And the great breakthrough came when Judge Rives and Judge Johnson and Judge Lynne, all from Alabama . . . sat as a three-judge district court where there was an attack on the constitutionality of the Montgomery ordinance requiring segregated seating in the bus. Judge Rives and Judge Johnson, in the majority opinion written by Judge Rives, applied the same principles that Brown-against-Topeka had applied in the schools to an ordinance requiring segregated seating on the buses. . . . From that time on our [Fifth Circuit] court almost without any serious hesitation applied it to courthouses and these other areas of activity.

445 • "Letter from a Birmingham Jail"

When Martin Luther King was arrested in Birmingham in 1963, he used newspaper corners and scraps of paper to answer eight white clergymen who called on him to avoid direct-action confrontation and allow the courts to resolve southern racial problems. His "Letter from a Birmingham Jail" became the movement's best theological defense of nonviolent direct action.

You deplore the demonstrations taking place in Birmingham. But your statement, I am sorry to say, fails to express a similar concern for the conditions that brought about the demonstrations. I am sure that none of you would want to rest content with the superficial kind of social analysis that deals merely with effects and does not grapple with underlying causes. . . .

There can be no gainsaying the fact that racial injustice engulfs this community. Birmingham is probably the most thoroughly segregated city in the United States. Its ugly record of brutality is widely known. Negroes have experienced grossly unjust treatment in the courts. There have been more unsolved bombings of Negro homes and churches in Birmingham than in any other city in the nation. . . . We know through painful experience that freedom is never voluntarily given by the oppressor; it must be demanded by the oppressed. Frankly, I have yet to engage in a direct-action campaign that was "well-timed" in the view of those who have not suffered duly from the disease of segregation. For years now I have heard the word "Wait!" It rings in the ear of every Negro with piercing familiarity. This "Wait" has almost always meant "Never." We must come to see, with one of our distinguished jurists, that "justice too long delayed is justice denied."

446 • "The Ballot or the Bullet"

From a speech by Malcolm X delivered April 3, 1964, at Cory Methodist Church in Cleveland, Ohio:

If we don't do something real soon, I think you'll have to agree that we're going to be forced either to use the ballot or the bullet. It's one or the other in 1964. It isn't that time is running out—time has run out! Nineteen sixty-four threatens to be the most explosive year America has ever witnessed. The most explosive year. Why? It's also a political year. It's the year when all of the white political crooks will be right back in your and my community with their false promises, building up our hopes for a letdown, with their trickery and their treachery, with their false promises which they don't intend to keep. As they nourish these dissatisfactions, it can only lead to one thing, an explosion; and now we have the type of Black man on the scene in America today . . . who just doesn't intend to turn the other cheek any longer.

447 • Wilson Baker on How SCLC Used Selma's Sheriff, Jim Clark

In 1965 Wilson Baker was Selma's director of public safety.

Dr. King either lost his briefcase or some way it was misplaced in Anniston—a copy of what he called Project Alabama. . . . They mentioned that it was a ready-made situation here for 'em with the posse that Jim Clark had. He had such a large posse. . . . He took his posse to Montgomery during the bus-riding days. . . . We were determined not to give 'em what they wanted and succeeded for two days that first week that they marched in here. We would try to set him down and talk with him.

We found out about two-thirty that morning they had decided that there had been too much homework going on in Selma, that they were going to march one mo' day, and they were going to make every effort to provoke someone in the posse or Jim Clark into committing some kind of violent arrest. And if they couldn't do it, then Dr. King would make a face-saving out and find another community in Alabama to do it in. . . . They were supposed to march at ten o'clock the next morning, and the city attorney, McLean Pitts, . . . came in and said that they could not control Jim, that he was in one of his wild rages . . . they [the marchers] came to the courthouse and when they got'chere Jim Clark started jerkin' 'em around and kicking 'em around. Jim he would want 'em to go in that *door of the courthouse, and they'd want to come in* this *door, and that's really the kind of situation it was. . . . He arrested some several of 'em here that day. . . . If he had made no arrests whatsoever that day, they would have moved out.*

448 • Wilson Baker After "Bloody Sunday"

I remember asking Mr. [Nicholas] Katzenbach after he got to be attorney general . . . what did the Justice Department expect if we had realistically registered Blacks as they came in under the existing laws. . . . he said, "About two thousand [Black voters], twenty-five hundred."

I said, "What do you expect if the Voter Rights Bill passes."

He said, "What do you mean if *it passes. You people passed that on that bridge. You people in Selma passed that on that bridge that Sunday." . . . And he pulled his finger over there a little further, and he said, "About ten thousand." And we wound up with about fifteen thousand.*

Murders and Other Violent Acts

449 • Emmett Till (1941–55)

Emmett Till left Chicago by train in the summer of 1955 for Mississippi, where he would be murdered for speaking to a white woman. Standing outside of a store in Money, Mississippi, on August 24, Till showed a group of Black boys a photograph of a white woman he said was his girlfriend. One of them dared him to prove his familiarity with white people by going into the store and speaking to the white woman working behind the counter. Reputedly Till entered the store, purchased some candy, and said "Bye baby" to Mrs. Carolyn Bryant, the wife of the store owner, who was out of town on a truck run to Texas. Till and the other boys ran off, thinking that the incident would blow over. It didn't. Different versions of the incident—that he whistled at her or asked her for a date—spread throughout the town. When Ray Bryant returned to town, he and his brother-in-law J. W. Milam drove to Mose Wright's home after midnight and demanded to see the boy "who done the talkin'." Although Wright tried to explain that the boy was from "up Nawth" and unfamiliar with southern ways, that did not stop Bryant and Milam from taking Till away in the night, and threatening Wright with death if he spoke a word of what happened that evening. Afterward, Bryant and Milam claimed to a reporter that they did not intend to kill Emmett, but when he would not repent his action or beg for forgiveness, they killed him. "What else could we do?" the brother-in-law recalled. "He was hopeless. I'm no bully; I never hurt a nigger in my life. . . . But I just decided it was time a few people got put on notice."

Emmett Till was discovered three days later at the bottom of a nearby river, with a seventy-five-pound cotton gin fan tied around his neck. The side of his skull had been crushed, an eye had been pushed in, and he had been shot in the head. Bryant and Milam were first charged with kidnaping and then murder, and many Mississippians tried to distance themselves from the murder. The sheriff wanted to bury the body immediately, but Mamie Till, his mother, demanded that the body be sent to Chicago, where she demanded an open-casket funeral so everyone could see what had been done to her son. The picture of the battered, horribly disfigured face was published by *Jet* magazine, and thousands of Black Americans became embittered. As national outrage built, white Mississippians rallied around Bryant and Milam. At the trial, a courageous Mose Wright stood up and did what no other Black Mississippian had ever done before: in open court, when asked to identify the men who had come and carried away Emmett, he rose and pointed to each man, and said, "Thar he." After an hour's deliberation, the jury re-

Emmitt Till. Prints and Photographs Division, Library of Congress, NYWT and S Collection

turned a verdict of not guilty. The Till murder mobilized the Black community, especially the young generation of Till's age, to activism more profoundly than the *Brown v. Board of Education* decision in 1954. The murder also convinced the nation that southern racism was a cancer that must be exorcised from American life.

450 • Martin Luther King, Jr.'s House Bombed

On January 30, 1956, at the height of the boycott against segregated buses in Montgomery, Alabama, Martin Luther King's home was bombed. His wife, Coretta King, jumped into the back room with her newly born child to avoid being injured. As Martin Luther King rushed home to find out if his family was hurt, dozens

of Black Montgomery residents flocked to his home with guns in their hands. After months of harassment by whites in cars and by the segregationist legal establishment, many had had enough and were ready to retaliate. But in this first real test of the resolve of the Montgomery Improvement Association that had begun the bus boycott, Martin Luther King articulated forcefully the philosophy of nonviolence as the ruling ideology of the movement. Coming outside of his house to face the growing crowd, he reassured them that all were safe and asked that those assembled go home peacefully. He told them it was for the higher goal of the dignity of their people that they had bound themselves together in this cause, and they must not let this incident take their eyes from that higher goal. The crowd dispersed and went home. And though the segregationists would still try to provoke—E. D. Nixon's home would be bombed on February 1—a corner had been turned in the direct-action movement.

451 • Martin Luther King, Jr., Stabbed in Harlem

On September 20, 1958, Martin Luther King was stabbed by a Black woman, Mrs. Izola Curry, with a letter opener in Blumstein's department store in New York City while he was autographing copies of his book *Stride Toward Freedom.* The woman's motives were never determined, but the stabbing, and the enforced convalescence, may have encouraged King to make a long-postponed pilgrimage to India, where he deepened his study of nonviolence in Gandhi's home country.

452 • Paul Guihard Murdered During the Ole Miss Riot

In the fall of 1962 James Meredith, a native of Mississippi and a veteran of the United States Air Force, tried to enroll in the University of Mississippi. He was blocked from attending by Mississippi Governor Ross Barnett, who continued to assert that no Negro would be a student at the University of Mississippi, even after a federal court ruled Barnett was wrong. After weeks of fruitless negotiations, President John F. Kennedy sent troops to enforce the enrollment of Meredith. But on Sunday evening, September 30, the three hundred federal marshals Kennedy sent were overwhelmed. Hundreds of whites massed around the main buildings of the campus in Oxford, Mississippi, and attacked federal marshals with bricks, rocks, bottles, and guns. On the morning of October 1, reinforcements of regular army troops poured into Oxford, and by the end of the week, close to two thousand federal troops occupied the city. More than two hundred people were arrested and more than forty guns were confiscated. Twenty-eight marshals had been shot and 130 injured. Two white men, one a French reporter named Paul Guihard (1932–62), were shot in the back. In one of his last dispatches from Mississippi, he wrote that "it is in these moments you feel there is a distance of a century between Washington and the segregationists of the South. . . . The Civil War has never ended."

453 • Herbert Lee (1912–61)

When Bob Moses came to Mississippi in 1961 to launch a voter registration drive, he found that there was only one registered Black voter in Amite County, but there was no shortage of Black people willing to help him start a registration drive. One of the most important was Herbert Lee, a longtime resident of the county who was also one of the few to own a car. Lee took Moses all over the county as the two of them encouraged often reluctant African Americans to try to register. Lee was invaluable in these ef-

forts because he knew the people and he was not afraid. That also made him a threat to the racial establishment in Mississippi. One day, when Lee brought his cotton to the local cotton gin outside of Liberty, Mississippi, he was accosted by Mississippi State Representative E. H. Hurst, who argued with Lee and shot him in the head in front of witnesses. Whites at the scene claimed Lee attacked Hurst with a tire iron. Another witness, a Black man named Louis Allen, was shotgunned later for fear that he might contradict that story. Following Lee's death, over one hundred African American high school students marched through McComb, Mississippi, to protest his senseless murder.

454 • William Moore's One-Man March

William Moore (1927–1963), a World War II Marine veteran, whose recovery from a nervous breakdown made him an idealistic and highly individualistic civil rights worker, was shot and killed outside of Reece City, Alabama, on April 23, 1963. A former social worker and postman, Moore combined elements of both jobs as he took long walks wearing signs that advocated integration. During a 1963 walk from Chattanooga, Tennessee, to Jackson, Mississippi, Moore was yelled at and stoned by motorists, and then shot and killed by a .22-caliber rifle as he sat resting by the side of the road. Although Floyd Simpson, the owner of the rifle, was identified, no one was ever indicted for Moore's murder. Even Governor George Wallace was forced to condemn the killing. But when twenty-nine marchers attempted to finish Moore's walk a month later, Alabama authorities arrested them, showing that the state was still not willing to allow public support for integration to be voiced by American citizens.

455 • Medgar Evers Killed

If relatively obscure citizens could be murdered with impunity in the South for supporting voting rights and integration, it is not surprising that the NAACP's field secretary in Mississippi since 1946 would be murdered as well. Medgar Evers (1925–63) had investigated the cases of George Lee, Emmett Till, and other victims of racist killings, and had even spirited Mose Wright out of Mississippi after he identified the killers of Emmett Till. Evers became more visible when he helped negotiate the successful conclusion of an integrated sit-in at downtown lunch counters in Jackson, Mississippi. Soon after, a Molotov cocktail was thrown into Evers's house, but no one was injured. Then, in the early morning hours of June 13, 1963, as he returned home after watching President John Kennedy's evening speech about the "moral crisis" of civil rights, Evers was shot in his drive-

Funeral procession for Medgar Evers proceeds to Arlington National Cemetery from downtown Washington, June 19, 1963. Courtesy of National Archives

way by White Citizens Council member Byron De La Beckwith. Although he was tried twice for murder soon after the shooting, neither jury convicted Beckwith. In 1994, more than thirty years later, Beckwith was finally convicted for the Evers murder.

456 • Murder of Four Children in a Birmingham Church

Three months after the victory of the 1963 Birmingham demonstrations, a Black church in that city was dynamited. The September 15th blast injured twenty-one and killed four little girls. National outrage and expressions of grief were immediate. President John Kennedy, in a television address the following day, expressed the hope that "if these cruel and tragic events can only awaken that city and state—if they can only awaken this entire nation . . . then it is not too late for all concerned to unite in steps toward peaceful progress before more lives are lost." Unfortunately the blast did not change the attitudes of Birmingham's white community: none of them attended the funeral.

457 • JFK Killed

Many theories have been advanced as to why President John F. Kennedy was murdered in Dallas on November 22, 1963. But many African Americans believed Kennedy's public advocacy of civil rights was a factor in his death. In 1963 Kennedy issued his strongest statement against segregation in his annual address to Congress and proposed sweeping civil rights legislation that was vehemently opposed by the South. Then, rather than oppose the March on Washington, Kennedy met its organizers and made the march part of his overall strategy to improve civil rights in America. Many African Americans interpreted such actions as proof of Kennedy's support for the Civil Rights Movement.

458 • Goodman, Schwerner, and Chaney Killed

On Sunday, June 21, 1964, three civil rights workers drove to Philadelphia, Mississippi, after the Mount Zion Methodist Church in Meridian was bombed. James Chaney, a native of Meridian and longtime CORE activist, was Black. The other two men, Michael Schwerner and Andrew Goodman, both from New York City, were white. All three were targeted by the Ku Klux Klan as troublemakers who deserved to be killed—Chaney because he was a local Black man who dared to challenge racism, and Schwerner and Goodman because they were outsiders. The three were arrested in Philadelphia, Mississippi, by Deputy Sheriff Cecil Price, then released at 10:00 that same evening. As the three continued on their way, they were stopped again—this time by Price and Klan members—placed in Price's police car, and transported to an isolated spot on Highway 19. Each was shot and placed in a ditch that was being converted into a dam. As soon as they were reported missing, a nationwide alarm went off, and President Lyndon Johnson committed the Justice Department and the FBI to finding the three men. After substantial rewards were offered for information on their whereabouts, the three bodies were finally located. Some Blacks and civil rights workers have noted that the FBI undertook the largest investigation in Mississippi only when two white men were killed and that hundreds of murdered Blacks were ignored by the agency. But the murder of the three civil rights workers was highly significant, because it exposed the system of terror operating in Mississippi at that time. Although reluctant to pursue a conviction at first, the Department of Justice indicted Price and several others on federal charges of violating the three workers' civil rights, since no indictment for murder was forthcoming. Seven Klan

members, including Price, were found guilty on October 20, 1967, of federal civil rights violations and sentenced to three to ten years in prison. This was the first time that Klansmen had been convicted in Mississippi on charges related to the murder of a black man.

459 • Lieutenant Colonel Lemuel Penn Killed

Lieutenant Colonel Lemuel Penn (1915–64) was driving north with two other Black officers after two weeks of Reserve training at Fort Benning, Georgia, when he was killed by two shotgun blasts fired point-blank by members of the Ku Klux Klan. These Klansmen were part of an Athens, Georgia, "security force" that had been formed to combat civil rights efforts with terror. Having previously beaten an older Black mechanic in March and blinded a teenage boy by shooting into a housing project, the "security force" was on the lookout for civil rights workers trying to change race relations in Georgia. Believing that the soldiers represented some possibly new effort at integration by President Lyndon Johnson, who had recently signed the Civil Rights Act of 1964, Joseph Howard Sims and Cecil William Myers shot Penn simultaneously with shotguns as he was driving the car. The murder, coming a week after the murders of James Chaney, Michael Schwerner, and Andrew Goodman, tested the federal government's resolve to prosecute such acts of violence. After years of legal wrangling, during which the Supreme Court overturned a lower court curtailment of the federal suit, Myers and Sims were convicted of civil rights violations and given the maximum sentences of ten years in jail.

460 • Jimmy Lee Jackson Killed

Jimmy Lee Jackson (1938–65) was beaten and shot on February 18, 1965, when he tried to protect his mother from being beaten by a state trooper who, with others, was attacking scores of civil rights demonstrators in Marion, Alabama. The march, led by SCLC veteran C. T. Vivan, was part of the Selma campaign for Black voter registration led by Martin Luther King. Shot in the stomach, Jackson continued to be beaten by state troopers until he collapsed on the street. He died days later. His killer was never indicted and the state trooper attack was vindicated. Jimmy Lee Jackson's death, however, inspired the March 21 march from Selma to Montgomery led by Coger Lee, Jimmy Lee's grandfather, and Martin Luther King.

461 • Malcolm X Killed

Following his removal as a minister of the Nation of Islam and his trip to Mecca, Malcolm X formed the Organization of Afro-American Unity, a Black nationalist group designed to

Police carry body of Malcolm X out of a New York ballroom on February 21, 1965, after he was shot attempting to address a meeting of his Organization of Afro-American Unity. Library of Congress, NYWT and S Collection

bring the injustices of American racism to the United Nations. Shortly after forming this organization, which allowed for more political involvement than he had enjoyed with the Nation of Islam, Malcolm X was assassinated by two former Black Muslims on February 21, 1965.

462 • Viola Gregg Liuzzo Killed

On March 7, 1965, Viola Liuzzo was so moved watching television reports of the beating of civil rights marchers on Pettus Bridge that she left her home in Michigan and drove to Selma, Alabama, to assist in the struggle. Viola was a remarkable person. After she was married and the mother of five, she went back to school and educated herself to be a lab technician. Then she quit her job as a lab technician to protest the abusive treatment of women secretaries on the job. She was also one of the few white members of the NAACP. Unfortunately, on March 25, 1965, she was on the road returning to Montgomery to pick up more marchers after the successful three-day march when she and LeRoy Moton, a Black civil rights worker, were spotted by Klansmen. Klansmen chased Mrs. Liuzzo and finally forced her off the road, where she was shot twice in the head. The Klan disseminated false information that Mrs. Liuzzo was having an affair with a Black civil rights worker, and the FBI reported these rumors without correction or qualification. In a survey, many readers of *Ladies' Home Journal* said they believed Mrs. Liuzzo had gotten "out of her place" when she went to Selma. Eventually Mrs. Liuzzo's family dispelled the rumors, and three Klansmen—Eugene Thomas, William Eaton, and Collie Wilkins, Jr.—were finally indicted and convicted for conspiring to violate Mrs. Liuzzo's civil rights, after two Alabama juries failed to convict them of murder. Viola Liuzzo became a martyr of the civil rights movement.

463 • Watts Riot

For six days in August 1965, rioting consumed the predominantly Black section of Los Angeles known as Watts. Fed up with years of neglect, impoverishment, and segregation from the rest of Southern California, African Americans in Watts threw rocks at windows and police, burned buildings, looted stores, and brought national attention to the problems of poverty, racism, and police brutality in Southern California. After the rioting was over, more than thirty African Americans had been killed, more than a thousand had been injured, and over $45 million in property had been destroyed.

464 • 1967 "Long Hot Summer"

In the summer of 1967 race riots broke out in Newark, New York, Buffalo, New Haven, Milwaukee, Atlanta, and Boston, with the worst occurring in Detroit. Hundreds of African Americans were killed, thousands injured, and property worth hundreds of thousands of dollars was destroyed.

465 • Martin Luther King, Jr., Killed

Traveling to Memphis in 1968 to champion the cause of striking sanitation workers, Martin Luther King, Jr. (1929–68), was assassinated on April 4 on the second-story balcony of the Lorraine Motel by a bullet fired by James Earl Ray. King had been the most important leader of the Civil Rights Movement, because he combined coolness under pressure, a gift for uplifting oratory, and a vision of an integrated America that enabled him to remain an eloquent spokesperson for the movement, even after nonviolence as a philosophy and a strategy had fallen out of favor. Some of King's critics argued that the movement had passed him by, especially after more radical elements took control of SNCC and CORE in 1966 and articulated a notion of Black

Martin Luther King, Jr., at press conference, Birmingham, Alabama, May 16, 1963. Library of Congress, U.S. News & World Report Collection. Photo by Marion Trikosko

Power and armed self-defense. Refusing to abandon nonviolence or embrace Black Power, King spoke out against the Vietnam War, addressed issues of world peace, and took on the thorny problem of the war against urban poverty in places like Chicago. Indeed, some speculate that it was precisely when King began to address the more fundamental issues of the inequitable distribution of wealth and power in America that he marched down the road toward his death.

466 • 1968 Rioting

As news of Martin Luther King's assassination spread, Black residents of urban ghettos in Washington, D.C., Baltimore, Chicago, and other major cities took to the streets and rioted—burning and destroying their own neighborhoods in a fury of frustration. In cities like Washington, blocks of urban development were destroyed overnight in a pillage of rage that set back the economic centers of largely African American inner cities for decades. King's death and the rioting that followed symbolically ended the great period of civil rights advancement.

Legal Decisions and Their Implications

467 • Civil Rights Act of 1957

The Civil Rights Act of 1957 was the first civil rights bill enacted by Congress since 1875. With this act, the U.S. Congress created a Civil Rights Commission of presidential appointees to investigate allegations that citizens were being deprived of their right to vote because of their race, color, religion, or national origin.

Aftermath of District of Columbia rioting, 1968. Prints and Photographs Division, Library of Congress, U.S. News & World Report Magazine Collection, Warren K. Leffler

468 • Civil Rights Act of 1960

The Civil Rights Act of 1960 was intended to strengthen compliance with the *Brown v. Board of Education* Supreme Court decision of 1954 to desegregate the South. The law addressed the growing recognition that southern Blacks were denied the right to vote. The act provided for the preservation of federal election records, extended the powers of civil rights commissions to take and administer oaths, and gave the courts the right to issue orders declaring persons qualified to vote who had been denied that right by state or local officials. The courts could even appoint voting referees to observe elections and discover whether potential voters were being deprived of their right to vote.

469 • Supreme Court Reinstates Dropped Names

In a major victory for voting rights, the United States Supreme Court ruled in 1960 in *United States v. Raines* that Louisiana must restore to the list of registered voters in Washington Parish thirteen hundred names of Black voters that were dropped for dubious reasons. This decision prefigures the oversight of voting that became the backbone of the Voting Rights Act of 1965.

470 • Interstate Commerce Commission Ruling

Under pressure from Attorney General Robert Kennedy after the Freedom Riders were brutally attacked for trying to integrate waiting rooms on interstate bus lines, the Interstate Commerce Commission barred all segregation in transportation terminals as of November 1, 1961. Afterward, signs that designated "white" and "colored" waiting and rest rooms were illegal, although they persisted in many southern towns.

471 • Civil Rights Act of 1964

In 1964 Congress passed the most important civil rights law of the century. The Civil Rights Act of 1964, signed by President Lyndon Johnson on July 2, created a mechanism to ensure compliance with the Fourteenth and Fifteenth Amendments, as well as the Supreme Court decision of 1954 in *Brown v. Board of Education.* This civil rights law outlawed literacy tests as a qualification for voting in any federal election and guaranteed equal access to "the full and equal enjoyment of the goods, services, facilities, privileges, advantages, and accommodations of any place of public accommodation without discrimination or segregation on the ground of race, color, religion, or national origin." This prohibition of discrimination applied to all hotels, restaurants, lunch counters, theaters, etc., though not to private clubs closed to the public, and empowered the U.S. attorney general to prosecute all those who sought to interfere with an individual's right to utilize such facilities freely with restriction based on his or her race, color, creed, or religion. If the attorney general received information that racially segregated schools did exist, he or she could sue the school district and demand they construct a plan to bring themselves into compliance. The law also appointed a commissioner to report on and approve plans by school boards to desegregate their school districts. The act specified that desegregation meant enrolling students in schools without regard to their race, color, religion, or national origin: it did not sanction assigning students to public schools in order to overcome racial imbalance.

Perhaps the most important part of the bill was Title VII, which outlawed discrimination in employment:

It shall be unlawful employment practice for an employer (1) to fail or refuse to hire or to discharge any individual, or otherwise discriminate against any individual with respect to his compensation, terms, conditions, or privileges of employment, because of such individual's race, color, religion, sex, or national origin; or (2) to limit, segregate, or classify his employees in any way which would deprive or tend to deprive any individual of employment opportunities... because of such individual's race, color, religion, sex, or national origin.

Again, the bill contained an important caveat that "nothing contained in this title shall be interpreted to require any employer, employment agency, labor organization, or joint labor-management committee... to grant preferential treatment to any individual or to any group because of the race, color, religion, sex, or national origin of such individual or group." The bill also created the Equal Employment Opportunity Commission to investigate charges of discrimination.

Federal registrar registers Black woman to vote in Canton, Mississippi, August 11, 1965. Photograph by Marion S. Trikosko. Prints and Photographs Division, Library of Congress, U.S. News & World Report Collection. Copyright © 1965 by Matt Herron/TAKE STOCK

472 • Voting Rights Act of 1965

Before the passage of the Voting Rights Act in 1965, most Blacks could not vote in the United States. Most Blacks still lived in the South and were denied the right to vote by a variety of covert restrictions and overt intimidation and violence. That fact was made clear by the famous Selma to Montgomery March in 1965, when Alabama state troopers mercilessly beat marchers on their way to the state capital to demand their right to vote. In response, Congress passed the Voting Rights Act of 1965, signed by President Lyndon Johnson on August 6, that declared unconstitutional any state law that imposed qualifications preventing citizens from voting in federal elections because of their "race or color." The act outlawed all "tests" and taxes required to vote. Moreover, the act created a mechanism for dealing with patterns of race discrimination in voting: if complaints reached the U.S. attorney general that residents of a certain state were denied the right to vote because of their race or color, or if the ratio of nonwhite persons to white persons registered to vote suggested that some voters were unregistered because of their race or color, then the attorney general was to instruct the Civil Service Commission to appoint examiners to maintain lists of persons eligible to vote. The act prevented states from changing their voting qualifications or their voting districts for a period of five years without review by the attorney general.

473 • Ban Against Intermarriage Unconstitutional

In *Loving v. Virginia* the United States Supreme Court ruled in 1967 that a Virginia state law against marriages between African Americans and European Americans was unconstitutional. In this case, a white man and a Black woman, both residents of Virginia, had been married in the District of Columbia. After returning to Virginia, the couple was arrested and convicted of violating the state's antimiscegenation law. Each faced a one-year jail term. The Supreme Court ruled that Virginia's statute violated both the equal protection and the due process clauses of the Fourteenth Amendment and was thus unconstitutional. All similar statutes were also declared unconstitutional. For the first time in three hundred years, marriages between the races were legal in Virginia and the rest of the United States.

474 • Civil Rights Act of 1968

The Civil Rights Act of 1968 contained provisions that banned discrimination in housing and provided penalties for crossing state lines to incite a riot. This bill became the basis for prosecuting civil rights leaders, such as H. Rap Brown, who advocated violence.

REACTION AND BACKLASH

People and Politics

475 • Nixon's Agenda

When Richard M. Nixon was elected president in 1968, he made it clear he represented the growing reactionary feeling in the white electorate against rapid civil rights change. One of his favorite targets was busing students to achieve desegregation, and he urged federal officials not to use "forced busing" to bring about desegregation of southern schools or to integrate across suburban and urban school districts. Nixon suggested such officials might lose their jobs if the practice continued. Nixon even went so far as to threaten to pass a constitutional amendment against the use of busing.

476 • Charleston Confrontation

In 1969, seeking to continue the work begun by Martin Luther King to broaden the Civil Rights Movement to include the working-class struggle, Ralph Abernathy and Coretta Scott King staged a march and demonstration by hospital workers protesting racism and discrimination in Charleston, South Carolina. Hundreds of people were arrested and the governor called in the South Carolina National Guard to restore order.

477 • Affirmative Action

Affirmative action actually began under a Republican administration. In 1969, Arthur A. Fletcher, a Black assistant secretary of labor in the administration of President Richard Nixon, developed the "Philadelphia plan": firms with federal government contracts in the lily-white construction industry would have to set and meet hiring goals for African Americans or be penalized. The plan became a model for other programs such as the "set aside" program, which reserved some contracts for minority-owned businesses; and hiring plans for white women, who gained the most job mobility from affirmative action plans. Because the setting of goals and timetables rationalized the process of compliance, large corporations embraced affirmative action plans in the 1970s; but affirmative action became a political target of the Ronald

Reagan Administration in the 1980s as white Americans faced rising unemployment for professional, middle management, and skilled labor positions. Proportional representation of minorities on jobs became known as "quotas" that took jobs from more qualified white males. The notion that Blacks and women in professional jobs were less qualified than whites became so pervasive that some educated African Americans criticized affirmative action as demeaning Black success. Affirmative action became a campaign theme in 1990 and remains a powerful, divisive national issue.

478 • Cornell Takeover

In 1969 armed Black students took control of campus buildings at Cornell University to protest racial attacks on campus. Students also protested the lack of Black Studies courses and professors. After days of negotiation and tension, the university administration granted student demands. In this period, numerous other elite college campuses experienced similar takeovers and demonstrations by students who had grown up during the Civil Rights Movement, and who were now demanding that their college education reflect the African American experience. These protests led to establishment of Black Studies programs on most major college and university campuses in the North and the West.

479 • Black Manifesto

In April 1969 civil rights activist James Forman led a conference in Detroit to discuss the state of Black America. The conference produced a Black Manifesto that demanded that "White Christian Churches and Jewish Synagogues" and other historically white institutions pay $500 million in reparations to Black people for the sacrifices of African Americans under slavery. The funding was to be used for economic rehabilitation of the urban ghettos. Although the sum was never paid, some churches and synagogues increased their outreach and funding to help the urban poor.

480 • Kenneth Gibson, Mayor of Newark

In 1970 Kenneth Gibson became the first African American mayor of Newark and the first African American mayor of a major industrial center in the North. Not long afterward, James McGhee was elected mayor of Dayton, Ohio, the first Black mayor of that city. Such elections began a trend toward the election of Blacks as mayors of northern cities experiencing "white flight" to the suburbs and an expanding African American population within the city.

481 • Angela Davis (b. 1944)

A brilliant graduate student in philosophy at the University of California at San Diego, where she studied under Herbert Marcuse, Angela Davis developed a powerful interest in the issues of race and class inequality. This led her first to embrace socialism and then to a career as an activist. Involved in the 1960s with both the nonviolent Civil Rights Movement (SNCC) and the more militant Black Panthers, she became disillusioned by the intense sexism she found in both groups. This shy but brilliant and popular professor at the University of California at Los Angeles became a household name when she was accused in 1970 of providing the weapon used in a failed prison escape by Jonathan Jackson. Once accused, she became a fugitive and topped the FBI's Ten Most Wanted list by the end of the year. She was eventually captured, and the furor around the trial led to the "Free Angela movement." She was acquitted of all charges. In 1980 and again in 1984 she ran

FREE ANGELA DAVIS NOW! Poster by New York Committee to Free Angela Davis, c. 1971. Artist unknown. Prints and Photographs Division, Library of Congress. Used by permission of Gary Yanker

for vice president on the Communist Party ticket. More recently, Angela Davis has lectured extensively on the issues of gender exploitation in America.

482 • Wilmington 10

Benjamin Chavis and nine other civil rights activists were arrested in Wilmington, North Carolina, in 1971 and charged with burning down a store. These activists received harsh sentences, but their cases were publicized by Amnesty International. In 1980 the convictions were overturned. One of the Wilmington 10, Ben Chavis, went on to become the head of the NAACP in 1993. He was removed from office over allegations of mismanagement and sexual harassment in 1995.

483 • Black Caucus

In 1971 the Congressional Black Caucus was created by the twelve African Americans elected to the House of Representatives in 1970. With such new representatives as Ron Dellums from Northern California, Parren Mitchell from Maryland, Ralph Metcalfe and George Collins from Illinois, and Charles Rangel (who defeated Adam Clayton Powell, Jr.) from New York, Black Americans had a critical mass of representation in the House of Representatives. The formation of the Congressional Black Caucus was an attempt to pressure President Richard Nixon and the Congress to secure better enforcement of civil rights legislation.

484 • PUSH

In 1971 the Reverend Jesse Jackson created PUSH, People United to Save Humanity, in Chicago. Jackson had founded Operation Breadbasket, the economic arm of the Southern Christian Leadership Conference, in 1966, and had resurrected the use of boycotts against businesses that discriminated against minorities. After his influence in SCLC waned, Jackson created PUSH as a personal political organization, although the group also continued the use of boycotts, usually highly publicized, to win concessions in the form of money and jobs from programs that discriminated against African Americans. PUSH also pioneered educational programs, such as a Los Angeles program to limit television viewing time of inner-city schoolchildren.

485 • Barbara Jordan (1936–96)

Barbara Jordan, considered one of the greatest speakers of modern times, is also known for being the first Black woman to win election to state office in Texas when she became a Texas state senator in 1966. She was also the first

African American to sit in the Texas senate in the twentieth century. In 1972 she won election to the House of Representatives in Washington, D.C., where she served until 1978. She gained national attention in 1973 as a member of the House Judiciary Committee when her speech on the House floor recommending impeachment of President Richard Nixon was carried on national television. Her keynote address at the 1976 Democratic National Convention was an outstanding example of inspired political oration, and led to speculation that she would be a candidate for vice president or president someday. But illness forced her to retire from political office in 1978, although she did give a keynote address in a wheelchair at the 1992 Democratic National Convention. In 1994 President Bill Clinton chose Jordan to head the Commission on Immigration Reform in America.

486 • Shirley Chisholm (b. 1924)

Shirley Chisholm was elected to the United States House of Representatives in 1968 as a Democrat after four years as a New York State assemblywoman. She served on the House Education and Labor Committee and instituted programs such as day care and minimum-wage increases to help her predominantly black constituency. Frustrated when President Richard Nixon vetoed much of the legislation, she decided to run for president herself. In 1972 Chisholm became the first African American and first woman to seek a major party's nomination for president. Although she lost the Democratic nomination, she remained in the Congress until her 1982 retirement from politics.

487 • Election of Ronald Reagan

The election of Ronald Reagan, a retired actor and former governor of California, to the presidency in 1980 brought to the White House a man who was hostile to many of the achievements of the Civil Rights Movement, including the use of the federal government to desegregate schools. In 1981 Reagan attempted to obtain federal funding for the Bob Jones College, a school that refused to allow African Americans as students. That effort failed after a storm of controversy confronted the Reagan administration's argument that the federal government should not legislate the practices of private institutions of higher education. In 1982 Reagan did not support renewal of the Voting Rights Act, although after controversy arose, he reluctantly signed the legislation. When Reagan appointed William Bradford Reynolds, a man who opposed most affirmative-action programs, to head the Civil Rights Division of the Department of Justice, he sent a message to African Americans that they should not look to the federal government for relief from discrimination in American society.

488 • Hostage Release

In 1983, in a dramatic demonstration of his international reputation among peoples of color around the world, Jesse Jackson negotiated the release of Lieutenant Robert O. Goodman, Jr., an African American pilot who had been shot down over Syria. Jackson, as a private citizen, had succeeded where the Reagan administration had failed, and his success was a testament to his close connections in the Arab world.

489 • Harold Washington, Mayor of Chicago

In 1983 Harold Washington became the first African American mayor of Chicago after an intense, racially polarized contest. Washington's election was more than the usual African American "first," for Washington represented both a successful mobilization of the Black citizens

into a powerful voting bloc and the arrival of a man with a leftist political agenda. With a clear racial mandate, Washington led a campaign to transform the patronage political system of Chicago ward politics. Unfortunately, after weathering another difficult campaign and winning reelection in 1987, Washington died of a heart attack on November 25.

490 • Martin Luther King Day

In 1983 musician Stevie Wonder successfully led a campaign to have Martin Luther King's birthday declared a national holiday. On November 2, in a dramatic White House Rose Garden ceremony, President Ronald Reagan signed the King holiday bill. The first celebration of the holiday took place on January 15, 1986, but some states, such as Arizona and New Hampshire, refused to make King's birthday a state-observed holiday. After these states lost millions of dollars in tourism and convention money because of a well-coordinated boycott, New Hampshire became in 1993 the last state to adopt the King holiday. In January 1995 President Bill Clinton declared Martin Luther King's birthday to be a federal holiday. But even some states that adopted the holiday did so only by combining celebration of King's birthday with those of others. For example, in Virginia, the holiday is officially known as Lee-Jackson-King Day, an amalgam that ironically linked the celebration of America's most successful desegregationist with those who fought to defend slavery.

491 • Jesse's Presidential Runs

In 1984 Jesse Jackson declared his candidacy for the Democratic Party's presidential nomination. While many were skeptical at first, Jackson drew impressive numbers of votes from African Americans and others, and came to the Democratic National Convention with three

Jesse Jackson, July 1, 1983. Photograph by Warren K. Leffler. Prints and Photographs Division, Library of Congress, U.S. News & World Report Collection

hundred delegates. He lost out to Walter Mondale. In 1988 Jackson ran again and in televised debates with other Democratic candidates, acquitted himself well. He received over 6 million votes in the 1988 contest and won seven primaries, but again, lacked enough support to challenge the front-runner, Michael Dukakis. Jackson was the third major African American candidate for the office of president, after James W. Ford, who ran on the Communist Party ticket in the 1930s, and Representative Shirley Chisholm.

492 • Million Man March

On October 16, 1995, roughly 870,000 Black men responded to the call of Nation of Islam Minister Louis Farrakhan and traveled from several states to the mall outside the United States Congress to stage the largest civil rights demonstration to date. Billed as a day of atonement and redemption for Black men to become better fathers, husbands, and citizens of their

communities, the Million Man March drew many African Americans who wished to protest the conservative trend in American politics epitomized in attacks on affirmative action, welfare programs, and aid to education. Many people argued that attendance at the march was an endorsement of Farrakhan's anti-Semitic and separatist racial views; but only 5 percent of those who attended the march, according to a *Washington Post* poll, said they came out of allegiance to Farrakhan. Most came to affirm the strength of the Black family, to show Black unity, and to challenge the negative images of Black men in the media by assembling peacefully on the mall. While Jesse Jackson, Congressional Representative Kweisi Mfume, Reverend Al Sharpton, Mayor Kurt L. Schmoke, and other political figures spoke, the poetry of Maya Angelou, the singing of Stevie Wonder, and the testimony of Rosa Parks resonated best with those assembled (which included small numbers of Black women, Hispanics, and whites). Indeed, Farrakhan's two-and-a-half-hour speech, with its mystical, numerological, and historical references, dazed rather than uplifted the crowd. It was his idea of a secular pilgrimage to the mall that had really energized Black men, who had come, seen their strength in numbers, and embraced one another.

493 • Marian Wright Edelman (b. 1939)

Marian Edelman began her involvement in the civil rights struggle during the SNCC voter registration drive in Mississippi in 1963, the same year she graduated from Yale Law School. After becoming the first Black woman to pass the Mississippi state bar in 1964, she decided to practice civil rights law ("mostly getting students out of jail") and to head the NAACP Legal Defense and Education Fund. She founded the Children's Defense Fund in 1973 to develop and provide long-term assistance to children at risk. It became one of the best known and most highly regarded organizations of the Civil Rights Movement. She achieved even greater prominence in 1992 when Bill Clinton, a close friend, was elected president of the United States. Edelman, a trusted adviser of the president, was consulted on numerous decisions made by the president and Mrs. Hillary Clinton.

494 • Myrlie Evers-Williams (b. 1932)

In February 1995, Myrlie Evers-Williams won an upset, one-vote victory over long-time NAACP chairman, William F. Gibson, and was elected the first chairwoman of the NAACP, the nation's oldest living civil rights organization. The former wife of slain NAACP field officer Medgar Evers, Evers-Williams represented a reform movement within the NAACP that sought to put the organization back on the road to financial solvency, after allegations that Gibson had misappropriated funds for his own benefit. Large financial gifts to the NAACP had already begun to dry up in the aftermath of the resignation of former NAACP president Benjamin Chavis amid charges of sexual harassment and financial improprieties. But perhaps most important, Evers-Williams's election in 1995 meant a moral victory for those advocating that the organization return to its original function as an activist, integrationist pressure group at a time when a Republican-led Congress was pushing through a rollback of social programs benefiting the poor and minorities. Beyond restoring financial credibility to the NAACP, Evers-Williams hopes to make the NAACP relevant to younger African American men and women who have been largely alienated from the organization since the 1960s.

Murders and Other Violent Acts

495 • Chicago Panthers Killed

In a raid on the Chicago headquarters of the Black Panther Party on December 4, 1969, police shot and killed Fred Hampton, chairman of the Illinois Black Panther Party, as he lay in bed. Another Panther, Mark Clark, was killed and four other Panthers were seriously injured in the attack. The Chicago police used the wounding of one police officer to substantiate its claim that police fired on Hampton and the others in self-defense. But a later federal grand jury investigation proved that police had massed such a concentration of machine-gun fire that it was impossible any of the police could have been hit by return fire. No police were indicted in the shooting.

496 • Jonathan Jackson's Shoot-out

In 1970 Jonathan Jackson, the brother of inmate George Jackson, kidnaped a judge during a botched attempt to free several Blacks on trial in a San Rafael, California, courtroom. Cornered by police, Jonathan Jackson, along with two defendants, was killed, but he managed to kill the judge before dying. One of the guns used by Jackson was registered to University of California at Los Angeles philosophy professor Angela Davis, who went underground rather than face charges of conspiracy in the murder. Davis was eventually arrested in disguise in New York.

497 • Attica

At the Attica correctional facility in upstate New York in 1971, Black and Puerto Rican inmates rioted, took over the prison, and issued a list of demands, including an end to racial discrimination and improvement in the prison facility. Eventually negotiations with New York Governor Nelson Rockefeller broke down and Rockefeller ordered state troopers to attack the prison. Forty people, including guards held as hostages, were killed in the worst prison riot in history.

498 • Howard Beach

On December 20, 1986, three Black men made the mistake of going to a pizza joint in Howard Beach, an overwhelmingly white section of New York City, to get help with their car. After verbal insults were exchanged, a gang of young whites attacked and chased the three. One of the Black men, Michael Griffith, was struck and killed by a speeding automobile while trying to flee the whites. Three of the white gang members were indicted on second-degree murder and other charges in the case. In 1988 they were convicted of misdemeanor riot charges.

499 • Ku Klux Klan Attack in Georgia

In 1987 four hundred members of the Ku Klux Klan attacked approximately ninety civil rights demonstrators in Forsyth County, Georgia, who were trying to conduct a "brotherhood walk" to honor Martin Luther King, Jr. When the walk was repeated a week later, the now twenty thousand people were guarded by three thousand members of the National Guard.

500 • Rodney King (b. 1966?)

On March 3, 1991, Rodney King, a young African American, was stopped while driving his car by Los Angeles police officers. Once out of the automobile, King was attacked by officers with nightsticks and electric prods, being struck over fifty times in one eighty-one-second period. What made this beating exceptional was

that it was captured by a bystander on videotape, which was repeatedly played over television stations throughout the nation and the world. Many who saw the videotape, including President George Bush, were horrified by it. But a predominantly white jury in Sylmar, California, found the officers not guilty, except for one minor charge. That verdict set off the worst race riot in American history, from April 29 to May 1, 1992, in Los Angeles, during which $2 billion of property was destroyed, fifty people were killed, and dozens of innocent people, such as Reginald Denny, were injured. The verdict and the riot forced the federal government to indict the officers on charges of violating Rodney King's civil rights. After another lengthy trial, three of the four officers were convicted and sentenced to jail. In May 1994 King was awarded $3.8 million in damages from the city of Los Angeles for the beating he received.

Legal Decisions and Their Implications

501 • Bobby Seale on Trial

Under the antirioting provisions of the 1964 Civil Rights Act, Black Panther leader and Chicago Eight member Bobby Seale was tried for conspiracy to incite a riot at the Democratic National Convention in 1968. The Chicago Eight were charged with coming to Chicago in August to incite a riot, for which the penalty was five years in jail. When Seale argued with Judge Julius Hoffman repeatedly in court, Hoffman had Seale chained, bound, and gagged, the only one of the eight defendants to be so treated. A storm of protest ensued as pictures of the gagged and chained Seale were beamed around the world. Seale claimed he had been denied the counsel of his choice because Hoffman refused to postpone the trial so that lawyer Charles R. Garry could attend the trial. Hoffman eventually separated Seale's case from the other defendants, and convicted Seale of contempt of court, for which Seale was sentenced to four years. The contempt charges, however, were overturned, and Seale served only two years.

502 • Busing

Since residential segregation was one of the most intractable causes of segregated schooling in urban areas, it was logical for federal courts in the late 1960s to require busing of Black children to historically white schools and white children to historically Black schools. But white opposition to busing was swift and virulent, especially after the Supreme Court's 1971 *Swann v. Charlotte-Mecklenburg Board of Education* decision expanded the use of busing to achieve desegregated education in America. Public criticism of busing galvanized Congress to place anti-busing amendments on many bills, and some even proposed a constitutional amendment against busing. Perhaps in response to the public outcry, the Supreme Court reversed itself in *Milliken v. Bradley* (1974) and concluded that busing was not allowable as a solution to the segregated schooling in Detroit and its surrounding suburbs. In the wake of that decision, busing was recommended less by lower federal courts, and desegregation slowed to a halt.

503 • *Bakke* Decision

In 1978 the Supreme Court ruled in the *Bakke* case that race alone could not be used by public schools in their affirmative-action programs to ensure a set number, or "quota," of places for Black students in their incoming classes. Allan Bakke, a Jewish applicant to the University of California at San Diego medical school, who had been turned down by numerous medical schools, was able to argue in this instance that he was denied admission because of his race. Bakke complained that Black students with lower grade point averages and test scores were admitted under a program in the medical school that set aside a "quota" of slots in each admitting class for African Americans. The Court ruled that such affirmative-action programs amounted to reverse discrimination against whites on the basis of race and were unconstitutional. This decision gave rise to the use of "quota" in connection with other civil rights legislation whenever it could be construed as potentially displacing whites. It also spawned new challenges to affirmative-action programs in schools and the workplace. Many in the Civil Rights Movement viewed this decision as the end of affirmative action in America. But affirmative-action programs did not end, because the Court did not say that race could not be one among many factors used by schools to construct a racially diverse student body or class.

504 • *City of Richmond v. J. A. Croson Co.*

In a continuation of the logic of the *Bakke* decision, the Supreme Court ruled in *Richmond v. Croson* (1989) that it was unconstitutional for a city to create a "set-aside program" to award a certain number of public contracts to minority contractors. Because white contractors could not compete for these slots, the set-aside program was deemed a violation of the civil rights of white contractors. This was another blow to affirmative action and to those city governments that had responded to civil rights agitation by awarding contracts to minority businesses.

505 • Civil Rights Act of 1991

The Civil Rights Act of 1991, signed by President George Bush on November 21, was the response of Congress to recent decisions handed down by the United States Supreme Court which limited the ability of victims of discrimination to easily sue for compensation. The act provided additional remedies for sexual harassment in the workplace in a response to sexual harassment claims by Anita Hill against Supreme Court Justice Clarence Thomas, and it made claims against employers for discrimination possible retroactively.

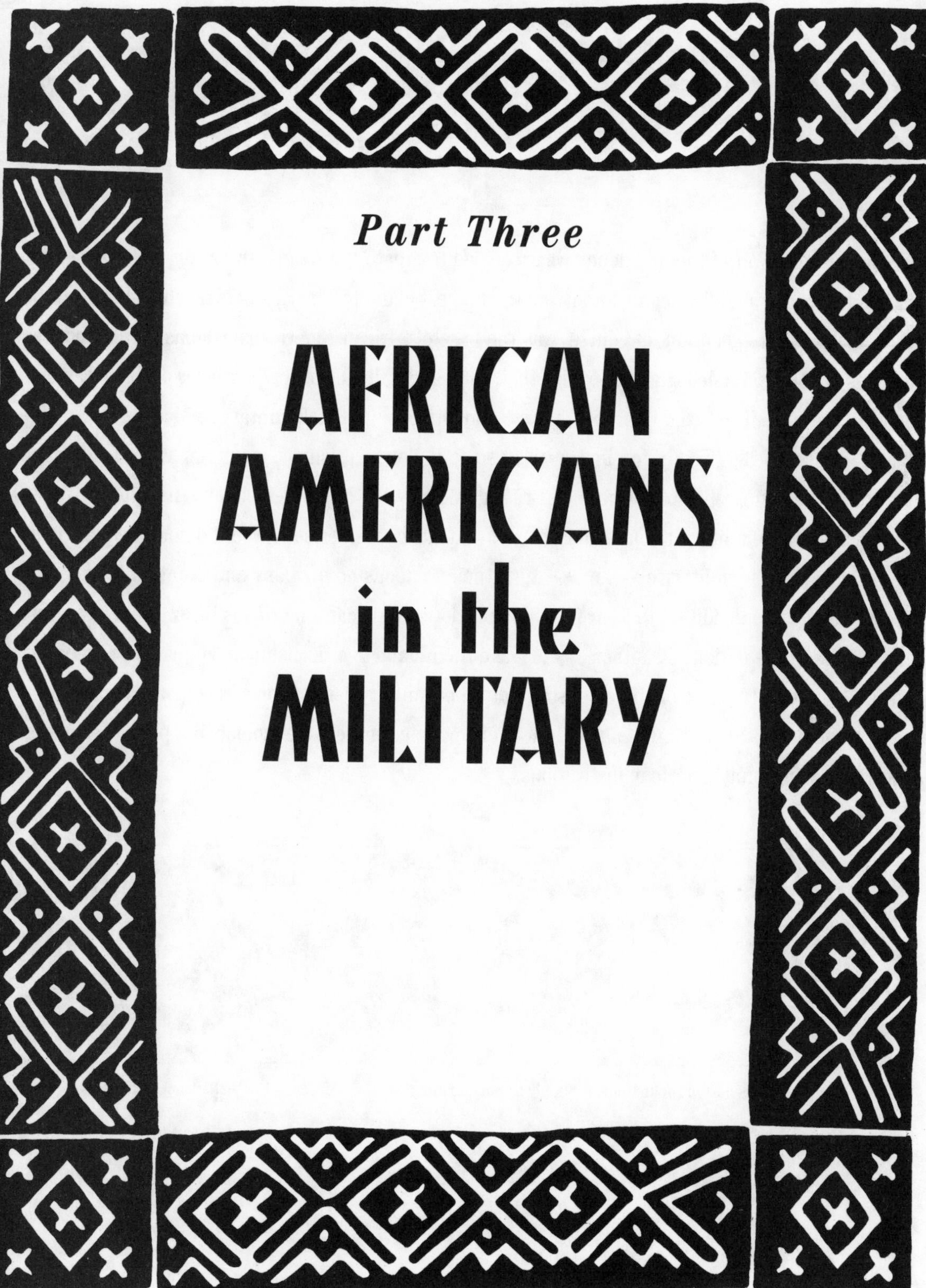

Part Three

AFRICAN AMERICANS in the MILITARY

Because the War of Independence was required to create the American nation, military service has had a special significance in conferring the highest claim to American citizenship on those who served. The great exception, of course, was the case of African Americans, who as slaves and free persons of color defended the nation with their lives and still lacked the privileges of American citizenship. Because it involved questions of race and citizenship, Black military service became a second front of civil rights agitation in American society. Not surprisingly, many American leaders, no less than the ruling elite of the former British colony, were ambivalent about the use of African Americans in the military. Such leaders feared that African Americans would demand equal rights after serving in the military or—worse—turn their weapons on a colony and a nation that denied their civil rights. In addition to their profound patriotism, African Americans threw themselves into the defense of the nation as another way to stake their claim to citizenship and equality in American society. One consequence of the contested nature of military service for African Americans is that the American military not only reflected the racial policies of the larger society but pioneered desegregation among many American institutions.

Black women nurses as part of Field Medical Supply Depot, Washington, D.C., March 22, 1919. National Archives

COLONIAL AND REVOLUTIONARY WARS

Engagements and Policy

506 • Seventeenth-Century Military Role of African Americans

The use of African Americans in military defense varied greatly from colony to colony. Virginia, the father of American slavery, was the first colony to reject the arming of African Americans for defense in the Act of 1639. Massachusetts pursued an ambivalent policy: in 1652 Massachusetts law required African Americans to train and serve in the colonial militia and in some cases, even freed slaves for meritorious service. Four years later, however, Massachusetts reversed itself and banned "Negroes and Indians" from the militia. But a 1660 Massachusetts law required "every person above the age of sixteen" to train, and in 1695 a law exempted African Americans and Indians from military training but provided them with arms and ammunition in case of an emergency! Surprisingly, given its vehement opposition to arming slaves in the Revolutionary War, South Carolina, in 1703, required slaves to serve in emergencies, for it was prudent "to have the assistance of our trusty slaves to assist us against our enemies." The Act of 1703 also promised to free all those who "kill or take one or More of our enemies in case of actual invasions."

507 • Bacon's Rebellion

African Americans fought in the first armed rebellion against British authority in the colonies, Bacon's Rebellion, in 1676. Nathaniel Bacon was a member of the rising generation of colonial planters who resented British rule and, particularly, the British protection of Indian lands that lay just outside of the Virginia settlement. As life expectancy increased in the second half of the seventeenth century, as more and more indentured servants lived beyond the end of their indentures, and as the king gave away huge tracts of arable land to his friends in England, increasing numbers of poor whites found they could not afford land to farm once their indentures were up. Bacon became the leader of a motley crew of poor whites who rebelled against the British governor, seized Williamsburg, and forced the governor to flee the capital. Bacon also offered freedom to any slaves who joined his rebellion. Bacon's substitute government lasted only a few weeks, but it showed the potential to gain the loyalty of the slaves by offering freedom.

508 • Slave Soldiers in the Yamasee War

When the Yamasees, the Creeks, and several other Indian tribes formed a confederation and attacked South Carolina in 1715, South Carolina recruited and armed a free and slave defensive force. Although the turning point in the war came when the Cherokees decided to fight on the side of the whites rather than the Creeks and Yamasees, armed slaves fought and died to defend the colony. Those who could prove that they had killed the enemy on the battlefield were rewarded with freedom and their owners were compensated by the colony. Although the actual number of slaves freed is unknown, there must have been enough to cause South Carolina authorities concern about linking armed service to manumission. In 1719 South Carolina changed the 1703 law and rewarded slaves who killed or captured the enemy with a cash payment, but not freedom.

509 • Black Servicemen in the French and Indian War

Even before the Revolutionary War, a pattern had been established in the British colonies whereby African Americans were enlisted to defend the colonies when they were attacked, but were excluded from military service in times of peace. When Major General Edward Braddock's forces were defeated in the French and Indian War in 1755, Virginia was forced to utilize free African Americans in its colonial military. Yet the colonial legislature refused to use African Americans in combat positions, preferring to relegate them to labor positions and service as scouts. Once armed, African Americans might, it was feared, turn their weapons on the colony in an attempt to free the slaves.

510 • George Gire

George Gire of Grafton, Massachusetts, fought in the French and Indian War (1754–63). Because of the injuries he received in that war, he was awarded an annual pension of forty shillings. Gire, along with Benjamin Negro and Caesar of Rhode Island, was part of an emerging class of free African Americans in the Northeast, where slavery was declining as an agriculturally profitable system of labor. Thus, unlike slaves who were often forced into service by their masters, Gire, along with his Black compatriots, represents the first example in American history of free African Americans fighting for the British colonies.

511 • Colonial Militia Integrated in the War of Independence

The first integrated army in American history was the colonial militia that fought the early battles of the War of Independence. Black minutemen fought on the front lines in the first battles against British authority: Blacks assembled at Lexington and Concord on April 19, 1775, to defend Boston against a threatened attack by His Majesty's regiments. One of the first to see combat was Prince Easterbrooks, a Lexington slave, who was a member of Captain John Parker's company and who was wounded at the battle of Concord. He survived, however, to fight in many other companies throughout the Revolutionary War. Another was Barzillai Lew, who joined the 27th Massachusetts Regiment, fought at Bunker Hill, and served in the army for seven years. Although the Continental Army tried to exclude African Americans at one time during the conflict, and some states raised all-Black units, free Black and slave militiamen served alongside of white militiamen in many battles from Bunker Hill to Yorktown.

512 • Peter Salem

A free Black man, Peter Salem, a private in Captain Simon Edgel's company at the battle of Bunker Hill, was the first military hero of the War of Independence. On June 17, 1775, at a crucial moment in the battle when British Major John Pitcairn had rallied the disorganized British troops and prepared a counterattack, Salem shot the major through the head just after the latter yelled, "The day is ours." Peter Salem, a former slave who had gained his freedom upon enlisting in the militia, had battled Pitcairn and his forces earlier at Lexington and was glad to have dispatched the hated major as he did. Now leaderless, the British lost their nerve and the battle. Afterward, Salem's fellow soldiers took up a collection for him. He was also honored by a visit to meet George Washington and by a monument placed over his grave in Framingham, Massachusetts, in 1882.

513 • Salem Poor

Salem Poor was an African American hero of

The Battle of Bunker Hill, 17 June 1775, detail, by John Trumbull, 1786. "Lt. Grosvenor and Peter Salem after Salem shot the British Major Pitcairne." Yale University Art Gallery

the Revolutionary War. He distinguished himself so in battle that fourteen American officers praised him before Congress. On December 5, 1775, a memorial was dedicated to him at Cambridge, Massachusetts, which carried the citation that "under our own observation, we declare that a negro man called Salem Poor, of Colonel Frye's regiment, Captain Ame's company, in the late battle at Charlestown, behaved like an experienced officer, as well as an excellent soldier."

514 • African Americans Excluded from the Continental Army

Shortly after George Washington took command of the American forces in July 1775, the

council of war decided informally not to enlist "any deserter from the Ministerial army, nor any stroller, negro, or vagabond" in the Continental Army. During the debate on the question in the Continental Congress, Edward Rutledge from South Carolina offered a resolution to "discharge all the Negroes, as well as slaves and freemen, in his army." That failed, but the general recommendation to prohibit African Americans from enlisting in the Continental Army was approved by the council of war on October 8, 1775, and by the delegates to the Continental Congress on October 23. General George Washington made it official on November 12, 1775, when he issued orders that "neither Negroes, boys, unable to bear arms, nor old men unfit to endure the fatigues of the campaign are to be enlisted." But this exclusionary policy would change after 1778.

515 • Black Man Captures British General Prescott

African Americans continued to serve in the colonial militias despite the ban on further enlistment in the Continental Army, and some, like Prince, a Black man in Lieutenant Colonel Barton's Rhode Island army, showed great daring and bravery. Early in August 1777, Colonel Barton conceived a plan to capture British Major General Prescott, commander of the Royal Army at Newport, Rhode Island, to effect a trade for a captured American general. Leading an army of forty men in two boats, Barton landed five miles from Newport and advanced on foot to the headquarters of General Prescott, where the colonel, with "a stout negro close behind him, and another at a small distance," confronted and then overwhelmed a sentry. While the other men surrounded the house, "a negro man, named Prince, instantly thrust his beetle head through the panel door, and seized his victim [Prescott] while in bed." While Colonel Barton received "an elegant sword" for his exploits, Prince, the actual captor of the general, received nothing. In that sense, Prince was not exceptional: throughout the war, African Americans played a pivotal, decisive role in battles only to have that role forgotten afterward.

516 • Africans Still Serve in Labor Battalions

Despite the ban on using African Americans as fighting soldiers, many of the colonies and the Continental Army used slaves and free African Americans as laborers to build fortifications to defend colonial cities. Even South Carolina, which later refused to raise an all-Black regiment, utilized African Americans to build batteries around Charleston. South Carolina leased such slaves from their masters at a cost of ten shillings a day, which the owners received if their "property" was killed or injured on such duty. The use of African Americans in labor battalions, a sign of their lack of the privileges of full citizenship, would continue until the Korean War.

517 • Lord Dunmore's Declaration

The royal governor of Virginia, John Murray, earl of Dunmore, decided to exploit a weakness of the colonial rebels when he issued a proclamation on November 7, 1775, that freed "all indented servants, negroes or others (appertaining to Rebels)" who joined the British forces. Approximately five hundred slaves rushed to join Dunmore, who organized an Ethiopian Regiment. According to Edmund Pendleton: "The Governor . . . marched out with three hundred and fifty soldiers, Tories and slaves. . . . Letters mention that slaves flock to him in abundance; but I hope it is magnified." It

wasn't: as Dunmore wrote the British secretary of state on March 30, 1776: "I have been endeavoring to raise two regiments here—one of white people, the other of black. The former goes on very slowly, but the latter very well. . . ." Defeated more by a smallpox epidemic than battle, Dunmore's Ethiopian Regiment was reduced to 150 by the disease six months after his call to action. In June 1776 rebel forces drove Dunmore and his troops from Gwynn's Island and ended the threat of a British-led slave rebellion in Virginia.

518 • African Americans Replace Reluctant Whites

By 1777 losses on the field of battle and rising white desertions had reduced the Continental Army's ranks of men. Northern colonies began to accept African Americans, free and slave, because these colonies could not fill their quotas with white men. In October 1777 Connecticut adopted a policy whereby masters could avoid service in the army by providing one of his slaves, who would receive his freedom for such service. The policy to allow slaves to substitute for masters spread throughout the northern colonies.

519 • Rhode Island's Black Army

As the war took a turn for the worse for the American forces at the end of 1777 at Valley Forge, the general assembly of Rhode Island passed an act in February 1778 to create a battalion of nonwhite troops. The act declared: "That every able-bodied negro, mulatto, or Indian slave in this State, may enlist into either the said two battalions to serve during the continuance of the present war with Great Britain; that every slave so enlisted shall be entitled to receive all the bounties, wages, encouragements allowed by the Continental Congress to any soldier enlisted in their service." The act also provided that all slaves offered by their masters would be free after the war and that the masters would receive up to 120 pounds per slave. Although many opposed the plan, in part because of its cost, Rhode Island formed a regiment of emancipated slaves that was one of the three that prevented the British from turning the flank of the American army at the battle of Rhode Island on August 29, 1778.

520 • Rev. Dr. Samuel Hopkins on Why Rhode Island Raised a Regiment of Black Troops

God is so ordering it in his providence that it seems absolutely necessary something should speedily be done with respect to the slaves among us, in order to [insure] our safety and to prevent their turning against us in our present struggle, in order to get their liberty. Our oppressors have planned to get the blacks and induce them to take up arms against us, by promising them liberty on this condition. . . . And should we attempt to restrain them by force and severity, keeping a strict guard over them, and punishing those severely who shall be detected in attempting to join our oppressors, this will only be making bad worse, and serve to render our inconsistence, oppression and cruelty more criminal, perspicuous and shocking, and bring down the righteous vengeance of Heaven on our heads. The only way pointed out to prevent this threatening evil is to set the blacks at liberty ourselves by some public act and laws, and then give them proper encouragement to labor, or take arms in the defense of the American cause, as they shall choose. This would at once be doing them some degree of justice, and defeating our enemies in the scheme that they are prosecuting.

Washington crossing the Delaware with his personal servant, James Armistead.
Prints and Photographs Division, Library of Congress

521 • Washington Accepts African Americans in the Continental Army

Facing mounting desertions and the possibility of losing the war, George Washington reversed himself in 1778 and approved the enlistment of free Negroes in the Continental Army. By the end of the war, over five thousand African Americans had served in the Continental Army. Though many had been assigned to labor units, nearly every battle of the Revolutionary War contained some African American soldiers. Washington's confidence in Black soldiers was such that several, including Oliver Cromwell and Prince Whipple, were among the troops Washington used in his daring nighttime crossing of the Delaware, December 25, 1776.

522 • Black Regiments for South Carolina and Georgia?

Because much of the War of Independence was fought in the South, where American forces were weakest, Henry Laurens and his son John proposed that South Carolina and Georgia arm African Americans for defensive purposes. Henry Laurens first proposed the idea to George Washington when Laurens wrote that "the country is greatly distressed, and will be so unless further reinforcements are sent to its relief. Had we arms for three thousand such black men as I could select in Carolina, I should have no doubt of success in driving the British out of Georgia, and subduing East Florida before the end of July." Colonel John Laurens lobbied both the

South Carolina and Georgia legislatures to raise companies of Black troops for defense of the colonies. But opposition to the plan was high in both states, perhaps because such slaves might have to be freed after the war. Even after Sir Henry Clinton, commander in chief of the British forces, announced on June 30, 1779, that all slaves of rebels who joined the British would be freed, and some slaves did enter the British lines, Colonel Laurens could not overcome South Carolina's opposition to arming Black troops. Evidently most South Carolinians preferred to risk enslavement by the British than end the enslavement of their fellow Americans. But despite the opposition of such southern colonies to arming Black soldiers, African Americans did serve in the army of the South in a variety of ways, as builders of breastworks, dams, and fortifications, as guides in forests, swamps, and waterways, as spies and drummers, and in some rare cases, as men who bore arms.

523 • George Washington on the Failure of South Carolina to Raise African American Troops for Defense

The following is an excerpt from a letter written by George Washington in 1782 to Colonel John Laurens about the latter's inability to persuade his fellow South Carolinians to raise a regiment of Black troops in an hour of desperate need.

I must confess that I am not at all astonished at the failure of your plan. That spirit of freedom, which, at the commencement of this contest, would have gladly sacrificed everything to the attainment of its object, has long since subsided, and every selfish passion has taken its place. It is not the public but private interest which influences the generality of mankind; nor can the Americans any longer boast an exception. Under the circumstances, it would rather have been surprising if you had succeeded; nor will you, I fear, have better success in Georgia.

524 • Black Reenslavement After Service in the Continental Army and Washington's Response

Many African American slaves were led to believe that if they joined the colonial militia or Continental Army and fought for American independence, they would be freed from slavery at the end of the war. But many slaves were reenslaved after the war by "stay at home" masters. One particularly poignant case was that of Simon Lee, the grandfather of William Wells Brown, the first African American novelist, and a Virginia slave when he joined the war effort. When discharged honorably from the army, Lee was returned to his master to work as a slave on his master's tobacco plantation.

Although himself a slave owner, George Washington was outraged at the practice of reenslaving those who had fought in the war. In one case where a slave owner, Mr. Hobby, demanded return of an African American who had fought in the Massachusetts army, Washington interceded in 1783 and appointed a commission of officers to investigate the claim and the African American's record of service. Eventually the Virginia legislature passed a law that those slaves who had enlisted in a regiment and who had been a substitute for a free person who was obligated to serve would be determined to be free, as if he had been specifically promised such freedom after service.

525 • Fate of African Americans Who Fought for British

As with slaves who fought with the colonies, the slaves who fought on the British side were not guaranteed their freedom or dignity after the war either. According to Thomas Jefferson:

Black sailor in crew of ship at the battle of Lake Erie, 1814. Prints and Photographs Division, Library of Congress

From an estimate I made at that time, on the best information I could collect, I supposed the State of Virginia lost, under Lord Cornwallis' hand, that year, about thirty thousand slaves; and that, of these, twenty-seven thousand died of the small-pox and camp fever; the rest were partly sent to the West Indies, and exchange of rum, sugar, coffee and fruit; and partly sent to New York, from whence they went, at the peace, either to Nova Scotia or England. From this last place, I believe they have lately been sent to Africa.

526 • African Americans Excluded After Revolutionary War

Even though African Americans had helped the Continental Army secure American independence, the new nation, in the Enlistment Act of 1792, limited the right to serve in the national militia only to "each and every free able-bodied white male citizen of the respective States, resident therein, who is or shall be of the age of eighteen years, and under the age of forty-five years."

WAR OF 1812

Engagements, Policy, and People

527 • *Chesapeake-Leopard* Affair

Although the U.S. Army did not enlist African Americans after the Revolutionary War, the U.S. Navy continued to use African Americans as seamen because of the perennial shortage of white sailors. The Black presence in the navy placed them at the center of the naval incident that led to the War of 1812. In 1807 the British frigate *Leopard* shelled the USS *Chesapeake* to locate four escaped British sailors. When the *Chesapeake* yielded and the British boarded the American ship, they took into custody four sailors, three of whom—William Ware, Daniel Martin, and John Strachan—were African Americans previously impressed by the British. Although it was obvious that these men were Americans, the British refused to return them for four years, inciting American public opinion and leading President Thomas Jefferson to close American harbors to British ships. The U.S. could not go to war then because it lacked a serious navy; but the seeds of resentment were sown, and in June 1812 the United States declared war on Britain, citing the impressment of American citizens as a principal reason for going to war.

528 • Integrated Navy During War of 1812

An exact accounting of the number of African

Americans in the U.S. Navy during the War of 1812 is unknown. But a surgeon, Usher Parsons, who served on board several ships during the war, recalled:

In 1814, our fleet sailed to the Upper Lakes to co-operate with Colonel Croghan at Mackinac. About one in twelve of the crew was black. In 1816, I was surgeon of the "Java," under Commodore Perry. The white and colored seamen messed together. About one in six or eight were colored. In 1819, I was surgeon of the "Guerriere," under Commodore Macdonough; and the proportion of blacks was about the same in her crew. There seemed to be an entire absence of prejudice against the blacks as messmates among the crew.

529 • American Navy Officers Debate Quality of Black Sailors

Throughout the War of 1812, Captain Oliver Hazard Perry of the American naval forces on Lake Erie complained about the lack of qualified officers and seamen available for his navy. In one instance, after receiving a new allotment of men from Commodore Isaac Chauncey, Perry complained about their quality. "The men that came by Mr. Champlin are a motley set,—blacks, soldiers, and boys. I cannot think you saw them after they were selected. I am, however, pleased to see any thing in the shape of a man." Upset by Perry's comments, Chauncey defended the quality of the men in his reply:

I regret that you are not pleased with the men sent you by Messrs Champlin and Forest; for, to my knowledge, a part of them are not surpassed by any seamen we have in the fleet: and I have yet to learn that the color of the skin, or the cut and trimmings of the coat, can effect a man's qualifications or usefulness. I have nearly fifty blacks on board of this ship, and many more of them are among my best men; and those people you call soldiers have been to sea from two to seventeen years; and I presume that you will find them as good and useful as any men on board of your vessel.

530 • Cyrus Tiffany

Black heroism was not daunted by Captain Oliver H. Perry's opinion of Black sailors; indeed, a Black sailor, Cyrus Tiffany, was instrumental in protecting the life of Perry. When the USS *Lawrence,* the flagship of the American navy on Lake Erie, was sunk during the battle at Put-in-Bay in July 1814, Tiffany and others were rowing Perry to the USS *Niagara,* the new flagship, when the British began to shoot at the rowboat. Tiffany shielded his captain with his body and allowed Perry to escape safely to the new ship.

531 • General Andrew Jackson Reverses U.S. Army Policy

Americans suffered several devastating losses in the first year of the War of 1812 with England. The failed American invasion of Canada, the cessation of the war in Europe, which allowed England to focus its military on the U.S., and the falling morale of American troops and volunteers set the stage for the employment of the African American in the army. When the British prepared to attack New Orleans, General Andrew Jackson issued the following proclamation on September 21, 1814:

To the Free Colored Inhabitants of Louisiana:

Through a mistaken policy, you have heretofore been deprived of a participation in the glorious struggle for national rights in which our country is engaged. This no longer shall exist. As sons of freedom, you are now called upon to defend our most inestimable blessing. As Americans, your country looks with confidence to her adopted children for a valorious support, as a faithful return for the advantages enjoyed under her mild and equitable government. . . . To every noble-hearted, generous freeman of color volunteering to serve during the present contest with Great Britain, and no longer, there will be paid the same bounty, in money and lands, now received by the white soldiers of the United States, vis: one hundred and twenty-four dollars in money, and one hundred and sixty acres of land. . . .

The free African Americans were to be enrolled in a separate regiment, commanded by white officers, and free from negative comments or "sarcasm" from fellow white officers.

532 • Black Battalions of Freemen Respond

African Americans in Louisiana had already organized their own battalion, which, in September 1812, had been recognized by the state legislature of Louisiana and organized as a corps of free African Americans as part of the state militia. After General Andrew Jackson's call to arms, the Battalion of Free Men of Color, as they were called, were joined by a second battalion of Black soldiers organized by a free Black Santo Domingan emigrant, Joseph Savary, and together they were pressed into service in December 1814 to defend New Orleans. While one battalion attended British forces at Chalmette Plains, the other built fortifications against the British attack in January 1815. Both were engaged on January 8 during the main attack by the British, and together they kept the center of the fortifications, the artillery batter-

Black riflemen at battle of New Orleans. Prints and Photographs Division, Library of Congress ies, from being taken. Although the African Americans had repulsed the British assault, British sharpshooters took up positions after the battle and picked off Americans trying to rescue their wounded on the field. Savary, now a captain, led a group of Black men who routed the British sharpshooters in the last major battle of the contest. Afterward, Jackson praised the Black soldiers as having "not disappointed the hopes that were formed of their courage and perseverance in the performance of their duty."

533 • General Jackson Reneges on His Promise

A negative view of Andrew Jackson's regard for Black troops emerges from *The Narrative of James Roberts,* written by a man who served in Jackson's army at New Orleans. Roberts was a slave who had been returned to slavery after serving in the Revolutionary War.

General Jackson, in order to prepare to meet Packenham, the British General, in the contest at New Orleans, came into our section of the country . . . to enlist five hundred negroes. Jackson came into the field and then addressed us thus: "Had you not as soon go into the battle and fight, as to stay here in the cotton field, dying and never die? If you will go, and the battle is fought and the victory gained on Israel's side, you shall be free."

But after the battle was won and "sixty or seventy or more of the colored men were killed . . . [who] were, without doubt, as Jackson himself acknowledged, the instrumental cause of the victory," Jackson told the men to "go home to your masters." Roberts challenged Jackson about his promise to free them, and Jackson answered: " 'If I were to hire you my horse, could you sell it without my leave? You are another man's property, and I have not money sufficient to buy all of you, and set you free." Infuriated at the betrayal, Roberts cocked his gun but discovered Jackson had had the guns of the African Americans unloaded. "Had my gun been loaded," Roberts recalled, "doubtless Jackson would have been a dead man in a moment. . . . Jackson asked me if I contended for freedom. I said I did. He said, 'I think you are very presumptuous.' I told him, the time had come for us to claim our rights. He said, 'You are a day too late.' Some of the whites standing round said, 'He ought to be shot.' Now, just think of that! Two days before, I had, with my fellow soldiers, saved their city from fire and massacre . . . now, 'he ought to be shot!' simply for contending for my freedom, which, both my master and Jackson had solemnly before high heaven promised, before I left home."

534 • African American Designs the "Cotton-Bag Fort"

When Andrew Jackson assembled his force at New Orleans, his soldiers, many of whom were African American slaves, were outnumbered by the British forces ten to one. Faced with this disadvantage, Jackson consulted with his men as to what was the best defense. According to *The Narrative of James Roberts,* "There was in Jackson's army a colored soldier named Pompey, who gave Jackson the first idea about the *cotton-bag fort,* and superintended the construction of it. We engaged in making it, and it was completed in the latter part of the second day. The cotton-bags were so placed as to leave port holes for three muskets to point through each." It would be from behind that makeshift cotton-bag fort that Jackson's outnumbered forces would mow down the onrushing British soldiers "like grass before the scythe," and achieve the initial destruction of the center of the British army.

535 • "Major" Jeffrey and American Racism

Among the brave blacks who fought in the battles for American liberty was Major Jeffrey, a Tennessean, who, during the campaign of Major General Andrew Jackson in Mobile, filled the place of "regular" among the soldiers. In the charge made by General Stump against the enemy, the Americans were repulsed and thrown into disorder,—Major Stump being forced to retire, in a manner by no means desirable, under the circumstances. Major Jeffrey, who was but a common soldier, seeing the condition of his comrades, and comprehending the disastrous results about to befall them, rushed forward, mounted a horse, took command of the troops, and, by an heroic effort, rallied them to the charge,—completely routing the enemy, who left the Americans masters of the field. He at once received from the General the title of "Major," though he could not, according to the American policy, so commission him.

A few years ago receiving an indignity from a common ruffian, he was forced to strike him in self-defense; for which act, in accordance with the laws of slavery in that, as well as many other slave States, he was compelled to receive on his naked person, nine and thirty lashes with a raw hide! This, at the age of seventy odd, after the distinguished services rendered his country,—probably when the white ruffian for whom he was tortured was unable to raise an arm in its defense,—war more than he could bear; it broke his heart, and he sank to rise no more, till summoned by the blast of the last trumpet. . . .

—Anonymous, from Joseph T. Wilson's *Black Phalanx*

536 • African Americans in the Navy

Although the U.S. Army returned to its "no African Americans" policy after the War of 1812, African Americans continued to be present in the navy, not only as cooks but also as seamen. The general lack of white enlistment in the navy disposed this branch of America's antebellum armed forces to not draw the color line. African Americans were so prevalent on American ships that in one case, four Europeans who had seen the USS *Constitution* in port in Trieste were convinced that all Americans were Black because all of the crew members they had seen on the American ship were African Americans!

CIVIL WAR

Engagements and Policy

537 • Black Soldiers Rejected at Beginning of Civil War

When the Civil War erupted in 1861, Blacks rushed forward to volunteer for the Union Army. But they were turned away. "This is a white man's war" was the popular cry. Many northerners believed that servitude rendered slaves unusable as soldiers. Newspaper writers and cartoonists reinforced these feelings by making outrageous examples of how African Americans could be used to aid the Union Army effort.

538 • Lincoln's Early Position

President Abraham Lincoln seemed to reinforce the view that African Americans were inappropriate as Union soldiers by refusing to enlist Black troops. Lincoln's decision was based less on any prejudice against Black soldiers than on his desire to entice the Confederate South back into the Union and to keep the border states from seceding. He believed the use of Black troops would infuriate the southern

368 FRANK LESLIE'S ILLUSTRATED NEWSPAPER. [Oct. 26, 1861.

DARK ARTILLERY; OR, HOW TO MAKE THE CONTRABANDS USEFUL.

Beadle's Military Hand-Book,
EMBRACING the Official Articles of War, U. S. Army Regulations, a Dictionary of Military Terms, Pay List, Rations, Equipments, Courtesies, etc. Price 25 cts.
For sale by all Book and News Dealers, and Army Sutlers.

No. 2. No. 2.
BEADLE'S
Dime Union Song-Book, No. 2.

THE
FINKLE & LYON
Sewing Machine Company,
538 BROADWAY,
New York,
Having greatly improved their SEWING MACHINES and REDUCED PRICES, invite examination. Circulars,

Stationery Packets.
NEW and Splendid Article, containing Engraved and Colored Stationery; also Packets of Plain Stationery containing a Gift of Jewellery. Sold on liberal terms to Agents. Send Stamp for Circular. PRESCOTT & CO., 118 William St.
309o

FOR THE ONLY IMPORTANT DISCOVERY FOR THE MARRIED—Send Stamp to D. A. WILLIAMS, Lowell, Mass. 000o

Friends of Soldiers!

A Lamp Chimney that will not Break.
Made for the Million.
The Patent Mica Chimneys for Coal Oil Lamps possess many advantages over the glass Chimneys. They do not break from the heat, falling, cleaning or any ordinary usage. When one is purchased, with care it will last as long as the Lamp. They fit all the Burners now in use.
AMOS HORNING,

Cartoon, "Dark Artillery; or, How to Make the Contrabands Useful." Prints and Photographs Division, Library of Congress

and border states. Moreover, by keeping African Americans out of the fighting, Lincoln hoped to keep the question of slavery out of the war as well.

539 • Slaves as Contraband

Slaves flocked to Union forces whenever they approached plantations, but early in the Civil War Lincoln ordered Union states to return such runaway slaves to their Confederate masters. That policy brought strong public criticism from abolitionist newspapers in the North. The first challenge to that policy came on May 27, 1861, when General Benjamin F. Butler issued an order that captured slaves coming into his lines would be retained as "contraband of war" and used to aid the Union Army. Butler argued that such confiscation was necessary to deprive the Confederates of their use to construct fortifications. Butler's rationale took hold, and afterward, slaves who had been used on Confederate military projects were not returned. Soon the entire policy of returning any contrabands was reviewed, and early in 1862 the War Department

reversed it and prohibited the use of federal troops to return runaway slaves.

540 • Confederates First to Accept Black Volunteers

Ironically the secessionists were the first to use African Americans as soldiers, although they were free Negroes, not slaves. Some of those who served were wealthy landowners in Louisiana and South Carolina who either supported the institution of slavery or believed they must show support of the Confederate cause in order to retain their property in the South. A November 23, 1861, review of Confederate troops at New Orleans showed that these forces contained a company of fourteen hundred free African Americans who were later praised for having supplied themselves "with arms without regard to cost and trouble."

541 • First Law to Enlist African Americans as Soldiers

On June 28, 1861, Tennessee became the first state to pass a law for the enlistment of "all male free persons of color between the ages of fifteen and fifty years." The wording of the law suggested that its primary intention was not to employ these men as soldiers, but to require them "to do all such menial service for the relief of volunteers."

542 • Pressure from Congress

After the Union Army suffered a series of military defeats in 1861 and 1862, pressure mounted on Lincoln to use African Americans as soldiers. As Charles Sumner put it: "I do not say carry the war into Africa; but carry Africa into the war." As desertions from the Union Army increased, and white enlistment plummeted, Congress passed the Confiscation Act of August 6, 1861, which authorized the president to enlist African Americans in the army. Lincoln still refused. Then, in October 1861, Secretary of War Edwin Stanton authorized General Thomas W. Sherman to use "all loyal persons offering their services for the defense of the Union" at Port Royal, South Carolina. On July 17, 1862, Congress amended the Enlistment Act of 1795 giving the president authority to enlist African Americans, but Lincoln still refused to act on Congress's recommendation. He even went so far as to state he would resign rather than use Negro regiments.

543 • The First African American Regiment

Events on the field of battle advanced ahead of Washington policymaking. In May 1862 General David Hunter, commander of the Department of the South, ordered the formation of the first armed and uniformed Black regiment in the Civil War, what became known as the 1st South Carolina Volunteer Regiment. "Volunteer" was something of a misnomer, since Hunter forcibly pressed into his army African Americans who appeared able-bodied. When news of the regiment reached the press, C. A. Wickliffe, congressman from Kentucky, demanded an explanation from Secretary of War Edwin M. Stanton, as to whether Hunter had raised a regiment of "fugitive slaves." Hunter wrote back that a regiment of "fugitive slaves" did not exist, but rather a "fine regiment of persons whose late masters are 'fugitive rebels.' " Given that these "loyal persons composing this regiment" wished to avoid their masters, the "loyal persons" were working now for the government and helping to "go in full and effective pursuit of their fugacious and traitorous proprietors." Hunter's letter constructed a brilliant argument for raising African American troops out of the language of Secretary Stanton's earlier directive to Sher-

Black soldiers on review, South Carolina. Prints and Photographs Division, Library of Congress

man, but it angered Wickliffe and Lincoln, who disbanded "Hunter's Regiment." Re-formed and reconstituted under Colonel Thomas Wentworth Higginson, the 1st South Carolina was mustered on November 7, 1862, and served throughout the Civil War.

544 • First Appeal for Black Troops in the North

The first northern appeal for African American troops was made on August 4, 1862 by General Sprague of Rhode Island, who asked Black men to enlist as soldiers in the state militia. Rhode Island then organized the first African American artillery regiment. Other appeals for Black soldiers followed, such as General Butler's appeal on August 22 to the free Negroes of New Orleans, which had recently fallen under Union control, to join the Union Army.

545 • Lincoln Approves

By August 1862, even President Lincoln knew that he could not win the war without the Negro soldier; he just did not want generals making the decision. Accordingly, when Lincoln issued his Emancipation Proclamation on January 1, 1863, he included a provision for enlisting Black troops. The War Department began to aggressively recruit African Americans. By the war's end, approximately 186,000 African Americans had served in the Union Army, with 30,000 casualties. Although all those in the army served in segregated units and mostly in labor battalions, Black soldiers fought in several important battles of the war.

546 • First Civil War Battles of African Americans

The first actual fighting done by Black troops occurred on October 28, 1862, by the 79th Colored Infantry from Kansas in a battle at Island Mound, Missouri. A week later, November 3–10, 1862, the 1st South Carolina engaged the enemy in the first extended action and pursuit of the war on St. Helena Island. Under the command of Captain Trowbridge and Lieutenant Colonel Oliver T. Beard, the 1st South Carolina also pursued the enemy along the coast of Georgia and east Florida. Even after these engagements, however, resistance to the use of Black troops in combat remained high. When Frederick Douglass asked Pennsylvania's governor, Andrew Curtin, whether he would accept African American troops, the answer was no—until General Robert E. Lee invaded southern Pennsylvania in

"Make Way for Liberty!" Prints and Photographs Division, Library of Congress

the summer of 1863. Suddenly the prohibition against the use of Black troops evaporated, and by June 23 the first eighty African Americans were recruited into the Pennsylvania forces.

547 • First Publicized Battle

The first publicly documented fighting of Black troops occurred on the night of January 26, 1863. It was part of a deliberate plan to get African Americans into battle so as to end speculation as to whether African Americans could

be good fighting men. At the battle of the Hundred Pines in South Carolina, war correspondents accompanied the expedition and reported back that the African American soldiers had acquitted themselves well in combat with the enemy.

548 • Louisiana's *Corps d'Afrique* Enter the Fray

On May 27, 1863, at Port Hudson, Louisiana, free African Americans and former slaves (The *Corps d'Afrique*) in the 1st and 3rd Louisiana Native Guards launched a valiant attack against the Confederate Army. Even though the Confederate stronghold at Port Hudson did not fall until two months later, the courage and heroism of these soldiers was widely reported.

549 • African Americans Repulse Confederate Army

On June 7, 1863, approximately one thousand African American soldiers repulsed an assault by the Confederate Army at Milliken's Bend, Louisiana. General Ulysses S. Grant had withdrawn troops from the garrison at Milliken's Bend to support his attack on Vicksburg. Brigadier General Dennis, who was in command of the troops in Milliken's Bend, was surprised when a Confederate force of three thousand attacked the garrison. When the Confederates mounted the works, Black soldiers fought vicious hand-to-hand combat with Confederate regulars after white Union soldiers had abandoned the field of battle. By the end of the day, the Black troops repulsed the Confederate forces and won the respect of Grant for holding Milliken's Bend.

550 • The 54th Massachusetts at Fort Wagner

Despite the gallantry of African American soldiers at Port Hudson and Milliken's Bend, the belief lingered in the North that African Americans were not fit for the most dangerous and courageous missions of the Civil War. It was with that prejudice in mind that Lieutenant Colonel Robert volunteered the all-Black 54th Massachusetts Volunteer Infantry to lead the largely suicidal assault on South Carolina's Fort Wagner on July 18, 1863. Highly publicized, this attack on a heavily fortressed symbol of Confederate resistance might have succeeded if white troops had reinforced the 54th's heroic assault. After advancing across the open beach side of the fort, during which they suffered many casualties, including the colonel, the 54th Massachusetts briefly took the fort before being

"Storming Fort Wagner." Chromolithograph by Kurz & Allison. Prints and Photographs Division, Library of Congress

repulsed by the Confederates. Still, the 54th's indisputable courage convinced many northerners that Black soldiers were capable of fighting gallantly in the Union Army.

551 • General Grant's Men

Even before the 54th Massachusetts charge against Fort Wagner, Black troops had won the respect of the Union Army's most important general, Ulysses S. Grant. Early in June 1863 Grant had had to withdraw troops from the garrison at Milliken's Bend and thereby left its defense to three infantry regiments of African American troops. The garrison, which then contained fourteen hundred men from the 9th and 11th Louisiana Regiments and the 1st Mississippi, plus a smattering of whites, was attacked on June 7 by three thousand Confederate soldiers. The African American troops repulsed the larger Confederate force, which had mounted the works, with musket fire, bayonets, and hand-to-hand fighting. African American troops gained Grant's respect for holding Milliken's Bend. When Grant left the western front to assume command of the entire Union forces in Virginia, he brought twenty thousand African American soldiers with him. During the last year of the war, thirteen African American regiments were a crucial part of the Union Army that brought victories at Chaffin's Farm, New Market Heights, and Fort Harrison in Virginia.

552 • Fort Pillow Massacre

Black soldiers, along with southern whites who had joined the Union Army, were especially hated by Confederate troops, who made that graphically clear in the spring of 1864 at Fort Pillow, Tennessee. Defended by 295 white men of the 13th Tennessee Union Cavalry and 262 African Americans of the 6th United States Heavy Artillery, Fort Pillow was surrounded on April 12 by a vastly superior force of Confederates. When Major General N. B. Forrest demanded surrender of the fort, Union commanders refused; when the Confederates overwhelmed the fort several hours later, the Confederates slaughtered the Union soldiers, along with women and children in the fort, even though they surrendered. The killing lasted until midnight, as Confederates vented their anger on helpless Black soldiers in the fort: several were shot down as they ran, and others, wounded, were burned alive. Afterward Major Forrest tried to stem the public outcry by claiming that the atrocities were exaggerated, but the massacre lived on in the memory of African American soldiers. In several later engagements, African American soldiers led their charges into battle with the cry "Remember Fort Pillow."

553 • Fatigue Duty

Despite the valor of African American soldiers under fire, most Black soldiers in the Civil War were consigned to labor or fatigue duty. Relegating African Americans to labor battalions reflected the belief that African Americans were second-class citizens and unfit for military service. However, in emergencies, as was true throughout the history of the African American soldier, the army would not hesitate to use African Americans in combat situations. For example, the 14th United States Colored Troops were consigned to fatigue duty until August 15, 1864, when General Joseph Wheeler attacked the Union forces garrisoned at Dalton, Georgia. General James B. Steedman sent the 14th Infantry of ex-slaves to rescue the white Union troops. After the battle had been turned in the Union forces' favor by the quickly dispatched African Americans, they were cheered by the white 51st as the 14th Infantry marched into

Dalton. In recognition of their valor, the 14th Infantry was joined with General Lovell H. Rousseau's command at Pulaski, Tennessee, on September 27, 1864.

Black and white sailors and marines mingle on deck of the U.S. gunboat *Mendota*, 1864. National Archives

554 • Colored Troops' Pay

Throughout the Civil War, Black troops were paid less than white troops. The July 1862 act that gave the president permission to enlist African Americans in the Union Army specified that they were to be paid ten dollars a week, rather than the thirteen a week paid to white soldiers. That act rationalized the lower payment for African Americans with the idea that African Americans were contraband of war and to be used exclusively in labor battalions. But when the 54th Massachusetts was formed, expressly for combat service, it was promised pay as other troops; but the men did not receive it. On June 15, 1864, Congress passed the Army Appropriation Bill that declared Black troops should receive the same uniform, arms, equipment, pay, and bounty as other soldiers. On July 14, 1864, Attorney General Edward Bates declared himself in favor of equal pay and bounty for Black soldiers. But Black soldiers were still paid ten dollars a week until the end of the war.

555 • Gabriel Young Receives Freedom for His Military Service

One of the incentives for military service was freedom. Gabriel Young became free after he joined Captain James Johnson's Regiment of Colored Infantry Volunteers. Subsequently his wife was also freed, and his son, Charles, was born into freedom in 1865 in Mayslick, Kentucky. Charles Gabriel eventually became the third African American to graduate from West Point.

556 • African Americans in the Navy

Although African Americans in the army were rigidly segregated in the Civil War, they served in the navy on several ships, often in integrated mess and living quarters. This liberalization of racial restrictions resulted from the prevalance of Blacks in the Civil War navy: one out of every four seamen (about 30,000 sailors in the Union Navy) were African American by the war's end; Blacks also served on the infamous Union ship, the *Monitor.*

557 • Robert E. Lee Requests African Americans

When Robert E. Lee became commander in

chief of the Confederate Army on January 31, 1865, one of the first things he did was to ask for the military use of African Americans by the Confederate government. The lower house of the Confederate Congress approved the resolution on January 28, but the senate rejected it. Again, the idea of using Black troops was reintroduced by Lee and again rejected by the Senate, but finally, on March 13, the Congress passed an act to recruit Black troops. On March 23 the 1st Company of Negro state troops joined Confederate active service.

People

558 • African American Leaders Served in the Civil War

Harriet Tubman, the former slave who led hundreds of African Americans North to freedom before the war, became a scout and a spy for the Union Army. Although Frederick Douglass did not accept a commission in the army, two of his sons, Charles and Lewis Douglass, served in the famous 54th Massachusetts, his oldest son, Lewis, becoming a sergeant major. Martin R. Delany, the prewar advocate of African American emigration, accepted commission as a major in the 104th Regiment at Charleston, South Carolina. The war also made some new political leaders. Captain P. B. S. Pinchback of the 2nd Louisiana Volunteers became lieutenant governor of Louisiana during Reconstruction.

559 • Robert Blake at Sea

On December 25, 1863, the USS *Marblehead* was shelled by Confederate batteries on John's Island, South Carolina, killing the powder boy and throwing the ship into confusion. Robert Blake, the commander's steward, rushed out of his quarters, substituted for the dead powder boy, and brought gunpowder boxes to the ship's artillery throughout the battle. Credited not only with bringing vitally needed gunpowder but also with a sense of humor during the tense battle, Blake was awarded the Navy Medal of Honor on April 16, 1864, for his heroism.

560 • Black Congressional Medals of Honor

During the Civil War, at least sixteen African Americans received the Congressional Medal of

Christian Fleetwood, Medal of Honor man. Prints and Photographs Division, Library of Congress

Honor, a commendation established by Congress on July 12, 1862, to recognize enlisted men of the armed forces who "distinguish themselves by their gallantry in action." Typical of the acts that were honored were those of two men who fought at New Market Heights and Chaffin's Farm in September 1864. Private James Gardner of the 36th United States Colored Troops rushed ahead of his brigade as they stormed the fort at New Market Heights: Gardner shot and bayoneted a rebel officer who was rallying his forces. At Chaffin's Farm, Christian A. Fleetwood, a sergeant major of the 4th United States Colored Troops, grabbed the Union flag after two color-bearers had been shot. With no officers present, Fleetwood then rallied a group of reserves to attack the fort during the final successful battle of the engagement.

POST–CIVIL WAR

Engagements and Policy

561 • Retained but Segregated

Because the army wished to demobilize white troops as quickly as possible and yet retain an effective fighting force after the Civil War, Black troops were retained in the army after the war. The 122,000 Black troops in the U.S. Army as of June 1865 comprised 13 percent of the total—the largest percentage of Blacks in the army in U.S. history. Congress gave official recognition to its continuing need for the African American soldier by passing, in March 1866, a law to create six exclusively African American regiments: four infantries (the 38th, 39th, 40th, and 41st) and two cavalries (the 9th and 10th). Although the infantry regiments were reduced to two—the 24th and 25th—in 1869, these all-Black regiments proved that the African American soldier had a right to serve in the United States Army. But congressional action also gave a legal basis to a segregated army and made more difficult the effort to desegregate the army in the future.

562 • African Americans in the Army of Reconstruction

After the Civil War, African American troops helped occupy the former Confederacy and enforce the policies of the Reconstruction Act of 1867. Although never a majority of the troops stationed in the South, the eighty thousand African American soldiers serving there became the target of southern white hostility to Reconstruction. Southerners complained bitterly during Reconstruction about Black soldiers who were "uppity" and "disrespectful" of southern whites during the occupation. Black troops had the unenviable task of protecting unpopular Reconstruction governments from the Ku Klux Klan, the White League, and other terrorist organizations. Black soldiers also supported efforts of Black southerners to vote, to hold office, and to organize farm and labor cooperatives. The withdrawal of Black troops in 1877 by President Rutherford B. Hayes ended such protections, but did not end white southerner hostility to Blacks in uniform. Even after World War II, the South greeted Black servicemen with violence, in part because Black soldiers symbolized the occupation of the South during Reconstruction.

563 • Buffalo Soldiers in the Indian Wars

With the decline of Reconstruction, the National Army dwindled in numbers, but African

Americans continued to serve in the U.S. Army and took an active part in the Indian wars in the West. Stationed at such outposts as Fort Snelling, Minnesota, in the 1880s, the 25th Infantry escorted western migrants, protected mail and stage routes, and fought in attacks on the Apaches, Kiowas, Cheyennes, Comanches, and Arapahos. The 10th Cavalry played an even more dramatic role: it was credited with capturing the feared Indian leader Geronimo in 1885. With fewer desertions than white counterparts and greater devotion to the army, the "Buffalo Soldiers," as the Indians named them, distinguished themselves and received fourteen Congressional Medals of Honor for their efforts.

564 • Lieutenant Powhatan Clarke

Congress awarded a Buffalo Soldier the Medal of Honor for a daring rescue during the 1886 campaign to recapture Geronimo. The Apache leader had escaped from the San Carlos reservation in Arizona in May 1885, and after a year-long pursuit that led into Mexico, the K Company of the 10th Cavalry had cornered Geronimo—or so they thought—in the Pinto Mountains, some thirty

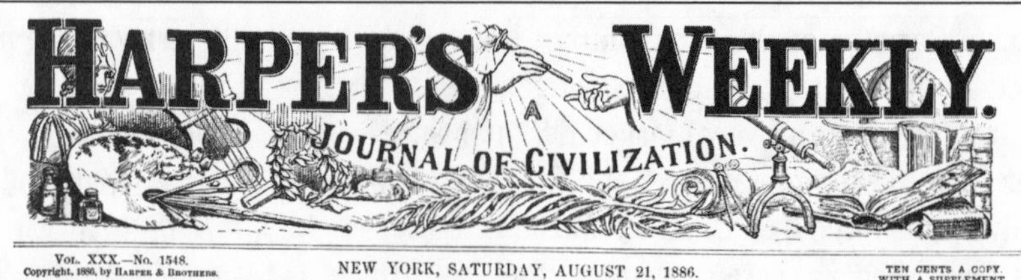

HARPER'S WEEKLY. A JOURNAL OF CIVILIZATION.

Vol. XXX.—No. 1548. Copyright, 1886, by Harper & Brothers. NEW YORK, SATURDAY, AUGUST 21, 1886. TEN CENTS A COPY. WITH A SUPPLEMENT.

Soldiering in the Southwest—the rescue of Corporal Scott. Prints and Photographs Division, Library of Congress

miles south of the Mexican border. But as the K Company marched forward to attack on foot, they found themselves pinned down by Apache rifle fire. Corporal Scott was wounded and lay exposed to enemy fire in an open field. Without regard to his own safety, Lieutenant Powhatan Clarke ran from behind a ridge and dragged Scott to safety. During the commotion created by the rescue, Geronimo escaped from the grasp of the Buffalo Soldiers. Four months later, after a renewed campaign, Geronimo surrendered to the 10th Cavalry.

565 • Why Blacks Out West?

The army stationed a disproportionate number of African Americans in the West for a variety of racially based reasons. First, African American troops were unpopular in the South and in the North, particularly in urban areas. Stationing African American troops in rural areas thus removed them from white opposition. Moreover, in an era of rising scientific racism, the army believed that African Americans were more adapted to the harsh conditions of life in the West. Not only were African Americans believed to survive better in the harsh climate, but also some people, like William Tecumseh Sherman, believed that Blacks survived attacks of typhoid fever better than whites. That such theories were mainly justification for sending African American troops to the worst possible duty, which most white troops would reject, was made plain when the 25th Infantry of presumably "tropical" African Americans was forced to spend ten years in the frigid conditions in Montana and the Dakotas.

566 • African American Heroes of the Spanish-American War

Teddy Roosevelt and his Rough Riders are credited with winning the Spanish-American War, but Black soldiers turned the most important battles in the Americans' favor. At Las Guásimas, Cuba, on June 23, 1898, the all-Black 10th Cavalry, with more experience from the Indian wars and better arms (machine guns), led the rest of the American forces and overwhelmed the Spanish. Afterward, Roosevelt remarked: "No troops could behave better than the colored soldiers." During the battle of El Caney, Teddy was even more grateful: the 9th and 10th Cavalries rescued his Rough Riders when they were pinned down by a heavily fortified garrison. Advancing quickly through the surrounding woods, the Black troops endured heavy losses from artillery and infantry fire, but freed the Rough Riders from their position. The 10th Cavalry joined with the rest in an assault that crushed the Spanish at El Caney and later

Battle of Las Guásimas. Prints and Photographs Division, Library of Congress

at Santiago. According to one white corporal: "If it had not been for the Negro cavalry, the Rough Riders would have been exterminated." Another put the racial implications of the victory more succinctly: "They can drink out of our canteens."

567 • What a Difference Five Months Makes

Lieutenant John J. Pershing, commander of the 10th Cavalry, heaped praise on his Black soldiers in July 1898 after their valorous assault on San Juan Hill, Cuba, another major engagement of the Spanish-American War. "They had fought their way into our affections, as they have fought their way into the hearts of the American people." But just five months later, in Huntsville, Alabama, two Black members of the same regiment were killed by a Black man. He killed them because local white citizens had announced that a reward would be paid for every Black cavalryman that was killed. As one member of the regiment put it, "Cuba was a paradise. There we expected and looked for trouble. Our enemies were there, but here it is among our supposed friends . . . that we face a more deadly enemy."

568 • Roosevelt's Brownsville Affair

On August 13, 1906, a gun battle broke out in Brownsville, Texas, a town near the Mexican border, that left a white bartender dead and a police lieutenant wounded. White townspeople blamed three companies of the 25th Colored Infantry stationed at nearby Fort Brown for the attack, believing it was retaliation for the town's harassment of the African American troops. The soldiers denied involvement in the affair, and an inspection of their weapons proved none had been fired. Still, when an army investigation concluded that the battalion's "conspiracy of silence" shielded the guilty parties, President Theodore Roosevelt ordered the dishonorable discharge, without a trial, of 167 of the 170 soldiers in the 1st Battalion of the 25th Infantry. His decision forfeited the pension of seasoned soldiers, including six Medal of Honor winners, who not only had fought bravely throughout the American West but also, ironically, had backed up Roosevelt's Rough Riders in their assault on San Juan Hill. Issued a day after African Americans had cast crucial votes for the Republican ticket in several state elections, Roosevelt's decision destroyed his reputation among African Americans, damaged the leadership of Booker T. Washington, a firm Roosevelt supporter, and helped deny Roosevelt and Taft the presidency in 1912.

569 • Colonel Benjamin Grierson

United States Army policy discouraged African Americans from serving as officers, even in all–African American regiments. In the eyes of the army, the stigma of slavery rendered African Americans unfit to lead. Since most whites viewed officer duty as a blight on their careers, African American troops were generally led by white officers who could not avoid such duty—the least qualified. An exception to that rule was Colonel Benjamin Grierson, a fine officer, who organized the 10th Cavalry, molded it into a highly trained fighting force, and led its campaigns against the Comanches, the Mescaleros, and the Chiricahuas in the Southwest.

570 • First Black West Point Cadets

The first African American cadet at West Point was not Henry Flipper or Benjamin O. Davis, as is often believed. Two others—Michael Howard from Mississippi and James Webster Smith from South Carolina—share

that distinction. Both entered in 1870, the result of the election of Blacks to Congress under Reconstruction, since entrance to West Point required the recommendation of a member of Congress. Unfortunately neither Howard nor Smith graduated. Smith went on to supervise the training of cadets at South Carolina State College.

571 • Henry Flipper and the Code of Silence

Henry Flipper is rightfully remembered as the first African American to graduate from West Point, on June 15, 1877. That was a considerable achievement, as Flipper's book on his life at West Point disclosed. During his entire four years at West Point, Flipper had to survive a psychological campaign of total isolation during which none of the other cadets would speak with him. Upon graduation, Flipper received a command of a Black unit, the 10th Cavalry "Indian fighters." Unfortunately Flipper was accused of embezzlement of funds and conduct unbecoming of an officer. Although the charge of embezzlement was dropped, he was convicted of the second charge and discharged from the army. He did not let his unfair treatment, however, defeat him. He worked as a special agent in the Justice Department and published several translations of Spanish and Mexican laws that are still used today. Although Flipper failed to vindicate his name by the time of his death in 1940, later investigations concluded he had been wrongfully accused, largely because of his race. He was granted, posthumously, an honorable discharge and burial in Arlington National Cemetery.

Lieutenant Henry Flipper. Arizona Historical Society, Tucson

572 • The Court-Martial of Johnson Chestnut Whittaker

The perils of being a Black cadet at West Point in the post–Civil War years are illustrated by the experience of Johnson Chestnut Whittaker. On April 6, 1880, this Black cadet was discovered delirious and bound to his bed in his room at West Point, with his ears cut as if he were a hog, his face covered with blood. Incredibly authorities' first reaction was that Whittaker had staged an attack to get "sympathy." A West Point court of inquiry concluded that there was no evidence to support Whittaker's contention that three masked cadets had attacked him. Even when evidence surfaced later in a court-martial that three masked cadets had been seen that evening, the court dismissed that evidence in favor of handwriting experts who claimed that Whittaker had written a threatening note to himself. Although Whittaker was found guilty, the attorney general threw out the decision on the inadmissibility of handwriting evidence. Nevertheless, Whittaker

was dismissed from the academy in 1882 for deficiencies on an exam he took shortly after the first verdict. Afterward Whittaker joined the faculty of the Colored Normal, Industrial, Agricultural and Mechanical College in South Carolina and refrained from publicly discussing the issue. His son served in World War I and a grandson in World War II.

573 • Colonel Charles Young

Charles D. Young was the third African American to graduate from West Point. During the Spanish-American War, he commanded the all–African American 9th Ohio Regiment. Then, during the Mexican campaign, he led the 10th Cavalry against Pancho Villa's army at Aguascalientes and Santa Cruz de Villegas. Young's brilliance in the field led to his promotion by John Pershing to lieutenant colonel. But when the United States entered World War I, the U.S. Army forced Colonel Young to retire because of unfounded high blood pressure, in order, many African Americans believed, to avoid giving him a commission as commander of an all-Black regiment. Colonel Young rode by horse from Ohio to Washington, D.C., to disprove such claims, but the army refused to change its decision.

WORLD WAR I

574 • African American Soldiers in World War I

On the eve of America's entry into World War I, approximately 20,000 African Americans were members of the regular army and National Guard, comprising merely 2 percent of the total number of men in the armed forces. Such a low percentage reflected a bias against use of African Americans as soldiers that continued into World War I. Although the United States Army was understaffed when President Woodrow Wilson declared war on Germany in April 1917, the army rejected most of the African Americans who volunteered once war was declared. The situation improved when Congress passed the Selective Service Act on May 18 that called for the enlistment of all able-bodied American citizens. Over 700,000 African Americans signed up on the first day of registration, and ultimately, over 2 million would be registered during World War I. Out of that number, over 360,000 African Americans would be accepted for service and nearly 40,000 of them would serve in two all-Black divisions, the 92nd and 93rd, formed in November and December, 1917, respectively.

575 • The Significance of the Houston Riot

African Americans were not accepted in the marines, or as combat personnel in the navy, which continued to confine African Americans to mess duty on ships. Even in the army, Black soldiers often received inadequate training, served in labor battalions, and languished under white officers who verbally and physically abused them. Perhaps the most negative aspect of joining the army was the experience of being stationed in the South, where white communities often resented and tormented Black troops from the North. In one instance, the constant abuse, goading, and beatings routinely endured by Black regiments flared into a riot. After weeks of harassment, the 24th Infantry retaliated when one of its members, Corporal Charles W. Baltimore, was beaten, shot at, and then arrested by policemen in Houston for having the temerity to ask the policemen about another ar-

Officers of the "Buffaloes," 367th Infantry, 77th Division, in France, c. 1918. National Archives

rested member of the battalion. On the night of August 23, 1917, approximately one hundred soldiers of the 24th marched on the town, opened fire on the police station, and killed sixteen whites, including five policemen, and wounded several others. The army quickly court-martialed sixty-three of the soldiers, convicted and hanged nineteen of them, without appeal, and jailed another sixty-seven. Like the Brownsville Affair, the punishment in the Houston Riot divided African Americans and raised, once again, the question of the kind of justice that African American soldiers could expect from a military that refused to protect them from southern attacks. Moreover, the Houston Riot may have led Secretary of War Newton Baker to abandon plans to recruit sixteen regiments of African Americans; he organized only four.

576 • African American Officers

African Americans were anxious to serve as officers in World War I but were blocked from receiving the training necessary for such service because of the army's refusal to integrate officer training facilities. Joel Spingarn, a board member of the NAACP, began lecturing on Black college campuses, drumming up support for his proposal that the army establish a separate officer training facility in Des Moines, Iowa. Although some African American newspapers criticized the idea as a capitulation to segregation, others, like W. E. B. Du Bois in the *Crisis,* argued that the alternative to a segregated facility was no African American officers at all. When General Leonard of the army promised to establish such a camp if two hundred college-trained African Americans could be found, a Central Committee of Negro College Men was established at Howard University in May 1917 and produced over fifteen hundred names within days. Eventually a camp was established at Fort Des Moines, Iowa, which commissioned 639 Black officers on October 17, 1917. By the end of the war, over fourteen hundred African Americans had received commissions as officers. Although many found themselves in command of labor battalions, others saw combat and distinguished themselves in Europe.

577 • Racial Violence Propels the 369th Abroad

Southern racism actually propelled one regiment, the 15th New York (later the 369th Infantry in France), overseas into combat. In

October 1917 Noble Sissle, the company's drum major and later a famous composer, was beaten viciously by a proprietor of a hotel in Spartanburg, South Carolina, near where the regiment was stationed. The African American militiamen resolved to attack the hotel, but were restrained by Lieutenant James R. Europe, the bandleader, who dispersed them. Later restrained again by their commanding officer, Colonel William Hayward, the regiment's resolve to obtain justice from the town forced the War Department to send the regiment abroad to avoid further trouble. As such, early in 1918 the 369th became the first African American regiment to enter the European war, where it served in the trenches longer than any other American outfit.

578 • The 369th in France and Welcomed Home

The 369th was welcomed when it arrived in France early in 1918, since French forces were exhausted from years of battling the Germans. As part of the American Expeditionary Force, the 369th was attached to a French unit, armed with French weapons, and thrown immediately into combat. Holding off the Germans at Bois d'Hauza and fighting their way to the Rhine, the 369th recorded one of the most impressive records of any American regiment, never retreating and never surrendering any of its men to capture by the enemy. The Germans called them *blutlustige Schwarze* (bloodthirsty Blacks) because of their zealous fighting; the French saw them as saviors, and broke with the American army's tradition of not rewarding black heroism by awarding 171 of them the French Legion of Honor for their bravery. When they returned home to New York, they were given a hero's welcome as they marched down Fifth Avenue to confetti and applause.

579 • U.S. Army Tries to Export Racism

W. E. B. DuBois located an official memorandum about how the U.S. Army advised the French to "deal" with African American troops.

French Military Mission
Stationed with the American Army
August 7, 1918

SECRET INFORMATION CONCERNING BLACK AMERICAN TROOPS

Conclusion

1. We must prevent the rise of any pronounced degree of intimacy between French officers and black officers. We may be courteous and amiable with these last, but we cannot deal with them on the same plane as with white American officers without deeply wounding the latter. We must not eat with them, must not shake hands or seek to talk or meet with them outside of the requirement of military service.

2. We must not commend too highly the black American troops, particularly in the presence of Americans. It is all right to recognize their good qualities and their services, but only in moderate terms, strictly in keeping with the truth.

3. Make a point of keeping the native cantonment population from "spoiling" the Negroes. Americans become greatly incensed at any public expression of intimacy between white women and black men.... Familiarity on the part of white women with black men is furthermore a source of profound regret to our experienced colonials who see in it an overweening menace to the prestige of the white race.

Military authority cannot intervene directly in this question but it can through the civil authorities exercise some influence on the population.

580 • "Close Ranks"

Because African Americans were subjected to racial discrimination when they attempted to join Woodrow Wilson's "War to Make the World Safe for Democracy," many African Americans remained ambivalent about the war effort. W. E. B. Du Bois, editor of the *Crisis,* the journal of the NAACP, addressed the issue in his editorial "Close Ranks," published July 1918, and called on African Americans to put the war effort before their own needs.

This is the crisis of the world.... For all the long years to come men will point to the year 1918 as the great Day of Decision.... We of the colored race have no ordinary interest in the outcome. That which the German power represents today spells death to the aspirations of Negroes and all the darker races for equality, freedom and democracy. Let us not hesitate. Let us, while this war lasts, forget our special grievances and close our ranks shoulder to shoulder with our white fellow citizens.... We make no ordinary sacrifice, but we make it glad and willingly with our eyes lifted to the hills.

Afterward, Du Bois's idealism was marred by the revelation that he wrote the editorial in part to secure an army commission in military intelligence, which, fortunately, he eventually declined.

581 • African American Women

African American women played an important role in World War I. Many Black women organized camps for men about to leave for Europe. Others served as nurses in the Field Medical Supply Depot in Washington, D.C. Although African American nurses were still segregated, in operations such as the Field Medical Supply Depot they were interspersed throughout the group.

WORLD WAR II

582 • Blacks in the Military Prior to World War II

In 1939, on the eve of World War II, African Americans were underutilized and segregated in the armed forces of the United States. In the army, African Americans were restricted to four Black units that had been allowed to decline to 3,640 men. In the navy, African Americans were still segregated and served only in the galley of ships. The Marine and Army Air Corps excluded African Americans altogether. But Black protest against discriminatory treatment, Allied war propaganda against fascism, and the demands of total American mobilization to win the war forced changes in American military policy and set the stage for desegregation of the armed forces after the war.

583 • Discrimination in Mobilization Effort

Having learned from World War I that simply demonstrating their loyalty and patriotism would not automatically improve African Americans' civil rights after the war, African Americans organized protest against discrimination in the armed forces even before the United States entered World War II. In May 1939 the Committee for the Participation of Negroes in National Defense was formed, headed by Howard University history professor Rayford W. Logan and supported by the *Pittsburgh Courier* and the NAACP. The committee secured its first victory when it inserted nondiscriminatory clauses in the Selective Service Bill that passed on September 14, 1940. The bill demanded that men be drafted without regard to race (since many draft boards underrecorded African Americans), and it declared that all servicemen should receive the same training without regard to color (in response to the claim that African Americans often received substandard combat training).

584 • African Americans Challenge the President

On September 17, 1940, the Brotherhood of Sleeping Car Porters' president, A. Philip Randolph, the NAACP's executive secretary, Walter White, and the acting secretary of the National Urban League met with President Franklin Roosevelt to present a seven-point program for African Americans in the American military mobilization. Among other things, the program demanded that African Americans be trained as Army Air Corps pilots, that Black women be admitted to the Red Cross and to army and navy nurse units, and that the fighting units be desegregated. But Roosevelt refused to end segregation in the armed forces, claiming in an October 9, 1940, statement that any change would hurt the national defense. Beyond his promise to enroll Black Americans in the armed forces at a rate equal to their percentage of the population, Roosevelt merely continued World War I policy. African Americans reacted angrily and publicly to the president's statement, especially when it became known that his press secretary, Stephen Early, had lied when he claimed that Randolph and the others had approved the president's statement.

585 • Roosevelt Yields—Somewhat

In response to pressure from African Americans and Republican politicians, the Roosevelt administration made a number of concessions on Black military policy during World War II. Colonel Benjamin O. Davis was promoted to a general, plans were launched to create the first Black flying units, more African Americans were drafted into the armed forces, and William H. Hastie, the law school dean of Howard University, was made an aide to the secretary of war. An African American, Colonel Campbell C. Johnson, became an adviser to the Selective Service. Perhaps most important, Roosevelt in 1942 ordered the navy and the Marine Corps to accept African Americans into their regular military service units. Blacks would still be segregated in the navy and the marines, and confined in the navy to work in the galleys of most ships.

586 • Protest Against Induction

Some African Americans felt strongly enough about the discriminatory nature of the United States war mobilization to refuse induction. The first man to do so was Ernest Calloway, who in January 1941 wrote his Chicago draft board that he could not "accept the responsibility of taking the oath upon induction into military service under the present anti-democratic structure of the United States Army." Calloway was a member of Conscientious Objectors Against Jim Crow, organized by J. G. St. Clair Drake, which sought to establish the right of African Americans to exempt themselves from service because of segregation. Calloway, however, was jailed, and the group disintegrated. Although organized resistance to induction based on racial grounds collapsed with the entry of the United States into World War II, individuals continued to protest U.S. Army racism by refusing to be inducted. The longest and most significant battle was presented by William Lynn of New York, who refused to be inducted by arguing that the army's induction of African Americans under its "quota" system violated the Selective Service Act's prohibition against racial discrimination. In June 1942 a federal judge demanded that Lynn allow himself to be drafted before the government would hear the case. After submitting

for induction and presenting a writ of habeas corpus for his release, Lynn was denied his request to be released because the U.S. Circuit Court of Appeals ruled in February 1944 that Section 4(a) of the Selective Service Act forbade racial discrimination but not segregation! Eventually Lynn's case was argued before the Supreme Court, which declined to rule in the case because Lynn was already serving in the Pacific War. Thus, the Court avoided ruling on a case that would very likely have forced it to overturn United States military policy as a violation of the Selective Service Act.

587 • Double V for Victory Program

Most African Americans responded enthusiastically and patriotically once America entered the war. But Black leaders and newspapers abandoned the World War I strategy advocated in W. E. B. Du Bois's editorial "Close Ranks," to put aside racial activism during wartime. Instead, even the NAACP as well as more militant groups adopted a two-front approach to the war, known as the Double V campaign: African Americans would fight for victory against racism abroad and at home. Black leaders continued to fight publicly against segregation of and discrimination against African Americans even as Blacks rushed forward to serve their country.

588 • Pearl Harbor's Hero

An African American was the first American hero of World War II. When the Japanese bombed Pearl Harbor on December 7, 1941, it was Dorie Miller, a messman on the USS *Arizona,* who rose to the occasion. Coming up from the ship's galley during the attack, Miller, who had had no previous shooting practice due to the segregated nature of navy training, commandeered an antiaircraft gun on his own and shot down four Japanese airplanes before the *Arizona* sank. Miller was awarded the Navy Cross for his heroism, pinned on his chest by Admiral C. W. Nimitz, on May 27, 1942. But that was not enough to make him a navy gunner. Miller died later in World War II during the Japanese attack on the *Liscome Bay,* an aircraft carrier on which he was still working as a messman.

Poster of Doris (Dorie) Miller by David Stone Martin, 1943. National Archives

589 • The Tuskegee Airmen

The first Black pilots in the U.S. armed forces were trained at Tuskegee Institute in Alabama. Beginning on July 19, 1941, African Americans received flying instruction on Booker T. Washington's campus and, on March 7, 1942, the first cadets received their wings. Led by their commander, Colonel Benjamin O. Davis, Jr., the Tuskegee Airmen, as they were known, flew their first combat mission in North Africa on June 2, 1942, and broke a barrier against Blacks

First Lieutenant Lee Rayford of the 99th Fighter Squadron. National Archives

in aerial combat that the army had maintained since World War I. Interestingly, the Tuskegee Flight Training Program was not restricted to males: several women, most notably Willa Brown, who trained pilots later, and Janet Waterford Brogs, a registered nurse, graduated from the program.

590 • "Never Lost a Bomber"

African American pilots amassed an excellent record in World War II. They flew over fifteen thousand sorties, over fifteen hundred missions, and shot down or damaged over four hundred enemy aircraft. Perhaps the most important contribution made by Black fighter pilots was in escort missions with heavy bombers over Germany. They flew two hundred such missions without losing one American heavy bomber to enemy fighter aircraft. The 450 Black pilots of the 99th, 100th, 301st, and 302nd Fighter Squadrons, known collectively as the 332nd Fighter Group, were honored on March 24, 1945, by receiving a Presidential Unit Citation for their " 'outstanding courage, aggressiveness, and combat technique.' "

591 • Capacities of Service

Although Blacks still served in segregated and support units during World War II, many did so in a variety of jobs that drew upon a wide range of capacities in combat and behind the lines. Not only did such African Americans as Benjamin O. Davis, Jr., fly the Mustang P-51 fighter plane in Europe, but African Americans also worked in maintenance crews in Italy.

592 • Black Women Integrated

Some integration crept into the American military despite official policy to the contrary. Interestingly, African American women were more integrated than African American men in the armed forces. In army hospitals and in the Waves, African Americans participated unsegregated in some activities. These islands of integration occurred especially when the number of trainees was so small as to make it grossly inefficient to segregate and when African Americans entered services for the first time.

Right, Lieutenant Harriet Pickens and Ensign Frances Willis, 1944, the first African American Waves to be commissioned. National Archives

593 • Racial Conflicts

Rather than ensuring peace between racial groups, segregation, particularly on and around military camps in the South, was often a source of racial violence. Segregation was strictly enforced on buses that ran between army camps and neighboring towns in the South, such that Black soldiers were often forced to wait until all the whites had boarded and then ride standing up for the duration of trips from town to bases. Resistance to such southern protocols led to Black servicemen being jailed, beaten, and sometimes killed in altercations. Some studies proved that segregation had a negative effect on Black morale. While the overwhelming majority of African Americans entered the military with a strong sense of patriotism, many chafed under segregated life in the military until by the end they were, in the words of Private Bert B. Barbero "indifferent to the whole affair." Many who wrote letters commented that the "very instrument which our government has organized and built, the United States Armed Forces, to fight for world democracy, is within itself 'undemocratic.' "

594 • Some Prefer Segregation

Not surprisingly, some African American servicemen preferred not to be trained or to serve in integrated units with whites. According to a War Department survey, 38 percent of African American servicemen voiced approval of separate military units, as opposed to 36 percent who demanded integration. While some African Americans certainly preferred to be separated from whites, the polling used to register these feelings was inherently unreliable, since many probably felt compelled not to criticize existing policy or risk harassment. For example, when asked whether they believed army policy was unfair, three-fifths of African American respondents had "mixed opinions."

595 • Morale Booster

The need to raise Black morale led William Hastie to recommend that the War Department launch an educational program about Black contributions in the history of American war efforts that led to the production of the film *The Negro Soldier* (1944), by Frank Capra. The movie detailed the role of African Americans in the American Revolution, the Civil War, and World War I, among others. When the film was shown to Black and white troops in 1944, most of both groups liked the film. An index of the success of the film was that only 4 percent of the whites and 3 percent of the Black servicemen thought the film lacked veracity. While Black critics thought the film romanticized Black life in the military and white critics thought it gave too much importance to the Black role, over 80 percent thought the film

"United We Win," poster by Howard Liberman of integrated aircraft factory workers, 1943. National Archives

ought to be shown publicly. White approval ratings suggest the film was most effective at challenging the belief held by many white soldiers that African Americans historically had not been patriotic and had not contributed to the nation's defense.

596 • Labor Battalions

Despite attempts to rehabilitate the image of Blacks as patriots, army officials continued to try to confine Black troops to labor units. Although the number of Black troops rose from 97,725 in the U.S. Army in November 1941 to 504,000 in 1943, over 425,000 of these troops remained in the United States. This allocation of man- and womanpower was especially perplexing given the widespread shortage of American personnel in war zones abroad. The administration claimed that keeping African Americans at home reflected the opposition of foreign governments to Black troops, but in reality, the prejudice came more from United States overseas commanders, who discouraged attempts to send Black troops early in the war. By 1944 the need for American troops was such that some of the barriers to Black combat units began to come down.

597 • The Port Chicago Mutiny

Segregation placed African Americans at the center of the worst home-front disaster in World War II and led to the Port Chicago Mutiny. On July 17, 1944, at the U.S. Navy loading depot at Port Chicago, ammunition being loaded by African Americans exploded, blowing up the dock and two ships, the *E. A. Bryan* and the *Quinalt Victory.* Of the 320 men killed, 202 were Black enlisted men; another 390 were injured. The explosion accounted for 15 percent of all of the casualties suffered by African Americans in World War II. After the explosion, when the Black sailors, who had not been trained in ammunition loading, were ordered to resume the same work, without any change in procedures, 258 refused, citing their fear of another explo-

sion. Fifty Black sailors were court-martialed for mutiny and sentenced to fifteen years, while the other 208 were tried and sentenced for lesser charges. After the war, the men were granted amnesty, but their convictions for mutiny were not overturned, even though their case was argued by Thurgood Marshall of the NAACP Legal Defense Fund. Some good did come out of their protest: historian Robert L. Allen found that the navy changed its policy of assigning only Black sailors to this dangerous assignment, and afterward assigning white sailors as well.

598 • Blacks in Combat

Despite the policy of segregating Blacks in labor units, many African Americans did serve in combat roles during World War II. Blacks served in the artillery and mortar units. The mortar company of the 92nd Infantry Division was given credit for wiping out numerous Italian and German machine guns in the Italian campaign of the U.S. Army in November 1944.

599 • Silver Star for Bravery

African Americans won distinction for their courage under fire from the elite of the American military. On October 13, 1944, Lieutenant General George S. Patton, commander of the United States Third Army, pinned a Silver Star on Private Ernest A. Jenkins for his bravery during the fierce fighting that liberated Châteaudun, France.

600 • Battle of the Bulge

The greatest challenge to segregation came from the demands of total war against the enemy. For example, in December 1944 in what became known as the Battle of the Bulge, the Germans overran Allied positions in a desperate last attempt to win the war. Faced with a shortage of white soldiers, General Dwight D. Eisenhower, commander of the Allied forces, accepted a recommendation from General John Lee of the Communications Zone to take volunteers from Black service units. More than five thousand African Americans volunteered, many of whom were noncommissioned officers who took reductions in grade to get an opportunity to fight the Germans. Twenty-five hundred men were accepted and trained for six weeks, after which they became thirty-seven platoons that were attached to white units. Such troops fought with valor until the end of the war in 1945; but even in this emergency, the

Black mortar company of the 92nd Infantry Division liquidates several German machine-gun nests near Massa, Italy, c. November 1944. National Archives

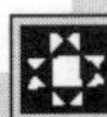

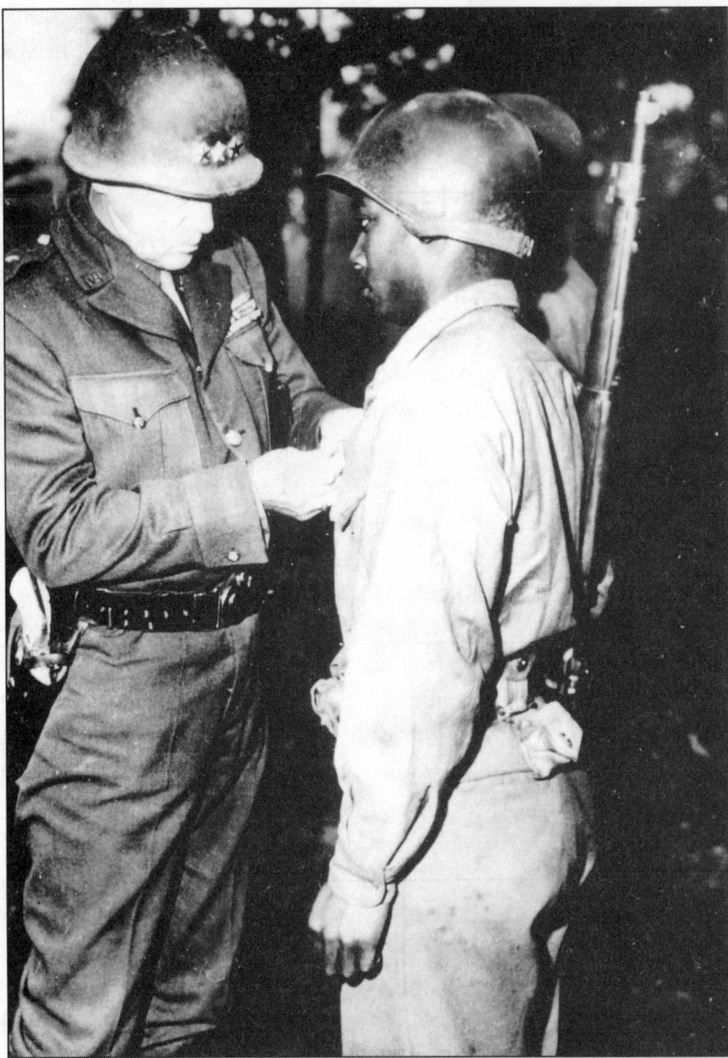

Lieutenant General George Patton pins Silver Star on Private Ernest Jenkins. National Archives

army rather awkwardly maintained its segregation policy by segregating African Americans into platoons of forty men that were "attached" to companies of two hundred white men.

601 • Black Ships!

The navy found an interesting way to maintain segregation toward the end of the war when the demands of total war dictated a wider use of Black seamen than simply in the ship's galley. A Special Programs Unit in the Bureau of Naval Personnel suggested that the navy staff entire ships with African Americans. In 1944 two ships, the USS *Mason* and PC 1264, the attack submarine, sailed with all-Black crews. On June 3 of that year, the SS *Harriet Tubman* was launched.

602 • Change at Navy

Much of the navy's zeal for segregation derived from Secretary of Navy Frank Knox, who was a staunch segregationist. His death in 1944 brought the considerably more humane James Forrestal to the helm at the navy. Forrestal established a program to integrate twenty-five ships. He then integrated the auxiliary fleet. In 1945 the Special Programs Unit concluded that integration made for a more effective fighting navy. Restrictions on African Americans in the navy would end in 1947, but the service would not be integrated until 1949.

People

603 • Benjamin Oliver Davis, Sr. (1877–1970)

Benjamin Oliver Davis was a dedicated soldier whose military career extended from the

Spanish-American War to World War II. Davis left Howard University in 1898 to join the army and fight in the Spanish-American War. He also fought in the Philippines and served in World War I. Partly in response to mounting criticism of its segregated army policy, the Roosevelt administration appointed Davis a brigadier general in 1940, the first Black man to become a general in the U.S. Army. He served in France during World War II.

604 • Benjamin Oliver Davis, Jr. (b. 1912)

Perhaps the most important of the Tuskegee Airmen was Benjamin O. Davis, Jr., who attended West Point, where he survived four years of "silencing" and from which he graduated in 1936, to become captain of the 99th Pursuit Squadron, the "Tuskegee Experiment." After personally supervising the training of the airmen at Tuskegee, Davis and his fliers were stationed on Sicily in June 1943, when they began to fly defense for American bombers. In September 1943 Davis left the 99th to begin organizing a new, larger flying unit, the 332nd Fighter Group in the United States. To do that, Davis had to make several presentations to military brass to disprove vicious, inaccurate rumors that the 99th had not performed well. Once the record of the 99th was vindicated, the 332nd Fighter Group and the 99th joined forces in escorting bombers over Germany from Italy. His success in those missions earned Davis the Distinguished Flying Cross.

605 • Estine Cowner

The demand for qualified labor in World War II opened up new opportunities for African American women to serve their country in industrial jobs previously closed to them. One of the women who experienced a radical change in her job description was Estine Cowner, a former waitress, who became a scaler on a construction crew at the Kaiser shipyards in Richmond, California, to construct the Liberty ship *George Washington Carver.* The Carver was launched on May 7, 1943.

606 • Warren Capers

African Americans were present when American forces landed on the coast of France on D-Day, August 18, 1944. One of the most important was Private Warren Capers. As a member of a medical detachment, Capers established a dressing station and treated more than 330 soldiers that day. This heroic devotion to wounded soldiers led his superiors to recommend him for a Silver Star.

General Benjamin O. Davis Sr. National Archives

Estine Cowner. National Archives

Josephine Baker sings the national anthem in the Municipal Theater, Oran, Algeria, May 17, 1943. National Archives

Warren Capers. National Archives

607 • African American Celebrities

Numerous African American celebrities, sports heroes, and entertainers lent their support to the war effort. In addition to the boxer Joe Louis, who joined the army, and Paul Robeson, who made numerous singing and public appearances, the internationally renowned singer and actress Josephine Baker helped build African support for the Allies by singing the national anthem on May 17, 1943, as the finale to her show in the Municipal Theater, Oran, Algeria.

KOREAN WAR

Engagements and Policy

608 • The Changing Military

Although Franklin Delano Roosevelt has been hailed as a liberal American president, it was Harry Truman, who became president when Roosevelt died in April 1945, who instituted substantial racial change in the American military following World War II. In 1946 Truman established the Committee on Equality of Treatment and Opportunity in the Armed Services, which recommended in its 1947 report, "To Secure These Rights," the elimination of segregation and discrimination within the military. Faced with unlikely reelection in 1948, Truman took the dramatic step of issuing Executive Order 9981, which called for equal treatment and opportunities for all armed services personnel. Despite these orders and recommendations, full integration of African Americans in the United States Army occurred slowly. Two years after Executive Order 9981, for example, the first African American troops sent to Korea still went in segregated units. But when North Korean attacks substantially reduced the forces of several all-white regiments, African American soldiers were sent in as replacements. By mid-1951, over 20 percent of the African American soldiers in Korea were assigned to integrated units.

609 • Black Troops in the Korean War

The oldest African American infantry, the 24th Regiment, spearheaded the first victory of American forces in Korea. Arriving in Korea on July 13, 1950, the unit, which was part of the 25th Army Division, saw its first action within a week. On July 20 the 24th led a successful drive to recapture Yechon, a vital transportation center overtaken by the North Korean Army. The regiment's victory improved morale for both Black and white troops, and was acknowledged in the *Congressional Record* "for shaming us out of our fears. They demonstrated, the hard way, their faith in a certain cause that has no room for the ignorance and selfishness of racism and bigotry." In later battles, soldiers reportedly yelled "Remember Yechon" as they attacked the enemy.

610 • Removal of Douglas MacArthur Speeds Integration

One of the greatest impediments to army integration was eliminated when President Truman removed for insubordination General Douglas MacArthur, an opponent of integrated forces, from his command of American forces in April 1951. MacArthur was replaced by Lieutenant General Matthew Ridgeway, who immediately sought to integrate every unit. Although Ridgeway's actions were publicly decried by several white southern congressmen, by July 1953, 90 percent of the African Americans serving in

Private Edward Wilson, 24th Infantry, wounded in action near front lines in Korean War. National Archives

Korea were assigned to integrated units. The air force and Marine Corps also integrated their forces during this period, but the navy did not take similar steps until the 1960s.

VIETNAM

Engagements and Policy

611 • Project 100,000

At the beginning of the Vietnam War, African Americans comprised 10 percent of the armed forces, but few served as officers. In 1967, for example, Blacks accounted for 10 percent of the U.S. Marine Corps, but less than 1 percent of the Marine Corps's officers. Throughout the war, the U.S. government tried to control the burgeoning Black Power movement by drafting or recruiting those African Americans to whom the Black nationalist message would most appeal. In mid-1966, for example, the Defense Department launched Project 100,000, aimed at reducing the high rejection rate of African Americans. Billed as a way to "rehabilitate" impoverished or wayward applicants, the project allowed recruitment offices to accept applicants with criminal records or other liabilities for which they would have traditionally been disqualified. The program is credited with supplying over 340,000 new recruits for Vietnam, 40 percent of whom were African Americans. The promised rehabilitation and training failed to materialize, however, as financial difficulties beset the program, and many of the Project 100,000 recruits ultimately saw more extensive combat duty than regular recruits.

612 • Black Opposition to the Vietnam War

Martin Luther King, Jr., strongly opposed the Vietnam War, and after 1965 he worked vigorously to persuade other civil rights leaders and the American public that the conflict was morally wrong. On April 4, 1967, King made a famous antiwar speech at Riverside Church in New York City and led a huge antiwar rally a few days later. King's firm stance caused discomfort among some in the Civil Rights Movement who feared his opposition would create an unwanted backlash or divert attention away from their cause. Other prominent African Americans opposed to the war included Julian Bond, who was denied his seat in the Georgia legislature because of his antiwar views until the courts ordered him seated, and Muhammad Ali, who argued he "had no quarrel" with the Viet Cong. As a Muslim, Ali claimed exemption from military service based on his religious beliefs, but he was convicted of draft evasion, stripped of his boxing title, and sentenced to five years in prison.

People

613 • Medal of Honor Man

Even though the Vietnam War was controversial, African Americans still served bravely and with distinction. This was certainly the case with Clifford C. Sims, a staff sergeant in Vietnam. On patrol with his men during the battle for Hue in 1968, Sergeant Sims heard an ominous click—the sound made by a tripped booby-trap bomb. Without hesitation, Sims leaped onto the bomb to shield his men from the blast. The explosion killed him, and he was awarded the Congressional Medal of Honor posthumously for having given his life to save his men.

Staff Sergeant Clifford Sims, who died saving the lives of his men near Hue, Vietnam. U.S. Army

614 • Colin L. Powell (b. 1937)

It was in Vietnam that Colin Powell won distinction as a hero. Born in Harlem to Jamaican parents, Colin attended the City College of New York, where he enrolled in the Reserve Officers' Training Corps (ROTC). After graduating in 1958, Powell entered the army and Ranger training and later served as a platoon commander in Germany. After becoming a captain, Powell was transferred to Vietnam. On patrol with

General Colin Powell. U.S. Army

his men one day, Colin stepped on a punji stake, a sharpened stick hidden in holes in rice paddies, and was severely injured. In spite of tremendous pain, Powell continued to lead his men to their destination, where they were needed to reinforce other troops. For his persistence and devotion to duty, he was awarded the Bronze Star. After a brief return to the United States, during which he enrolled in the Command and General Staff College at Fort Leavenworth, Kansas, Powell returned to Vietnam. While serving as an operations chief for the Americal Division, Powell again showed his bravery when a helicopter he and his men were flying in crashed in the Vietnam jungle. Being the only member of the craft not to be knocked unconscious by the crash, Powell, with "complete disregard for his own safety, and while injured himself," dragged his injured fellow soldiers from the smoldering craft. For this act of courage, he received the Soldier's Medal. In 1989 Powell became the first African American to be selected Chairman of the Joint Chiefs of Staff, and he orchestrated the successful Operation Desert Storm in 1990. He retired from the army in 1993, published his autobiography, *My American Journey,* in September 1995, and declined to be a candidate for any political office in 1996 at a graceful November 1995 news conference.

Quotation

615 • Return from Vietnam

Those brave soldiers that did make it back from Vietnam did not receive a hero's welcome. African American soldiers, in particular, returned to find that surviving combat on behalf of their country had done little to improve their status. Specialist 4 Richard J. Ford III, who served with the 25th Infantry Division of the army in 1967–68, described his experiences after he was wounded:

You know, they decorated me in Vietnam. Two Bronze Stars. The whiteys did. I was wounded three times. The officers, the generals, and whoever else came out to the hospital to see you. They respected you and pat you on the back. They said, "You brave. And you courageous. You America's finest. America's best." Back in the States the same officers that pat me on the back wouldn't even speak to me. They wanted that salute, that attention, 'til they holler at ease. I didn't get the respect that I thought I was gonna get. . . . They just wanted another black in the field. Uncle Sam, he didn't give me no justice. You had a job to do, you did it, you home. Back where you started. They didn't even ask me to reenlist.

PERSIAN GULF WAR

Engagements and Policy

616 • African American Participation in the Gulf War

The Persian Gulf War helped publicize the disproportionate representation of African Americans serving in the armed forces, especially in combat positions. Led by General Colin Powell, the first African American to chair the Joint Chiefs of Staff, African Americans comprised 25 percent of the troops deployed in the Persian Gulf, yet accounted for only 13 percent of the U.S. population. During the war, many African Americans pointed to these statistics as evidence that career and educational opportunities for young African Americans in American society are still too limited. According to this argument, rather than serving out of a sense of patriotism, many African Americans are forced to consider military service because it is one of the few ways to acquire adequate training or financial support. In times of conflict, then, such as the Persian Gulf War, African Americans disproportionately risk their lives because of economic necessity.

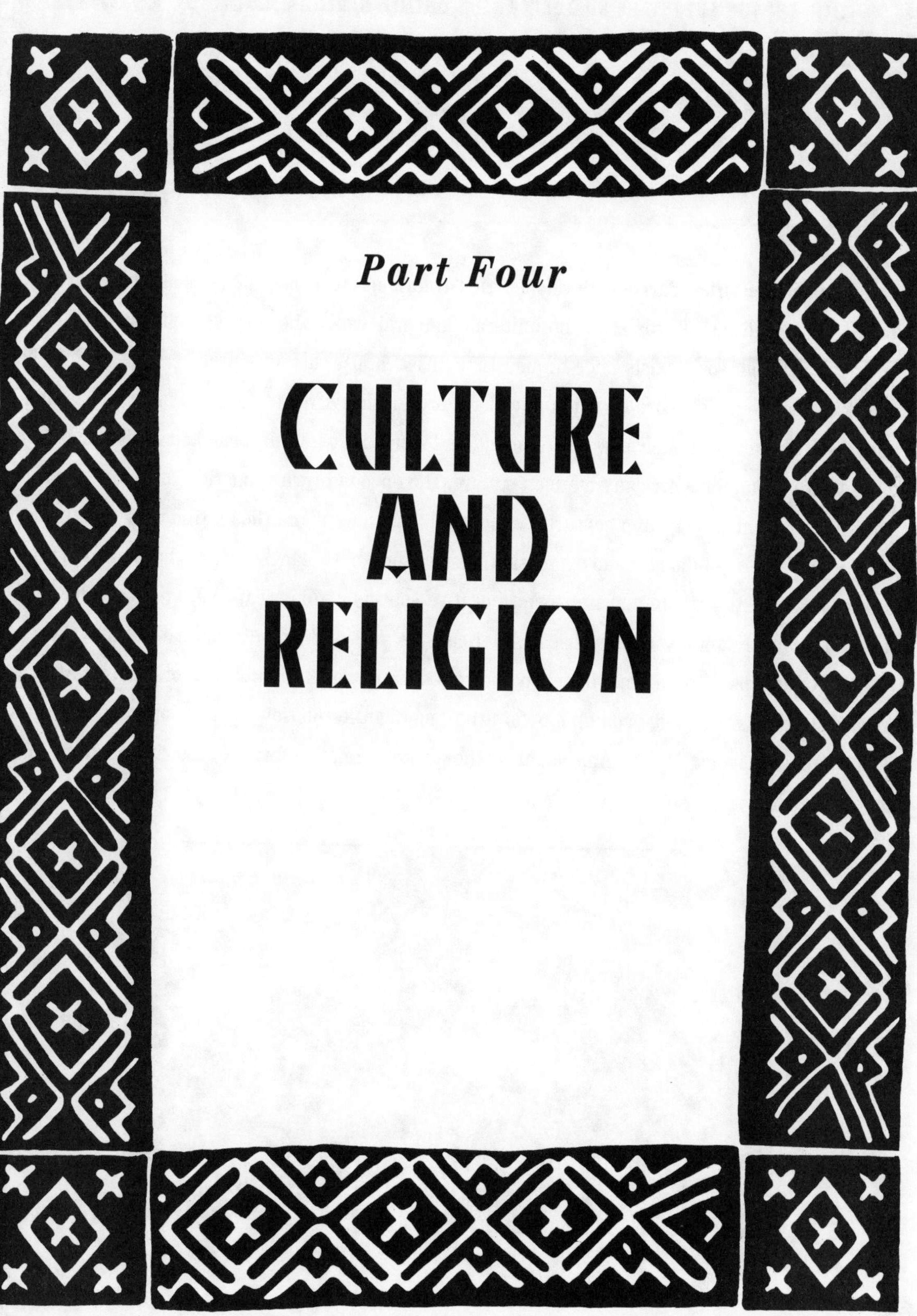

Part Four

CULTURE AND RELIGION

Over the centuries, Africans developed rich traditions in music, dance, sculpture, weaving, mask making, and verbal expression, both literate and oral, which they brought with them to North America. Although sociologists once argued that Africans lost this ancestral heritage during the "shock of enslavement," more recent studies have proven that Africans retained much of that heritage, used it to adapt to their new environment, and melded it with European and Native American forms to create a unique African American culture. The encounter with America, of course, exposed Africans to racism, slavery, and centuries of cultural degradation and thus introduced new themes into African American thought and expression. Generations of African Americans have utilized their culture to contest, satirize, and transcend negative aspects of American life, and some have attempted to win greater respect for African Americans because of their cultural vitality. But while European Americans have often mimicked, borrowed from, and otherwise appropriated African American expressive styles, beginning before the American Revolution, such "adoptions" have seldom resulted in seeing African Americans as the pivotal formative force in American culture that they have been.

Domino Players, 1943. Horrace Pippin (1888–1946). Courtesy of the Phillips Collection, Washington, D.C.

FROM AFRICA TO COLONIAL AMERICA, 1619–1770

Music and Dance

617 • Band and Concert Tradition of African Societies

Music was an integral part of rites, festivals, and ceremonies in West African societies, especially for dignitaries. After Thomas Edward Bowditch led a group of explorers to Africa to meet the king of the Ashanti, he reported:

. . . more than a hundred bands burst at once on our arrival, [all playing] the peculiar airs of their several chiefs; the horns flourished their defiances [i.e., fanfare melodies], with the beating of innumerable drums and metal instruments, and then yielded for a while to the soft breathings of their long flutes, which were truly harmonious; and a pleasing instrument, like a bagpipe without the drone, was happily blended. . . .

He also noted that "the drummers threw their 'white-washed drums' into the air and caught them again, 'with much agility and grimace,' as they walked along." Bowditch's recollections show the origins not only of the long tradition of African American marching bands and folk music but also the music of African American concert tradition, which is often commissioned for special occasions.

618 • Dance in Africa

The English explorer John Barbot recalled African dances he observed on the coast of Nigeria:

Their dances are commonly in a round, singing the next thing that occurs, whether sense or nonsense. Some of them stand in the middle of the ring, holding one hand on their head, and the other behind their waist, advancing and strutting out their belly forwards, and beating very hard with their feet on the ground. Others clap their hands to the noise of a kettle, or a calabash fitted for a musical instrument.

John Barbot, visiting a West African king, from Awnsham Churchill's *A Collection of Voyages and Travels, Some Now First Printed from Original Manuscripts* (1704; London, 1732). Courtesy of Henry E. Huntington Library, San Marino, California

619 • Dancing on Ships

Sometimes the Africans' love of dance was used against them. In some cases, they were tricked into bondage by being asked to dance on European ships docked off the coast of Africa. This request, often with the promise of pay, was usually made just before the ship was to depart. Once the ship set sail, Africans would be forced to dance, in a practice called "dancing the slaves," reputedly for health reasons. Dr. Thomas

Trotter, the surgeon assigned to the *Brookes* on its 1783 voyage, recalled that after the morning meal every day, "those who were in irons were ordered to stand up and make what motions they could, leaving a passage for such as were out of irons to dance around the deck." Often, it was difficult to make those in chains dance, so the crew would frequently whip the slaves.

620 • The Atlantic Tradition of Dance

Traditional African dances crossed the Atlantic with the slave trade, landed in the Caribbean, and flourished. Generally, African culture met with less overt opposition from the white planter class in the Caribbean than on the mainland of North America and was able to maintain itself more freely and for a longer time in the West Indies. Conditions of life in West Indian slavery—absentee white ownership of plantations, consequently a low level of concern by whites about the recreational activities of the slaves, frequent arrivals of new Africans due to the higher mortality rate of slaves in the West Indies, and the numerical superiority of Blacks over whites—aided the retention of African culture. Although different African peoples preferred particular dance traditions, four major dances were widespread in the Caribbean. The *calenda,* performed by several couples who circled one another, was a shuffling advance and retreat between partners, who moved mainly with their hips. The *chica* involved mainly the rotation of the hips while the rest of the body was immobilized. The *bamboula,* likely an offshoot of the *chica,* was named after the bamboula drum and performed by a couple inside of a ring. The *juba* was a dance of competition and skill, in which a woman, moving slowly with shuffling feet and contorted limbs, challenged several men to enter the ring and best her dancing, often with the result that they retired exhausted. Although such dances flourished in the West Indies—and drew African American choreographers such as Katherine Dunham to the islands to study them in the 1930s—some variations of them made it to North America. The *chica* spread with the West Indian migration to New Orleans, while the *juba* was danced in selected areas of the southern United States.

621 • Music and Dances for the Masters

Although African American musicians were rarely known nationwide in the seventeenth century, they did perform regularly within the slave quarters and at the plantation owners' homes, also known as the Big Houses. When guests visited plantations, masters often summoned slaves to play music and dance. On these occasions, certain dances were considered appropriate entertainment for the "white folks." The *buck-and-wing* was often performed on such occasions, the "wing" sometimes referred to as the *pigeon wing.* In this dance, slaves flapped their arms and legs, and held the head and neck stiff, like a bird. Some slaves performed the *Irish jig* so well as to be entered in contests with the slaves of other masters. The *cakewalk,* in which couples walked on a straight path with sharp, precise turns, was often danced by slaves at harvesttime. Its name derived from the tradition on some plantations where the mistress would award a cake as a prize to the couple who danced the best. Some learned to play music and dance so well that they were allowed to teach others and to participate in parades for events such as 'Lection Day, a carryover from the days before captivity, in which slaves chose their own officials.

622 • Dirty Dancing

Some dances were considered too risqué to be performed in front of the masters and thus

were generally confined to private occasions in the slave quarters. One dance considered particularly primitive was the *ring dance,* which resembled the Congo dances of West Indians. Following a circular path, slaves danced individually in an animated shuffle that vibrated the entire body. Another popular dance was the *buzzard lope,* an animal dance that retained African tradition and sought to represent the behavior of a turkey buzzard "carrying on" about a hen. The *water dance* was performed by slaves who danced while carrying a bucket or glass of water on their heads. This dance looked back to the Africans' tradition of carrying goods on their heads. The West Indian juba became known as the *djouba* in the United States and was a secular dance in which participants "patted" out the juba by clapping, slapping one's chest, thighs, or legs when drums were prohibited. The djouba became the renowned *hambone* dance in modern times.

623 • House Servants' Dances

Caste divisions existed among slaves in the South and were reflected in the kinds of dances that the house servants would perform. Given that the house servants on large plantations in the South often thought of themselves as superior to the field servants, these domestic servants performed dances that integrated West African dance elements with steps from the English square dances and the French quadrille. In New Orleans and Charleston, house servants (and the free persons of color who occupied the "brown societies" of those cities) held balls and cotillions where such "dignified" dancing as the *figure dance* and the *sixteen-figure dance* were popular.

The Old Plantation, watercolor by unknown artist, c. 1800. Courtesy of Abby Aldrich Rockefeller Folk Art Center, Williamsburg, Virginia

624 • Masters' Ambivalence Toward Dancing

While some masters believed that encouraging dance among their slaves was an effective way to keep them happy and contented, other masters refused to allow slaves to hold such dances on their plantations. Some of these masters allowed their slaves to travel to other plantations for dances, but others would not—a restriction that posed difficulties for slaves who enjoyed dancing. Some slaves, however, found ingenious ways to surmount these obstacles. In 1937 a former plantation slave interviewed by the Alabama Writers' Project recalled that

young Massa told Tom . . . one time not to go to de frolic. . . . Tom said "Yassuh" but Marse Nep watch Tom th'oo de do' and atter while Tom slip out and awy he went, wid young Massa right 'hin' him. He got dere and foun' Tom cuttin' groun' shuffle big as anybody. Young Massa called him, "Tom," he say, "Tom, didn't I tell you you couldn't come to dis frolic?" "Yassuh," says Tom, "you sho' did, and I jes' come to tell 'em I couldn't come!"

625 • Alternatives to Drums

Like their West Indian neighbors, southern whites generally prohibited slaves from playing drums, because drums were believed to be used to send signals during a revolt. This prohibition became widespread in the South after the Stono Rebellion in 1739 when Angolan slaves beat drums as they moved through the South Carolina countryside murdering whites. Because of the prohibition, African Americans developed other percussive instruments on which to play. Patting knees, arms, backs, and heads, hand clapping, clinking of spoons, and "playing the bones" became alternative ways for slaves to beat out the time at dances or while generally passing the time on the plantation.

The Bone Player, 1856. Museum of Fine Arts, Boston. Bequest of Martha C. Karolik for the M. and M. Karolik Collection of American Paintings, 1815–65

626 • Coastal Drums

Despite its general prohibition, use of drums did persist in the coastal areas of Georgia, where slaves lived at great distances from one another and from disapproving whites, and in a social environment in which other African-influenced traditions, such as the Gullah language, also survived. Drum use could also be found in parts of Louisiana, because of the nineteenth-century migration of large numbers of West Indian slaves who had been able to practice drum playing in the Caribbean. Both West Indians and native-born African Americans generally made drums by stretching rawhide over one end of hollow logs.

627 • Line Singing

The practice of "line singing" came from the Dutch Reformed Church in colonial New York, where in 1645 church law decreed that the precentor "tune the psalm" for congregational

singing. The precentor chanted one or two lines at a time, ended it on a definite pitch, and the congregation followed the precentor's lead with the singing of the same line. This practice became the distinctive feature of African American hymn singing.

628 • Banjar

The "banjar," or banjo, was an African contribution to American music in the eighteenth century. Thomas Jefferson commented on the banjo in his *Notes on Virginia* and acknowledged that it had been "brought hither from Africa, and . . . is the original of the guitar, its chords being precisely the four lower chords of the guitar."

629 • Fiddle

Because masters encouraged its use, the fiddle was probably the most popular instrument played by the slaves in the eighteenth and nineteenth centuries. Some owners purchased fiddles for their slaves to play, hired out talented fiddle players for profit to other slave owners or public functions, and paid more money for slaves who could play the instrument. Such demand was a factor in the enslavement of Solomon Northrop, a free Black man from the North, who was captured and sold into slavery. That African Americans were proficient at fiddle (or violin) playing is attested by the slave orchestras formed in the South, comprised largely of fiddlers and supplemented with tambourine or bones players. Some women fiddlers existed as well. One fiddler, an enslaved woman named Clarinda, was cited by missionaries in the middle of the eighteenth century for having learned the violin, eschewed Christian piety, and played for men and women dancers on the first day of each week.

630 • Whites Act Black

Although Thomas Rice is often credited as the first American white man to perform in Black character on the American stage in 1828, the truth is that white Americans in blackface had been performing on the stage from before the American Revolution. In 1767 the *New York Journal* ran an announcement of a performance by a Mr. Bayly and a Mr. Tea on April 14: at the end of the third part of the performance, Mr. Tea (perhaps the original Mr. T?) offered to the audience a "*Negro Dance, In Character.*" A white woman appeared on stage in Boston on November 25, 1796, and performed "*A Comic Dance, In Character of a Female Negro.*" A year earlier, the first portrayal of the African American in a serious American drama, *The Triumph of Love,* graced the American stage, containing a "shuffling, cacklin, allegedly comic Negro servant." Ironically the birth of an American political identity coincided with the emergence of a need among American whites to denigrate African American characters through a caricature of Black dance.

Art

631 • African Craft Tradition in the United States

Enslavement destroyed many African artistic traditions, because it rendered obsolete the production of ceremonial masks, throne stools, and musical instruments for kings and rulers by village artists. But the shortage of craftsmen in the colonies created a demand for talented Africans to express their aesthetic sensibilities in pottery, cloth, wood, metal, and architectural production. Some slave owners recruited Africans specifically as artisans rather than agricultural laborers, and profited from their

skill under a hiring-out system that rented artisan slaves to white craftsmen. Some enslaved artisans even profited under such a system, moved up from apprentices to journeymen to master craftsmen, and even purchased their freedom in some cases. By the mid-eighteenth century Africans dominated crafts production in such colonies as Maryland, Georgia, South Carolina, and Louisiana.

632 • Personal-Use Artifacts

When slave artisans from West Africa were not working for their masters, they often adorned everyday objects with designs and forms of aesthetic and spiritual significance. The so-called grotesque jugs in slave pottery and the dramatic, carved-wood grave markers are forms that resemble similar objects in West Africa and serve spiritual purposes in North America. Faces on jugs or markers on graves were often designed to frighten away evil spirits.

Folklore, Language, and Literature

633 • African American Folklore

Africans brought to America a body of folklore in the form of humor, poetry, proverbs, and stories that were handed down from generation to generation, but also changed over time to incorporate numerous aspects of the American experience. Satire about the ways and foibles of masters, commentary about the love and marriage relations on the plantation, and slave wisdom of the type that would later be collected in the nineteenth century abounded in African American communities of the seventeenth and eighteenth centuries.

634 • Gullah and Other Pidgin Languages

In all of the southern colonies, the constant importation of Africans via the slave trade brought diverse peoples who spoke different languages into close proximity on plantations. Several generations of Africans continued to see the world through an African worldview and to call objects by their African names and could speak in unadulterated African languages. But most first- and certainly second-generation Africans developed a pidgin language made up of elements from several African languages and English. That process of pidginization began in Africa when speakers from different language groups were thrown together while they awaited deportation to America. It continued and increased once Africans reached colonial North America. In some colonies, such as South Carolina, where Africans were a majority for most of the eighteenth century, such pidginization resulted in Africans developing a distinctive New World language, Gullah, which has survived into the twentieth century.

635 • Koran-Reading Slaves

From 1711 and lasting into the nineteenth century, Muslims, sometimes referred to as Mandingoes, became more numerous in the Atlantic slave trade. These Africans brought with them a literate culture, as reading the Koran was essential to worship. In the 1730s, for example, Job Ben Solomon, the prince of Boudou in the land of Futa, lived as a slave for two years in Maryland. Then, after he wrote a letter in Arabic to his father and it came to the attention of Sir Hans Sloane, an Oxford don, a process began that resulted in Solomon's freedom and return to Africa. Yarrow Mamount was another Muslim who had been kidnaped in Africa and brought to the United States. He purchased his freedom,

Portrait of Yarrow Mamount by Charles Willson Peale. The Historical Society of Pennsylvania

lived to be over a hundred years, and had his portrait painted by the artist Charles Wilson Peale.

Religion

636 • West African Religion

West Africans brought to America a variety of religious beliefs and practices, some of which were shared despite the diversity of African peoples who came to America. One belief was that spirits could take possession of individuals and could be embodied in charms. In the early colonial period, African Americans buried charms with the dead to ensure that the ancestors, some of the most powerful spirits, would not be angered as they passed into the next world. African Americans who also believed in a supreme God continued their West African burial practices well into the nineteenth century. Funeral rites involved a long period of mourning and great feasting as Africans believed that upon dying one went "home." Such a view of death may have accounted for the frequency of attempted suicides on the journey to America.

637 • First Baptized

The first African child baptized in English America was christened William in the Church of England at Jamestown in 1624. By the English law of the colony in effect at that time, that child became free with the baptism.

638 • Cotton Mather and the First Black Church Service

In 1693 the first recorded church service for Black slaves occurred in Massachusetts. Cotton Mather, a Puritan clergyman, responded to a request from slaves for guidance and produced *Rules for the Society of Negroes* for their benefit. Later Mather published *The Negro Christianized* (1701). In this, he chastised masters who were reluctant to offer religious training to

Cotton Mather. Prints and Photographs Division, Library of Congress

their slaves: "You deny your *Master in Heaven* if you do nothing to bring your Servants into the Knowledge and Service of that glorious Master." However, as he was a slaveholder, he believed that Christianity helped them accept their lot in life and become more obedient slaves: "that is God who has caused them to be *Servants,* and that they serve Jesus Christ, while they are at work for their *Masters.*"

639 • Society for the Propagation of the Gospel in Foreign Parts

Established by the Church of England in 1701 to aid the growth of the church in the colonies, the Society for the Propagation of the Gospel in Foreign Parts focused religious instruction on Blacks and Indians. Many planters resisted, as they already allotted their slaves the Sabbath day to tend to their personal chores, such as planting and harvesting food for their own families; the planters had no intention of allowing slaves additional time off. In an effort to persuade the slaveholders to provide religious education for their slaves, the SPG distributed pamphlets indicating that Christian training would convince slaves to be obedient and accept their lot in life: "Scripture, far from making an alteration in Civil Rights, expressly directs that every man abide in the condition wherein he is called, with great indifference of mind concerning outward circumstances." The SPG cited Ephesians 6:5, "Servants, be obedient to them that are your masters," ad nauseam. Slaves were also required to recite the following oath:

You declare in the presence of God and before his congregation that you do not ask for the Holy Baptism out of any design to free yourself from the duty and obedience you owe to your masters while you live; but merely for the good of your soul and to partake of the grace and blessings promised to the members of the Church of Christ.

640 • The First Great Awakening

It was not until the Great Awakening, which began in the 1730s and climaxed in the 1740s, that large numbers of African Americans were baptized in the English colonies. John and Charles Wesley, who were responsible for founding the Methodist faith in England, traveled to southern colonies in the 1730s to revive religious consciousness and especially to convert African Americans. The Great Awakening rejected the established church, resurrected the notion that anyone could experience God's grace, and stressed the egalitarian nature of Christianity. As such, it rejected the tendency of American Protestantism to avoid conversion of Blacks and Indians. Methodism held that being a Christian was a disposition of the heart, rather than of the head, and thus undermined not only the learned clergy in America but also the intellectual racism that decreed Blacks and Indians were not smart enough to be Christians. The Great Awakening drew many Blacks into white churches for the first time, allowed "called ministry," including Blacks, to preach, and fostered some of the first integrated churches in America.

641 • Black Harry (?–1810)

One of the men most responsible for the spread of Methodism in the United States was Black Harry (Harry Hosier), a close personal assistant of Francis Asbury, the man who increased by 150 percent the number of Methodists in the United States. Sent by Charles Wesley from England in 1771, Asbury took such long and arduous journeys across the United States that the white preacher often broke down under the strain. Asbury turned

many of the preaching duties over to Black Harry, including the giving of sermons. Black Harry became one of the most popular draws on the camp meeting circuit of the Great Awakening because of his excellent preaching and rapport with the audiences.

642 • Religious Separatism

An African American desire for religious autonomy and cultural self-determination led to the founding of the first Black churches in the South. These separatists, or Baptists, planted the idea of separate and independent congregations of southern Blacks who saw religion as a way to establish their own social independence. Based on plantation congregations, the first southern Black churches emerged in Virginia and South Carolina.

643 • Black Catholicism

Black Catholicism was established in 1724 by Governor M. Bienville of Louisiana, who encouraged masters to educate and baptize their slaves in the Catholic tradition. Catholicism among slaves had its greatest success in Louisiana and Maryland, states that had sizable Catholic populations before large numbers of slaves had arrived. But even in these states, Catholicism did not flourish among African Americans as it did among slaves elsewhere in the hemisphere. Most notably, the nature of Catholicism—its rituals (difficult for the uninitiated to comprehend), the exclusive nature of its priesthood, and its lessened reliance on the Bible as primary authority—weakened its appeal. Only in the twentieth century did large numbers of African Americans move toward Catholicism.

REVOLUTIONARY AWAKENING, 1760–1820

Movements and Organizations

644 • African American Enlightenment

A generation of African American writers, artists, petitioners, and inventors born around the middle of the eighteenth century produced the first recorded African American intellectual movement. To varying degrees, these thinkers fashioned Protestant Christianity, Enlightenment rationalism, and the revolutionary ideology of equality of opportunity into an argument that Africans were fully human, possessed of all of the human faculties, including reason and the higher emotions, and lacked civilization only because of being forced to live as slaves. This generation believed that displays of ability in literature, the arts, and the sciences would prove that Africans deserved the rights accorded to other American citizens in the new republic. However, Enlightenment African Americans were not glued to one path to freedom. While some, like the slave-born poets Jupiter Hammon and Phillis Wheatley, accommodated to slavery and assimilated Anglo-American traditions and practices, others, like the Black petitioners, used republican ideology to demand their rights as citizens in the new nation. Some, like Richard Allen and Absalom Jones, eschewed remaining in increasingly segregated white churches after the Revolution and established independent churches and fraternal associations that were called African by name. Others, like Prince Hall, first allied with British institutions and then

contemplated expatriation from America. Perhaps what was most striking about this generation was its giving voice, unequivocally, to the humanity of African people and their right to be treated with human dignity and respect like other American citizens.

645 • Black Masons Movement

On March 6, 1776, Prince Hall, a well-respected African American, and fourteen other African Americans joined the Masons fraternal organization that was part of a Boston British regiment. After fighting broke out at Lexington and the British soldiers evacuated Boston, Hall and his men retained their permit to have a lodge. Prince Hall may have seen in the Masons the possibility of unity and of support for Black self-determination from the British. In January 1777 Hall would be among eight African Americans who petitioned for the abolition of slavery by citing the need to restore "the Natural Right of all men." After the war, "African Lodge No. 1, Dedicated to St. John," applied for and received a charter in 1787, with Prince Hall as the master. That same year, Hall sent a petition to the general court of Boston to provide "Africans . . . one day in a week to work for themselves" to purchase themselves and transport themselves "to some part of the Coast of Africa, where we propose a settlement." This petition of emigration to Africa was written almost a quarter of a century before Paul Cuffee's voyage to Sierra Leone.

646 • African Union Society

In the fall of 1789 African Americans in Newport, Rhode Island, joined together to ensure their security in the new nation by forming the African Union Society. In one sense, this institution was designed to preserve the identity of the Black community by keeping records of births, deaths, marriages, lawsuits, and diaries and to provide references and opportunities for employment for the Black citizenry. It was also an organization committed to improvement of the character of African Americans by encouraging them to adopt "good conduct" as the best way for Blacks to raise the esteem of the group in the eyes of the nation.

647 • Literary Society Movement

Free African Americans in the North during the early nineteenth century founded literary and improvement societies in order to elevate the moral and intellectual condition of free Blacks. Separate intellectual institutions, often supported by and based in separate Black churches, were required because African Americans were excluded from participation in benevolent societies and public libraries in the North. Hence, such groups as the Reading Room Society, founded in 1828, collected books, sponsored debates, hosted musical programs and poetry readings, and presented lectures in which a popular history of Africa was invoked to inspire African American achievement.

648 • African Grove Theater Company

Established in 1820 in New York City by James Hewlett, America's first Black tragic actor, the African Grove Theater Company, at Grove and Bleecker Streets in New York, performed Shakespearean plays before African American and white audiences. Hewlett, a West Indian, built an audience for the Grove Theater by acting and singing for parties in homes of the upper classes of New York. Reacting against the segregated audience policy at New York's Park Theater, Hewlett founded the African Grove Theater as a space in which African Americans could present and see such plays as *Richard III* without segregation, and receive training in the dramatic arts. Unfortunately the African Com-

pany performed at a time of increasing white working-class hostility toward educated African Americans as "uppity" and English plays as "aristocratic." African Grove Theater performances were negatively reviewed by the press, disrupted by white hoodlums, and shut down by police, who arrested actors for allegedly causing disturbances. Eventually this abuse destroyed the African Company and convinced Ira Aldridge, who studied at the African Grove Theater, that his future as a serious actor lay in Europe and not America.

Some Important Books and Poems

649 • *An Evening Thought* (1760)

The first African American to publish a poem was not Phillis Wheatley but Jupiter Hammon (1711–1800), whose broadside *An Evening Thought. Salvation by Christ, with Penitential Cries: Composed by Jupiter Hammon, a Negro belonging to Mr. Lloyd, of Queen's-Village, on Long Island* was printed more than a dozen years before Wheatley's book of poems appeared. Hammon was a preacher whose poetry reflected the intense religious fervor of African Americans who had converted to Christianity during the Great Awakening. Born a slave on Long Island on October 17, 1711, Jupiter was allowed to attend school and learn to read his master's books, especially the Bible, before moving with his master to Connecticut during the Revolution. Hammon witnessed the tragic 1741 New York slave plot that resulted in the burning of thirteen slaves and hanging of eighteen others, an event that may have conditioned his recommendation in his eighty-eight-line poem (to other slaves?) that humanity seek freedom in heavenly salvation, and not on earth. Hammon's other published poems included *An Address to Miss Phillis Wheatley, Ethiopian Poetess* (1778).

650 • *Poems on Various Subjects, Religious and Moral* (1773)

Before being able to publish her book *Poems on Various Subjects, Religious and Moral,* Phillis Wheatley (1753?–1784), a recent African immigrant and Boston house slave, had to pass an oral examination administered by eighteen of the most important white citizens of Boston at the courthouse. She submitted herself to this examination, as her book had been rejected by Boston publishers the year before. Though no transcript of the examination has survived, it appears likely that Wheatley was questioned on her knowledge of the neoclassical as well as biblical references that appear in her poems. More important, this group of examiners, which included Thomas Hutchinson, the governor of the colony, and John Hancock, a future signer of the Declaration of Independence, sought to determine whether she was capable of writing the poems she claimed to have written. No one, they assured her, would believe that a Negro could write poetry. She passed this examination, for in 1773 her book of poems was published in London (Boston publishers still refused the book!) with a preface that included a written "Attestation" from these citizens that she "is thought qualified to write them." It was the first book to be published that was authored by an African American. "On Being Brought from Africa to America" (1773), perhaps its most famous poem, attested to her faith that although "Some view our sable race with scornful eye . . . Remember, *Christian* Negros, black as *Cain,* May be refin'd, and join th' angelic train."

651 • *The Interesting Narrative of the Life of Olaudah Equiano, or Gustavus Vassa, the African* (1789)

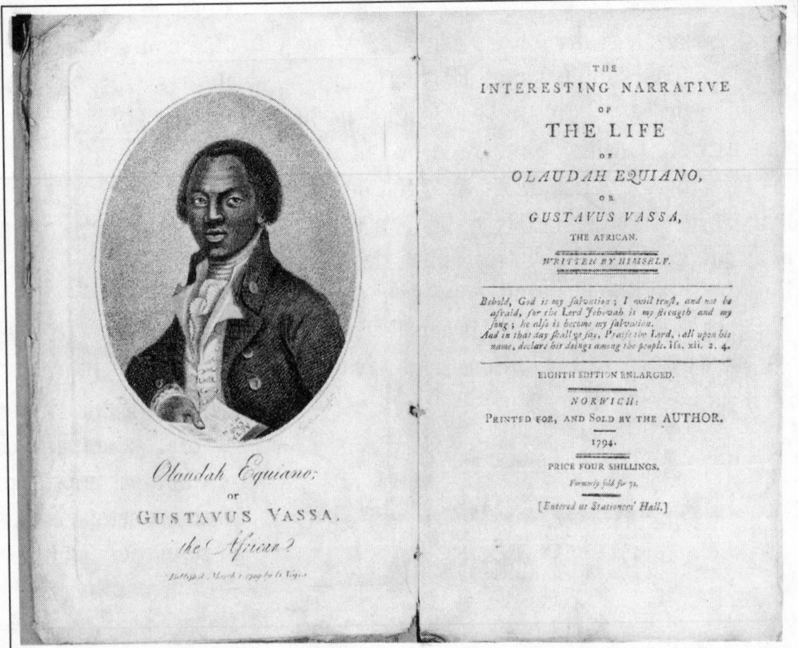

Olaudah Equiano; or GUSTAVUS VASSA, the African.

THE
INTERESTING NARRATIVE
OF
THE LIFE
OF
OLAUDAH EQUIANO,
OR
GUSTAVUS VASSA,
THE AFRICAN.

WRITTEN BY HIMSELF.

Behold, God is my salvation; I will trust, and not be afraid, for the Lord Jehovah is my strength and my song; he also is become my salvation.
And in that day shall ye say, Praise the Lord, call upon his name, declare his doings among the people. Isa. xii. 2, 4.

EIGHTH EDITION ENLARGED.

NORWICH:
PRINTED FOR, AND SOLD BY THE AUTHOR.
1794.
PRICE FOUR SHILLINGS.
Formerly sold for 7s.
[*Entered at Stationers' Hall.*]

Frontispiece engraving of Olaudah Equiano and title page of *The Interesting Narrative of the Life of Olaudah Equiano, or Gustavus Vassa, the African.* Prints and Photographs Division, Library of Congress

The Narrative by Olaudah Equiano (1745–97) provides a dramatically different perspective from Phillis Wheatley's on the slave trade. Written by an Ibo nobleman, *The Narrative* provides a graphic and detailed account of how African slavery differed from the Atlantic variety, how deeply hurt he was by his separation from his homeland and his sister, and how terrified he was by the huge ships that greeted him when he was brought to the coast of Africa. Vassa, who became an abolitionist, also writes movingly of how he learned to read and write and ultimately acquired enough money to purchase his freedom in Philadelphia in 1766.

Art

652 • Scipio Moorhead

Scipio Moorhead was the painter to whom Phillis Wheatley dedicated her poem "To S.M. a young *African* Painter, on seeing his Works" in her *Poems on Various Subjects, Religious and Moral.* Moorhead was an African slave whose Massachusetts master, like Miss Wheatley's, indulged the talent of his slave. Wheatley's poem describes the effect of seeing two of Moorhead's paintings—one of Aurora and another on the myth of Damon and Pythias. Perhaps because Moorhead shared Wheatley's interest in classical figures, she lauded his work and hinted it showed the emotional depth of the "bosom" of the African.

To show the lab'ring bosom's deep intent,
And thought in living characters to paint,
When first thy pencil did those beauties give,
And breathing figures learnt from thee to live,
How those prospects give my soul delight,
A new creation rushing on my sight?

Some art historians believe that Scipio Moorhead may have rendered the copperplate engraving of Phillis Wheatley.

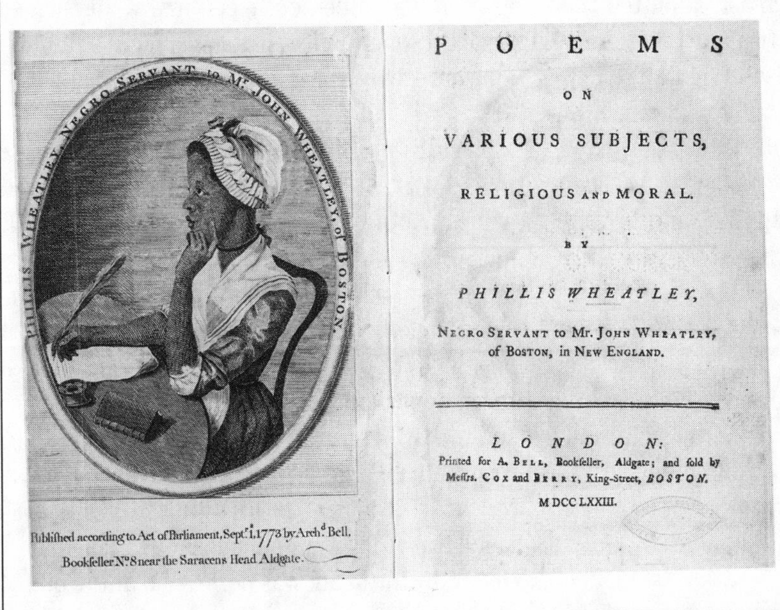

PHILLIS WHEATLEY, NEGRO SERVANT to Mr. JOHN WHEATLEY, of BOSTON.

Published according to Act of Parliament, Sept. 1, 1773 by Arch.d Bell, Bookseller No. 8 near the Saracens Head Aldgate.

POEMS

ON

VARIOUS SUBJECTS,

RELIGIOUS AND MORAL.

BY

PHILLIS WHEATLEY,

NEGRO SERVANT to Mr. JOHN WHEATLEY, of BOSTON, in NEW ENGLAND.

LONDON:

Printed for A. BELL, Bookseller, Aldgate; and sold by Messrs. COX and BERRY, King-Street, BOSTON.

M DCC LXXIII.

Frontispiece engraving after Scipio Moorhead and title page of *Poems on Various Subjects, Religious and Moral* (London, 1773). Prints and Photographs Division, Library of Congress

653 • Joshua Johnston (active 1795–1825)

Although absolute proof of his racial identity has not been found, most art historians regard Joshua Johnston (or Johnson) as the first well-known African American portrait painter. Johnston, who lived and worked in Baltimore, painted primarily affluent European Americans. He may have been influenced by Charles Wilson Peale or Peale's son Rembrandt, also Maryland-based artists. Although his portraits were not signed or dated—a common practice of the day—Johnston nonetheless depicted his subjects in a distinctive, signature style: his figures, both adults and children, appeared stiff, motionless, and posed, with oversize heads that lent a primitive quality to his work. Johnston also produced several portraits of prominent African Americans, whose more relaxed and sympathetic treatment perhaps suggests his identification with these subjects as an African American. In his *Portrait of a Cleric,* Johnston depicts a neatly dressed African American whose smile, reminiscent of Leonardo da Vinci's *Mona Lisa,* is slight yet warm and inviting.

654 • Gilbert Stuart's Tutor

The famous American portrait painter Gilbert Stuart reputedly received his first lesson in painting from an African American slave named Neptune Thurston. According to Edward Peterson's *History of Rhode Island* (1853), Stuart "derived his first impression of painting from witnessing Neptune Thurston, a slave, who was employed in his master's cooper-shop, who sketched likenesses on the heads of casks." Thurston may have been the same African whose advertisement appeared in the *Boston Newsletter* on January 7, 1775: "At Mr. M'Lean's, Watchmaker near the Town-House, is a Negro man whose extraordinary genius has been assisted by one of the best Masters in London; he takes fares at the lowest rates. Specimens of his Performances may be seen at said Place."

655 • Slave Artisans

Although enslaved artisans were generally treated better than agricultural laborers, some masters exploited, bartered, and sold them just as vigorously as plantation owners treated their

slaves. John Allerwood, an artist, admitted the profitability of enslaving artisans when he advertised his desire to "dispose of his Negro Fellows, Painters. On Wednesday, the Seventh of April Next. . . . As to their abilities . . . they have transacted the Whole of His Business, without any hired Assistance." Perhaps Joe, another enslaved artisan, suspected a similar fate awaiting him when he decided to flee captivity. His master's advertisement in the *South Carolina and American General Gazette* in 1772 sought the return of a runaway silversmith who "is near sixteen years old, . . . is very arch and sensible, and wrought at the silversmith's trade many years, being at work with Mr. Oliphant, jeweller, when he absented himself. . . ."

Music and Drama

656 • Musicians in the Militia

Africans in America were permitted to enter the militia during the colonial period, where many of them learned to play musical instruments. The instruments most commonly played were the fiddle or violin, the French horn, and the drums. Drum-playing soldiers were common throughout the colonial militias and the Continental Army. But, as the late historian Sidney Kaplan observed, seldom was their participation recorded in drawings or portraits from the era.

657 • The First Hymnal

The first hymnal intended for an all-Black religious congregation was *A Collection of Spiritual Songs and Hymns Selected from Various Authors by Richard Allen, African Minister* and was printed in 1801. Such a hymnal was a natural complement to the emergence of an independent church and a sign that by the first year of the nineteenth century, a distinctive African American religious singing tradition may have already existed.

658 • The Camp Meeting Shout

African Americans improvised upon hymns at camp meetings during the latter part of the Second Great Awakening (1770–1815), and these improvisations were the forerunners to the camp meeting spiritual form. Although most people have assumed that Blacks assimilated these songs from whites, it is not known for sure. Most likely, the camp meeting experience was the first time many slaves were introduced to Christianity, and in this atmosphere, it was much easier for worship and song to take place. Generally the shout was performed at the end of the meeting as the camp was disassembling. Shouting was the climax of this style of music, which included a type of dance step, thigh slapping, and various religious texts mixed with hymn texts, but set to tunes that were more secular in nature.

659 • Ira Aldridge (1807–67)

Recognized as one of the greatest Shakespearean actors, Ira Aldridge was the first African American to perform *Othello* on the English stage. Although the early details of his life are in dispute, Ira Aldridge was apparently born in New York City, where he attended the African Free School and studied at Hewlett's African Theater before he left for England in 1824. On October 10, 1825, Aldridge opened at the Royal Coburg in London and gave his first performance in the play *The Revolt of Surinam or A Slave's Revenge.* But he became internationally famous in 1833 when he debuted at the Theatre Royal, Covent Garden, London, in the title role of *Othello* and won the acclaim of the English press. Nicknamed the African Roscius,

Portrait of Ira Aldridge (as Othello) by Henry Perronet Briggs, c. 1830. National Portrait Gallery, Smithsonian Institution

Aldridge was even more acclaimed when he embarked on his first continental tour in 1852, playing such roles as Mango, Macbeth, Shylock, King Lear, and Richard III, as well as Othello. In 1863 he became a citizen of Great Britain; he was married twice to European women. Though he planned to return to the United States for an acting tour on the eve of his death, Aldridge never set foot in America. A chair dedicated to Ira Aldridge is located in the fourth row of seats of the rebuilt Shakespeare Memorial Theatre at Stratford-upon-Avon.

Religion

660 • First African Baptist Church in Savannah, Georgia

The First African Baptist Church was founded in 1778 by Andrew Bryan (1737–1812), a black pastor and slave. Upon one of the numerous occasions when his gatherings were disrupted by the "pattyrollers" (slave patrols), he "told his persecutors that he rejoiced not only to be whipped, but *would freely suffer death for the cause of Jesus Christ.*" Fortunately his master sought his release and permitted Bryan to continue his ministry in the plantation barn. He soon gained respect as white ministers examined his congregation and found them to be well instructed. Upon his death in 1812, the white Baptist Association of Savannah issued a memorial statement noting his good works.

661 • Lemuel Haynes (1753–1833)

Born in West Hartford, Connecticut, on July 18, 1753, Lemuel Haynes was the first Black minister certified by a predominantly white denomination and licensed to preach in the Congregational Church. His term began on November 29, 1780. Haynes was also the first Black pastor of a white church. In 1785 he was ordained and named pastor of a white church in Torrington, Connecticut. In 1787 he was called to a white church in Rutland, Vermont.

662 • Mother Bethel and St. Thomas Episcopal Church

Racial discrimination caused Blacks to form separate churches in the North. Though Blacks had been a part of St. George's Methodist Church since 1767, the year it was founded, these members found themselves segregated by class from the leadership of the church and by race from common Methodists. As early as the summer of 1791, the society approached several white philanthropists for aid in purchasing two lots on which to erect a church. These plans became more urgent after an incident at St. George's during the summer of 1792. The gallery had just been erected and Richard Allen, Absa-

Bethel African Methodist Episcopal Church. Schomburg Center for Research in Black Culture, New York Public Library, Astor, Lenox and Tilden Foundation

lom Jones, and other Blacks were directed to sit there. As prayers began, the Blacks were ordered to the rear of the gallery. Instead of doing so, Allen states, "all went out of the church in a body and they were no more plagued with us in the church." The Blacks who walked out formed two new congregations: most who left formed St. Thomas Episcopal Church, of which Absalom Jones became pastor; others, followers of Allen, formed Mother Bethel, perhaps the most famous Black church in the early nineteenth century.

663 • Second Great Awakening

Although the First Great Awakening led white masters to encourage conversion of their slaves, it was during the Second Great Awakening (1770–1815) that large numbers of African Americans began joining mainstream Christian churches, in part because many were allowed to attend large camp meetings in which a passionate faith was instilled in those attending. Moreover, the millennialism of the Second Great Awakening, which emphasized universal sin and the coming of God, motivated many to prepare for that event. Such millennialism was a factor in the emergence of spiritual leaders among slaves like Sojourner Truth.

ANTEBELLUM EXPRESSION, 1820–60

Movements, Organizations, and Celebrations

664 • Antislavery Testimony

During the middle of the nineteenth century, several former slaves published autobiographies, called slave narratives, which transformed not only American politics but also American literature. Drawing on eighteenth-century forms of the picaresque novel and nineteenth-century folk and oral traditions, Frederick Douglass, William Wells Brown, Harriet Jacobs, Nat Turner, Harriet E. Wilson, and Sojourner Truth created a new American genre of the heroic slave who discovers an identity

through romantic rebellion against American society. David Walker, Martin Delany, and Henry Highland Garnet wrote confessional novels and nonfictional exhortations of rebellion which shaped the work of Henry David Thoreau and other romantic rebels. In folk literature and music, especially the spirituals, African Americans gave voice to the spiritual transcendence of those whose freedom is deferred and the coded escape of those driven to seize freedom now. Such narratives shaped even the expressions of free persons of color who came to believe that none could be free, especially after the Fugitive Slave Act of 1850, as long as the masses remained enslaved.

665 • Slave Festivals

Throughout the nineteenth century, slaves held festivals and carnivals in the United States and throughout the Caribbean. The noisy public performances sometimes lasted for days and included dancing, singing, and music, often with banjos and other slave-made instruments. One of the most famous festivals was Jonkonnu, believed to have originated in Jamaica and been re-created, perhaps by migrating slaves, in North Carolina in 1828. Festivals were occasions on which slaves often reclaimed some of their African heritage: they simulated sounds made by drums, instruments forbidden by slave masters, created and wore outlandish masks and costumes, and danced with "pagan" ringlets, cowbells, and spectacular headdresses. The revelry of Jonkonnu was allowed by masters in part because it took place during Christmas holidays, after the planting of the crop was concluded. While masters looked upon such festivities as merely opportunities for slaves to "let off some steam," the slaves' adornment of masters' and mistresses' clothing, holding of mock courts, and the exchange of gifts symbolized that slaves also saw the festivals as opportunities to act as if they were free.

666 • Literacy Efforts

Frederick Douglass argued that the only way to permanently keep someone a slave was to keep him or her ignorant. Most antebellum southern states agreed and considered it a crime to teach African Americans, slave or free, to read or write. In Norfolk, Virginia, Margaret Douglass conducted reading lessons in her home for a group of free Black children. Soon a warrant was issued for her arrest and she was indicted by a grand jury and tried for breaking the Virginia law that prohibited assembly of African Americans for religious worship unless the services were led by a white, the gathering of African Americans for instruction in reading and/or writing, and any congregation of Blacks at nighttime for any purpose. Any white person assisting in these assemblies was to be fined and imprisoned. Mrs. Douglass received a one-dollar fine and a one-month jail sentence.

Some Important Books

667 • *Narrative of the Life of Frederick Douglass: An American Slave* (1845)

Frederick Douglass (1818–95), an escaped slave and abolitionist speaker, wrote the *Narrative* to prove to skeptical audiences that he had actually been a slave. When published in June 1845, the *Narrative,* accompanied by William Lloyd Garrison's preface and Wendell Phillips's letter of recommendation, became a best-seller, selling 4,500 copies by the fall and 30,000 by 1850. The book's popularity derived from its having been written by a former slave rather than transcribed by a white abolitionist, and from its compelling story of one man's struggle

to emancipate himself mentally and physically from American enslavement. Because it was written by a slave who had taught himself how to read and write, the book not only launched the runaway slave as a powerful figure in American literature but established the self-made African American as a central character in American autobiography. Although Douglass revised his life story in *My Bondage and My Freedom* (1855) and *The Life and Times of Frederick Douglass* (1881), he retained the powerful form of the earlier narrative.

Frances Ellen Watkins Harper. Prints and Photographs Division, Library of Congress

668 • *Clotel; or, The President's Daughter: A Narrative of Slave Life in the United States* (1853)

Clotel, William Wells Brown's allegorical novel of Thomas Jefferson, democratic hypocrisy, and slave life in America, is the first novel published by an African American, appearing in 1853 in London, where Brown (1815–84), a fugitive slave and intellectual expatriate, had been staying for four years. Brown's melodramatic story of the life of three generations of African American descendants of Thomas Jefferson mixes fact, fiction, and political assertion to establish what would become a predominant form for African American fiction—the protest novel. Because of the controversial nature of Brown's assertion that Thomas Jefferson had kept an African American mistress and that he allowed the children from that liaison to remain enslaved, the American edition of the book, published in 1864, substituted a senator for the president. It was not until 1969 that the original version of this inflammatory novel appeared in print in the United States.

William Wells Brown. Prints and Photographs Division, Library of Congress

669 • *Poems on Miscellaneous Subjects* (1854)

Poems on Miscellaneous Subjects, the first book of poems by Frances Ellen Watkins Harper (1825–1911), contained her classic depiction of

the travail of motherhood under slavery ("The Slave Mother") and her indictment of social disdain for women who had slept with men out of wedlock ("A Double Standard"). Although Harper was much more than a poet—a founder of the National Association of Colored Women and a participant in the Equal Rights Association Convention in 1869—she was foremost a writer who is credited with authoring, in addition to her several volumes of poetry, the first short story by an African American, "The Two Offers" (1859).

670 • *Our Nig* (1859)

Harriet Wilson's novel *Our Nig; or, Sketches from the Life of a Free Black, in a two-story white house, North: showing that slavery's shadows fall even there* is the first novel written by an African American woman to be published. Jacobs's novel, which was discovered by literary scholar Henry Louis Gates, Jr., is an engaging study of the conditions of life in the antebellum North, where "slavery's shadows fall even there" with discrimination, segregation, and abuse the staple of lives led by African American women and men.

671 • *Blake, or the Huts of America* (1859)

Martin Delany's novel of a slave rebellion remains the only revolutionary novel of the antislavery movement. Breaking with the slave narrative tradition of the long-suffering victims of the system and the solitary Frederick Douglass–like rebel, Delany, who was a freeborn African American and student at Harvard Medical School, crafted a novel that imagined what a mass revolt against slavery would look like. Delany's protagonist is an insurrectionist slave who moves stealthily between plantations, being hidden by friendly slaves and informed of developments by the slave "underground," to organize a full-scale rebellion. Serialized originally in the *Anglo-African,* Delany's novel was one of the most popular novels of the period with the African American reading public.

672 • *Incidents in the Life of a Slave* (1861)

Incidents in the Life of a Slave, the autobiographical novel written by Harriet Jacobs (1813–97), is the best narrative account of slave life from the perspective of a black woman. Jacobs tells the story of Linda Brent (a pseudonym for Jacobs herself), who is sexually harassed by her master and then victimized by her jealous mistress. Jacobs provides an insider's view of the struggles to avoid ongoing rape and reprisal, a conflict that leads Linda to try to escape by entering into a relationship with another white man. When that relationship also becomes problematical, Brent decides to hide in a crawl space on the property for seven years until she can finally escape by boat to the North. Her story also details the prejudice up North, the Fugitive Slave Law in action, and Black women's relationships.

Art

673 • Patrick Henry Reason (1817?–1850?)

Patrick Henry Reason was an engraver from Philadelphia who is most famous for his engraving *Am I Not a Woman and a Sister*—an emblem that signified his commitment to the abolitionists' movement and Black women's rights. He was educated in the African Free School, apprenticed to a white craftsman, and became a skilled engraver himself. Beyond his famous emblem, he contributed

numerous images in many antislavery magazines, created the frontispiece for Charles C. Andrews's *The History of the African Free Schools,* published in 1830, and produced portraits of several of the more important abolitionists, including a lithograph (1840) and an engraving (1848) of Henry Bibb.

674 • Julien Hudson (active 1830–40)

Julien Hudson was a freeman of mixed race from New Orleans. Born into the so-called mulatto group, Hudson partook of the French-influenced, flamboyant, upper-class lifestyle that was available to well-born free African Americans in New Orleans. One of his most important works was his painting *Battle of New Orleans* (1815), which documented the contribution made to the War of 1812 by the famous corps of free Black soldiers and its white commander, Colonel Michel Jean Fortier, Jr. Hudson is also distinguished for painting, in 1839, the only known self-portrait of an African American artist in the antebellum period.

Julien Hudson, *Self-Portrait*, 1839. Courtesy of Louisiana State Museum

Advertisement featuring stereotypes "uncle," "auntie," and "pickaninnies." The Warshaw Collection, National Museum of American History, Smithsonian Museum

675 • Caricatures

Racial caricatures flooded the American press in the antebellum period. While caricatures had existed earlier in the eighteenth-century press, the number and viciousness of Black caricatures increased dramatically in the late 1820s and continued to grow through the rest of the nineteenth century. Caricatures seemed to grow in popularity as Blacks made advances in free society, whether northern or southern. Edward Clay began a series of cartoons in the late 1820s called *Life in Philadelphia* that ridiculed the "airs" and conspicuous consumption of Philadelphia's Black elite. These caricatures were very popular because they captured the attention of working-class whites who felt looked down upon by upwardly mobile Blacks, and

emerged around the time of the horrendous anti-Black riots in cities like Philadelphia and Cincinnati. Caricatures abounded in the 1840s and 1850s in response to the abolitionist movement and continued to spread after the Civil War as a way to critique the ex-slaves and the extension of political rights to Blacks. Racial caricatures were so widely disseminated in the nineteenth century that they came to define the public image of African Americans and limit the publishing opportunities for alternative images created by Black artists.

676 • Robert Scott Duncanson (1821–72)

Robert Scott Duncanson was the first African American landscape painter to gain national and international attention. Born to a Scottish Canadian father and a free woman of color in Seneca County, New York, Duncanson grew up in Canada but moved to a community outside of Cincinnati in the 1840s. In 1842 Duncanson was included in an exhibition sponsored by the Society for the Promotion of Useful Knowledge and secured several important portrait commissions of abolitionists, including that of James G. Birney, the former slave owner and Liberty Party presidential candidate. But Duncanson's true love was landscape painting in the Hudson River School romantic-naturalistic tradition and was distinguished by his use of atmospheric effects in his landscapes. Moving between Detroit and Cincinnati, Duncanson was able to exhibit his work in the annual Western Art and Union exhibitions and was well regarded by his fellow artists. After going abroad in 1853, he returned to the United States and produced a series of murals of Cincinnati for his patron, Nicholas Longworth. Perhaps Duncanson's most impressive work was his series of American landscapes, of which *Landscape with Rainbow* is a fine example. Because of his need for money and his interest in daguerreotypes, Duncanson began working in 1849 with daguerreotypist J. P. Ball.

677 • J. P. Ball (1825–1904)

Born in Cincinnati, J. P. Ball worked as a waiter on a riverboat and remained something of a showman and entrepreneur for the rest of his life. In 1851 he had one of the most elaborate and fashionable daguerreotype studios in Cincinnati. He did portraits of famous personalities, such as Jenny Lind, and employed Robert Duncanson to transform the daguerreotypes into oil paintings. Ball's most ambitious work, however, was a panoramic history of slavery that consumed a half mile of canvas. Although the work of art has been lost, Ball's lecture notes survived and were published in 1855. The panorama began, according to the notes, with an African village and ended with the recent Cincinnati riots of 1841. Not until Aaron Douglas in the 1930s would another African American artist attempt as sweeping a mural project as that executed by J. P. Ball.

Music and Dance

678 • Work Songs

Sung by both slaves and free people of color in the South, African American work songs were first described by Fanny Kemble in her *Journal of a Residence on a Georgia Plantation in 1838–1839.* Kemble noted that the Black men rowing her boat down a stream

set up a chorus, which they continued to chant in unison with each other, and in time with their stroke, till their voices were heard no more from the distance. . . . [T]hey all sing in unison, having never, it appears, attempted or heard any-

thing like part-singing. Their voices seem oftener tenor than any other quality, and the tune and time they keep something quite wonderful.

Work songs were used extensively in West Africa, in Dahomey and Yoruba, as well as in Haiti, Brazil, and Trinidad, to harmonize the work rhythms mainly of agricultural laborers. In the antebellum South, such songs were sung not only by agricultural laborers but by domestic servants, industrial workers, and steamboat laborers. With one man usually providing the "call" by announcing the verses of the song, the group then echoes those verses in the tempo of his first call. Work songs survived slavery and became characteristic of the "chain gangs" of the convict lease system after the Civil War and can still be heard in certain southern prisons.

679 • Congo Square

Located just outside the northeast limits of New Orleans, Congo Plains (later known as Congo Square) was a vacant plot of land that became a site of Black dancing and music playing in the nineteenth century. After 1805, the year that the United States took over administration of New Orleans from the French, African American slaves began to congregate in Congo Square, along with Indians and Creoles, to play competitive field games, hold dog- and bullfights, and generally carouse. The proximity of Congo Square to a brickyard where voodoo rites were held also lent a West Indian quality to the square. But Congo Square became famous after the New Orleans City Council ruled in 1817 that "assemblies of slaves" would be confined to Sundays and designated Congo Square as the place for slave entertainments. Although the original impetus was to confine immoral and potentially insurrectionary activities to a particular site where they could be watched carefully, the ordinance turned the square into a tourist attraction where out-of-towners regularly came to see Jamaicans and southern African Americans play drums, dance with long animal tails, and perform complex dances. Congo Square declined after 1880, when the area was divided up into lots.

The Love Song, drawn in Congo Square, New Orleans, by E. W. Kemble, in *Century Magazine*, 1886. From *Black Dance: 1619 to Today* by Lynne Fauley Emery

680 • Frank Johnson (1792–1844)

Frank Johnson was a fiddler, bugler, horn player, and bandleader who acquired a national reputation. Based in Philadelphia, he was sought after for his improvisational, compositional, and orchestration skills. He and his band traveled the country at the request of rich patrons who had heard of his talent to call a tune. The Frank Johnson organization also toured

England and gave a command performance for Queen Victoria at Buckingham Palace.

681 • Elizabeth Taylor Greenfield (182?–76)

Known as the Black Swan, Elizabeth Greenfield was the most celebrated Black concert singer of the antebellum period. Born in the 1820s, and given very little training, she was reputed to be the first African American musician to earn a reputation both in the United States and abroad. After a successful singing tour throughout the free states from 1851 to 1853, Greenfield dazzled audiences on her tour of England in 1854, where she gave a command performance before Queen Victoria. With a singing range of three octaves, she was a vocal curiosity as well as an appreciated singer of classical music songs. Although she toured the U.S. again in 1863 and sang often at charitable events, her singing career was limited by her inability, because of race prejudice, to obtain the kind of training she needed to become a first-rate opera singer. Hence, most of her career was spent as an instructor of music.

682 • Blacks Composed "Dixie"

In 1859 Dan Emmett, a white man in blackface, sang "I Wish I Was in Dixie Land," and the song brought tears to southern eyes and became the Confederate national anthem. But although Emmett claimed to have written the song, historians have now proved that the song was actually composed and sung by a Black musical family from Ohio. The Snowdens, former slaves in Maryland who had migrated to and settled in Knox County, Ohio, were a family of farmers who performed songs for Black and white audiences, usually accompanying themselves on the banjo and the fiddle. Apparently Dan Emmett traveled through Knox County, heard the song, memorized it, and then made himself famous—for the song. Ironically the song of the South was composed "up North" by African Americans.

683 • Jim Crow Rice

In 1828 Thomas Dartmouth Rice was the first white man to create a successful one-man show based on reputedly dancing like an African American. Rice claimed to have seen a crippled African American sing and dance. Rice's representation of a Black man dancing became known as "to jump Jim Crow." In addition to shuffling in a contorted posture, wheeling his body around to jump high in the air, Rice also dressed in tattered, outlandish clothes, wore a crumpled hat, and rolled his eyes grotesquely. Historians debate whether Rice's performance was an accurate depiction of African American dancing. Some have argued that it was a fusion of a jig and a shuffle. Others have argued that at best it was Rice's imitation of a "lame Negro," and at worst, simply a caricature of Black dance exaggerated and ridiculed in order to entertain a white audience. Whatever its origins, Jim Crow became an instant hit, was hugely successful, and ingrained a stereotype of African American behavior in nineteenth-century American popular culture.

684 • Ethiopian Minstrelsy

Thomas Rice's success spawned numerous imitators and led to the creation of a major American dance and theatrical institution, that of Ethiopian minstrelsy—usually two and sometimes three or more whites performing in blackface several skits, scenes, and songs. Although the performances were supposedly based on African American slave life, the minstrelsy troupes actually provided social commentary upon the events of the day and social issues con-

Juba performing at the Vauxhall Gardens in London, 1848. From *Black Dance: 1619 to Today* by Lynne Fauley Emery

fronting the masses. Patronized mainly by working-class whites, including many immigrants, the Ethiopian minstrelsy became the most important form of popular entertainment during the pre–Civil War period. It challenged in some instances legitimate theater in America. Eventually Blacks were allowed to form and tour their own minstrel shows, but like the whites, Black performers had to cover their faces with burnt cork and follow closely the pantomimed traditions of the white minstrels, or risk violence. Ironically Blacks by the middle of the century could only perform on the American stage by copying the routines of whites who had mimicked other African Americans.

685 • Juba, the Real Thing

The most famous and most authentic interpreter of African American dance styles in the antebellum period was Master Juba (William Henry Lane), a freeborn African American who emerged in the 1840s on the American popular stage. Juba was an expert in dancing the jig, and his outstanding skill was attested to by many. Marian Winter, who saw Juba dance, stated in 1845 that "it was flatly stated by members of the profession that Juba was beyond question the very greatest of all dancers." In 1846 Juba joined a minstrel show, White's Serenaders, which traveled to London in 1848. Dancing at the Vauxhall Gardens in London, Juba stunned English reviewers, who could not believe they were witnessing such "mobility of muscles, such flexibility of joints, such boundings, such slidings, such gyrations, such toes and heelings, such backwardings and forwardings, such posturings. . . ." A "school of Juba" emerged in the United States, but Master Juba died in London in 1852 before ever returning to his native land. Some critics credited Juba with reviving Black dance on the stage as an authentic rather than a caricature performance.

686 • Blind Tom (1849–1908)

Born near Columbus, Georgia, Thomas Greene was sold with his mother, Charlotte Wiggins, from the Oliver family to the Bethune family while still a baby. When Tom was four, the Bethunes acquired a piano. Tom heard Mrs. Bethune teaching her daughters every day for three years. One day, at age seven, he sat down to the piano and played perfectly the tunes he had heard the previous day. Recognizing his genius, the Bethune family decided to hire out Tom for activities that required music. Armed with a strong memory, Tom developed a huge repertory, on which he could improvise, without formal

Blind Tom. Prints and Photographs Division, Library of Congress

musical training. Tom was such a concert draw between 1857 and 1898 that the Bethunes became wealthy. After the war, reformers sued the Bethunes to gain Tom's freedom, but Tom objected that freedom would not help him, given his sightless condition. He remained a ward of the Bethune family until his death.

687 • Spirituals

For generations prior to the Civil War, African Americans had sung songs based on religious hymns, some of which were the English Wesleyan hymns. These "sorrow songs," as they were called by W. E. B. Du Bois, were sung in a distinctive style that was different from the standard phrasing and emphases of the English renditions. European and religious in origin, these songs were distinctively African American in style, and the choice and emphasis of certain songs by the slaves made them into plaintive commentary on the slave system. Moreover, some songs, like "Swing Low, Sweet Chariot" and "Steal Away," possessed a double meaning: the possibility of escape to freedom on earth as well as that promised in heaven. These songs first gained national attention during the Civil War when they were commented on by Thomas Wentworth Higginson in his articles on his service with a Black regiment, and in 1867 when William Allen, Charles Ware, and Lucy McKim Garrison published the first collection of the songs, entitled *Slave Songs of the United States.* Then in 1916 Harry T. Burleigh, an African American singer and arranger, published the first arrangement of a spiritual for solo voice and piano when he arranged "Deep River." With additional arrangements of "Weepin' Mary," "You May Bury Me in the East," and others in 1917, a new period for concert performance of the spirituals began.

688 • Slave Songs as Commentary

One former slave recalled how some of the slave songs emerged from the experience of enslavement.

I'll tell you, it's dis way. My master call me up, and order me a short peck of corn and a hundred lash. My friends see it, and is sorry for me. When dey come to de praise-meeting dat night dey sing about it. Some's very good singers and know how; and dey work it in—work it in, you know, till you get it right; and dat's de way.

689 • Underground Railroad Songs

Travelers of the underground railroad used many of the slave songs to pass messages and communicate over long distances. Some songs were used to keep spirits up. Some were meant as a signal to get ready, while others warned of danger. And there were those such as the well-known "Follow the Drinking Gourd" that were intended as maps for the fugitives.

Religion

690 • On White America as Egypt

Maria Stewart, a free Black minister, reform activist, and the first Black woman to give a speech in public, used a speaking occasion in Boston in 1831 to make the biblical connection between Egypt and

America, America, foul and indelible is thy stain! Dark and dismal is the cloud that hangs over thee, for thy cruel wrongs and injuries to the fallen souls of Africa. The blood of her murdered ones cries to heaven for vengeance against Thee. . . . You may kill, tyrannize, and oppress as much as you choose, until our cry shall come up before the throne of God; for I am firmly persuaded, that he will not suffer you to quell the proud, fearless and undaunted spirits of the Africans forever; for in his own time, he is able to plead our cause against you, and to pour out upon you the ten plagues of Egypt.

691 • Those Separate Churches

After the Nat Turner Rebellion in 1831, many independent Black churches in the South, such as the African Baptist Church of Williamsburg, Virginia, responded to white fears by merging with white churches. In the North, hostility toward independent Black churches in Philadelphia led to riots in which the most prominent churches, such as Mother Bethel, were attacked by white mobs. Working-class whites felt that such independent churches were the reason for the success and wealth of Blacks.

692 • The Invisible Institution

The Invisible Institution is the name used by some scholars to describe the secret worship services of African American slaves prior to the Civil War. These secret services took place in "hush harbors," makeshift meeting places in the swamps and bayous away from the plantations. Wet quilts and rags were hung up in the trees around the services in an effort to stifle the sound of the worship. Here they interpreted Christianity according to their personal experience, which inevitably contradicted the messages their masters taught.

693 • Voodoo

Although voodoo, or *vodun* as it was called in Haiti, was never as strong a presence in North America as in the West Indies, it did become quite popular in Louisiana after the eighteenth-century importation of French West Indian slaves. The ruling elite of Louisiana sought to suppress voodoo because they believed it incited rebellion against whites and because prominent voodoo priests or priestesses, such as the renowned Marie Laveau, were free persons of color, who operated outside the social control of planters. Voodoo, called hoodoo by slaves who lived on plantations, involved conjuration, the creation of charms, potions, or other magic, and the prediction of the future. In New Orleans, voodoo was primarily worship of the snake-god, Damballa or Da, from the Dahomey tradition, and involved rituals of spirit possession and animal sacrifice. Voodoo conjurers claimed an ability to predict the future and to fashion charms that protected slaves from masters, but most slaves and free Blacks used voodoo against other African Americans. In the nineteenth century certain voodoo priests, including Marie Laveau, even had a large clientele of whites, especially those who wished to get information, such as on a spouse, loved one, or recently departed relative or friend. Voodoo reached its height in popularity in the 1850s.

Marie Laveau (1794–1881), known as the Voodoo Queen of New Orleans. From the collection of the Louisiana State Museum

POSTBELLUM BLUES, 1865–1915

Movements, Organizations, and Celebrations

694 • Historical Associations

In the post–Civil War environment, a popular theme in African American culture was the celebration of African American heroes, most notably Frederick Douglass. As a former slave who had become a famous and influential abolitionist and citizen, Douglass epitomized the ideology of self-improvement that became dominant in African American intellectual circles. When Douglass died in 1895, his second wife, Helen Pitts Douglass, a white woman, was instrumental in gaining the support of prominent African Americans who joined her in forming the Frederick Douglass Memorial and Historical Association to preserve his Anacostia home at Cedar Hill. Other historical associations and societies, such as the New York Society for Historic Research (1890) and the American Negro Historical Society (1897), were formed during this period, along with such research collections as the Jesse Moorland collection at Howard University, to document the history of exemplary African American individuals and the contributions of Blacks to world history.

695 • African American Folklore Movement

Although African American historical associations represented themselves as preserving the history of all African Americans, the history of the Black masses and the history of slavery were usually understudied in mainstream African American historical associations before the twentieth century. But in the 1890s a group of intellectuals interested in studying the unique qualities of folk culture of the formerly enslaved masses of southern Black people came together and founded the Boston Society for the Collection of Negro Folklore in the 1890s. Similarly, African American historian W. E. B. Du Bois established the significance of African American folk culture in his pathbreaking essay on the "sorrow songs" in *The Souls of Black Folk.* His work and the work of the Boston Folklore Society set the stage for other scholars to collect and preserve the myths, jokes, toasts, and tales of southern Black vernacular culture.

Some Important Books

696 • *A Voice from the South* (1892)

Anna J. Cooper's *A Voice from the South by a Black Woman of the South* is the most forceful indictment of the sexism and racism of late-nineteenth-century reform movements written by an American intellectual. The daughter of a slave and her master, Cooper (1858–1964) graduated from Oberlin College with a B.A. and M.A., became principal of Washington, D.C.'s M Street School (later Dunbar High), and eventually earned a Ph.D. from the Sorbonne in Paris. As a contemporary of W. E. B. Du Bois and Booker T. Washington, Cooper criticized the tendency of Black reform movements to marginalize the plight and potential of Black women in discussions of the "race problem." *A Voice from the South* details the bias against educating women in Black colleges, seminaries, and high schools and critiques the women's movement, especially its leaders, Susan B. Anthony and

Anna B. Shaw, for being unwilling to oppose racism in the women's clubs. *A Voice from the South* also provides an impassioned indictment of the industrial education movement as a conspiracy to deny the humanity of African Americans, both female and male.

697 • *Lyrics of Lowly Life* (1896)

Paul Laurence Dunbar (1872–1906) was an elevator boy in a New York City hotel when he began to compose and publish poetry and short stories, many of which were written in dialect. But it was the publication of 1896 of *Lyrics of Lowly Life,* his third book of poems, with its introduction written by the dean of American letters, William Dean Howells, that made Dunbar famous. While Dunbar's poems were shackled to a degree by dialect he used, they also manifested a directness of expression and sincerity of emotion that eluded dialect poetry produced by Thomas Nelson Page and others. Moreover, in some of his "standard English" poems, Dunbar registered his sense of African American doubleness ("We Wear the Mask") and the bitterness of not being able to live fully in a segregated world.

698 • *The Conjure Woman* (1899)

Charles Chesnutt's first collection of short stories is a subtle and complex retelling of folktales told to a northern carpetbagger and his wife by "Uncle Julius," a trickster ex-slave who worked for the northerner as a coachman. Julius's tales within the northerner's seven tales are written in a North Carolina dialect and conform outwardly to the popular plantation stories written by George W. Cable, Thomas Nelson Page, and others in the late nineteenth century. But unlike those stories, Chesnutt's reveal the tragedy of slavery. In "Sis Becky's Pickaninny," Julius tells of a slave mother sold away from her family and home because of a greedy slave owner, while "Po' Sandy" narrates the tragedy of a slave whose wife turns him into a tree so that he won't be sold away only to have their master cut down the tree for lumber. Perhaps most important, the stories in *The Conjure Woman* narrate an African American folk mysticism in which slaves and ex-slaves identified with supernatural forces and relied on them to gain advantage on white folks. That folk mysticism would become an enduring theme in African American fiction, developed best in the writings of Zora Neale Hurston and Toni Morrison.

699 • *Up from Slavery* (1901)

Up from Slavery, the autobiography of Booker T. Washington (1856–1915), built upon the Black self-made-man genre of Frederick Douglass's *Narrative* but eliminated the earlier book's fiery indictment of American society. Although *Up from Slavery* condemns slavery, it does so mainly for its miseducation of African Americans in a philosophy of labor at odds with the capitalist ethic that one profits from one's labor. Made famous by his 1895 Atlanta Exposition Address that encouraged Blacks to postpone demands for social and political equality for the promise of independent economic development, Washington recounts his rise from slavery to world fame as an allegory of African American success in America if Blacks adopt his philosophy that hard labor is always rewarded. Washington's Horatio Alger–like autobiography not only disseminates his political program for Black advancement in post-Reconstruction America but also, like Benjamin Franklin's *Autobiography,* teaches an ethic of public behavior considerably less sophisticated than the man himself.

700 • *The Souls of Black Folk* (1903)

W. E. B. Du Bois's collection of essays, *The Souls of Black Folk* (1903), is not only one of the most inspiring books in the entire African American canon but also a book that created a genre—the poetic, autobiographical collection of essays—of African American letters. Containing the famous pronouncement "the problem of the twentieth century is the color-line," and the introspective exploration of the "double-consciousness" of the African American, *The Souls of Black Folk* revealed how the educated class of Black Americans felt and thought about life under racism in America. Perhaps even more important than declaring his political independence from the thought of Booker T. Washington, Du Bois (1868–1965) used this book to declare the existence of an African American folk culture that should not be sacrificed to integration. Concluding the book was one of Du Bois's most influential essays, "On the Sorrow Songs," the first published analysis of the spirituals as the building block of African American culture.

701 • *Autobiography of an Ex-Colored Man* (1912)

James Weldon Johnson's only novel is a superb treatment of the problem of the African American identity, which is forced to choose between the material and social success of the white world and the warmth and creativity of the black. On one level, Johnson's novel is the story of an African American light-skinned enough to pass for white. But on another, the *Autobiography of an Ex-Colored Man* is the first cultural pluralist novel of the twentieth century, because it portrays passing into the white world as the choice of personal anonymity and cultural failure for the talented African American. Leaving behind the spirited bohemian New York jazz scene, where his talent as a musician and performer was recognized and celebrated, the narrator laments the rich and vibrant African American culture he is forced to abandon. The *Autobiography of an Ex-Colored Man* is also an excellent guide to the urban folk culture of bohemian New York, which James Weldon and his brother J. Rosamund knew intimately from their days as composers of lyrics and songs for the theater.

Art

702 • Edward Bannister (1828–1901)

Edward Bannister was born and educated in Canada, and when he moved to Boston in 1848, he already possessed a highly developed interest in painting. Working as a barber, he took evening classes at the Lowell Institute and was inspired by the paintings of William Morris Hunt. Exposed to the French Barbizon paintings, Bannister developed into an excellent landscape artist in the heavy-palette style of French naturalism. He gained fame when one of his paintings was accepted in the Philadelphia Centennial Exposition of 1876 and won the first prize bronze medal. The judges wanted to reconsider once they learned that Bannister was African American, but the protest of fellow painters forced the committee to award him the prize. Afterward, he became a leading painter in Providence, Rhode Island. Although the bulk of his work was landscapes, his most sensitive painting remains *Newspaper Boy* (1869), where he captures the expectancy, tentativeness, and mood of a possibly African American newspaper boy.

703 • Edmonia Lewis (1843?–after 1911)

Edmonia Lewis was the first professional African American sculptor. Born of a free

Edmonia Lewis. Photograph by Henry Rocher, c. 1870. National Portrait Gallery, Smithsonian Institution

African American father and a Chippewa Indian mother, Lewis attended Oberlin College in Ohio in 1859, from which she was dismissed because of unsubstantiated accusations that she had poisoned several of her white female schoolmasters. Moving to Boston, she began to do portrait busts of white abolitionists. In 1865 she took a trip to Europe, settled in Rome, and perfected her neoclassical style. Joining an American community in Rome that consisted of Charlotte Chuman, an actress, and Harriet Hosmer, a sculptor, Lewis remained in Rome in part because of the excellent marble she was able to obtain. Her sculpture of Hagar, an Old Testament Egyptian maidservant of Sarah, the wife of Abraham, who was cast into the wilderness, is one of her most compelling works. It exemplifies her ability to use the neoclassical style to create a dignified rendition of this African and Biblical subject.

704 • Henry Ossawa Tanner (1859–1937)

Henry O. Tanner was the best African American artist of the nineteenth and early twentieth centuries. Born in Philadelphia into the upperclass elite, Tanner enrolled in the Pennsylvania Academy of Fine Arts at age twenty-one and studied with the legendary teacher Thomas Eakins. Eakins steered Tanner away from his first love, landscape painting, toward genre painting. After working for a short while as an art teacher at Clark College, Tanner traveled during the summer of 1889 in North Carolina, where he made numerous sketches of the landscape and its people. Perhaps his most famous work grew out of that trip. *The Banjo Lesson* (1893) depicted a sensitive relationship of an elder teaching a young African American child

The Banjo Lesson, 1893. Courtesy of Hampton University Museum, Virginia

to play a banjo. But Tanner eschewed African American genre studies after the 1890s, went to Paris, and became enthralled with the city, eventually settling there as an expatriate. In the early twentieth century Tanner turned increasingly to religious painting of scenes from the Bible. During World War I he again returned to genre studies of the impact of the war on the people. He received numerous awards in his career, perhaps the most impressive being the French Legion of Honor in 1923.

705 • Collection of African Art

In the late nineteenth century, a museum at Hampton Institute, a Black institution of higher education in Hampton, Virginia, began to collect African art as a way to promote self-knowledge among Black students. Under the direction of curator Cora Mae Folsom, the museum purchased a collection of African artifacts from the Kuba people of the Congo that had been collected by William Sheppard. Sheppard had gone to Africa in 1890 to spread Christianity and European values among the natives but had found himself fascinated by the sophistication and complexity of African civilization. Amassing a large collection of African art and anthropological artifacts, Sheppard came to believe, along with Folsom, that Black Americans needed a positive identification with Africa in order to create a healthy identity. The collaboration of Sheppard and Folsom resulted in Hampton Institute becoming the only American college in the early twentieth century to possess a comprehensive collection of African art.

706 • Meta Warrick Fuller (1877–1968)

Born in Philadelphia and educated in its public schools, Meta Warrick Fuller graduated from the Pennsylvania School of Industrial Art with honors in 1898. After winning a scholarship to study sculpture for a year, she chose to venture across the Atlantic to Paris, where she was mentored by another Philadelphia-born painter, Henry Ossawa Tanner. Her sculpture *The Wretched* was exhibited at the Paris Salon in 1903 and gained her local acclaim and the attention of French sculptor Auguste Rodin, who took her on as a student. She returned to the United States after three years and opened a studio in her hometown. Her work received little attention until she secured a commission to produce 150 historical Black figures for the Jamestown Tercentennial Exposition of 1907. Although much of her work from this period was destroyed in a fire that consumed a Philadelphia warehouse, she was able to produce a series of historical sculptures when she received another commission from the New York Semi-Centennial of Emancipation. Fuller's commitment to African American portrayal set her apart from the majority of late-nineteenth-century African American artists. Her *Ethiopia Awakening* (1914), a life-size bronze of an Egyptian woman emerging from a mummy's wrapping, testifies to an identification with Africa that looks forward to the Harlem Renaissance.

Music and Theater

707 • Georgia Minstrels

After the Civil War, the first successful all–African American minstrel troupe emerged. The *Georgia Minstrels* was founded by Geo. B. Hicks, a Black Georgian, in 1865. Reorganized by a white manager under the name *Callender's Original Georgia Minstrels* and then in 1878 as *Haverly's European Minstrels,* it was finally known from 1882 on as *Callender's Consolidated Minstrels.* The *Georgia Minstrels* was dis-

Billy Kersands of Callender's Georgia Minstrels. Courtesy of Billy Rose Theater Collection. The New York Public Library for the Performing Arts. Astor, Lenox, and Tilden Foundations

tinguished not only by its all–African American personnel but also by its attempt to elevate minstrelsy to a serious art form. With several outstanding musicians, such as banjoists the Bohee Brothers, the *Georgia Minstrels* excelled at playing serious music and working it into the minstrelsy form. At its peak in 1876, the troupe contained twenty-one performers. It also contained two of the most outstanding minstrels in the history of the form—Billy Kersands and Sam Lucas.

708 • James Bland (1854–1911)

The composer of "Carry Me Back to Old Virginny" and "Oh, Dem Golden Slippers" was a Black minstrel named James Bland, who was born in Flushing, New York, on October 22, 1854. Reared in a mixed-race middle-class family, Bland taught himself to play the banjo as a child. After the family moved to Washington, D.C., and Bland graduated from high school, he entered Howard University to study law, but became infatuated with the songs of the former slaves after hearing them on campus. He dropped out of school to join a minstrel troupe, over the objections of his family, and eventually became famous as a minstrel singer, composer, and performer in the United States and abroad. Quite popular in Europe, where he traveled with the *Haverly Minstrels,* Bland remained abroad by himself in part because he could perform without blackface. This he did for almost ten years until his popularity began to wane with the advent of vaudeville, and he returned to the United States. Of the more than seven hundred songs composed by Bland, the most familiar tunes included "In the Evening by the Moonlight," "There's a Long, Long Trail a-Winding," and "Carry Me Back to Old Virginny," which became the Virginia state song in 1940.

709 • Sissieretta Jones (1868–1933)

Known as the Black Patti, Sissieretta Jones was arguably the most celebrated African American vocalist of the nineteenth and early twentieth centuries. Born into a musical family, she loved to perform from the time she was a toddler. She was a regular entertainer at the White House (she sang for four presidents), performed at several U.S. world expositions, worked with Antonin Dvořák and Harry Burleigh, and toured the West Indies in her early career. Now established, Jones's later career was buoyed by her work with *Black Patti's Troubadoures.* Organized by Jones's managers, the group was created as a vehicle and a platform for her operatic performances. The Troubadoures disbanded and Jones left the stage in 1916.

The first Fisk Jubilee Singers. National Archives

710 • Fisk Jubilee Singers

The Fisk Jubilee Singers emerged in 1871 when George L. White, the European American music teacher at Fisk School in Nashville, Tennessee, decided to present his singing students in a series of fund-raising concerts. Initially White, a fan of Negro music, had the group of five men and four women sing classical music and popular ballads, but these songs received only a lukewarm reception. Gradually White added plantation songs and spirituals to the repertoire, and the white audiences became enthusiastic. By the end of their first tour in 1871, the Singers were able to raise $20,000 after singing in several northern cities and performing before President Ulysses S. Grant. The Fisk Jubilee Singers became world-famous when they sang at the World Peace Jubilee concert in Boston in 1872 and were able to sing "The Battle Hymn of the Republic" flawlessly even though the band had started the song much too high for most of the assembled singers. By the end of their tour in 1878, which had taken them to Europe, the Singers had raised $150,000.

711 • The Blues

Although the exact origin of the blues is a mystery, this type of music appears to have emerged in the Mississippi Delta after the Civil War when African American musicians could travel around the South for the first time and create a repertoire of songs by singing in several towns and cities. Unlike the pre–Civil War spirituals, the blues were sung by solo musicians, and unlike prewar popular Black musicians, the blues singers preferred the guitar to the banjo and fiddle. It was the music of African Americans who had been freed from slavery only to experience perpetual poverty by sharecropping. Actually the blues were more closely related to the work songs of the early nineteenth century, which have been traced back to the work songs heard in West Africa from the seventeenth century forward. Although the blues songs are commonly about such themes as betrayal in love, they are also a poignant commentary on the sadness of African Americans in the post–Civil War period.

712 • Black Musical Comedy

After 1875, minstrelsy declined as a medium for serious African American musical expression, but a new medium emerged in 1891 that revitalized Black theatrical performance. The shift began with *The Creole Show,* which opened in 1891 with Sam Lucas, Fred Piper, Billy Jackson, and Irving Jones, all minstrels, who created something new when they added a chorus of beautiful dancing African American women to the show. With its fancy costumes and new songs, *The Creole Show* was the first modern musical comedy because it emphasized Black music and dancing talent over the buffoonery and caricature of minstrelsy. In 1895 another show, *The Octoroons,* appeared with the same blend of talent and repertoire, and was followed in 1896 by *Oriental America* and later *Black Patti's Troubadoures,* starring the serious concert singer Sissieretta Jones. A new period of the Black musical comedy had emerged, which lured audiences with the promise of comedy but won over their hearts with the music.

713 • Ragtime

The first "rags" appeared in the 1890s in the "coon songs," those humiliating ditties about chicken, watermelon, and razor-wielding Blacks that defined the worst of the minstrel era. But once the "ragging," a speeded-up, jerky, syncopated rhythm, was extracted and fused with new lyrics, such as in "Clorindy, the Origin of the Cake Walk" (1898), by Will Marion Cook and Paul Laurence Dunbar, ragtime emerged as a distinctive form. Ragtime became popular as a piano style after Ben Harvey transcribed it for piano in his 1897 "Ragtime Instructor" and Scott Joplin created his series of rag compositions like "Maple Leaf Rag" (1898) and "Palm Leaf Rag" (1903). Ragtime attained perhaps its greatest musical expression in the May 1912 Carnegie Hall concert of the Clef Club Orchestra of 125 African American musicians.

Religion

714 • John Jasper's "Visible" Black Church

When the Civil War emancipated millions of slaves, it also freed African Americans from having to worship in white congregations or in secret, and many slave preachers established their own independent congregations. One of the most colorful was John Jasper, an ex-slave, who started a church in a stable but built Sixth Mount Zion Baptist Church into a nationally known congregation. It was famous because of his impassioned, emotional sermons, especially his 1878 sermon "The Sun Do Move," a defense of the Bible against the scientific view that the earth moved around the sun. Although most who heard the sermon were skeptical of Jasper's astronomical views, many, Black and white, liked his preaching style and it made him a popular religious figure until the end of the century.

715 • Benjamin Tucker Tanner (1835–1923)

More respected than John Jasper by fellow African American ministers of the postwar period was Benjamin Tanner, initially a preacher and later a bishop of the African Methodist Episcopal Church. Born in Pittsburgh into a privileged African American family, Tanner had been educated at the historically white Avery College and trained in the ministry in the Western Theological Seminary. Ordained as a minister in the AME Church at the beginning of the Civil War, Tanner went to Washington, D.C., after the war, where he took over the First Colored Presbyterian Church of Washington. He took the lead in bringing religious training and education to freedmen who flocked to Washington from the former slave states of the upper South. During his missionary work, he organized several African American congregations, ministered at Baltimore's Bethel Church, and became the editor of the intellectually oriented AME journal, the *Christian Recorder.*

716 • Militant Black Missionaries

Even Black preachers in northern white congregations went South to minister to the needs of the freedmen, and some of them became involved in the political struggle to advance African American rights. One of the most courageous was the Reverend Jonathan Gibbs (1827–74), a Presbyterian minister from Philadelphia, who traveled to South Carolina in 1865 and assumed leadership of Zion Presbyterian Church and built a school for the freedmen in Charleston. Moving on to Florida, he expanded his efforts as a missionary and was chosen by his peers to serve as state superintendent of public instruction. But in 1874, while running for the United States Congress, he was found dead. Many suspected that he had been murdered by the Ku Klux Klan, which had threatened him several times.

717 • Women's Day

As the pivotal leader in the National Baptist Convention, Nannie Helen Burroughs sought a way to institutionalize recognition of the contribution of Black women in African American religious circles and found a novel device in Women's Day. At the 1906 meeting of the National Baptist Convention, she proposed a special Sunday be designated as national Women's Day, when women would lead and speak in the

Nannie Helen Burroughs. 1909. Prints and Photographs Division, Library of Congress

worship service of Baptist churches around the nation. Women's Day was a way for women's voices to be heard at least one day of the year in even the most sexist church. Over the years, Women's Day grew into a series of events, such as a meal served to the women by men of the church, that provided recognition for the essential role played in the Black church by women.

THE NEW NEGRO, 1916–39

Movements

718 • Harlem Renaissance

The Harlem Renaissance emerged after World War I when black writers and artists created poetry, plays, music, painting, sculpture, and cultural criticism that celebrated African American life and captured national attention. Originally called the New Negro Movement, the Harlem Renaissance reflected a sense of racial pride and self-confidence that flourished in Black urban communities of the North as hundreds of thousands of poor Blacks migrated out of the South and into the urban North during World War I. The travail and struggle of such migrants to create lives for themselves in New York City, Chicago, and Washington, D.C., supplied the poems and stories written by Langston Hughes, Claude McKay, and Rudolph Fisher during the period. The Harlem Renaissance benefited from the interest of white American writers in the Black experience, the rise of jazz as America's popular musical form, and the domination of American popular theater by Black musical comedies. Toward the end of the 1920s, another flowering of creativity occurred in the visual arts when Aaron Douglas, Richmond Barthe, Archibald Motley, William H. Johnson, and Lois Mailou Jones created African American art based on African forms. The Harlem Renaissance plummeted after the stock market crash of 1929, but such African American artists as Zora Neale Hurston, Paul Robeson, and Jacob Lawrence continued to produce powerful works of art that influenced later generations.

Some Important Books

719 • *Bronze* (1922)

Georgia Douglas Johnson's book of racial poetry announced the Black woman's modern voice in poetry. Johnson was the foremother of twentieth-century Black modernism, with close personal relationships with Alain Locke and Jean Toomer. That role comes through clearly in *Bronze,* her collection of racial poetry, in which she constructs, in opposition to the "mammy" stereotype rampant in the early twentieth century, a new, powerful image of the Black mother whose courage and devotion "sandals the feet" of her offspring, balming them against the pain of life in a racist America. At the same time, her poems signal a call for independent womanhood, released from the doldrums of being someone else's caretaker. Carefully crafted and lovingly expressed, Johnson's poems outline paths taken and extended by such later poets as Gwendolyn Brooks.

720 • *Cane* (1923)

Cane, Jean Toomer's modernist homage to African American life and culture, was the Harlem Renaissance's first work of genius and one of the most innovative works of American fiction. Authored by the grandson of P. B. S.

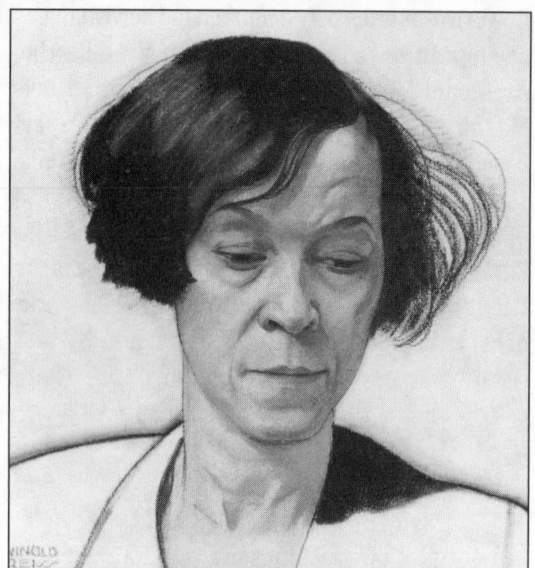

A Poetess (Georgia Douglas Johnson) by Winold Reiss. Copyright Reiss Estate. Collection of J. P. Speed Art Museum, Louisville, Kentucky

Pinchback, the Louisiana Reconstruction lieutenant governor, *Cane* is Toomer's attempt to capture the rhythm and mood of African American life by weaving together short fiction, imagistic poetry, and theatrical dialogue. Divided into three parts, *Cane* begins with a series of impressionistic sketches of southern Black women that Toomer began writing on his return from a summer spent in 1921 as the temporary head of an industrial school in Sparta, Georgia. The second section uses mainly poetry to portray Black life in the North, most powerfully the street life of 7th and T Streets in Washington, D.C., where recent southern migrants congregated, sang songs, and told their life stories. A third section, also sited in the South, narrates the frustrations of an educated African American with religious and educational efforts in the South. Toomer sought to stretch literary form and rebel against the accepted homilies of African American racial politics in *Cane*, which succeeds best in creating a haunting mood of languid rural life and folk culture in the Black South.

721 • *The New Negro* (1925)

Alain Locke's compendium of poetry, prose, critical and social essays, artwork, and historical commentary is the bible of the New Negro Movement. Announcing a "New Negro," who is culturally self-conscious, racially proud, politically militant, yet socially open to interracial contact, Locke created one of the first mixed-media anthologies in American literary history. With pastel portraits of famous and working-class African Americans, with poems by Countee Cullen, Claude McKay, Langston Hughes, and Jean Toomer, with short fiction by Rudolph Fisher, Zora Neale Hurston, and others, Locke created an open space for the many lights of the

Alain LeRoy Locke, 1925, by Winold Reiss. Courtesy of Reiss Estate

"renaissance" to shine brightly. Moreover, by bringing in such political figures as W. E. B. Du Bois, James Weldon Johnson, and Robert Moton, Locke sought to pose the artistic revival of the twenties as a synthesis of older discourses about how African Americans could win acceptance in American culture.

722 • *The Weary Blues* (1926)

Langston Hughes's (1902–67) first book of poetry may have been his best. It was certainly the best single book of poetry published in the 1920s that captured so powerfully the spirit of the Harlem Renaissance. With poems written on the blues form and in free verse, *The Weary Blues* broke with the traditional English verse forms that dominated the work of Hughes's rivals, Claude McKay and Countee Cullen. By transliterating the speech and music of the urban poor into free-verse poetry, Hughes fulfilled the Harlem Renaissance dictum that the artist should become the voice of his people.

723 • *Home to Harlem* (1928)

Claude McKay (1889–1948), a Jamaican immigrant to the United States, whose book of poetry *Harlem Shadows* (1922) was one of the first books of poems published by one of the new Harlem Renaissance poets, turned to the novel form in the later twenties and produced perhaps the best single novel of the Black twenties. *Home to Harlem* served McKay better than his poetry as a vehicle to portray the color, class, and moral conflicts of the Harlem Renaissance period. Perhaps more than any other novel of the period, *Home to Harlem* captured the urbanism of the Black twenties. It also finds Jake, the urban proletarian, and Ray, the young Black intellectual, to be the perfect pair to carry on a dialogue about the question of Black identity in a modern, urban, American world. The novel also excelled at weaving discussion of the identity conflicts of African Americans into a complicated yet exciting plot of Black conflict in Harlem during the 1920s.

724 • *The Walls of Jericho* (1928)

Rudolph Fisher's first novel was written on a bet that no one could blend the lives of working- and middle-class Harlemites of the 1920s into one excellent short novel. Fisher did it and thereby portrayed the conflicts of class and skin color better than any other Harlem Renaissance writer. Written from the perspective of working-class men at Padmore's pool hall, Fisher's novel pokes satirically at all of the major characters of the Harlem Renaissance, from race- but not class-conscious striving Black professionals to well-meaning but misguided white philanthropic patrons. Even the working-class pair of Bubber and Jinx do not escape a critique in narrative of the color and class foibles that form their "walls of Jericho." What this novel provides is an excellent portrait of the color and class tensions that divided and sustained Harlem in the twenties.

725 • *Passing* (1929)

Nella Larsen's second novel remains one of the most haunting, suggestive, and contemporary novels written during the Harlem Renaissance. The story is more than just another rehash of the trauma of light-skinned African Americans who can masquerade as white. The story reveals the chance encounter between Irene Redfield and an old neighborhood friend, Clare Kendry. Clare is married to a white man from whom she has hidden her Black ancestry, and in the hands of Larsen, this secret is shaped into a subtle commentary on the "perfect" marriage of an upper-class Black woman of the 1920s. Clare comes to symbolize much that is

missing from Irene's bourgeois lifestyle and suggests that the Black bourgeoisie are more fascinated with those who live the double life than this class usually admits. Clare's social and possibly sexual attractiveness for Irene comes from the former's daring energy and boldness of feeling, both of which Irene discovers she needs to survive as a creative woman. More than any other Black writer of the 1920s, Larsen is willing to probe the psychological territory of difference to convey the sense of unexpressed yearning of early-twentieth-century Black middle-class life. As such, *Passing* is a subtle, provocative critique of the Black Victorian propriety in the 1920s.

726 • *Southern Road* (1932)

In his review of *Southern Road,* Alain Locke lauded Sterling Brown for being able to "compose with the freshness and naturalness of folk balladry" and thereby convince skeptics that a Negro poet can achieve an authentic folk-touch. *Southern Road* deserved such praise. For in such poems as "Maumee Ruth," "Sam Smiley," and "Strong Men," Brown captured the poetry and the militancy of the African American blues. Leaving behind the somewhat vague political voice of Hughes's *Weary Blues, Southern Road* possesses the toughness of the 1930s southern folk identity face-to-face with the Great Depression. Perhaps most remarkable, *Southern Road* avoids a note of despair. For in such poems as "Strong Men," Brown constructed a strong male voice that could declare, "The strong men keep a-comin' on, The strong men git stronger."

727 • *Their Eyes Were Watching God* (1937)

Zora Neale Hurston's *Their Eyes Were Watching God* is the first feminist novel of the twentieth century. Situated in Hurston's fictional Eastonville, a kind of idealized world in other Hurston short stories and novels, *Their Eyes Were Watching God* showed that the world of all-Black southern towns was hardly an idyllic one for African American women. Readers follow Hurston's protagonist, Janie, through a series of learning experiences that begin with adopting and then rebelling against the advice given her by her mother. Moving through two marriages, Janie learns to assert her identity in the face of husbands and townspeople who utilize men as "mules." Eventually Janie seizes her right to define her own identity outside of the strictures imposed by such communities. Remarkably Hurston tells her liberation story without portraying these communities as pathological.

Art

728 • Winold Reiss (1886–1953)

In 1924 Paul Kellogg, editor of the *Survey Graphic,* teamed Winold Reiss, the German portraitist and graphic artist, with Alain Locke to illustrate the special Harlem issue of the *Survey Graphic* that appeared March 1, 1925. That issue contained sympathetic pastel studies of Harlem's working class and flattering portraits of Harlem Renaissance Black artists and intellectuals from an artist better known in America for his Indian portraits and commercial design. The latter helped, however, too, for Reiss also produced sharply etched abstract imaginatives of life in Harlem that became the signature design style of the Black twenties. His pastel portraits were exhibited at the 125th Street Harlem Branch of the New York Public Library, and color reproductions enhanced Locke's *The New Negro* (1925). During the late twenties, Reiss

Cover of March 1, 1925, issue of *Survey Graphic*, designed by Winold Reiss, featuring portrait of Roland Hayes.

produced sensitive portraits of African Americans from the Sea Islands in South Carolina and continued to explore the African American subject in the 1930s. Before his death, Reiss donated most of those Harlem Renaissance and South Carolina portraits to Fisk University, while several others are at the Smithsonian's National Portrait Gallery.

729 • Aaron Douglas (1899–1979)

Aaron Douglas rose to prominence in the 1920s because of his willingness and ability to produce Africanist illustrations and designs that satisfied the Harlem Renaissance's need for racially representative images. Migrating to New York from Kansas in the early twenties, Douglas studied with Winold Reiss, whose cover and illustrations for the *Survey Graphic* had inspired Douglas. Encouraged by Reiss to study African sculpture and motifs, Douglas developed a unique African American interpretive design style that captured the rhythm and energy of African American dances, postures, and consciousness in the twenties. Douglas developed his own signature style that avoided stereotypical images and portrayed a positive and proud African American subject and culture. During the 1920s, Douglas's illustrations graced the covers of many books, journals, and magazines. One of Douglas's best was his cover for *Fire!!*, the aesthetically radical Black journal of the 1920s that produced only one scandalous issue. Douglas's flat, geometric designs were often centered by a monumental, Africanized head and embellished with smaller stylized Africanist motifs. During the 1930s Douglas produced more paintings and murals, especially the marvelous New York Public Library mural of African American history at the 125th Street Harlem Branch (1934).

730 • Richmond Barthe (1901–89)

Richmond Barthe was first a painter who studied at the Chicago Art Institute, but became a sculptor when encouraged to produce some sculptures for the Negro Art Week organized in Chicago in 1927. Like Douglas, Barthe became known for his willingness to produce African American sculpture that utilized African principles of design, particularly the elongation of body forms, to portray African American people. Moreover, in such sculptures as *Blackberry Woman* (1932) and *African Dancer* (1933), which were purchased by the Whitney Museum in 1935, Barthe excelled at capturing motion in clay.

African Dancer, 1933. Photograph by Catharine Kneeland at a one-man show of Richmond Barthe at the Arden Gallery, March 1939. Courtesy of National Archives, the Harmon Foundation Collection

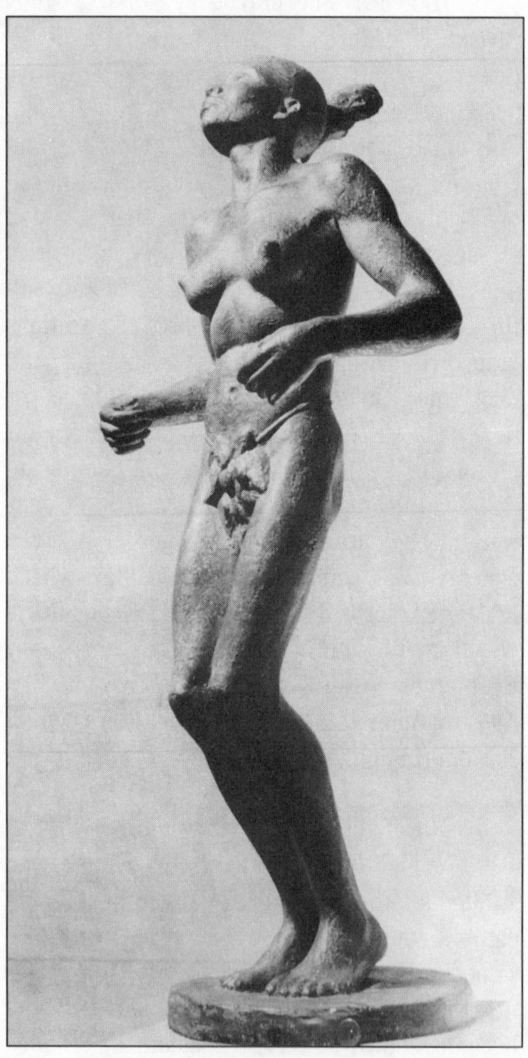

731 • James Van Der Zee (1886–1983)

James Van Der Zee was the most important documentary photographer of the Harlem Renaissance, the man whose photographs have become records of the look, feel, and self-consciousness of Harlem residents between the wars. Migrating to Harlem in 1906, Van Der Zee was at first a pianist, but in 1917 opened a portrait studio on 135th Street in New York City, where he earned a good living by crafting sensitive, often retouched photographs of Black residents, returning servicemen, and white visitors to Harlem. Approaching photography as an art, Van Der Zee used atmospheric effects, soft-focus techniques, and elaborate backdrops to capture the dignity of his subjects, whether they were part of the working class or the educational and financial elite.

732 • Archibald Motley (1891–1980)

Archibald Motley was one of the most versatile artists of the 1920s and 1930s, a man who began with exquisitely detailed portraits of African Americans and then broke into a modernist style of portraying Black urban life that one art historian has called the "blues aesthetic." Born in New Orleans into the Catholic elite of that city, Motley nevertheless acknowledged a Pygmy ancestry and a commitment to documenting African American life. During study at the Art Institute of Chicago, Motley began the type of work that early distinguished his career, portraiture of what might be called the "Old Negro." With his sensitive treatment of an elderly Black woman, *Mending Socks* (1923), Motley evoked an era of the southern servant and grandmother who achieved enduring dignity by helping others. But during the late 1920s Motley's style underwent a dramatic transformation, leaving behind realistic portraiture for modernistic, almost caricaturist, studies of working-class urban African Americans dancing in rent parties; howling in church; and crawling the street in *Chicken Shack* (1936). What these latter pictures conveyed was the energy of African American communities in rich syncopation and color.

Chicken Shack, 1936. National Archives, the Harmon Foundation Collection. Courtesy of Archie Motley

733 • William H. Johnson (1901–70)

Born in Florence, South Carolina, William H. Johnson was one of the most prolific artists of the twentieth century, and a man whose work went through several styles of expression in his lifetime. Migrating North, he enrolled in the National Academy of Design in New York City, spent summers at the Cape Cod School of Art in Provincetown, Massachusetts, and won several prizes for his work before going to Paris in 1926. There he was influenced by the work of Cézanne and Chaim Soutine, and produced contorted, colorful landscapes that were examples of his expressionist cubism. Returning to the South, he used this technique to produce several studies of southern architecture as well as its people. But it was only after his return to Denmark, his marriage to Holcha Krake, and his subsequent return to the United States in 1938 that Johnson began to paint in his most successful style—that of his silkscreens from the 1930s and 1940s. As in *Going to Church,* Johnson excelled at creating humorous, graphically complex pictures that seemingly reduced his subjects to the bare essentials of design and form.

734 • Horace Pippin (1888–1946)

Horace Pippin was a self-taught African

American artist who stopped painting for years after an injury during service in World War I cost him the use of his right arm. Learning to draw in 1929 by using a hot poker on wood, Pippin developed a technique that communicated his deep emotional response to subject matter. He became well known when one of his paintings was discovered in a shoe repair window in Pennsylvania in 1937 by art critic Christian Brinton. His work was supported by such influential figures as the art dealer Robert Carlen and the flamboyant art collector Albert Barnes. Pippin's painting ranged from arresting winter landscape scenes to such historical narratives as *John Brown Going to His Hanging* (1942) and genre studies as *Domino Players* (1943). Pippin excelled at rendering scenes of life with a combination of warmth and social irony.

735 • Sargent Johnson (1887–1967)

One of the most versatile artists to emerge from the New Negro Movement was Sargent Johnson, who became one of the most provocative sculptors of the 1920s and 1930s. Born in Boston, Johnson was an orphan who moved among several foster homes and cities before taking up residence in San Francisco in 1915, where he studied at the A. W. Best School of Art and the California School of Fine Arts. Through the Harmon Foundation exhibitions, he gained national attention when his bust *Sammy* won a medal in the 1928 exhibition. Self-consciously committed to producing "Negro Art," Johnson adeptly mined the mask traditions of West Africa as inspiration for some of his best sculptures, such as his terra-cotta *Girl's Head* (1929) and *Copper Mask* (1935). His masterpiece *Forever Free* (1933), with its evocation of both African sculpture and African American folk traditions, has become almost iconic in African American art history. But Johnson was not limited to small-scale sculpture. During the thirties he worked for the Federal Arts Project and created several monumental and stone relief sculptures. Johnson also created numerous sensitive lithographs, of which *Lenox Avenue* (1938), with its fusion of African American figural and musical elements, is especially beautiful.

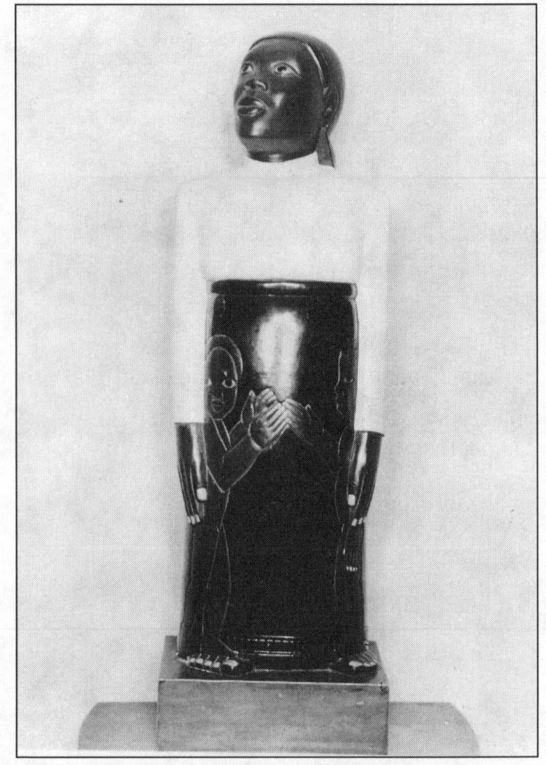

Sargent Johnson's *Forever Free*, 1933. 36″ × 11½″ × 9″ × ½″. Courtesy of San Francisco Museum of Art. Gift of Mrs. E. D. Lederman. Photo by Marjorie Griffiths. National Archives

736 • Augusta Savage (1900–62)

Despite Augusta Savage's lack of support from her father to become an artist, she persevered to become a well-known portrait sculptor of the 1920s in Harlem, New York. Moreover, Savage was not only a productive sculptor but also an arts administrator who coordinated the Harlem Community Art Center in the 1930s. She

was responsible, for example, for promoting the careers of younger artists, most notably Jacob Lawrence, whom she befriended when he was an adolescent. Among her most famous artistic works is *Gamin* (ca. 1930). This piece was modeled in clay, cast in plaster, and then painted. This gamin, or anonymous boy on the street, is a portrait of an individual yet represents the temperament and savvy style of numerous young people during the Harlem Renaissance era. The boy appears to be tough yet compassionate, to have a jaunty sense of self, and to possess the requisite determination to make it.

737 • Lois Mailou Jones (b. 1905)

As an artist who has traversed several historical periods in African American art, Lois Mailou Jones was discovered during the late 1930s by James Herring, James Porter, and Alain Locke as a promising, engaging artist. Born in Boston, Jones attended the Boston Museum School of Fine Arts, New York's Teachers College, and the Académie Julien in Paris. Influenced by the French impressionists, her early work consisted of marvelous studies of French urban life distinguished by their color and design. She took up African American subject matter after Alain Locke's suggestion of "doing something of your own people." Jones responded with the sensitive realism of *Jennie* and the cubistic Africanism of *Les Fétiches* (1938). During several years in Haiti, Jones developed a palette and a technique that combined the aesthetics of Haitian, African, and French cultures, captured in such paintings as *Marche Haiti* (1963). Moreover, as an art teacher at Howard University, she not only taught several generations of African American students but reacted to the emergence of racial self-consciousness in the 1960s and 1970s with such invigorating compositions as *Deux Coiffeurs d'Afrique* (1982).

Music and Dance

738 • *Shuffle Along* (1921)

Shuffle Along was the first musical revue written, produced, and performed by African Americans. It opened in New York to rave reviews. With music by Eubie Blake and lyrics by Noble Sissle, the revue sported a number of hits, including "I'm Just Wild About Harry" and "Love Will Find a Way," and launched the careers of Josephine Baker and Florence Mills. *Shuffle Along* was such a sensation because it showcased African American dance, music, and acting on Broadway that was not imitative of white American musicals. Eubie Blake and Noble Sissle followed up *Shuffle Along* with another Broadway hit in 1923, *Runnin' Wild*, which launched the signature dance of the twenties—the Charleston.

739 • William Christopher Handy (1873–1958)

W. C. Handy, as he was generally known, was a cornet player, a minstrel musician, and a bandleader, but is best known as the composer who first wrote down the blues. Actually, Handy grew up in Alabama hearing spirituals, cakewalks, and minstrel music, and when he began playing the cornet, he performed in what were called novelty music bands, such as the Hampton Cornet Band. He also learned to sing the spirituals and sang with the Mahara's Minstrels. While working as a director of a Black band in Tutwiler, Mississippi, in 1903, Handy first heard the blues, and later came up with the idea of composing and arranging them. In 1912 he published the first blues composition, *The Memphis Blues,* although some interpreters have suggested it was more of a cakewalk than a blues. He quickly followed with *St. Louis Blues* (1914),

Joe Turner's Blues (1915), and *Beale Street Blues* (1917). His autobiography, *Father of the Blues* (1941), made him famous, although it fueled the resentment of some, such as Jelly Roll Morton, who believed that Handy claimed too much in his title.

740 • Jelly Roll Morton (1890–1941)

Jelly Roll Morton became widely known in 1938 when he heard a *Ripley's Believe It or Not!* claim that W. C. Handy was the father of jazz and wrote back that New Orleans was the "cradle of jazz and I, myself, happened to be the creator in 1902." Although many disputed Morton's claim to have originated jazz, he is generally acknowledged as the first complete jazz pianist and the first full-fledged composer of New Orleans–style jazz. Born into the self-consciously superior Creole class that had absorbed French and Spanish musical traditions, Morton got his musical education in the red-light district of New Orleans called Storyville, where he worked as a "house pianist" and won recognition as a "piano professor" by age seventeen. Migrating to Chicago in the early 1920s, he worked briefly for a music company but gained a greater recognition as an intimidating pianist who would elbow lesser players off the piano stool at clubs to teach them and the audience a few piano "lessons." Borrowing from ragtime, the blues, and New Orleans band style, Morton perfected a two-handed piano style that in his own words "imitated a band." With multiple themes, breaks, counterrhythms, and even Latin American accents, Morton's piano playing was incredibly rich. Unfortunately, by the time Morton recorded his music with the Red Hot Peppers in 1926, the New Orleans piano style was falling out of favor. But that did not deter him: Jelly Roll apparently brought a pistol to recording sessions to ensure that his younger sidemen did not stray too far from the New Orleans jazz line. After his reminiscences, *Mister Jelly Roll,* were published in 1950, Morton's music enjoyed a brief revival, and more recently, has been given fresh reinterpretation by Marcus Roberts. His piano work remains one of the foundations of twentieth-century jazz piano.

741 • King Oliver's Creole Jazz Band

The reputed king of cornet playing in New Orleans in the 1910s, King Oliver (1885–1938) was the first African American to introduce New Orleans jazz to a northern audience. After leaving New Orleans for Chicago in 1918, Oliver formed a band that established itself at the South Side's Lincoln Gardens. The band became a major jazz-performing operation when Louis Armstrong joined the band in 1922. In a series of recordings from April to December 1923, the high-water mark of early Chicago jazz playing was set.

742 • James P. Johnson (1894–1955)

The legendary pianist James P. Johnson was the originator of the Harlem Stride piano playing style that marked the transition from ragtime to jazz. Growing up in the so-called San Juan Hill area of New York City early in the twentieth century, Johnson listened to European music played by middle-class New York African Americans, to ring shouts and gutbucket music favored by Gullah migrants from South Carolina, who danced the original Charleston in the alleyways, and to quadrilles played by New Orleans visitors, and he developed a piano playing style that could appeal to all of these audiences. He became famous while playing piano for the Jungles Casino, a dance hall masquerading as a school. James P., as he was known, created a tradition of piano playing that was continued by Duke Ellington, Fats

Waller, Count Basie, Thelonius Monk, and Herbie Hancock.

743 • Fletcher Henderson (1897–1952)

Fletcher Henderson organized the premier dance band of the 1920s. Initially a studio piano musician, Henderson had numerous publishing and recording connections by the early 1920s, when he put together a pickup band and molded it into a complete orchestra. Dropping the banjos and violins that earlier orchestras such as James Europe's had contained, Henderson streamlined the jazz orchestra and developed the practice of featuring a soloist, such as the legendary Coleman Hawkins, on saxophone. With Don Redman as his arranger, the Fletcher Henderson Orchestra held forth at the Roseland, a whites-only dance establishment, and was the first New York jazz band to play arrangements. But the band really came into its own after September 29, 1924, when Henderson lured Louis Armstrong away from King Oliver and Chicago to come to New York and play with the Henderson Orchestra. Armstrong taught the orchestra to swing, and by the time of Armstrong's departure several months later, the Fletcher Henderson Orchestra had become the most popular dance band in New York.

Louis Armstrong. Prints and Photographs Division, Library of Congress. Used by permission of the Louis Armstrong Educational Foundation

744 • Louis Armstrong (1898–1971)

Louis Armstrong was the single most important musical innovator of the 1920s. When King Oliver invited Armstrong to join his band in Chicago in 1923, Oliver knew that Armstrong had already eclipsed the "king's" position in New Orleans cornet playing. And although the sidemen in Fletcher Henderson's band laughed at Louis Armstrong's country-bumpkin manners and his simple, ready grin, they listened with awe once he began to play the cornet. Armstrong came out of the same New Orleans tradition of cornet playing that had produced King Oliver, but Armstrong was superior to others of his time in his ability as an improvising soloist. Louis played predictable passages of music with such inventive phrasing, such imagination, such rhythm, and such remarkable accuracy and speed that he pushed bands not only to keep up but also to change their approach to the music. Some of his greatness was lost to later audiences and listeners who were only familiar with him from recordings and broadcasts from the 1940s and 1950s, when his performances were less demanding musically and his contribution clouded by his sometimes obsequious demeanor on stage. But during the 1920s, particularly in the legendary Hot Fives recordings, Armstrong

recorded some of the outstanding small combo music in the history of jazz.

745 • Bessie Smith (1894–1937)

The only musical equal of Louis Armstrong in the 1920s was Bessie Smith, the premier blues and jazz singer of the decade, who changed the way that jazz was played with her singing. Although legend has it that Bessie Smith was discovered and taught the blues by Ma Rainey and her husband, the truth is that no one was responsible for the remarkable musical intelligence that Bessie Smith brought to the singing of songs. As a teenager singing in the theater circuit of the 1910s, Bessie Smith first became popular as a stage performer in a vaudeville-like theater world in which Black women performers were required to dance, act, and play the fool before Black and white audiences. But Bessie Smith really came into her own in 1923, when, following Mamie Smith's recording of "Crazy Blues," the first blues record, in August 1920, Bessie began recording songs for the Okeh record company. Her version of "Downhearted Blues" sold 780,000 copies and propelled her into stardom. When she recorded "St. Louis Blues," W. C. Handy's composition and Ethel Waters's signature piece, with Louis Armstrong in January 1925, Bessie Smith slowed down the tempo, simplified the phrasing, and introduced such depth of feeling that she made hers the definitive version of the song. Bessie Smith's quick rise to popularity was followed by a quick decline in the early 1930s, when her records no longer sold as well. A hard-drinking and verbally abusive woman, Bessie Smith communicated the "hurt" she carried inside in her singing of songs and her acting performance in the film *St. Louis Blues* (1929). Bessie Smith died tragically in 1937 as a result of an automobile accident in Clarksdale, Mississippi, but contrary to what Edward Albee's play *The Death of Bessie Smith* (1960) reported, it was not a racially motivated tragedy. She did not die because she was refused treatment at a southern hospital. Rather, she was treated for shock by a physician at the scene of the accident and transported to an African American hospital where she died.

Bessie Smith. Photograph by Carl Van Vechten, February 3, 1936. Prints and Photographs Division, Library of Congress. Gift of Carl Van Vechten

746 • Duke Ellington (1899–1974)

Edward Kennedy Ellington was a pianist and composer who emerged in the late 1920s and 1930s to become America's most accomplished jazz bandleader during the so-called swing era. Born into the Black middle class of Washington, D.C., Ellington attended excellent public

schools, but left high school in 1917 to devote himself fully to playing music, often solo but increasingly in small combos around town. Early in 1923 he left for New York, where as a pianist he absorbed everything he could from ragtime, Harlem Stride piano, and New Orleans jazz band music, and transmuted it into a remarkably subtle, orchestral piano playing style. Performing initially with a five-piece band known as the Washingtonians, Ellington began writing songs for the group and began recording in 1924. He also expanded the size of the band to ten pieces and moved it to the famous Cotton Club in 1927. By then, it was clear that Ellington was an innovator in his approach to the jazz orchestra. Rather than using the band to feature his piano playing or imposing strict control over the sidemen's playing, Ellington approached the entire orchestra as an instrument, allowed each sideman to develop his own voice, and then used his piano to tie together the overall performance. Ellington was also gaining a reputation for his personal style and sophistication—hence, the title "Duke"—and that was increasingly represented in what could be called his own "sophisticated style" of jazz, which would later be called swing. Having begun recording in 1924, Ellington produced numerous popular songs over the years, including "Mood Indigo," "Down Beat," "Sentimental Lady," and "Harlem Air Shaft." Ellington kept his band alive in the Depression years by touring the South and the North and adding complexity to his compositions. In the 1940s he teamed up with arranger and songwriter Billy Strayhorn to produce a string of hits, including "Take the A Train," "Just a-Settin' and a-Rockin'," and "I Got It Bad and That Ain't Good." After World War II, Ellington was one of the few swing-era musicians and composers who continued to hold the respect of the younger "bebop" generation of jazz musicians and to record with them.

747 • Count Basie (1904–84)

The real master of swing in American jazz during the 1930s was William "Count" Basie, a pianist, but more importantly a jazz bandleader who remained popular with dancers throughout his long career. Born in Red Bank, New Jersey, Basie began playing piano as a teenager, being early influenced by "Fats" Waller. After a stint with the Benny Moten Orchestra in Kansas City in 1926, Basie started his own band and toured the United States from the 1930s on. Known for his distinctive, up-tempo style, Basie not only performed standards but composed such originals as "One O'Clock Jump." Despite the decline of many big bands in the 1940s with the advent of bebop, Basie's brand of swing remained popular. In 1957, he became the first American bandleader to perform before the Queen of England. In the 1970s, he enjoyed a revival of interest in his music by a young generation returning to dancing because of disco music.

748 • William Grant Still (1895–1978)

William Grant Still was the first African American to have a symphony performed by a white American orchestra, the Rochester Philharmonic, conducted by Howard Hanson, in 1931. The son of a bandleader, Grant Still was a medical student at Wilberforce College when he decided to take up music seriously. He studied classical music at Oberlin College; but he played oboe in the orchestra for the musical revue *Shuffle Along.* Further study in composition with such teachers as George Chadwick and Edgard Varèse strengthened his knowledge of musical form. His Symphony no. 1, or the *Afro-American* Symphony, as it is commonly known, was a synthesis of what Still had learned of traditional

Portrait of Lillian Evanti by Lois Mailou Jones, 1940.
Courtesy of National Portrait Gallery, Smithsonian Institution

European symphonic form and what his ear heard in the Black community of the 1920s. Though the dominant tune is not a folk song, Still's melody is nevertheless an improvisation on the blues, especially as they were played by jazz bands in New York. The four movements of the symphony—Longings, Sorrows, Humor, and Aspirations—could be metaphors of the African American outlook on life in the mid-twentieth century. Although known mainly for his *Afro-American* Symphony, Still composed a number of other pieces—*Africa* (1928), *Swanee River* (1939), and a ballet score, *Lenox Avenue* (1936). He received many awards during his career, including the Guggenheim Fellowship in 1934.

749 • Lillian Evanti (1891–1967)

Lillian Evanti was the first African American to sing opera with a major opera company. A coloratura soprano, Evanti (born Lillian Evans) grew up in Washington, D.C., the daughter of the founder of the Armstrong Technical High School. After earning a bachelor of music from Howard University in 1917, she studied voice with Frank La Forge in New York and Madame Ritter-Ciampi in Paris, before singing with the Paris Opéra in 1925. Her debut with the Paris Opéra in Nice in the opera *Lakmé* was acclaimed by those who heard her. She also gained rave reviews for singing in *The Barber of Seville* in Milan in 1930. Perhaps her greatest performance in America came on February 9, 1934, when she sang for President and Mrs. Roosevelt at the White House.

750 • Josephine Baker (1906–75)

Josephine Baker became an internationally famous dancer, singer, and nightclub performer in the 1920s. Fleeing East St. Louis after the pogromlike attack of whites on the Black neighborhoods in 1917, Baker went to Philadelphia, where she obtained her first break as a dancer in the *Dixie Steppers.* Moving to New York, she took a job as a dresser and then filled in for a sick chorus girl in Noble Sissle and Hubie Blake's *Shuffle Along* (1923). After becoming a star in their *Chocolate Dandies,* she gained an international reputation performing the *Danse Sauvage* in *La Revue Nègre* in Paris in 1925. The next year, she created pandemonium among French audiences with her erotic dancing and singing in a banana skirt in the Folies-Bergère. During the 1930s she transformed her image into a more dignified, if no less spectacular, French music hall performer, beginning with her engagement at Casino de Paris in 1931–32. Baker also made several movies. During the 1940s she was awarded the French Legion of Honor for her work during World War II.

Having adopted numerous orphaned children of various nationalities in the 1950s, she came out of retirement to perform in *Paris, Mes Amours* at the Olympia in Paris in 1959.

751 • Marian Anderson (1902–93)

Born in Philadelphia, Marian Anderson was the most accomplished singer of her generation. Having obtained her early music training in church choirs, she studied voice with Giuseppe Boghetti and appeared before the New York Philharmonic Orchestra in 1925. After winning a Rosenwald Fellowship, she traveled to and sang in Berlin in 1930. During the next five years, she studied and performed in Europe before returning to the United States and giving recitals at New York's Town Hall and Carnegie Hall. But her reputation soared in 1939, when the Daughters of the American Revolution (DAR) refused to allow her to sing at Constitution Hall in Washington, D.C., because she was African American. In the uproar that followed, Mrs. Eleanor Roosevelt resigned from the DAR and arranged for Anderson to sing at the Lincoln Memorial on Easter, an outdoor performance witnessed by over 75,000 people. Despite her reputation as a superb contralto, however, not until 1955 did the Metropolitan Opera Company invite Marian Anderson to sing with the company in Verdi's *Un Ballo in Maschera.* She became the first African American invited to perform with the Metropolitan.

752 • Leadbelly (1885–1949)

Born Huddie Ledbetter, Leadbelly, whose nickname referred to his deep-throated singing voice, was the most moving blues singer and guitar player of the 1940s. Early acknowledged as Louisiana's best guitar player, Leadbelly became more widely known when he accompanied Blind Lemon Jefferson to Texas in the 1910s. Regarded as a "dangerous Negro," who always carried a pistol, charmed and assaulted women, and attempted several murders, Leadbelly spent much of his young adulthood in jail or on the chain gang. Working and singing as the lead man on chain gangs strengthened the work-song elements in his music and added a poignant realism to his crying laments. He literally sang himself to freedom in 1925 when Texas Governor Pat M. Neff freed him in 1925 after hearing him sing. In 1930 Leadbelly was back on a chain gang, this time in Louisiana, but was freed again in 1934 after being discovered and recorded by Alan Lomax for the Library of Congress. Thereafter, Leadbelly became a celebrity entertainer who performed in New York, Hollywood, and at Harvard University, and who influenced such singers as Pete Seeger, Bob Dylan, and Paul McCartney. His songs "Good Night Irene," "Rock Island Line," and "Midnight Special" are classics.

Some Important Plays and Films

753 • *Within These Gates* (1919)

Within These Gates was the second film produced by Oscar Micheaux, the most prolific Black independent filmmaker of the twentieth century, whose Micheaux Film and Book Company was founded in Chicago in 1918. A film of many plots, *Within These Gates* is, on one level, the love story of Jennie, a Black woman with a hidden, compromised past who finds redemption in raising funds for Piney Woods School for African American children. But *Within These Gates* is also Oscar Micheaux's answer to D. W. Griffith's racist Reconstruction film *Birth of a Nation* (1915), because Micheaux shows how a

Oscar Micheaux. Schomburg Center, New York Public Library, Astor, Lenox and Tilden Foundation

white landowner cheats his Black sharecropper, who in turn is lynched after challenging the landowner's figures. *Within These Gates,* whose only surviving print was recently discovered by Thomas Cripps, also details early-twentieth-century Black Victorian color and class consciousness.

754 • *The Emperor Jones* (1920)

The Emperor Jones, written by white playwright Eugene O'Neill, opened by the Provincetown Players in New York in 1920 and starred the African American actor Charles Gilpin. O'Neill's play details how Brutus Jones, an ex–Pullman car porter and former criminal, becomes an evil emperor of a Caribbean island. Ultimately Brutus suffers a nervous breakdown for brutalizing the island people just as the whites. When O'Neill opened *The Emperor Jones* in London in 1924, he replaced the unreliable Gilpin with Paul Robeson in the title role. The film version of *The Emperor Jones* appeared in 1937, also starring Paul Robeson. *The Emperor Jones* became the signature play of the Harlem Renaissance for its psychological depiction of an African American. It played less well in Harlem, according to Langston Hughes, who recalled that when Jules Bledsoe ran across the Lafayette Theater stage as if in the jungle, Blacks in the audience yelled, "Man, you come on outa that jungle! This is Harlem!"

755 • *The Chip Woman's Fortune* (1923)

The first Broadway play by an African American was *The Chip Woman's Fortune,* which opened in May 1923. Written by playwright Willis Richardson, *The Chip Woman's Fortune* was produced by Chicago's Ethiopian Art Players. The Players were originally brought to Harlem, but after the community reception was lukewarm, the producers moved the serious play to Broadway, where it was well received.

Religion

756 • Storefront Church

During the Great Migration, which began in World War I and continued into the 1940s, southern Blacks abandoned the South for the greater opportunity of the urban North. While many of these migrants were absorbed into established Baptist and Methodist congregations in the North, some found northern styles of worship to be too formal. As some of the southern ministers left behind followed their flock northward, these clergy founded churches in homes or in storefronts—usually rented commercial properties on busy streets in the major northern cities. Visitors to the city on Sundays could regularly hear organ music, tambourine playing,

and emotive singing coming from such storefronts, where parishioners found not only a more emotional style of worship but also temporary housing, food, and fellowship with other southerners.

757 • Longest-Running Radio Program: *Church of God*

Elder "Lightfoot" Solomon Michaux was persuaded by his wife, Mary, in 1917, to build a church to house "Everybody's Mission," a nondenominational, interracial church, in Newport News, Virginia. Although Michaux became an ordained evangelist and Everybody's Mission became affiliated with the Church of Christ, Michaux broke away from the Holiness mother church in 1921 and organized the independent Church of God. Michaux's Church of God became nationally known in 1929, when he decided to begin a radio broadcast to bring religion to those who did not attend church. With a theme song, "Happy I Am," Michaux combined a call for repentance with a message of the power of positive thinking and thereby ensured that his radio message had something for everyone. The popularity of his program declined after 1937 after a scandal over his reputed mismanagement of funds. Undaunted, Michaux continued to broadcast until his death in 1960, making his the longest-running radio program in American history.

758 • Moorish Science Temple of America

The Moorish Science Temple fused Black nationalist ideology and Islamic faith in the United States and laid the groundwork for the Nation of Islam. Derived from the Canaanite Temple that was founded in Newark, New Jersey, in 1913 by Noble Drew Ali (born Timothy Drew), the Moorish Science Temple of America emerged after Ali and his followers broke with the original temple and set up the Moorish Holy Temple of Science in Chicago in 1925. Ali taught that African Americans needed a nationality before a religion, that they were not Negroes but "Asiatics" who had lost their identity through the domination of Europeans. Ali encouraged followers to replace slave surnames with Islamic ones, identify themselves as Moors on federal, state, and local forms, and practice economic self-sufficiency. Other temples popped up in Milwaukee, Pittsburgh, and Detroit, but the Chicago temple was the most active: followers sometimes challenged "Europeans" on the streets of Chicago with carrying cards that announced the bearers were not Negroes but Moors. In 1930, after a rival was murdered, Ali died mysteriously shortly after being indicted for the other man's murder.

759 • Sweet Daddy Grace (1882?–1960)

Bishop Charles Emmaniel "Sweet Daddy" Grace was the founder of the United House of Prayer for All People who turned his claims of being able to raise the dead into a messianic movement among poor African Americans during the 1930s and 1940s. Born in the Cape Verde Islands in 1881, Sweet Daddy moved to New Bedford, Massachusetts, in 1900 and worked as a short-order cook before he founded the United House of Prayer in 1921. Although the church was located in New Bedford, Grace traveled in North Carolina, South Carolina, Georgia, Michigan, and other states recruiting followers, claiming that he had revived his sister after she had been pronounced dead by doctors. In his famous admonition, Sweet Daddy stated, "Never mind about God. Salvation is by Grace only." He was perhaps most famous for his outstanding appearance—shoulder-length hair, colorful

suits, flashy jewelry, and three-inch-long fingernails—and his superb merchandising. He sold such items as Daddy Grace soap, which supposedly cleansed the body and reduced fat, and the *Grace* magazine, which reputedly could cure a cold or tuberculosis if it was placed on one's chest. Grace was also adept at collecting contributions: in 1956 the Internal Revenue Service estimated his net worth at over $4 million.

Sweet Daddy Grace, 1938, by James Van Der Zee. Courtesy of Donna Van Der Zee

760 • Father Divine's Peace Mission Movement

Born George Baker, on Hutchinson Island, Savannah, Georgia, Father Divine (1880–1965) became a nationally known religious figure in 1932, when residents of Sayville, Long Island, had him arrested. Calling himself God, Divine had established a nondenominational, interracial religious commune on Long Island, and nearby wealthy residents did not like it. But a few days after New York Supreme Court Justice Lewis J. Smith sentenced Divine to one year in Suffolk County Jail on Long Island, the judge died, leading Divine's followers to conclude: "The judge sentenced God to jail, and God sentenced the judge to hell!" Even Divine said from his jail cell, "I hated to do it!" Divine's appeal was based on more than the belief that he was really God: during the Great Depression, Divine's Peace Missions fed hundreds of hungry African Americans and whites, and gave hope when all else seemed to be failing. Divine combined an intensely religious movement with a practical program of action: he ran a lodging house for the homeless, an employment bureau for the unemployed, and several schools for both adults and children. He also registered members to vote in local and national elections, and in 1936 he helped launch the All People's Party by bonding together with Communist Party representatives to run a slate of radical candidates. But when it no longer served his purpose, he repudiated the communists, for Divine was actually an economic conservative. He criticized Franklin Roosevelt's New Deal programs for creating dependency among the people and advocated instead a strict program of self-reliance and Protestant work ethic values. He advised members to pay their debts, to avoid drinking and gambling, and to save, and even held up Andrew Carnegie and Henry Ford as models to be emulated by the masses. Divine also taught that race and color were incidental and developed a strong following among whites. Indeed, he developed at least three movements in one: an eastern United States movement mainly among Blacks; a western movement, sited mainly in California, that appealed largely to the white middle class; and a foreign movement that attracted working-class whites in Canada, Australia, and western Europe. Although the actual scope of his movement is unknown, his membership ranged from 10,000 to 100,000, 75 percent of whom were women.

BLACK SOCIAL REALISM, 1940–63

Some Important Books

761 • *Native Son* (1940)

Born in Mississippi, Richard Wright (1908–60) migrated North to Chicago, where he worked at odd jobs until the Great Depression, when he obtained work on the Federal Writers' Project. His short story "Big Boy Leaves Home," about the racial prejudice and brutality of the South, won the *Story Magazine* prize for the best WPA Writers' Project story, and another, "Fire and Cloud," won a second prize in the O. Henry awards. But it was the publication of *Native Son* that catapulted Wright to national and international prominence. *Native Son* chronicled the tragic trajectory of a working-class Black man in Chicago who finds his manhood in the murder of a white woman, and whose case becomes a cause célèbre for the Communist Party. Part social realist document

Sunday morning breakfast of Richard Wright in his Left Bank apartment, July 1948. National Archives.

and part critique of the communist movement of the 1930s, Wright's *Native Son* ushered in a whole new genre in which racial anger and retaliation against whites was frankly discussed in Black fiction. Moreover, the tremendous popularity of *Native Son* brought Wright recognition as America's leading Black author and showed that social indictment fiction by Blacks could find an audience among white readers.

762 • *The Street* (1946)

Ann Petry's novel of Lutie's struggle to create a life for herself and her son in a disintegrating slum neighborhood did for African American women's fiction what *Native Son* did for Black males. Providing vivid detail about life in Harlem, Petry extracted from the sociological situation of a single Black woman's struggle a measure of universal transcendence. Again, similar to *Native Son,* Lutie's murder of her lover becomes an indictment of the society in which she is forced to live, and not simply a defeatist caving into environmental forces. Moreover, Petry's use of poetic language to describe life in Harlem and Lutie's psychological motivations gives a narrative elegance to this novel.

763 • *Annie Allen* (1949)

Gwendolyn Brooks's Pulitzer Prize–winning book of poems, *Annie Allen,* is a lyrical masterpiece. Divided into three sections—"Notes from the Childhood and the Girlhood," "The Anniad," and "The Womanhood"—*Annie Allen* narrates the story of a Black woman from the inside. Moreover, in such lines as

It is brave to be involved,
To be not fearful to be unresolved.
Her new wish was to smile
When answers took no airships, walked
a while.

Gwendolyn Brooks. Courtesy of the Contemporary Forum. Photo by Bill Tague

her lyricism touched something universal in the struggle of this young woman for dignity in a Black world. The poems read as well today as they did when they made Brooks the first African American to win the Pulitzer Prize.

764 • *Invisible Man* (1952)

Ralph Ellison's classic novel of the African American as the Underground Man has become the iconic African American novel, particularly so given that its author did not publish another novel in his lifetime. Perhaps one masterpiece was enough, for *Invisible Man* had it all—an existential central character whose alienation from both the white and Black worlds of racial accommodation was nearly complete, an incisive critique of the world of Black education and its compromising hypocrisies, and the probing investigation of the language and culture of the African American folk, still caught in the webs of resistance and accommodation to white power structures. *Invisible Man* still reads today as the indictment of the ways in which the sensitive African American youth habitually have their creativity destroyed by the structures of racial politics in America.

765 • *Go Tell It on the Mountain* (1953)

James Baldwin's first novel about growing up in Harlem as the son of a preacher is his best. It re-creates in excruciating detail the terrors of being reared in a Black slum world that looks on in contempt at the talented young man whose sensibilities unfit him for the stereotypical roles to success available to midcentury Negroes. The central struggle with religion, sexuality, and a sense of community with other African Americans provides a sophisticated, psychological introduction to what life offered the talented exception in modern, pre-integration America. Moreover, Baldwin's personal style of expression takes this novel to a different level of narrative than that of Ellison's *Invisible Man*, showing the emergence of a fictional versatility in Black letters that had been missing before the advent of this new, social realist generation of the 1940s and 1950s.

Art

766 • Jacob Lawrence (b. 1917)

Recognized as one of America's best artists of the twentieth century, Jacob Lawrence was introduced to art at the Utopia Children's Center in Harlem, New York, and later trained by Augusta Savage at the Harlem Community School. When Savage obtained a position for him on the Works Progress Administration Arts Project, Lawrence began to produce powerful paintings. Lawrence possesses a unique, cubistic style of painting that he uses to comment on the social conditions of Black life. Although he has painted numerous single works in his career, Lawrence is distinguished by his artistic series on Black historical themes, such as his Toussaint l'Ouverture, Frederick Douglass, and Harriet Tubman series. Best known is his sixty-panel Migration Series, with historical captions written by Lawrence, that depict the exodus of African Americans into the North beginning in World War I. His stylized renderings of figures, powerful simplification of forms, and bold use of color make each panel a uniquely artistic interpretation of the social issues. Lawrence's larger theme in the Migration Series and his other works is the necessity of struggle for spiritual realization in this life.

767 • Elizabeth Catlett (b. 1915)

Elizabeth Catlett is one of America's best

sculptors and printmakers. Her large wood and marble sculptures, and stunning linocuts and lithographs, possess remarkable social realism and political significance. Born into a middle-class family in Washington, D.C., Elizabeth Catlett attended Howard University, where she studied under James Herring and Lois Mailou Jones. After graduating in 1937, she continued her art study at the University of Iowa, becoming the first person to receive a master's degree in fine art from that university, in 1940. She then headed the art department at Dillard University in New Orleans before attending the Art Institute of Chicago, where she met and married artist Charles White. She later moved to New York, divorced White, and married Mexican painter Francisco Mora, moving to Mexico City, where she taught art at the National University. Enormously prolific, Catlett has produced numerous strongly modeled portrait sculptures of women. She has also produced fine linocuts, one of the most sensitive being *Sharecropper* (1968). Like all of her studies of African American women, her subject here is tall, strong, and resolute in her eyes and bearing, with her brim straw hat. Her sharecropper has the strength and faith needed to endure the social and economic conditions of tenancy in the rural South.

Music and Dance

768 • Katherine Dunham (b. 1910)

This master dancer, choreographer, anthropologist, teacher, and activist launched the trend among African American modern dancers to ground their choreography in the African dance traditions still alive in the folk culture of the Caribbean. Dunham first gained attention when a dance group she had organized, Ballets Negres, presented one of her compositions, *Negro Rhapsody,* at the Beaux Arts Ball in Chicago in 1931. Her dancing and choreography reflected not only her race consciousness but her anthropological curiosity about African survivals in the Western Hemisphere, which she researched first at the University of Chicago as a student and then on site in the Caribbean as a Rosenwald Fellow in 1935. Study of African dance in Maroon villages in Jamaica, in urban communities on Martinique and Trinidad, and in voodoo communities on Haiti led to several publications, most notably *Journey to Accompong* (1946), and also to several compositions, such as *Tropics, Tropical Revue,* and *Bal Negre.* While she and her troupe also performed in mainstream productions, such as George Balanchine's *Cabin in the Sky* with Ethel Waters, her heart and creativity went increasingly into her Katherine Dunham School of Arts and Research, founded in 1945. In recent years, she has not only been an authority on the diasporic traditions of African American dance, but also an activist whose hunger strike in 1994 (along with that of Randall Robinson of TransAfrica) forced President Bill Clinton to change American policy toward Haiti, introduce U.S. troops, and restore democracy to her beloved island.

769 • Pearl Primus (1919–94)

Judged by dance critic John Martin to be one of the best dancers in America "regardless of race," Pearl Primus took the American dance scene by storm in 1943 as a dancer in *Folk Dance, Hard Times Blues,* and *African Ceremoniad.* Born in Trinidad, Primus had graduated from Hunter College with a degree in biology before being discovered in a dance unit of the National Youth Administration. After studying briefly with the New Dance Group, she was cast in several productions that she dominated with her remarkable strength and technical abil-

Pearl Primus. The Astor, Lenox and Tilden Foundations. Dance Collection, New York Public Library for the Performing Arts

ity—the "audience audibly gasped," according to Martin, at some of her extremely high leaps. Primus also possessed great dramatic ability and in 1946 was cast in the revival of *Show Boat.* Like Katherine Dunham, however, Primus was interested in the roots of African American dance. She did graduate work in anthropology and psychology before spending nine months in Africa in 1948 on a Rosenwald grant. That experience transformed her into an Africanist, who thereafter molded her dancing, her teaching, and her choreography around the performatory and spiritual benefits of African dance.

770 • Billie Holiday (1915–59)

Billie Holiday (born Eleanor Fagan) was a jazz singer of the blues in the 1930s and 1940s. Born in Baltimore, where she was raped at ten, Billie (a nickname she reputedly got for her tomboyish manner) seemed to carry the scars of a tragic childhood for the rest of her life. As a mature woman, she was also a drug addict who had her cabaret license in New York revoked after an arrest for heroin addiction in 1947. But what made Billie Holiday special was the way she used her personal pain to shape a new lyrical interpretation of the blues song. After listening to the records of Bessie Smith and Louis Armstrong while working in a bordello, Holiday began singing for ten dollars a week in New York in the late 1920s. Her big break came when she met John Hammond, who arranged for her to record with Benny Goodman in 1933 and with small studio bands, most notably Teddy Wilson's. After singing with Count Basie's Orchestra in 1937 and Artie Shaw's in 1938, she recorded her first albums, *Fine and Mellow* and *Strange Fruit,* with its title protest song against lynching, in 1939. During the 1940s she toured as a solo performer and gained a reputation as a unique jazz singer, who changed the rhythm, harmony, and meaning of popular songs as creatively as any jazz instrument player. After her arrest and incarceration in 1947, she emerged to give a triumphant performance at Carnegie Hall; but restricted to playing outside of New York because of her drug problems, she was forced to perform in sleazy nightclubs in California and in Europe for little more than cigarette and drug money. Then, in 1958, two years after the publication of *Lady Sings the Blues,*

Billie Holiday. Photograph by Carl Van Vechten, March 23, 1949. Courtesy of Prints and Photographs Division, Library of Congress. Gift of Carl Van Vechten

her autobiography, and a year before her death, Billie Holiday rallied from deteriorating health to produce—despite her voice's technical limitations—perhaps her best album, *Lady in Satin.* With the dignified treatment of string accompaniments, the autobiographical character of the songs, and the emotional intimacy of her singing, Billie Holiday produced an album not only about love but also her life.

771 • Charlie "Byrd" Parker (1920–55)

Charlie Parker was an improvisational genius on the alto saxophone and one of the main architects of the bebop style that transformed jazz during the 1940s. Born in Kansas City, Missouri, Parker started playing the alto saxophone in 1933, then went to New York in 1939, where he participated in numerous jam sessions and carved out his individual style. Bored with the traditional swing movement changes for the saxophone, Parker hit upon the idea of composing new melodic themes in songs using chord progressions he borrowed from other popular songs. Charlie Parker also broke the pulse and meter of songs, introduced a succession of subdivisions into them, and played the changes at breakneck speed. After playing in Earl Hines's and Billy Eckstine's bands during World War II, Parker emerged as a leader of his own band in New York in 1945 and became nationally recognized after a stint in Los Angeles. But Parker was also suffering from drug and alcohol addiction, and in June 1946 had to be hospitalized at the state hospital in Camarillo, California. Returning to New York in 1947, he entered upon his most productive period. But when the New York narcotics department caused his cabaret license to be revoked in July 1951, he could not work, and entered into a decline of further hospitalization, suicide attempts, and his death in New York on March 12, 1955.

772 • John "Dizzy" Gillespie (1917–93)

Dizzy Gillespie first became well known as the preferred trumpeter sideman for Charlie Parker, whom he had met when the latter joined Earl Hines's band in 1942. Dizzy was the other crucial architect of bebop, whose bent horn, lightning-fast playing, and numerous compositions were the natural complement to Parker's improvisational style. But Dizzy left Charlie Parker's band in Los Angeles in 1946, returned to New York, and became a leader in his own right, recording his own compositions. Even more than Parker, Dizzy worked with

Cuban musicians, wrote compositions utilizing Caribbean themes, and served as a musical bridge between African American and other music of the African diaspora.

773 • Thelonius Monk (1920–82)

Everything about Thelonius Monk—his odd name, curious hats, quirky piano playing, and outlandishly titled compositions—seemed to epitomize bebop, the dominant African American jazz idiom of the 1940s and 1950s. Born in Rocky Mount, North Carolina, Monk learned to play the piano as a child in New York, where he acquired the reputation as the most innovative of the young pianists at Minton's Playhouse in Harlem who, along with Dizzy Gillepsie, Charlie Christian, and Kenny Clarke, created bebop. Monk's piano work was important not only for its strong harmonic structure but also for the creative timing, offbeat syncopation, and uninhibited joy with which he played the piano. Monk was also one of the more memorable bebop composers, whose songs, such as "Round Midnight," "Ruby, My Dear," "Straight, No Chaser," "Well, You Needn't," "Misterioso," "Criss Cross," and "Crespuscule with Nellie," are classics. Relegated to supportive accompaniment of better known beboppers in the forties and fifties, Monk emerged as a star in his own right after his 1959 Town Hall concert in New York. He enjoyed his greatest recording and performance successes in the 1960s when he welded Charlie Rouse (tenor sax), John Ore (bass), and Frankie Dunlop (drums) into the Thelonius Monk Quartet.

774 • Miles Davis (1926–91)

As the man who replaced Dizzy Gillespie in Charlie Parker's Quintet in 1947, Miles Davis became famous as the young boy trumpeter of the bebop generation. But early in the 1950s Miles Davis stepped out from under Dizzy's influence, developed a unique trumpet "voice," and as a bandleader himself, led the way out of the bebop style with his "birth of the cool" movement in the 1950s. During that decade and the next, Davis established himself as the premier bandleader in American jazz, who attracted the best sidemen to work with him, including John Coltrane, Cannonball Adderley, Gerry Morgan, Max Roach, Wayne Shorter, Bill Evans, Herbie Hancock, Chick Corea, Keith Jarrett, Joe Zawinul, Ron Carter, and Tony Williams, and who produced a series of big-band albums using arrangements by Gil Evans. Miles also wrote numerous now classic jazz songs, including "So What," "All Blues," Freddie Freeloader," and "Four," to name only a few. By the early 1960s Miles was more than a musician—he had become a model for young Blacks of how to walk, and talk, and carry oneself in a "cool" manner. In the late 1960s Miles became controversial with fans and critics because he incorporated electric pianos, electric basses, and guitars into his band and began to play a fusion jazz that incorporated the funky rhythms of Jimi Hendrix, James Brown, and Sly and the Family Stone into his music. Yet Miles created some excellent fusion jazz albums, such as "Filles de Kilimanjaro," "Miles in the Sky," "In a Silent Way," and the astonishing 1970 two-record set "Bitches Brew," before a physical and mental decline led him to abandon recording and performing in 1975. Returning in 1980, Miles pursued a mellower electronic synthesis of popular and serious jazz tunes before his death in 1991.

775 • Gospel Music

While African American gospel music has obscure roots in the spirituals, it is a modern form of religious singing that emerged in the 1890s,

Thomas A. Dorsey, the father of gospel music, was known as Georgia Tom in the 1920s blues world. Calyton Hannah Collection, Hogan Jazz Archive, Tulane University Library

predominantly in Holiness or Pentecostal churches of the urban North and South. The formal birth date of gospel music is generally given as 1907, when during a famous revival tent meeting in Los Angeles, Black religious gospel singing came to greater attention. Gospel music got its name from this meeting, designed to recreate the moment when the spirit or gospel came down from heaven to the multitude. Unlike the spirituals, gospel music is an urban rather than rural music, and an instrumental music—with pianos, tambourines, and drums—instead of the often a cappella singing of the spirituals. Initially, Baptist churches, with whom this music is now associated, resisted the new music as a challenge to the authority of ministers. But because of the role of C. Albert Tindley, who wrote gospel songs in the early 1900s, and Thomas Dorsey, who not only wrote many songs but distributed single sheets of music for sale to singers in churches, the movement spread until at the 1930 National Baptist Convention in Chicago two gospel songs—"How About You" and "Did You See My Savior"—written by Thomas Dorsey were allowed to be performed. The overwhelming enthusiasm for the music broke down the resistance, and gospel music—"feeling" music—spread to Baptist and Methodist church services. Of individual gospel singers, Mahalia Jackson has been the most popular, with the Mighty Clouds of Joy being the most popular gospel singing group.

776 • Leontyne Price (b. 1927)

Leontyne Price was the first African American woman to sing with the Metropolitan Opera when she performed the role of Leonora in *Il Trovatore* on January 27, 1961. Having received a Julliard School of Music scholarship in 1949, Price's first big break came in 1952, when Virgil Thompson chose her to sing in his Broadway revival of *Four Saints in Three Acts.* Soon after followed her singing the role of Bess in the production of Gershwin's opera, her role as Madame Lidoine in the San Francisco production of Poulenc's *Dialogues des Carmélites,* and her debut at the Verona Arena, Vienna, and Covent Garden. After her debut at the Metropolitan Opera, she returned as Cleopatra in Barber's *Anthony and Cleopatra* at the opening of the new Metropolitan Opera in 1966. Known especially for her singing in Verdi's music, she has been renowned for her ability as a musical interpreter.

777 • Chuck Berry (b. ca. 1926)

Chuck Berry was the principal architect of

fifties rock and roll. Despite the accolades and mass popularity given to Elvis Presley, it was Berry, as a songwriter and a performer, who ushered in the transition from rhythm and blues to rock and roll. Growing up in St. Louis, Berry worked as an automobile assembler and then a hairdresser before starting to sing and play the guitar to make extra money. Berry did not forget his cosmetology experience when he went to New York and recorded his first hit song with Chess Records: it was titled "Maybellene" (1955), the name of a popular hair preparation. Berry followed that with a host of other hits, including "Roll Over Beethoven" (1957) and "Johnny B. Goode" (1958). Berry also became an outstanding stage performer, especially noted for his "duck walk"—skating across stage, in a crouched position, while playing the electric guitar. But a conviction under the Mann Act for taking a fourteen-year-old hatcheck girl across state lines almost destroyed his life and career, for after a two-year imprisonment, he emerged in 1964 with a broken family and a different rock music environment. Then, in 1972, his opening in Las Vegas to tremendous ovations signaled a return of attention to this star; and his song "My Ding-a-Ling" shot to number one in October. In 1986 he was still going strong, with a birthday concert in St. Louis with Keith Richards, guitarist of the Rolling Stones, in which Chuck Berry rolled out on stage in a red convertible. A film biography, *Chuck Berry: Hail! Hail! Rock 'n' Roll,* was issued in 1987, the same year that *Chuck Berry: The Autobiography* appeared.

778 • Little Richard (b. 1932)

Little Richard (Richard Wayne Penniman) was born in Macon, Georgia, the grandson of a Baptist minister and the son of a bootleg liquor salesman. That tension between the religious and the nefarious gave his music its special energy. He started singing in a family gospel group, later in church, where he gained a reputation for his tendency to "rock" the gospel—to sing it wildly and extravagantly. When he went on the road at fourteen, he sang rhythm and blues with all the energy of a Holiness church meeting. After touring the South with a variety of rhythm and blues groups, he landed in New Orleans in 1955 with a demo tape and promptly recorded his first hit, "Tutti Frutti." With his pounding keyboard playing and high-energy, punchy singing, "Tutti Frutti" captured the attention of teenage America, who promptly made it number seventeen on the *Billboard* pop chart in January 1956. Reputedly, Elvis Presley was able to record "Hound Dog," his signature song, only after he heard "Tutti Frutti." Richard quickly followed with such hits as "Long Tall Sally," "Slippin and Slidin," "Good Golly, Miss Molly," and an appearance with Jayne Mansfield in a movie, *The Girl Can't Help It* (1956). A sensational performer, with his hair piled high, his makeup packed on, and his eyebrows penciled in, Little Richard did something other Black performers had not yet done—he proved that an African American could enthrall audiences with large numbers of white females, who were attracted by a sexually ambiguous persona that was less threatening than such blatantly heterosexual figures as Chuck Berry. Richard's homosexuality, though hidden in the 1950s, burdened him increasingly as he became more successful, and in 1957 he renounced "sinful" rock and roll and retreated into the church. When Little Richard returned to commercial music in the 1960s, rock music had changed, and his music sounded dated. White artists, such as Pat Boone, had made careers out of "covering"—singing—his songs, but Richard could not collect royalties, because unprincipled recording

executives held the ownership rights to his songs. In the 1990s, however, he reemerged as an icon of redemption, who handed out Bibles on talk shows and claimed—as Jelly Roll Morton did before him—that he had invented it all. His 1992 album for children, *Shake It All About,* sold well, and in 1993 the National Academy of Recording Arts and Sciences honored him with a lifetime achievement award.

779 • Motown

Begun in a frame house in Detroit with the sign "Hitsville, U.S.A." outside, Motown Records blossomed into a multimillion-dollar entertainment corporation that produced the best music in America during the 1960s. Motown launched the careers of Mary Wells, Smokey Robinson and the Miracles, Diana Ross and the Supremes, Martha and the Vandellas, the Temptations, the Four Tops, the Jackson 5, Stevie Wonder, Marvin Gaye, Gladys Knight and the Pips, Lionel Richie, and a host of others. Motown's stable of singers produced from 1961 to 1972 over one hundred songs that reached the Top 10 on the pop music charts, with thirty-one of them ranked number one in the country. Such songs as "Please, Mr. Postman," "My Guy," "Baby Love," "Stop! In the Name of Love," "My Girl," "You Keep Me Hanging On," "Reach Out, I'll Be There," "Dancing in the Streets," and "I Heard It Through the Grapevine" became classics still listened and danced to today. Motown was the brainchild of Berry Gordy, Jr., a Ford assembly plant worker, who wrote songs, managed Black rhythm and blues groups, and marketed their music to a national, largely white pop audience. With the songwriting team of Eddie Holland, Lamont Dozier, and Brian Holland, Gordy created the "Motown Sound" of strong bass lines, lush harmonies, and squeaky-clean lyrics that made the music and the groups acceptable to radio and television audiences. A masterful institution builder, Gordy had a knack for attracting new talent just as older groups left the company or broke up. Such strategies netted Motown Records $40 million in sales in 1971 and made it the most profitable Black-owned company in the United States. Motown also contributed to the Civil Rights Movement by creating a spoken-word label that recorded speeches by political leaders, most notably the 1971 Grammy-winning speech, *Why I Oppose the War in Vietnam,* by Martin Luther King, Jr. In 1988 Gordy sold Motown to MCA, Inc., for $61.8 million.

Some Important Plays and Films

780 • *A Raisin in the Sun* (1959)

A Raisin in the Sun, Lorraine Hansberry's first play, made brief appearances in Philadelphia and Chicago before it opened March 11, 1959, on Broadway with Ruby Dee, Sidney Poitier, and Claudia McNeil in the leading roles. *A Raisin in the Sun* won the Drama Critics Circle Award and brought Lorraine Hansberry (1930–65) national acclaim. It was the longest-running play on Broadway by an African American up to that date (847 performances). Opening on Broadway just five years after the Supreme Court's *Brown v. Board of Education, Topeka, Kansas* decision, the play gave theatergoers an insider's look at one Black family's struggle with the costs of residential integration. Transformed in 1973 into a musical, *Raisin* won the Tony Award for the best musical.

781 • *Lilies of the Field* (1963)

Sidney Poitier's portrayal of Homer Smith in this film earned him an Oscar for best actor and

made him the first African American to win this award. *Lilies of the Field* epitomized Poitier's emergence as a Hollywood archetype—some might say a new stereotype—of the superlative Negro whose sterling selflessness and devotion to others allowed him to avoid being mistaken for the shiftless, stupid, and incompetent Negro of old Hollywood movies. The film narrates an accidental meeting between Homer Smith (Poitier), a good-natured drifter driving through the western United States, and a group of German immigrant nuns whose leader, played by Lilia Skala, commandeers Smith to build the nuns a chapel. At first, he resists. But after a local boss asks Smith his profession, he replies "a contractor" and builds the church as a way to create a new identity for himself. Criticized by some Black audiences in the 1960s for its saccharine image of a Black man and the implication that he could only find his identity by helping white people, *Lilies of the Field* nevertheless contains memorable scenes. In one, Poitier confronts a man who calls him "boy" by calling *him* "boy"; in another, Poitier teaches the nuns to sing the spirituals and shows that African Americans possess a distinct and vibrant culture. Poitier's portrayal announced to a mass white audience that a new, more prideful Negro had emerged for the 1960s.

Religion

782 • Black Social Gospel Movement

During the 1930s and 1940s a Social Gospel Movement developed in the African American ministry that stressed the need to remember the social dimension of the Christian doctrine and to apply it to transforming the racial situation in America. Black ministers, many of them educated or practicing in Protestant churches in the North, sought to apply the moral reform theology of Reinhold and Richard Niebuhr to transform the Black church into a social reform institution. Religious leaders as diverse as Howard Thurman, Adam Clayton Powell, Jr., and Martin Luther King, Sr., and many others, carved out an engaged ministry that argued Black Christianity was not confined to advocating freedom in the next world, but committed to bringing about social freedom in this one. As a consequence, Black churches became sites of interracial fellowship, community organizing, and protest organizing that brought about the Civil Rights Movement.

BLACK ARTS MOVEMENT, 1959–80

Movements, Organizations, and Celebrations

783 • Black Arts Movement

During the 1960s a new generation of writers, artists, and dramatists emerged in the North to express a Black sensibility in the arts. The movement began in 1959, when Elmer Lewis, Margaret Burroughs, Ossie Davis, Ruby Dee, and LeRoi Jones founded the American Negro Repertory Company, which, like the National Conference of Negro Artists (later the National Conference of Artists), Margaret Burroughs's Ebony Museum of Negro Culture in Chicago, and the San Francisco Negro Historical and Cultural Association, led the way to the 1960s Black Pride movement. Although these institutions

grew out of the Civil Rights Movement's belief in integration, they were also committed to the idea that art and history should promote racial self-appreciation. By 1965 this "Black Pride" viewpoint, and a related identification with Africa, led younger artists like LeRoi Jones to change his name to Imamu Amiri Baraka and establish the Black Arts Theater in Newark, New Jersey. Other little theater and writers' groups spurted up around the country in African American ghettos and encouraged young urban Blacks to write about their experiences. By the mid-sixties Black poets, playwrights, and fiction writers linked art to political expression, and articulated a Black aesthetic in the arts that was unavailable to white artists. Influenced by the Pan Africanist Negritude movement of Leopold Senghor and the revolutionary politics of Frantz Fanon, such writers as Larry Neal, Hoyt Fuller, Addison Gayle, Don L. Lee, and Harold Cruse argued for a self-consciously cultural nationalism. The movement was characterized by its multiple media, with groups such as "The Last Poets," which recorded rather than published poetry. In cinema, Gordon Parks, Melvin Van Peebles, and Gordon Parks, Jr., emerged as pro-Black directors in Hollywood. The proliferation of soul music, urban street gangs, and the urban rebellions of the late sixties gave a political urgency to the works of art produced in this period.

Some Important Books

784 • *The Autobiography of Malcolm X* (1965)

Malcolm X's autobiography, ghostwritten by Alex Haley, is a classic Black life story of personal corruption, then redemption through the Nation of Islam, the Honorable Elijah Muhammad's Black nationalist organization. Tracing his life from those early days hustling on the streets of Detroit, Malcolm X chronicles his descent into crime and his personal rejuvenation by the Black Muslim religion, which created a code of behavior as well as a rhetoric of indictment of white racism. As a spokesperson for the Nation in the late 1950s and early 1960s, Malcolm X became more famous and more political than Elijah Muhammad, and when Malcolm disobeyed Muhammad's command and commented on the death of President John F. Kennedy, Malcolm X was censured and eventually left the Black Muslims. He then traveled to the Middle East, and his encounter with Muslims who were white and yet not racist transformed him and led Malcolm to advocate a nonracist but radical critique of American institutions. The story of this transformative life is arrestingly told by Haley, who published the book after Malcolm's assassination in 1965.

785 • *The Man Who Cried I Am* (1967)

John A. Williams's novel *The Man Who Cried I Am* is the most powerful novel of the 1960s. Its power derives from its narrative, which is economic, pungent, fast-paced, and sparkingly provocative. Williams weaves together a forties story of the expatriate Black author who, like Richard Wright and James Baldwin, is vainly searching for African American meaning in Europe, and a sixties plot of the protagonist's encounters with political activism, extremist Black nationalism, and government intelligence programs. As such, Williams turns the problem of the Black intellectual and writer into an engaging narrative. For his central character, Max, pursues the contradictions of the Civil Rights Movement, expatriation, interracial romantic

relationships, and rising Black nationalism with an intellectual energy and sophistication that is rare in African American fiction.

786 • *The Crisis of the Negro Intellectual* (1967)

Harold Cruse's autobiographical critique of twentieth-century African American intellectuals became a classic the moment it was published. Cruse defined the problem of the Black intellectual as the failure to develop strong Black cultural nationalism in America. Beginning with the Harlem Renaissance of the 1920s, Cruse traced that failure to the desire in most African American intellectuals to integrate into white cultural institutions, rather than to develop autonomous, self-sustaining Black institutions. According to Cruse, the failure of the Harlem Renaissance was that it allowed Black art and thought to be controlled by white patrons, while the Black intellectuals on the left in the 1930s were guilty of being hoodwinked by Jewish communists into abandoning Black institutions as "chauvinistic," even as such communists maintained their own ethnic identity and institutions. Cruse called on younger Black artists and intellectuals of the 1960s to develop a healthy cultural nationalism that grounded its art and culture in the Black consumer audience. Cruse's book influenced a generation of African American scholarship, much of it dedicated to refuting some of his historical claims.

787 • *The Black Aesthetic* (1971)

This anthology became the bible of the Black Arts Movement because it published in one book the best critical writing of the movement. With essays by LeRoi Jones, Larry Neal, Hoyt Fuller, Don L. Lee, Loften Mitchell, and editor Addison Gayle, the book asserts that a Black aesthetic exists which is distinctive to African American expression. The book was designed to counter arguments by mainly white critics that the new Black arts of the 1960s were an aberration, and merely a capitulation to racial anger. Editor Addison Gayle sought to establish the intellectual canon of ideas in the Black Arts Movement by including in the book's sections "Theory," "Music," "Poetry," "Drama," and "Fiction" essays on Black aesthetics written by Alain Locke, Langston Hughes, J. A. Rogers, and Richard Wright earlier in the century. Moreover, such contemporaries as Larry Neal and Don L. Lee, for example, assert that the Black aesthetic is more than simply a distinctive sense of beauty—it is a characteristic worldview that derives from African culture and differs fundamentally from the Western aesthetic that has dominated American expression.

788 • *Song of Solomon* (1977)

Although Toni Morrison's first two novels, *The Bluest Eye* and *Sula,* were excellent works of fiction, her third novel, *Song of Solomon,* is her masterpiece. In *Song of Solomon,* Morrison creates the world of a Black community that exists, struggles, and nourishes itself completely independent of white control. The novel weaves together the world of myth, ghosts, and African American burial practices, and particularly shows the power of African American naming patterns: characters are named "Macon Dead" and "Milkman" and function in a world where the will of the dead is as important, at times, as that of the living. *Song of Solomon* also shows that such African American naming patterns exist as an act of resistance, as when the Black community first names a street "Doctor" and then "Not Doctor" after the white community attempts to take back the power to name

Toni Morrison. Photo © 1978 by Helen Marcus

streets in the Black part of town. *Song of Solomon* is distinguished by the power of its language, its remarkable detail in description of scenes and surroundings, combined with an imaginative sweep and emotional intensity unseen in American fiction. Perhaps more than any other African American novel of the 1970s, Toni Morrison's *Song of Solomon* drew upon African American folklore not only for the setting but also for the turns of plot.

Art

789 • Romare Bearden (1912–88)

Though born in Charlotte, North Carolina, Bearden grew up in Harlem, where he met such writers, artists, and musicians of the Harlem Renaissance as W. E. B. Du Bois, Countee Cullen, Aaron Douglas, and Duke Ellington. After developing an interest in art, Bearden became controversial in the 1930s for his criticism of the Harmon Foundation, a white foundation that held annual exhibitions of Black art, for some of the shoddy art it selected for exhibition. Bearden started as a relatively typical social realist painter who, during the 1930s and early 1940s, documented African American rural and urban life. But in the 1940s and 1950s he broke with current trends: first, he produced small oil paintings on literary themes; but by the late 1950s and early 1960s, he had, belatedly, embraced abstract expressionism. It seemed that Bearden was lurching from one style to another in a vain search for his own distinctive medium when in 1961 he began to construct collages out of cutout photographs of African American figures and other images. In his 1964 series *The Prevalence of Ritual,* Bearden combined disparate elements—photos of African masks, working-class African Americans, rural and urban landscapes, cutouts of teeth, hands, and noses—into a new visual language that evoked Picasso, Braque, Matisse, and the surrealists and embodied African American themes and images. His numerous collages and later his photomontages signaled not only a return to the African American figure but also an ability to use cubistic principles of abstraction to evoke the rhythm and pattern of African American folk culture. Perhaps more than any other artist of his generation, Bearden's work represented the fractured yet triumphant spirit of the Black community in the 1960s, from the optimism of the Civil Rights Movement to the alienation of the urban riots. Something of the richness, complexity, and sophistication of Bearden's artistic vision comes through in his posthumously pub-

lished art history, *A History of African-American Artists* (1988), which he coauthored with journalist Harry Henderson.

790 • John Biggers (b. 1924)

Born in Gastonia, North Carolina, John Biggers early developed an ability to translate his affective appreciation for African American people and culture into lush, engaging paintings. A trip to Africa under the auspices of Unesco occasioned a process of self-discovery that he chronicled in the book *Ananse, the Web of Life in Africa* and in the painting *Jubilee-Ghana Harvest Festival* (1959), a mixed-media composition that portrayed a public celebration he witnessed in West Africa. More recently, Biggers has combined his sense of the dignity of Black people with his increasing knowledge of African cultural traditions in several stunning compositions, such as *Shotguns* (1987), a tribute to the visual patterns of African American shotgun houses, and *Starry Crown* (1987), his luscious representation of the three Marys of African antiquity—from Egypt, Benin, and the Dogon of Mali.

791 • Ed Love (b. 1936)

This Los Angeles–born artist recalled that conversations between his father and uncles about Marcus Garvey first inspired in him an interest in things African. Then, in the 1960s, he began to research Egypt, especially Egyptian mythology, and discovered the complexity of Africa. In such powerful steel sculptures as *Osiris* (1972) and *Mask for Mingus* (1974), Love molds scraps of steel, usually from car bumpers he collects, into sculptures that are anthropomorphic and evocative of West African masks and sculptures. Love responds as well in his sculpture to African American music, the violent American traditions of lynching and foreign wars, and the artwork of David Alfaro Siqueiros. Perhaps his masterpiece is the multiple-figure sculpture *Arkestra* (1984–88) that celebrates African American musicians in twenty-seven kinetic steel sculptures. After teaching art for many years at Howard University, Love moved to Miami in 1987 to become dean of the Visual Arts Division of the New World School of the Arts.

The Prevalence of Ritual: Baptism. Photograph by Lee Stalsworth, 1964. Hirshhorn Museum and Sculpture Garden, Smithsonian Institution. Gift of Joseph H. Hirshhorn, 1966. Courtesy of Estate of Romare Bearden

Music and Dance

John Coltrane. Prints and Photographs Division, Library of Congress

792 • John Coltrane (1926–67)

John Coltrane eventually occupied the improvisational space vacated by the death of Charlie Parker. Born in Hamlet, North Carolina, Coltrane studied music in Philadelphia in 1945 and then with the Dizzy Gillepsie Orchestra from 1949 to 1951. In 1955 he was recruited by Miles Davis to join his quintet. After a brief stint with Thelonius Monk in 1957, Coltrane rejoined Miles's band in 1958 and made some of his best and most innovative soloing with Davis's band. Leaving Miles Davis again in 1960, he formed his own band, with Elvin Jones, McCoy Tyner, and Paul Chambers. In a series of recordings, Coltrane defined the avant-garde of the early sixties with his rapid-fire delivery of notes and long, complex modal solos on both the tenor and the soprano saxophones.

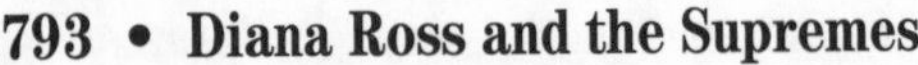

793 • Diana Ross and the Supremes

The Supremes set the high-water mark of hit productions for Motown music from July 1964 to April 1965 when they had five consecutive number one singles. That established the Supremes (with Diana Ross as lead singer and Mary Wilson and Florence Ballard as backups) as the most popular American singing group in the 1960s. As if to emphasize the point, the Supremes returned to the number one hit parade in 1966, when the group had another run of four hit songs that lasted until 1967. Singing songs written by the team of Eddie Holand, Lamont Dozier, and Brian Holland, the Supremes epitomized Berry Gordy's ideal of the crossover group: their sweet, sparkling singing of catchy lyrics endeared them to thousands of white Americans. When they appeared successfully on Ed Sullivan's television show on October 10, 1965, they established the mass appeal of the Motown Sound and opened doors for other African American musical groups in the white commercial market. Not surprisingly, their incredible success led to dissension in the Supremes: in July 1967 the group's name was changed to Diana Ross and the Supremes, and Florence Ballard was booted out of the group and replaced by Cindy Birdsong. Then, in January 1970, Diana Ross left the group to pursue what became a very successful solo career: she herself had five number one hit songs over the next ten years and became a popular motion picture actress, starring in *Lady Sings the Blues* (1972), *Mahogany* (1975), and *The Wiz* (1978).

794 • The Temptations and the Four Tops

Most who listened to the Temptations and the Four Tops had a strong preference for one or the other group as the best Black male singing group in America. But together they were clearly the best male singing groups in Motown and the top Black male singing groups in the United States during the 1960s. The Temptations—with a string of Top 10 hits, including "The Way You Do the Things You Do," "The Girl's Alright With Me," and "My Girl," along with such number one hits as "Ain't Too Proud to Beg" and "Just My Imagination"—were considered the top act in Motown, and they were protected as such: in 1970, Gordy gave the Vietnam protest song "War" to Edwin Starr for fear it was too controversial for the Temptations. The Temptations were both polished and versatile, with complex harmonizing, intricate dance routines, flashy clothing, and the ability to sing fast-paced dance tunes and ballads. Interestingly, the Temptations were the only Motown singing group to break out of the conservative Motown Sound formula and embrace (with some criticism) electric, acid rock in the early 1970s. The breakthrough album *Psychedelic Shack* (1970) was the result. Moreover, by singing songs like "Papa Was a Rolling Stone" (1972), the "Temps" (as they were sometimes called) moved beyond simple romantic ballads to social commentary songs. By contrast, the Four Tops (Renaldo Benson, Abdul Fakir, Lawrence Payton, and Levi Stubbs) never abandoned the Motown Sound and remained the undisputed masters of romantic ballad singing. Although their 1965 number one hit "I Can't Help Myself" was an up-tempo tune, the Four Tops are mainly remembered for "Baby I Need Your Loving," "Reach Out, I'll Be There," and "Still Water"—the latter the title of their best album. In contrast with the numerous personnel changes in the Temptations, the Four Tops have remained the same four singers for over thirty years. Both groups still tour, sometimes together.

795 • Smokey Robinson and the Miracles

The Miracles were formed in 1957 and signed by Motown in 1959, and in 1961 they recorded Motown's first million-unit seller, "Shop Around." The original Miracles contained Warren Moore, Claudette Rogers, Bobby Rogers, Ronnie White, and leader William "Smokey" Robinson, but recorded as a quartet after Claudette Rogers married Smokey in 1965. Not only was Smokey Robinson's smooth, almost falsetto voice the key to the Miracles' beautiful harmonies, but Smokey was an incredibly prolific writer of songs—over one thousand—many of which, like "My Girl," were recorded by other Motown groups. He was also the only artist to become a vice-president of Motown (1963) and to produce other music groups. Smokey left the Miracles in 1972 and the group disbanded in 1978.

796 • James Brown (b. 1928)

James Brown was the most influential bandleader in soul music during the 1960s. He was also a superb performer in concert, with many of his moves, gestures, and antics being copied by hundreds of performers. Born in Pulaski, Tennessee, Brown moved at an early age with his family to Augusta, Georgia. After being arrested as a young man, Brown took up singing, initially with some gospel music groups, during the 1940s, and then expanded his musical knowledge by studying the organ; he also played the drums, and in the 1950s, backed by his

James Brown, 1968. National Archives, photo by Emiloi Grossi

group, the Famous Flames, he got a recording contract and became known to the inner-city ghetto listeners when he recorded "Please, Please, Please" in 1956. After such hits as "Papa Got a Brand New Bag" (1965) and "It's a Man's World" (1966), Brown developed a following among hip young white listeners of rhythm and blues. But his biggest achievements came at the end of the 1960s with "Say It Loud, I'm Black and I'm Proud" (1968), "Mother Popcorn" (1969), and "Give It Up and Turn It Loose" (1969).

797 • Jimi Hendrix (1942–70)

Jimi Hendrix was the greatest guitarist of the 1960s. It was not simply his gifted technical skills that made him great—it was that Hendrix permanently changed the way that electric guitar was played and influenced an entire generation of musicians, guitarists, and others. Born in Seattle, Hendrix listened to records of Muddy Waters and other blues guitarists, learned to reproduce their style of playing, and after a brief stint as a paratrooper in the 101st Airborne Division, began to play guitar with numerous rhythm and blues groups during 1961–66, including James Brown. Then, late in 1966, he began singing, went to England, and created the Jimi Hendrix Experience with drummer Mitch Mitchell and guitarist Noel Redding, who played bass. After playing to sellout crowds in England, the Jimi Experience took the United States by storm after its performance during the 1967 Monterey Pop Festival, where the highly amplified music, lurid lyrics, and Jimi's onstage burning of his guitar made the group an "Experience!" During the next two years, the group toured the United States and produced three platinum albums, *Are You Experienced?* (1967), which included such classics as "Purple Haze," "Hey Joe," and "Foxey Lady," *Axis: Bold as Love,* and *Electric Ladyland,* both in 1968, that set a high-water mark for musical creativity. Famous early for his tight, punchy rock songs and his fast, intense, and metallic guitar playing, Hendrix in his later albums expanded his mastery of electric guitar feedback and created special effects that turned the guitar into the most important musical instrument of the decade. He influenced such divergent musicians as the jazz musician Miles Davis and the traditional soul group the Temptations. Unfortunately, at the height of his fame, he became addicted to heroin and died of an overdose in England in 1970.

798 • Stevie Wonder (b. 1950)

At the tender age of eleven, Stevie Wonder joined Motown in 1961 and within two years had a number one hit on the pop charts, "Fingertips, Pt. 2," a live performance recorded at the Regal Theater in Chicago. His *12 Year Old Genius* was Motown's first number one album. After that tri-

umph, Stevie Wonder was a bona fide early-sixties star, who toured the country with the Rolling Stones as his opening act in 1964. In 1972, ironically, it would be Stevie Wonder who would be the Rolling Stones' opening act as he introduced to a new and largely white audience his new album, *Talking Book*, which for the first time in history entered the pop charts at number one. That album was followed by *Innervisions* in 1973, *Fulfillingness First Finale* in 1974, and the critically acclaimed double album *Songs in the Key of Life* in 1976. These albums established Wonder as one of the most creative musical artists in America, for his ability to weave poetic lyrics and electronic effects into moving songs. In the course of his career, Stevie Wonder has won more than sixteen Grammy Awards and an Oscar for best original song ("I Just Called to Say I Love You," 1985) and has produced eight number one hits, twenty-six in the Top 10. He has also been devoted to social and political causes, participating in the "We Are the World" video and recording to help Africa, and becoming a leader in the campaign to make Martin Luther King's birthday a national holiday.

799 • Alvin Ailey (1931–91)

Alvin Ailey was influenced by, and continued the tradition of, Katherine Dunham in modern dance. In 1953 he gained attention by choreographing two pieces, *Creation of the World* and *Work Songs,* that drew upon the African American folk tradition. Then, in 1954, he appeared as a dancer in *Carmen Jones* with Carmen de Lavallade. Responding to the upsurge in Black consciousness in the late 1950s, Alvin Ailey began giving dance concerts in Harlem at the YMCA and in 1960 formed his own company. During the 1960s he choreographed numerous ballets for his own and other companies, creating a distinctive signature style of African American modern dance. Ailey was adept at mining the African American religious tradition for compositions, of which his most famous is *Revelations.* In 1974 he created a series of works based on the music of Duke Ellington. By the mid-1970s Ailey had expanded to become a comprehensive dance theater institution, with not only the Alvin Ailey American Dance Theater but also the Alvin Ailey Repertory Ensemble and Dance Center. Since his death, his company has been guided by his featured dancer, Judith Jamison.

Alvin Ailey dance troupe in a modern, sensual number, 1972. National Archives. Photo © by Jack Mitchell

800 • The Dance Theater of Harlem

Founded by Arthur Mitchell in 1969, the Dance Theater of Harlem explored the possibilities of a Black classical ballet rather than modern dance. Mitchell had gained national attention in 1956 in the signature role of George Balanchine's *Agon.* Mitchell then became one of the premier soloists of the New York City Bal-

let. But Mitchell wanted to be more than simply a featured dancer: after teaching ballet at the Harlem School of the Arts in the 1960s and realizing that considerable interest existed among Black youth for ballet, he, along with Karel Shook, founded the Dance Theater of Harlem. With financial support from many whites who championed his work, Mitchell was able to build the Dance Theater into a major company. With a diverse repertoire that drew upon his Balanchine roots, the Ballet Russe tradition, and the African American heritage of dance, Mitchell developed a distinctive series of compositions that reinterpreted the classical tradition through the lens of African and African American dance expression. His *Firebird* and *Giselle* became signature works; but Mitchell also developed compositions, such as *Streetcar Named Desire,* that blended dramatic and ballet form into truly innovative and provocative performances.

Some Important Plays and Films

801 • *The Dutchman* (1963)

LeRoi Jones's *The Dutchman* was a landmark play that launched a trend in Black drama toward open discussion of racism in American life. The play tells the story of a white woman who makes advances toward a Black man on a subway and then insults him when he begins to respond. Overcome with anger, Clay, the previously soft-spoken African American, ridicules her and all white people for their racism. Lula, the white woman, kills Clay and dumps his body from the subway car. The powerful play suggested that Blacks who told white America the truth about racism and the anger that it produces would be eliminated. The play ended the period of oblique criticism in Black American literature and ushered in the more direct social criticism associated with the Black Arts Movement.

802 • *Putney Swope* (1969)

This film imagines what happens to a faltering white advertising agency when Putney Swope, the sole Black member of its board of directors, is accidentally elected in a vote of no confidence for its white members. Instead of kowtowing to the white board members, Swope turns the company into a Black-oriented agency whose "Truth and Soul" advertisement really tells the truth about products. In addition to its remarkably funny mock commercial, *Putney Swope* also parodies typical Black characters familiar to participants in the Black Power movement of the 1960s and suggests that even those included in a skin color revolution will sell out to get ahead in capitalist America.

803 • *Sweet Sweetback's Baadassss Song* (1971)

Melvin Van Peebles produced and financed this classic African American escape saga using credit cards. Peebles recalled that when Hollywood studios turned down his requests for funding, he simply looked in the mirror one morning and stated: "I think I am a studio, therefore I am a studio." Peebles also starred in the movie, which tells the story of an escaped prisoner whose name derives from his expertise as a sexual partner, an expertise that helps him escape capture as he gains the support of numerous women in the Los Angeles ghetto because of his ability as a lover. Eventually Sweetback runs on foot to Mexico. His rebellion against the police, their brutal relationship to the Black community, and the criminal justice system in Los Angeles expressed a militant Black critique of

American race relations. Its angry, unapologetic, and working-class lead character broke sharply with the saccharine assimilationism of Sidney Poitier's roles in major Hollywood movies. The box-office success of the movie alerted Hollywood that movies marketed to a predominantly African American audience would make money. Ironically *Sweet Sweetback's Baadassss Song* ushered in the wave of less critical blaxploitation films of the 1970s.

804 • *Shaft* (1971)

Directed by Gordon Parks, Sr., and starring Richard Roundtree, *Shaft* epitomizes the blaxploitation films of the early 1970s. It chronicles the adventures of a Black private detective in New York who is hired by a Harlem underworld boss to find his kidnaped daughter. In the course of finding this daughter, Shaft fights the bad guys, woos the women, and "stands up to the Man" in predictable ways; but the movie is embellished by Parks's cinematic ability to portray his hero with a kind of lush adulation. The story is also interesting for its depiction of the dilemma of the "Black spade detective" who must balance his commitment to law enforcement with his loyalty to the Black community. Though Shaft is fundamentally honest and legal in his dealings, he also refuses to "sing a song to the police, baby!" For all its crass commercialism, *Shaft* is a 1970s study of the "double consciousness" that W. E. B. Du Bois decreed in *Souls of Black Folk* as dogging the careers of all thinking African Americans in the twentieth century.

805 • *Superfly* (1972)

This engaging film by Gordon Parks, Jr., takes up where *Shaft* leaves off, but this time from the other side of the legal fence, by glorifying the lifestyle of Superfly (aka Youngblood Priest), who is a cocaine dealer, flashy dresser, and lover man who develops an inappropriate passion—for freedom from working for the Man and the whole system of living in the underworld. What makes this movie more than the usual formulaic blaxploitation film is the way in which it subtly convinces us that Priest is not typical, that he is, in fact, a highly socially competent, intelligent man who has mastered his environment; and the final act of mastery will be to leave it, despite the fact that everyone, from his partner to the white police official who "owns" drug dealers, wants to thwart if not kill him. The film is also interesting for its nonstereotypical portrayal of Black inner-city life and the interesting, atypical angles that the director films the movie. Finally the movie benefits from one of the best movie scores of the period, written and performed by Curtis Mayfield, formerly of the Impressions. Songs such as "Freddie's Dead," "Pusherman," and "Superfly" were outrageously popular during their time, and are enjoying a comeback in the 1990s as they are sampled by rap musicians and television commercial music writers.

806 • *For Colored Girls Who Have Considered Suicide When the Rainbow Is Enuf* (1976)

Ntozake Shange's bold, Black feminist play stunned audiences throughout the United States with its sustained, raplike critique of destructive Black male attitudes and behaviors toward Black women. Shange's play infused the preachy, monologic drama style of Black Arts Movement theater with Black women's anger at the failure of Black men to live up to the rhetoric of Black manhood. By portraying the pain of hurt, tricked, and disillusioned Black women in America, Shange struck a chord with the Black feminist audience searching for its

Poster for play at Booth Theater, 1976. Prints and Photographs Division, Library of Congress. Used by permission of Paul Davis

voice in the mid-1970s. This play's sharp articulation of women's frustrations has kept it alive in the repertory of little theater and college theater groups.

807 • *Roots* (1977)

When Alex Haley translated his fictionalized reconstruction of his family history from West Africa to North America into a television miniseries shown on eight consecutive nights in 1977, he transformed American television as well as America's knowledge and perspective on American slavery. The television series earned the highest ratings of any network program in history as millions of Americans, including Blacks, learned about the evils of slavery for the first time. Dramatic acting by Lou Gossett, Oprah Winfrey, Ruby Dee, Chuck Connors, and many others transformed Haley's powerfully written personal story into an epic narrative of American history, as it brought to a popular audience what historians and other scholars had been writing about the history of slavery for years. Moreover, Haley's story on the little screen became a profoundly American story as it documented the Black family's struggle toward freedom and dignity over generations, while maintaining the tenuous but inspiring folk traditions brought from Africa.

Religion

808 • Nation of Islam

The modern Nation of Islam emerged from the earlier movement of Noble Drew Ali, who founded the Moorish-American Science Temple. When Ali died in 1929, W. D. Fard assumed leadership of the movement, but was replaced, in 1933, by Elijah Muhammad, who was imprisoned in 1942 for refusing to serve in the Army during World War II for his religious beliefs. After his time in jail, during which he recruited many jailed Blacks to the movement, Muhammad organized fifty temples by 1959 and had over one thousand members in his Chicago Temple by 1965. Muhammad restricted mem-

bership to nonwhites and rejected the term "Negroes," preferring to call Blacks Muslims (rather than Moslems) in order to emphasize their special religious status as a separate chosen people, whose mission was to redeem the Black nation. Muhammad taught that an apocalypse would occur in the future in which Allah would destroy the United States for its sins against Black people and make nonwhite peoples the sole rulers of the world. While awaiting this apocalypse, Blacks should separate socially and politically from whites, who would never accept Blacks on equal terms, live in autonomous communities, control the institutions in those communities, and live a virtuous Muslim lifestyle. Muhammad sought to create a new positive profile for Blacks by requiring them to be clean cut, businesslike, well dressed, and socially conservative, while confidently articulating a radical critique of white people as permanently racist. From the 1950s onward, Muslims were known for selling a newspaper, *Muhammad Speaks,* and bean pies on the corners of urban ghettos dressed in suits, with white shirts, bow ties, and short haircuts. The Nation became famous in the United States during the 1950s and 1960s, largely because of hostile media coverage and the articulate spokesperson Malcolm X. After Malcolm X's assasination in 1965 and the death of Elijah Muhammad in 1975, Elijah's son, Imam Warith Deen Muhammad, took over the organization, lifted its ban on white membership, and moved it closer to being a traditional Islamic organization. But then Louis Farrakhan revived the older Elijah Muhammad philosophy in a splinter group that has come to be known as the Nation of Islam in the 1990s. Although criticized for his attacks on Jews as "bloodsuckers" and Judaism as a "gutter religion," Farrakhan has gained new respectability with his October 1995 "Million Man March" on Washington, D.C., to protest the demonization of Black men in late twentieth-century America.

809 • Black Theology

Dated usually from the publication of James Cone's seminal books, *Black Theology and Black Power* (1969) and *A Black Theology of Liberation* (1970), a Black theology movement emerged that interpreted Christianity as a theology of liberation for the Black community. Occurring before the formal emergence of the Latin American liberation theology movement, the Black Theology Movement built upon the momentum of the Black Social Gospel Movement, but drew its immediate inspiration from the Black Power Movement of the late 1960s and the tradition of urban Black ministers such as Adam Clayton Powell, Jr., Albert B. Cleage, Nathan Wright, and Ben Chavis who interpreted the urban riots of the 1960s as a stage in the Black revolution. Abandoning the Martin Luther King "turn the other cheek" tradition of Christian social struggle, Cone, C. Eric Lincoln, Leon Watts, and Bill Jones (known for his provocatively titled book, *Is God a White Racist?*) critiqued Christian theology from the perspective of the Black revolutionary movement, interpreted the Bible in terms of the history of the Black community, and argued that a Black theology was necessary because white American Christian theology defended the racial status quo and ignored the Black freedom struggle. After its institutional arm, the National Committee of Black Churchmen, was founded in 1969, the Black Theology Movement spread among young Black ministers and seminarians during the 1970s. But by the beginning of the 1980s, the movement was in decline, in part because of a sustained counterattack against radical Black theology in mainstream American religious organizations and the rise of conservative televangelists, many of whom, like Jerry Falwell and Jim and Tammy Baker, successfully wooed Black worshipers away from Black radicalism with an appeal to family values and interracial reconciliation through Christian fellowship. Nevertheless, the movement spawned several spin-offs in the late 1970s and early 1980s, including a Black womanist theology and an alliance between African Americans and Third World theologians in the World Council of Churches' Commissions on Faith and Order.

810 • Kwanzaa

Kwanzaa is a holiday celebrated from December 26 through January 1 that was initiated in 1966 by Maulama Karenga, now a professor of African American studies, who founded US, a sixties paramilitary cultural nationalist organization. The word "Kwanzaa" means "first fruits" in Swahili and reflected Karenga's belief that African Americans needed a holiday of their own that celebrated what he held as core African values. On each day of Kwanzaa, by eating certain foods, telling stories, and taking part in collective activities, celebrants affirm their commitment to the following values: *umoja* (unity), *kujichangulia* (self-determination), *ujima* (collective work and responsibility), *ujamma* (cooperative economics), *nia* (purpose), *kuumba* (creativity), and *imani* (faith). Although relatively ignored by the masses of African Americans when first proposed, Kwanzaa has become quite popular in the 1990s, and Kwanzaa cards, candles, and other supporting paraphernalia are now commercially available.

AFRICAN AMERICAN RENAISSANCE, 1981–95

Movements, Organizations, and Celebrations

811 • The Second African American Renaissance

The second African American Renaissance began in the early 1980s, largely due to an outpouring of literature, plays, and belles lettres by Black women writers—Toni Morrison, Alice Walker, Toni Cade Bambara, Ntozaka Shange, Terry McMillan, bell hooks, and others—who wrote about racism, sexism, and the Black women's experience with energy, honesty, and imagination not seen before. Their works appear precisely at the time when the production of literature by Black male writers seemed in decline and interest in Black Studies generally seemed to wane. Because these women writers discussed sexism and feminism through Black women's eyes, their works found a white women readership that boosted sales and took some to the top of the best-seller lists. Indeed, in 1993, two African American women garnered recognition never before bestowed on any African American when Toni Morrison became the first African American to win the Nobel Prize for literature and Maya Angelou became the first Black writer to read a poem during a presidential inauguration.

Four other developments have helped usher in the latest renaissance. First, as in the Harlem Renaissance, a sense of the importance of the African past emerged in the 1980s, reflected in the popularity of books such as Martin Bernal's

Black Athena (1987), which documented the influence of Africa on early Western civilization, and in consumer culture items such as videotapes, clothes, educational programs, and paraphernalia that celebrated Africa. Second, an increase in the educated Black middle class during the 1970s and 1980s created a reading and theatergoing audience for books and plays by such authors as Terry McMillan and August Wilson that had been absent, largely, during the first renaissance. Third, and in almost diametrical opposition to the first factor, there emerged in the late 1980s and early 1990s a new freedom among the critical mass of African American writers and artists to create without ideological concerns as their main motivation.

The emergence of figures like Rita Dove, who was the first African American chosen poet laureate of the United States in 1993 on the basis of largely nonracial poetry is a case in point. Fourth, in the early 1990s, a diasporic consciousness that African Americans are part of a worldwide dispersion of African peoples fueled interconnections and "samplings" from the Caribbean and Europe. That development has been evidenced by the increased popularity of reggae music—especially reggae rap artists—in America and the popularity of writings by cultural historian Paul Gilroy that assert African Americans are part of a larger, "Atlantic community." Together, these diverse forces have led to the production of more works of quality than were produced during the first renaissance of the 1920s.

812 • Afrocentricity

Afrocentricity, or Afrocentrism, is a philosophy of culture that revaluates American and world history by looking at it from an African perspective. Afrocentrism emerged in the 1970s in Black Studies programs as a way to challenge Eurocentric values and perspectives in American educational and cultural institutions and to argue that contemporary Black American values, behaviors, and aspirations are only understandable when they are traced back to their African roots. Afrocentrists reject the notion that America can ever be a colorblind society and suggest that successful assimilation into American society by Blacks requires them to abandon their African identity. Afrocentrists see all Black people around the globe as one people and assert that the African past before European contact was a golden age that was preferable to the present. Afrocentrism emerged as a belief system in the early 1970s as professors and students in Black Studies departments searched for a new paradigm to replace outdated notions that Black Studies curricula were needed simply to fill in gaps in Eurocentric college courses or to critique systemic institutional racism in America. Just as feminists in Women's Studies began to demand to look at American history from the perspective of gender, Afrocentrists, such as Molafi Kete Asante, professor at Temple University and author of *Afrocentricity* (1980), argued that retelling the history of America and the world from an African viewpoint would transform our way of understanding history. Such a reinterpretation was already occurring in the work of such scholars as Robert Ferris Thompson, Charles Joyner, Vincent Franklin, Ben Johannon, Janheinz Jahn, Vincent Harding, and many others. Asante's movement met strong resistance in the academic community, but won acceptance in numerous Black Studies programs and among secondary and primary school teachers who saw it as a way to teach African American children and adults a history they could be proud of. With its focus on African kingship and empires, particularly the

glorious days of the Egyptian empire, Afrocentric courses gained popularity in the late 1980s. It also spawned a huge commercial industry that produced kente cloth hats, necklaces with African medallions, African beads, dresses, and walking sticks that promoted a positive identification with Africa. Afrocentricity was also helped by its adoption by rap groups in the late 1980s, whose videos and other promotional materials evidenced an African consciousness.

Some Important Books

813 • *The Color Purple* (1982)

Alice Walker borrowed from the nineteenth-century tradition of women's confidential letter writing to construct a powerful novel of two Black women's psychic bonding in the face of male physical and psychological abuse. The novel's innovative form and the power of its focus on gender rather than racial conflict garnered its author a Pulitzer Prize in fiction and instant fame as the woman novelist who temporarily supplanted Toni Morrison's position as the top African American woman novelist writing in contemporary America. The issue of the novel's representation of Black male figures became the focus of a national debate when Steven Spielberg turned Alice Walker's novel in 1985 into a hit movie and made the careers of such new actors as Whoopi Goldberg, Oprah Winfrey, and Danny Glover.

814 • *Ain't I a Woman: Black Women and Feminism* (1981)

In her landmark study of sexism, African American women, and feminism, bell hooks provides a trenchant analysis of the history of sexist treatment of African American women from the beginnings of African enslavement to the contemporary feminist movement. hooks argues that even in West Africa, Black women were oppressed by sexism, and that this oppression was observed and appropriated by white enslavers who conceptualized that African women could be both agricultural laborers and sexual objects in colonial America. Even more, hooks critiques those historians and sociologists who have described Black women's rape by white men as primarily a feature of slavery, who have perpetuated the myth of Black matriarchal dominance of Black males, and who have failed to delineate the ways in which Black men have participated in and perpetuated oppression of Black women. She provides a theoretical discussion of the relationship between racism and sexism, and the racism of the contemporary feminist movement.

Alice Walker, 1982. National Archives

815 • *Beloved* (1987)

While supervising the publication of *The Black Book* (1974) as an editor at Random House, Toni Morrison came across the story of an enslaved woman who ran away from slavery and then kept slave hunters from recapturing her two children by killing them. That story lodged in Morrison's mind and later emerged as the focal point for her *Beloved*, a novel about slavery and the persistence of its memory in African American women's lives. It is her most extraordinary novel to date. *Beloved* weaves together realistic detail and dreamlike stream-of-consciousness writing that explores the psychological ramifications of enslavement for Black women. In the process, Morrison shows how transfiguring was the struggle of Black women to achieve a sense of dignity in the face of slavery and how even resistance to slavery's oppression often warped those who resisted. The novel engages such universal questions as whether the enslaved life is worth living and the moral question of infanticide, seen through the eyes and heard through the ears of a community aghast at one woman's protest against the system of slavery. By switching point of view, Morrison is able to voice the anger, sympathy, horror, and inhumanity felt by the entire community as a witness to slavery's ultimate inhumanity—its infection of the humanity of the enslaved. *Beloved* brings to light how the memory of slavery, preserved in African American myth and folkore, remains a powerful way of understanding the tortured context of African American experience.

816 • *The Schomburg Library of Nineteenth-Century Black Women Writers* (1988)

Oxford University and Schomburg Library's republication of thirty books in a single edition brought the writings of nineteenth-century Black women writers to an entirely new generation of readers and signaled that African American women writers had come of age. General editor Henry Louis Gates, Jr., blended well-known works by Phillis Wheatley, Harriet Jacobs, and Anna J. Cooper with lesser known writings by Alice Dunbar-Nelson, Elizabeth Keckley, and Pauline Hopkins that balanced efforts in fiction, poetry, autobiography, and social criticism by Black women. Numerous university libraries purchased the entire set and provided a new generation of students and general readers with access to the Black women's literary voice of the nineteenth century. Moreover, the republication of these classics during a period in the 1980s when contemporary Black women writing was flowering signaled that indeed an African American women's renaissance had emerged toward the end of the twentieth century that was as self-conscious and confident of its literary origins as the predominantly male Harlem Renaissance of the early twentieth century.

817 • *Neon Vernacular* (1993)

Yusef Komunyakaa's *Neon Vernacular*, a collection of new and selected poems from other publications, won the Pulitzer Prize for poetry in 1994. The new poems in *Neon Vernacular* continue his autobiographical exploration of years spent in Bogalusa, Louisiana, and thus these poems convey a powerful sense of place and tragedy for a young Black man growing up in the South. But all of Komunyakaa's poems are distinguished for the remarkable physical and emotional detail that they convey. Komunyakaa works as a collagist who layers jazz references, segregationist hypocrises, religious allegories, and a strong, politicized voice into compositions such as "February in Sydney":

Dexter Gordon's tenor sax
plays "April in Paris"
inside my head all the way back
on the bus from Double Bay.

I emerge from the dark theatre,
passing a woman who grabs her red
purse
& hugs it to her like a heart attack.

A loneliness
lingers like a silver needle
under my black skin,
as I try to feel how it is
to scream for help through a horn.

Art

818 • Richard Hunt (b. 1935)

Richard Hunt is one of the nation's most prolific and sought-after sculptors. In fact, because Hunt produces mainly large, abstract metal sculptures, most who see his provocative public installations probably do not realize that he is African American. Nevertheless, as a young student at the Art Institute of Chicago, Hunt was introduced to and influenced by the work of fellow sculptor Richmond Barthe. Something of Barthe's elongation of form and rich, vibrant verticality can be seen in Hunt's work, not only his small sculpture but his monumental metal sculptures. There is a rhythm and vitality to Hunt's sculptures that is organic and powerful. Some of his more recent work, such as the projected installation *Middle Passage,* promises an even more strongly narrative response to African American history.

Collard Greens. Photograph by Jarvis Grant. Courtesy of Martha Jackson-Jarvis

819 • Martha Jackson-Jarvis (b. 1952)

Martha Jackson-Jarvis is a remarkably creative sculptor who uses clay to create complex, evocative, and rhythmic installations. Beginning as a child with a love for fashioning small clay sculptures, Jackson-Jarvis has continually refined and expanded her control of this medium until she can populate entire galleries with her thematically interesting objects. With pieces on walls as well as floors, she creates a synergy among the objects that makes the installation rooms into vibrant environments. *The Gathering,* installed at the University of Delaware in 1988, was one of her most heralded early works. More recently, Jackson-Jarvis has used her clay sculptures to model one of African American culture's favorite foodstuffs in *Collard Greens,* a provocative set of sculptures that affirm the need of all people to sustain a

healthy relationship with our agricultural heritage and ecological future.

820 • Renee Stout (b. 1958)

Renee Stout is one of those contemporary African American artists who seek in their work and the work of West African artists a means to address issues of spirituality in their lives. After obtaining a B.F.A. from Carnegie Mellon University in 1980, Stout's first shift in focus came on a six-month artist-in-residence at Northeastern University in 1984–85, when she shifted from painting to sculpture. She also moved more self-consciously into the study of West African art and culture, especially the *vodun* religion, and began to create box forms and assemblages out of found objects, old photographs, and Kongo spirit-script. An excellent example of this type of sculpture is *Instructions and Provisions: Wake Me Up on Judgment Day* (1987), a mixed-media box containing the instructions and provisions needed for someone to pass through the afterlife. Much of her work seems driven by the desire to bridge the division between life and death, and find in West African ancestral symbols the power to mobilize the self in this world. That project is epitomized in *Fetish #2,* Stout's mixed-media body sculpture. Here the artist cast her own body in plaster, painted the mold with black paint, and added medicine bags, a medicine pouch, a stamp from Niger, a picture of a young girl, dried flowers, cowrie shells for eyes, and monkey hair for the headdress. In effect, Stout has created a full-size West African *nkisi* figure out of her own body that challenges Western conceptions of the female nude and creates instead a powerful symbol of African American womanhood.

821 • David Hammons (b. 1943)

Born in Springfield, Illinois, Hammons began his career as an innovator who utilized the monoprint or body print to create a series of haunting images of African Americans, such as *Injustice Case* (1970). But in the 1980s Hammons expanded into the use of found objects to fashion artwork that challenged prevailing notions of race. His *How Ya Like Me Now?* (1989), a sixteen-foot-high portrait of Jesse Jackson as a white man, was designed to question whether Jesse Jackson would have been an acceptable 1988 presidential candidate if he had been white. But when the portrait was installed over a Metro subway stop in Washington, D.C., as part of an exhibition, "The Blues Aesthetic," created by curator Richard Powell for the Washington Project for the Arts, the portrait was torn down by a group of Black men who believed it was an insult to Jackson and the race. Such provocative, double-meaning art is the specialty of Hammons, who sees the purpose of art to provoke, not to enshrine positive Black images. He has received a MacArthur Foundation Fellowship, twice been awarded National Endowment for the Arts fellowships, and has been a fellow at the American Academy in Rome.

822 • Lorna Simpson (b. 1960)

This multimedia artist has created installations that challenge African Americans as well as European Americans to consider the ways in which control is exercised over African Americans in the American past and the present. In *Self-Possession* (1992), Simpson uses a photograph of a Black woman's body to challenge the structures of domination of Black women's bodies in modern American culture. In *Places with a Past* (1991), Simpson works with an actress, appropriates historical artifacts, and utilizes audiotapes to symbolize the effects of the slave trade as it operated in eighteenth- and nineteenth-century South Carolina. Simpson is con-

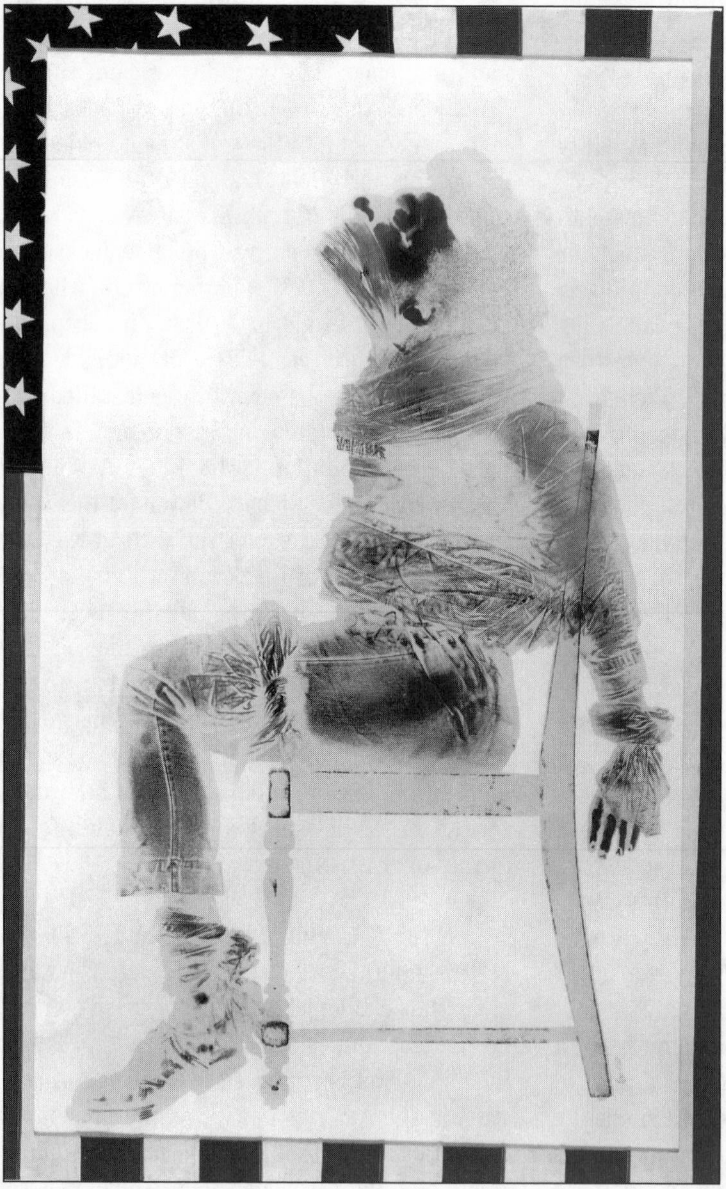

Injustice Case, David Hammons (after Bobby Seale Chicago riot trial in 1968), 1970. Los Angeles County Museum of Art. Museum Purchase Fund

cerned with the ways in which Western culture has objectified both women and African Americans, and her installations force us to face those forces and thereby restore to us a sense of agency in a world of continuing alienation. In her much discussed installation *Wigs,* Simpson challenges us to rethink how notions of what is a proper hairstyle for women are contested by Black women today. She has received numerous honors in her career, perhaps the most important being the first African American woman artist to represent the United States at Venice Biennale.

Music and Dance

823 • Wynton Marsalis (b. 1961)

Wynton Marsalis, whose younger brother, Branford, plays the saxophone, is a trumpeter who has led the neoclassical movement in jazz that has done much to make jazz acceptable again to middle-class audiences in the 1980s and 1990s. Born in New Orleans, Marsalis brought back the sound of the New Orleans trumpeter, made famous earlier by King Oliver and Louis Armstrong, and sought to replace the fusion jazz sound of Miles Davis, his nemesis. Marsalis studied both jazz and classical music, performed both publicly while still a young man in

New Orleans, and attended the Berkshire Music Center at Tanglewood (Massachusetts) and the Juilliard School of Music in New York. He played with Art Blakey, Herbie Hancock, Ron Carter, and Tony Williams in the 1980s before forming his own quintet in 1982 with Kenny Kirkland, Charles Fambourgh, Jeff Watts, and Branford Marsalis. Then, in 1984, he won Grammys in both jazz and classical music recording categories, becoming the first musician ever to do so. Marsalis's trumpet playing has been distinguished for its speed, brilliance, and sophistication, while his best albums, with the exception of the stunning *Black Codes (from the Underground)* (1985), have been reinterpretations of jazz classics. In 1995 he authored a book about jazz, *Sweet Sing Blues on the Road.*

824 • Michael Jackson (b. 1958)

Michael Jackson was a mere eleven years old when the Jackson 5 (Tito, Jermaine, Marlon, Jackie, and Michael Jackson) signed with Motown Records and had its first single, "I Want You Back." As the Jackson 5 developed into stars in the 1970s, Michael matured from a child dancing attraction into the lead singer and then star of what became by 1975 America's hottest teenage singing group. That year the Jacksons (as they would later be called) left Motown to sign with Epic Records, in part so that they could begin writing and singing their own material. Michael Jackson's solo career blossomed under the new regime: after his first hit, "Got to Be There" (1971), rose to number five on the *Billboard* charts, Michael followed with the number one hit "Ben" (1972), the lead song on the sound track of the movie that chronicled the exploits of a heroic rat. Michael then teamed with talented composer and arranger Quincy Jones to produce two stunning albums, *Off the Wall* (1979) and *Thriller* (1982), which broke industry records for sales and number of singles (four and six respectively) to become number one from a single album (both of which were also number one). Perhaps as important, *Off the Wall* and *Thriller* were cultural successes: both albums won the approval of white audiences, young and old, garnered praise from pop music critics, and yet retained strong followings among the urban, Black audience. Subsequent albums, *Bad* (1987) and *Dangerous* (1991), were not as popular or critically successful. Among Michael Jackson's other accomplishments are that he was the first to develop the music video format, now a staple with rap and pop artists, and that he is a superb popular dancer whose performances have been praised by such dance experts as Bob Fosse and Fred Astaire. Jackson's decline in music popularity paralleled his increasingly controversial personal life, which included lightening of his skin color and alteration of his face through plastic surgery, a child sex abuse suit lodged against him and settled out of court, and his marriage in 1994 to Lisa Marie Presley, the daughter of Elvis Presley.

825 • Rap Music

Rap was the most influential and controversial Black music form of the 1980s and remains a powerful expression of Black youth culture in the 1990s. Rap music is the rhyming storytelling by one or more speakers over a musical selection often borrowed or "sampled" from another artist. Such rapping has a long pedigree in African American, Caribbean, and African culture, such as the familiar African American "dozens" (rhyming verbal jousts), or the less familiar Jamaican art of "toasting," perhaps introduced to the United States by the DJ Kool Herc, who moved from Jamaica to the West Bronx in New York in 1967. As a musical form, rap began

in the 1950s with the "scat" singing of such bebop jazz groups as Lambert, Hendricks, and Ross and the disc jockey innovation of "Jocko," a fifties "emcee," who used the breaks between songs he played over the radio to deliver rhyming ditties to his listening audience. In the 1960s a kind of rap music could be heard in the Last Poets and Gil Scott-Heron; but it was not until the 1970s that a core group of rapping DJs emerged in New York who also cut between various records to create new songs out of parts of records. At the same time, Black youth street rappers in New York began to narrate stories of love, violence, and betrayal in rhyme over music played on huge cassette players, or "ghetto blasters." Then, in 1979, this art form burst onto radio and the nation when the first rap record hit, "Rapper's Delight," by the Sugar Hill Gang, was released and rose to number forty-one on the disco chart, and coincided with the introduction of the term "hip-hop" to characterize the ability to jump between catchy jingles. Afterward successive waves of rap artists swept American listening audiences, such as Grandmaster Flash, Kurtis Blow, Afrika Bambaataa, and the Fatback Band of the "Old School" in the early 1980s, Run D.M.C., LL Cool J, Public Enemy, and Doug E. Fresh of the "New School" of the mid-1980s, and KRS-ONE, Heavy D, Big Daddy Kane, Queen Latifah, and 2 Live Crew of the "Newer New School," and so on. Rap music became controversial because of its connection with the street culture of Black America during a period of rising racial retrenchment and its reflection of Black youth anger in political, critical, and sometimes offensive lyrics. At the same time, rap music has had a tremendous influence on mainstream white American culture, from dress and car styles—the Jeep became an urban vehicle of choice because it was a favorite of rap artists—to television, where such shows as *The Fresh Prince of Bel-Air* and *Living Single* have been very popular.

826 • Grandmaster Flash

Grandmaster Flash, originally named Joseph Sadler, originated in 1974 the disc jockey technique of "scratching"—moving a record back and forth underneath a needle to produce a rhythmic, jarring sound that has become a staple sound of rap records. His album *The Adventures of Grandmaster Flash on the Wheels of Steel* (1981) exhibited this technique for the first time. Flash is also credited for the innovation of hooking two turntables up to the same set of speakers and, by putting different records on the turntables, switching quickly from one to the other to mix musical elements from both records into a third, original composition. Such a technique made the disc jockey into a creative musician, whose ability to switch quickly between records required skill and concentration. As Flash became more adept at this technique in the 1970s, he realized that he could not "compose" at the turntable as creatively as he wanted and also rap. He then recorded his first rap song using a group of rappers, the Furious Faive, out front to carry the rap, while he managed the music. The group received little airplay on radio stations, fueling the view among rappers that the "true" rappers are underground artists who are "dissed" by the commercial radio industry.

827 • Queen Latifah (b. 1970)

Queen Latifah (Dana Owens) is an example of how rap music has created its own oppositions: she achieved prominence in the late 1980s as both a critic of male dominance and the glorification of conspicuous consumption that was a hallmark of the early 1980s when rappers talked about their material possessions,

wore gold chains and gold tooth caps, and drove expensive cars. Reared in East Orange, New Jersey, she broke into the rap scene in 1989 with her first album, *All Hail the Queen,* a powerful statement of both Afrocentrism and female self-respect. Often photographed wearing her Nefertiti headdress, the Queen, as she styles herself, goes further, and has created an identity of female authority to contest the rise of anti-women lyrics in rap music of the late 1980s and early 1990s. Her second album, *Nature of a Sistah* (1991), contains several cuts that state, unequivocally, that the Queen has "had it up to here" with both commercialism in rap and anti-women lyrics and violence. But Queen Latifah is known more today as the star of the television series *Living Single,* on which she plays, in keeping with the Afrocentric economic message, the owner of a magazine called *Flavor*. Reputedly Queen Latifah manages her own economic empire, perhaps realizing better than any other current rap artist the ideology of economic self-sufficiency implicit in both Black feminism and Afrocentrism.

828 • Anthony Davis (b. 1951)

In 1985 Anthony Davis composed an opera, *X: The Life and Times of Malcolm X,* that is a provocative fusion of classical, jazz, and gospel music styles around the theme of the African American hero Malcolm X. Davis, a trained classical pianist, had composed two smaller works—"Hemispheres" (a work in five parts composed for Molissa Fenley's theatrical dance *Hemispheres*) (1983) and "The Ghost Factory" (1984), a violin concerto—before attempting the much larger, three-part opera. The opera form allows Davis to use his romantic music to explore the life of an exemplary African American. By grounding his music in such a narrative, Davis can evoke jazz, gospel, and other African American musical styles within a basically classical operatic format. In chanted songs like "Africa's Time Has Come," Davis choruses champion ideals that were dear to Malcolm X. The entire piece has the feeling of a requiem to a fallen hero. When it was performed by the New York City Opera in 1986, it helped to sustain the growing infatuation with Malcolm X as a source of creative commentary on what it means to be Black in America. Since *X,* Davis has produced *Lost Moonas Sisters for Soprano, Violin, Keyboards, Marimba & Vibraphone* (1990) for the "Urban Diva" and "Emergency Music" series. His *X* was performed by William Henry Curry, Pisteme & Orchestra of St. Luke's and is recorded.

829 • Garth Fagan (b. 1940)

Born in Jamaica, Garth Fagan developed as a dancer in that Caribbean island. He got his start in dance with the Ivy Baxter Company. Upon coming to New York, Fagan studied with Martha Graham, among others. In 1970 he began the Bucket Dance Company in upstate New York, to

Garth Fagan. Photograph by Ron Wu. Courtesy of Garth Fagan Dance

tap urban African American talent. The company has continued to perform compositions choreographed by Garth Fagan and has toured nationally. Working within the tradition of Pearl Primus, Fagan has evolved an abstract but socially relevant choreography. His most important work to date is his critically acclaimed modern ballet *Griot New York*, a sensual full-evening tribute to the energy and frustrations of the modern city that opened at the Brooklyn Academy of Music in 1991 and toured several cities. Wynton Marsalis composed the music, and Martin Puryear sculpted the sets on this collaborative production.

830 • Bill T. Jones (b. 1952)

Bill Jones has emerged as the most inventive modern dance choreographer of the 1990s. Unlike Garth Fagan, Jones has never seen himself as a Black dancer or choreographer. Early in his career, Jones developed an abstract and provocative choreography that was performed by a company started by Jones and Arnie Zane. The most famous of these is *Fever Swamp* (1983), which was also performed by the Alvin Ailey company. After being diagnosed as HIV positive in 1985, and the death of Zane from AIDS in 1988, Jones produced numerous compositions, not only for his own company but also for the Berlin Opera Ballet. Jones has also explored new media in adapting dance to the postmodern aesthetics of the late twentieth century. His multimedia dance composition *Last Supper at Uncle Tom's Cabin/The Promised Land* is a fifty-person extravaganza that begins by interpreting *Uncle Tom's Cabin* and ends with a dialogue between Jones and a clergyman on whether AIDS is a heaven-sent punishment. Rather than seeing himself as working within the Alvin Ailey or Katherine Dunham tradition, Jones seeks to sample all cultural forms to create a more universalist choreography. His company, for example, contains more non-Black dancers than African American.

Some Important Plays and Films

831 • *A Soldier's Story* (1981)

This award-winning play narrated the internal conflicts in a Black army unit training in the South during World War II. As such, it documented the pathological and psychological ramifications of racism for African American soldiers, particularly the diversity of social strategies among Black males during segregation for dealing with racism. Written by Charles Fuller, *A Soldier's Story* opened at the Negro Ensemble Company and starred Adoph Caesar, Charles Brown, and Denzel Washington.

832 • *Purple Rain* (1984)

Prince's thinly autobiographical film about an obsessively self-involved rock bandleader and his dysfunctional family life broke new ground in African American rock cinematography. By probing the psychological roots of the lead character's physical abuse of his girlfriend, his psychological abuse of his band members, and his tense relationships with a frustrated Black father and a victimized white mother, Prince's maiden voyage as a film actor engaged many of the issues that still plague the lives of talented media heroes. Confronting such issues as wife abuse, egocentricity, and the sexual politics of success in the commercial world of rock club entertainment, *Purple Rain* suggested that a healing catharsis was possible for those willing to confront the devils in their pasts. The movie was distinguished by its sound track,

which was not only one of Prince's best albums but won an Academy Award for best sound track of the year.

833 • *She's Gotta Have It* (1986)

Spike Lee's *She's Gotta Have It* was more than a great film about Black relationships in the 1980s. It also inaugurated the modern era of movies directed by African Americans that were successful at the box office. Produced for $175,000 over twelve days of filming, *She's Gotta Have It* is the story of sexual competition among three Black males—a completely self-involved pretty boy, a frustrated, violent middle-class guy, and a ghetto bicycle homeboy played by Spike Lee—for the love (and sexual fidelity) of one woman, Nola Darling. Because the woman refuses to choose a monogamy that her suitors insist upon, the movie reverses the typical pattern of noncommittal men versus commitment-oriented women; but it also goes further and critiques all of the available options confronting Nola Darling, whose character is far more complex, creative, and likable than any of the males she is pressured to choose. The film introduces several formal cinematic innovations in the way that it is shot in tight close-ups by Ernest Dickerson in gritty black and white. What Lee achieves is a remarkably funny examination of the foibles of sex and love among seemingly overly serious Black people whose characters seem more real than the overly stereotyped and conventionalized representations of Black people coming from mainstream Hollywood in the 1980s.

834 • *Do the Right Thing* (1989)

Spike Lee's mosaic of racial and generational conflict in Brooklyn is a bold challenge to the prevailing genre of race conflict films produced by Hollywood. With outstanding performances by Ossie Davis, Danny Oryeda, and Rosie Perez, the movie shows the depth of interracial attraction in America, the ways in which whites worship Black stars while despising Black people, and the class nature of racial conflict in America. Lee's portrait of the Brooklyn ghetto fused hot sexual scenes, poignant confrontations between the elders and respectless youth of the Black community, and the explosiveness of racial confrontations across class lines. *Do the Right Thing* was also a commercial success as well as extremely popular with Black audiences. The movie grossed over $27 million at the box office, received the accolades of reviewers, and snagged an Oscar nomination for best screenplay.

835 • *The Piano Lesson* (1990)

August Wilson's second Pulitzer Prize–winning play (the first was *Fences,* 1987) is a tight family drama of conflict between a brother and sister over a piano; but it is also conflict over what price African Americans should pay for success, especially if that price is the sacrifice of African American heritage. Set in the Hill neighborhood of Pittsburgh, where Wilson grew up, the drama unfolds in a family's living room after a brother returns home with a not-so-hidden agenda—to sell the family heirloom, a piano with African-inspired carvings that record the family's history, which he co-owns with his sister. He wants to sell the piano, which will bring a good price, in order to buy some land and achieve his economic freedom. But his sister refuses to sell the piano, and the subsequent family argument revolves around whether the piano, which represents the family's past, ought to be sold to create a viable future. What distinguishes August Wilson's plays is not so much their plots, but the powerful poetical language with which his characters argue their case and

struggle with their personal demons. After the hot, fast-paced dialogue reaches a peak in which the resolution of the dispute seems to require bloodshed, a spiritual presence, representing the family spirit, makes itself known to the family and resolves the dilemma. Directed by Lloyd Richards, the play opened on Broadway in 1990 with Charles Dutton playing the lead; it was adapted to television (again with Dutton in the lead) and broadcast on CBS on February 5, 1995.

836 • *Boyz N the Hood* (1991)

John Singleton's premier movie about the violence of black urban life in Los Angeles opened to more theater violence than any other movie in American history. It also grossed $55 million and starred Ice Cube, a rapper, in one of its lead roles. The film narrates the struggle of a young urban Black male to be a success, despite growing up in one of the most dangerous neighborhoods in America. With the support of a single-parent father, who instills a dignity and a sense of self-worth in his son, the young man is a success. He is nevertheless constrained by the social dislocation and anomie of his surroundings.

837 • *Twilight: Los Angeles, 1992* (1993–94)

Playwright and performer Anna Deavere Smith's one-woman theater performance *Twilight: Los Angeles, 1992,* which she created, wrote, and performed, is a provocative engagement of the many issues surrounding the Rodney King rebellion. Commissioned by Gordon Davidson of Los Angeles' Mark Taper Forum, Smith conducted interviews with over two hundred people, including African Americans, Koreans, and whites, who were directly or indirectly involved with the beating, the case, or the rioting. She then edited those remarks and skillfully wove them into a stage performance that consists solely of the interviewee's remarks. With numerous costume changes, Smith mimics those interviewed and effectively suggests their personalities without simply duplicating them. The result is a dramatic cross section of America's mind on race. Although the immediate focus is the Los Angeles conflict, Smith's actual goal is to dredge up and expose the terrors, pains, hurts, and angers that fuel contemporary American racial divisiveness. Through her performance, she offers audiences an avenue of catharsis through which they can see themselves and others engaged in the often futile struggle to make America work for them and their ethnic group. *Twilight: Los Angeles, 1992* originally premiered on May 23, 1993, at the Center Theater Group/Mark Taper Forum in Los Angeles, produced by Gordon Davidson, and then opened at the New York Public Theater in March 1994, directed by George C. Wolfe. *Twilight: Los Angeles, 1992* is part of a ten-year-long series of performances on real events called *On the Road: A Search for American Character.* Although the performance could only represent twenty-five of those interviewed, the book script, *Twilight: Los Angeles, 1992: On the Road: A Search for American Character* (1994), by Anna Deavere Smith, contains all of the interviews. Some of those interviewed in the book include Angela King, Rodney's aunt, a Los Angeles Police Department expert on "use of force," a juror in the Simi Valley trial, and Reginald Denny, the white truck driver dragged from his truck and beaten during the rioting.

838 • *Sankofa* (1992)

The movie *Sankofa* is an independently produced and distributed story about a Black fashion model who visits Elmina, the island fortress

built by the Portuguese to house Africans before sending them into the Middle Passage. On this visit, this woman, who is considerably lacking in Black consciousness, is suddenly transported back into history to become her ancestor who was shipped from this island into slavery in the sugar islands of the Caribbean. The story is captivating for its frank portrayal of the cruelty and oppression of slavery, the complexity of social relationships between house and field slaves, and the resistance of Africans to the masters. Filmmaker Haile Gerima, a Howard University professor, states that he produced the film without studio support because Hollywood would not approve the script with such frank criticism of the slave institution. Gerima was also locked out of distribution networks, but rented a Washington, D.C., theater to put on the film. The strategy succeeded: the film garnered critical acclaim and has reaped a profit for the filmmaker, who made the film for $1 million.

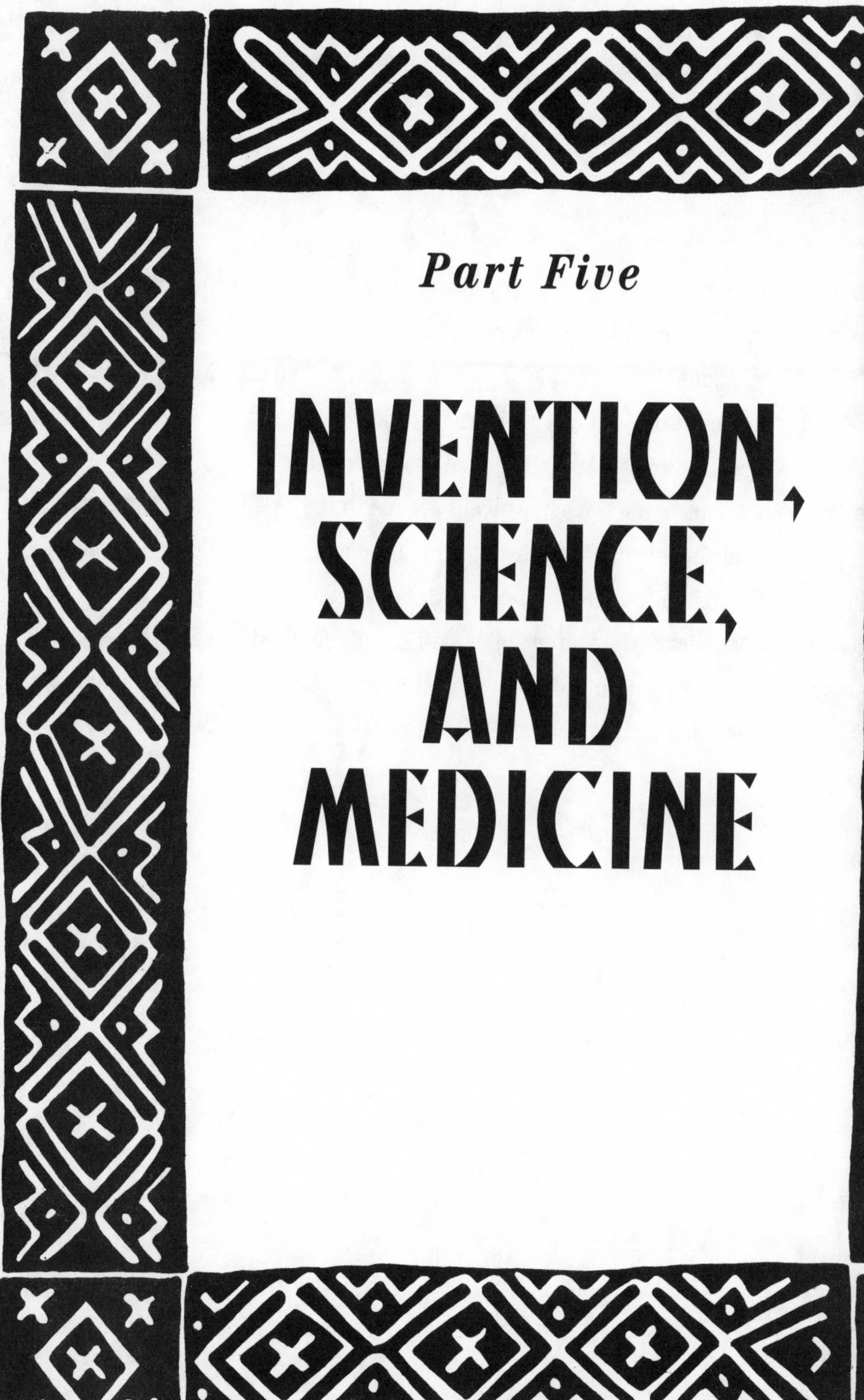

Part Five

INVENTION, SCIENCE, AND MEDICINE

Because of a Eurocentric perspective on the world history of science and technology, the belief has persisted for centuries that Africans lacked scientific and technological sophistication. In addition, many believed that the Middle Passage and subsequent brutal assimilation into a Euro-American culture erased whatever cultural heritage Africans had possessed. But recent research has shown that Africans were creative and inventive problem-solvers in science, medicine, metallurgy, and agriculture prior to European contact. When Africans arrived in the New World, they used their technical knowledge of agriculture, boatbuilding, fishing, iron production, medicine, and textile production to solve many of the problems facing America, both before and after the American Revolution. Slave and free African Americans were often highly skilled and recruited specifically because of those skills. The resultant American culture was less a "white man's culture," and more a multicultural product of African American, Native American, and European American innovation.

INVENTION

Colonial Innovation

839 • Rice and Rice Technology Introduced

West Africans introduced the rice plant and its cultivation to North America. English settlers had no knowledge of rice cultivation until West Africans, who had grown the rice plant since A.D. 100, were transported by English planters on Barbados to South Carolina in the late seventeenth century. Once West Africans showed the English how to plant rice seed in the spring, hoe it in rows during the summer, and harvest it West African style in the fall, the English realized that rice could turn South Carolina into a profitable colony. Indeed, rice became so important to South Carolina's economy that it continued to be that colony's major crop long after the rest of the South had turned to cotton farming in the nineteenth century. Not only did West Africans introduce rice to the colonial American economy, but they also introduced the technology to process the crop. The technique of irrigating the crop by flooding the rice fields was West African in origin. West African mortars and pestles were used to break the husks from around the grains. Then coiled-grass fanner baskets—wide, flat, circular baskets about two feet in diameter—were employed to separate the chaff from the edible grains. Slaves tossed the rice into the air, the wind blew away the lighter husks, and the heavier rice grains fell back into the baskets. Baskets made of grasses and palmetto were produced by both Africans and Indians, and some fusion of technologies occurred to create South Carolina's great basket-weaving tradition.

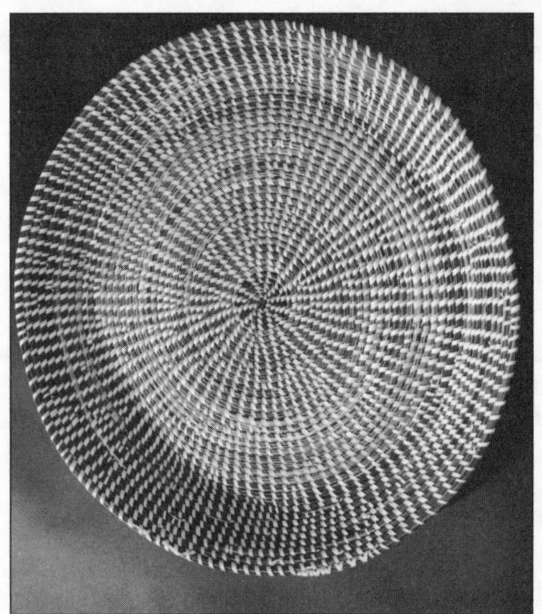

Rice fanner basket. Photograph by Harold Dorwin. Courtesy of Anacostia Museum

840 • Dugout Canoe

West Africans, along with the Indians, introduced the English in the seventeenth century to dugout canoes, but the English had difficulty learning to row and steer them. Slaves built the narrow canoe by hollowing out a large cypress log, burning the insides so that it could be held open by sticks, and then, after the hull hard-

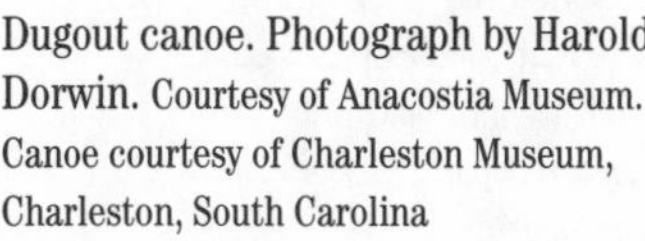

Dugout canoe. Photograph by Harold Dorwin. Courtesy of Anacostia Museum. Canoe courtesy of Charleston Museum, Charleston, South Carolina

ened, adding log planks to the sides. Two or three such hollowed-out logs would be joined to make the larger and more stable pettiauger, or piragua, a multiple-log dugout canoe. In South Carolina, a colony of numerous narrow waterways and without adequate roads or bridges, African Americans became expert boatmen who used the canoes to fish, hunt, scout, and escape from slavery.

841 • Poisoning Fish

Africans were also some of the colony's best fishermen, in part because of their practice of poisoning fish. Drugging fish was a common West African practice. A particular stream would be dammed up and then quicklime and other plant juices would be added to the water. The intoxicated fish could be captured by hand, and they were still edible. The practice spread so widely in South Carolina that the assembly passed a law in 1725 to publicly whip any slave convicted of the "pernicious practice," but it continued. Africans also introduced net fishing to the colonies and sometimes combined the two techniques: standing in dugout canoes, Africans hauled in large amounts of drugged fish by flinging nets out into the many waterways of South Carolina. Fishing supplied a lucrative income for slaves and was an important trade source for South Carolina.

842 • Ironsmithing

Ironsmithing was a highly developed technology in West Africa by the sixteenth century when the slave trade began, and Africans brought that technology with them when they crossed the Atlantic. African Americans were highly valued in the South as blacksmiths, not only because they created effective tools but also because of the ironwork they contributed to the decorative architecture in places like New Orleans. Indeed, many of the most famous New Orleans ironworkers employed large numbers of slaves, skilled iron craftsmen, who actually performed the jobs the white supervisors contracted. Often the African American workers in white shops were given the freedom to inscribe motifs in gates and fences that reveal African influences.

Net fishing. Photograph by Harold Dorwin, Anacostia Museum, Smithsonian Institution. From *Dictionary of Black African Civilization*

843 • Shotgun Houses

The "shotgun" house found extensively in African American neighborhoods throughout the American South was an African American invention. Such rectangular houses are called shotgun houses because if one stood on the porch and fired a shotgun, its pellets would go straight through the house with ease. Usually these houses contain three or more small rooms in succession from the front to the back, the gabled or small end of the house facing the street. This arrangement promotes a great deal of interaction among residents, since one must pass others to get out of the house. These houses led to the southern African American practice of sitting on front porches, one of the few ways to escape the intense interaction within, and also promoted more neighborhood interaction among residents sitting on front porches. Some historians argue that the front porch, an anomaly in English houses, is an African American contribution.

844 • Quilting Language

Although other groups had developed quilts, Africans were some of the most prolific quiltmakers, a testament to their mastery of textile production. But Africans also developed something unique: a language of quilt signs designed to convey messages to those traveling. By the middle of the eighteenth century, a well-developed language of signs had emerged by which quilts could be hung outside a house to impart information surreptitiously to other African Americans, especially runaway slaves. The hanging of the quilt outside of a house meant this was a safe house for a slave to stop at to gain rest and refreshment before going on to the next station on the underground railroad to freedom.

Free Inventors

845 • Benjamin Banneker (1731–1806)

In 1791 inventor and mathematician Benjamin Banneker produced the first scientific book written by an African American. Banneker's almanac consisted of weather data, tidal information for Chesapeake Bay, recipes, medical remedies, poems, abolitionist essays, and information about festivals and holidays. Such almanacs were popular in late-eighteenth-century America when books on natural phenomena were the only secular reading material available. Banneker was already famous in Baltimore for building a wooden clock in 1753, without any instruction, from a pocket watch loaned to him. The clock was still working upon his death. Encouraged by Quaker abolitionists, Banneker sent his almanac, along with a letter offering himself as proof of African American ability, to Thomas Jefferson prior to publishing it. Jefferson's reply was published in the almanac, which was reissued annually until 1797. Jefferson recommended Banneker to Major Andrew Ellicott and Banneker served as an astronomical assistant to Ellicott (not, as some contend, to Major Pierre Charles L'Enfant) during the preliminary survey of the ten-mile square that became the District of Columbia.

846 • Benjamin Banneker and Thomas Jefferson Debate the Doctrine of Racial Inequality

On August 19, 1791, Banneker sent Thomas Jefferson the following letter along with a copy of Banneker's almanac:

I suppose it is a truth too well attested to you, to need a proof here, that we are a race of beings, who have long laboured under the abuse and censure of the world; that we have long been looked

upon with an eye of contempt; and that we have long been considered rather as brutish than human, and scarcely capable of mental endowments. . . . I apprehend you will embrace every opportunity, to eradicate that train of absurd and false ideas and opinions, which so generally prevail with respect to us; and that your sentiments are concurrent with mine, which are, that one universal Father hath given being to us all; . . . and endowed us all with the same faculties; and that however variable we may be in society or religion, however diversified in situation or colour, we are all of the same family, and stand in the same relation to Him. . . . but sir, how pitiable it is to reflect, that although you were so fully convinced of the benevolence of the Father of Mankind, and of His equal and impartial distribution of these rights and privileges, which He hath conferred upon them, that you should at the same time counteract His mercies, in detaining by fraud and violence, so numerous a part of my brethren under groaning captivity, and cruel oppression, that you should at the same time be found guilty of the most criminal act, which you professedly detest in others, with respect to yourselves.

On August 30, 1791, Jefferson wrote back:

I thank you most sincerely, for your letter of the 19th instant, and for the Almanac it contained. Nobody wishes more than I do, to see such proofs as you exhibit, that nature has given to our black brethren talents equal to those of the other color of men; and that the appearance of want of them is owing merely to the degraded condition of their existence, both in Africa and America. I can add with truth, that nobody wishes more ardently to see a good system commenced, for raising the condition, both of their body and mind, to what it ought to be, as far as the imbecility of their present existence, and other circumstances, which cannot be neglected, will admit.

I have taken the liberty of sending your Almanac to Monsieur de Condorcet, Secretary of the Academy of Sciences, at Paris and Member of the Philanthropic Society, because I considered it as a document to which your whole colour have a right for their justification against the doubts which have been entertained of them.

Curiously, Condorcet never received a copy of Banneker's almanac.

847 • Thomas Jennings (1791–1859)

On March 3, 1821, Thomas Jennings became the first African American to receive a patent. As the owner of a New York dry-cleaning business, Jennings invented and patented a new process for cleaning clothing. Jennings used the money he earned with his invention to buy his family out of slavery. Active as an abolitionist, Jennings published petitions that advocated the end of slavery in New York.

848 • Henry Blair (1804?–60)

On October 14, 1834, Henry Blair of Greenosa, Maryland, became the second African American to obtain a patent. Blair received his first patent for a corn harvester. On August 31, 1836, he obtained his second patent for a cotton seed planter. Blair's entry in the patent registry identifies him as "a colored man," the only entry of this period to do so. It seems likely that other African Americans had received patents, but simply were not identified by race.

849 • Norbert Rillieux (1806–94)

A freeborn African American from New Orleans revolutionized the sugar industry when he invented the multiple-effect evaporator for re-

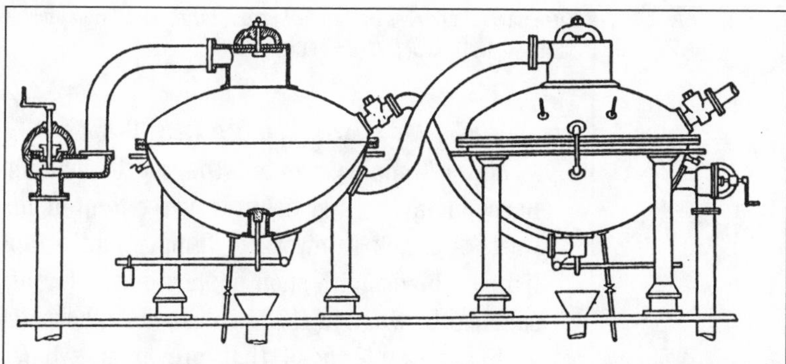

Diagram of the multiple-effect evaporator invented by Norbert Rillieux. Schomburg Center for Research in Black Culture, New York Public Library, Astor, Lenox and Tilden Foundation

Norbert Rillieux. Courtesy of Schomburg Center for Research in Black Culture, New York Public Library, Astor, Lenox and Tilden Foundation

fining sugar. The son of Constant Vivant, a free Black woman, and Vincent Rillieux, an engineer and plantation owner who recognized his son's extraordinary mechanical ability, Norbert was sent to Paris to study engineering. Rillieux also taught at the L'Ecole Central in Paris and authored scholarly papers on the steam engine and steam processes that were well received by European scientists. Familiar with the expensive, slow, and dangerous "Jamaica Train" process of refining sugar in use in New Orleans, which at best produced a sugar like molasses in color and texture, Rillieux designed a new process, the multiple-effect evaporation system, in Paris in 1830. Returning to the United States to get funding for his invention, Rillieux operated his new system on a Louisiana plantation in 1845. By 1848 Rillieux's system was successfully producing finer, whiter sugar with a huge reduction in costs and labor. His system was adopted by factories throughout Louisiana, Cuba, and Mexico, and its steam principles found much broader application in manufacturing industries for condensed milk, soap, gelatin, and glue products. Heralded for his work and accepted professionally by the scientific community, Rillieux was nonetheless isolated socially and denied equal access to public accommodations. When Louisiana began to require that every black, free or slave, carry an identification pass, Rillieux returned to Paris in 1861 and studied Egyptology, deciphered hieroglyphics, and continued to perfect his invention until the 1880s. He worked on several other, smaller inventions until his death in 1894.

850 • Sail Positioning Device

James Forten was a sailmaker from Philadelphia who invented and sold an improved version of a sail positioning device, a product that made his company one of the most prosperous sailmaking companies in antebellum Philadelphia. As a young boy, Forten served in the navy during the Revolutionary War and then apprenticed to

AN ADDRESS

DELIVERED BEFORE THE

LADIES' ANTI-SLAVERY SOCIETY

OF

PHILADELPHIA,

On the Evening of the 14th of April, 1836,

By JAMES FORTEN, Jr.

PHILADELPHIA:
PRINTED BY MERRIHEW AND GUNN,
No. 7 Carters' Alley.
......
1836.

Title page of address by James Forten, sailmaker. Prints and Photographs Division, Library of Congress

Robert Bridges, a Philadelphia sailmaker, whose company Forten purchased in 1798. Forten used the fortune he made as a sailmaker to support the abolitionist movement and fund the activities of the emigrationist Paul Cuffee.

Toggle whaling harpoon. Photo by Harold Dorwin, Anacostia Museum. Courtesy of the National Museum of American History

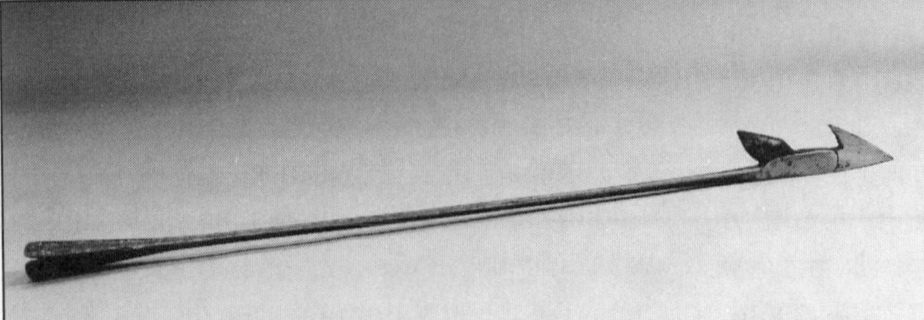

851 • Lewis Temple (1800–54)

Lewis Temple invented the toggle whaling harpoon in the 1840s but never patented his work. A Black ironworker, Temple had established a blacksmith shop in New Bedford, Massachusetts, when in 1848 he designed a harpoon with a movable head that prevented whales from slipping loose from the hook and escaping. The head of the harpoon became "locked" in the whale's flesh, and the only way to remove it was to cut it loose after the whale was killed. Known as the toggle iron, Temple's harpoon became standard whaling equipment; but Temple's failure to patent his work allowed others to reproduce the harpoon themselves, reducing his profits. When he died in 1854, his estate was valued at less than $1,500.

Slave Inventors

852 • Ned and Intellectual Property

The U.S. Patent Office's refusal to award patents to slaves reinforced the predominant view that African Americans were incapable of significant contributions to technology. The policy also kept slave owners from obtaining patent rights for inventions made by their slaves. Such was the result when Oscar J. E. Stuart, a white Mississippi planter, wrote to Secretary of Interior Jacob Thompson, also a southerner, on August 25, 1857, to request a patent for a labor-saving cotton scraper that Ned, a slave blacksmith on Stuart's plantation, had invented. Stuart claimed the invention was his because of his belief that

all products of Ned's labor "both intiliectual [*sic*] and manual" belonged to Ned's master. But the commissioner of patents, who ruled on the case, disagreed, contending that the recipient of a patent must be a citizen, and since slaves were not regarded as citizens by the United States government, patents could not be issued in their name. That reading of the matter angered Stuart, who wrote back that he had not applied for the patent in Ned's name but rather his own. The attorney general concurred with the commissioner, however, ruling in 1858 that "a machine invented by a slave, though it be new and useful, cannot, in the present state of the laws, be patented. I may add that if such a patent were issued to the master, it would not protect him in the courts against persons who might infringe it." Nevertheless, Stuart began to sell the cotton scraper in 1860, and even justified the invention as a sign that slavery did not corrupt the intellect of slaves. Neither Ned's intellect nor person was ever heard of again.

HENRY BOYD,

MANUFATURER of Patent Right and Left Wood Screw and Swelled Rail Redsteads, North-west corner of Broadway and Eighth streets, Cincinnati, Ohio, would respectfully invite those wishing to purchase a superior article of furniture in Bedsteads, to call at his ware room and examine for themselves This newly invented Bedstead is warranted superior to any other ever offered in the West; possessing the following decided advantage over all others heretofore used, they can be put up or taken apart in one fourth the time required to do the same with others, without the possibility of a mistake—are more firm, less apt to become loose and worthless, and without a single harbor for vermin.

CERTIFICATES:

The undersigned, having used the above named Patent Bedsteads, feel no hesitation in recommending them to be the best now in use.

Hon. N. C. Reed,
Hon. Henry Morse,
Hon. Richard Ayres,
I. G. Burnett,
M. Allen,
Rev. L. G. Bingham,
D. L. Rusk,
S. B. Hunt,
Wm. D. Gallagher,
P. Evens,
Isaiah Wing,
J. B Russell,
P. Grandin, Esq,
B. Tappin,
Daniel Burritt,
Sam'l L'Hommedieu.
Milton McLean, Esq,
G. W. H. Evans, Cincinnati Hotel,
Samuel Berresford,
Wright Smith, Sr,
James Eshelby,
Wm. Holmes,
Wm. H. Henrie, Henrie House,
T. M. Cockrell, Pearl st House,
Wm. Marsh, Galt House,
J.W. Mason, 4th st House,
Wm. Crossman, } Trus.
Josiah Fobes, } of the Com. Hospital.

Caution: There are imitations of this Bedstead in market very much resembling it. The genuine, which only he warrants, are all stamped "H. Boyd."

may 18 12-4m

Certificate advertising Henry Boyd's bedstead. Prints and Photographs Division, Library of Congress

853 • Whose Reaper?

Black slave Jo Anderson seldom received credit for his development of the reaper. Instead, Cyrus McCormick is usually given credit for the invention of the automatic reaper. Although McCormick himself gave Anderson some credit for coming up with the idea, it was still McCormick who reaped the financial rewards for the invention.

854 • Brains Buys His Freedom

Henry Boyd invented a bed whose wooden rails screwed into both the headboard and footboard, giving it a much stronger structure than other early-nineteenth-century beds. He used his carpentry skills and his new bedstead idea to purchase his freedom in 1826. In 1836 he opened his own company using his bed frame design as the foundation. Boyd never patented his device, but he did try to have it protected by having a white man apply for the patent. In addition, Boyd stamped his name on every frame he made to ensure authenticity to his clients. By 1843 he was among Cincinnati's most successful furniture makers with a staff of twenty-five to fifty employees.

855 • Benjamin Montgomery and Jefferson Davis

Benjamin Montgomery (1819–77), while

working as a mechanic on Joseph Davis's plantation in the 1850s, designed an angled blade propeller that enabled steamboats to move efficiently through shallow waters around the plantation. Joseph, along with his brother, Jefferson Davis, who later became president of the Confederacy, tried to obtain a patent for Montgomery's invention. But the attorney general's decision in the Stuart case kept the Davises from profiting from the mental creativity of their slave. Once Jefferson Davis became president of the Confederacy, he had the Confederate Congress pass a law enabling masters to obtain patent rights for slave inventions.

Black Inventions After 1865

856 • Black Patents

Passage of the Thirteenth and Fourteenth Amendments to the Constitution brought a generally unrecognized benefit to African Americans: these amendments gave African Americans the right to patent their inventions. As a result, in the period following the Civil War, the number of patents for inventions filed by Blacks increased dramatically as innovators from all walks of life—farmers, blacksmiths, and scientists—sought recognition for their technological ingenuity. Still, we do not know exactly how many patents were obtained by African Americans, since racial identity was not recorded by the Patent Office.

857 • Agricultural Inventions

Because most African Americans became tenant farmers and continued to work the land after the Civil War, many of the inventions patented by Blacks in the postwar period were agricultural or domestic implements. Former slave Peter R. Campbell, who, like Benjamin Montgomery, had been a slave on Joseph Davis's plantation, patented a screw press in 1879. Charles T. Christmas, another former slave in Mississippi, received a patent in 1880 for a device to simplify the baling of cotton. Lockrum Blue received a patent in 1884 for a corn sheller.

858 • Gong and Signal Chair

Little is known about the Washington, D.C., teacher Miriam E. Benjamin, who received an 1888 patent for a chair with a small flag and a bell that an occupant rang using a rod attached to the seat of the chair. These chairs were used in many hotel dining rooms to summon a waiter. And with the support of a Black congressman, George Washington Murray, Benjamin recommended them to the United States House of Representatives as a way for congressmen to signal for a page.

859 • "The Real McCoy"

The term "the Real McCoy" comes from the automatic engine lubricator that Elijah McCoy (1843–1929) invented to continuously oil train and ship engines, which was immediately adopted by railroad and shipping lines. But soon imitations appeared that did not work as well as McCoy's lubricator and that led many would-be purchasers to inquire, "Is this the real McCoy?" Eventually the phrase was coined as a way to ask whether an item was genuine and of the highest quality. McCoy, born in Canada in 1844 and educated in Scotland, was unable to find work as an engineer after he moved to the United States. Taking a job as a fireman on the Michigan Central Railroad, he noticed that the fireman's duty of oiling the train's engine while stationary added tremendously to the length of

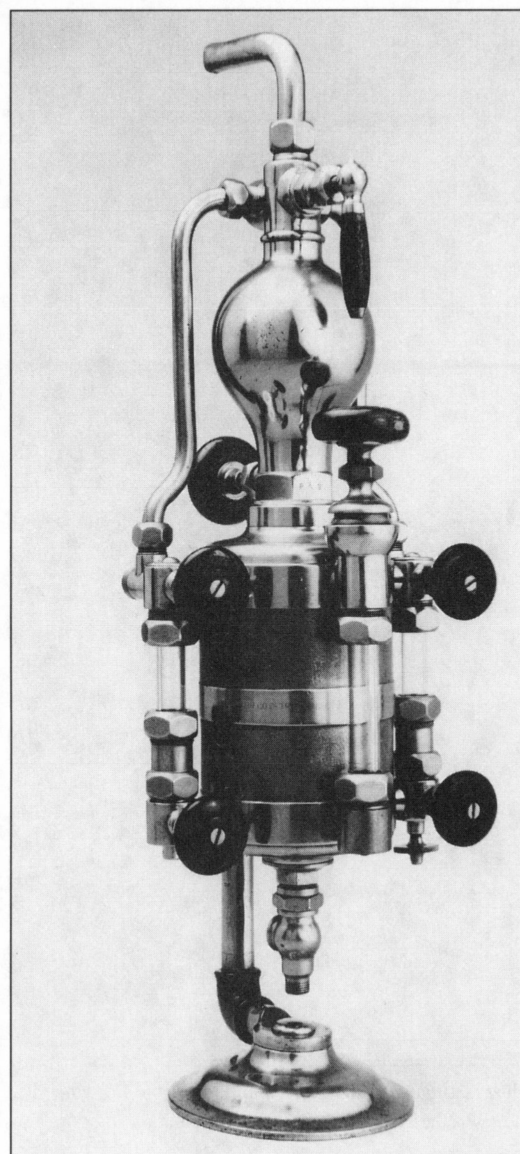

Elijah McCoy's automatic engine lubricator. Photograph by Harold Dorwin. Courtesy of Greenfield Village and the Henry Ford Museum

train trips. McCoy's first invention, a "lubricating cup," patented in 1872, provided a continuous flow of oil over the gears and thus eliminated "the necessity of shutting down the machine periodically." McCoy acquired fifty-seven other patents for devices designed to streamline the automatic lubrication process of machinery. He is also credited with inventing the ironing board, the lawn sprinkler, and, what McCoy considered his best invention, a graphite lubricator. In April 1915 he received a patent for a graphite lubricator that eliminated the problems of oiling a superheater engine that used large amounts of steam to operate. In 1920 McCoy established the Elijah McCoy Manufacturing Company to manufacture and sell the lubricator.

860 • The "Jenny" Automatic Coupler

Elijah McCoy was not the only African American railroad worker to create innovative solutions to railway problems. In 1897 Andrew J. Beard (1849–1941), an Alabama worker who had seen many men injured while manually coupling train cars, developed the best device for automatically coupling cars. Before Beard's invention, railroad workers had to brace themselves between railway cars while the cars were moved close enough together to drop a metal spike into a slot. The Jenny coupler secured two railroad cars once they were bumped together. Beard was one of the few inventors to actually profit from his invention—receiving $50,000 for his design.

861 • Pullman Car Ventilator

Even those who worked inside the train cars were ingenious in solving some of the mundane problems of riding the railroad. One man, Pullman porter H. H. Reynolds, responded to the constant requests of passengers to open windows by designing a ventilator that allowed air to flow into cars and at the same time kept out dust and soot. When he told his manager about the idea, Reynolds learned what many inventors have learned—that some will try to steal the idea of unsuspecting inventors. After his manager had a working model made, Pullman tried to obtain patent rights for Reynolds's idea. But Reynolds sued the Pullman Company and won the right to profit from his invention.

862 • Shoe Lasting Machine

The shoe manufacturing process in America was revolutionized by a Black immigrant, Jan Ernst Matzeliger (1852–89), who nevertheless died in poverty. Born in Surinam, Matzeliger apprenticed in government machine shops, joined onto an East Indian merchant ship at the age of nineteen, and then left the ship in 1870 to settle in Philadelphia and apprentice as a shoe cobbler. While learning the machinery used in the industry, he noticed that the most difficult part of the production process—"lasting," or connecting the upper to the sole of the shoe—had to be done by hand. After he moved to Lynn, Massachusetts, a center of shoe manufacturing, Matzeliger used a discarded forge in the factory where, for five years, he worked to develop a

Shoe lasting machine. Photograph by Harold Dorwin. Courtesy of the United Shoe Machinery Corporation

Jan Ernest Matzeliger. Schomburg Center for Research in Black Culture, New York Public Library, Astor, Lenox and Tilden Foundation

prototype of his shoe lasting machine. In exchange for two-thirds interest in the product, Matzeliger obtained from Melville S. Nichols and Charles H. Delnow the financial assistance he needed to perfect the machine. Finally Matzeliger received a patent on March 20, 1883, for a machine that cut costs in half while greatly increasing production. Not surprisingly, demand for his invention was high, and even though Matzeliger, Nichols, and Delnow formed the Union Lasting Machine Company to produce the machine, the company was too small to handle the huge number of requests. Two more investors were brought in, a larger Consolidated Lasting Machine Company was formed, and Matzeliger had to exchange his patents for a block of stock. Matzeliger lived only six years after his patent was granted, and he bequeathed his stock in the company to the North Congregational Society in Lynn. Apparently Matzeliger had attempted to join several white churches upon his arrival in Massachusetts, and all but the North Congregational Society rebuffed him.

863 • "The Black Edison"

Granville T. Woods (1856–1910) was known as the Black Edison, in part because he competed successfully with the celebrated Thomas Edison to market a telegraph system. Earlier, in 1884, Woods had lost a struggle with Alexander Graham Bell to market an advanced telephone transmitter for which Woods had received a patent. Without the requisite funding to market his device, Woods sold it to the Bell Telephone Company. But later, when Woods's telegraphic device for transmitting messages between moving trains was challenged by a similar device designed by Edison, a court ruled that Woods's design deserved the patent. After that victory, Woods secured the funding in the 1890s to form his own company, the Woods Electrical Company, to market his inventions, including air brakes and an egg hatching machine. But Woods's career also shows the effects of racism on talented Black inventors: Woods circulated a story in *Cosmopolitan* magazine that he was descended from "full-blooded savage Australian aborigines." Apparently Woods believed that his inventions would not be recognized if it was known that he was an African American.

864 • Carbon Filaments for Lamps

Lewis Latimer received a patent on January 17, 1882, for his unique design of carbon filaments for the electric incandescent lamp sold by Hiram Maxim's U.S. Electric Lighting Company. Primarily a patent illustrator, Latimer had

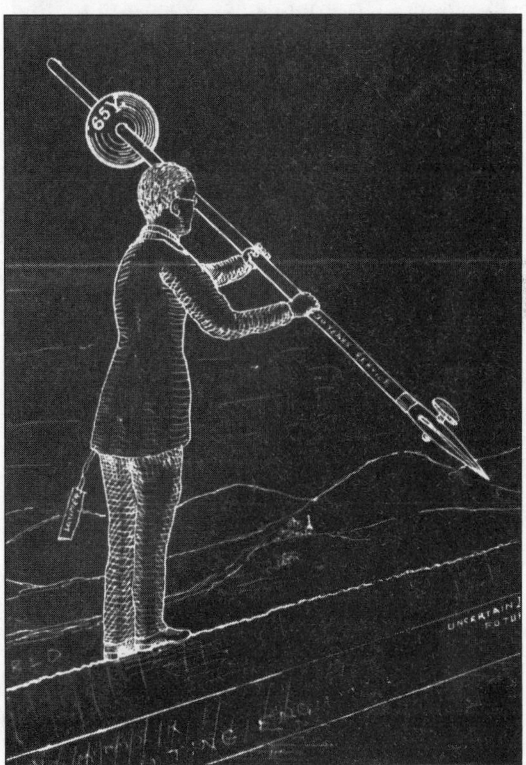

Drawing by Lewis Latimer to highlight the precariousness of his position as a consulting engineer. Photograph by Harold Dorwin. Courtesy of Dr. Winifred Norman Latimer, the Latimer Collection

begun work on an improved and cheaper carbon filament to make it possible for more people to enjoy electric lighting. His invention also made it possible for U.S. Electric to operate lights safely at a higher temperature.

865 • Edison Pioneers

The changing nature of invention in the late nineteenth century is revealed by the career of Lewis Latimer, who in 1884 was hired away from Maxim's U.S. Electric to join what eventually became known as the Edison Pioneers. As inventions became more scientific and technical in the late nineteenth century, inventors like Thomas Edison and Alexander Graham Bell formed research labs that coordinated a diversity of functions from pioneer research to product development to distribution and patent defense under one roof. Lewis Latimer's multifaceted genius for invention, patent drawing, and legal writing, made him a natural choice for Edison. Unlike at Maxim's, where Latimer served mainly as an inventor, Latimer became Edison's chief litigator in patent conflicts against those, like Granville Woods, who challenged Edison's patents. Latimer documented his experience working with Edison by writing the first book on electrical lighting, *Incandescent Electric Lighting: A Practical Description of the Edison System,* in 1890. Then, on January 24, 1918, Latimer was chosen to be the only Black member of the Edison Pioneers, the name Edison gave to the group of distinguished scientists and inventors he had assembled at Menlo Park, New Jersey. Generally speaking, the transition in American invention toward teams of researchers working in labs was not advantageous to Black inventors because it coincided with the rise of segregation in American life, which prevented many talented African Americans from living and working in proximity with other scientists and inventors in research and development labs. Nevertheless, independent Black inventors continued to develop inventions out of their work.

Edison Pioneers. Photograph by Harold Dorwin. Courtesy of Dr. Winifred Norman Latimer, the Latimer Collection

866 • Wrinkle-Preventing Trouser Stretchers

This invention emerged out of Archia Ross's work as a laundress. Wrinkles, obviously, were a problem for laundry and dry-cleaning establishments, and during her work in one, Ross came up with the idea of a wrinkle-preventing trouser stretcher. She received a patent for that invention in 1899. Not only did Ross design this work-saving device, but she also invented a device for keeping handbags closed and a runner to be used on doorsteps.

867 • Bread Crumbing Machine

Master cook Joseph Lee's invention emerged from his work. Lee thought too much bread became stale and was

discarded each day. To address this problem, he created the bread crumbing machine to reduce bread to crumbs through a tearing and grinding process. Lee then used the crumbs to make croquettes, escalloped oysters, cutlets, dressing for poultry, cake batter, fried meats, and puddings. He received a patent for his invention on June 4, 1895. Lee sold the patent to the Royal Worcester Bread Crumb Company of Boston, the machine's manufacturer, and the bread crumbing machine became standard equipment in top restaurants around the world. Lee also invented a bread making machine which mixed the ingredients through a more sanitary method than kneading the dough by hand. Variations of this design are still in use today.

Seven African Americans in Hampton Institute exhibit area of the African American Building at the Atlanta Exposition, 1895. Prints and Photographs Division, Library of Congress

868 • Recognition for Black Inventions

Congressman George Washington Murray championed the accomplishments of Black inventors to refute the argument that African Americans should be excluded from the proposed Cotton States Exhibition because African Americans had contributed nothing to American technological progress in the nineteenth century. On August 10, 1894, Murray stood in the House of Representatives and read the names of Black inventors into the *Congressional Record* from a list supplied him by Henry A. Baker, an African American who worked in the Patent Office. Together, Murray and Baker sought to use African American inventiveness as a weapon in the war against Social Darwinist claims of African American racial inferiority. African American invention gained national attention in 1895, when Black inventions were part of the exhibitions in the African American building at the Atlanta Exposition, and received international attention in 1900, when the Paris Exposition featured approximately 350 African American inventors in the African American section of the United States exhibit. The U.S. Patent Office had collected the information on Black inventors in creating the latter exhibit, which was seen by approximately 39 million visitors, many of which had probably never known that any Black inventors existed.

869 • The Gas Mask

The invention of the protective hood or gas mask in 1912 shows the pathos endured by African American inventors. Garrett Augustus Morgan (1877–1963) was a self-trained sewing machine mechanic who in 1909 had accidentally discovered a chemical solution that straightened hair. Morgan devised a protective hood and smoke protector that enabled firefighters and other personnel to enter smoky or toxic environments without breathing contaminated air. The protective hood covered the head and upper torso and supplied clean air to the

Garrett Augustus Morgan's advertisement for his gas mask. Photograph by Harold Dorwin, courtesy of Anacostia Museum. Used by permission of Western Reserve Historical Society, Cleveland, Ohio

wearer through two tubes from a bag of air that hung on the back of the hood. Garrett patented his invention in 1914 and staged an event in New Orleans where he entered a tent filled with smoke from burning tar sulfur, formaldehyde, and manure and remained for twenty minutes. The *New Orleans Times–Picayune,* reporting the event, described Morgan as "Big Chief Mason," a "full-blooded Indian from the Wolpole Reservation in Canada." Morgan believed that the public and New Orleans officials would be more disposed to believe an Indian had created his safety hood than an African American. His invention gained national attention when the Cleveland Waterworks exploded on July 25, 1916, trapping more than twenty workmen inside with poisonous smoke and gases, and Morgan and his brother donned their masks, entered the tunnel, and retrieved the men. Morgan was celebrated afterward as Cleveland's "most honored and bravest citizen" and his gas mask went into production; but Morgan used white salesmen to promote the mask in the South. Ultimately it was discovered that an African American had invented the mask and it fell into disuse. But Morgan's mask did save the lives of hundreds of American soldiers who wore it in World War I. Its design resembles modern-day suits worn by hazardous chemical fire personnel.

870 • The Stop Sign

Garrett Augustus Morgan was the inventor of a three-way automatic stop sign, a precursor of the present-day traffic light. Before Morgan's invention, traffic signals only had two commands—"Go" and "Stop"—and were generally known as "Go-Stop" signals. Morgan's invention was a tall pole with a bell on top and two flags with "stop" printed on them; the signal controlled traffic by raising and lowering the flags by rotating a hand crank located near the base of the mechanism. Paused in a half-mast position, the flags alerted drivers and pedestrians to prepare to stop. Morgan's traffic light received a U.S. patent on November 20, 1923, and was patented in Great Britain and Canada. So successful was his design that General Electric paid Morgan $40,000 for the rights to his automatic stop sign.

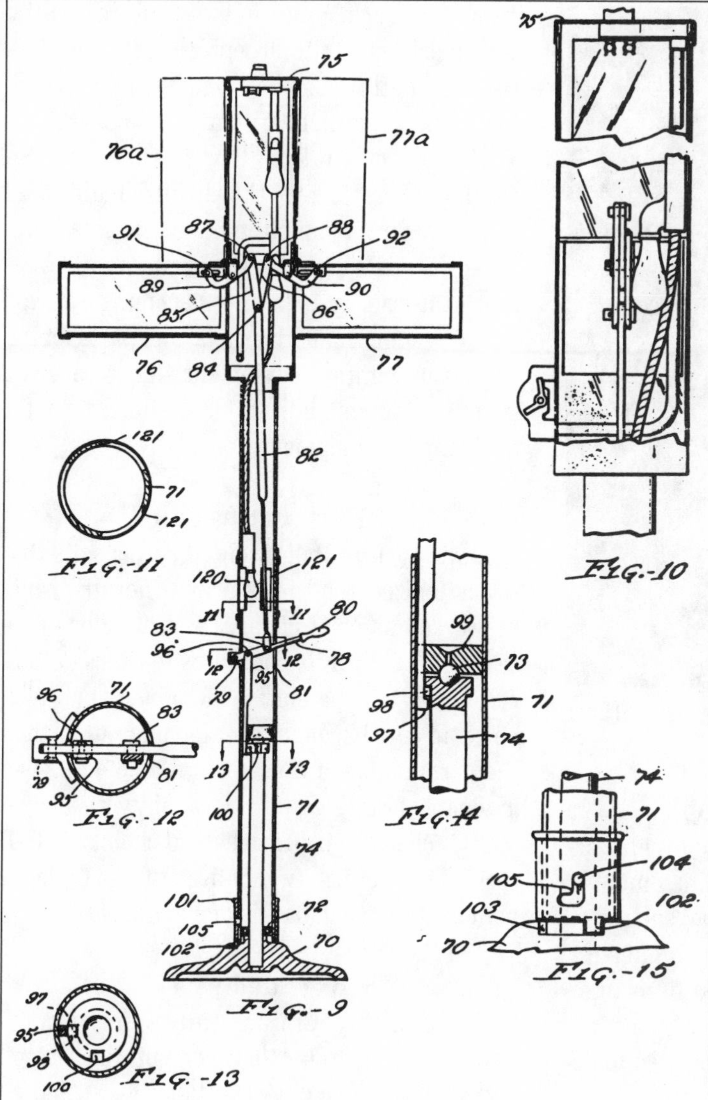

Patent drawing for Morgan's traffic signal. Photograph by Harold Dorwin, courtesy of Anacostia Museum. Used by permission of Western Reserve Historical Society Cleveland, Ohio

871 • Hair Straightening

Sarah Breedlove Walker (1867–1919) discovered a process that would ultimately lift her out of poverty as a washerwoman and make her a millionaire. In 1905, in St. Louis, Missouri, Madam C. J. Walker, as she was later known, perfected a chemical and the use of the hot comb to straighten African American women's hair. She also developed a facial cream for lightening African American skin color. Marrying C. J. Walker and moving to Denver in 1906, she sold her products door-to-door and taught African American women how to use these products in beauty salons. She then established a manufacturing plant and headquarters in Indianapolis, Indiana, and began to distribute her products nationwide. Her marketing techniques were just as innovative as her chemical techniques, and she used demonstrations and advertising, especially in African American newspapers, to outsell her competitors, while her "beauty shop" network created independent jobs for thousands of African American women.

872 • Adding Machine

Shelby J. Davidson (1869–1931) developed his invention, the adding machine, out of his efforts to make work in the U.S. Postal Service more efficient. Davidson began work in a Washington, D.C., post office in 1893 and found the adding of long columns of figures a tedious task. After an intensive study of applied mechanics, Davidson first sketched, then modeled in cardboard, a working version of his invention.

Photograph of James Andrew Jones. Photograph by Harold Dorwin. Courtesy of Jacqueline Jones Grammer

873 • Convertible Top

On January 21, 1919, James A. Jones of Jackson, Tennessee, received a patent, number 1,292,330, for "The Jones" vehicle spring—a mechanism to raise and lower a top for an automobile. Jones, who had worked as a fireman on the railroad, was a skilled mechanic and designed the device at a time when most automobiles lacked tops.

874 • X-Ray Machine and Refrigerator Equipment

The portable X-ray machine, a refrigerator for military field kitchens, and mechanical refrigeration techniques applied to railroad cars and trucks were invented by Frederick McKinley Jones. Before he started experimenting with refrigeration devices in the late 1930s, truck refrigeration units were too big and wasted space inside the truck. Jones reduced the size of the unit and began, with Joseph Numero, the U.S. Thermo Control Company to manufacture these automatic air coolers for trains, ships, and airplanes in order to keep food fresh. Jones also developed ways to keep the air surrounding food at a constant temperature, devices that produced special atmospheric conditions to prevent fruit from drying out or becoming overripe before reaching supermarkets, and parts for existing refrigeration equipment. Jones received over sixty patents during his lifetime, forty for refrigeration equipment.

875 • Curing Salts

Lloyd Augusta Hall invented curing salts that revolutionized the meatpacking industry while he worked as chief chemist and director of research for Griffith Laboratories in Chicago. Hall received a 1951 patent for the process by which he could cure bacon in several hours rather than the normal time of from six to fifteen days. As a graduate of Northwestern University with a bachelor of science in pharmaceutical chemistry, Hall received more than twenty-five other patents for manufacturing and packing food products.

876 • Medtek 410

It took Michael Croslin nearly twenty years to perfect the Medtek 410, a computerized blood pressure measuring device. Before the Medtek 410, most blood pressure devices relied on the sound of blood pumping to determine blood pressure, but extraneous sounds sometimes disturbed the readings. Croslin's device relied on the motion of the blood, provided almost instantaneous readings, and could be easily calibrated digitally. Unlike many other Black inventors, Croslin successfully created a company—Medtek Corporation—in 1978, and he directly distributed and profited from his invention.

Science

877 • George Washington Carver (1865–1943)

George Washington Carver was an agricultural chemist who won international fame for his research into the uses of peanuts and sweet potatoes. Known as the Peanut Man for his discoveries of 300 products that could be made from the peanut, including a milk substitute, face powder, soap, and printer's ink, Carver also developed 118 uses for the sweet potato, including the production of rubber. Carver was hailed as the pioneer in the new applied science of chemurgy, which involved finding industrial uses for agricultural products. Unfortunately for his later reputation, Carver's career emerged when applied science was increasingly viewed as less respected than theoretical science. Carver was viewed as a mere concocter of products instead of a "real" scientist by the American scientific community, and his relationship with Booker T. Washington and the Tuskegee Institute, which he joined in 1896, diminished his standing among early-twentieth-century militant Black leaders. Nevertheless, Carver's numerous innovations in the applications of peanuts, sweet potatoes, and soybeans revolutionized agriculture in the South particularly, as he used his base at Tuskegee to encourage Black farmers to practice agricultural techniques to increase the yield of and add nutrients to their farmland. In 1923 Carver received the NAACP Spingarn Medal.

878 • Bessie Coleman (1893–1926)

The first licensed African American pilot was Bessie Coleman, a pioneer in women's aviation. Although she was prevented from entering flight school in America, she refused to give up on her passion for flying and traveled to France, where she studied the science of aviation and

George Washington Carver in his laboratory. Photograph by Harold Dorwin. Anacostia Museum, Smithsonian Institution, Tuskegee University Library

Bessie Coleman. Courtesy of Arizona Historical Society, Tucson

received the necessary instruction to get her license. Back in the United States, she flew in many flight exhibitions to raise money for her next dream, a flight school for African Americans. Unfortunately, Coleman died in a plane crash before she could make her flight school into a reality.

879 • Ernest E. Just (1883–1941)

Howard University professor of biology Ernest E. Just was the first to establish, through laboratory experiments, the importance of ectoplasm to the functioning of cells. Born in South Carolina and educated in Charleston's public elementary schools, Just and his family believed he would receive a better education in the North. Just took a job aboard a small ship working its way up the East Coast and eventually arrived in New York City. Once there, he worked long hours to save enough money for tuition and expenses at the Kimball Academy in New Hampshire. After completing the four-year academy curriculum in three years, Just entered Dartmouth, where he became the only person in his class to graduate *magna cum laude* in 1907. That fall, Just accepted a position teaching English at Howard University, but encouraged by President Wilbur Thirkield, Just entered graduate work in biology at the marine biological laboratories in Woods Hole, Massachusetts, where, after 1912, he spent twenty-two of his twenty-four summers. In 1915 Just was awarded the first NAACP Spingarn Medal, less for his accomplishments than for his potential for bringing prestige to Blacks at a time when science was the penultimate arena of intellectual distinction. But Just lived up to his potential after he began receiving an $80,000 Julius Rosenwald grant from 1920 to 1925 that enabled him to spend six months out of every year in research. During the twenties, Just published numerous research papers on cell fertilization, coauthored a book, *General Cytology*, published by the University of Chicago Press in 1924, and conducted experiments in parthenogenesis, cell division, and cell mutation. Prior to Just's research, scientists believed a cell's nucleus was the key to the cell's functions and the outer membrane was only of minor importance. But in a series of experiments carried out at Woods Hole Marine Biological Laboratory on Cape Cod, Massachusetts, Just proved that the ectoplasm is just as important as the nucleus to cell function, that ectoplasm regulates the cell's relationship to the external environment, and that without the ectoplasm, cell fertilization is impossible. Perhaps most remarkably, Just established that the nucleus is not the source of hereditary material in a cell. Rather, hereditary factors are located in the cytoplasm and are extracted from the cytoplasm by the genes in the nucleus. Just's research, published in *The Biology of the Cell Surface* (1939), transformed our picture of cells, cell functioning, and human reproduction. Despite numerous discoveries in the field of biology, he was denied appointment to any of the major U.S. laboratories including the Rockefeller Institute for Medical Research, and was never appointed as a full-time faculty member at any historically white American university. Bitter and disheartened, Just, in 1929, accepted an invitation from Max Hartmann to pursue research at the Kaiser Wilhelm Institute for Biology in Germany. After Hitler came to power in 1933, Just continued his research at the Sorbonne in Paris and the Naples Zoological Station in Italy. Despite his tremendous accomplishments, Just felt hampered by the lack of adequate laboratory facilities at Howard University and the institutional racism that constrained his career in the United States. As Frank R. Lillie wrote in an obituary in 1942,

"that a man of his ability, scientific devotion, and of such strong personal loyalties as he gave and received, should have been warped in the land of his birth must remain a matter of regret."

880 • Science Doctorates

Although the first doctorate degree in physics was awarded as early as 1876 to an African American, Edward Bouchet (1825–1918), by Yale University, only thirteen African Americans earned doctorate degrees in the biological and physical sciences before 1930, because continuing segregation in higher education meant that African Americans had to attend Black universities that lacked both the faculties and the facilities to sustain Ph.D. programs in science. But during the thirties and forties the breakdown of segregation in postgraduate education and the increased sophistication of faculties at historically Black universities enabled more than one hundred African Americans to receive doctorates in science. By 1972 over eight hundred African Americans had earned doctorates in the natural sciences. Yet even in 1981 most African American science doctorates were confined to teaching positions in historically Black colleges and universities, which still continue to train most Black scientists in America.

881 • Georgia Caldwell Smith

Even those without doctorate degrees have played a significant role in Black scientific education. Born in 1909 in Atchison, Kansas, Georgia Caldwell Smith graduated Phi Beta Kappa from the University of Kansas in 1928 with a bachelor of science in mathematics and earned a master's degree in math at the same university in 1929. That year she began a long and distinguished career as a teacher at Spelman College, the women's college of Atlanta University, where she taught, with brief teaching appointments at other colleges and universities, for over twenty years.

882 • Atomic Negro

Ralph Gardner was a pioneer chemist whose research into plastics led to the development of so-called hard plastics. His innovations in the manipulation of catalytic chemicals led to products for the petrochemical and pharmaceutical industries as well as plastics. Born in Cleveland, Ohio, on December 3, 1922, Gardner was the son of educated parents who provided him with the chemistry set that led to his career. After receiving a B.S. in chemistry from the University of Illinois in 1943, Gardner joined the University of Chicago Argonne National Laboratories and worked on development of the atomic bomb as part of the so-called Manhattan Project. Two other African Americans who worked on the development of the first atomic bomb were William J. Knox and J. Ernest Wilkins. But even though Gardner worked directly under the famed nuclear scientist Dr. Enrico Fermi on the Manhattan Project, Gardner could not find employment when he left the project in 1947.

883 • Earl Shaw, the Laser Man

Born in Mississippi in 1937, Earl Shaw was part of the Second Great Migration North to Chicago, where he enrolled in Crane Technical High School, went on to get a B.A. from the University of Illinois, a master's in physics from Dartmouth, and a doctorate from the University of California at Berkeley in 1969. After teaching for many years at Howard University in Washington, D.C., Shaw joined the Bell Labs in the 1970s where he developed an accelerator that adjusted the wavelength of an electron laser more easily than others did. Shaw, who retired in 1991, was not only an inventor but a pioneer

in opening up research labs like Bell to Black participation: after he entered in the 1970s, other Black physicists, such as Shirley Jackson, Roosevelt Peoples, Kenneth Evans, and Walter P. Lowe, were also hired by Bell.

884 • Shirley Jackson (b. 1946)

Shirley Jackson was the first African American woman to be awarded a doctoral degree from the Massachusetts Institute of Technology. An expert on the study of particle physics, Jackson was hired as a theoretical physicist by the Bell Laboratories in 1976. She joined the faculty of Rutgers University in 1991 as a professor of physics. Her particular interest in physics has been the study of how electrons in atoms behave under different experimental conditions, which has yielded her insights into the ways that certain substances conduct electricity. Dr. Jackson has been elected to the American Academy of Arts and Sciences and as a fellow of the American Physical Society.

885 • Black Mathematician (b. 1919)

The first African American mathematician to be elected to the National Academy of Sciences was David H. Blackwell. Blackwell pioneered the study of mathematical game theory, wrote a textbook in the field, and in 1979 received the Von Neumann theory prize. He is best known for his work in the theory of games, especially that of "duels"—military games for deciding when sides in a conflict ought to fire on their enemy. His research has been underwritten by the Rand Corporation.

886 • Carruthers's Ultraviolet Camera/Spectrograph

George E. Carruthers, born in 1939, was one of two naval research laboratory workers responsible for the placement of the ultraviolet camera/spectrograph on the lunar surface. Carruthers designed the instrument that went up on *Apollo 16* in April 1972. Instrumentals designer William Conway adapted the device for the mission. The spectrographs, obtained from eleven targets, include the first photograph of the ultraviolet equatorial bands of atomic oxygen that surround the earth. The spectrograph was the first moon-based observatory and was the first man-made instrument to detect the existence of hydrogen deep in space. Carruthers received a NASA Exceptional Scientific Achievement medal for his work.

887 • Ronald McNair (1950–86)

Dr. Ronald McNair was not the first African American astronaut. That honor goes to U.S. Air Force Colonel Guion "Guy" Bluford, who aboard the shuttle *Challenger* became in August 1983 the first African American to leave the earth's atmosphere. With an M.A. and a Ph.D. in aero-

Ronald McNair. National Archives. Photograph courtesy of NASA

space engineering, Bluford had become an astronaut in 1979 and had flown on the shuttle *Challenger* in 1983 and 1986 before McNair's fatal flight on the *Challenger* on January 28, 1986. McNair was one of America's most accomplished scientists. As a laser physicist who advanced the use of lasers in satellite communications, McNair had flown on earlier *Challenger* missions and was the second African American to orbit the earth on a space mission. On a 1984 *Challenger* flight, McNair had activated the Manned Maneuvering Unit, deployed the Canadian Arm used to move crew members around the *Challenger*'s payload, and assisted the flight crew in the first runway landing of the space shuttle at Kennedy Space Center. On the 1986 mission, McNair was to have deployed the Spartan-Halley satellite which utilized lasers to track Halley's comet. A saxophone player, McNair used his free time aboard the shuttle to become the first person to play the instrument in space.

888 • Dr. Mae C. Jemison (b. 1956)

A pioneering African American astronaut, Mae Jemison, a mission specialist, graduated from Stanford University in 1977. After completing the requirements for a doctor of science in chemical engineering, she entered medical school at Cornell University in September 1977 with the intent on becoming a medical engineering researcher. With a grant from the International Traveling Institute for Health Studies, Jemison went to Africa in January 1983 and became a medical area Peace Corps specialist. After the *Challenger* explosion and the death of Ron McNair, she applied for a position as an astronaut. In 1987 she was accepted into the astronaut program and in 1992 flew on the shuttle *Endeavor,* a joint project of Japan and the United States.

Medicine

889 • Inoculation

Africans introduced the practice of inoculation in America as a cure for smallpox. During the smallpox epidemic of 1721, a Boston slave named Onesimus instructed Cotton Mather, the Puritan cleric, about the technique. Mather injected some infected fluid from a smallpox victim into the blood of another person and found that the second person was immune from catching the disease. In order to overcome white opposition to Mather's use of the technique, he authored the pamphlet "An Account of the Medho and Success of Inoculating the Small-Pox," to show its origin and effectiveness:

A gentleman well known in the City of Boston, had a Garamanee *Servant, who first gave him an Account of a Method frequently used in* Africa, *and which had been practis'd on himself, to procure an* easy Small-Pox, *and a perpetual security of neither* dying *by it, nor being again infected with it. . . . in their Country (where they use to die like* Rotten Sheep, *when the* Small-Pox *gets among them) it is now become a* common Thing *to cut a Place or two in their Skin, sometimes one Place, and sometimes another, and put a little of the Matter of the* Small-Pox; *after which, they, in a few Days, grow a* little Sick, *and a few* Small-Pox *break out, and by and by they dry away; and that no Body ever dy'd of doing this, nor ever had the* Small-Pox *after it: Which last Point is confirm'd by their constant Attendance on the Sick in our Families, without receiving the Infection.*

890 • African Pharmacists

Africans also made important contributions to pharmacological knowledge in colonial America. The use of herbs and other plants to

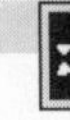

heal afflictions was widespread and sophisticated in Africa and became very popular in the United States. Sometimes slaves received their freedom for curing the ills of their masters.

891 • Caesarean Midwives

African American women enjoyed a widespread reputation in the eighteenth century for being excellent midwives, practitioners of the art and science of assisted childbirth. From Africa, these midwives brought with them the knowledge of caesarean section, which made them highly valued for their treatment of white as well as Black women. Masters often designated certain African American women as midwives who used their knowledge of various herbs and vegetables to speed healing in women after childbirth. Sometimes midwives' duties were extended into feeding and nursing newborn children whose mothers were forced to return rapidly to plantation labor. At the same time, African American midwives also used their skills to abort unwanted pregnancies, especially those of young slave women raped by their masters or overseers. The tradition of Black women as midwives extends into modern times. A few outstanding midwives are Mattie D. Brewer, born in Tennessee in 1882, who delivered more than one thousand children in her career. She delivered her last child when she was eighty-one years old. Another was Marie Jones Francis from Dublin, Georgia, who was an expert in premature childbirth. And then there was Julia M. Shade, who started midwifing in 1925 in Mississippi and who was known to have delivered over four thousand babies. Her career as a midwife led her to formal study and she earned a degree in nursing from Wayne State University in 1952. In 1939, in recognition of the significance of Black midwives, Tuskegee Institute created a school of nurse-midwifery.

892 • James Derham (b. 1762 or '67?)

The first African American widely recognized as a doctor was James Derham. As a teenage slave owned by John Kearsley, Jr., a Philadelphia doctor, Derham mixed and administered medicines for Dr. Kearsley's patients. Kearsley was impressed with Derham's intelligence and provided him with the beginnings of a medical education. Kearsley was a Tory, however, and he was arrested and imprisoned as a traitor during the Revolutionary War. Kearsley eventually went insane and died in captivity. After Kearsley's death, Derham was sold to a British army surgeon fighting in the war, and with his new owner, he helped care for injured soldiers. After the war, Dr. Robert Dove of New Orleans purchased Derham, and again, Derham acted as a doctor's assistant. Soon, Dove freed Derham as a reward for his outstanding work, and Derham opened his own practice, which served both blacks and whites. Derham was regarded as one of the preeminent doctors in New Orleans and eventually made as much as $3,000 per year. He was recognized as an authority on the relationship between disease and climate. Derham's talents were not limited to the medical field—he was also known as a superb linguist who spoke both French and Spanish fluently.

893 • Black Doctors

In the antebellum South, slaves and free African Americans served as doctors to their masters and other members of the white population. In some cases, Blacks were preferred over white doctors because of the herbal knowledge and the higher success rates of Black doctors. Nevertheless, a prejudice against using Black doctors persisted among whites. Even during the Civil War, the War Department was initially reluctant to use African American medical personnel. That unwillingness to admit

African Americans as doctors and nurses may have contributed to the 35 percent greater total casualties that African American troops suffered in the war as compared to white troops. This greater percentage is particularly striking given that African American troops were not used in the war until 1863. The higher death rate also suggests that white physicians and nursing personnel were not adequately treating African American troops. Only eight African American doctors were commissioned in the Army Medical Corps, and seven of these eight were assigned to hospitals in Washington, D.C.

894 • Medical Schools Discriminate

Medical schools in the South and the North discriminated against prospective African American medical students. Martin Delany, for example, applied to the University of Pennsylvania, Jefferson Medical College, and medical schools in Albany and Geneva, New York, before finally gaining acceptance at Harvard University in 1850. In 1860 eight northern medical schools admitted African Americans: Bowdoin, the medical school of the University of New York, Caselton Medical School in Vermont, Berkshire Medical School in Massachusetts, Rush Medical School in Chicago, the Eclectic Medical School of Philadelphia, the Homeopathic College of Cleveland, and Harvard University Medical School.

895 • James McCune Smith Critiques Craniology

Some African Americans opted to travel abroad for their education. Dr. James McCune Smith (1813–65) received his early education in New York City but, rebuffed by American colleges, went to the University of Glasgow and received his B.A., M.A., and M.D. by 1837. Smith returned to New York and opened a successful practice, but he devoted the majority of his time to abolitionist activities. He edited both the *Colored American* and the *North Star.* Smith dedicated himself to refuting popular theories of racial inferiority, especially those espoused by Senator John C. Calhoun and Dr. Samuel Cartwright. Cartwright offered a biological justification for slavery in 1843:

> *. . . the brain being ten percent less in volume and weight, he [the Negro] is, from necessity, more under the influence of his instincts and animality than other races of men and less under the influence of his reflective facilities. . . . His mind thus depressed . . . nothing but arbitrary power, prescribing and enforcing temperance in all things, can restrain the excesses of his mental nature and restore reason to her throne.*

In addition to Cartwright's theory, Calhoun pointed to the census of 1840 as evidence of African American inferiority. The census allegedly showed that the rate of mental illness among free Blacks was eleven times that of Black slaves—indicating an inability to handle the "burden of freedom." Dr. Smith refuted Calhoun by proving that the results of the 1840 census were fraudulent. Smith showed, for example, that several northern towns said to contain mentally incompetent African Americans had no African American residents at all. In a series of lectures entitled "Comparative Anatomy and Physiology of the Races," Smith successfully repudiated Cartwright's biological arguments.

896 • Freedmen's Hospital

In 1868 General O. O. Howard ordered the Freedmen's Hospital to be established at Fifth and W Streets N.W. in Washington, D.C. The hospital was to serve the thousands of African Americans who had flocked to Washington at the conclusion of the Civil War. Dr. Charles Purvis was chosen to head the three-hundred-

bed facility, thereby becoming the first African American to head a civilian hospital. The hospital was vital to improving the health of the African American community. In 1866 some 23,000 of the city's 31,500 African Americans were said to be suffering with some type of illness, and the extraordinary efforts of the hospital and its medical staff helped reduce the number of sick.

897 • Medical Schools Established at Black Universities

In 1868 a medical school was established to serve both white and black students at Howard University. The student body was diverse; in 1871, for example, students came from thirteen states, the District of Columbia, six foreign countries, and the West Indies. The school term lasted almost six months, with classes held from 3:30 to 10:00 P.M. to accommodate those students who worked for the government. Howard was unique because it admitted not only Black and white students but also women. Initially the faculty included several white professors who at the same time held similar positions at the Georgetown University Medical School. Another important medical school was established in Nashville, Tennessee, for the education of African American doctors. Called Meharry Medical College, it differed from Howard in that it educated only African Americans. Between 1877 and 1890, Meharry Medical College awarded medical degrees to 102 students. Many of these students remained in the South following their graduation and provided much-needed services to local African American communities.

898 • William H. Barnes (1887–1945)

In 1887 Dr. William H. Barnes became chief of otolaryngology at Frederick Douglass Hospital in Philadelphia. Born into poverty in Philadelphia, Barnes was awarded a scholarship to the University of Pennsylvania Medical School based on his outstanding score on a competitive exam. Dr. Barnes is most famous for his bloodless operative techniques, and he created several new or improved surgical instruments to make surgeries easier and cleaner. A firm believer in the relationship between health and environment, as well as racial equality, Barnes fought actively for better housing and living conditions for African Americans in Philadelphia.

899 • Daniel Hale Williams (1856–1931)

Dr. Daniel Hale Williams, who founded the Provident Hospital and Training School on May 4, 1891, was the first person to perform a successful open-heart operation. On July 9, 1893, a man stabbed in the chest during a bar brawl was brought to Provident with a wound considered fatal. Without the benefit of X-rays, breathing apparatus, or blood transfusions, Williams

Daniel Hale Williams. Photograph Courtesy of Schomburg Center for Research in Black Culture, New York Public Library, Astor, Lenox and Tilden Foundation

opened a small trapdoor in the patient's chest, assessed the wound, repaired the damage to the left internal mammary artery, and closed a second wound in the quivering pericardium, which covered the heart. The patient was pronounced healthy and discharged fifty-one days later. Williams wanted to see nurses, both white and Black, trained with high standards and with the newest methods of cleanliness. He also wanted to see training for doctors, especially Black surgeons, improved. At the time, even if Black doctors went to good medical schools, they were not allowed to operate in most hospitals, which prevented them from getting practical experiences or finding consistent work on a hospital staff. Provident insisted on high standards, and only doctors from accredited medical schools were allowed to practice there. Similarly, only the most well-educated women were accepted by the nursing school.

900 • Louis T. Wright (1891–1952)

In 1919 Dr. Louis T. Wright became the first Black physician to be appointed to the staff of a New York hospital when he was hired by Dr. Cosmo O'Neal, the superintendent of Harlem Hospital. At the time, Harlem was a wealthy white community. Dr. O'Neal had heard of Wright's successful work in the army with a smallpox vaccination, using an injection method rather than the previously used scratching method. His reputation enabled him to break the barriers to Black doctors in New York hospitals. In 1948 Dr. Wright entered the field of cancer research. He founded the Harlem Hospital Cancer Research Foundation and dealt with the effectiveness of chemotherapeutic agents to attack and destroy cancer cells. He received a grant from the Damon Runyon Fund to engage in cancer research. He wrote fifteen papers on his work on the effects of various drugs and hormones on cancer cells. Perhaps the crowning achievement of his career came in 1949, when Dr. Wright became the first physician in the world to experiment on humans with the drug Aureomycin. He used it for treatment of patients with lymphogranuloma venereum, a venereal disease caused by a virus that can weaken the body to make the patient an invalid for life. Wright found the drug that helped the patients and cured other diseases such as typhus, pneumonia, and intestinal infections. He published thirty papers on his discoveries with Aureomycin. Dr. Wright is also credited with developing the neck brace used to care for a patient with a broken neck without moving the person and causing further damage to the spinal cord. His successful work on skull trauma led editor Charles Scudder to ask him to contribute a section on skull fractures to the eleventh edition of *The Treatment of Fractures,* published in 1938. Wright also invented a blade plate for surgical treatment of fractures above the knee joint.

901 • Solomon C. Fuller (1872–1953)

Dr. Solomon Carter Fuller was known throughout the medical community for his work on physical or organic changes in the body that cause different forms of mental disorders. Carter was born in Liberia in 1872, the son of a coffee planter and a government official. Educated at Livingstone College in North Carolina, he received his M.D. from Boston University in 1897. Following graduation he was appointed to the faculty at Boston University and remained on staff for over thirty years. His research investigated schizophrenia, old-age mental illness, alcoholism disorders, and inherited brain diseases. It was Fuller who suggested in 1911 that Alzheimer's was caused by something other than the conventional explanation of arteriosclerosis, or hardening of the arteries. Fur-

ther testing confirmed his theory. Fuller was also credited as a pioneer in adapting European psychological research and knowledge in the United States. During his forty-five-year career at the Westborough State Hospital for the Insane in Massachusetts, for example, Fuller was one of the first to practice psychotherapy—the treatment of patients through counseling and discussion to help the patient analyze his own behavior and feelings.

902 • William Hinton (1883–1959)

Dr. William Hinton developed the Davies-Hinton test for syphilis detection that dramatically improved the ability of doctors to accurately test patients for the disease. Born in Chicago, Hinton attended Harvard as an undergraduate and as a medical student, graduating with an M.D. in 1912. Because of his race, he could not obtain an internship at a Boston hospital, but he did secure a position at the Wasserman Laboratory, where he was appointed assistant director in 1915. There he became one of the world's foremost authorities on venereal disease and authored, in 1936, *Syphilis and Its Treatment*, the first medical textbook published by an African American. He also taught at Harvard University, becoming in 1949 the first African American professor at the university. But Hinton's real contribution was to revolutionize the detection of syphilis. Hinton's test was faster, more accurate, and more easily replicated. The U.S. Public Health Service concluded in 1934 that his test was the most efficient for early detection of the disease. In 1931, Hinton started a school at the Boston Dispensary to train women and men to become laboratory technicians. The program grew into one of the country's leading schools for medical technician training. The Hinton program—which continues today as part of the medical training program at Northeastern University in Boston—was one of the first to help meet the growing demand for technicians well versed in new laboratory techniques, and graduates of the school were hired by laboratories and hospitals nationwide. This brilliant man was also modest: when offered the NAACP's Spingarn Medal in 1938, he refused it because he felt he had not accomplished enough.

903 • Charles R. Drew (1904–50)

Dr. Charles Richard Drew was the first African American to receive the doctor of science degree in medicine. After earning his bachelor's degree at Amherst College in 1925 and graduating from McGill University Medical School in Canada in 1933, Drew came to Columbia University to do research on blood preservation. At the time, blood transfusion was already an established medical procedure, but much remained to be learned about the best ways to

Portrait of Charles R. Drew by Betsy Graves Reyneau, c. 1953. National Portrait Gallery, Smithsonian Institution. Gift of the Harmon Foundation

preserve and handle donated blood. Whole blood, for example, could be stored for no longer than ten days before the blood cells began to break down. Drew's research demonstrated that plasma, or blood fluid, with the cells and platelets separated out, was much easier to preserve than whole blood. His thesis, "Banked Blood," addressed the evolution of the blood bank, the transformations that occur in preserved blood, and the success of the blood bank established at Presbyterian Hospital (New York City) in August 1939 by Drew and Dr. John Scudder.

904 • "Blood for Britain"

In August 1940 the "Blood for Britain" project, designed to generate blood for transfusions for the growing number of men wounded in World War II, was organized. Much of the blood arriving in England from the United States was contaminated and useless. Dr. Charles Drew was offered the position of medical supervisor to address the problem, and upon his acceptance, he immediately standardized blood drawing and storing procedures at all participating hospitals to avoid contamination. He also increased the volunteer pool for blood donation. At the conclusion of this project, the American Red Cross set up a similar program and appointed Drew as the director in January 1941. Ironically, because the U.S. Army prohibited blood donations from African Americans, Drew could not contribute to his own program.

905 • Percy L. Julian (1899–1975)

Dr. Percy Lavon Julian overcame considerable obstacles to make valuable contributions to both organic chemistry and the treatment of arthritis. Born in 1899, the grandson of a former slave, Julian received an inadequate education at the segregated schools of Alabama. Accepted

Percy L. Julian. Courtesy of National Archives

to DePauw University in 1916, Julian was forced to take remedial and supplemental courses during his first two years to make up for the deficiencies of the Alabama system. A tireless worker (the desire for education ran strong in his family—his grandfather was missing two fingers as punishment for learning to read and write as a slave), Julian soon caught up and graduated as a class valedictorian and a Phi Beta Kappa. Discouraged from entering graduate school because of the lack of postgraduate jobs available for African Americans with advanced degrees, Julian accepted a teaching position at Fisk University and remained there until he won the Austin Fellowship in Chemistry position at Harvard University. Again he graduated at the top of his class, and again he was discouraged from further study. After a two-year faculty position at Howard University, Julian

traveled to Vienna, where he earned a Ph.D. in organic chemistry. Julian returned to the United States and accepted a position at DePauw, where he conducted research until he was offered the position of chief chemist and director of research at the Glidden Company. Dr. Julian developed inexpensive copies of many costly drugs, making them accessible to the general population. In 1935 he developed an exact copy of the rare and expensive drug used to treat glaucoma. His writings about the discovery were the first papers with a Black individual as the senior author to appear in respected American chemistry journals. Julian also produced synthetic cortisone, which cost several hundred dollars less per gram to produce than the cortisone, significantly reducing the cost of treating arthritis and other muscle and bone disorders.

906 • Julian's Struggles

I shall never forget a week of anxious waiting in 1920 to see if I could get to graduate school. I had worked hard for four years. I stood by as day by day my fellow students in Chemistry came by saying, "I am going to Illinois"; "I am going to Ohio State"; "I am going to Michigan"; "I am going to Yale." "Where are you going?" they asked, and they answered for me, "You must be getting the Harvard plum." I could stand the suspense no longer. I went to Professor Blanchard, as staunch a friend as he knew how to be then, and certainly later my most unforgettable friend, and asked timidly, "Professor, did you get me a fellowship?" And then this dear fellow with resignation told me "Now, now, Julian, I knew you would be asking me that. Come in to my office." There he showed me numerous letters from men who had really meant "God" to me—great American chemists of their day. And they had written to him, "I'll take your Mr. ———, but I'd advise you to discourage your bright colored lad. We couldn't get him a job when he's done, and it'll only mean frustration. In industry, research demands co-work, and white boys would so sabotage his work that an industrial research leader would go crazy! And, of course, we couldn't find him a job as a teacher in a white university. Why don't you find him a teaching job in a Negro college in the South? He doesn't need a Ph.D. for that!" There went my dreams and hopes of four years, and as I pressed my lips to hold back the tears, I remembered my breeding, braced myself, and thanked him for thinking of me.

907 • *Chicago Sun-Times* on Fire Bombing of Julian's Home

As the first black family to move into an all-white community in Oak Park, a suburb of Chicago, Dr. Percy L. Julian and his family were often the targets of racial violence. The following is an editorial that appeared in the *Chicago Sun-Times,* November 23, 1950, after an arson attempt on the Julian home on Thanksgiving Day:

Arsonists tried to burn down the newly purchased home of Dr. Percy Julian to keep him out of Oak Park because he is a Negro. We wonder whether these cowards whose mad prejudice drove them to commit a felony would refuse to use the lifesaving discoveries of Dr. Julian because they came from the hand and brain of a Negro. Would they refuse to take synthetic cortisone if they were wracked with the pain of arthritis? Would they forbid their wives the use of synthetic female hormone now abundantly available because of Dr. Julian's work? Would they refuse to use his synthetic physostigmine if they were afflicted with the dread eye disease, glaucoma? If they themselves were caught in a raging gasoline fire such as they tried to set, would they order the fireman not to use Dr. Julian's great discovery, chemical foam? This stuff

saved the lives of thousands of American airmen and sailors after crash landings during the war. No! The bigots welcome the discoveries of Dr. Julian the scientist, but they try to exclude Dr. Julian the human being.

908 • Samuel L. Kountz

Dr. Samuel L. Kountz, noted for his research in immunology, founded the largest kidney transplant research center and participated in the first West Coast kidney transplant in 1959. He worked on methods to combat organ transplant rejection and performed five hundred kidney transplants during his career. In 1964 Dr. Kountz made history by transplanting a kidney from mother to daughter. This was the first transplant between two humans who were not identical twins.

909 • Rebecca Lee

Rebecca Lee was the first African American woman to receive a medical degree. She received her doctorate of medicine degree from the New England Female Medical College in 1864. She conducted a successful practice in Richmond, Virginia, for several years before relocating back to Boston. In 1883 Lee published *A Book of Medical Discourses* that counseled women on how to care for themselves and their children.

910 • Jane Cooke Wright (b. 1919)

Dr. Jane Cooke Wright was appointed associate dean of the New York Medical College in July 1966, attaining the highest post ever granted to an African American woman. She is credited as the first doctor to see remissions in skin cancer mycosis fungoides patients and in solid breast cancer tumor patients. Dr. Wright is an accomplished author, with writings appearing in professional journals and medical textbooks. Wright originally worked with her father, Dr. Louis Wright, at the Cancer Research Foundation testing new alkylating agents for treatment on cancer patients.

Dr. Jane C. Wright, cancer researcher, professor of surgery, and associate dean of the New York Medical College. New York Medical College

911 • Levi Watkins, Jr.

Dr. Levi Watkins, Jr., performed the first surgical implantation of the automatic implantable defibrillator in the human heart in 1980. The device corrects arrhythmia, which prevents the heart from pumping blood.

912 • Ben Carson (b. 1951)

A graduate of Yale University and the University of Michigan Medical School, Ben Carson gained worldwide recognition for his part in the first successful separation of Siamese twins joined at the back of the head, an extremely complex and delicate operation that was planned for five months and took twenty-two hours of actual surgery.

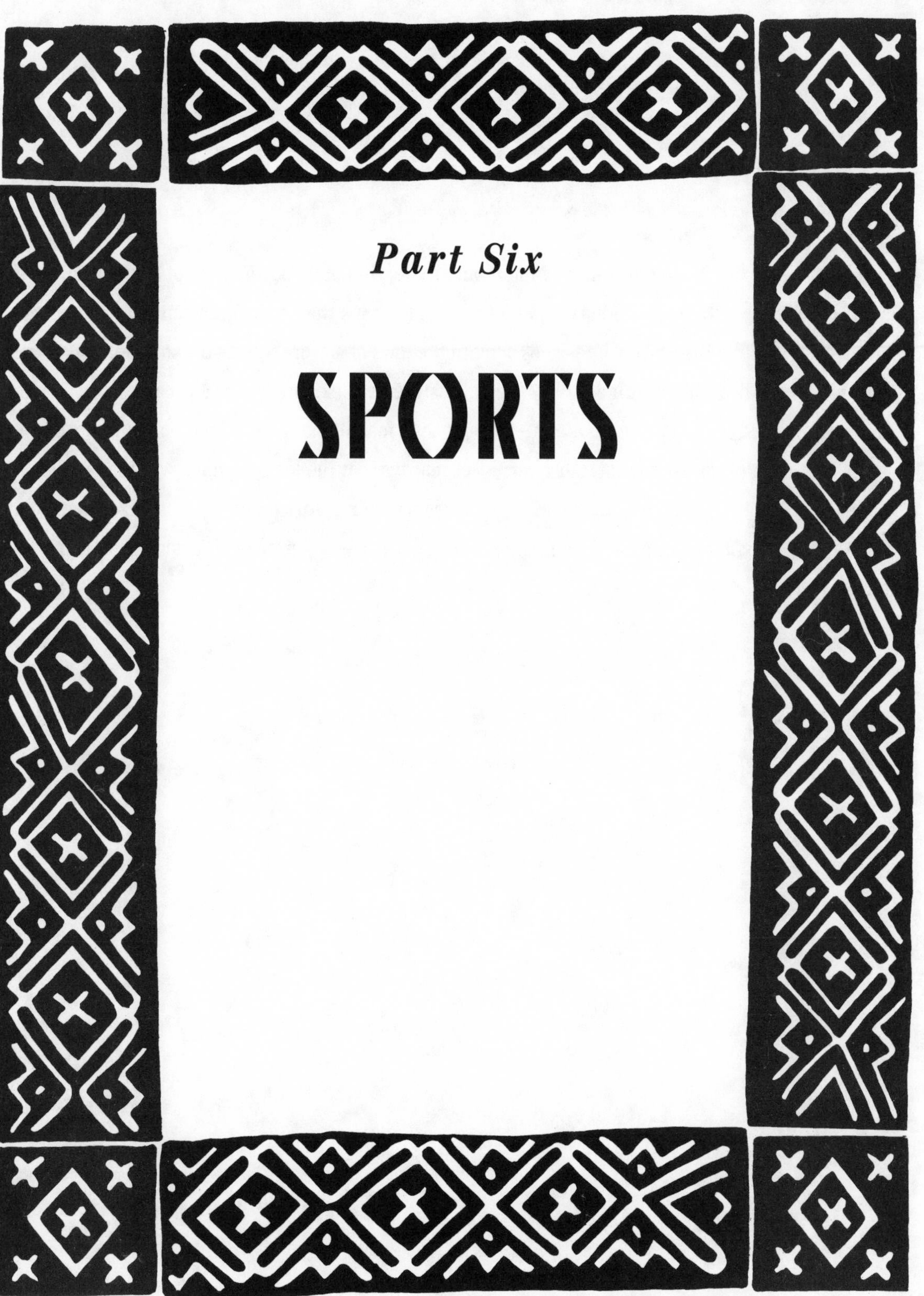

Part Six

SPORTS

Sport in America is not only entertainment and recreation but also an arena of competition that is highly charged with racial stereotypes and feelings. Perhaps the first conflicts over Black participation in sports activities with whites goes back to the days of slavery when African Americans were thought of as bodies without minds. This ideology justified the exploitation of African Americans for the cultivation of tobacco, rice, and cotton; but it also meant that Black Americans would be respected for their physical prowess. For a variety of reasons, not the least of which was that sports offered upward mobility (and in some cases freedom from slavery), African Americans seized on sports as a way to prove first equality and then, in selected sports, the superiority of African American athletes.

913 • Mixed Participation Banned

By the early 1800s the inferiority of slaves in "both body and mind" was accepted as fact. States began to vigorously discourage social interaction between slaves and whites. In 1830, for example, North Carolina enacted legislation making it unlawful "for any white person or free Negro or mulatto, or persons of mixed blood to play at any game of cards, dice, nine-pins, or any game of chance or hazard whether for money, liquor, or property or not, with any slave or slaves."

914 • Slave Participation in Sports

Despite their banishment from organized sports, enslaved African Americans still found opportunities to participate in sports activities. One ex-slave recalled, "Us tho'ed horse shoes, jumped poles, walked on stilts, an' played marbles." Another explained, "Shinny [baseball] was de thing dat I like best." Slave owners considered sports activities disruptive to the daily routine, but they did allow sports and games during holidays. Frederick Douglass believed "those holidays were among the most effective means in the hands of the slaveholders in keeping down the spirit of insurrection." He noted that "everything of rational enjoyment was frowned upon, and only those wild and low sports peculiar to semi-civilized people were encouraged." These wild sports included cockfighting, boxing, and gambling.

915 • Black Colleges and Sports

Black colleges in the post–Civil War period lacked well-developed athletic facilities. Fearing the displeasure of their white patrons, Black college officials were often reluctant to allocate funds to athletic programs. Often, there were no funds to distribute to the athletic department anyway. In 1890, for example, a congressional act appropriated funds to establish land-grant colleges for African Americans (now the Big Ten schools) and earmarked some of the money for recreational facilities. However, the money had to be channeled through the state legislatures, and for more than seventy years, most of these funds were given instead to white land-grant schools.

Boxing

916 • First Black to Contend for a World Title in Any Sport

On October 8, 1805, William Richmond became the first African American to contend for a world title in any sport. Richmond, a free Black born in 1763 on Staten Island, grew up fighting soldiers on the docks of New York Harbor during the British occupation. Richmond's fighting prowess was noticed by the British commander, Hugh Percy, and he brought Richmond with him when he returned to England. Once in England, Richmond accumulated enough semiprofessional wins to challenge then-champion Tom Cribb to a bout. On October 8, 1805, Richmond and Cribb boxed for more than ninety minutes before Cribb was declared the winner. Despite his loss, Richmond continued to box professionally until he was fifty-two. He also gave boxing lessons in London and was responsible for training Tom Molineaux, the next African American to challenge Cribb for the championship.

917 • Tom Molineaux (1784–1818)

Slavery directly influenced the boxing career of Tom Molineaux. Molineaux, born into slavery on March 23, 1784, won thousands of dollars for his owner in matches against other slaves. Slave owners frequently pitted their slaves against

Tom Molineaux, hand-colored etching by Robert D. Dighton, 1812. National Portrait Gallery, Smithsonian Institution

one another, placing huge wagers on the outcome, and Molineaux and his brothers often won double their market worth for their owner. In 1809, in recognition of his service, Molineaux's master agreed to set him free if he won a final bout. After his victory, Molineaux, with $500 in his pocket, sailed first to New York and then to London, where he met William Richmond.

Once in London, Molineaux trained diligently. After winning six bouts against lesser known opponents, William Richmond placed an ad in the *London Times* for Molineaux, challenging Tom Cribb to "unretire" and "meet the Moor." On December 10, 1810, Cribb and Molineaux met in Copthall Hall in Sussex, England. Although Cribb officially won the fight after forty-four exhausting rounds and collected a $2,000 purse, Molineaux clearly deserved the victory. In the twenty-eighth round, Molineaux had knocked Cribb down and Cribb did not rise within the required thirty seconds. Cribb's trainer leaped into the ring to accuse Molineaux of hiding weights in his gloves, and referee Ap Phys Price, defending the honor of white Britain, waived the rules and gave Cribb two more minutes to revive himself. A disappointed Molineaux finally succumbed fifteen rounds later.

918 • First Black to Hold an American Title

On March 31, 1891, George "Little Chocolate" Dixon became the first Black man to hold an American title in any sport. Dixon, born in Halifax, Nova Scotia, in 1870, became interested in boxing after he moved to Boston with his parents and began an apprenticeship with a photographer specializing in boxing photography. After training in a local gym, the 5′3″ 100-pound bantamweight turned professional at age sixteen. In 1888 Dixon fought seventy rounds to a draw against Cal McCarthy for the bantamweight title. In a rematch three years later, on March 31, 1891, he captured the title with a knockout in the twenty-second round. Dixon became the first Black boxer to win an international title on June 27, 1890, when he knocked out British featherweight champion Nunc Wallace for the international bantamweight title. Then, on June 27, 1892, he won the featherweight world title and $4,500 by knocking out Fred Johnson. Buoyed by his victories, Dixon decided to try his luck in the South. On September 6, 1892, Dixon fought the white amateur boxer Jack Skelly at the private New Orleans Olympia Club. At the time, New Orleans was racially very divided and it was assumed that any experienced white boxer in good condition could beat any Black fighter. Through eight rounds on September 6, 1892, Dixon beat Shelly badly. The white community was horrified and discouraged southern white boxers from fighting in future interracial bouts.

919 • White Boxers Refuse to Fight African Americans

It was difficult for African American boxers to challenge for titles against white boxers. John L. Sullivan, one of the country's first national sports heroes and the world heavyweight champion in 1889, for example, refused to fight against Black boxers: "I will not fight a negro. I never have, and I never shall."

John Sullivan's refusal to fight Black boxers was supported by many in the white sports community. Charles Dana, an influential sports editor writing for the *New York Sun,* decried the rise of African Americans in boxing and warned that unless others followed Sullivan's example, Blacks would soon dominate the sport:

We are in the midst of a growing menace. The Black man is rapidly forging to the front ranks in athletics, especially in the field of fisticuffs. We are in the midst of a Black rise against white supremacy. . . . There are two negroes in the ring today who can thrash any white man breathing in their respective classes [George Dixon and Joe Walcott]. . . . What America needs now is another John L. Sullivan. . . . Wake up, you pugilists of the white race! Are you going to permit yourself to be passed by the Black race?"

920 • First Black Man to Beat a White World Heavyweight Champ

John Arthur "Jack" Johnson, born in Galveston, Texas, in 1878, sought adventure from an early age. Leaving home after finishing fifth grade, Johnson worked on a milk wagon, as a baker's apprentice, and as a cook's helper on a steamship. While working for an ex-boxer in a Dallas carriage shop, Johnson entered his first match and took home twenty-five dollars even though he lost. For the next several years, Johnson traveled the country entering matches, participating in battles royal and serving as a sparring partner for better fighters. On February 3, 1903, Johnson took the Negro heavyweight crown from "Denver" Ed Martin. Not

Jack Johnson. Photograph by Otto Sarony, 1909. Prints and Photographs Division, Library of Congress

content to fight within the ranks of African American boxers, Johnson tried to arrange bouts with the 1903 white heavyweight champion, Jim Jeffries, and Canadian Tommy Burns. Burns drew the color line and refused a match, but Johnson followed him to England, France, and Australia, publicly demanding that he fight. Finally Burns agreed, and on December 26, 1908, Johnson and Burns fought for a $40,000 purse—$35,000 for Burns and $5,000 for Johnson. Johnson clearly dominated the fight, staggering Burns with rights to the head and combinations, and in the fourteenth round, with Burns bleeding from the mouth and his eyes swollen almost completely shut, the fight was stopped and Johnson declared the winner.

921 • Johnson vs. Jeffries

Following Jack Johnson's victory over Tommy Burns in 1908, public pressure mounted for Jim Jeffries to come out of retirement and reclaim the crown and white honor. Author Jack London wrote, "... one thing now remains. Jim Jeffries must emerge from his alfalfa farm and remove the golden smile from Jack Johnson's face. Jeff, it's up to you!" Jeffries reluctantly agreed, and the fight was set for July 4, 1910, in San Francisco. The fight sparked enormous interest, and six promoters vied for the right to handle the contest. The negotiations with the potential promoters signified the largest legitimate business deal ever conducted by an African American up to that time. Ultimately the $101,000 purse was issued in four installments: $20,000 immediately after signing the contract; $20,000 sixty days after signing; $50,000 forty-eight hours before the bout; and the rest following the fight. The money was split sixty-forty, with the larger percentage allocated to Jeffries.

Jeffries, a 5 to 3 favorite despite his more than five-year absence from the ring, was billed as the Great White Hope. Throughout the match, Johnson easily outboxed Jeffries and verbally taunted him with remarks about his ability. Early in the fifteenth round, Jeffries was knocked to the ground twice. After a third knockdown several seconds later, he was counted out and Jack Johnson awarded the world heavyweight title. Jeffries was gracious in his loss: "I guess it's my own fault.... They started calling for me and mentioning me as 'the white man's hope.' I guess my pride got the better of my judgment." He later acknowledged, "I never could have whipped Johnson at my best. I couldn't have hit him." The Johnson-Jeffries bout was one of the most racially charged fights in history.

922 • Fallout from Johnson vs. Jeffries

The 1910 defeat of Jim Jeffries by an African American infuriated whites. Nationwide, thirteen African Americans were murdered and hundreds injured in postfight racial incidents. The July 5 edition of the *New York Times* contained numerous stories describing the violence, including "Three Killed in Vidalia [Georgia] ... Omaha Negro Killed ... Two Negroes Slain ... Blacks Shoot up Town ... Houston Man Kills Negro ... Negro Shoots White Man ... Negro Hurt in Philadelphia ... Outbreaks in New Orleans ... Police Club Rioting Negroes ... Mob Beats Negroes in Macon ... 70 Arrested in Baltimore."

923 • The Brown Bomber (1914–81)

It took twenty years after Jack Johnson's victory over Jim Jeffries before another African American was allowed a shot at the heavyweight title. When he was seventeen, Joe Louis, born Joe Louis Barrow, was given fifty cents by his mother to pay for his violin lessons. Instead, Louis used the money to rent a locker at the

Joe Louis. Photograph by Carl Van Vechten. Prints and Photographs Division, Library of Congress. Gift of Carl Van Vechten

Brewster East Side Gymnasium in Detroit, where he began to train as a boxer. After fighting fifty-four matches as an amateur, Louis turned professional on July 4, 1934. Aided by John Roxborough, a local Black businessman, and Jack Blackburn, an ex-boxer, Louis prepared to break into the heavyweight division. Anxious to elude the fate of Jack Johnson, Louis made every effort to avoid activities that would encourage racial discord. He was given lessons in manners and diction, advised to always seek a knockout rather than depend on the judges' decisions, and was repeatedly admonished, "For God's sake, after you beat a white opponent, don't smile." By May 5, 1935, Louis's heavyweight professional record was 22–0. No match had lasted more than ten rounds.

Louis's popularity within the Black community skyrocketed after his defeat of Primo Carnera on June 25, 1935. Making his New York debut, Louis knocked the 6′7″ 275-pound Italian out in the sixth round. Louis described his bewilderment at the attention he received:

When I walked in the church, you'd have thought I was the second coming of Christ.... Rev. J. H. Maston ... talked about how God gave certain people gifts ... and through my fighting I was to uplift the spirit of my race. I must make the whole world know that Negro people were strong, fair, and decent.... He said I was one of the chosen. I thought to myself, "Jesus Christ, am I all that?"

924 • Louis vs. Schmeling

The fights that brought Joe Louis his greatest fame came against the German fighter Max

Schmeling. On June 19, 1936, Louis was knocked out in the twelfth round by Schmeling, and Nazi Germany celebrated Louis's defeat. A German magazine, *Der Weltkampf,* printed an article that said "France, England, and white North America—cannot thank Schmeling enough for his victory, for he checked the arrogance of the Negro and clearly demonstrated to them the superiority of white intelligence." This time, however, white Americans were more hesitant to support a boxer solely because of his race. Schmeling was a German, and as news of Nazi atrocities began to cross the Atlantic, the defeat of fascism and a victory for America became more important than racial solidarity. On June 22, 1938, Louis knocked Schmeling out just two minutes and four seconds into the first round. In contrast to the violence that followed Gans's and Johnson's victories over white men, this time the entire country celebrated Louis's feat. Louis would hold the heavyweight title for eleven years, eight months, and seven days.

925 • Sugar Ray Robinson (1920–89)

Born Walker Smith, Jr., Sugar Ray Robinson recorded eighty-nine amateur fights with sixty-nine knockouts, forty-four coming in the first round. Winner of the 1939 featherweight and the 1940 lightweight Golden Gloves titles, Robinson turned professional in 1940 and won his October 4 debut at Madison Square Garden with a second-round knockout of Joe Echeverria. He went on to win thirty-nine consecutive fights, twenty-eight by knockout. Finally, on February 5, 1943, in their second meeting, Jake LaMotta beat Robinson in ten rounds for his first loss. Rebounding, Robinson won ninety-six straight matches over the next eight years.

At age thirty, on February 14, 1951, Sugar Ray Robinson won his first world middleweight crown from Jake LaMotta in a thirteenth-round technical knockout. He lost the crown to Randy Turpin in England on July 10, 1951, in a fifteen-round bout. In the rematch at the Polo Grounds on September 12, 1951, Robinson regained the title with a tenth-round technical knockout. After retiring to a two-and-a-half-year show business career, Robinson returned to the ring at age thirty-four and won the middleweight crown for the third time from Carl "Bobo" Olson in a second-round knockout. On May 1, 1957, he became the first man to win a world title four times when he scored a fifth-round knockout over Gene Fullmer. Fullmer later beat Robinson in a fifteen-round bout, but Robinson won his fifth middleweight crown on March 25, 1958, against Carmen Basilio. Robinson finally retired in 1965 and was elected to the Boxing Hall of Fame in 1967.

926 • First Heavyweight Champion to Regain Title

Floyd Patterson learned to box at the Wiltwyck School for troubled youngsters in New York City. As an amateur, he developed a peekaboo style of defense and won the 1952 Golden Gloves middleweight title, a gold medal in the 1952 Olympics as a middleweight, and the National AAU middleweight title in 1952. Patterson won the heavyweight title from Archie Moore in a fifth-round knockout in 1955. He lost the title to Swede Ingemar Johansson on June 26, 1959, at Yankee Stadium. Johansson knocked Patterson down seven times during the match on his way to a technical knockout in the third round. Patterson became the first heavyweight to regain the title in June 1960 in a fifth-round knockout over Johansson at the Polo Grounds. He defeated Johansson a second time at Miami Beach on March 13, 1961, on a sixth-round knockout.

927 • Sonny Liston (1932–70)

Charles Liston learned to box in the Missouri State Penitentiary when he was incarcerated for robbing a service station. After his release, Liston won the 1952 Golden Gloves heavyweight title. In 1956 his boxing license was revoked when he was arrested for assaulting a policeman and sentenced to nine months in a workhouse. Liston's prison record and alleged ties to organized crime made it difficult for him to secure matches, but he finally obtained a shot at the heavyweight title in February 1962 after he hired Jack Nilon as a manager. After his second defeat of Floyd Patterson, Liston fought Cassius Clay on February 25, 1964. Liston, a 7 to 1 favorite, alleged Clay "couldn't lick a Popsicle." At the beginning of the seventh round, however, Liston threw in the towel, claiming he was unable to move his left arm. Many speculated Liston threw the fight to pay off a debt to an organized crime figure. A second fight was held on May 25, 1965, with Liston being knocked out two minutes and twelve seconds into round one.

928 • Muhammad Ali Wins Heavyweight Title Four Times (b. 1942)

One day after winning the world heavyweight title by defeating Sonny Liston, Cassius Clay, who had been befriended by Malcolm X, announced his conversion to the Muslim faith and changed his name to Muhammad Ali, which means "worthy of all praise." As part of his new religious faith, Ali refused to submit to the Vietnam War draft because of his opposition to war. He spent twenty-nine months in jail, was stripped of his championship title, and lost his license to fight professionally. He was finally declared free on June 28, 1970, by the United States Supreme Court, and his license was restored. He began training once again and used victories over Jerry Quarry and Oscar Bonavena to prepare for his fight with the new WBA heavyweight title holder, Joe Frazier.

On March 28, 1971, 20,000 fans at Madison Square Garden and 1.3 million fans before closed-circuit televisions watched Muhammad Ali fight Joe Frazier for the WBA heavyweight title. Frazier won the fifteen-round bout but did not fight for ten months following the match. Both boxers were taken to the hospital following the fight. In their second meeting for the NABF title on January 28, 1974, at Madison Square Garden, 20,746 live fans and 1.1 million closed-circuit television viewers witnessed a

Muhammad Ali battling Joe Frazier in their first championship fight, March 18, 1971. Associated Press. Courtesy of Wide World Photos, Inc. National Archives

twelve-round Ali victory. The gross receipts for the second fight totaled $25 million.

Muhammad Ali became the second man in history to regain the world heavyweight title on October 30, 1974. An eighth-round knockout over George Foreman was witnessed by 62,000 fans in Kinshasa, Zaire. Ali used what he described as his "rope-a-dope" strategy to defeat Foreman. By leaning back against the ropes, protecting his head, and allowing Foreman to throw numerous punches, Ali correctly guessed Foreman would tire himself out.

Ali's third and final meeting with Joe Frazier came on September 30, 1975, in Manila, the Philippines. Also called Super Fight II, the match was hailed as the greatest fight in the history of the sport. After fourteen difficult rounds, Frazier's trainer, Eddie Futch, refused to let him come out for round fifteen, cutting his gloves off him and telling him, "Sit down, son. It's all over. No one will ever forget what you did here today."

Muhammad Ali lost the world title on February 15, 1978, at age thirty-six to Leon Spinks in a fifteen-round split decision in Las Vegas. Ali became the first man to win the world heavyweight title three times with a fifteen-round unanimous decision over Spinks in the New Orleans Superdome. He retired and then returned at age thirty-nine to lose in eleven rounds to WBC heavyweight champion Larry Holmes on October 2, 1980. Muhammad Ali was elected to the Boxing Hall of Fame in 1987.

929 • One of the Most Financially Successful Boxers

"Sugar" Ray Charles Leonard won the 1973 National Golden Gloves lightweight title, the 1974 National Golden Gloves light-welterweight title, the 1974 and 1975 United States AAU light-welterweight titles, and the light-welterweight gold medal in the 1975 Pan-American Games and the 1976 Olympics. In his first professional fight, Leonard won $38,000. He won the NABF welterweight title from Pete Banzany on August 12, 1979, in Las Vegas. On November 30, 1979, Leonard won the WBD welterweight title in a fifteenth-round knockout over Wilfredo Benitez. Leonard had earned more than $3 million in his first three years as a professional boxer. He lost his title in a close decision to Roberto Duran on June 20, 1980. In the rematch on November 25, Leonard regained the title. These two bouts grossed Leonard over $16 million, more than the combined career winnings of Joe Louis, Sugar Ray Robinson, Floyd Patterson, and Archie Moore. Leonard elevated to the junior middleweight class and captured the world title from Ayub Kalule in Houston on June 25, 1981, in a ninth-round knockout. After a victory over Thomas Hearns on September 16, 1981, Leonard underwent surgery for a detached retina and retired in 1984.

930 • The "Hit Man" (b. 1958)

Thomas Hearns won the United States National AAU light-welterweight championship and the National Golden Gloves welterweight championship in 1977. His first seventeen professional bouts were won by knockout and he won thirty out of thirty-two fights. Hearns won the WBA title from Pipino Cuevas on August 2, 1980, in a second-round knockout. He lost the bid to unify the WBA and WBC world titles in a fourteenth-round loss to Ray Leonard on September 16, 1981. Hearns did unify the world titles in the junior middleweight class by capturing the WBC title over Wilfredo Benitez on December 3, 1982, and the WBA title over Roberto Duran on June 15, 1984.

931 • Mike Tyson (b. 1966)

Mike Tyson entered the fighting world of the heavyweights as the enfant terrible, and he has lived up to his billing. Nurtured from the age of thirteen by his father surrogate, Cus D'Amato, Tyson developed early into a very aggressive fighter: in his first sixteen fights, he knocked out twelve of the boxers before the first round was over. With the same ferociousness, he won the heavyweight championship in 1985 and consolidated the heavyweight crown by beating Tony Tucker in 1987. He reached the zenith of his career when he devastated Michael Spinks in less than one round. But things began to go downhill for Tyson shortly thereafter. After he wed actress Robin Givens in 1988, the highly publicized marriage came to an end a year later. Then, uncharacteristically, Tyson seemed listless and unfocused when he was knocked out by the unspectacular Buster Douglas on February 16, 1990. Then, in February 1992, he was convicted of raping an eighteen-year-old contestant in the 1991 Miss Black America pageant in Indianapolis, and was sent to jail in April. Released in April 1995, he plans a return to boxing as a heavyweight.

George Foreman waves American flag after winning the Olympic heavyweight boxing gold medal, October 26, 1968, in Mexico City. United Press International. Courtesy of Bettmann Archives. National Archives

932 • George Foreman (b. 1948)

George Foreman won the heavyweight Olympic gold medal in the 1968 Olympics. With a second-round knockout of Joe Frazier in January 1973, he became only the second man in history to win both an Olympic gold medal and a world title in the heavyweight division. He defended his title against Jose Roman and Ken Norton in two bouts which together totaled only three rounds. These victories made Foreman eligible for his "Rumble in the Jungle" with Ali, the first-ever heavyweight title match to take place in Africa. After his loss to Ali in that fight, Foreman retired from boxing and became a minister before returning to boxing in 1987. He became the oldest fighter to regain a boxing title when, at age forty-five, he defeated Michael Moorer in November 1994 and took Moorer's International Boxing Federation heavyweight championship belt.

Baseball

933 • The Integrated National Association of Baseball Players

The first national organization of baseball clubs included Blacks. When the National Association of Baseball Players (NABBP) was formed in 1858, it did not exclude Blacks who were members of clubs in the association. However, in 1867, just when African Americans were winning the right to vote, the NABBP banned all Blacks from participation. The guidelines barred both African Americans and any clubs that had African Americans as members, thus creating an incentive for local clubs to refuse to allow Blacks on their teams. The pressure to eliminate Blacks came from Irish and German clubs that did not want to compete with Black players. In 1871 that organization was replaced by the National Association of Professional Baseball Players (NABP), which continued the ban through an unwritten "gentleman's agreement" among club owners. But because professional baseball was relatively unorganized, Black players continued to play for the numerous local all-Black teams that flourished in the post–Civil War period. Often these teams were comprised of members of the Black upper class who had the time and leisure to travel playing baseball. Bud Fowler, a player from one of these Black teams, the Washington Mutuals, became the first African American to play professional baseball full-time. He joined a local white team from New Castle, Pennsylvania, in 1872, before Reconstruction ended and the national organizations consolidated their control over baseball.

934 • First Black Player in Organized Baseball

Rivalry between national organizations helped create an opportunity for Moses Fleetwood Walker to become the first African American to play what is known as organized baseball. When the National League of Professional Baseball Clubs (NLPBBC) arose in 1876 to replace the NABP, the NLPBBC continued the earlier clubs' ban on Blacks. But in 1880 rebels against what became the National League formed their own competing American Association. Moses Walker was the Toledo Mudhens' full-time catcher when the team joined the Northwestern League of the American Association of Baseball Clubs in 1884. Walker had been the first African American to play on a white college varsity team, catching in 1878 for Oberlin College in Ohio and later at the University of Michigan Law School. Racism still blunted his baseball career, however. He had a nasty run-in with Adrian Cap Anson, the star of the Cincinnati Red Stockings and a known racist. Walker was also jeered by fans when the team played in Louisville and threatened with bodily harm when the team planned to play in Richmond, Virginia. Despite such harassment, Walker compiled an excellent record in 1884: he batted .251 over forty-six games, including four doubles and two triples, and was a superb fielding catcher.

935 • Blacks Forced out of Professional Baseball

African American players were becoming popular in the league again in 1887 when Cap Anson, the manager of the Chicago White Stockings, refused to field his team against Newark until Moses Walker and George Stovey left the field. Anson's personal boycott galvanized the opposition of several white players who refused to play against Black players. The same year, players on the St. Louis Browns, a white team, sent a letter of protest to the team president on the eve of a scheduled game before fifteen thou-

sand against the Cuban Giants that read: "We, the undersigned members of the St. Louis baseball club, do not agree to play against negroes tomorrow. We will cheerfully play against white people at anytime, and think by refusing to play we are only doing what is right, taking everything into consideration." The protest worked, the game was called off, and the St. Louis Browns played against and lost to the Detroit Tigers instead. It was then understood throughout the league that no Black players would be signed in the future.

Most Black baseball players were paid much less than white players. This pay disparity was one of the reasons white players increasingly objected to playing with Blacks. White players feared large numbers of Black players on a team might lower the salaries for all.

936 • The Negro National League

At the urging of Rube Foster, a select group of Black baseball club owners met at the Colored YMCA in Kansas City on February 13–14, 1920, to form the Negro National League. The owners present were Rube Foster of the Chicago American Giants; C. I. Taylor of the Indianapolis ABCs; Joe Green of the Chicago Giants; J. L. Wilkerson, a white owner of the Kansas City Monarchs; Lorenzo S. Cobb of the St. Louis Giants; and J. T. Blount of the Detroit Stars. The NNL was the first long-term Black league in any professional sport. In the league's debut game on May 2, 1920, the Indianapolis ABCs defeated the Chicago Giants 4–2 in front of eight thousand fans at home. The NNL disbanded in 1931 due to bickering among owners, weak financial backing, few stars for the Black press to write about, and the death of Rube Foster on December 9, 1930. The NNL finally received serious competition in 1937 when the Negro American League was formed. The NAL consisted of the Kansas City Monarchs, the St. Louis Stars, the Indianapolis Athletics, the Cincinnati Tigers, the Memphis Red Sox, the Detroit Stars, the Birmingham Black Barons, and the Chicago American Giants.

While Black baseball teams often played each other, more often they barnstormed, traveling from town to town in the United States, Cuba, Mexico, and the Dominican Republic to play local Black teams and semiprofessional white teams. While no records of these contests have survived, evidence suggests such Black teams were competitive with white professional baseball teams. In 1911 Ty Cobb and the Detroit Tigers played a Black baseball team in Cuba. Cobb batted .370 for the five-game series, but the Black team's John Lloyd averaged .500. Cobb refused to play any more Black teams after the series was concluded.

937 • Josh Gibson (1911–47)

Known as the Black Babe Ruth, Josh Gibson, born in Buena Vista, Georgia, on December 21, 1911, was probably the most powerful baseball player of his time. Roy Campanella, who played with both Hank Aaron and Josh Gibson, once said: "I think Josh was the greatest home-run hitter I ever saw. Now it's true, nobody ever counted the home runs this man has hit, but I'll say one thing, I'll put him with anybody, not taking anything away from Babe Ruth. I think Josh Gibson was the greatest home run hitter that ever lived." He was easily the best player on his favorite team, the Homestead Grays, where he played catcher. In one game, he hit four home runs out of Griffith Stadium. According to his teammate Buck Leonard, "I saw him almost hit one out of Yankee Stadium. At the Polo Grounds I saw him hit one between the upper deck and the roof. It hit an elevated train track outside the park. Josh hit seventy to seventy-two home

Josh Gibson. Photograph by Charles "Teenie" Harris, c. 1942. Courtesy of Pittsburgh Courier Photographic Archives

runs in one year. In 1939 he hit more home runs in Griffith Stadium than all the right-handed hitters in the American League combined." Unfortunately there are no official records of Gibson's performances and he died before the desegregation of baseball.

938 • Judy Johnson

Another outstanding player was third baseman Judy Johnson of the Pittsburgh Crawfords. Johnson was regarded as one of the best all-around players in baseball. He was an excellent fielder, able to roam to the right and left to catch balls, he bunted and hit well, and he was a defensive punisher who often threw out men at the plate with his powerful arm. In March 1975 Judy Johnson was inducted into the Baseball Hall of Fame.

939 • Satchel Paige (1906–82)

Leroy Paige earned his nickname while carrying satchel bags at the train station in Mobile, Alabama. He began pitching at age eighteen in 1924 with the Mobile Tigers. In 1926 Paige pitched for the Chattanooga Black Lookouts and the New Orleans Black Pelicans for $50 to $200 a month. Legendary as a pitcher in the Negro Leagues, Paige played in the 1948 World Series in game five between the Cleveland Indians and the Boston Braves at Cleveland. Paige pitched relief for two-thirds of an inning. He went on to play for the St. Louis Browns in 1951–53. To qualify him for a major league pension, the Kansas City Athletics signed Paige in 1965 for one game in which he pitched three innings. He was fifty-nine years old at the time. Satchel Paige was inducted into the Baseball Hall of Fame in 1971.

940 • First African American to Play in the Major League

On October 23, 1945, Branch Rickey, owner of the Brooklyn Dodgers of the National League, announced the signing of Jack Roosevelt Robinson to the organization. Robinson, who lettered in football, baseball, track, and basketball at UCLA, had been playing for the NNL's Kansas City Monarchs since March 1945 for $400 a month. In August 1945 Robinson signed with the Dodgers and was assigned to the Dodgers' minor league affiliate, the Montreal Royals, for a $3,500 signing bonus and $600 a month. On April 9, 1947, Rickey announced Robinson

African American baseball players of the Brooklyn Dodgers (from left to right): Roy Campanella, catcher, Don Newcombe, pitcher, and Jackie Robinson, second base, 1949. Courtesy of Bettmann Archives. National Archives

would be moved up to the Dodgers. In his first season, he batted .297 with twelve home runs, forty-eight runs batted in, and sixteen errors at first base. He led the National League in stolen bases with twenty-nine. He dominated on the field despite name-calling, racial epithets, a Black cat being thrown at him in Philadelphia, and brushback pitches from opposing pitchers.

Jackie Robinson's best year came in 1949, when he finished first in the National League in batting average (.342) and stolen bases (37). He finished second in RBIs (124) and hits (203). In 1951 Robinson set a new National League record for double plays by a second baseman with 137. He retired in 1956 and during his ten years in the league, he completed six World Series and played every position except pitcher and catcher. In 1962 he became the first African American inducted into the Baseball Hall of Fame in his first year of eligibility.

941 • MVP Three Different Years

Roy Campanella was the only Black baseball player to be named Most Valuable Player for three separate years (1951, 1953, and 1955). In 1948 he became the fourth Black player in the modern major leagues after he signed with the Brooklyn Dodgers. Campanella was originally asked by Branch Rickey to join the Dodgers organization in October 1945 because he did not want Robinson to be the only Black player, but Campanella declined because he thought Rickey was referring to the Brooklyn Brown Dodgers. In the 1955 World Series, he had two home runs, four runs batted in, and seven hits. On January 28, 1959, Campanella's car skidded into a pole on an icy road in New York and left him paralyzed from the chest down. After intensive physical therapy, he returned as an instructor with the Dodgers. In May 1959, 93,000 fans, a league record, crowded into the Los Angeles Coliseum to honor Campanella's courage and accomplishments. He was inducted into the Baseball Hall of Fame in 1969.

942 • Willie Mays (b. 1931)

Willie Howard Mays joined the Birmingham Black Barons in the late 1940s. His contract was bought by the Giants for $10,000 from the Barons. He joined the Giants on May 25, 1951, and signed for $5,000 a year. Mays was chosen as the National League's Rookie of the Year in 1951. Mays was known for his basket-style technique of catching fly balls, holding the glove waist-high and palms-up. His over-the-head bas-

ket-style nab of Cleveland Indian Vic Wertz's long fly ball in the first game of the 1954 World Series at the Polo Grounds was his most famous catch. The score was tied 2–2 in the top of the eighth with two men on base and Mays saved a run. Mays was named the National League Most Valuable Player in two seasons over ten years apart—1954 and 1965.

In 1954 Willie Mays won the major league batting title and made the cover of *Time* magazine. He hit 30 home runs and stole 30 bases in the 1956 and 1957 seasons. Mays was also the first man to hit 200 home runs and steal 200 bases. He spent his last two seasons, 1972 and 1973, with the New York Mets. Over his career, Mays played in 2,992 games, had 3,283 hits, 660 home runs, led the league three times in triples, four times in home runs, five times in slugging average, and four times in stolen bases. He was inducted into the Baseball Hall of Fame in 1979. Although Mays had an outstanding career, he received some criticism for not using his position as a premier athlete to speak out against racial injustice. Mays explained in 1960: "I don't picket in the streets of Birmingham. I'm not mad at the people who do. Maybe they shouldn't be mad at the people who don't."

943 • Discrimination in the Major Leagues

Although both the American and National Leagues were successfully integrated by the 1960s, Black baseball players still faced discrimination and limited opportunities. A December 1970 report by the Rand Corporation found that no Black baseball player prior to 1959 had received a signing bonus over $20,000, although such bonuses had been paid to twenty-six white players during the same period. Between 1959 and 1961, forty-three whites and only three Blacks received $20,000 or greater signing bonuses. Black baseball players were often forced to accept less favorable terms because even fewer opportunities existed for them off the field. Hank Aaron remembered, "I'd always been easy to deal with. They'd offer me a contract and I'd nearly always sign without any argument." Black players were also handicapped by lack of education. Few white colleges recruited Black baseball players and few Black colleges had baseball programs, so African American baseball players had more limited access to higher education than their white counterparts, who often played on scholarships at white colleges.

944 • Hank Aaron (b. 1934)

On March 13, 1954, Hank Aaron broke into the Braves lineup when Bobby Thompson injured his leg. In his third year with the Braves, Aaron led the National League with a batting average of .328, 200 hits, 340 total bases, and 34 doubles. He was second in the National League with 14 triples, third in slugging average with .558, and third in runs scored with 106. In 1957 Aaron was named National League Most Valuable Player and he helped the Braves win the World Series.

On Monday, April 8, 1974, Hank Aaron hit his 715th home run, breaking Babe Ruth's record. At the time of his retirement, he had 755 home runs. Aaron was named captain of the Braves in 1969 and retired after the 1976 season. Over his career, Aaron hit 40 or more home runs eight times, had 100 or more RBIs eleven times, and had a batting average of .300 or higher fourteen times. He set a record with twenty consecutive years of hitting at least 20 home runs. He was inducted into the Baseball Hall of Fame in 1982.

945 • First Black Major League Manager

On October 3, 1974, Cleveland Indians General Manager Phil Seghi announced that Frank Robinson would become a player-manager for the Indians with a one-year, $180,000 contract. Robinson had played for the Cincinnati Reds, had led the league with 38 home runs, and 122 runs scored, and won National League Rookie of the Year honors. In 1956 he was the only major league baseball player to be voted Most Valuable Player in both the National and American Leagues. In 1966 he won the triple crown, finishing the season first in batting average, home runs, and runs batted in. Robinson became the first player to hit the ball completely out of Baltimore's Memorial Stadium in 1966 with a 451-foot home run. As the Cleveland Indians manager, he hit a home run in his first at-bat. Ejected three times and suspended once over the season, Robinson felt the officiating was biased against him because he was Black. His first season record was 79–80, a fourth-place finish. Robinson was fired by the Indians and hired by the San Francisco Giants in 1981 and was replaced in 1984 after a 268–277 record.

946 • Baseball's Complete Integration

The Boston Red Sox finally completed the total integration of Black players in every major league franchise when they signed Elijah "Pumpsie" Green in 1959. It had been twelve years since Jackie Robinson's first day in the majors. Nineteen fifty-nine was also the first year that Black players dominated the record books. Black players led the league in nine of twelve batting categories and two of twelve pitching categories. The top five stolen-base leaders—Willie Mays, Jim Gilliam, Orlando Cepeda, Tony Taylor, and Vada Pinson—were Black.

947 • "The Stacking Phenomenon"

From 1960 to 1971, Black players were limited on team rosters by position. African Americans were mostly confined to the outfield, first base, or second base. In 1968, Black players made up the following proportions of major-league positions: 53 percent of outfielders, 40 percent of first basemen, 30 percent of second basemen, 26 percent of shortstops, 14 percent of basemen, 12 percent of catchers, and 9 percent of pitchers. This stacking phenomenon was originally described by Black University of California at Berkeley professor Harry Edwards. Reasons given for the arrangement were that (1) Blacks were thought of as untrustworthy in the crucial positions of pitcher and catcher, (2) pitchers and catchers required more pre–major league experience and interaction with coaches and many Black players found it difficult to relate to their white coaches, and (3) aspiring young Black players wanted to emulate their heroes and had few non-outfield examples to follow.

Distinctions were also made among African Americans when assigning positions. According to the June 1969 issue of *Ebony,* the skin tone of Black players also determined a player's position. It reported that 80 percent of very light-skinned Black players were assigned non-outfield roles; 67.9 percent of light brown players; 56.8 percent of medium brown players; 53.5 percent of dark brown players; and 25 percent of very dark-skinned players.

948 • Reggie Jackson (b. 1946)

Reginald Martinez Jackson began his career in 1967 with the Kansas City Athletics. The Athletics moved to Oakland in 1968. Jackson became a first-string player in his rookie season with the A's after thirty-five games. Through 1984, Jackson led the American League in home

runs four times. In the 1977 World Series in the sixth game, Reggie Jackson walked in his first at-bat, hit a two-run homer in his second, hit another two-run homer in his third, and hit a solo home run in his fourth at-bat. No one had ever hit three consecutive home runs in World Series competition on three consecutive pitches. Jackson is known for his outstanding play during play-offs. He tied or set seven World Series records: most homers in a World Series (five); most runs scored (ten); highest slugging average in a six-game Series (1.250); most total bases (twenty-five—tied with Willie Stargell); most extra-base hits in a six-game Series (six); most home runs in consecutive at-bats (four); most total bases in one Series game (twelve—tied with Babe Ruth); and most homers in one game (three).

949 • Youngest All-Star to Win Cy Young Award

In his first year with the New York Mets in 1984, Dwight "Doc" Gooden compiled a 17–9 record, a 2.60 earned-run average, and a league-leading strikeout total of 276. He broke the rookie strikeout record of 245 by Herb Score. In September 1984 Gooden set the National League record by striking out thirty-two total batters in two consecutive games. He also set a record of 11.39 strikeouts-per-nine-innings performed over the 1984 season. Gooden was the youngest player to ever appear in an All-Star game at age twenty and was voted National League Rookie of the Year. In his second season in the major leagues, Doc Gooden became the youngest pitcher to win at least twenty games with his 24–4 record. Gooden's 268 strikeouts and 1.53 ERA led the major leagues and helped him become the youngest player to win the triple crown, leading the major leagues in wins, strikeouts, and ERAs.

950 • Why Blacks Were Kept Out

Judy Johnson recalled asking Connie Mack, the owner of the Philadelphia Athletics, why he did not field a Black player on his team. "He told me, 'There were too many of you to go in. It would have taken too many jobs away from the white boys.' "

951 • The Significance of Jackie Robinson (1919–72)

In 1947, my mother couldn't wait to see Jackie Robinson play, so we wandered up to the Polo Grounds one hot July day to see a Giant-Dodger double-header. It was a really weird feeling to see so many Blacks in a major-league park at one time. My mother laughed and said, "Who's playing today, the Black Yankees and the Homestead Grays?" Man, my people were raising hell in the ballpark that day. I think they would have applauded if Robinson had urinated on home plate. But what the hell, it had been a long time coming. A Black ballplayer in the major leagues!

—Art Rust, *Get That Nigger off the Field!*

I don't know anyone who could have stood all the abuse Jackie had to take in breaking into baseball and stuck it out to become the great player he was. When you know the true nature of Jackie . . . what a fighter he was and how he had to keep it inside of him . . . it's just unbelievable. Thinking back on it, I'm just glad I got to play alongside Jackie and be a part of history.

—Pee Wee Reese

Basketball

952 • First Full-Salaried Pro Team

Robert J. Douglas, the father of Black basketball, organized the Spartan Braves of Brooklyn,

which became the New York Renaissance (the Rens) in 1923. Douglas's talent and business sense enabled the team to survive until the late 1940s. The players earned $800 to $1,000 per month and traveled annually in the spring through the South to play Black college teams. On March 30, 1932, the Rens won their first world professional championship against an all-white squad, the Original Celtics, beating them 37–34. In a rematch on April 3, the Rens prevailed again, 30–23. The New York Renaissance was inducted into the Professional Basketball Hall of Fame in 1963.

953 • The Harlem Globetrotters

In 1927 Black basketball was enhanced by the organization of the Harlem Globetrotters team. By 1940 the Globetrotters were considered better than the Rens, but both teams were handicapped by the lack of a Black league. After the integration of the National Basketball Association in the 1960s, the Globetrotters lost their monopoly on the best Black players, and they switched to playing as an entertainment team using comical routines and fancy ball handling.

954 • First African Americans to Play in NBA

In 1951 the Boston Celtics signed Chuck Cooper out of Duquesne University and made him the first African American to play in the National Basketball Association. Cooper played in sixty-six games, had 562 rebounds and 174 assists, and scored 615 points in his first season. Nathanial "Sweetwater" Clifton of Xavier University was also signed in 1950 by the New York Knickerbockers. He played in sixty-five games and had 491 rebounds, 162 assists, and 562 points.

955 • First Rookie to Win NBA All-State MVP Award

Elgin Gay Baylor attended Spingarn High School in Washington, D.C., and the College of Idaho on a football scholarship. He transferred to Seattle University and was the MVP of the 1958 NCAA Tournament. He was chosen in the first round of the 1958 draft by the Los Angeles Lakers and was the first player to impress crowds with his seeming ability to defy gravity. Over his fourteen-year career, Baylor was a member of a championship team once. The Lakers lost to the Celtics in the play-offs six times during Baylor's career. He was inducted into the Basketball Hall of Fame in 1976 and was chosen to the NBA 35th Anniversary All-Time Team in 1980.

The Harlem Globetrotters against the Boston Whirlwinds, 1958. National Archives. Courtesy of A.P./Wide World Photos, Inc.

956 • Wilt the Stilt (b. 1936)

Wilton Norman Chamberlain played for the University of Kansas for two seasons and played for the Harlem Globetrotters in the 1958–59 season. He later signed with the Philadelphia Warriors. In his first NBA game, October 24, 1959, Chamberlain scored 43 points and had 28 rebounds against the New York Knicks. He was the first and only NBA player to score 100 points in a game. In what was his finest year, 1960, he was chosen NBA Rookie of the Year, the Most Valuable Player in the NBA All-Star Game, and the NBA's Most Valuable Player. He was again the league's Most Valuable Player in 1966, 1967, and 1968. Chamberlain is the all-time leading NBA rebounder with 23,924. He was inducted into the Basketball Hall of Fame in 1978 and was chosen to the NBA 35th Anniversary All-Time Team in 1980.

957 • Women Basketball Players

In 1931 the *Philadelphia Tribune* Black newspaper sponsored a female basketball squad that became the first Black female sports team to experience success in the United States. The team rarely lost behind star center Ora Washington. The typical style of women's basketball until the 1960s was six players per team with separate threesomes for offense and defense. The squad was named national champion by most Black newspapers throughout most of the 1930s.

Cheryl Miller played on the 1984 Olympic gold medal women's basketball team. In one game at Polytechnic High School in Riverside, California, Miller scored 105 points. She was a member of two NCAA championship teams at the University of Southern California and the All-America team in 1983 and 1984.

958 • "The Russell Rule"

Consistently voted the most valuable player in NBA history, William Fenton Russell (born 1934) led his University of San Francisco basketball team to two NCAA titles, while suffering only one loss in his college career. He was chosen Most Outstanding Player of the 1955 NCAA Tournament and was a member of the 1956 United States Olympic basketball team. So dominant was Russell as a rebounder that the NCAA adopted what was known as the Russell Rule: at the end of 1955, the NCAA doubled the width of the field goal lane, from six to twelve feet. Still, Russell dominated NCAA rebounding.

Bill Russell has more championship titles than any other American athlete in major

Bill Russell succeeds Arnold "Red" Auerbach as coach of the Boston Celtics and becomes the first African American head coach of a major-league sport in the United States, 1966. United Press International. National Archives. Courtesy of Bettmann Archives

sports. As a Celtic, Russell led the team to eleven NBA titles, beginning in 1957. Russell was named Most Valuable Player of the National Basketball Association in 1958, but was not named by sportswriters to the all-NBA team. He also won the MVP award in 1961, 1963, and 1965 and the NBA All-Star Game MVP award in 1963. For the 1966–67 season, Russell was named player-coach of the Celtics and later coached the Seattle Supersonics and the Sacramento Kings. He was inducted into the Basketball Hall of Fame in 1974 and chosen to the NBA 25th Anniversary All-Time Team in 1970 and the 35th Anniversary Team in 1980.

959 • Kareem (b. 1947)

In 1967, 1968, and 1969, Ferdinand Lewis Alcindor, Jr., was an NCAA All-America selection and Most Outstanding Player in the NCAA Tournament. He was United Press International's Player of the Year in 1967 and 1969. Alcindor was 1970 NBA Rookie of the Year, NBA All-Star 1970–74 and 1976–88. He was NBA MVP 1971, 1972, 1974, 1976, 1977, and 1980. Alcindor changed his name to Kareem Abdul-Jabbar and at one time held the NBA all-time lead in points scored with 38,387, field goals made with 15,837, and games played with 1,560. Because of Lew Alcindor, the NCAA changed its rules and outlawed the "dunk." Later the ruling was reversed.

Lew Alcindor (Kareem Abdul-Jabbar) as a member of the Milwaukee Bucks, 1972. National Archives. Courtesy Milwaukee Bucks

960 • Dr. J (b. 1950)

With his huge Afro, his frenetic, fast-paced drives to the basket, and his monster dunks, Dr. J (Julius Erving) came to symbolize the new style of basketball and personal appearance of the American Basketball Association (known as the ABA, founded in 1967) when he began to play for the New York Nets in 1972. During his ABA career, Erving was clearly the best player on the best ABA team: he was chosen MVP of the ABA three times and led the Nets to two ABA championship titles (1974–76). With the merger of the four ABA teams—the Denver Nuggets, Indiana Pacers, San Antonio Spurs, and the New York (now New Jersey) Nets—into the NBA, Dr. J. faced and met a new challenge—to prove that the open, hectic, fast-paced ABA style of basketball that he played could be successful in the more plodding, defense-minded NBA. Growing with the change,

Erving developed into an excellent defensive player and outside shooter, to go along with his slashing, driving style of offense. He was selected five times as a member of the All-NBA first team, was MVP of the league in 1981, and in 1983 he led the Philadelphia 76ers to the NBA championship title. Perhaps just as important, the "Doctor," as he was affectionately called by teammates and fans, became a graceful, debonair, and respectable businessman and spokesperson after he decided to end his professional basketball-playing career in 1987.

961 • Magic (b. 1959)

In Lansing, Michigan, Earvin Johnson guided his Everett High School team to the state title. As a sophomore at Michigan State University in 1979, Johnson led the team to the NCAA title. In 1981 he was signed by the Los Angeles Lakers to a twenty-five-year, $25-million contract, the largest total sum in team sports history at that time. Within five years, Magic had helped the Lakers win two NBA titles. In the fall of 1991 he announced that he had contracted the AIDS virus and was retiring from professional basketball. He went on to play on the 1992 Olympic gold medal basketball "Dream Team." Johnson coached the Los Angeles Lakers for a temporary period in the 1993–94 season.

962 • Michael Jordan (b. 1963)

At the University of North Carolina at Chapel Hill, Michael Jordan earned the College Player of the Year Award two years in a row. His final shot won UNC its first title in twenty-five years. In 1983 Jordan helped the United States team win a gold medal at the Pan-American Games. A member of the 1984 and 1992 gold medal U.S. Olympic teams, Jordan was named the 1985 NBA Rookie of the Year, led the NBA in scoring for 1987–93, won the Most Valuable Player award in 1988, 1991, and 1992, and set the record for points scored in a play-off game (63). Jordan led the Chicago Bulls to three consecutive NBA titles in 1991, 1992, and 1993 and was voted MVP of the play-offs for those years. Jordan led the NBA in all-time scoring average at 32.2 points per game, before retiring from professional basketball in 1993. He returned to basketball in 1995 after a year and a half of trying to play professional baseball. His comeback as the star of the Chicago Bulls was spoiled when the Orlando Magic defeated the Bulls in the 1995 semi-finals championship.

Rodeo

963 • Bill Pickett (1860?–1932)

Bill Pickett is renowned as the inventor of the modern art of bulldogging, which became the most popular act at rodeos in the late nineteenth century. Historians differ on the origin of Pickett's special technique. Some argue that when a steer escaped its pen one day around 1900 on a farm where Pickett was working, he jumped on his horse and gave chase. Rather than roping the runaway animal from his perch on his horse, Pickett jumped onto the steer's back from his horse while moving, grabbed the steer's horns, and by turning them, forced the steer over onto the ground. Reputedly, he would also bite into the steer's lip while wrestling it over onto its side. Others suggest that Pickett may have imitated a bulldog of the type that was used to extricate steers from underbrush by jumping up and biting the steers on their necks. Whichever version one accepts, Pickett was a brave, innovative wrestler of steers, and he perfected his technique into a popular rodeo act. In 1908, Pickett even bulldogged a bull in Mexico in a stunt that almost took his life. That he lost in 1932 when he was kicked in the head by a horse. Pickett's exploits lived on in the entertainment careers of Will Rogers and Tom Mix, both of whom worked as Pickett's assistants.

Bicycling

964 • Fastest Bicyclist in the World

Marshall W. "Major" Taylor (1878–1934) was literally "the fastest bicyclist in the world" from 1898 to 1910, the year he retired from professional bicycling competition. Beginning in 1898, he was champion of America for several years; in 1899, he established a new one-mile world record and secured the world championship in Montreal. On his first European tour in 1901, he competed in sixteen cities, raced against the best European riders on their own courses, and won all but two single man-to-man races; returning to Europe in 1902, he topped his earlier record by winning every single man-to-man match race he entered, and beating the former world champion, Thorwald Ellegaard, in Paris. Taylor raced against and beat all of the outstanding bicyclists of his time in the United States, Canada, Europe, Australia, and New Zealand. He was so good that the League of American Wheelmen (L.A.W.) tried to ban him from its races; and when that failed, his white competitors, especially Americans, used a combination of dirty tricks—from running him off of the track to surrounding him with other riders, creating "pockets"—to keep him from winning. But Taylor, whose strategic ideas and competitive will equaled his physical skills, learned to avoid and escape such traps, and dominated bicycling for sixteen years. Taking three years off from compe-

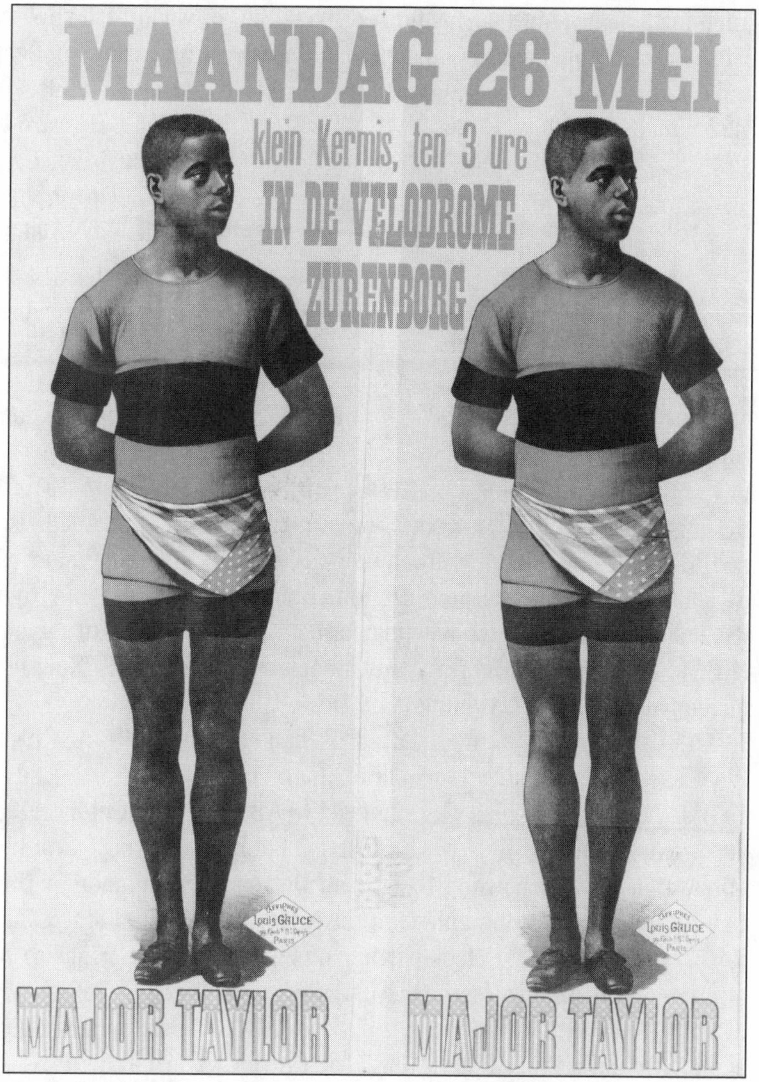

Poster announces the appearance of Marshall W. "Major" Taylor at a fair in Antwerp, Belgium, 1902, the year he beat the Belgium national champion. National Portrait Gallery, Smithsonian Institution tition in 1905, he staged a thrilling comeback in 1908 when he regained his championship form and established two world records, before retiring for good in 1910.

Bowling

965 • Black Bowling Association Formed

The National Negro Bowling Association was organized on August 20, 1939, in Detroit because of the ban on Black bowler participation in the American Bowling Congress (ABC) and the Women's International Bowling Congress (WIBC). The first NNBA tournament was held in 1939, and in 1944 the organization changed its name to the National Bowling Association (NBA). The best bowlers in the association hailed from Chicago, Cleveland, and Detroit. In 1950 the ABC and WIBC finally lifted the ban on Blacks because of the threat of a lawsuit, and by 1951 any qualified bowler was admitted to ABC and WIBC events. On May 24, 1951, in St. Paul, Minnesota, a Black bowling team from Detroit finished in seventy-second place in the ABC national competition. The Black participants were awarded $600 in prizes and became the first African Americans to participate in any ABC competition. In 1960, Fuller Gordy of Detroit became the nation's first Black professional bowler, and the first to have a career on the Professional Bowlers' Association (PBA) tour.

Golf

966 • Patent for Golf Tee

In 1899 Dr. George F. Grant received United States patent number 638,920 for his invention of a golf tee, a small cone-shaped, solid piece of wood with slightly concave tops. Before Grant's invention in Boston, golfers had to construct small mounds of dirt on which to place their balls. A Harvard University graduate and prominent dentist, Grant never made an attempt to capitalize on his invention. The tees used in modern golf games were adapted from Grant's invention.

967 • First African American Member of PGA

The Professional Golfers' Association had no formal restrictions on membership when it formed in 1916, but it banned Black membership in 1943. Dewey Brown became the first Black member of the PGA in the 1920s, but he was too old to play competitively in tournaments. He served as a golf teacher and caddy in southern New Jersey country clubs.

968 • First Case in Black Sports to Reach Supreme Court

In October 1950 Joseph Rice and his NAACP attorney, Franklin Williams, appealed a decision made by the Florida Supreme Court to the United States Supreme Court. Rice had sued Miami Springs to protest the restriction of Black golfers to one day per week of play on the city's only public golf course. The U.S. Supreme Court ordered the Florida Supreme Court to reconsider its decision to uphold the rights of Miami Springs as opposed to the rights of Black golfers. The case encouraged more Black golfers across the country to press for equal access to public facilities.

969 • First African American to Win a Major PGA Event

By winning the Los Angeles Open in 1969, Charlie Sifford became the first African American to win a major PGA event. He also won the

1964 Puerto Rico Open, the 1967 Hartford Open, the 1975 PGA Seniors Open, and the 1980 Suntree Seniors. His career earnings were $339,000 on the PGA tour and $251,000 on the PGA Senior tour.

970 • First African American to Play in the Masters

Robert Lee Elder won the UGA Professional title four times, turned professional in 1959, and received his PGA card in 1967 and played as a thirty-three-year-old rookie. Elder was financially successful in his first nine PGA events in 1968. In 1971 he won the Nigerian Open and became the first African American to play in the South African Open. Elder became the Masters Tournament's first Black entrant when he teed off at the Augusta, Georgia, course on April 10, 1975, his seventh year on the PGA tour. His admittance to the Masters was heralded as a breakthrough of the color line in golf. Yet, twenty years later, the country club that hosts the Masters has only one Black member.

Calvin Peete. Copyright *Washington Post.* Reprinted by permission of D.C. Public Library

971 • Most Successful 1980–84 Player on the PGA Tour

In 1983 Calvin Peete won the PGA Georgia-Pacific Atlantic Classic and the Anheuser-Busch Classic. He was placed on the Ryder Cup Team, won the Golf Writer's Association's Ben Hogan Award and *Golf Digest* magazine's 1983 All-America Team. In 1982 Peete won the Greater Milwaukee Open for the second time, the Anheuser-Busch Classic, the BC Open, and the Pensacola Championship, and finished third in the PGA championship. He won the Vardon Trophy in 1984 for lowest scoring average with a 70.56 score. Peete ended 1984 as the winningest player on the PGA tour for the preceding four years. Calvin Peete had never been a caddy, never played in the UGA, and had not played golf until he was in his early twenties. Many had believed he would never succeed as a golfer because a childhood injury had limited his arm swing.

972 • Youngest U.S. Amateur Champion

In 1994, at age eighteen, Tiger Woods became the youngest amateur golfer to win the United States Amateur Championships. Because he was the U.S. Amateur Champion, he was automatically invited to the Masters, becoming the second Black golfer to play in that tournament.

Horse Racing

973 • First Black Jockey

African Americans played an important role in the early years of horse racing in the United States. Aware that a horse's success was often dependent on the skills of its jockey, southern horse owners turned to their Black slaves, who had long been responsible for the physical care of their owners' horses. These slaves proved extremely adept at riding, and by 1800 diminutive Blacks accounted for almost all the jockeys in the southern United States. The first known African American jockey was 4′6″ Monkey Simon. Considered the country's best jockey in the early 1800s, Simon was able to earn more than $100 per ride for himself or his master. Despite the slave jockeys' achievements, credit was usually given to the horses' owners instead.

974 • Isaac Murphy (1861–96)

After the Civil War, African American jockeys became active again. Between 1880 and 1905, Black riders won more than 110 major races, including 13 Kentucky Derbys. Isaac Murphy, born in Kentucky, was one of the best jockeys of the time, Black or white. When he was twelve, Murphy obtained his jockey apprentice license and began his career as an exercise rider. After developing excellent skills as a hand rider, a jockey who rarely needed a whip to motivate his horse, Murphy won his first major victory aboard Lady Greenfield at Louisville in 1875. By 1882 he was earning $10,000 per year, $25 per winning ride and $15 for every loss. In 1884, with four different horses, Murphy won six races, including the Kentucky Derby. He was the first jockey to win three Kentucky Derbys, a record that stood until 1948. In 1891 the *Louisville Times* said of Murphy, "His integrity and honor are the pride of the Turf, and many of the best horsemen pronounce him the greatest jockey that ever mounted a horse." Murphy died in 1896 of pneumonia at the age of thirty-five.

Isaac Murphy, three-time winner of the Kentucky Derby. Prints and Photographs Division, Library of Congress

As the nineteenth century drew to a close, segregation and discrimination in American society worsened. This development was reflected in events on the horse track. An observer noted:

> *The white riders retaliated [against the victories of Black jockeys] ganging up against the black riders on the rails. A black boy would be pocketed, thrust back in a race; or his mount would be bumped out of contention on a white boy's stirrup, and toss him out of the saddle . . . those white fellows would slash out and cut the nearest Negro rider. . . . they literally ran the black boys off the track.*

975 • The Jockey Club

African Americans were essentially forced out of racing with the establishment of the Jockey Club in 1894 to license riders. The Jockey Club refused to grant Black jockeys their licenses, and Jess Conley, who finished third aboard Colston in 1911, became the last African American to ride in the Kentucky Derby. Although unable to ride, Blacks remained in the

sport working as trainers, dockers, hot walkers, exercise boys, stable hands, and groomers.

Some Black riders turned to steeplechase events after being forced out of "flat" racing events. Water jumps, hedgerows, and railings served as obstacles in steeplechase riding, and many African Americans proved adept at the sport. Charlie Smoot, the most successful and visible African American steeplechase rider, won the Beverwyck Steeplechase in 1916, 1926, and 1933.

Gymnastics

976 • First Internationally Ranked Black Woman Gymnast

Diane Durham was the first Black gymnast to achieve prominence at an early age. She was the 1981 and 1982 United States Junior Champion in the floor exercise, vault, parallel bars, and balance beam. In 1983 Durham was named National Senior Champion in the same four events. She was injured just before beginning the 1984 Olympic competition.

977 • 1994 U.S. Champion

In the 1992 Seoul Olympics, Dominique Dawes helped the United States gymnastics team win a bronze medal. Dawes was the 1994 United States champion in the all-around competition. She also placed first in individual competition in the uneven bars, beam, floor, and vault events.

Ice Skating

978 • First Black Winter Olympic Medalist

In 1980 Debra Thomas finished second in the United States Novice Ladies ice skating competition. She finished thirteenth in the 1983 Senior Ladies competition and won the 1983 Critérium International du Sucre in France. She placed sixth in the 1984 National Seniors event and second in 1985 competition. Thomas won the United States and World Figure Skating titles in 1986 and the United States championship in 1988. The first African American woman figure skater to be widely covered in the media in 1988, she won a bronze medal in the 1988 Winter Olympics.

Weight Lifting

979 • First Man to Win Eight Straight World and Olympic Weight Lifting Championships

John Davis won the 1938 world light-heavyweight championship when he was seventeen years old. He won the 1946–47 and 1949–51 world heavyweight titles, the 1939–40 U.S. light-heavyweight title, and the 1941–43, 1946–48, and 1950–53 U.S. heavyweight titles. In 1951 he became the first amateur weight lifter to clean and jerk more than 400 pounds. The first man to win eight consecutive world and Olympic championships, Davis was elected to the Helms Hall of Fame and the Black Athletes Hall of Fame.

Football

980 • First-Team All-American

In 1915 Paul Leroy Robeson began attending Rutgers University on an academic scholarship. In his second year, Robeson was promoted to first string on the football team at the tackle and guard positions, but was left off the team for Rutgers' game against Washington and Lee

University because that school refused to play against Blacks. In 1918 Walter Camp, the initiator of the All-America team, said that Robeson was the finest end to ever play the game and named him to his first-team All-America roster. Robeson graduated Phi Beta Kappa with honors, and after graduation, played professional football to support himself through Columbia University Law School. Robeson later became a successful concert singer, stage and motion picture actor, and civil rights activist. Because Robeson had the temerity to criticize American racial practices and voice support for the Soviet Union during the McCarthy era, he became the target of a blacklisting campaign that affected the record of his football accomplishments. When lists of football All-Americans were published in the 1950s, there was a blank space where Robeson's name had been.

981 • First African American to Win Bert Bell Trophy

In his first year with the Cleveland Browns in 1957, Jim Brown led the National Football League with 942 rushing yards and was selected as NFL Rookie of the Year. He led the league in rushing for eight seasons. In seven of his nine career seasons, Brown rushed for 1,000 yards or more. He was selected as a football All-Pro in 1957, 1958, and 1959. His 12,312 total career rushing yards was the record in the National Football League for nineteen years. Brown was given the Bert Bell Trophy as the Most Valuable Player in the NFL in 1963, becoming the first African American to win the award. Brown was voted Football Back of the Decade for 1950–60. He was elected to the Professional Football Hall of Fame in 1971.

982 • First African American in Hall of Fame

In 1968 Marion Motley became the first African American player to be inducted into the National Football Hall of Fame. A running back out of the University of Nevada at Reno, Motley began his professional career with the Cleveland Browns of the All-American Football Conference (AAFC) in 1946 and played with the Pittsburgh Steelers in 1954–55.

983 • Rookie of the Year in 1965

University of Kansas running back Gale Sayers was voted Rookie of the Year in his first season in 1965 with the Chicago Bears. In a November 5, 1965, game versus the San Francisco 49ers, Sayers scored six touchdowns. He led the league in rushing in 1969 with 1,032 yards and was the highest-paid player in the league. Sayers retired in 1970 and was inducted into the Professional Football Hall of Fame in 1977.

984 • O.J. Simpson (b. 1947)

While at the University of Southern California, running back Orenthal James "O.J." Simpson won the 1968 Heisman Trophy. He signed a three-year, $250,000 contract with the Buffalo Bills in 1969.

On December 16, 1973, O.J. Simpson set an NFL record of 2,003 rushing yards in one season. On November 25, 1976, in a game against the Detroit Lions, he set a new single-game rushing record of 273 yards. Over his eleven total seasons in the National Football League, he rushed for 1,000 yards or more in five seasons. Simpson received the 1973 Bert Bell Trophy as Most Valuable Player in the National Football League. He was the United Press International's American Football Conference Player of the Year in 1972, 1973, and 1974. Simpson was in-

O.J. Simpson playing for the University of Southern California in the Rose Bowl, January 1, 1969. National Archives. Courtesy of USC Sports Information

ducted into the Professional Football Hall of Fame in 1985.

Arrested and charged with the June 12, 1994, murder of his former wife, Nicole Brown Simpson, and her friend Ronald Goldman, Simpson was found not guilty on all murder charges by a Los Angeles jury on October 3, 1995.

985 • All-Time Leading NFL Rusher

Walter "Sweetness" Payton broke Jim Brown's career rushing record on October 7, 1984, in a game with the New Orleans Saints. Payton, out of Jackson State University, became the only runner to set the all-time rushing record for his college conference and for the National Football League.

Walter Payton broke O.J. Simpson's single-game rushing record on November 20, 1977, by rushing for 275 yards on forty carries against the Minnesota Vikings. Over his ten-year career,

Jim Brown playing lacrosse. 1957 Onondagan, Syracuse University Archives

Althea Gibson, the first African American to win women's singles at Wimbledon, rides up Broadway in New York during ticker-tape parade in her honor, 1957. Courtesy of the *New York Times.* National Archives

Payton rushed for 1,000 yards or more in eight seasons. He finished his career with 13,309 total rushing yards.

Lacrosse

986 • First African American to Play in Lacrosse's North-South Game

Jim Brown, the star football player, was also a Syracuse lacrosse midfielder in 1955–56. He initially tried the sport out of curiosity and came to be known for his speed on the field. In 1957 Brown became the first African American to participate in the North-South game. He played for half the game, scoring five goals and making two assists to lead the North squad to a 14–10 upset victory.

Arthur Ashe in action during the United States National Tennis Championship, September 8, 1965. Courtesy of Wide World Photos, Inc. National Archives

Tennis

987 • Althea Gibson (b. 1927)

Althea Gibson was given her first tennis racket in 1940. In 1955 she won eighteen of the nineteen tennis events she participated in. In the spring of 1956 Gibson became the first Black to win a Grand Slam event when she won the singles and doubles title at the French Open. In 1956 she also won the doubles title at Wimbledon and the Asian Championships in Ceylon. In 1957 and 1958 Althea Gibson was ranked as the number one female tennis player in the world. She won her first Wimbledon singles title in 1957 over Darlene Hard 6–3, 6–2.

Gibson had become the first Black athlete to appear on Wimbledon courts in 1951. She was the first Black tennis player to play at Forest Hills in 1950. Gibson won the U.S. Lawn Tennis Association Nationals at Forest Hills in 1957 by beating Louise Brough 6–3, 6–2. Gibson repeated these victories in 1958. She was a member of the 1957–58 United States Wightman Cup Squad and was awarded the Female of the Year Babe Didrickson Zaharias Trophy.

988 • Arthur Ashe, Jr. (1943–93)

Arthur Ashe, Jr., became the first African American to receive a USLTA national ranking when he ranked fifth among all United States junior players in 1958. Ashe won three ATA Boys' titles. From 1960–62 Ashe won three consecutive ATA men's singles titles. He became the first Black member of the United States Junior Davis Cup Team in 1960 and won the 1960 USLTA National Junior Indoors title. After winning the U.S. Open Singles Championship in 1968, Ashe appeared on the cover of *Life* magazine and was the first African American athlete to appear on the talk show *Face the Nation.* In 1975 Ashe defeated Jimmy Connors at Wimbledon and took over the World Championship Tennis singles title from Bjorn Borg. Ashe retired on July 31, 1979, after suffering a mild heart attack. He died in 1993 after suffering with the AIDS virus contracted through blood transfusions during heart surgery.

Track and Field

989 • First Black Medals in Modern Olympics

George Coleman Poage won a bronze medal in the 400-meter hurdles in the 1904 St. Louis Olympics, becoming the first African American to receive a medal in the Olympic Games. The next day, Poage won a bronze medal in the 200-meter hurdles. At the University of Wisconsin, Poage set the collegiate record for the 440-yard sprint and low hurdles.

At the 1908 London Olympics, John Baxter Taylor, Jr., ran the third leg of the 1,600-meter relay, which the American team won by twenty-five yards. Taylor's gold medal in this event was the first gold received by any Black member of the United States Olympic team.

990 • First Black Individual Gold Medal Olympian

At the 1924 Paris Olympics, William Hubbard won a gold medal in the long jump with a leap of 24 feet 5⅛ inches. He tied the 100-yard dash world record at 9.6 seconds in a meet against Ohio State and later won the national title in the 100-yard dash. Hubbard set the world record in the long jump on June 13, 1925, at 25 feet 107/8 inches at the Stagg Field NCAA Championships.

991 • Jesse Owens (1913–80)

James Cleveland "Jesse" Owens won a then-unprecedented four gold medals at the 1936 Berlin Olympics. On Monday, August 3, Owens tied the Olympic record in the 100-meter dash with a time of 10.3 seconds. On Tuesday, August 4, he set an Olympic record in the long jump with a leap of 26 feet 5½ inches. In the college conference championships in 1935, Owens had set the world record in the long jump at 26 feet 8½ inches. On Wednesday, August 5, Owens set an Olympic record in the 200-meter dash at 20.7 seconds. In his last competition on Friday, he helped set a world record in the 400-meter relay at 39.8 seconds. Jesse Owens won as many track and field events alone as did any other country.

In 1950 the Associated Press named Jesse

Jesse Owens sprints to an easy victory in the 200-meter race during the 1936 Summer Olympics. United Press International. Courtesy of Bettmann Archives. National Archives

Owens the Athlete of the Half-Century. He was given an honorary award from his alma mater, Ohio State University, in 1971. The NCAA presented Owens the 1974 Theodore Roosevelt Award for collegiate contribution, and he was made a charter member of the Track and Field Hall of Fame. In 1976 President Gerald Ford awarded Owens the highest award a civilian could receive, the Presidential Medal of Freedom.

992 • First Black Woman to Win Olympic Gold

Alice Coachman (Davis) was the only United States woman to win a gold medal in a track and field event at the 1948 Olympics. She set an Olympic record in the high jump with a leap of 5 feet 6 inches. Between 1939 and 1948, Coachman set a record for the most victories in the National AAU Outdoor High Jump without a loss at 10. She is a member of the National Track and Field Hall of Fame, the Helms Hall of Fame, the Tuskegee Hall of Fame, the Georgia State Hall of Fame, and the Bob Douglas Hall of Fame.

993 • Decathlon Olympic Record

In the 1956 Olympics, Rafer Johnson won a silver medal in the decathlon with 7,568 points in ten events: the 100-meter dash, the broad jump, the shot put, the high jump, the 400-meter run, the 100-meter hurdles, the discus throw, the pole vault, the javelin toss, and the 1,500-meter run. In the 1960 Olympics, Johnson set an Olympic record in the decathlon, capturing the gold medal with 8,001 points. He carried the American flag in the 1960 Olympics and lit the Olympic torch above the Coliseum in the 1984 Olympics in Los Angeles.

994 • First Black Female Sprinter to Win Gold

Wilma Rudolph, out of Tennessee State University, won a bronze medal in the 440-meter relay in the 1956 Olympics. She returned in 1960 to win three gold medals, becoming the first African American female to win a gold medal in a sprint event at the Olympic Games. She had sprained her ankle the day before her first race, but won the 100-meter dash in 11.0 seconds, the 200-meter dash in 24.0 seconds, and the 400-meter relay in 44.5 seconds. Rudolph won the AAU Outdoor 100-meter title from 1959 to 1962.

Wilma Rudolph wins the 200-yard dash at the 1960 Summer Olympics in Rome. Copyright *Washington Post.* Reprinted by permission of the D.C. Public Library

995 • "Arch of Unity and Power"

Tommie Smith and John Carlos finished first and third respectively in the 200-meter dash at the 1968 Olympic Games. In a victory stand demonstration during the playing of the American national anthem, Smith raised his right Black-gloved fist high above his head. Both men bowed their heads and closed their eyes during the entire national anthem. Afterward, Smith explained to Howard Cosell, "My raised right hand stood for the power in Black America. Carlos' raised left hand stood for the unity of Black America. Together they formed an arch of unity and power." Both runners were ejected by the International Olympic Committee from the Olympic Village.

996 • Long Jump Too Long

Before the 1968 Olympic Games, Bob Beamon had won twenty long jump titles in twenty-one meets. He set an indoor world record of 27 feet 1 inch at the NAIA Indoors and extended the record to 27 feet 2¾ inches at a later meet. At the 1968 Olympics, he noticed a rain cloud approaching and wanted to accomplish a good jump before the rain started. After Beamon's jump, the meet marshals discovered that their optical equipment was not designed to measure a jump of that distance. They got a new tape and officially measured his jump twice at 29 feet 2½ inches. Beamon's new Olympic and world record extended the previous world record by almost 2 feet.

Tommie Smith crosses finish line in 200-meter dash at 1968 Olympics in Mexico. Associated Press. Courtesy of A.P./Wide World Photos, Inc. National Archives

997 • Unbeaten in 102 Races

Edwin Moses, out of Morehouse College, set an Olympic and world record in the 400-meter hurdles at 47.64 seconds in the 1976 Olympics. He went on to lower this record on several occasions. Before the 400-meter hurdle final in the 1984 Los Angles Olympic Games, Moses had an unbeaten streak of 102 races, with 89 consecutive wins in the finals. He won the gold medal in 1984.

998 • Six Olympic Medals

Jackie Joyner-Kersee won gold medals in the long jump and high jump in the 1988 Olympics and gold in the heptathlon and high jump in the 1992 Olympics. Her bronze medal in the long jump in 1992 and her silver in the heptathlon in 1984 brought Joyner-Kersee's total medal count through the 1992 Olympics to six. After her silver medal performance in the 1984 Olympics, Jackie Joyner-Kersee was awarded the 1986 James E. Sullivan Award for Most Outstanding Amateur Athlete.

999 • Carl Lewis (b. 1961)

Carl Lewis, out of the University of Houston, became the first Olympian since Jesse Owens in 1936 to win four gold medals in one Olympiad at the 1984 Olympics. Lewis won the 100-meter dash in 10.97 seconds, the long jump in 8.54 meters, and set an Olympic record in the 200-meter dash at 19.80 seconds. He helped set a new Olympic and world record in the 400-meter relay at 37.83 seconds. Lewis won the 100-meter by eight feet, the largest winning margin in history. His winning long jump was achieved on his first attempt. In the 1988 Olympics, Carl Lewis was awarded the gold medal in the 100-meter dash after the disqualification of Canadian Ben Johnson for steroid use. Lewis also won the gold medal in the long jump. Lewis returned to the 1992 Olympics to defend his long title and won the event for the third straight time. He also anchored the record-setting United States 400-meter relay.

1000 • Three Golds, One Silver

In the 1988 Seoul Olympics, Florence Griffith-Joyner won gold medals in the 100-meter dash (10.54 seconds), the 200-meter dash (21.34 seconds—world record), and the four by one hundred-meter relay. Flo-Jo had set the world record for the 100-meter dash at 10.49 at the United States Olympic Trials. She won the James E. Sullivan Trophy in 1988.

1001 • Long-Jump Record

In the 1988 Olympics, Mike Powell won the silver medal in the long jump. In fifteen attempts, Powell had never beaten Carl Lewis. Finally, at the 1991 World Track and Field Championships in Tokyo, Powell beat Lewis for the first time. He also broke Bob Beamon's twenty-three-year-old world record. Powell's jump of 29 feet 4¼ inches came on his fifth attempt in the meet. He won the 1991 James E. Sullivan Trophy.

SELECT BIBLIOGRAPHY

This bibliography is by no means a complete record of all the works and sources I have consulted in making this book. Rather, this bibliography indicates the substance and range of my readings and my suggestions for those who wish to pursue further the study of African American history.

Allen, Robert L. *The Port Chicago Mutiny.* New York: Amistad, 1993.

Applegate, Katherine. *The Story of Two American Generals: Benjamin O. Davis, Jr., Colin Powell.* New York: Dell, 1992.

Aptheker, Herbert. *American Negro Slave Revolts.* New York: Columbia University Press, 1944.

———. *A Documentary History of the Negro People in the United States.* Vol. 2. New York: Citadel Press, 1968.

Ashe, Arthur. *A Hard Road to Glory: A History of the African-American Athlete, 1619–1918.* New York: Warner Books, 1988.

Baer, Hans A., and Merril Sanger. *African American Religion in the Twentieth Century.* Knoxville: University of Tennessee, 1971.

Bedini, Silvio. *The Life of Benjamin Banneker.* New York: Charles Scribner's Sons, 1972.

Bennett, Lerone. *Before the Mayflower: A History of Black America.* Chicago: Johnson Publishing Co., 1969.

Bianco, David. *Heat Wave: The Motown Fact Book.* Ann Arbor: Popular Press, 1988.

Black Art Ancestral Legacy: The African Impulse in African-American Art. New York: Harry N. Abrams and Dallas Museum of Art, 1989.

Blaustein, Albert P., and Robert L. Zangrado, eds. *Civil Rights and the American Negro: A Documentary History.* New York: Washington Square Press, 1969.

Bogle, Donald. *Blacks in American Films and Television.* New York: Garland Publishing, 1988.

Brier, Stephen, et al. *Who Built America?* Vol. 1. New York: Pantheon Books, 1992.

Brodie, James. *Created Equal: The Lives and Ideas of Black American Innovators.* New York: Morrow & Co., 1993.

Bullard, Sara. *Free at Last: A History of the Civil Rights Movement and Those Who Died in the Struggle.* Montgomery: Civil Rights Education Project, Southern Poverty Law Center, 1989.

Bussey, Lt. Col. Charles M. *Firefight at Yechon: Courage and Racism in the Korean War.* Washington, D.C.: Brassey, 1991.

Carson, Clayborne. *In Struggle: SNCC and the Black Awakening of the 1960s.* Cambridge: Harvard University Press, 1981.

Clarke, John Henrik. *Harlem: A Community in Transition.* New York: Citadel Press, 1969.

Cohen, Bernard, ed. *Cotton Mather and American Science and Medicine.* Vol. 2. New York: Arno Press, 1980.

Conniff, Michael. *Africans in the Americas: A History of the Black Diaspora.* New York: St. Martin's Press, 1994.

Curtin, Philip D. *Atlantic Slave Trade: A Census.* Madison: University of Wisconsin Press, 1969.

David, Jay, and Elaine Crane, eds. *The Black Soldier: From the American Revolution to Vietnam.* New York: William Morrow & Co., 1971.

Davis, David Brion. *The Problem of Slavery in the Age of Revolution.* Ithaca: Cornell University Press, 1995.

Davis, Marianna W., ed. *Contributions of Black Women in America.* Vol. 2. Columbia, S.C.: Kenday Press, 1982.

Dawson, Joseph G., III. *Army Generals and Reconstruction: Louisiana, 1862–1872.* Baton Rouge: Louisiana State University Press, 1982.

Dees, Morris. *A Season for Justice: The Life and Times of Civil Rights Lawyer Morris Dees.* New York: Simon & Schuster, 1991.

Donaldson, Gary. *The History of African-Americans in the Military: Double V.* Malabar, Fl.: Krieger, 1991.

Driskell, David. *Two Centuries of Black American Art.* Venice, Calif.: Environmental Communications, 1976.

Dumond, Dwight L. *Anti-Slavery: The Crusade for Freedom in America.* Ann Arbor: University of Michigan Press, 1961.

Emery, Lynne Fauley. *Black Dance: From 1619 to Today.* 2nd rev. ed. Princeton, N.J.: Princeton Book Co., 1988.

Fletcher, Marvin. *The Black Soldier and Officer in the United States Army, 1891–1917.* Columbia: University of Missouri Press, 1974.

Foner, Eric. *Reconstruction: America's Unfinished Revolution, 1863–1877.* New York: Harper & Row, 1988.

Franklin, John Hope, and Alfred A. Moss. *From Slavery to Freedom: A History of African Americans.* New York: McGraw-Hill, 1994.

Frazier, Thomas, ed. *Afro-American History: Primary Sources.* New York: Harcourt, Brace & World, 1970.

Goldman, Martin S. *Nat Turner and the Southampton Revolt of 1831.* New York: Franklin Watts, 1992.

Grant, Joanne. *Black Protest: History, Documents, and Analyses, 1619 to the Present.* Greenwich, Conn.: Fawcett Publications, 1974.

Greene, Robert E. *Black Defenders of the Persian Gulf War.* Fort Washington, Md.: privately printed, 1991.

Grossman, James R. *Land of Hope: Chicago, Black Southerners, and the Great Migration.* Chicago: University of Chicago Press, 1989.

Haber, Louis. *Black Pioneers of Science and Invention.* New York: Harcourt, Brace & World, 1970.

Ham, Debra Newman, ed. *The African-American Mosaic: A Library of Congress Resource Guide for the Study of Black History and Culture.* Washington, D.C.: Library of Congress, 1993.

Hayden, Robert L. *7 African American Scientists.* Frederick, Md.: Twenty-First Books, 1992.

Higgenbotham, Leon, Jr. *In the Matter of Color: Race & the American Legal Process: The Colonial Period.* New York: Oxford University Press, 1978.

Hine, Darlene Clark. *Black Women in America: An Historical Encyclopedia.* New York: Carlson, 1993.

Hughes, Langston, and Milton Meltzer. *A Pictorial History of the Negro in America.* 3rd ed. New York: Crown Publishers, 1968.

James, Portia. *The Real McCoy: African-American Invention and Innovation, 1619–1930.* Washington, D.C.: Smithsonian Institution Press, 1989.

Johnson, Paul E. *African-American Christianity: Essays in History.* Berkeley: University of California Press, 1994.

Jones, Howard. *Mutiny on the Amistad: The Saga of a Slave Revolt and Its Impact on American Abolition, Law and Diplomacy.* New York: Oxford University Press, 1987.

Kaplan, Sidney. *The Black Presence in the Era of the American Revolution, 1770–1800.* Washington, D.C.: Smithsonian Institution, 1973.

Kate, William Loren. *Black People Who Made the Old West.* New York: Crowell, 1977.

King, Donald. *Legal Aspects of the Civil Rights Movement.* Detroit: Wayne State University Press, 1965.

Klein, Aaron. *The Hidden Contributors: Black Scientists and Inventors in America.* Garden City, N.Y.: Doubleday & Co., 1971.

Leckie, William H. *The Buffalo Soldiers: A Narrative of the Negro Cavalry in the West.* Norman: University of Oklahoma Press, 1967.

Lee, Irvin H. *Negro Medal of Honor Men.* New York: Dodd, Mead & Co., 1967.

Lewis, Samella. *African American Art and Artists.* Berkeley: University of California Press, 1990.

Lincoln, C. Eric. *Race, Religion, and the Continuing American Dilemma.* New York: Hill & Wang, 1984.

Locke, Alain. *Race Contacts and Inter-racial Relations.* Washington, D.C.: Howard University Press, 1992.

Logan, Rayford W., and Michael R. Winston, eds. *Dictionary of American Negro Biography.* New York: W. W. Norton & Co., 1982.

Long, Richard A. *The Black Tradition in American Dance.* New York: Rizzoli, 1990.

Lyttelton, Humphrey. *The Best of Jazz: Basin Street to Harlem.* New York: Taplinger, 1979.

McClendon, Robert Jr. James. *The Origin of Rap Music.* Del Rio, Tex.: "We the Negro People" Film and Non-Commercial Venture, Etc., 1994.

McCloud, Aminah Beverly. *African American Islam.* New York: Routledge, 1995.

McPherson, James. *The Negro's Civil War.* New York: Vintage Books, 1965.

Mannix, Daniel P., and Malcolm Cowley. *Black Cargoes: A History of the Atlantic Slave Trade, 1518–1865.* New York: Viking, 1972.

Marszaler, John F. *Assault at West Point: The Court Martial of Johnson Whittaker.* New York: Macmillan, 1972.

Maultsby, Portia. *Afro-American Religious Music.* Springfield, Ohio: Hymn Society of America, 1981.

Mitchell, Loften. *Black Drama.* New York: Hawthorn Books, 1967.

Morgan, Edmund. *American Slavery, American Freedom.* New York: Norton, 1975.

Nalty, Bernard C., and Morris J. MacGregor, eds. *Blacks in the Military: Essential Documents.* Wilmington, Del.: Scholarly Resources, 1986.

———. *Strength for the Fight: A History of Black Americans in the Military.* New York: Free Press, 1986.

Pierson, William Dillon. *Black Legacy: America's Hidden Heritage.* Amherst: University of Massachusetts Press, 1993.

Quarles, Benjamin. *Black Abolitionists.* New York: Oxford University Press, 1969.

———. *The Black American: A Documentary History.* Glenview, Ill.: Scott, Foresman, 1976.

Raboteau, Albert J. *Slave Religion.* New York: Oxford University Press, 1978.

Raines, Howell. *My Soul Is Rested: The Story of the Civil Rights Movement in the Deep South Told by the Men and Women Who Made It Happen.* New York: Bantam Books, 1978.

Rawley, James A. *The Transatlantic Slave Trade: A History.* New York: W. W. Norton & Co., 1981.

Reagon, Bernice Johnson. *We'll Understand It Better By and By: Pioneering African-American Gospel Composers.* Washington, Smithsonian, 1992.

Redkey, Edwin S. *Black Exodus: Black Nationalist and Back-to-Africa Movements, 1890–1910.* New Haven: Yale University Press, 1969.

Rust, Art. *"Get That Nigger off the Field!": A Sparkling, Informal History of the Black Man in Baseball.* New York: Delacorte Press, 1976.

Sacks, Howard L. *Way Up North in Dixie: A Black Family's Claim to the Confederate Anthem.* Washington, D.C.: Smithsonian Institution Press, 1993.

Smith, Edward D. *Climbing Jacob's Ladder: The Rise of Black Churches in Eastern American Cities, 1740–1877.* Washington, D.C.: Smithsonian Institution Press, 1988.

Smith, Jessie Carney. *Notable Black American Women.* Detroit: Gale Research, 1992.

Sollors, Werner, and Maria Diedrich, eds. *The Black Columbiad: Defining Moments in African American Literature and Culture.* Cambridge: Harvard University Press, 1994.

Southern, Eileen. *The Music of Black Americans.* New York: W. W. Norton & Co., 1971.

Still, William. *The Underground Railroad.* New York: Arno Press and the New York Times, 1968.

Story, Rosalyn M. *And So I Sing: African American Divas of Opera and Concert.* New York: Warner Books, 1990.

Tate, Claudia, ed. *The Selected Works of Georgia Douglas Johnson.* New York: G. K. Hall, 1996.

Terry, Wallace. *Bloods: An Oral History of Vietnam by Black Veterans.* New York: Random House, 1984.

Vlach, John. *The Afro-American Tradition in Decorative Arts.* Athens: University of Georgia Press, 1990.

Williams, Eric. *Capitalism and Slavery.* Chapel Hill: University of North Carolina Press, 1944.

Williams, George W. *Negro Troops in Rebellion, 1861–1865.* New York: Kraus Reprint, 1969.

Williams, Juan. *Eyes on the Prize: America's Civil Rights Years, 1954–1965.* New York: Penguin, 1988.

Wilson, Joseph T. *The Black Phalanx.* New York: Da Capo, 1994.

Wolff, Miles. *Lunch at the 5 & 10.* Chicago: Ivan R. Dee, 1990.

Wood, Peter H. *Black Majority: Negroes in Colonial South Carolina from 1670 Through the Stono Rebellion.* New York: W. W. Norton & Co., 1974.

Wuthenau, Alexander von. *Unexpected Faces in Ancient America.* New York: Crown Publishers, 1975.

INDEX

Page numbers in italics refer to illustrations.

Aaron, Hank, 363, 366
Abdul-Jabbar, Kareem, 371, *371*
Abeokuta (Yoruba king), 47
Abernathy, Ralph, 149, 157, 172
Abyssinian Baptist Church, 144
Academy Awards, 315
Adams, Henry, 52
Adams, John Quincy, 27
Adderley, Cannonball, 287
"Address on Non-Resistance to Offensive Aggression" (Whipper), 76
Affirmative action 172–73, 179–80
Africa, 10, 15, 27, 44, 46, 47, 141, 159, 227–28, 236
  ethnic/tribal warfare in, 10, 11
  repatriation to, 130
  slavery in, 10, *11*
African American(s)
  acceptance into mainstream, 103
  colonization schemes, 42–50
  prohibition of state immigration, 52, 90–91, 102
  Renaissance, 304–17
  social ranking system, 108
  strikebreakers, 55
  western settlement of, 50–53
African Free School, 240, 245
African Grove Theater Company, 236–37, 240
African Methodist Episcopal Church, 49, 119, 128, 155, 242, 252, 262
African Union Society, 236
African Zion Church, 74
Afro-American Council, 127
Afro-American Steamship and Mercantile Company, 47–48
Afrocentricism, 305–6, 313
Agricultural Adjustment Act (1933), 59, 133
AIDS, 372, 381
Ailey, Alvin, 299, 314
Air brakes, 331
Alabama Christian Movement for Human Rights, 152, 153, 157
Albany Movement, 151–52
Alcindor, Ferdinand Lewis, Jr., 371, *371*`
Alcorn, James L., 120
Aldridge, Ira, 237, 240–41, *241*
Ali, Muhammad, 222, *359*, 359–60
Ali, Noble Drew, 279, 302–3
All African Peoples Revolutionary Party, 159
Allen, Louis, 165
Allen, Richard, 235, 241
Allen William, 251
Allerwood, John, 240
All People's Party, 281
American Academy of Arts and Sciences, 340
American and Foreign Anti-Slavery Society, 76, 77, 84
American Anti-Slavery Society, 38, 41, 70, 75, 77, 79–80, 80, 83, 84
American Colonization Society, 44, 45, 47, 78
American Convention for Promoting the Abolition of Slavery, 70
American Federation of Labor, 131
American Moral Reform Society, 80, 81
Ameican Negro Academy, 127
American Negro Historical Society, 254
American Negro Repertory Company, 291
American Physical Society, 340
American Railway Union, 55
Amistad Rebellion, *26*, 26–27
Anderson, Jo, 327
Anderson Marian, 277
Andrews, Charles C., 246
Angelou, Maya, 177, 304

Annie Allen (Brooks), 282–83
Anti-Slavery Women, 75
Arlington National Cemetery, 4, 165, 207
Armistead, James, 188, *188*
Armstrong, Louis, 272, *273*, 273–74, 285, 310
Arnold, Matthew, 141–42
Art, 245–47
  Black Arts Movement, 294–95, 308–10
  caricatures, 246–47
  colonial period, 231–32, 238–40
  Harlem Renaissance, 266–71
  multimedia, 309–10
  post-Civil War, 256–58
Asante, Molafi Kete, 305
Asbury, Francis, 234–35
Ashe, Arthur, *380*, 381
Astronauts, *340*, 340–41
The Atlantic Slave Trade (Curtin), 5
Attica correctional facility, 178
Attucks, Crispus, 68–69, *69*
Austin, James T., 83

Bacaroons, 12
Back to Africa scheme, 50
Bacon, Nathaniel, 183
Baker, Ella, 150, *151*
Baker, George, 281
Baker, Henry A., 333
Baker, Josephine, *220*, 221, 271, 276–77
Bakke decision, 179–80
Baldwin, James, 283
Ball, J. P., 247
Ballard, Florence, 296
Ballets Negres, 284
Baltimore, Charles W., 208
Bambaataa, Afrika, 312
Bambara, Toni Cade, 304
Banneker, Benjamin, 323–24
Bannister, Edward, 256
Baraka, Imamu Amiri, 292
Barnes, William H., 344
Barnett, Ross, 152, 164
Barry, Marion, 160, *160*
Barthe, Richmond, 263, 267, 308
Baseball, 362–68
Basie, William "Count," 275, 285
Basketball, 368–72
Bass, Charlotta Spears, 140
Bass, John, 140
Bates, Daisy, 157
Baylor, Elgin, 369
Beamon, Bob, 383
Beard, Andrew J., 329
Bearden, Romare, 294–95
Beckwourth, James, 4, *4*
Beecher, Edward, 88
Bell Labs, 339, 340
Benezet, Anthony, 63, 74, 80
Benjamin, Miriam E., 328
Bernat, Martin, 304–5
Berry, Chuck, 288–89
Bestes, Peter, 69
Bethel African Methodist Episcopal Church (Mother Bethel), 242, *242*, 252
Bethune, Mary McCleod, 143
Bicycling, 373–74
Big Daddy Kane, 312
Biggers, John, 295
Birdsong, Cindy, 296
Birney, James G., 75, 84, 88, 247
Birth of a Nation (film), 140, 277–78
Black Arts Movement, 291–304
Black Arts Theater, 292
Black Athletes Hall of Fame, 377
Blackburn, Jack, 357
Black Caucus, 174
Black Codes, 106, 108, 110–11, 122
Black Harry, 234–35
Black Laws, 102, 103
Blacklisting, 143
Black Manifesto, 173
Black Masons, 71, 236
Black Muslims, 156, 157, 168, 232, 292, 303
Black nationalism, 143, 167, 222
Black Panthers, 156, 157, 159, 173–74, 178, 179
Black Patti, 259
Black Patti's Troubadoures, 259, 261
Black Phalanx (Wilson), 194
Black Power, 150, 159, 168–69, 222, 303
Black Pride, 49, 291
Black Seminoles, 35
Black separatism, 150
Black Star Line, 48, 49, 130
Black studies, 154, 173, 305–6
Black theology, 303–4
Blackwell, David H., 340
Blair, Henry, 324
Blake, Eubie, 271, 276
Blake, Robert, 202
Blakey, Art, 311
Bland, James, 259

Blind Tom, 250–52, *251*
Blow, Kurtis, 312
Blue, Lockrum, 328
Bluford, Guion "Guy," 340–41
Bohee Brothers, 259
Bond, Julian, 159, 222
Boston Massacre (1770), 69
Boston Massacre (1858), 90
Bouchet, Edward, 339
Bowditch, Thomas Edward, 227
Bowling, 374
Boxing, 353–61
Boycotts, 133, 144, 148–49
Boyd, Henry, 327
Bradley, Joseph P., 114
Brewer, Mattie D., 342
Brogs, Janet Waterford, 214
Brooke, Edward, 120
Brooks, Gwendolyn, 263, *282*, 282–83
Brooks, Preston S., 119
Brotherhood of Sleeping Car Porters, 131, 134, 142–43, 153, 212
Brown, Charles, 314
Brown, Elaine, 157
Brown, H. Rap, 159, 172
Brown, Henry "Box," 37–38, *38*
Brown, James, 287, 297–98, *298*
Brown, Jim, 378, 379, *379*, 380
Brown, John, 78, 90
Brown, Willa, 214
Brown, William Wells, 189, 242, 244, *244*
Brown Fellowship Society, 108
Brownsville Riot, 138
Brown v. Board of Education, 91, 123, 142–43, 145, 148, 160–61, 170
Bruce, Blanche K., 120, 121
Bryan, Andrew, 241
Bucket Dance Company, 313–14
"Buffalo Soldiers," 203–5
Bunche, Ralph J., 145
Burleigh, Harry T., 251
Burns, Anthony, 88–89
Burroughs, Margaret, 291
Burroughs, Nannie Helen, *262*, 262–63
Bush, George, 179, 180
"Buying Power" movement, 133

Cable, George W., 255
Caesar, Adoph, 314
Cain, Richard H., 103
Caldwell, James, 69
Callender's Original Georgia Minstrels, 258–59
Camp, Walter, 143
Campanella, Roy, 363, 365, *365*
Campbell, Peter R., 328
Camp meetings, 242
Canaanite Temple, 279
Cannibalism, 19
Canoes, dugout, 321–22
Capers, Warren, 219, *220*
Cardozo, Francis L., 103
Caribbean islands, 25, 26, 50
Carlos, John, 383
Carmichael, Stokely, 150, 159
Carnegie Hall, 285
Carpetbaggers, 108
Carruthers, George E., 340
Carson, Ben, 349
Carter, Ron, 287, 311
Cartwright, Samuel, 36
Carver, George Washington, 337, *337*
Catlett, Elizabeth, 283–84
Central Committee of Negro College Men, 209
Cepeda, Orlando, 367
Chaffee, Calvin C., 93
Chamberlain, Wilt, 370
Chambers, Paul, 296
Chaney, James, 165, 167
Chavis, Benjamin, 174, 177, 303
Chesnutt, Charles, 255
Chicago Defender (newspaper), 56, 58, 139–40
Chino, Bob, 135
Chisholm, Shirley, 175, 176
Christian, Charlie, 287
Christian Recorder (newspaper), 49
Christmas, Charles T., 328
Chuman, Charlotte, 257
Church of God (radio program), 279
Civil Rights Act (1866), 111, 112, 122
Civil Rights Act (1871), 113, 114
Civil Rights Act (1875), 113, 114, 123
Civil Rights Act (1957), 169
Civil Rights Act (1960), 170
Civil Rights Act (1964), 113, 153, 167, 170
Civil Rights Act (1968), 172
Civil Rights Act (1991), 180
Civil Rights Movement, 60, 148–72, 294
Civil War, 33, 47, 52, 54, 82, 83, 94–100, 194–203
Clark, Jim, 155, 162
Clark, Mark, 178
Clarke, Kenny, 287

Clarke, Powhatan, 204–5
Clarkson, Thomas, 74
Clay, Cassius. *See* Ali, Muhammad
Clay, Henry, 44
Cleage, Albert B., 303
Cleaver, Eldridge, 155, 157
Clifton, Nathanial "Sweetwater," 369
Clinton, Bill, 175, 176, 177, 284
Clinton, Hillary, 177
Clotel (Brown), 244
Coachman, Alice, 382
Cobb, Charles, 154
Coercive Acts, 23
Coffin, Levi, 40
Coffle, 12, *12*
Coleman, Bessie, *337*, 337–38
Collingwood, Luke, 17
Collins, George, 174
Colonization, 42–50, 102
Colored American (magazine), 81
A Colored Woman in a White World (Terrell), 142
Coltrane, John, 287, 296, *296*
Coming of Age in Mississippi (Moody), 150
Committee for the Participation of Negroes in National Defense, 211
Communist Party, 132, 141, 142, 174, 176, 281
Compromise of 1850, 37, 77–78, 91, 92
Compromise of 1877, 110
Cone, James, 303
Confiscation Act (1861), 96, 196
Confiscation Act (1862), 99
Congo Free State, 48
Congo Square, 248
Congress of Racial Equality, 135, 144, 151–52, 159, 165, 168
Conkling, Roscoe, 120
Conley, Jess, 376
Conner, Estine, 219, *220*
Connor, Eugene "Bull," 152
Conscientious Objectors Against Jim Crow, 212
Consolidated Lasting Machine Company, 331
Constitutional Conventions, 73, 117–18
Continental Congress, 23, 24
Convention of the Colored Peoples, 87, 117
Coolidge, Calvin, 50, 131
Cooper, Anna J., 254, 307
Cooper, Chuck, 369
CORE. See Congress of Racial Equality
Corn
  harvesters, 324
  shellers, 328
Cornish, Samuel, 76
Cotton balers, 328
Covenant Blocks, 59
Covey (the "Negro breaker"), 33
Cowboys, 51–52
Cox, Minnie, 138
Craft, Ellen, 36–37, 41
Craft, William, 36–37, 41
Creek war (1813), 34
Cripps, Thomas, 278
Crisis (newspaper), 56, 130, 141, 209, 211
Crittenden Compromise, 95, 118
Cromwell, Oliver, 188, *188*
Croslin, Michael, 336
Crum, William, 138
Cruse, Harold, 292, 293
Cuba, 25, 27
Cuffee, Paul, 44, *44*, 236, 326
Cullen, Countee, 264, 265, 294
Curry, Izola, 164
Curtin, Philip, 5

Dance, 284–85
  African, 227–28
  ballet, 313–14
  Black Arts Movement, 299–300, 313–14
  buck-and-wing, 228
  cakewalk, 228, 271
  Caribbean, 228
  colonial period, 228–31
  Congo Square, 248
  djouba, 229
  hambone, 229
  house servants', 229
  jigs, 250
  multimedia, 314
  risqué, 228–29
Dance Theater of Harlem, 299–300
Davidson, Gordon, 316
Davidson, Shelby J., 335
David Walker's Appeal (Walker), 31, 74, 76, 86
Davies-Hinton test, 346
Davis, Angela, 173–74, *174*, 178
Davis, Anthony, 313
Davis, Benjamin O., Jr., 212, 213, 214, 219
Davis, Benjamin O., Sr., 206, 218-19, *219*
Davis, Henrietta Vinton, 143
Davis, Hugh, 64
Davis, Jefferson, 119, 327–28
Davis, John, 377
Davis, Miles, 287, 296, 298, 310

Davis, Ossie, 291, 315
Dawes, Dominique, 377
Deadwood Dick, 51–52
Declaration of Independence, 23–24, 89
Dee, Ruby, 290, 291, 302
De La Beckwith, Byron, 166
Delany, Martin R., 47, 48, 78, 122, 202, 243, 245, 343
De Large, Robert Carlos, *121*, 121–22
Dellums, Ron, 174
Denny, Reginald, 179
DePriest, Oscar, 140–41
Derham, James, 342
Desegregation. *See also* Segregation
  busing in, 172, 179
  school, 149, 152, 153, 157, 170
Discrimination. *See also* Segregation
  economic, 122
  employment, 134, 170
  housing, 137, 172
  military, 211–13
  protests, 143
  public, 123
  racial, 127, 212, 241
  reverse, 179–80
  in sports, 355, 356, 362–63, 366, 374 , 376–77
Disfranchisement, 91, 122, 124
Dislondes, Charles, 30–31
Dixon, George "Little Chocolate," 354–55
Djulea peoples, 34
Dorsey, Thomas A., 288, *288*
Douglas, Aaron, 247, 263, 267, 294
Douglas, Buster, 361
Douglas, Robert J., 368–69
Douglas, Stephen A., 93, 119
Douglass, Charles, 202
Douglass, Frederick, 33, 36, 42, *43*, 45, 47, 54, 77, 78, 82, *82*, 84, 89, 94, 96, 97, 103, 197, 202, 242, 243, 254, 255
Douglass, H. Ford, 94
Douglass, Helen Pitts, 254
Douglass, Lewis, 202
Douglass, Margaret, 243
Douglass' Monthly, 96
Dove, Rita, 305
Downing, George, 9
Dozier, Lamont, 290, 296
Drake, J. G. St. Clair, 212
Drama, 290, 314
  colonial period, 240–41
  Harlem Renaissance, 278
"Drapetomania," 36
Dred Scott decision, 73, 78, 91, 93, 103
Drew, Charles Richard, *346*, 346–47
Drew, Timothy, 279
Dry-cleaning process, 324
Du Bois, W. E. B., 50, 56, 126, 128, 129, 130, 141, *141*, 142, 143, 209, 210, 211, 213, 251, 254, 256, 265, 294, 301
Due process. *See* Fourteenth Amendment
Dunbar, Paul Laurence, 255, 261
Dunbar-Nelson, Alice, 307
Duncanson, Robert Scott, 247
Dunham, Katherine, 228, 284, 299, 314
Dunlop, Frankie, 287
Durham, Diane, 377
Du Sable, Jean Baptiste Point, 50
Dutton, Charles, 316
Dyer, C. C., 131

Eagle (newspaper), 140
Easterbrooks, Prince, 184
Eaton, William, 168
Eckstine, Billy, 286
Edelman, Marian Wright, 177
Edison Pioneers, 332, *332*
Edwards, Harry, 367
Eisenhower, Dwight D., 149, 217
Elder, Robert Lee, 375
Elijah McCoy Manufacturing Company, 329
Ellington, Edward Kennedy "Duke," 272, 274–75, 294, 299
Ellison, Ralph, 283
Emancipation Proclamation, 98–100, 102, 107, 110, 197
Emigration. *See* Colonization
The Emperor Jones (film), 278
Employment
  competition for, 54, 100
  contracts, 110, 111, 117, 122
  demands for, 156, *156*
  discrimination, 134, 170
  factory, 58
  nonagricultural, 54, 58
  quotas, 173
  unionization in, 131, 134, 142–43
Engine lubricators, 328–29, *329*
Enlistment Act of 1792, 190
Enlistment Act of 1795, 196
Equal Rights Association, 245
Equiano, Olaudah, 19, 238
Erving, Julius "Dr. J," 371–72
Estevanico, 3
Ethiopian Art Players, 278
Europe, James R., 210, 273
Evans, Kenneth, 340

Evanti, Lillian, 276, *276*
Evers, Medgar, 165–66, 177
Evers-Williams, Myrlie, 177
"Everybody's Mission" (church), 279
Explorers, 2–5
Eyes on the Prize (TV documentary), 159

Fagan, Eleanor, 285–86
Fagan, Garth, 313–14
Fambourgh, Charles, 311
Famous Flames, 298
Fanon, Franz, 156, *156*, 292
Farmer, James, 135, 158, 159
Farrakhan, Louis, 176, 177, 303
Father Divine, 281
Faubus, Orval, 149
Federal Bureau of Investigation, 130–31, 156, *156*, 157, 165, 168, 173–74
Federal Employment Practices Commission, 134
Federal Writers' Project, 281
Fellowship of Reconciliation, 135
Fenley, Molissa, 313
Fifteenth Amendment, 105, 106, 112–13, 124, 170
Fisher, Rudolph, 263, 264, 265
Fishing, 322
Fisk Jubilee Singers, 260, *260*
Fisk University, 141, 158, 347
Flanders, Benjamin F., 110
Fleetwood, Christian, *202*, 203
Flipper, Henry, 206, 207, *207*
Folklore, 232–33, 254
Folsom, Cora Mae, 258
Football, 377–80
Ford, Gerald, 382
Ford, Richard J., III, 224
Foreman, George, 360, 361, *361*
Forman, James, 173
Forrest, Nathan Bedford, 109
Fort Brown, 206
Forten, James, 71, 79, 80, *80*, 325–26
Fort Negro, 27–28
Fort Pillow, 200
Fort Snelling, 204
Fort Wagner, 199, *199*
Foster, Rube, 363
Fourteenth Amendment, 105, 106, 111–12, 114, 121, 122, 146, 147, 148, 170, 172
Four Tops, 290, 297
Francis, Marie Jones, 342
Franklin, Benjamin, 70, 81
Franklin, Vincent, 305
Frazier, Joe, 359, *359*, 361
Free African Society, 71
Freedman's Savings Trust Company, 120
Freedmen's Bureau, 54, *104*, 104–5, 106, 112, 119, 122
Freedmen's Hospital, 343–44
Freedmen's Relief Association, 53
Freedom Rides, 135, 151, *151*, 158, 159, 170
Freedom Schools, 153–54
Freeman, Elizabeth "Mumbet," 72, *72*
Freeman, Sambo, 69
Freemen, 31, 51, 68, 90–91, 102, 107, 119, 196
  slave ownership, 67
Free-Soil Party, 85, 86
French and Indian War, 184
Fugitive Slave Act (1793), 35–36, 71, 73
Fugitive Slave Act (1850), 36, 37, 39, 47, 77–78, 80, 82, 88–89, 119, 243
The Fugitive Blacksmith (Pennington), 37
Fuller, Charles, 314
Fuller, Hoyt, 292, 293
Fuller, Meta Warrick, 258
Fuller, Solomon C., 345–46
Funeral rites, 233

Gabriel, Charles, 201
Gaines v. Missouri, 147
Gardner, James, 203
Gardner, Ralph, 339
Garnet, Henry Highland, 30, *30*, 84, 103, 243
Garrett, Thomas, 40
Garrison, Lucy McKim, 251
Garrison, William Lloyd, 42, 45, 74–75, *75*, 76, 77, 79, 80, 81, 83, 85, 243
Garvey, Marcus, 48, *49*, 49–50, 130–31, 295
Gas masks, 333–34, *334*
Gates, Henry Louis, Jr., 245, 307
Gaye, Marvin, 290
Gayle, Addison, 292, 293
Genius of Universal Emancipation (newspaper), 79
Georgia Minstrels, 258–59
Gerima, Haile, 317
Germantown Protest, 62
Gibbs, Jonathan C., 103, 262
Gibson, Althea, *380*, 380–81
Gibson, Josh, 363–64, *364*
Gibson, Kenneth, 173
Gibson, William F., 177
Gillespie, John "Dizzy," 286–87, 296
Gilliam, Jim, 367

Gilpin, Charles, 278
Gilroy, Paul, 305
Gire, George, 184
Givens, Robin, 361
Glover, Danny, 306
Goldberg, Whoopi, 306
Golden Gloves titles, 358, 359, 360
Golf, 374–75
Gooden, Dwight "Doc," 368
Goodman, Andrew, 165, 167
Gordy, Berry, Jr., 290, 296, 297
Gordy, Fuller, 374
Gorsuch, Edward, 39
Gossett, Lou, 302
Go Tell It on the Mountain (Baldwin), 283
Grace, Charles Emmaniel "Sweet Daddy," 279–80, *280*
Grace (magazine), 280
Grammy Awards, 299, 311
Grandmaster Flash, 312
Grant, George F., 374
Grant, Ulysses S., 107, 112–13, 199, 200, 260
Gray, Samuel, 69
Great Awakening, 234, 235, 237, 240, 242
Great Migration, 52–60
Greeley, Horace, 50, 86, 97
Green, Elijah "Pumpsie," 367
Greene, Thomas, 250–52, *251*
Greener, Richard T., 127
Greenfield, Elizabeth Taylor, 249
Grierson, Benjamin, 206
Griffith, Michael, 178
Griffith-Joyner, Florence, 384
Grimes, Leonard A., 41
Grimké, Angelina, 85
Grimké, Sarah, 85
Guihard, Paul, 164
Guinn v. United States, 130
Gullah, 232
Gymnastics, 377

Hair-straightening process, 335
Haiti, 24, 26, 29, 30–31, 78
Haley, Alex, 292, 302
Hall, Lloyd Augusta, 336
Hall, Prince, 235, 236
Hall of Fame
  baseball, 364, 365, 366
  basketball, 369, 370
  boxing, 358, 360
  football, 378, 379
Hall v. DeCuir, 112
Hamer, Fannie Lou, 154, *154*, 155
Hamilton, Alexander, 70
Hamilton, William, 87
Hamlet, James, 37
Hammon, Jupiter, 235, 237
Hammond, John, 285
Hammons, David, 309, 310
Hampton, Fred, 178
Hampton, Wade, 30
Hampton Cornet Band, 271
Hancock, Herbie, 273, 287, 311
Handy, W. C., 271–72, 274
Hansberry, Lorraine, 290
Harding, Vincent, 305
Harlem Community Art Center, 270
Harlem Community School, 283
Harlem Globetrotters, 369, *369*
Harlem Hospital, 345
Harlem Renaissance, 263–81, 278, 293, 294
Harlem School of the Arts, 300
Harmon Foundation, 294
Harper, Frances Ellen Watkins, *244*, 244–45
Harpers Ferry, 78
Harris, Enoch, 50
Harvard College, 127, 128, 141, 245, 343, 346, 347, 374
Harvey, Ben, 261
Hastie, William H., 212, 215
Haverly Minstrels, 258–59
Hawkins, Coleman, 273
Hayes, Rutherford B., 109, 110, 123, 203
Haynes, Lemuel, 241
Hearns, Thomas, 360
Heavy D, 312
Henderson, Fletcher, 273
Henderson, Harry, 295
Hendrix, Jimi, 287, 298
Henson, Josiah, 78
Henson, Matthew A., 4–5, *5*
Herring, James, 271, 284
Hewlett, James, 236, 240
Hicks, George B., 258–59
Higginbotham, Leon, 64, 67, 68
Higginson, Thomas Wentworth, 251
Hill, Anita, 180
Hilliard, David, 157
Hines, Earl, 286
Hinton, William, 346
Holbrook, Felix, 69
Holiday, Billie, 285–86, *286*
Holland, Brian, 290, 296

Holland, Eddie, 290, 296
Holly, James Theodore, 78
Holmes, Larry, 360
Homosexuality, 289
Hood, James, 153
hooks, bell, 304, 306
Hoover, Herbert, 132
Hopkins, Pauline, 307
Hopkins, Samuel, 187
Horse racing, 375–77
Hose, Sam, 128
Hosier, Harry, 234–35
Hosmer, Harriet, 257
Housing, 59
  demands for, 156, *156*
  discrimination, 137, 172
  front porches, 323
  ghettos, 60
  restrictive covenants, 59
  shotgun, 323
Houston, Charles, 132–33, 145
Howard, Michael, 206
Howard University, 132, 137, 209, 212, 219, 254, 259, 271, 276, 284, 295, 317, 338, 344, 347
Hubbard, William, 381
Hudson, Julien, 246, *246*
Hughes, Langston, 263, 264, 265, 293
Hunt, Richard, 308
Hunter, David, 97, 118, 196
Hurston, Zora Neale, 255, 263, 264, 266

Ice Cube, 316
Ice skating, 377
"I Have a Dream" (King), 153
Incidents in the Life of a slave (Jacobs), 245
Indian wars, 203–5
Intermarriage, 65, 172
Inventions, 321–36
Invisible Man (Ellison), 283
Ironsmithing, 322
Ivers, Barkley, 41
Ivy Baxter Company, 313–14

Jackson, Andrew, 191–92, 194
Jackson, Billy, 261
Jackson, Jesse, 174, 175, 176, *176*, 177
Jackson, Jimmy Lee, 167
Jackson, Jonathan, 173–74, 178
Jackson, Mahalia, 288
Jackson, Michael, 311
Jackson, Reggie, 367–68
Jackson, Shirley, 340
Jackson 5, 290, 311
Jackson-Jarvis, Martha, 308
Jacobs, Harriet, 242, 245, 307
Jahn, Janheinz, 305
Jamison, Judith, 299
Jasper, John, 261
Jay, John, 70, 74
Jefferson, Blind Lemon, 277
Jefferson, Thomas, 23–24, 25, 42, 44, 73, 189–90, 231, 244, 323–24
Jemison, Mae C., 341
Jenkins, Ernest A., 217, *218*
Jennings, Thomas, 324
Jim Crow, 55–56, 84, 113, 118, 122–25, 135–36, 145–46, 212, 249
Jimi Hendrix Experience, 298
Jockey Club, 376–77
Johannon, Ben, 305
Johnson, Andrew, 82, 105, 106, 110, 119
Johnson, Anthony, 20
Johnson, Ben, 384
Johnson, Campbell C., 212
Johnson, Earvin "Magic," 372
Johnson, Frank, 248–49
Johnson, Georgia Douglas, 263, *264*
Johnson, James P., 272–73
Johnson, James Weldon, 256, 265
Johnson, John Arthur "Jack," *355*, 355–56
Johnson, Judy, 364, 368
Johnson, Lyndon B., 145, 155, 165, 167, 170, 171
Johnson, Rafer, 382
Johnson, Reverend Daniel E., 47–48
Johnson, Sargent, 270
Johnson, William H., 38, 263, 269
Johnston, Joshua, 239
Joie, Chester, 69
Jones, Absalom, 71, 235, 241–42
Jones, Bill, 303
Jones, Bill, 314
Jones, Elvin, 296
Jones, Frederick McKinley, 336
Jones, Irving, 261
Jones, James Andrew, 336, *336*
Jones, John, 102
Jones, LeRoi, 291, 292, 293, 300
Jones, Lois Mailou, 263, 271, 284
Jones, Quincy, 311
Jones, Sissieretta, 259, 261

Jones, William Peel, 38
Jonkonnu, 243
Joplin, Scott, 261
Jordan, Barbara, 174–75
Jordan, Michael, 372
Joyner, Charles, 305
Joyner-Kersee, Jackie, 384
Julian, Percy Lavon, *347*, 347–49
Jungles Casino, 272
Just, Ernest E., 338–39

Kansas-Nebraska Act, 92–93, 119
Karenga, Maulama, 304
Katzenbach, Nicholas B., 153, 162
Keckley, Elizabeth, 307
Kemble, Fanny, 247–48
Kennedy, John F., 152, 153, 158, 164, 165, 292
Kennedy, Robert, 151, 158, 170
Kersands, Billy, 259, *259*
King, Coretta Scott, 157, 163, 172
King, Martin Luther, Jr., 149, 152, 153, 155, 157, 158, 161, 163–64, 167, 168, *169*, 178, 222, 290, 299
King, Martin Luther, Sr., 291
King, Rodney, 178–79, 316
Kirkland, Kenny, 311
Knight, Gladys, 290
Knox, William J., 339
Komunyakaa, Yusef, 307
Kool Herc, 311
Korean War, 221–22
Kountz, Samuel L., 349
KRS-ONE, 312
Ku Klux Klan, 109–10, 112, 113, 114, 120, 135, 140, 155, 165, 167, 168, 178, 203, 262
Kwame Ansa (Asante king), 6
Kwanzaa, 304

Lacrosse, 380
Lane, William Henry, 250
Lane Theological Seminary, 80
Langston, John Mercer, 53, 103, 137–38, *138*
Langston University, 53
Languages, 232, 323
Larsen, Nella, 265–66
Last Poets, 312
Latimer, Lewis, 331, 332
Laurens, John, 188–89
Laveau, Marie, 252, *253*
Lawrence, Jacob, 263, 271
Leadbelly, 277
Ledbetter, Huddie, 277
Lee, Coger, 167
Lee, Don L., 292, 293
Lee, George, 165
Lee, Herbert, 164–65
Lee, Joseph, 332
Lee, Rebecca, 349
Lee, Robert E., 78, 197, 201–2
Lee, Simon, 189
Lee, Spike, 315
Legal decisions
  abolition laws, 72–73
  colonial period, 64–68
  Revolutionary period, 72–73
  See also Supreme Court decisions
Leonard, Buck, 363
Leonard, "Sugar" Ray Charles, 360
"Letter from a Birmingham Jail" (King), 152, 161
Lew, Barzillai, 184
Lewis, Carl, 384
Lewis, Edmonia, 256–57, *257*
Lewis, Elmer, 291
Lewis, John, 153, 155, *158*, 158–59
Lewis, William H., 128
Liberator (newspaper), 74, 76, 79, 82
Liberia, 44, 46, 47, 48
Liberian Exodus Joint Stock Steamship Company, 48
Liberty Party, 77, *77*, 84, 86, 247
Lilies of the Field (film), 290–91
Lincoln, Abraham, 47, 83, 84, 85, 86, 94, 96, 97, 98, *98*, 99, 102, 105, 118, 194, 196, 197
Lincoln, C. Eric, 303
Liston, Sonny, 359
Literature, 236
  Black Arts Movement, 292–94
  colonial period, 232–33, 242–43
  folk, 243
  Harlem Renaissance, 263–66
  post-Civil War, 254–56
  protest novels, 244
  social indictment fiction, 282
Little Richard, 289–90
Little Rock Nine, 149, 157
Liuzzo, Viola Gregg, 168
LL Cool J, 312
Locke, Alain, 263, 264, *264*, 266, 271, 293
Lodge, Henry Cabot, 145–46
Logan, Greenbury, 51
Logan, Rayford W., 211
Lomax, Alan, 277

Long, Jefferson F., 120
Longworth, Nicolas, 247
Louis, Joe, 221, 356–58, *357*, 360
Louisiana Murders (1873), 109
L'Ouverture, Toussaint, 29, *29*
Love, Ed, 295
Love, Nat, 51–52
Lovejoy, Elijah, 76, 83, 88
Loving v. Virginia, 65
Lovingwood, R. S., 136
Lowe, Walter P., 340
Lucas, Sam, 261
Lucy, Autherine, 145, *145*
Lundy, Benjamin, 45, 79, 81
Lynching, 56, 57, *57*, 122, 123–24, *124*, 126, 128, 130, 131, 141, 142, 147, 285
Lynd, Staughton, 154
Lynn, William, 212

McCoy, Elijah, 328–29
McCrummell, James, 75, 79
McGhee, James, 173
McKay, Claude, 263, 264, 265
McKissick, Floyd, 159
McMillan, Terry, 304, 305
McNair, Ronald, *340*, 340–41
McNeil, Claudia, 290
Mahara's Minstrels, 271
Malcolm X, 156, 161, *167*, 167–68, 292, 303, 359
Malone, Vivian, 153
Mamount, Yarrow, 232–33, *233*
Manhattan Project, 339
March on Washington (1941), 134–35, 136
March on Washington (1963), 153, 158, 165
Mark Taper Forum, 316
Maroon colonies, 34, 35, 284
Marsalis, Branford, 310, 311
Marsalis, Wynton, 310–11, 314
Marshall, Thurgood, 133, 145, *145*, 217
Martha and the Vandellas, 290
Martin, Daniel, 190
Martin, "Denver" Ed, 355
Martin Luther King Day, 176, 299
Marx, Karl, 99, 156, *156*
Mason, George, 23, *23*
Massachusetts Anti-Slavery Society, 83
Massachusetts Bay Colony, 20
Master Juba, 250
Mather, Cotton, *233*, 233–34, 341
Matzeliger, Ernst, *330*, 330–31
Maverick, Samuel, 20, 69
Mayfield, Curtis, 301
Mays, Willie, 365–66, 367
Medicine, 341–49
Medtek Corporation, 336
Memphis Free Speech and Headlight (newspaper), 125
Mennonites, 62
Meredith, James, 152, 164
Metcalfe, Ralph, 174
Metropolitan Opera Company, 277, 288
Mexican War, 35, 83, 92
Mfume, Kweisi, 177
Michaus, Elder "Lightfoot" Solomon, 279
Micheaux, Oscar, 277–78, *278*
Middle Passage, 74
Midwives, 342
Mighty Clouds of Joy, 288
Migration, urban, 53–60
Military awards, 202–3, 204, 213, 214, 217, 219, 223, 224
Military service, 182–224, *197*
  Battalion of Free Men of Color, 192
  "Buffalo Soldiers," 203–5
  Civil War, 95, 99, 194–203
  conscientious objection to, 212–13
  cotton-bag forts, 193
  Ethiopian Regiments, 186–87
  fatigue duty, 200–1
  French and Indian War, 184
  integrated branches, 190–91, 194, 201, 218
  Korean War, 221–22
  labor battalions, 186, 188, *188*, 200–1, 208, 216
  pay differentials, 201
  Persian Gulf War, 224
  post-Civil War, 203–8
  racial conflict in, 215
  reenslavement after, 189, 193
  regiments, 184
  Revolutionary War, 183–90
  Selective Service Act, 208, 211, 212, 213
  Spanish-American War, 205–8
  substitution, 187
  Vietnam War, 222–24
  War of 1812, 190–94
  western, 205
  women in, 211, 214, *215*
  World War I, 208–11
  World War II, 211–21
  Yamasee War, 183
Miller, Cheryl, 370
Miller, Dorie, 213
Million Man March, 176–77, 303

Mills, Florence, 271
Minstrelsy, 249–50, 258–59, 261, 271
Minton's Playhouse, 287
Miscegenation, *101*, 101–2, 172
Mississippi Freedom Democratic Party, 154–55
Missouri Compromise, 90, 91, 93
Mitchell, Arthur, 299
Mitchell, Loften, 293
Mitchell, Parren, 174
Molineaux, Tom, 353–54, *354*
Monk, Thelonius, 273, 287, 296
Monroe, James, 30
Montgomery, Benjamin, 327–28
Montgomery Bus Boycott, 135, 148–49
Montgomery Improvement Association, 149, 164
Moody, Anne, 150, *150*
Moore, Archie, 358, 360
Moore, William, 165
Moorer, Michael, 361
Moore v. Dempsey, 130
Moorhead, Scipio, 238
Moorish American Science Temple, 302–3
Moorish Holy Temple of Science, 279
Morgan, Garrett Augustus, 333–34
Morrison, Toni, 255, 293–94, *294*, 304, 307
Morton, Jelly Roll, 272, 290
Moses, Bob, 164
Moses, Edwin, 383–84
Moten, Benny, 275
Motley, Archibald, 263, 268
Motley, Marion, 378
Moton, LeRoy, 168
Moton, Robert, 265
Motown, 290, 296, 297, 311
Mott, Lucretia, 85
Mountain Fur Company, 4
Muhammad, Elijah, 292, 302–3
Muhammad, Imam Warith Deen, 303
Mulattoes, 29, 30, 65, 107–8, 246
Murphy, Isaac, 376, *376*
Murray, Anna, 42
Murray, Donald Gaines, 133
Murray, George Washington, 328, 333
Murray, John, 186–87
Music, 285–90
  banjar (banjo), 231
  bebop, 286, 287, 312
  Black Arts Movement, 296–99, 310–13
  blues, 260–61, 274, 277, 285, 298
  bones playing, 230, *230*, 231
  classical, 311, 313
  colonial period, 227–31, 240–41
  cool, 287
  "coon songs," 261
  drum playing, 230, 240
  fiddle, 231, 240
  fusion, 287, 310, 313
  gospel, 287–88
  Harlem Renaissance, 271–77
  Harlem Stride, 272, 275
  hip-hop, 312
  hymns, 240
  jazz, 263, 272, 274, 275, 285, 286, 287, 310, 311, 312, 313
  line singing, 230–31
  minstrelsy, 249–50
  opera, 276, 277, 288
  post-Civil War, 258–61
  ragtime, 261, 272
  rap, 311–12, 313
  reggae, 305
  rhythm and blues, 289, 298
  rock and roll, 289, 290
  "scat," 312
  sorrow songs, 251, 254, 256
  soul, 292
  spirituals, 251, 256, 271, 287–88
  underground railroad songs, 251
  videos, 311
  work songs, 247–48, 261
Myers, Cecil William, 167

NAACP. *See* National Association for the Advancement of Colored People
Narrative of the Life of Frederick Douglass (Douglass), 42, 82, 243
Nash, Diane, 158
National Association for the Advancement of Colored People, 56, 129–30, 131, 132, 133, 137, 141, 142, 144, 148, 149, 151–52, 157, 165, 168, 174, 177, 209, 211, 212, 213, 217, 337, 338, 346
National Association of Colored Men, 127
National Association of Colored Women, 127, 129, 142, 245
National Colored Democratic League, 139
National Committee of Black Churchmen, 303
National Conference of Negro Artists, 291
National Convention of Colored Citizens (1864), 102–3
National Council of Negro Women, 143
National Equal Rights League, 103
National Federation of Women's Clubs, 128
National Independence Equal Rights League, 139
National Negro Bowling Association, 374

National Negro Business League, 128
National Negro Congress, 143
National Reformer (magazine), 81
National Youth Administration, 143
Nation of Islam, 156, 167, 168, 176, 279, 292, 302–3
Native Americans, 3, 22, 34, 35, 183, 204–5, 206
Native Son (Wright), 281–82
Naturalization Act (1790), 73
Navigation Acts, 22
Neal, Larry, 292, 293
Negro, Benjamin, 184
Negro Ensemble Company, 314
Negro National League, 363, 364
The Negro Soldier (film), 215
Newcombe, Don, 365, *365*
New Dance Group, 284
New Deal, 59, 133–34, 147
New England Anti-Slavery Society, 79, 86
New England Female Medical College, 349
New Negro Alliance, 133
New Negro Movement, 264, 270
Newton, Huey P., 156, *156*, 157
New York Bowery Theater, 122
New York City Manumission Society, 70
Niagara Movement, 126, 129, 141
Nicodemus (Black town), 53
Nixon, E. D., 164
Nixon, Richard, 157, 159, 172, 174, 175
Nobel Prize, 145, 304
North Congregation Society, 331
Northrop, Solomon, 39, 231
North Star (newspaper), 42, 45, 87
Northwest Ordinance, 73
Norton, Ken, 361
Notes on the State of Virginia (Jefferson), 42
Numero, Joseph, 336

Oberlin College, 141, 254, 257, 275, 362
Observations on the Inslaving, Importing and Purchasing of Negroes (Benezet), 63
Oglethorpe, James, 68
Oliver, King, 272, 273, 310
Olympics, 360, 361, 370, 372, 377, 381, 382, 383, 384
"On Being Brought from Africa to America" (Wheatley), 237
Ore, John, 287
Organization of Afro-American Unity, 156, 167
Oryeda, Danny, 315
Otis, Harrison Gray, 71
Our Nig (Jacobs), 245
Ovington, Mary White, 129, *129*, 130
Owens, Dana, 312–13
Owens, Jesse, 381–82, *382*, 384

Page, Thomas Nelson, 255
Paige, Leroy "Satchel," 364
Palmares Maroon colony, 34
Pan-Africanism, 159, 292
Pan-American Games, 360, 372
Panther (film), 157
Parker, Charlie "Byrd," 286, 296
Parker, John H., 132
Parks, Gordon, 292, 301
Parks, Rosa, 149, 160, 177
Parsons, Usher, 191
Patents, 326–27, 328, 334
Paternalism, 110–11
Patterson, Floyd, 358, 359, 360
"Pattyrollers," 241
Paulsen, Martin H. K., 48
Payton, Walter "Sweetness," 379–80
Peace and Freedom Party, 157
Peete, Calvin, 375, *375*
Penn, Lemuel, 167
Penniman, Richard Wayne, 289–90
Pennington, James W. C., 37, 76, *76*
Pennsylvania Abolition Society, 70
Pennsylvania Society for Promoting the Abolition of Slavery, 81
Peonage, 123
Peoples, Roosevelt, 340
People United to Save Humanity, 174
Perez, Rosie, 315
Perry, Oliver Hazard, 191
Persian Gulf War, 224
Petry, Ann, 282
Pharmacy, 341–42
Phillips, Captain Thomas, 18
Phillips, Wendell, 83, 243
Phipps, Benjamin, 32
Phyllis Wheatley Club, 127
Pickens, Harriet, 214, *215*
Pickens, William, 50
Pickett, Bill, 372–73
Pike, James, 106, 115
Pinchback, P. B. S., 121, *121*, 202
Pinson, Vada, 367
Piper, Fred, 261
Pippin, Horace, 269–70
Plantations

- coffee, 25–26
- rice, 21
- sugar, 7–8, 9, 25
- tobacco, 21

Planter (ship), 33–34
Plessy, Homer, 146
Plessy v. Ferguson, 146, 148
Poage, George Coleman, 381
Poems on Miscellaneous Subjects (Harper), 244–45
Poitier, Sidney, 290, 301
Poll taxes, 56, 124
Poor, Salem, 184–85
Poor People's Campaign, 157
Porter, James, 271
Powell, Adam Clayton, Jr., 133, 144–45, 291, 303
Powell, Colin L., *223*, 223–24
Powell, Mike, 384
Powell v. Alabama, 146–47
Price, Cecil, 165, 167
Price, Leontyne, 288
Prigg v. Pennsylvania, 91
Primus, Pearl, 284–85, *285*, 314
Prince, 314–15
Prioleau, Devany, 31
Pritchett, Laurie, 151–52
Proclamation on Amnesty and Reconstruction. *See* Reconstruction
Professional Bowlers' Association, 374
Professional Golfers' Association, 374
Progressive Party, 140
Project C, 152
Prosser, Gabriel, 29–30
Protests
- antebellum period, 74–78
- Civil Rights Movement, 148–57
- colonial period, 62–63
- military, 212–13
- Revolutionary period, 68–72

Public Enemy, 312
Pulitzer Prize, 282, 306, 307, 315
Punch, John, 64
Puritans, 22
Purvis, Charles, 343–44
Purvis, Robert, 75, 80, 81, *81*
Puryear, Martin, 314
PUSH. *See* People United to Save Humanity

Quakers, 40, 44, 46, 62, 63, 70, 85, 323
Queen Latifah, 312–13
Quilombos, 34
Quilting, 323
Quotas, 173, 179–80, 212

Rainey, Ma, 274
A Raisin in the Sun (Hansberry), 290
Randolph, A. Philip, 131, 134, *135*, 136, 142–43, 153, 212
Rangel, Charles, 145, 174
Rape, 125, 140, 146–47
Ray, Charles B., 76
Ray, James Earl, 168
Rayford, Lee, 214, *214*
Reading Room Society, 236
Reagan, Ronald, 172–73, 175, 176
Reapers, 327
Reason, Patrick Henry, 245–46
Rebellions, 24, 26–34
- Amistad incident, 26–27
- effect of, 67
- fear of, 27, 32
- Haitian, 26, 29, 30–31
- hidden, 33
- Nat Turner's Rebellion, 31–32
- New York City, 27, 28
- Stono Rebellion, 28–29, 67, 230

Reconstruction, 48, 52, 101, 102, 105–10
- Black, 106–7, 115, 121
- congressional, 106
- presidential, 105–6, 110, 117, 118
- radical, 106, 107, *107*, 108, 109

Reconstruction Act of 1867, 105, 106, 109, 112, 115, 117, 118, 122, 203
Redeemers, 109
Red Hot Peppers, 272
Redman, Don, 273
Reiss, Winold, 266–67
Religion, 252–54, 278–81
- baptism, 233
- camp meetings, 242
- Church of England, 234
- colonial period, 233–35, 241–42
- Great Awakening, 234, 235, 240, 242
- mainstream churches, 242
- post-Civil War, 261–63
- separate churches, 241–42, 252
- spirits, 233
- storefront churches, 278–79
- voodoo, 252
- West African, 233

Remond, Charles Lenox, 77, *77*, 78, 83–84
Remond, Sarah Parker, 84

Resurrection City, 157
Revels, Hiram Rhoades, 119–20, *120*
Reynolds, H. H., 329–30
Rice, 21, 321
Rice, Joseph, 374
Rice, Thomas, 122, 231, 249
Richards, Lloyd, 316
Richardson, Willis, 278
Richie, Lionel, 290
Richmond, William, 353, 354
Rights
  citizenship, 90–91, 147
  civil, 91, 93–94, 101, 106, 111, 112, 114, 115, 118, 119, 131, 141, 144, 147, 148–72
  equal, 103
  equality of opportunity, 147
  human, 156
  legal, 93
  political, 93–94, 101, 115, 119, 126, 146
  safety, 147
  social, 114–15
  voting, 91, 94, 102, 111, 112–13, 117, 119, 124, 145–46, 147, 155, 171
  women's, 76, 81, 83, 89, 103, 174
Rillieux, Norbert, 324–25, *325*
Riots, 122
  anti-Black, 91, 100–1
  Atlanta (1906), 128
  Boston (1903), 128–29
  Brownsville, 138
  Harlem (1935), 134
  Houston (1917), 208–9
  race, 134, 168, *169*, 179
  urban, 294, 303
  Watts, 168
Roberts, Joseph Jenkins, 46
Roberts, Marcus, 272
Roberts v. the City of Boston, 91
Robeson, Paul, 143–44, *144*, 221, 263, 278, 377–78
Robinson, Frank, 367
Robinson, Jackie, 364–65, *365*, 367, 368
Robinson, Randall, 284
Robinson, Smokey, 290, 297
Robinson, Sugar Ray, 358, 360
Rock, John, 90, 103
Rodeo, 372–73
Rogers, J. A., 293
Roosevelt, Eleanor, 276, 277
Roosevelt, Franklin D., 133–34, 143, 212, 221, 276
Roosevelt, Theodore, 128–29, 138, 139, 205–6, 206
Roseland, 273
Ross, Alexander, 40
Ross, Archia, 332
Ross, Diana, 290, 296
Roundtree, Richard, 301
Rouse, Charlie, 287
Roxborough, John, 357
Royal Adventurers, 21
Royal African Company, 15, 17, 21, 22
Rudolph, Wilma, 382, *383*
Ruggles, David, 82
Rush, Christopher, 76
Russell, Bill, *370*, 370–71
Rustin, Bayard, 153
Rutledge, Edward, 186
Ryder Cup Team, 375

Sadler, Joseph, 312
Salem, Peter, 184, *185*
Salter, John, Jr., 150, *150*
Saramaccan peoples, 34
Savage, Augusta, 270–71, 283
Savary, Joseph, 192–93
Sayers, Gale, 378
Scalawags, 108, 135
Schmeling, Max, 357–58
Schmoke, Kurt, 177
Schwerner, Michael, 165, 167
Science, 337–49
Scott, Dred, 73, 78, 91, 93, *93*
Scott-Heron, Gil, 312
Scottsboro Boys, 132, 142, 146–47
Seale, Bobby, 156, *156*, 157, 179
Sedgwick, Theodore, 72
Segregation, 55–56, 84
  in education, 91, 93, 132–33, 147–48, 149, 339
  in federal employment, 139
  Jim Crow, 118
  military, 147, 208, 209, 210, 212, 221
  in public accommodations, 103, 135, 170
  in transportation, 103, 104, 112, 118, 123, 125–26, 127, 135–36, 146, 149, 151
  in women's clubs, 127
The Selling of Joseph (Sewall), 62
Selma March, 155, 159, 168
Senghor, Leopold, 292
Servants, indentured, 20, 34, 183, 186
Sewall, Judge Samuel, 62, 63
Sex, interracial, 64–65
Sexism, 306
Shadd, Abraham, 75

Shade, Julia M., 342
Shange, Ntozake, 301–2, 304
Sharecropping, 59, 108, 123, 133, 260
Sharpton, Al, 177
Shaw, Earl, 339–40
Sheppard, William, 258
Shiloh Church, 77, *77*
Shoe lasting machine, *330*, 330–31
Shook, Karel, 300
Shuttlesworth, Fred, 157–58
Sifford, Charlie, 374–75
Simon, Monkey, 376
Simpson, Lorna, 309–10
Simpson, O. J., 378–79, *379*
Sims, Clifford C., 223
Sims, Joseph Howard, 167
Singleton, Benjamin "Pap," 52, 53
Singleton, John, 316
Sissle, Noble, 210, 271, 276
Sit-ins, 135, 149–50, 158, 165
Slave Act (1712), 27–28, 66
Slave Act (1722), 68
Slave Act (1740), 67
Slavery
- abolition of, 72–73, 74
- "living out," 54
- mortality rates in, 8, 13, 14, 15, 25
- opposition to, 62
- plantation, 54
- prohibition of, 102, 110
- in South America, 25–26
- urban, 53

Slave(s)
- betrayal by other slaves, 31
- catchers, 35, 37, 39
- as contraband, 195–96
- emancipation, 96–100
- "fattening up," 19
- festivals, 243
- fugitive, 34–42, 47, 68–69, 71, 73, 77–78, 80, 82, 88–89, 91, 92
- inspection of, 19–20, *20*
- occupations of, 10
- rebellions by, 26–34
- "refuse," 19
- runaway, 34–42, 68–69
- self-reproduction of population, 25
- sports participation, 353

Slave ships, 13–19
- *Albion-Frigate*, 27
- *Amistad*, *26*, 26–27
- *Arthur*, 15
- *Brookes*, 13, *14*
- *Creole*, 26
- *Elizabeth*, 13, 16
- *Le Rodeur*, 16
- *Little George*, 18
- murder on, 17
- packing on, 13–15, 17
- *Prince of Orange*, 18
- rebellions on, 27
- *St. Jan*, 13
- *Undine*, 9
- *Wildfire*, 5
- *Zong*, 17

Slave trade, 5–19
- in Africa, 10, *11*
- asiento system, 6–7
- in Caribbean, 8–9
- in colonial America, 20–26
- condemnation of, 63
- disease in, 16
- end of, 46–47
- escape attempts in, 18
- gang-labor method, 22
- head money in, 16
- internal, 50–51
- Middle Passage, 13–19
- mutinies in, 18, 19
- numbers of slaves, 5–6
- origins of, 10
- prohibition of, 24, 26, 92
- psychological trauma in, 15–16
- and relations with England, 22–26
- in South America, 7–8
- suicide in, 16, 18
- task system, 22
- triangle trade, 22
- for weapons, 11–12
- white mortality in, 16–17

Sly and the Family Stone, 287
Smalls, Robert, *33*, 33–34, 103
Smith, Anna Deavere, 316
Smith, Bessie, 274, *274*, 285
Smith, Georgia Caldwell, 339
Smith, Gerritt, 77
Smith, James A., 38
Smith, James McCune, 343
Smith, James Webster, 206
Smith, Mamie, 274
Smith, Tommie, 383, *383*
Smith, Walker, Jr., 358

Smoot, Charlie, 377
SNCC. *See* Student Nonviolent Coordinating Committee
Social Gospel Movement, 291
Society for the Promotion of Useful Knowledge, 247
Society for the Relief of Free Negroes Unlawfully held in Bondage, 70
Solomon, Job Ben, 232
Some Considerations on the Keeping of Negroes (Woolman), 63
The Souls of Black Folk (Du Bois), 128, 141, 301
Southern Christian Leadership Conference, 149, 150, 151–52, 153, 155, 157, 167, 174
Southern Horrors (Wells), 126
Southern Tenant Farmers' Union, 133–34
Spanish-American War, 205–8
Spingarn, Joel, 130, 209
Spinks, Leon, 360
Spinks, Michael, 361
Spirituals, 251, 256, 271
Sports, 353–84
  baseball, 362–68
  basketball, 368–72
  bicycling, 373–74
  bowling, 374
  boxing, 353–61
  football, 377–80
  golf, 374–75
  gymnastics, 377
  horse racing, 375–77
  ice skating, 377
  lacrosse, 380
  rodeo, 372–73
  tennis, 380–81
  track and field, 381–84
  weight lifting, 377
  women in, 370
Spirituals, 287–88
Stanton, Edwin M., 47, 196
Stanton, Henry B., 75
Starr, Edwin, 297
Steeplechase, 377
Stereotyping, 140, 249, 352
Stevens, Thaddeus, 118–19
Stewart, Maria, 252
Still, William Grant, 39, 41–42, *42*, 275–76
Stono Rebellion, 28–29, 67, 230
Stout, Renee, 309
Stovey, George, 362
Stowe, Harriet Beecher, 78, *85*, 85–86
Strachan, John, 190
The Street (Petry), 282
Stride Toward Freedom (King), 164
Student Nonviolent Coordinating Committee, 144, 150, 151–52, 153, 154, 155, 158, 159, 160, 168, 173–74, 177
Sugar, 7, 8, 9, 25, 324–25
Sugar Act, 22
Sugar Hill Gang, 312
Summer Project, 154
Sumner, Charles, 92, 119, 196
Supreme Court decisions
  Bakke decision, 179–80
  Brown v. Board of Education, 91, 123, 142–43, 145, 148, 160–61, 170
  Gaines v. Missouri, 147
  Guinn v. United States, 130
  Hall v. DeCuir, 112
  on intermarriage, 65
  Loving v. Virginia, 65
  Moore v. Dempsey, 130
  Plessy v. Ferguson, 146, 148
  Powell v. Alabama, 146–47
  Sweatt v. Painter, 147–48
  United States v. Cruikshank, 112
  United States v. Harris, 114
  United States v. Reese, 113
Sweat, Robert, 64
Sweatt v. Painter, 147–48
Sweet, Ossian, 131

Taney, Judge Roger B., 73, 78
Tanner, Benjamin Tucker, 49, 261–62
Tanner, Henry Ossawa, 257–58
Tappan, Arthur, 75, 76, 77, 80
Tappan, Lewis, 45, 75, 77, 80
Taylor, John Baxter, Jr., 381
Taylor, Marshall W. "Major," *373*, 373–74
Taylor, Tony, 367
Tea Act, 23
Telegraph system, 331
Temple, Lewis, 326
The Temptations, 297
Tennis, 380–81
Terrell, Mary Church, 141
Terrell, Robert, 142
Thirteenth Amendment, 107, 110, 146
Thomas, Clarence, 180
Thomas, Debra, 377
Thomas, Eugene, 168
Thompson, Robert Ferris, 305
Thompson, Virgil, 288
Thurman, Howard, 291